COMPUTERIZED ACCOUNTING
WITH
QUICKBOOKS® 5.0

COMPUTERIZED ACCOUNTING WITH QUICKBOOKS® 5.0

Janet Horne, M.S.
Los Angeles Pierce College

PRENTICE HALL, Upper Saddle River, New Jersey 07458

Acquisitions Editor: *Diane deCastro*
Editor-in-Chief: *P.J. Boardman*
Production Editor: *Lynda Paolucci*
Managing Editor: *Katherine Evancie*
Manufacturing Buyer: *Lisa DiMaulo*
Senior Manufacturing Supervisor: *Paul Smolenski*
Production Coordinator: *Cindy Spreder*
Cover Designer: *Lorraine Castellano*

QuickBooks is a registered trademark of Intuit, Inc. Screen shots reprinted with permission from Intuit, Inc. This book is not sponsored or endorsed by or affiliated with Intuit, Inc.

 © 1998 by Prentice Hall, Inc.
A Simon & Schuster Company
Upper Saddle River, NJ 07458

Library of Congress Cataloging-in-Publication Data
Horne, Janet.
    Computerized Accounting with QuickBooks 5.0 / Janet Horne.
       p.   cm.
    Includes index.
    ISBN 0-13-755307-2
    1. Quickbooks for Windows. 2. Small business--Accounting--Computer
    programs. 3. Small business--Finance--Computer programs.
  I. Title.
  HF5679.H663   1998
  657'.9042'02855369--dc21   97-42866
                                    CIP

Printed in the United States of America

10 9 8 7 6

ISBN 0-13-755307-2

Prentice-Hall International (UK) Limited, *London*
Prentice-Hall of Australia Pty. Limited, *Sydney*
Prentice-Hall Canada Inc., *Toronto*
Prentice-Hall Hispanoamericana, S.A., *Mexico*
Prentice-Hall of India Private Limited, *New Delhi*
Prentice-Hall of Japan, Inc., *Tokyo*
Simon & Schuster Asia Pte. Ltd., *Singapore*
Editora Prentice-Hall do Brasil, Ltda., *Rio de Janiero*

To my husband and our sons
with thanks for their support, patience, and understanding

TABLE OF CONTENTS

Chapter 3—Payables and Purchases: Service Business

Chapter 4—General Accounting and End-of-Period Procedures: Service Business

End of Section 1—Helping Hands Practice Set: Service Business

SECTION 2

Chapter 5—Sales and Receivables: Merchandising Business

Chapter 6—Payables and Purchases: Merchandising Business

Chapter 7—General Accounting and End-of-Period Procedures: Merchandising Business

End of Section 2—Golf World Practice Set: Merchandising Business

SECTION 3
Chapter 8: Payroll

Chapter 9: Computerizing a Manual Accounting System

End of Section 3—College Town Book Store Practice Set: Comprehensive Problem

Appendix A: Importing and Exporting Data

Appendix B: QuickBooks On-line

Index

PREFACE

Computerized Accounting with QuickBooks® 5.0 is a comprehensive instructional learning resource. This text has been designed to respond to the growing trend toward adopting Windows applications and computerizing accounting systems. As a result of this trend, the text provides training using *Windows® 3.1/95* and the popular *QuickBooks® 5.0* accounting program.

ORGANIZATIONAL FEATURES

Computerized Accounting with QuickBooks® 5.0 is organized into three sections. Accounting concepts and their relationship to *QuickBooks® 5.0* are presented in each chapter. In addition to accounting concepts, students use a fictitious company and receive hands-on training in the use of *QuickBooks® 5.0* within each chapter. At the end of every chapter, the concepts and applications learned are reinforced by the completion of true/false, multiple-choice, fill-in, and essay questions plus an application problem using a different fictitious company. At the end of each section, there is a comprehensive practice set that reviews all the concepts and applications presented within the section. The final practice set is a comprehensive problem utilizing all the major concepts and transactions presented within the textbook.

The first section introduces students to the computer, Windows, and QuickBooks accounting for a service business. The second section of the text focuses on merchandising businesses. The third section of the book concentrates on payroll and creating a company using QuickBooks. The appendices review the import/export and on-line capabilities of *QuickBooks® 5.0*.

DISTINGUISHING FEATURES

Throughout the text, emphasis has been placed on the use of QuickBooks' innovative approach to recording accounting transactions based on a business form rather than using the traditional journal format. This approach, however, has been correlated to traditional accounting through adjusting entries, end-of-period procedures, and use of the "behind the scenes" journal.

Unlike many other computerized accounting programs, QuickBooks is user-friendly when corrections and adjustments are required. The ease of corrections and the ramifications as a result of this ease are explored thoroughly.

Accounting concepts and the use of *QuickBooks® 5.0* are reinforced throughout the text with the use of graphics that show completed transactions, reports, and QuickBooks screens.

The text provides extensive assignment material in the form of tutorials, end-of-chapter questions (true/false, multiple-choice, fill-in, and essay), and comprehensive practice sets.

Students develop confidence in recording business transactions using an up-to-date commercial software program designed for small to mid-size businesses. With thorough exploration of the program in the text, students should be able to use *QuickBooks® 5.0* in the "real world" at the completion of the textbook training.

Students will explore and use many of the features of QuickBooks extensively, including recording transactions, applying customer and vendor discounts, tracking inventory, ordering merchandise, preparing a multitude of reports, assigning passwords, and compiling charts and graphs. In addition, QuickBooks on-line features and data import/export capabilities are explored.

In the last practice set, students will have an opportunity to create a company. They will then record transactions, customize business forms and reports, and use a logo for the company.

COURSES

Computerized Accounting with QuickBooks® 5.0 is designed for a one-term course in microcomputer accounting or for use in any accounting course requiring introductory work on an integrated computerized accounting package. Students should be familiar with the accounting cycle and how it is related to service and merchandising businesses. No prior knowledge of or experience with computers, Windows, or QuickBooks is required.

SUPPLEMENTS FOR THE INSTRUCTOR

Solutions Manual and Teaching Guide with Tests is a comprehensive answer key to all questions, exercises, and practice sets. All computer assignments are printed in full and included for use in grading or as a student answer key. In addition to answers to text assignments, the *Solutions Manual and Teaching Guide with Tests* for *Computerized Accounting with QuickBooks® 5.0* contains master data disks for all the companies in the text, a sample course outline, lectures for each chapter, written exams for each section, and suggestions for grading. Lecture materials include a lecture outline for the chapter plus a hands-on demonstration lecture.

ACKNOWLEDGMENTS

I wish to thank my colleagues for testing and reviewing the manuscript. Their comments and suggestions are greatly appreciated. These individuals are

Marilyn Lammers, California State University, Northridge; Jean Gutmann, University of Southern Maine; Mark Henry, Victoria College; Kay Walker Hauser, Beaufort County Community College; Joseph W. Wilkinson, Arizona State University; Roger K. Doost, Clemson University; Andrea Deebach, Lake Washington Technical College; Dan R. Ward, University of Southern Louisiana; Anne M. Oppegard, Augustana College; Tom Land, Bessimer State Technical College; Bruce England, Massasoit Community College; Stephen C. Schaefer, Contra Costa College; Barbara Reider, University of Alaska at Anchorage; and Patricia H. Holmes, Des Moines Area Community College.

COMPUTERIZED ACCOUNTING
WITH
QUICKBOOKS® 5.0

INTRODUCTION TO COMPUTERS AND QUICKBOOKS®

LEARNING OBJECTIVES

At the completion of this chapter, you will be able to:

1. Turn on your computer, open and close Windows, and open and close QuickBooks.
2. Recognize system requirements for using QuickBooks and Windows.
3. Use a mouse.
4. Identify QuickBooks desktop features and understand the QuickBooks Navigator.
5. Recognize menu commands and use some keyboard shortcuts.
6. Open, copy, back up, and close a company on disk.
7. Turn QCards on and off and use on-screen help.
8. Recognize QuickBooks forms and understand the use of lists and registers in QuickBooks.
9. Access QuickBooks reports and be familiar with QuickZoom.
10. Prepare QuickBooks graphs and use QuickReport within graphs.
11. Use QuickMath and the Windows calculator.

COMPUTERS HAVE BECOME A WAY OF LIFE

In today's world computers are appearing in many different places—from the desktop in the home or office to someone's lap on an airplane or at a sporting event. No longer is a computer simply a large, bulky piece of equipment used for "crunching numbers." Computers are used to process documents such as letters, memos, and reports; to perform financial planning and forecasting; to draw pictures and design equipment; to play games; and, of course, to keep the financial records of a company. A computer system is actually a group of hardware components that work together with software to perform a specific task. The steps involved in the processing cycle are input, processing, output, and storage.

INTRODUCTION TO COMPUTER HARDWARE

 "Computer hardware" refers to the equipment used as part of a computer system. While there are several computer classifications, this text will focus on the personal computer and its use in computerized accounting applications.

The hardware components used in today's computer system are as follows.

Input Devices

Input devices are used to enter data or commands into the computer. Essentially, during the input process the computer receives information coded in electrical pulses that indicate an on or an off state. The electrical pulses are called bits, which stands for binary digit, indicating either the on or off electrical pulse. The bits are grouped into a series of eight pulses to form a byte. In essence, one byte is equal to one character typed on the keyboard.

As information is input, it is temporarily stored in the random access memory (RAM) of the computer. Program instructions are also stored temporarily in RAM. Even though it is a temporary storage area, RAM storage is measured in bytes (remember, one byte is equal to one keyboard character). Because of the graphics used in today's software programs, RAM storage must also be quite large and is usually in the range of 4 megabytes (abbreviated MB; a MB equals 1 million bytes) or greater.

The most common input devices are the keyboard, the mouse, and a scanner. Of all the input devices, the keyboard is used most frequently. The keyboard allows the user to key in text, numbers, and other characters for use by the computer to process the data and provide information. Many times software commands or instructions are given via the keyboard.

Another popular input device, primarily used to give software commands, is the mouse. Many program instructions are given by pointing to an icon (picture) and clicking the primary (usually left) mouse button.

To input entire documents at once, a scanner can be used to scan the document and insert an image of the document into the computer.

Processing Devices

The data that have been input into the computer and the necessary program instructions are sent to the central processing unit (CPU) for processing by the computer. The control unit of the CPU directs the transfer of information from RAM into the ALU (Arithmetic/Logic Unit). Using program instructions, the ALU performs the necessary mathematical and logical computations on the data and formulae entered. The results of processing are sent to RAM, and the control unit of the computer sends these results to output or storage devices.

Output Devices

 As indicated, the result of processing is output. Output can be shown on the monitor, it can be printed on paper, and/or it can be stored on disk or other media. The most common output device is a monitor. Monitors can be monochrome or color. Today, most computer systems use color monitors to display output.

 Output is frequently in the form of a printed or "hard" copy. Several types of printers are available for printing output. The three most common types of printers used are dot matrix, which form characters in groups of dots; ink jet, which spray small droplets of ink on paper to create characters; and laser, which use a combination of a laser beam, static electricity, and ink toner to produce high-quality text.

Storage Devices

The most common storage device is a disk. The disk can be a removable floppy disk, which is either 5¼-inches wide or 3½-inches wide. The amount of storage space is measured in bytes. Remember, one byte is equal to one keyboard character. Storage space is calculated

 exponentially, so 1 kilobyte (abbreviated K) of memory is 1,024 bytes. For ease in calculations, the storage capacity is rounded to the nearest 1,000. A double-density 5¼-inch disk stores approximately 360K, a double-density 3½-inch disk holds a little over 720K, and a high-density 3½-inch disk holds more than 1.44MB. New types of floppy-disk drives that hold 100MB or more are currently on the market and are becoming popular as installed drives in computers.

5¼-inch disk   **3½-inch disk**

Most computers have internal storage on a hard disk. These permanent disks hold a great deal of information inside the computer. Most of the hard-disk space is used to store software programs; however, data may also be stored on the hard disk. In a classroom environment data are usually stored on the removable floppy disks. Storage space on a hard disk is also measured in bytes. Because of the size of the programs residing on it, the hard disk is becoming larger and larger. Hard disks are measured in megabytes and gigabytes. (A gigabyte is approximately 1 billion bytes. The abbreviation for gigabyte is GB.)

INTRODUCTION TO SOFTWARE

Data can be keyed on the keyboard and sent to RAM, but the central processing unit will not know what to do with the data unless it is given instructions via a computer program. The computer programs are called software and are divided into two different categories—operating system software and application software.

Operating System Software

System software gives the computer basic operating instructions and is required no matter what application software is used. The operating system software allows data to be input using a keyboard. The operating system software sends the data and program instructions to the central processing unit for processing, and it allows the results of processing to be shown on the monitor, sent to the printer, or stored on a disk. In addition to being the controlling program for the computer, the operating system software is used for disk and file management and organization.

When IBM-PC microcomputers started to appear in the office in the early 1980s, the operating system for these personal computers used a text-based command structure and was called PC-DOS. Because DOS (Disk Operating System) was developed by Microsoft, versions of DOS for IBM-clone computers were called MS-DOS; however, PC-DOS and MS-DOS are almost identical. Apple computers, which actually started the microcomputer revolution, had a more user-friendly operating system that used icons (pictures) to give commands. In order to compete with the Apple computers in ease of use, Microsoft developed an operating environment used in conjunction with DOS. This operating environment is Windows. It uses the principle of a graphical user interface (GUI) with pictures or icons representing software programs, hardware, and commands. Rather than rely on typed-in commands as is done in DOS, Windows receives instructions or commands when the user points to and clicks on an icon with a mouse.

To eliminate such cumbersome limitations such as the 8.3 DOS file-naming rule (a file name may have up to eight characters, a decimal point, and an optional three-character extension) and to allow the operating system to have "plug and play" recognition of software and hardware components, Windows 95 was developed and released by Microsoft in 1995.

There are many other operating systems on the market today. Most of the time you are working, you will not have much direct contact with the operating system; however, it is always important to know which system you are using. This chapter will illustrate both the Windows 3.1 operating environment and the Windows 95 operating system.

Application Software

Application software is task-specific software. In other words, if you want to keep the books for a company, you use a program such as QuickBooks to enter information regarding your business transactions and to produce your financial reports. If you want to type a term paper, a word processing program will be the application program to use. To do financial forecasting and perform "what if" scenarios, a spreadsheet program will be used. If you want to play a game of pinball using the computer, a computer game will be the application. Each application program is designed to respond to the commands you give. In some programs the use of a function key will give a completely different result than the use of the same function key in another program.

In the Windows 3.1/95 operating environment/system, program commands may be given by pointing to an icon and clicking the primary (usually left) mouse button. For example, no matter what Windows program or application software you use, clicking on the picture of a printer sends a copy of your document to the printer, or it may take you to another screen on which you can set printing options.

One of the exciting features of Windows is OLE (object linking and embedding). OLE allows you to work with a document in one application program and retrieve it and use it in another program. This text will provide information regarding OLE and QuickBooks.

MANUAL VERSUS COMPUTERIZED ACCOUNTING

The work to be performed to keep the books for a business is the same whether you use a manual or a computerized accounting system. Transactions need to be analyzed, recorded in a journal, and posted to a ledger. Business documents such as invoices, checks, bank deposits, and credit/debit memos need to be prepared and distributed. Reports to management and owners for information and decision-making purposes need to be prepared. Records for one business period need to be closed before one moves to the next business period.

In a manual system, each transaction that is analyzed must be entered by hand into the appropriate journal and posted to the appropriate ledger. A separate business document such as an invoice or a check must be prepared and distributed. In order to prepare a report, the accountant/bookkeeper must go through the journal or ledger and look for the appropriate amounts to include in the report. Closing the books must be done item by item via closing entries, which are recorded in the journal and posted to the appropriate ledger accounts. After the closing entries are recorded, the ledger accounts must be ruled and balance sheet accounts must be re-opened with Brought Forward Balances being entered. All of this is extremely time consuming.

In a computerized system, the transactions must still be analyzed and recorded; however, posting is done automatically or by giving the command to post. Reports are generated based on an instruction given to the computer—for example, by clicking on a menu item: "Report—Trial Balance." Some computerized accounting systems require the accountant/bookkeeper to enter each transaction as a debit and a credit in a General Journal. Other programs allow the use of special journals such as Cash Disbursements, Cash Payments, Sales, and Purchases journals.

Only QuickBooks operates from a business document point of view. As a transaction occurs, the necessary business document (an invoice or a check, for example) is prepared. Based on the information given on the business document, QuickBooks records the necessary debits and credits behind the scenes. If an error is made when entering a transaction, QuickBooks allows the user to return to the business document and make the correction. All recording in debits and credits is automatically performed behind the scenes. If you want to see or make a correction using the actual debit/credit entries, QuickBooks allows you to view the transaction register and make corrections directly in the register or use the traditional Journal. Reports and graphs are prepared by simply clicking "Report" on the menu bar.

SYSTEM REQUIREMENTS FOR QUICKBOOKS® 5.0 AND WINDOWS® 3.1/95

Hardware

The hardware requirements are an IBM-compatible computer, 486 (or higher) processor; 8MB RAM (16 MB recommended); 32 MB of hard-disk space available for QuickBooks, an additional 6.2 MB of hard-disk space for Netscape Navigator or Internet access, and 10.5 MB of hard-disk space available for Windows 3.1 or 35 MB of hard-disk space available for Windows 95; VGA or SVGA monitor; modem if using Online Banking or Netscape Navigator; printer supported by Windows 3.1 or Windows 95.

Software

The software requirements are Windows 3.1 or 95 and QuickBooks® 5.0.

INTRODUCTION TO WINDOWS® 3.1—SCREENS AND TERMINOLOGY

If you do not have a menu system or automatic batch file to start Windows, do the following:

*DO: If needed, turn on your computer and monitor
At the **C:** prompt, type **WIN** (Your screen will show: **C:\>win**)
Press the **Enter** key

Windows will begin running and **Program Manager** will show on the desktop (screen).

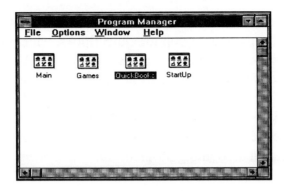

In order to use Windows effectively, it is helpful to understand the terminology used in describing the various Windows elements.

Desktop is the work area outside any open window—in other words, the screen.

Windows borders are the borders around the outside of open windows. You may point to a border, get a double arrow, then hold down the primary mouse button and drag the border to resize a window.

Control-menu box is always in the upper left corner of every window. Clicking on this allows you to access a drop-down menu, which is used for resizing, moving, maximizing, minimizing, closing, or switching a window. Double-clicking on the control-menu box will close the window without showing the drop-down menu.

Title bar displays the name of the application and/or the name of the document in use.

Minimize button is a downward-pointing arrow on the right side of the title bar. Clicking on this allows you to shrink or minimize a window into an icon. When a window is minimized, the program/document is still open and usable; it is just placed on the desktop as an icon so it is out of the way.

Maximize button is an upward-pointing arrow on the right side of the title bar. Clicking on this allows you to fill the entire screen with the contents of the window.

Restore button is a two-headed arrow that appears when a window is maximized. The original maximize button changes into the restore button. Clicking on this restores the window to its previous size.

A menu bar provides several options and will drop down a menu when a menu item is clicked. These different menus allow you to access most of the commands within a program.

Closed document window is a small icon representing a program or a group of programs. For example, you could have a program group for QuickBooks, which would contain a program item icon QuickBooks; or you could have a program group for Accounting, which would contain program item icons for QuickBooks and any other accounting programs that you use.

Open document window shows the program item icons that allow you to access a program. For example, clicking on the Accounting group icon opens that window. You will see program item icons for the individual accounting programs on your system.

A program group icon is an icon that represents a specific category of programs. For example, a program group icon for Accounting should contain program item icons for all the accounting programs available on your computer.

A program item icon is an icon that represents an individual program. When you have the Accounting group icon opened into a window, clicking on the program item icon for QuickBooks opens the QuickBooks program.

Application window holds or contains the application software program that is running.

Document window holds or contains the document being used. The document window fits within the application's window.

INTRODUCTION TO WINDOWS® 95—SCREENS AND TERMINOLOGY

When you turn on the computer, Windows 95 will automatically be in use and icons will be visible on the desktop. (Some computer laboratories require the use of passwords in order to access Windows 95 and the various application programs available. Check with your instructor regarding the configuration of your classroom computers.)

*DO: If needed, turn on your computer and monitor
Windows 95 will begin running, and the desktop will be displayed on the screen.

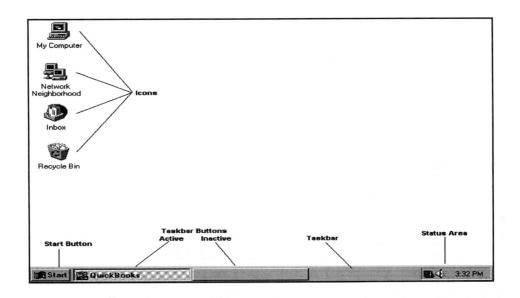

In order to use Windows 95 effectively, it is helpful to understand the terminology used in describing the various Windows elements.

Desktop is the primary work area and covers the entire screen.

Icons are pictorial representations of objects. Some icons on the desktop are "shortcuts" used to access programs and/or documents. Other icons are used to access information regarding your computer or to delete files/programs from the computer.

Taskbar is the major focal point of Windows 95. It usually appears at the bottom of your screen. The taskbar contains the **Start** button, which is used to launch (open) programs, access documents, alter the appearance of the desktop, and shut down the computer when you are finished working.

Taskbar buttons indicate the names of any programs/files that are currently open.

Status area is on the right side of the taskbar. Programs can place information or notification of events in the status area. Windows 95 places information in the status area: the time and (if available on your computer) a sound icon, which is used to control the volume of the computer's sound system.

ToolTip is a definition, instruction, or information that pops up when you point to something. For example, pointing to the time in the status area of the Taskbar gives you a ToolTip that displays the full date; pointing to the Start button gives you the ToolTip "Click here to begin."

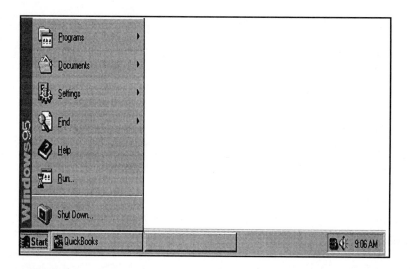

Start button is used to access the primary menu in Windows 95. This menu lists the main functions available.

    Programs is a menu listing the application programs available on your system. Frequently, you must make selections from several menus to access a program. For example, to access Calculator, which is a Windows 95 Accessory Program, you point to **Program** menu, then point to **Accessories** menu, and finally point to and click on **Calculator**.

    Documents lists the names of documents recently in use on the computer. (In a classroom environment, the documents listed may not be your documents; they may have been in use by another student.)

    Settings allows you to alter the Windows 95 environment.

    Find allows you to locate files, folders, computers or a network.

    Help takes you to a program to obtain on-line help for Windows 95.

    Run allows you to execute a program by name.

    Shut Down is *always* used to exit Windows 95 or restart the computer.

Once you have opened a program and are ready to work, Windows 95 will provide several items that are similar to those shown in the following QuickBooks window.

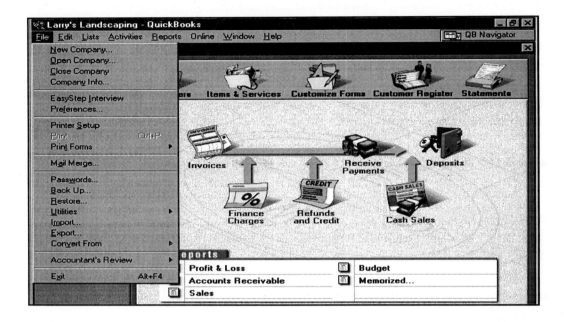

Control-menu icon is always in the upper left corner of every window. Clicking on this allows you to access a drop-down menu, which is used for resizing, moving, maximizing, minimizing, closing, or switching a window.

Title bar indicates the name of the program and the file in use.

Minimize button is located on the upper right side of the screen. It appears as a button with a minus sign. Clicking on this allows you to shrink or minimize a window into a button, which appears on the taskbar. When a window is minimized, the program/document is still open and usable; it is just placed on the taskbar as a button so it is out of the way.

Maximize button is a button with a single window as the icon. This is the middle button on the right side of the title bar. Clicking on this allows you to fill the entire screen with the contents of the window. (This is not shown on the QuickBooks window above.)

Restore button appears when a window is maximized, the maximize button changes into a button with two-windows. (This is shown on the QuickBooks window above). Clicking on this restores the window to its previous size.

Close button is on the far right side of the title bar. This button has an **X** on it. Clicking on this button closes both the document and the program. (The document window may also have its own minimize, maximize, and close buttons to be used only with the document. If so, these buttons will usually appear below the program minimize, maximize, and close buttons.)

Windows borders are the borders around the outside of open windows. You may point to a border, get a double arrow, then hold down the primary mouse button and drag the border to resize a window.

Menu bar will drop down a menu when clicked. These different menus allow you to access most of the commands within a program.

Dialog box is a box that appears in the middle of your screen and presents information to you or requests information from you.

Message box is a type of dialog box that informs you of a condition—a question, information, a critical error. Most message boxes require you to confirm, cancel, or retry an action by clicking on a command button.

Command button is a button used to answer the questions within a dialog box.

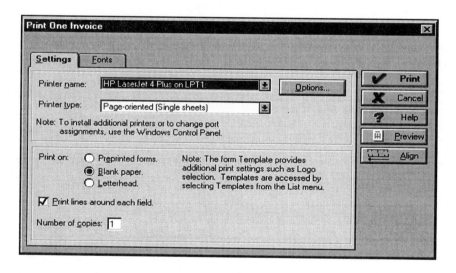

Other items in dialog boxes are:

Drop-down list or box contains the default choice. If you wish to make another selection, click the arrow next to the drop-down list box. If your choice is displayed, simply click on the desired item. (Look at the arrow next to the text box for "Printer name" in the "Print One Invoice" dialog box above.)

Option buttons present more than one choice; however, only one item may be chosen. The selected option contains a black dot. Options that are unavailable are dimmed. (Look at the section for "Print On" in the "Print One Invoice" dialog box.)

Text box allows you to key in information. (Look at the box next to "Printer name".)

Check box provides a choice that may be enabled or disabled. More than one item may be selected. If an option is unavailable, it is dimmed. (Look at the check box for "Print lines around each field.")

Spin box allows you to key in a number or to click on up or down arrows to increase or decrease a number. (Not shown on the illustration.)

BEGIN USING THE COMPUTER

At this point you will begin to use the computer. If you are not able to finish the chapter in one session, refer to the sections later in this chapter on How to Exit QuickBooks and/or How to Close or Shut Down Windows.

HOW TO USE A MOUSE

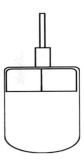

A mouse is an input device that is primarily used to issue commands within a software program. When working in a graphical user interface environment such as Windows 3.1 and Windows 95, the user sends instructions to programs by simply using the mouse to position the mouse pointer and clicking either the right or left mouse button. A mouse pointer is an arrow that can be used to point to an icon. When you are in a document or a dialog box that requires typing, the mouse pointer turns into an I-beam so it may be positioned more easily.

MOUSE TERMINOLOGY

When using a mouse, terms such as "click," "double-click," "right-click," "drag," and "drag and drop" will be used.

Mouse pointer is the arrow used when pointing to icons.

I-beam is the shape of the mouse pointer when being positioned within a document or a dialog box requiring typing.

Click means pressing the primary (usually left) mouse button one time.

Right-click means pressing the secondary (usually right) mouse button one time.

Double-click means to press the primary (usually left) mouse button two times very quickly.

Drag means to hold down the primary mouse button while dragging the mouse pointer through something (usually text) to highlight.

Drag and drop means to reposition something. This is achieved by pointing to an object or highlighted text with the mouse pointer, holding down the primary mouse button, and moving the mouse pointer/object by moving the mouse. When the item is repositioned, release the mouse button to "drop" the item into the new position.

PRACTICE USING A MOUSE

Practice with Windows® 3.1

*DO: Turn on computer and monitor, if not already on
At the C:\> prompt type **WIN**
- If you are working in a laboratory environment, the steps you follow to start the computer and access Windows 3.1 may be different. See your instructor for directions.

Point to the **Control-menu box**, click the primary mouse button
Point to **Minimize**, click **Minimize**
- Always use the primary mouse button when the instructions are *click*.

Program Manager is now a small icon on the desktop
Point to the **Program Manager** icon, double-click the primary mouse button
- This will enlarge the icon and open the Program Manager window.

Point to the **Maximize** button, click the button
- If you need to click to activate a command, future instructions will not indicate that you point to the item first. The above instructions will be given as: Click the Maximize button.

Program Manager covers the entire screen
Click the **Restore** button
Resize the window:
  Point to the **right border**
  - The mouse pointer will change into a double arrow.
  Hold down the primary mouse button
  Drag the window border to the right
  - Notice the dotted line indicating the new size.
  Release the primary mouse button
Move the window:
  Point to the **Title bar**

Hold down the primary mouse button
Drag the window to a new location on the desktop
- Notice the dotted window outline indicating the new position.
Release the primary mouse button

Practice with Windows® 95

 *DO: Turn on the computer and monitor, if not already on
You should see the Taskbar at the bottom of the screen and several icons on the desktop
- If you are working in a laboratory environment, the steps you follow to start the computer and access Windows 95 may be different. Check with your instructor for directions.
Point to the **Time** in the lower right corner of your screen
You will see the full date as a ToolTip
Point to the **Start** button
- Notice ToolTip: Click Here to Begin.
Open the **Notepad** program:
    Click the **Start** button
    Point to **Programs**
    Point to **Accessories**
    Point to **Notepad**, click the primary mouse button
    - If you need to click the primary mouse button to activate a command, future instructions will not tell you to point to the item first or to click the primary mouse button. The above instruction will be given as: Click Notepad.
Click the **Control-menu icon** in the upper left corner of the Notepad title bar
Click **Minimize** on the menu
- Notepad appears as a button on the Taskbar.
Click the **Notepad button** on the Taskbar
- This opens the same Notepad window.
- A button for Notepad remains on the Taskbar.
- Notice the difference in the button's appearance when the program is in use.
Click the **Maximize** button in the upper right corner of the Notepad window
- Notepad covers the entire screen.
Click the **Restore** button
- The Notepad window is restored to its former size.
Resize the window:
    Point to the **right border** of the Notepad window
    - The mouse pointer will turn into a double arrow.
    Hold down the primary mouse button

Drag the window border to the right
- Notice the dotted line indicating the new size.

Release the primary mouse button

Move the window:

Point to the **Title bar**

Hold down the primary mouse button

Drag the window to a new location on the desktop
- Notice the dotted window outline indicating the new position.

Release the primary mouse button

Click **Close** button to close Notepad

HOW TO OPEN QUICKBOOKS®

Once you are in Windows 3.1 or Windows 95, opening QuickBooks is as easy as point and click.

Open QuickBooks® in Windows® 3.1

 *DO: Program Manager should be open

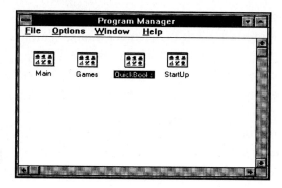

Double-click the **QuickBooks** program group icon
- Note: If you are working in a laboratory environment, the name of the program group icon may be different. Check with your instructor to obtain the name of your program group icon.
- The program group window for QuickBooks is now open.

Double-click the **QuickBooks** program item icon to access the program

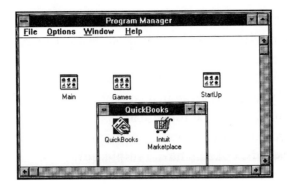

Open QuickBooks® in Windows® 95

*DO: Click **Start**
Point to **Programs**
Point to **QuickBooks**
Click **QuickBooks**

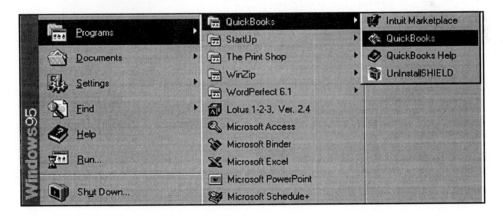

HOW TO OPEN A COMPANY

To explore some of the features of QuickBooks, you will work with the sample company that comes with QuickBooks. The company is Larry's Landscaping and is stored on the hard disk (C:\) inside the computer.

*DO: Click **File**
Click **Open Company**
Check **Drives** at the bottom of the screen

Make sure it indicates **Drive C:**
- If C: is not indicated, click the drop-down list arrow next to Drives, click **C:**

Check **Folders**, which is located above the Drives text box

Make sure Folders indicate: C:\qbooksw
- Note: If you are working in a laboratory environment, the folder names may not be the same as the folder names indicated here. Check with your instructor for specific information on accessing the sample company.

File name text box should have **sample.qbw**

If it is not in the text box:

If it appears beneath the text box, point to **sample.qbw** and click
- This should insert the file name into the text box.

If **sample.qbw** is not in the list beneath the text box, click in the text box and type the name

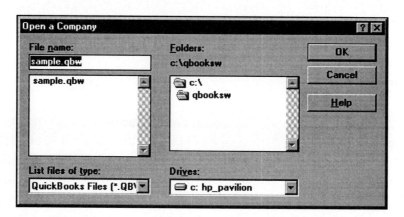

Click **OK** button on the right side of the dialog box

When using the sample company for training, a warning screen will appear. This is to remind you NOT to enter the transactions for your business in the sample company.

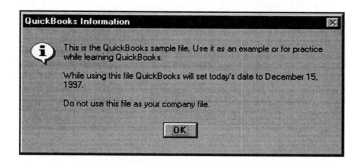

Click **OK** to accept the sample company data for use

- If Inside Tips or Reminders appears, click the **Close** button in the upper right corner of the title bar for Inside Tips or Reminders.

VERIFY AN OPEN COMPANY

It is important to make sure you have opened the data for the correct company. Always verify the company name in the title bar.

 *DO: Check **Title bar** to make sure it includes the company name.
The title bar should show:
> **Larry's Landscaping - QuickBooks**

> Larry's Landscaping - QuickBooks

INTRODUCTION TO QUICKBOOKS® DESKTOP FEATURES

Once the computer has been turned on, Windows has been accessed, and QuickBooks has been started, you will see QuickBooks on the desktop. As with Windows 3.1/95, QuickBooks displays a title bar. If a company is open, the title bar displays the **Company Name - QuickBooks**. The Windows 3.1/95 minimize, maximize, close, and control buttons are available in QuickBooks and appear on the screen. Beneath the title bar is the menu bar. Pointing and clicking on a menu item or using the keyboard shortcut of Alt+the underlined letter in the menu item will give QuickBooks the command to display the drop-down menu. For example, the File menu is used to open and close a company and may also be used to exit QuickBooks.

Below the menu bar is an optional iconbar. This "button" bar has a row of buttons that are labeled with the name of the item to be used. For example, clicking on the Invoice button will bring a blank invoice onto the desktop.

A new addition to QuickBooks® 5.0 is the QuickBooks Navigator. While using QB Navigator is optional, it is a quick and easy way to give commands to QuickBooks based on the type of transactions being entered.

This text will use various methods of giving QuickBooks commands, including use of QuickBooks Navigator, iconbar, menu bar, and keyboard shortcuts.

QUICKBOOKS® NAVIGATOR

QuickBooks Navigator allows you to give commands to QuickBooks according to the type of transaction being entered. QuickBooks Navigator appears in the center of the main QuickBooks window when you open QuickBooks.

 *DO: If not already open, click **OK** button to open QuickBooks Navigator
- Before you will be able to see all of QuickBooks Navigator on the screen, you may have to close a Reminders screen. A Reminders screen appears whenever you open QuickBooks and, as the name indicates, is used to remind you of things that need to be done.

Close the Reminders screen if it appears:

Click the **Control-menu box or icon** located in the upper left corner of the Reminders screen title bar

Click **Close**

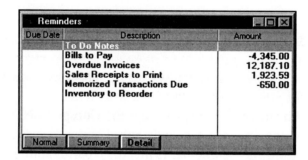

- Once Reminders has been closed, QuickBooks Navigator will fill the screen.

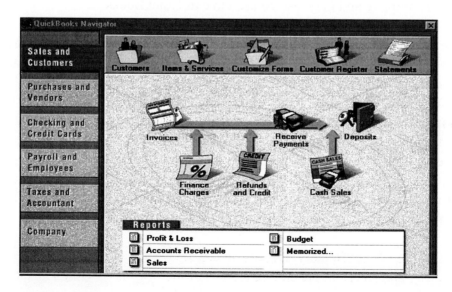

On the left side of the Navigator are six tabs. Each tab represents a different area of the program and different types of transactions.

Sales and Customers tab allows transactions associated with cash sales, credit sales, cash receipts, and bank deposits to be entered. Customer accounts and sales item lists may be accessed and updated. It also provides quick, easy access to reports associated with sales activities.

Purchases and Vendors tab allows you to enter your bills and to record the payment of bills. Vendor accounts and lists may be accessed and updated. Quick, easy access to reports associated with accounts payable activities is provided.

Checking and Credit Cards tab allows you to write checks, transfer money between accounts, use on-line banking, make bank deposits, reconcile the bank statement, and record credit card transactions. The check register may be accessed. Reports associated with the checking account may be generated.

Payroll and Employees tab allows paychecks to be created, payroll tax liabilities to be paid, and Forms 940, 941, and W2 to be printed. Employee information, payroll items, liability adjustments, and tax tables may be accessed. Payroll reports may be prepared.

Taxes and Accountant tab allows a disk to be prepared as an accountant's copy of company data and transactions. Journal entries may also be recorded. The Chart of Accounts may be accessed, and 1099s may be printed. A variety of reports including Profit and Loss, Balance Sheet, Tax Reports, Transaction Detail Reports, Journal, General Ledger, Trial Balance, Income Tax Summary, Income Tax Detail, and an Audit Trail may be prepared.

Company tab allows system preferences to be customized, backup disks to be made, budgets to be established, supplies to be ordered, QuickBooks update service to be accessed, and mail merge to be used. The Company tab also provides company information and information regarding QuickBooks and your industry. Employee information, the Chart of Accounts, To Do's, and Reminders may be accessed and updated. Reports such as Profit and Loss, Balance Sheet, and Budgets may be prepared.

When a tab is highlighted for use, the upper area of QuickBooks Navigator will show icons for lists and occasional activities performed in the area of focus. For example, Sales and Customers tab will show the list icons for Customers and Items & Services. It will also show icons for Customize Forms, Customer Register, and Statements.

The central area of the QuickBooks Navigator screen shows a flow chart with icons indicating the major activities performed in the area of focus. For the Sales and Customers tab, the center area of the screen shows a flow chart with icons indicating Invoices, Finance Charges, Refunds and Credit, Receive Payment, Cash Sales, and Deposits. You'll notice that the icons are arranged in the order in which transactions usually occur. You would not record a refund prior to creating an invoice for a sale, so the icon for invoice appears before the icon for refund and credit.

At the bottom of the QuickBooks Navigator screen is a list of reports that are usually prepared within the area of focus. In Sales and Customers the reports shown are Profit & Loss, Accounts Receivable, Sales, Budget, and Memorized. Each of these report areas will have several report options available. (You may have to turn off the iconbar to see the list of reports available.)

*DO: Click on **Sales and Customers** side tab
- View the lists and occasional activities, flow charts for main activities, and reports available.

Repeat for each of the other side tabs:

Purchases and Vendors, Checking and Credit Cards, Payroll and Employees, Taxes and Accountant, Company

MENU COMMANDS

Menu commands can be the starting point for issuing commands in QuickBooks. The following menus are available for use in QuickBooks® 5.0:

File menu is used to access company files—new company, open company, close company, and company information; begin the EasyStep interview to setup a company; back up and restore company files; make accountant's copy of company files; set system preferences; printer setup and printing; use mail merge; create passwords; import and export information; and convert files from previous accounting software.

Edit menu is used to make changes such as: undo, revert, cut, copy, paste, insert a line, delete a line, edit information, delete information, memorize transactions, void transactions, copy transactions, show lists, change colors, go to Notepad program.

Lists menu is used to show lists used by QuickBooks. These lists include: chart of accounts (also the general ledger), items, payroll items, customers:jobs (also the accounts receivable ledger), vendors (also the accounts payable ledger), employees, memorized transactions, to do notes, and templates.

Activities menu is used to enter transactions via business forms. The types of activities performed include: create invoices, receive payments, make deposits, enter cash sales, create credit memos/refunds, create statements, write checks, transfer money, enter bills, pay bills, enter credit card charges, make journal entries, payroll, reconcile bank statement.

Reports menu is used to prepare reports including: profit and loss (income statement), balance sheet, accounts receivable reports, sales reports, accounts payable reports, budget reports, transaction reports, transaction detail reports, payroll reports, list reports, custom reports, and graphs showing graphical analysis of business operations.

Online menu provides access to on-line services such as on-line banking, QuickBooks update service, and Intuit web sites.

Window menu is used to switch between documents that have been opened, to arrange icons, and to show more than one open window in cascade, vertical, or horizontal arrangements.

Help menu is used to access Help. The Help menu includes topics such as: Help, Ask Intuit: Q and A, How to use Help, Inside Tips, QuickBooks and Your Industry, New Features for QuickBooks 5.0, Hide/Show Qcards, About QuickBooks, About Tax Tables.

 *DO: Click on **Edit** menu
View the commands available
- Many commands will remind you of commands you can make using QuickBooks Navigator.
- Notice that available keyboard shortcuts are listed next to the menu item
Click outside the menu to close

KEYBOARD SHORTCUTS

Frequently, it is faster to use a keyboard shortcut to give QuickBooks a command than it is to point and click the mouse through several layers of menus. The following charts list common keyboard shortcuts available for use in QuickBooks.

GENERAL	KEY
Start QB without a company file	Ctrl+double-click
Suppress desktop windows (at Open Company window)	Alt (while opening)
Display information about QuickBooks	Ctrl+1 (one)
Cancel	Esc
Record (when black border is around OK, Next, or Prev button)	↵ (Press Enter key)
Record (always)	Ctrl+↵

HELP WINDOW	KEY
Display Help in context	F1
Select next option or topic	Tab
Select previous option or topic	Shift+Tab
Display selected topic	↵
Close pop up box	Esc
Close Help window	Alt+F4

DATES	KEY
Next day	+ (plus key)
Previous day	- (minus key)
Today	T
First day of the Week	W
Last day of the weeK	K
First day of the Month	M
Last Day of the montH	H
First day of the Year	Y
Last Day of the yeaR	R

EDITING	KEY
Edit transaction in selected register	Ctrl+E
Delete character to right of insertion point	Del
Delete character to left of insertion point	Backspace
Delete line from invoice in detail area	Ctrl+Del
Insert line in invoice or detail area	Ctrl+Ins
Cut selected characters	Ctrl+X
Copy selected characters	Ctrl+C
Paste cut or copied characters	Ctrl+V
Increase check or other from number by one	+ (plus key)
Decrease check or other form number by one	- (minus key)
Undo changes made in field	Ctrl+Z

MOVING AROUND A WINDOW	KEY
Next field	Tab
Previous field	Shift+Tab
Report column to the right	→ (Right arrow)
Report column to the left	← (Left arrow)
Beginning of current field or report row	Home
End of current field or report row	End
Line below in detail area or on report	Down arrow
Line above in detail area or on report	Up arrow
Down one screen	Page Down
Up one screen	Page Up
Next word in field	Ctrl+→
Previous word in field	Ctrl+←
First item on list or previous month in register	Ctrl Page Up
Last item on list or next month in register	Ctrl Page Down
Close active window	Esc or Alt+F4

ACTIVITY	KEY
Account list, display	Ctrl+A
Check, write	Ctrl+W
Copy transaction in register	Ctrl+O
Customer:Job list, display	Ctrl+J
Delete check, invoice, transaction, or item from list	Ctrl+D
Edit lists or registers	Ctrl+E
QuickFill and Recall (type first few letters of name and press Tab, name fills in)	abcxyz Tab
Find transaction	Ctrl+F
Go to register of transfer account	Ctrl+G
Help in context, display	F1
Hide/Show Qcards	Ctrl+F1
History of A/r or A/P Transaction	Ctrl+H
Invoice, create	Ctrl+I
List (for current field), display	Ctrl+L

Memorize transaction or report	Ctrl+M
Memorized transaction list, display	Ctrl+T
New invoice, bill, check, or list item	Ctrl+N
Paste copied transaction in register	Ctrl+V
Print	Ctrl+P
QuickBooks overview	F2
QuickZoom on report	←
QuickReport on transaction or list item	Ctrl+Q
Register, display	Ctrl+R
Use list item	Ctrl+U
Transaction journal, display	Ctrl+Y

KEYBOARD CONVENTIONS

When using Windows, there are some standard keyboard conventions for the use of certain keys. These keyboard conventions also apply to QuickBooks and include the following.

Alt key is used to access the drop-down menus on the menu bar. Rather than click on a menu item, hold down the Alt key and type the underlined letter in the menu item name. Close the menu by simply pressing the Alt key.

 *DO: Access the File menu: **Alt+F**, view the menu choices, close File menu: **Alt**
Access the Edit menu: **Alt+E**, view the menu choices, close Edit menu: **Alt**
Access the Lists menu: **Alt+L**, view the menu choices, close Lists menu: **Alt**
Access the Activities menu: **Alt+A**, view the menu choices, close Activities menu: **Alt**
Access the Reports menu: **Alt+R**, view the menu choices, close Reports menu: **Alt**
Access the Online menu: **Alt+O**, view the menu choices, close Online menu: **Alt**
Access the Window menu: **Alt+W**, view the menu choices, close Window menu: **Alt**
Access the Help menu: **Alt+H**, view the menu choices, close Help menu: **Alt**

Tab key is used to move to the next field or, if a button is selected, to the next button.

Shift+Tab is used to move back to the previous field.

Esc key is used to cancel an active window without saving anything that has been entered. It is equivalent to clicking the Cancel button.

> ***DO:** Access Activities menu: **Alt+A**, access Create an Invoice: type **I**
> Press **Tab** key to move forward through the invoice
> Press **Shift+Tab** to move back through the invoice
> Press **Esc** to close the Invoice

QUICKBOOKS® ICONBAR

Another way to give commands to QuickBooks is to use the optional iconbar. If activated as a system preference, the iconbar will be placed below the menu bar. The iconbar has a list of buttons that may be clicked in order to access activities, lists, or reports. For example, to see a list of customers and the balances they owe, you click the Cust icon.

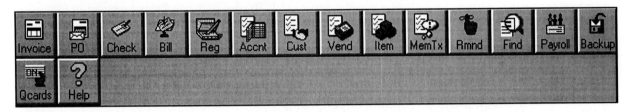

> ***DO:** Access activities using the iconbar:
> If the iconbar is not on the screen:
> Click **File** menu
> Click **Preferences**
> Click Iconbar on the left side of the screen
> • If the Iconbar is not visible, click on Preferences title bar, drag to bring into view.
> Click **Show Icons and Text**
> Click **OK** button
> • Iconbar appears beneath the menu bar. The reports available on QuickBooks Navigator may not be in view when using the iconbar.
> When the iconbar is on the screen, click **Cust** icon
> • You will see a list of customers and the balances they owe.

QUICKBOOKS® QCARDS

Qcards are pop-up screens that give information about items that appear as you work in Quick-Books. For example, the Qcard for the Customer List pops up when you click the Cust icon.

> The Customer:Job list stores information about your customers and the jobs you perform for each customer.
>
> To set up a customer, click the Customer:Job menu button at the bottom of the window and choose New.

*DO: Click the minus sign in the upper left corner of the Qcard to close this Qcard

Because QuickBooks allows you to work with or without Qcards, the Qcard option may be turned on or off. This is known as a toggle command. By default, the Qcard option is ON. One way to turn off the Qcard option is to click the Qcard icon on the iconbar. To turn on the Qcard option, click the Qcard icon again.

*DO: Turn off the Qcard option, click **Qcard** icon
Turn on the Qcard option, click **Qcard** icon
Press **Esc** or click the Close button to close the Customer List

Other methods of turning off Qcards are:

Click File on the menu bar, click Preferences, click General, click Hide Qcards for All Windows, click OK button
Click Company tab on QuickBooks Navigator, click Hide Qcards for All Windows, click OK button
Click Help on the menu bar, click Hide/show Qcards
Ctrl+F1

ON-SCREEN HELP

QuickBooks has on-screen help, which is similar to having the QuickBooks reference manual available on the computer screen. Help can give you assistance with a particular function you are performing. QuickBooks help also gives you information about the program using an on-screen index. Help can even give you instructions on how to use help.

Help may be accessed to obtain information on a variety of topics, and it may be accessed in different ways:

To find out about the window in which you are working, press F1, click Help icon on iconbar, or click Help menu and click Help on the drop-down menu

To obtain answers to commonly asked questions, click Help menu, click Ask Intuit: Q and A

To obtain information and learn how to use QuickBooks for your type of business, click Help menu, click QuickBooks and Your Industry

To learn about the new features available in QuickBooks® 5.0, click Help menu, click New Features for QuickBooks 5.0

Once Help has been opened, you may obtain information regarding any topic. To do this, click Contents at the top of the screen. QuickBooks Help screen appears. There are three tabs at the top of the QuickBooks Help screen.

Contents tab is clicked to access the table of contents for QuickBooks help. Help is divided into main topics with book icons next to the topic name. To find out about subtopics, click the book icon next to the main topic name. When you find the topic you need, double-click it; and you will get a help screen with information regarding that topic.

Index tab will provide an on-screen index. There is a text box where you may type the first few letters of the name of the item with which you need help. As you key in the item name, QuickBooks index displays items alphabetically. When the topic you need appears on the screen, double-click the topic to display it.

Find tab is used to search for every occurrence of a word or a phrase. It is a very thorough search, but it may provide topics that are not as relevant as those that appear in the index.

When the topic for help has been located, information about the topic is provided in the Help window. If there is more information than can be shown on the screen, scroll bars will appear on the right side of the help screen. A scroll bar is used to show or go through information. As you scroll through help, information at the top of the help screen disappears from view while new information appears at the bottom of the screen.

Sometimes words appear in green in the QuickBooks Help screen. Clicking on the green words will take you to other topics. If the word is underlined with a dotted line, clicking on the word will give you a pop-up definition of the word.

If you want to see a different topic, you may click Search at the top of the screen. Search will give you the QuickBooks index and allow you to search for a different topic.

If you want to print a copy of the QuickBooks Help screen, click the Print button at the top of the Help screen. Another way to print the QuickBooks Help screen is to click the File menu at the top of the Help screen then click Print Topic.

You may close a QuickBooks Help screen by clicking the Close button in the upper right corner of the screen, or click the File menu and click Exit.

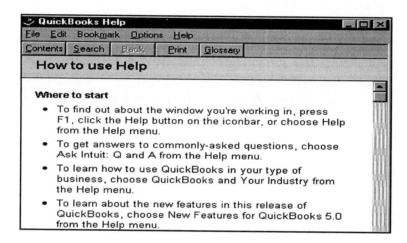

 ***DO:** Click **Help** menu
Click **How To Use Help**
Read the QuickBooks Help screen
Scroll through the Help window to see information that is not displayed
- This may be done in several ways:
  To advance the screen one line at a time, click the down arrow on the scroll bar.
  To go back up one line at a time, click the up arrow on the scroll bar.
  To move through sections of the screen, point to the scroll button, hold down the primary mouse button, and drag the scroll button down a little at a time.
Click **Contents** at the top of the screen

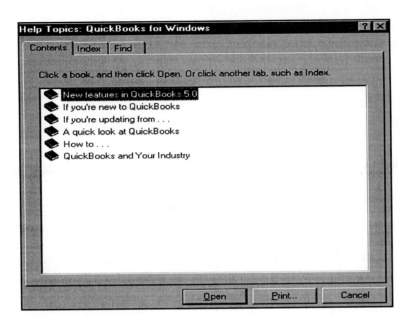

Click **Contents** tab on the QuickBooks Help screen

Click **QuickBooks and Your Industry**

Click **Open**

Click **Consulting**

Click **Display**

Scroll through QuickBooks and Your Industry help screen

Click on the green heading **Understanding Income and Profitability with Reports**

Click **Back** at the top of the screen to go back to the previous help screen

Click **Contents** at the top of the help screen

Click **Index** tab

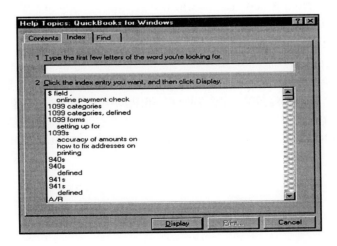

Key in **pr**
Preferences will be highlighted
Click **Display** button
Click the topic **Setting General Preferences**
Click **Display** button
Click the green underlined words **What the desktop options do**
Read the pop-up definitions
Click in the Help window to close the pop-up definitions
Close Help using one of the following methods:
   Alt+F4
   Click **Control-menu Icon**, click **Close**
   Click **File Menu**, click **Exit**
   Click **Close button** in the upper right corner of the screen

QUICKBOOKS® FORMS

The premise of QuickBooks is to allow you to focus on running the business, not deciding whether an account is debited or credited. Transactions are entered directly onto the business form that is prepared as a result of the transaction. For example, a sale on account is recorded by completing the invoice for the sale. Behind the scenes, QuickBooks enters the debit and credit to the Journal and posts to the individual accounts.

QuickBooks has several types of forms used to fill in your daily business transactions. They are divided into two categories: forms you want to send or give to people and forms you have received. Forms to send or give to people include invoices, cash sales receipts, credit memos, checks, deposit slips, and purchase orders. Forms you have received include payments from customers, bills, credits for a bill, and credit card charge receipts.

You may use the forms as they come with QuickBooks, you may change or modify them, or you may create your own custom forms for use in the program.

When preparing a form, you move from one field to the next to enter the information needed. To move from one field to the next, press the tab key or position the mouse pointer within a field and click the primary mouse button. While each form does require different types of information, there are several common features within forms. Examine the invoice that follows.

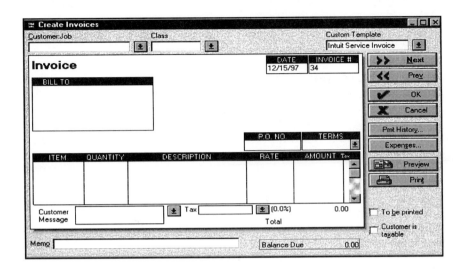

Field is an area on a form requiring information. Customer:Job is a field.

Text box is the area within a field where information may be typed or inserted. The area to be filled in to identify the Customer:Job is a text box.

Drop-down list arrow appears next to a field when there is a list of options available. On the invoice for Larry's Landscaping, clicking on the drop-down list arrow for Customer:Job will display the names of all customers who have accounts with the company. Clicking on a customer name will insert the name into the text box for the field.

Buttons on the right side of the invoice are used to give commands to QuickBooks.

Next button is clicked to go to the next invoice. When the Next button is clicked, the invoice is saved and a blank invoice appears on the screen. This is used when you are entering more than one invoice at a time. Grouping invoices together and entering them all at one time as a "batch" of transactions is an efficient way to work.

Prev button is clicked to go back to the previous invoice. This is used when you want to view, print, or correct the previous invoice. Each time the Prev button is clicked, you go back one invoice. You may click the Prev button until you go all the way back to Invoice 1.

OK button is clicked when all information has been entered for the invoice and you are ready for QuickBooks to save the invoice and exit the Create Invoices screen.

Cancel button is clicked if you want to exit the Create Invoices screen without saving the information entered on the current invoice.

Pmt History... button allows you to view information regarding any payments that have been made on the invoice.

Expenses button shows information regarding reimbursable expenses incurred for this transaction.

Preview button allows you to view a printed copy of the invoice on the screen prior to printing it on paper.

Print button is used to print the invoice on paper.

*DO: Click the **Invoice** button on the iconbar
OR
Use QuickBooks Navigator:
　Click **Sales and Customers** tab
　Click **Invoices**
Locate the invoice features described previously
Click the **Prev** button to view invoices that have been completed
Click the **Cancel** button to close the Create Invoices screen
Look at some of the other forms used in QuickBooks:
　Click **Check** button on the iconbar to view checks, click **Cancel** to exit checks
　Click **Bill** button on the iconbar to view Enter Bills screen, click **Cancel** to exit bills
　Click **Sales and Customers,** click **Cash Sales** in QuickBooks Navigator to view a sales receipt, click **Cancel** to exit sales receipts
　Click **Checking and Credit Cards,** click **Make Deposits** in QuickBooks Navigator to view a deposit slip, click **Cancel** to exit deposit slip

QUICKBOOKS® LISTS

In order to expedite entering transactions, QuickBooks uses lists as an integral part of the program. Customers, vendors, sales items, and accounts are organized as lists. In fact, the chart of accounts is considered to be a list in QuickBooks. Frequently information can be entered on a form by clicking on a list item. For example, a customer name can be entered on an invoice by clicking the drop-down list arrow next to the Customer:Job text box and clicking on the customer name from the Customer:Job list.

Most lists have a maximum of 14,500 items, so there is room to add list items as you work. In fact, QuickBooks allows items to be added to lists "on the fly." This means, if you are preparing an invoice for a new customer, QuickBooks allows you to add the new customer to the

Customer:Job list while you are filling in the Customer:Job text box for the invoice. QuickBooks allows you to do a "Quick Add" to add a customer name or to use "Set Up" to add complete customer information.

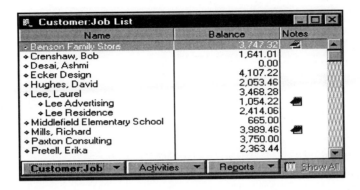

 *DO: Use the iconbar to examine several lists:

    Click **Cust** button to view the Customer:Job list, click **Control-menu box or icon**, click **Close** to exit

    Click **Accnt** button to view the Chart of Accounts, click **Close** button to exit

    Click **Vend** button to view the Vendor list, **Ctrl+F4** to exit

    Click **Item** button to view the Sales Item list, click **Close** button to exit

Use QuickBooks Navigator to examine other lists:

    Click **Payroll and Employees** tab, click **Employees** icon to view a list of employees, **Ctrl+F4** to exit the list

    With Payroll and Employees Navigator screen showing, click **Payroll Items** icon to view payroll items and categories, click **Control-menu icon**, click **Close**

Use Lists Menu to examine lists:

    Click **List** menu, click **Other Names** to see a list including names of owners, partners, and other miscellaneous names and descriptions used in transactions, double-click **Control-menu box or icon** to exit

QUICKBOOKS® REGISTERS

QuickBooks prepares a register for every balance sheet account. An account register contains records of all activity for the account. Registers provide an excellent means of looking at transactions within an account. For example, the Accounts Receivable register maintains a record of every invoice, credit memo, and payment that has been recorded for credit customers.

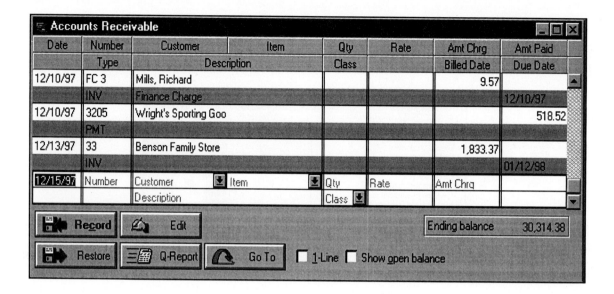

Date	Number	Customer	Item	Qty	Rate	Amt Chrg	Amt Paid
	Type		Description	Class		Billed Date	Due Date
12/10/97	FC 3	Mills, Richard				9.57	
	INV	Finance Charge					12/10/97
12/10/97	3205	Wright's Sporting Goo					518.52
	PMT						
12/13/97	33	Benson Family Store				1,833.37	
	INV						01/12/98
12/15/97	Number	Customer	Item	Qty	Rate	Amt Chrg	
		Description		Class			

Ending balance   30,314.38

Record   Edit   Restore   Q-Report   Go To   ☐ 1-Line ☐ Show open balance

*DO: Click **Accnt** button on iconbar

Click on **Accounts Receivable**

Click **Activities** button at the bottom of the screen

Click **Use Register**

Scroll through the register

Look at the **Number/Type** column

- Notice the types of transactions listed:

    INV is for an invoice.

    PMT indicates a payment received from a customer.

Click **Close** button on the Register to exit

Click **Checking** account in the Chart of Accounts

Click **Activities** button

Click **Use Register**

Scroll through the register

- Notice the types of transactions listed:

    CHK is for a check we wrote

    PAY CHK is a paycheck for an employee

    PMT is a check received for accounts receivable

    BILL PMT records an accounts payable payment

    DEP records a bank deposit

    TRANSFER records a transfer of funds from one account to another

Close the Register using **Ctrl+F4**

Close the Chart of Accounts list using **Ctrl+F4**

QUICKBOOKS® REPORTS

Reports are an integral part of a business. Reports enable owners and managers to determine how the business is doing and to make decisions affecting the future of the company. Reports can be prepared showing the Profit and Loss for the period, the status of the Balance Sheet (assets equal liabilities plus owner's equity), information regarding accounts receivable and accounts payable, and the amount of sales for each item. QuickBooks has a wide range of reports and reporting options available. Reports may be customized to better reflect the information needs of a company. Reports may be generated in a variety of ways.

Reports menu includes a complete listing of the reports available in QuickBooks and is used to prepare reports including: profit and loss (income statement), balance sheet, accounts receivable reports, sales reports, accounts payable reports, budget reports, transaction reports, transaction detail reports, payroll reports, list reports, custom reports, and graphs showing graphical analysis of business operations.

QuickBooks Navigator at the bottom of each Navigator window is a list of reports available for the selected tab. (If the iconbar is on, you may not be able to see this.)

Reports button at the bottom of lists allow reports for specific accounts and list items to be prepared.

 *DO: Prepare reports from the Reports menu:
Click **Reports** menu
Point to **Profit & Loss**, click **Standard**
Scroll the Profit and Loss Statement for Larry's Landscaping
- Notice the Net Income for the period.
Click the **Close** button to exit the report
Prepare reports using the Report button at the bottom of a list:
    Click **Accnt** button on the iconbar
    Checking account will be highlighted
    Click **Report** button at the bottom of the list window
    Point to **Reports on All Accounts**
    Point to **Balance Sheet**
    Click **Standard**
Scroll through the report
- Notice that assets equal liabilities and equity.
Click **Control-menu box or icon**, click **Close** to exit the report
Prepare reports using QuickBooks Navigator
- If necessary, close iconbar, click **Company** tab, click **Preferences**, click **iconbar**, click **Don't show iconbar**.

Click **Sales and Customer** tab
Click **Sales** icon under Report tab
Click **By Item Summary**
Scroll through the report to see the amount generated by each sales item
Ctrl+F4 to exit the report

QUICKZOOM

QuickZoom allows you to view transactions that contribute to the data on reports or graphs. When viewing a report, place the mouse pointer over an amount. The pointer will turn into a magnifying glass with a Z inside. To see detailed information, double-click the mouse. For example, double-clicking on a fixed asset shown on the balance sheet will provide information regarding depreciation and the original cost of the asset.

 *DO: Click **Reports** menu
Click **Balance Sheet**
Click **Standard**
Scroll through the Balance Sheet until you see the fixed asset Truck
Position the mouse pointer over the amount for **Total Truck**
• The mouse pointer turns into a magnifying glass with a Z.
Double-click the mouse to see the transaction detail for the Truck
Click the **Close** button to close the Transaction Detail Report
Click the **Close** button to close the Balance Sheet

QUICKBOOKS® GRAPHS

Using bar charts and pie charts, QuickBooks gives you an instant visual analysis of different elements of your business. You may obtain information in a graphical form for Income & Expenses, Sales, Accounts Receivable, Accounts Payable, Net Worth, and Budget vs. Actual. For example, clicking on the Report menu, pointing to Graphs, and clicking on Net Worth allows you to see an owner's net worth in relationship to assets and liabilities. This is displayed on a bar chart according to the month. To obtain information about liabilities for a given month, you may zoom in on the liabilities portion of the bar, double-click, and see the liabilities for the month displayed in a pie chart.

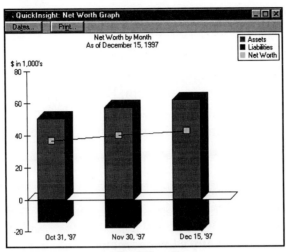

Net Worth

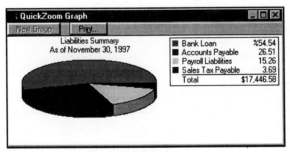

Liabilities

*DO: Click the **Reports** menu

Point to **Graphs**

Click **Net Worth**

Zoom in on the Liabilities for October

Double-click

View the pie chart for October's liabilities

Click the **Close** button to close the pie chart

Zoom in on the Net Worth for December

Double-click

View the pie chart for December's Net Worth Summary

Ctrl+F4 to close the pie chart

Click **Control-menu box or icon**, click **Close** to close the Net Worth graph

QUICKREPORT

QuickReports are reports that give you detailed information about items you are viewing. They look just like standard reports that you prepare but are considered "quick" because you don't have to go through the Reports menu to create them. For example, when you are viewing the employee list, you can obtain information about an individual employee simply by clicking on the employee's name in the list, clicking the Reports button, and selecting QuickReports from the menu.

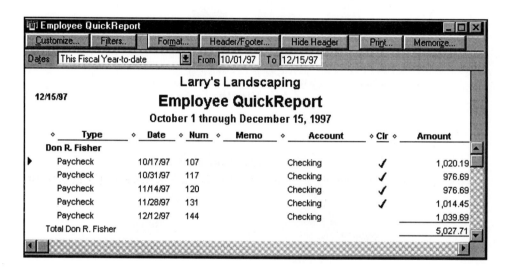

*DO: Click **Lists** menu
Click **Employees**
Click **Jenny Miller**
Click **Reports** button
Click **QuickReport: Jenny Miller**
Click **Control-menu box or icon**, click **Close** to close the QuickReport
Click **Control-menu box or icon**, click **Close** to close the Employee List

HOW TO USE QUICKMATH

QuickMath is available for use whenever you are in a field where a calculation is to be made. Frequently, QuickBooks will make calculations for you automatically; however, there may be instances when you need to perform the calculation. For example, on an invoice, QuickBooks will calculate an amount based on the quantity and the rate given for a sales item. If for some reason you do not have a rate for a sales item, you use QuickMath to calculate the amount. To do this, you tab to the amount column, type an = or a number and the +. QuickBooks will show a calculator tape on the screen. You may then add, subtract, multiply, or divide to obtain a total or a subtotal. Pressing enter ↵ inserts the amount into the column.

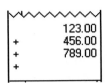

 *DO: Click the **Invoice** button on the iconbar
Click in the **Amount** column on the Invoice
Press the =
Enter the numbers: **123+**
                                    456+
                                    789+

Press **Enter**
The total **1,368** is inserted into the Amount column
Click **Cancel** button on the Invoice to close the invoice without saving

HOW TO USE WINDOWS® CALCULATOR

Windows 3.1 and Windows 95 include accessory programs that may be used when working. One of these accessory programs is Calculator. Using this program gives you an on-screen calculator.

Using Calculator in Windows® 3.1

To use Calculator in Windows 3.1, double-click the Main Program Group icon to open, then double-click Calculator. A calculator appears on your screen.

 *DO: Open Calculator:
Double-click the **Main Program Group** icon to open

Double-click **Calculator**

Change from a standard calculator to a scientific calculator, click **View** menu, click **Scientific**

Change back to a standard calculator, click **View** menu, click **Standard**

Numbers may be entered by:

    Clicking the number on the calculator

    Keying the number using the numeric keypad

    Typing the keyboard numbers.

Enter the numbers: **123+**

                       456+

                       789+

The amount is added after each entry

After typing 789+, the answer 1368 appears automatically

To clear the answer, click the **C** button on the calculator

Enter: **55*6**

Press **Enter** or click = to get the answer

Click **Control-menu box**, click **Close** to close the calculator

Using Calculator in Windows® 95

To use Calculator in Windows 95, click Start, point to Programs, point to Accessories, click Calculator. A calculator appears on your screen.

 *DO: Open Calculator:

    Click **Start**

    Point to **Programs**

    Point to **Accessories**

    Click **Calculator**

Change from a standard calculator to a scientific calculator, click **View** menu, click **Scientific**

Change back to a standard calculator, click **View** menu, click **Standard**

Numbers may be entered by:

    Clicking the number on the calculator

    Keying the number using the numeric keypad

    Typing the keyboard numbers

Enter the numbers: **123+**

                       456+

                       789+

The amount is added after each entry

After typing 789+, the answer 1368 appears automatically

To clear the answer, click the **C** button on the calculator

Enter: **55*6**
Press **Enter** or click **=** to get the answer
Click **Control-menu icon**, click **Close** to close the calculator

ACCESS WINDOWS® CALCULATOR THROUGH QUICKBOOKS®

When you are working in QuickBooks, you may access the Windows calculator by clicking the Activities menu, pointing to Other Activities, and clicking Use Calculator.

 *DO: Access Windows Calculator through QuickBooks
Click **Activities** menu
Point to **Other Activities**
Click **Use Calculator**
Close the calculator using the keyboard shortcut **Alt+F4**

HOW TO CLOSE A COMPANY

The sample company—Larry's Landscaping—will appear as the open company whenever you open QuickBooks. In order to discontinue the use of the sample company, you must Close the Company.

 *DO: Click **File** menu, click **Close Company**

HOW TO COPY A FILE

A data disk containing company files should be kept as a master disk. A master disk is never used, it is set aside in case something happens to the disk you are using to do your work. Work within the text will always be performed on a duplicate copy of the company data.

Windows® 3.1

 *DO: Make a duplicate of Creative Computer Consulting
Check with your instructor to obtain a disk containing the data for Creative
Computer Consulting. Insert this disk in **A:** and a blank, formatted disk
labeled **Creative** in **B:**
Double-click **File Manager** icon
Click the **Drive A** icon
Click **Creative.QBW**

Click **File**
Click **Copy**
In the Copy textbox for **To:** Enter **B:**
- If you have only an A: drive or are copying the company files from the hard disk, see your instructor for directions.

Windows® 95

 *DO: Make a duplicate of Creative Computer Consulting
Check with your instructor to obtain a disk containing the data for Creative Computer Consulting. Insert this disk in **A:** and a blank, formatted disk labeled **Creative** in **B:**
Right-click **Start**
Click **Explore**
Scroll through the **All Folders** side on the left side of the Explorer screen
Click **3½ Floppy (A:)**
On the right side of Explorer right-click **Creative.QBW**
Click **Send To** on the pop-up menu that appears
Click **3½ Floppy (B)**
- If you have only an A: drive or are copying the company files from the hard disk, see your instructor for directions.

HOW TO BACK UP DATA

As you work with a company and record transactions, it is important to back up your work. This allows you to keep the information for a particular period separate from current information. A backup also allows you to restore information in case your data disk becomes damaged. Before entering transactions for Creative Computer Consulting (CCC) in Chapter 2, make a backup of the company data from the Creative disk created above.

 *DO: Insert the **Creative** disk in A:\
Click **File**
Click **Open Company**
Click **Drive drop-down list**
Click **A:**
Click **Creative.qbw** under file name
Click **OK** button

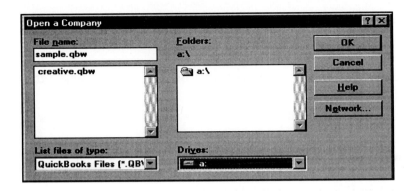

- If the dialog box to open Navigator appears, click **OK** button. Close Reminders if it appears.

Click **File Menu**

Click **Back Up...**

The **Back Up Company To...** dialog box appears

File name for the backup copy of the company files is:

    Creative.qbb

Verify that the drive is A:\

- QuickBooks will back up the information for Creative Computer Consultants on the **Creative** data disk in the A:\ drive
- If you wish to use a separate backup disk, place the backup disk in the B:\ drive. When you see the name Creative.qbb on the Back Up Company To... screen, click drop-down list arrow next to Drives, click B:\. If you have only one disk drive, see your instructor.

Click **OK** button on the **Back Up Company To...** dialog box

- QuickBooks displays a dialog box stating that the backup was successful

Click **OK**

Click **File Menu**

Click **Close Company**

HOW TO EXIT QUICKBOOKS®

When you complete your work, you need to exit the QuickBooks program. If you are saving work on a separate data disk (in A:\), you must not remove your disk until you exit the program. Following the appropriate steps to close and exit a program is extremely important. There are program and data files that must be closed in order to leave the program and company data so that they are ready to be used again. It is common for a beginning computer user to turn off the computer without exiting a program. This can cause corrupt program and data files and can make a disk or program unusable. Always close the company as you did on page 1-44 before exiting QuickBooks.

*DO: There are several ways to exit QuickBooks properly. Select the method of choice and close/exit QuickBooks:

Click **Control-menu box or icon** in the upper left corner of title bar, click **Close**

Double-click **Control-menu box or icon** in the upper left corner of title bar

Click **Close** button in upper right corner of title bar

Click **File** menu (or **Alt+F**), click **Exit** (or type **X**)

Alt+F4

HOW TO CLOSE OR SHUT DOWN WINDOWS®

When you have exited your application program and are ready to close Windows, you need to follow proper exit/closing procedures. Simply turning off the machine is *not* the method to follow when exiting Windows. This might corrupt files that are needed to make the program work properly. When you close or shut down, Windows must close certain files and write information to disk so it will be ready for use the next time the computer is needed. Always be sure to follow the appropriate steps for closing/shutting down Windows.

Closing Windows® 3.1

*DO: There are several ways to close Windows. Select the method of choice and close/exit Windows:

Click **Control-menu box** in the upper left corner of title bar, click **Close**

Double-click **Control-menu box** in the upper left corner of title bar

Click **File** menu (or **Alt+F**), click **Exit** (or type **X**)

Alt+F4

Remove the disk from drive A:

Shut Down Windows® 95

*DO: Click **Start**

Click **Shut Down**

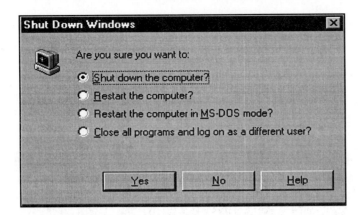

Select **Shut down the computer?**
• Unless you are instructed to follow a different procedure by your instructor.
Click **Yes** button
When the message **"It is now safe to turn off your computer"** appears, turn off
the computer and the monitor
Remove the disk from drive A:

SUMMARY

Chapter 1 provides general information regarding Windows 3.1, Windows 95, and QuickBooks.
In this chapter the mouse was used, the computer was turned on, different menus were accessed,
a company was opened and closed, reports were examined, and a backup was made.

END-OF-CHAPTER QUESTIONS

TRUE/FALSE

ANSWER THE FOLLOWING QUESTIONS IN THE SPACE PROVIDED BEFORE THE QUESTION NUMBER.

_____ 1. There are various methods of giving QuickBooks commands, including use of QuickBooks Navigator, iconbar, menu bar, and keyboard shortcuts.

_____ 2. In QuickBooks the Window menu is used to switch between documents that have been opened, to arrange icons, and to show more than one open window.

_____ 3. RAM storage is measured in bytes.

_____ 4. The mouse is the most frequently used input device.

_____ 5. In a computerized accounting system, each transaction that is analyzed must be entered by hand into the appropriate journal and posted to the appropriate ledger.

_____ 6. QuickBooks Navigator appears beneath the title bar and has a list of drop-down menus.

_____ 7. Windows borders are the borders around the outside of buttons.

_____ 8. The Alt key + a letter are used to access the drop-down menus on the menu bar.

_____ 9. When you have exited your application programs and are ready to close Windows, you need to follow proper exit/closing procedures.

_____ 10. Customers, vendors, sales items, and accounts may be added only after the end of the period has been closed.

MULTIPLE CHOICE

WRITE THE LETTER OF THE CORRECT ANSWER IN THE SPACE PROVIDED BEFORE THE QUESTION NUMBER.

_____ 1. QuickBooks gives you an instant visual analysis of different elements of your business using ___.
  A. line graphs
  B. pie charts
  C. bar charts
  D. both B and C

_____ 2. QuickMath displays ___.
  A. a calculator
  B. adding machine tape
  C. a calculator with adding machine tape
  D. none of the above

_____ 3. QuickBooks keyboard conventions ___.
  A. are keyboard command shortcuts
  B. use the mouse
  C. use certain keys in a manner consistent with Windows
  D. incorporate the use of QuickBooks Navigator

_____ 4. Buttons on the right side of an invoice are used to ___.
  A. give commands to QuickBooks
  B. exit QuickBooks
  C. prepare reports
  D. show graphs of invoices prepared

_____ 5. The Help Index tab provides ___.
  A. step-by-step instructions for using Help
  B. an on-screen index used for finding Help topics
  C. a search of all occurrences of a word or a phrase
  D. all of the above

_____ 6. QuickBooks iconbar ___.
  A. is optional
  B. must be used in conjunction with QuickBooks Navigator
  C. appears above the menu bar
  D. appears at the bottom of the screen

_____ 7. An icon is ___.
   A. a document
   B. a picture
   C. a chart
   D. a type of software

_____ 8. The QuickBooks program is a type of ___ software.
   A. operating system
   B. forecasting
   C. application
   D. word processing

_____ 9. There are ___ side tabs in QuickBooks Navigator.
   A. 5
   B. 7
   C. 6
   D. 4

_____ 10. To verify the name of the open company, look at ___.
   A. the iconbar
   B. QuickBooks Navigator
   C. the menu bar
   D. the title bar

FILL-IN

IN THE SPACE PROVIDED, WRITE THE ANSWER THAT MOST APPROPRIATELY COMPLETES THE SENTENCE.

1. The most common input devices are_____, _____, and _____.

2. The information processing cycle comprises _____, _____, _____, and _____.

3. Two types of software used are _____ software and _____ software.

4. In Windows 3.1 or Windows 95 a window can be resized by clicking on the _____, _____, or _____ buttons in the upper right corner of the title bar.

5. Most lists used in QuickBooks have a maximum of _____ items.

SHORT ESSAY

Describe the term "on the fly" and tell how it is used in QuickBooks.

_____

_____

_____

_____

_____

END-OF-CHAPTER ASSIGNMENTS

ASSIGNMENT 1

Complete the Windows 3.1 or the Windows 95 tutorial.

Complete the Windows® 3.1 Tutorial

　　　*DO: Open Windows 3.1 as instructed in the chapter
　　　　　Click **Help** on the **Program Manager** menu bar
　　　　　Click **Windows Tutorial**
　　　　　Complete the Lesson on Using a Mouse:
　　　　　　　Type **M**
　　　　　　　Read the screen, press **Enter** key ↵
　　　　　　　Type **R** if you will be holding the mouse with the right hand
　　　　　　　Type **L** if you will be holding the mouse with the left hand
　　　　　Continue the Lesson:
　　　　　　　Read the screen
　　　　　　　Do what the tutorial says
　　　　　　　Press keys indicated
　　　　　Continue with the Windows Basic Lesson when you complete the practice with
　　　　　　　the mouse:
　　　　　　　Click **Instructions** button, read the screen with instructions
　　　　　　　Click **Continue** button
　　　　　Continue the Lesson:
　　　　　　　Read the screen
　　　　　　　Do what the tutorial says
　　　　　　　Press keys indicated
　　　　　Continue with the next assignment

If you are finished working for the day and plan to complete the next assignment during your next training session, do the following:

> **Ctrl +F4** to close Help
> Click **Control-menu box** to close Windows
> Unless you have other instructions, turn off your monitor and your computer

Complete the Windows® 95 Tutorial

 *DO: Click **Start** button
Click **Help**
Click **Contents** tab
Click **Tour: 10 Minutes to Using Windows**
- You may not have the Tour available on your computer. If it is not available, skip this section and continue with "If you've used Windows before" below.

Click **Display**
Take the tour and complete all the items:
> Starting a Program
> Exploring your Disk
> Finding a File
> Switching Windows
> Using Help

- When you are taking the tour, if you are not sure what to do, click the **Show Me** button.

When you complete the Tour or if you do not have the tour available, click on the **Window's Help Topics** and display **"If you've used Windows before"**
Open and read each of the following topics and their subtopics:
> Introducing Windows
> How to
> Tips and Tricks
> Trouble Shooting

Click **Exit**
Continue with Assignment 2
- If you are finished working for the day and plan to complete the next assignment during your next training session, do the following:
  > Click **Start**
  > Click **Shut Down**
  > Click on **Shut down the computer?** to select
  - If your instructor has provided different instructions, follow those instructions.
  > Click **Yes**

Turn off the computer and monitor when windows displays **It's now safe to turn off your computer.**

ASSIGNMENT 2

Complete the QuickBooks Tutorial.

 *DO: Open QuickBooks as you were instructed in Chapter 1
Click **Help** on the menu bar
Click **How to Use Help**
Click the **Contents** button at the top of the screen
Click **Contents** tab, click **A Quick Look at QuickBooks**
Click Open, click **Sales**
Click **Display** button
Click on each of the business forms shown
Read the information provided on the pop-up screen
Click the pop-up screen to close the screen
Click **Contents** at the top of the Help screen
Repeat the above procedures for each of the remaining items:
    Bills and Expenses
    Sales Tax
    Inventory
    Payroll Setup
    Pay Checks and Payroll Taxes
Obtain information about a specific industry, click **Contents** at the top of the Help screen, click **QuickBooks and Your Industry**
Click on any industry of interest
Click the **Close** button to exit Help
Exit QuickBooks and Windows as instructed in Chapter 1

SALES AND RECEIVABLES: SERVICE BUSINESS

LEARNING OBJECTIVES

At the completion of this chapter, you will be able to use QuickBooks to:

1. Create invoices and record sales transactions on account.
2. Create sales receipts to record cash sales.
3. Edit, void, and delete invoices/sales receipts.
4. Create credit memos/refunds.
5. Add new customers and modify customer records.
6. Record cash receipts.
7. Enter partial cash payments.
8. Display and print invoices, sales receipts, and credit memos.
9. Display and print Quick Reports, Customer Balance Summary Reports, Customer Balance Detail Reports, and Transaction Reports by Customer.
10. Display and print Summary Sales by Item Reports and Itemized Sales by Item Reports.
11. Display and print Deposit Summary, Journal Reports, and Trial Balance.
12. Display and print Accounts Receivable Graphs and Sales Graphs.

ACCOUNTING FOR SALES AND RECEIVABLES

Rather than use a traditional Sales Journal to record transactions using debits and credits and special columns, QuickBooks uses an invoice to record sales transactions for accounts receivable in the Accounts Receivable Register. Because cash sales do not involve accounts receivable, QuickBooks puts the money from a cash sale into the Undeposited Funds Register until you record a deposit to a bank account. Instead of being recorded within special journals, cash receipt transactions are entered as activities. However, all transactions regardless of the activity are placed in the general journal behind the scenes. A new customer can be added "on the fly" as transactions are entered. Unlike many computerized accounting programs, in QuickBooks error correction is easy. A sales form may be edited, voided, or deleted in the same window where it was created. Customer information may be changed by editing the Customer list. A multitude of reports are available when using QuickBooks. Accounts receivable reports include Customer Balance Summary or Balance Detail reports. Sales reports provide information regarding the amount of sales by item. Transaction Reports by Customer are available as well as the traditional accounting reports such as Trial Balance, Profit and Loss, and Balance Sheet. QuickBooks also has graphing capabilities so you can see and evaluate your accounts receivable and sales at the click of a button.

TRAINING TUTORIAL

The following tutorial is a step-by-step guide to recording receivables (both cash and credit) and cash receipts for a fictitious company with fictitious employees. This company is called Creative Computer Consulting (CCC) and is sometimes referred to as "CCC." In addition to recording transactions using QuickBooks, we will prepare several reports and graphs for CCC. The tutorial for Creative Computer Consulting will continue in Chapters 3 and 4, when accounting for payables, bank reconciliations, financial statement preparation, and closing an accounting period will be completed.

TRAINING PROCEDURES

To maximize the training benefits, you should:

1. Read the entire chapter *before* beginning the tutorial within the chapter.
2. Answer the end-of-chapter questions.
3. Be aware that transactions to be entered are given within a **MEMO**.
4. Complete all the steps listed for the Creative Computer Consulting tutorial in the chapter. (Indicated by: ▨ ***DO:**)
5. When you have completed a section, put an **X** on the button next to ***DO:**.
6. As you complete your work, proofread carefully and check for accuracy. Double-check amounts of money.
7. If you find an error while preparing a transaction, correct it. If you find the error after the invoice, sales form, credit memo, or customer list is complete, follow the steps indicated in this chapter to correct, void, or delete transactions.
8. Print as directed within the chapter.
9. You may not finish the entire chapter in one computer session. Always back up your work at the end of your work session as described in Chapter 1.
10. When you complete your computer session, always close your company. If you try to use a computer for CCC and a previous student did not close the company, QuickBooks may freeze when you put in your disk. If you close the company as you leave, QuickBooks will allow other students to work with CCC.

COMPANY PROFILE: CREATIVE COMPUTER CONSULTING (CCC)

As the name indicates, Creative Computer Consulting (CCC) is a company specializing in computer consulting. CCC provides program installation, training, and technical support for today's business software as well as getting clients "on-line" and giving instruction in Web browsing. In addition, Creative Computer Consultants will set up computer systems for customers and will install basic computer components, such as memory, modems, sound cards, disk drives, and CD-ROM drives.

Creative Computer Consulting is located in Southern California and is a sole proprietorship owned by Roger Owens. Mr. Owens is involved in all aspects of the business and has the responsibility of obtaining clients. CCC has three employees: Carolyn Masters, who is responsible for software training; Samuel Yee, who handles hardware installation and technical support; and Carmen Mendoza, whose duties include being office manager and bookkeeper and providing technical support.

CCC bills by the hour for training and hardware installation with a minimum charge of $95 for the first hour and $80 per hour thereafter. Clients with contracts for technical support are charged a monthly rate for service.

BEGIN TRAINING IN QUICKBOOKS®

As you continue this chapter, you will be instructed to enter transactions for Creative Computer Consulting. The first thing you must do in order to work is "boot up" or start your computer.

 *DO: Turn on computer and monitor, if not already on

OPEN WINDOWS®

Open Windows® 3.1

If you do not have a menu system or automatic batch file to start Windows, do the following:

 *DO: At the **C:** prompt, type **WIN** or **win**
Your screen will show: **C:\>WIN** or **C:\win>**
Press **Enter** key
- If you are working in a laboratory environment, the steps you follow to start the computer and access Windows 3.1 may be different. See your instructor for directions.

Windows will begin running and **Program Manager** will show on the desktop (screen).

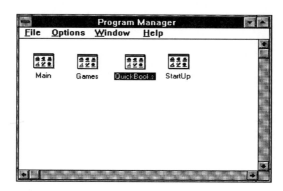

Open Windows® 95

Rather than display a C: \> prompt, Windows 95 will automatically be in use and icons will be visible on the desktop when you turn on the computer. (Some computer laboratories require the use of passwords in order to access Windows 95 and the various application programs available. Check with your instructor regarding the configuration of your classroom computers.)

 *DO: When you turn on the computer, Windows 95 will begin running and the desktop will be displayed on the screen
- You should see the Taskbar at the bottom of the screen and several icons on the desktop.
- If you are working in a laboratory environment, the steps you follow to start the computer and access Windows 95 may be different from those discussed in the test. See your instructor for directions.

HOW TO OPEN QUICKBOOKS®

As you learned in Chapter 1, once you are in Windows 3.1 or Windows 95, opening QuickBooks is as easy as pointing and clicking.

Open QuickBooks® in Windows® 3.1

 *DO: Program Manager should be open
Insert **Creative Data Disk in A:**

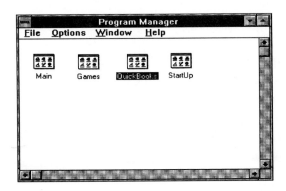

Double-click the **QuickBooks** program group icon

- Note: If you are working in a laboratory environment, the name of the program group icon may be different. Check with your instructor to obtain the name of your program group icon.
- The program group window for QuickBooks is now open.

Double-click the **QuickBooks** program item icon to access the program

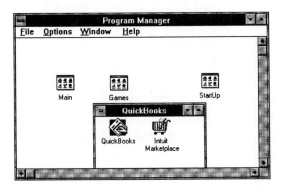

- **Note:** Refer to Chapter 1 if you require more detailed instructions.

Open Quickbooks® for Windows® 95

 *DO: Insert **Creative Data Disk in A:**
Click **Start**
Point to **Programs**
Point to **QuickBooks**
Click **QuickBooks**
- **Note:** Refer to Chapter 1 if you require more detailed instructions.

OPEN A COMPANY—CREATIVE COMPUTER CONSULTING (CCC)

In Chapter 1 Creative Computer Consulting (CCC) was opened and a backup of the company files was made. CCC should have been closed in Chapter 1. Open the company for this work session by clicking on File menu and Open Company. Verify this by checking the title bar.

 *DO: Open **Creative Computer Consulting**
Click **File**
Click **Open Company**

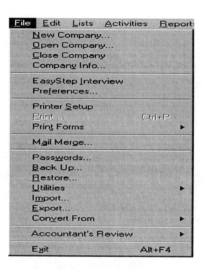

Click the arrow for drop-down list box for **Drives**
Click **A:**
Locate **Creative.qbw** (Under the File Name Text Box)
Double-click **Creative.qbw** to open

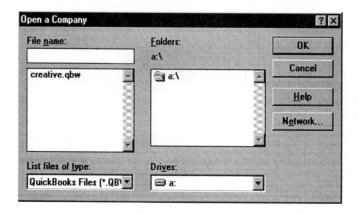

VERIFYING AN OPEN COMPANY

 *DO: Verify the title bar heading:

- **Note:** Unless you unless you tell QuickBooks to create a new company, open a different company, or close the company, Creative Computer Consulting (CCC) will appear as the open company whenever you open QuickBooks.
- If you do not close the company at the end of your computer session and another student tries to work for CCC using the Creative disk he or she created in Chapter 1, QuickBooks may freeze.
- Always close your company at the end of the work session.

ADD YOUR NAME TO THE COMPANY NAME

Because each student in the course will be working for the same companies and printing the same documents, personalizing the company name to include your name will help identify many of the documents you print during your training.

 *DO: Add your name to the company name
Click **File** menu
    OR
Click **Company** tab on QuickBooks Navigator
Click **Company Info**
Click to the right of **Creative Computer Consulting (CCC)**
Type **--Your Name**
- Type your real name, *not* the words Your Name. For example, Raul Reynolds would type **--Raul Reynolds**.
Click **OK**
- The title bar now shows Creative Computing Consultants (CCC)--Your Name.

Creative Computer Consulting (CCC)--Student's Name - QuickBooks

QUICKBOOKS® NAVIGATOR

QuickBooks Navigator is a graphic screen you may use to enter information/transactions in QuickBooks. You may also choose to use the menu bar, the iconbar , or the keyboard to give commands to QuickBooks. When you first open QuickBooks, you may see a message box for "Opening QuickBooks Navigator." For more detailed information regarding QuickBooks Navigator, refer to Chapter 1. Instructions in this text will be given for the Navigator and the menu bar, iconbar, and/or keyboard methods.

   *DO: To use the Navigator, click **OK** button on the message box

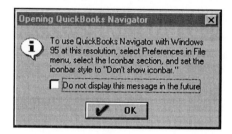

- If you did not want to see this dialog box each time you open QuickBooks, you would click **Do not display this message in the future.** (Do not do this.)

QUICKBOOKS® INSIDE TIPS

The QuickBooks Inside Tips screen, which contains helpful hints about QuickBooks, may appear on the screen whenever you begin QuickBooks. To turn off this feature, click the box next to **"Show Tips When QuickBooks Starts Up."** To access Inside Tips at another time, click **Help** then click **Inside Tips**.

   *DO: You will be working without Inside Tips when you begin QuickBooks. If there is a check mark in the check box next to **"Show Tips When QuickBooks Starts Up,"** click the check box to remove it.

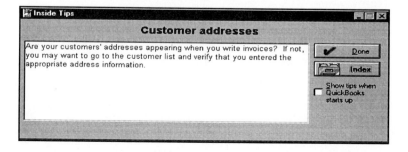

QCARDS

QuickBooks has built-in pop-up screens that give information about fields as you move the mouse pointer around in each window or work within a business document. The first Qcard pops up when the Reminders screen is open.

 *DO: Click the minus sign in the upper left corner of the Qcard to turn it off.

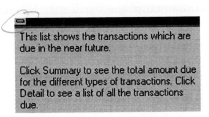

You may also choose to work without using the Qcard option. If you wish to do this, click the Qcard icon on the iconbar to turn off the Qcard.

CLOSING THE REMINDERS SCREEN

The Reminders screen is on by default when you open QuickBooks. This screen reminds you of things that need to be done. These items include checks to print, invoices to print, overdue invoices, sales receipts to print, bills to pay and money to deposit. Once you have seen the Reminders screen, you may close it.

 *DO: If it is showing, close **Reminders** by clicking the close button in the upper right corner of the **Reminders** screen.

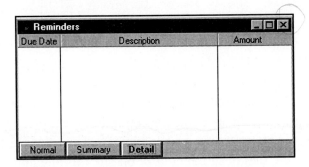

BEGINNING THE TUTORIAL

In this chapter you will be entering both accounts receivable transactions and cash sales trans-actions. Much of the organization of QuickBooks is dependent upon lists. The two primary types of lists you will use in the tutorial for receivables are a Customer:Job list and a Sales Item list.

The names, addresses, telephone numbers, credit terms, credit limits, and balances for all established credit customers are contained in the Customer:Job list. The Customer:Job list can also be referred to as the Accounts Receivable ledger. QuickBooks does not use this term; however, the Customer:Job list does function as the Accounts Receivable ledger. A transaction entry for an individual customer is posted to the customer's account in the Customer:Job list just as it would be posted to the customer's individual account in an Accounts Receivable ledger. The balance of the Customer:Job list will be equal to the balance of the Accounts Receivable account in the Chart of Accounts, which is also the General Ledger. Invoices and accounts receivable transactions can also be related to specific jobs you are completing for customers. You will be using the following Customer:Job list for established credit customers.

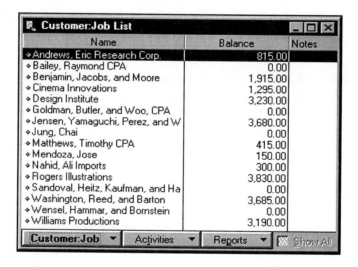

Various types of income are considered to be sales. In CCC there are several income accounts. In addition, there are categories within an income account. For example, CCC uses Training Income to represent revenues earned by providing on-site training. The sales items used for Training Income are Training 1 for the first or initial hour of on-site training and Training 2 for all additional hours of on-site training. As you look at the Item list, you will observe that the rates for both items are different. Using lists for sales items allows for flexibility in billing and a more accurate representation of the way in which income is earned. The following Item list for the various types of sales will be used for CCC.

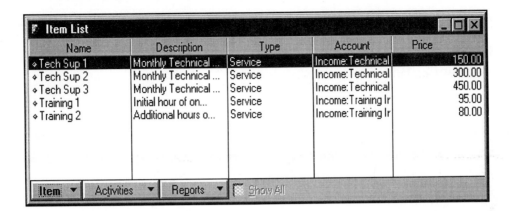

In the tutorial all transactions are listed on memos. The transaction date will be the same date as the memo date unless otherwise specified within the transaction. Customer names, when necessary, will be given in the transaction. All terms for customers on account are Net 30 days unless specified otherwise. If a memo contains more than one transaction, there will be a horizontal line separating the transactions.

MEMO

DATE: The transaction date is listed here

Transaction details are given in the body of the memo. Customer names, the type of transaction, amounts of money, and any other details needed are listed here.

Even when you are instructed how to enter a transaction step by step, you should always refer to the memo for transaction details. Once a specific type of transaction has been entered in a step-by-step manner, additional transactions will be made without having instructions provided. Of course, you may always refer to instructions given for previous transactions for ideas or for steps used to enter those transactions.

ENTER SALES ON ACCOUNT

Because QuickBooks operates on a business form premise, a sale on account is entered via an invoice. You prepare an invoice, and QuickBooks records the transaction in the Journal and updates the customer's account automatically.

MEMO

DATE: January 2, 1998

Bill the following: <u>Invoice 1</u>—Jose Mendoza has had several questions regarding his new computer system. He spoke with Roger Owens about this and has signed up for 10 hours of technical support (Tech Sup 2) for January. Bill him for this and use "Thank you for your business." as the message.

*DO: Record the sale on account shown in the invoice above. This invoice is used to bill a customer for a sale using one sales item:
Click **Invoice** button on the iconbar
    OR
Use **QuickBooks Navigator**:
    Click **Sales and Customers** tab
    Click **Invoice** icon

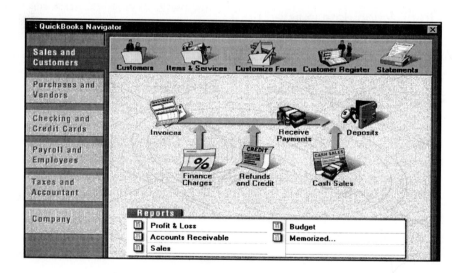

- A blank invoice will show on the screen.

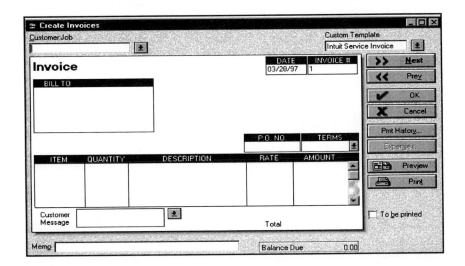

Click the drop-down list arrow next to **Customer:Job**

Click **Mendoza, Jose**

- Name is entered as Customer:Job and Bill To: information is completed automatically.

Tab to **Custom Template**

- Intuit Service Invoice should be showing. If it is not, click the drop-down arrow beneath Custom Template, click **Intuit Service Invoice**.

Tab to **Date**

- When you tab to the date, it will be highlighted. When you type in the new date, the highlighted date will be deleted.

Type **01/02/98** as the date

Invoice No. 1 should be showing in the **Invoice No.** box

- The Invoice No. should not have to be changed.

There is no PO No. to record

Terms should be indicated as **Net 30**

- If not, click the drop-down list arrow next to **Terms** and click **Net 30**.

Tab to or click the first line beneath **Item**

Click the drop-down list arrow next to **Item**

- Refer to the memo above and the Item List for appropriate billing information.

Click **Tech Sup 2** to bill for 10 hours of technical support

- Tech Sup 2 is entered as the Item.

Tab to or click **Qty**

Type **1**

- The quantity is one because you are billing for 1 unit of Tech Sup 2. As you can see on the Item List, Tech Sup 2 is for 10 hours of support. The total for the item and for the invoice is automatically calculated when you tab to the next item or click in a new invoice area.

Click in box for **Customer Message**
Click the drop-down list arrow next to **Customer Message**
Click **Thank you for your business.**
- Message is inserted in the Customer Message box.

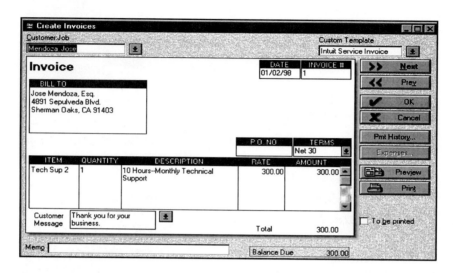

EDIT AND CORRECT ERRORS

If an error is discovered while entering invoice information, it may be corrected by positioning the cursor in the field containing the error. You may do this by tabbing to move forward through each field or pressing Shift+Tab to move back to the field containing the error. If the error is highlighted, type the correction. If the error is not highlighted, you can correct the error by pressing the backspace or the delete key as many times as necessary to remove the error, then typing the correction. (Alternate method: Point to error, highlight by dragging the mouse through the error, then type the correction.)

     *DO: Practice editing and making corrections to Invoice 1:
Click the drop-down list arrow next to **Customer:Job**
Click Matthews, Timothy CPA
- Name is changed in Customer:Job and Bill To: information is also changed.
Click to the left of the first number in the **Date**—this is **0**
Hold down primary mouse button and drag through the date to highlight.
Type **10/24/99** as the date
- This removes the 01/02/98 date originally entered.
Click to the right of the **1** in **Quantity**
Backspace and type a **2**

To eliminate the changes made to Invoice 1, click the drop-down list arrow next
    to **Customer:Job**
Click **Mendoza, Jose**
Click the cursor so it is in front of the **1** in the **Date**
Press the Delete key until the date is removed
Type **01/02/98**
Click to the right of the **2** in **Quantity**
Backspace and type a **1**
Press Tab key
- This will cause QuickBooks to calculate the amount and the total for the
  invoice and will move the cursor to the Description field.
- Invoice 1 has been returned to the correct customer, date, and quantity.
  Compare the information you entered with the information provided in the
  memo.

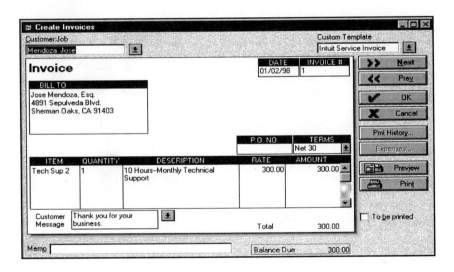

PRINT AN INVOICE

*DO: With Invoice 1 on the screen, print the invoice immediately after entering
    information
Click **Print** button on the **Create Invoices** screen
Check the information on the **"Print One Invoice" Settings** tab:
    Printer Name: (Should identify the type of printer you are using)
    - This may be different from the printer identified in this text.
    Printer Type: Page-oriented (Single sheet)
    Print On: Blank Paper

- The circle next to this should be filled. If it is not, click the circle to select.

Print Lines Around Each Field check box:

- Should be empty. If it is not, click the box to deselect.
- If there is a check in the box, lines will print around each field.
- If a check is not in the box, lines will not print around each field.

Number of Copies should be 1

- If a number other than 1 shows:

  Click in the box

  Drag to highlight the number

  Type **1**

Click **Print** button

- This initiates the printing of the invoice through QuickBooks. However, because all classroom configurations are not the same, check with your instructor for specific printing instructions.

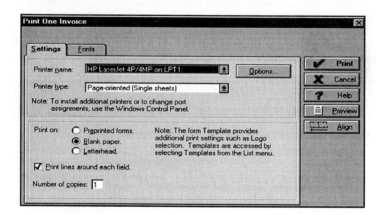

While the invoice is printing, a dialog box "Did form(s) print OK?" will appear
When the form has been correctly printed, click **OK** button on the dialog box

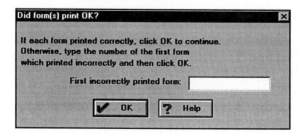

Click **OK** button on the right side of the **Create Invoices** screen to record and close the invoice

ENTER TRANSACTIONS USING TWO SALES ITEMS

MEMO:

Date: January 3, 1998

Bill the following: Invoice 2—Timothy Matthews, CPA, spoke with Roger Owens regarding the need for on-site training to help him get started using the Internet. Bill him for a 5-hour on-site training session with Carolyn Masters. Use "Thank you for your business." as the message. (Remember to use Training 1 for the first hour of on-site training and Training 2 for all additional hours of training.)

*DO: Record a transaction on account for a sale involving two sales items:
Click **Invoice** button on the iconbar
   OR
Use **QuickBooks Navigator**:
   Click **Sales and Customers** tab
   Click **Invoice** icon
Click the drop-down list arrow next to **Customer:Job**
Click **Matthews, Timothy, CPA**
• Name is entered as Customer:Job. Bill To: information is completed automatically.
Tab to or click **Date**
Delete the current date
• Refer to instructions for Invoice 1 or to editing practice if necessary.
Type **01/03/98** as the date
Make sure that Invoice No. 2 is showing in the **Invoice No.** box
• The Invoice No. should not have to be changed.
There is no PO No. to record
Terms should be indicated as **Net 30**
Tab to or click the first line beneath **Item**
• Refer to memo and Item list for appropriate billing information.
Click the drop-down list arrow next to **Item**
Click **Training 1**
• Training 1 is entered as the Item.
Tab to or click **Quantity**
Type **1**
• Total is automatically calculated when you go to the next line. Notice the amount is $95.00.

Tab to or click the second line for **Item**
Click the drop-down list arrow next to **Item**
Click **Training 2**
Tab to or click **Quantity**
Type **4**
- The total amount of training time is five hours. Because the first hour is billed as Training 1, the remaining four hours are billed as Training 2 hours. The total amount due for the Training 2 hours and the total for the invoice are automatically calculated when you go to Customer Message box.

Click **Customer Message**
Click the drop-down list arrow next to **Customer Message**
Click **Thank you for your business.**
- Message is inserted in the Customer Message box.

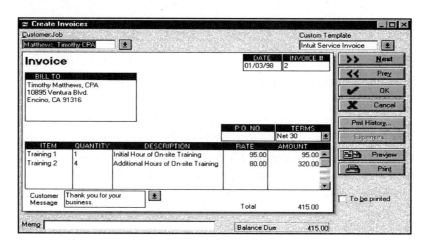

PRINT AN INVOICE

*DO: With Invoice No. 2 on the screen, print the invoice immediately after entering invoice information
Click **Print** button on the **Create Invoices** screen
Check the information on the **"Print One Invoice" Settings** tab:
Printer Name: (Should identify the type of printer you are using)
- This may be different from the printer identified in this text.

Printer Type: Page-oriented (Single sheet)
Print On: Blank Paper
- The circle next to this should be filled. If it is not, click the circle to select.

Print Lines Around Each Field check box:
- Should be empty. If it is not, click the box to deselect.

Click **Print** button
- This initiates the printing of the invoice through QuickBooks. However, because all classroom configurations are not the same, check with your instructor for specific printing instructions.

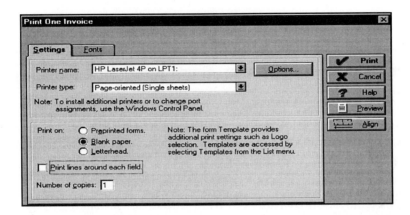

While the invoice is printing, a dialog box "Did form(s) print OK?" will appear
When the form has been correctly printed, click **OK** button on the dialog box

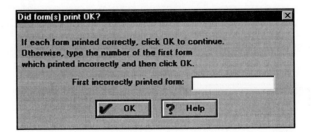

Click **OK** button on the right side of the **Create Invoices** screen to record and close the invoice.

PREPARE INVOICES WITHOUT STEP-BY-STEP INSTRUCTIONS

MEMO
DATE: January 5, 1998

Bill the following: <u>Invoice 3</u>—Chai Jung needed to have telephone assistance to help her set up her Internet connection. Prepare a bill for 10 hours of technical support for January. (Remember customers are listed by last name in the Customer List. Refer to Items list to select the correct income account for billing.)

<u>Invoice 4</u>—Sandoval, Heitz, Kaufman, and Hardin have several new employees that need to be trained in the use of the office computer system. Bill them for 40 hours of on-site training from Carolyn Masters.

<u>Invoice 5</u>—Goldman, Butler, and Woo, CPA, need to learn the basic features of QuickBooks, which is used by many of their customers. Bill them for 10 hours of on-site training provided by Carolyn Masters and 15 hours of technical support for January so they may call and speak to Samuel Yee regarding additional questions. (Note: You will have three sales items in this transaction.)

<u>Invoice 6</u>—Wensel, Hammar, and Bornstein has a new assistant office manager. Carolyn Masters is providing 40 hours of on-site training for Beverly Williams. To provide additional assistance, the company has signed up for 5 hours technical support for January.

*DO: Enter the four transactions in the memo above. Refer to instructions given for the two previous transactions entered.

- Remember, when billing for on-site training, the first hour is billed as Training 1, and the remaining hours are billed as Training 2.
- Always use the Item list to determine the appropriate sales items for billing.
- Use "Thank you for your business." as the message for these invoices.
- If you make an error, correct it.
- Print each invoice immediately after you enter the information for it.
- To go from one invoice to the next, click **>>NEXT** button on the right side of the Create Invoice screen rather than **OK**.
- Click **OK** after Invoice 6 has been entered and printed.

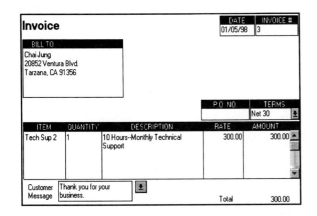

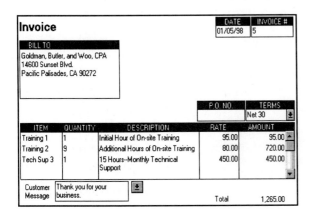

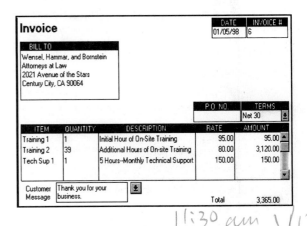

11:30 am 1/17

PRINT A/R REPORTS

QuickBooks has several reports available for accounts receivable. One of the most useful is the Customer Balance Summary report. It shows you the balances of all the customers on account.

 *DO: Click **Reports** on the menu bar

Point to **A/R Reports**

Click **Customer Balance Summary**

To remove the current date from the report:

Click **Header/Footer** button

Click the check box next to **Date Prepared** to deselect this option

Click **OK**

Change the Dates for the report:

Click the drop-down list arrow next to **Dates**

Click **Custom**

- You may need to scroll down the list until you see Custom.

Tab to **From**

Enter **01/01/98**
Tab to **To**
Enter **01/05/98**
Press Tab key
- After you enter the date, pressing the tab key will generate the report.
- This report lists the names of all customers on account with balances. The amount column shows the total balance for each customer. This includes opening balances as well as current invoices.

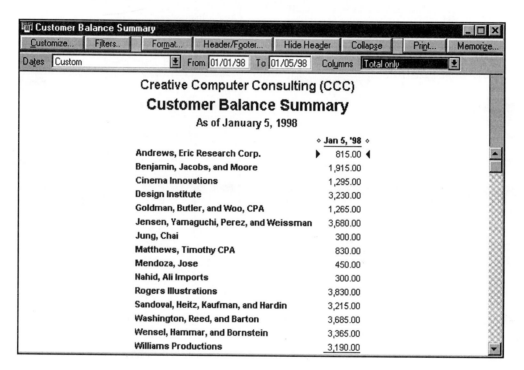

Click **Print** button at the top of the Customer Balance Summary Report
Complete the information on the **Print Reports Settings** tab:
Print To: The selected item should be **Printer**
- Printer name should appear in the printer text box. This may be different from the printer identified in this text.
  If the printer name is not in the text box:
    Click the drop-down list arrow
    Click the correct printer
Orientation: Click **Portrait** to select Portrait orientation for this report
- Portrait orientation prints in the traditional 8½- by 11-inch paper size.
Page Range: **All** should be selected; if it is not, click **All**
If necessary, click on "Fit report to one page wide" to deselect this item

- When selected, the printer will print the Journal using a smaller font so the report will be one page in width.

Click **Print** on the **Print Reports** screen

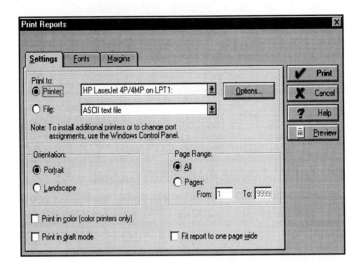

Click **Close** button to close **Customer Balance Summary Report**

USE THE QUICKZOOM FEATURE

Roger Owens asks the office manager, Carmen Mendoza, to obtain information regarding the balance of the Sandoval, Heitz, Kaufman, and Hardin account. To get detailed information regarding an individual customer's balance while in the Customer Balance Summary Report, use the **Zoom** feature. With the individual customer's information on the screen, you can print a report for that customer.

*DO: Click **Reports** on the menu bar
Point to **A/R Reports**
Click **Customer Balance Summary**
- Once again, you will see the balances for all customers on the screen.
Point to the balance for **Sandoval, Heitz, Kaufman, and Hardin**
- Notice that the mouse pointer turns into a magnifying glass with a **Z** in it.
Click once to mark the balance
▸**3,215.00**◂
- Notice the marks on either side of the amount.
Double-click to **Zoom** in to see the details
Remove the current date from the header

- Follow the instructions previously listed for removing the current date from the header for the Customer Balance Summary report.

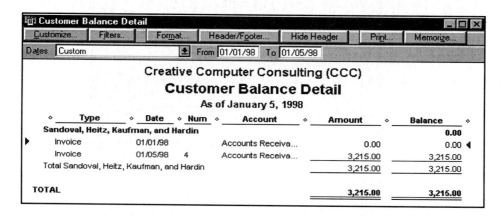

- Notice Invoice 4 was recorded on 01/05/98 for $3,215.
- To view Invoice 4, simply double-click on this transaction, and the invoice will be shown on the screen.
- To exit Invoice 4 and return to the Customer Balance Detail report, click the Cancel button on the right side of the Create Invoices screen for Invoice 4.

Print the **Customer Balance Detail** report for Sandoval, Heitz, Kaufman, and Hardin

- Follow the steps previously listed for printing the Customer Balance Summary report.

The report dates used should be from **01/01/98** to **01/05/98**

Creative Computer Consulting (CCC)
Customer Balance Detail
As of January 5, 1998

Type	Date	Num	Account	Amount	Balance
Sandoval, Heitz, Kaufman, and Hardin					0.00
Invoice	01/01/98		Accounts Receiva...	0.00	0.00
Invoice	01/05/98	4	Accounts Receiva...	3,215.00	3,215.00
Total Sandoval, Heitz, Kaufman, and Hardin				3,215.00	3,215.00
TOTAL				**3,215.00**	**3,215.00**

Click **Close** button to close Customer Balance Detail Report
Click **Close** to close Customer Balance Summary Report

CORRECT AN INVOICE AND PRINT THE CORRECTED FORM

Errors may be corrected very easily with QuickBooks. Because an invoice is prepared for sales on account, corrections will be made directly on the invoice. We will access the invoice via the register for the accounts receivable account.

MEMO

DATE: January 11, 1998

The actual amount of time spend for on-site training increased from 10 hours to 12 hours. Change Invoice No. 5 to Goldman, Butler, and Woo, CPA, to correct the actual amount of training hours to show a total of 12 hours.

---

*DO: Correct the error indicated on the above memo and print a corrected invoice:
Click the **Accnt** button on the iconbar
    OR
Use QuickBooks Navigator:
    Click **Company** side tab

        Click **Chart of Accounts**
In the Chart of Accounts, click **Accounts Receivable**

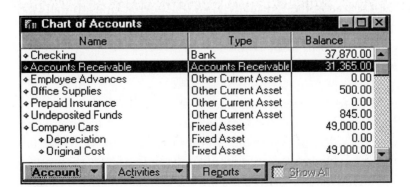

    Click **Activities** button
    Click **Use Register**

- The Accounts Receivable Register appears on the screen with information regarding each transaction entered into the account.

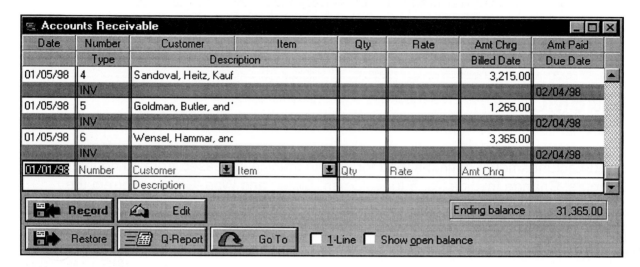

Date	Number	Customer	Item	Qty	Rate	Amt Chrg	Amt Paid
	Type	Description				Billed Date	Due Date
01/05/98	4	Sandoval, Heitz, Kauf				3,215.00	
	INV						02/04/98
01/05/98	5	Goldman, Butler, and'				1,265.00	
	INV						02/04/98
01/05/98	6	Wensel, Hammar, anc				3,365.00	
	INV						02/04/98
01/01/98	Number	Customer	Item	Qty	Rate	Amt Chrg	
		Description					

Record   Edit   Ending balance   31,365.00

Restore   Q-Report   Go To   ☐ 1-Line ☐ Show open balance

If necessary, scroll through the register until the transaction for **Invoice No. 5** is on the screen
- Look at the **Number/Type** column to identify the number of the invoice and the type of transaction.
    - On the <u>Number line</u> you will see a <u>check number</u> or the <u>invoice number</u>.
    - On the <u>Type line</u>, <u>PMT</u> indicates a payment was received on account, and <u>INV</u> indicates a sale on account.

Click anywhere in the transaction for Invoice No. 5 to Goldman, Butler, and Woo, CPA

Click **Edit** at the bottom of the register
- Invoice No. 5 appears on the screen.

Click the line in the **Quantity** field that corresponds to the **Training 2** hours

Change the quantity from 9 hours to 11 hours

Position cursor in front of the 9

Press Delete

Type **11**

Press Tab to generate a new total

Click **Print** button on the **Create Invoices** screen to print a corrected invoice

Check the information on the "**Print One Invoice**" **Settings** tab:

   Printer Name: (Should identify the type of printer you are using)
   - This may be different from the printer identified in this text.

   Printer Type: Page-oriented (Single sheet)

   Print On: Blank Paper

- The circle next to this should be filled. If it is not, click the circle to select.

   Print Lines Around Each Field check box:
- Should be empty. If it is not, click the box to deselect.

Click **Print** button

Click **Print** button on **Print One Invoice** screen

Click **OK** to answer **Did form(s) print OK?**

Click **OK** to record changes and close invoice

VIEW A QUICKREPORT

After editing the invoice and returning to the register, you may get a detailed report regarding the customer's transactions by clicking the Q-Report button.

 *DO: After closing the invoice, you return to the register.

Click **Q-Report** button to view the **Goldman, Butler, and Woo** account

Verify the balance of the account. It should be **$1,425.00**
- Note: You will get the current date in your QuickReport.

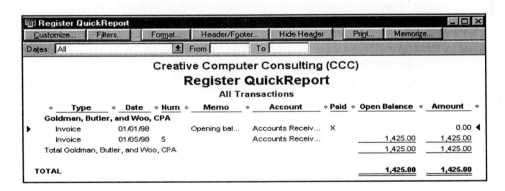

ANALYZE THE QUICKREPORT FOR GOLDMAN, BUTLER, AND WOO

 *DO: Notice that the total of Invoice 5 is $1,425.00

Close the QuickReport without printing

Close Accounts Receivable Register

Close Chart of Accounts

VOID AND DELETE SALES FORMS

Deleting an invoice or sales receipt permanently removes it from QuickBooks without leaving a trace. If you would like to correct your financial records for the invoice that you no longer want, it is more appropriate to void the invoice. When an invoice is voided, it remains in the QuickBooks system, but QuickBooks doesn't count it.

Void an Invoice

MEMO

DATE: January 13, 1998

Chai Jung called on January 5 to cancel the 10 hours of technical support for January. (This was the same day the invoice was recorded.) Because Invoice No. 3 to Chai Jung was prepared in error, void the invoice.

---

 *DO: Void the invoice above by going directly to the original invoice:
Click **Invoice** button on the iconbar
    OR
Use **QuickBooks Navigator**:
    Click **Sales and Customers** tab
    Click **Invoice** icon
• You may also access the invoice via the register for accounts receivable.
Click **<<Prev** button until you get to Invoice 3
With Invoice 3 on the screen, click **Edit** menu

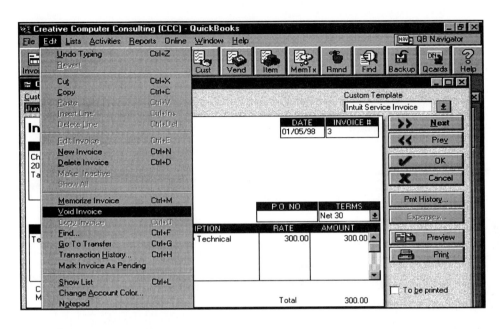

Click **Void Invoice**

- Notice that the amount and total for the invoice shown above are no longer 300. They are both **0.00**

Click **OK** on the **Create Invoices** screen

Click **Reports** menu

Point to **Transaction Reports**

Click **By Customer**

To remove the current date from the report:

Click **Header/Footer** button

Click the check box next to **Date Prepared** to deselect this option

Click **OK**

Change the Dates for the report:

Click the drop-down list arrow next to **Dates**

Click **Custom**

- You may need to scroll down the list until you see Custom.

Tab to **From**

Enter **01/01/98**

Tab to **To**

Enter **01/13/98**

Tab to generate the report

Print transactions for **January**:

Click **Print** button at the top of the **Transactions by Customer Summary** Report

Complete the information on the **Print Reports Settings** tab:

Print To: The selected item should be **Printer**

- Printer name should appear in the printer text box. This may be different from the printer identified in this text.

    If the printer name does not appear:

        Click the drop-down list arrow

        Click the correct printer

Orientation: Click **Portrait** to select Portrait orientation for this report

- Portrait orientation prints in the traditional 8½- by 11-inch paper size.

Page Range: **All** should be selected; if it is not, click **All**

If necessary, click on "Fit Report to one page wide" to deselect this item

- If selected, the printer will print the report using a smaller font so it will be one page in width.

Because you are not using the option to fit the report to one-page wide, this report will print on two pages.

Click **Print** on the **Print Reports** screen

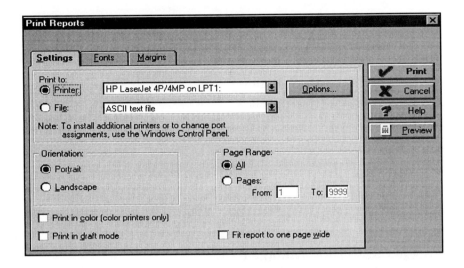

- This report gives the amount for each transaction with the customer—including opening balances.
- Notice that Invoice 3 is marked VOID in the Memo column and has an **X** in the **Clr** column.
- The **SPLIT** column tells you which account was used to record the income. If the word **-SPLIT-** appears in the column, this means the transaction amount was "split" among two or more accounts.

Close the **Transactions by Customer** report

Delete an Invoice

MEMO

DATE: January 14, 1998

Because of the upcoming tax season, Timothy Matthews has had to reschedule his 5-hour training session with Carolyn Masters three times. Timothy Matthews finally decided to cancel the training session and reschedule it after April 15. Delete Invoice No. 2 to Timothy Matthews.

---

*DO: Delete the above transaction using FIND to locate the invoice:
- Find is useful when you have a large number of invoices and want to locate an invoice for a particular customer.

- Using Find will locate the invoice without requiring you to scroll through all the invoices for the company. For example, if customer Sanderson's transaction was on Invoice 3 and the invoice on the screen was 1,084, you would not have to scroll through 1,081 invoices because Find would locate Invoice 3 instantly.

To use Find:

Click **Find** button

OR

Click **Edit** menu

Click **Find**

In the list displayed under **Filter**, click **Name**

In the **Name** dialog box, click the drop-down list arrow

Click **Matthews, Timothy CPA**

- This allows QuickBooks to find any transaction recorded for Timothy Matthews. This is sufficient for now.
- If, however, there were several invoices and several payments recorded for Timothy Matthews, another filter would need to be defined in order to find all invoices but no payments.
- This would be done by selecting a second filter: "Transaction Type" and identifying the type of transaction as an "Invoice."
- Notice that the Current Choice Box shows "Filter: Name" and "Set to: Matthews, Timothy CPA."

Click the **FIND** button on the FIND dialog box

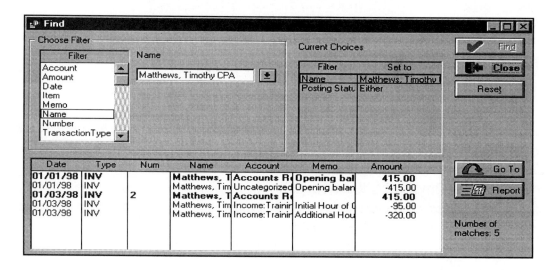

Click the line for **Invoice 2**

Click **Go To** button

- Invoice No. 2 appears on the screen.

With the invoice on the screen, click **Edit** menu

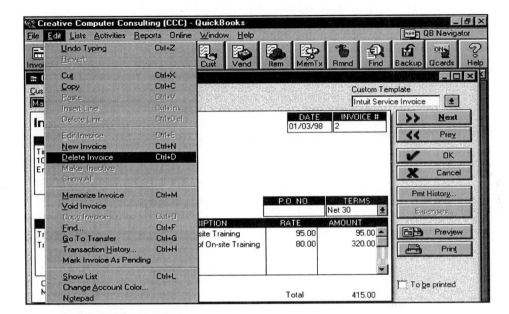

Click **Delete Invoice**
Click **OK** in the **Delete Transaction** dialog box

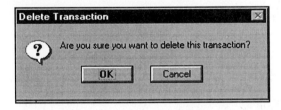

- Notice that the cursor is now positioned on Invoice 3.
Click **OK** button on the **Create Invoices** screen to close invoice
- Notice that Invoice 2 no longer shows on Find.
Click **Close** button to close Find
Click **Reports**
Point to **A/R Reports**
Click **Customer Balance Detail**
To remove the current date from the report:
    Click **Header/Footer** button
    Click the check box next to **Date Prepared** to deselect this option
    Click **OK**
Dates should be **All**
Click **Print** to print report
    Click **Print** button at the top of the **Customer Balance Detail** report

Complete the information on the **Print Reports Settings** tab:

Print To: The selected item should be **Printer**

- Printer name should appear in the printer text box. This may be different from the printer identified in this text. If the printer name does not appear:

    Click the drop-down list arrow, click the correct printer

Orientation: Click **Portrait** to select Portrait orientation for this report

- Portrait orientation prints in the traditional 8½- by 11-inch paper size.

Page Range: **All** should be selected; if it is not, click **All**

Click on **Fit report to one page wide** to select this item

- Because this option has been selected, the printer will print the report using a smaller font, and the report will be one page in width.

Click **Print** on the **Print Reports** screen

- Look at Timothy Matthews' account.
- Notice that Invoice No. 2 doesn't show up in the account listing. When an invoice is deleted, there is no record of it anywhere in the report.
- Notice that the Customer Balance Detail report does not include the information telling you which amounts are opening balances.
- The report does give information regarding the amount owed on each transaction plus the total amount owed by each customer.

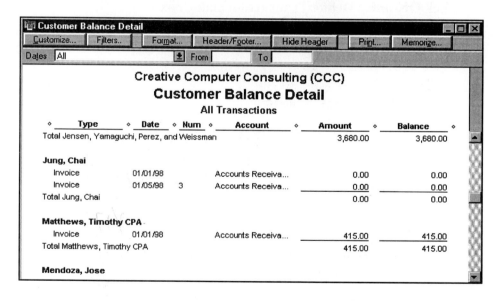

Close the Customer Balance Detail Report

PREPARE CREDIT MEMOS

Credit memos are prepared to show a reduction to a transaction. If the invoice has already been sent to the customer, it is more appropriate and less confusing to make a change to a transaction by issuing a credit memo rather than void the invoice and issue a new one. A credit memo notifies a customer that a change has been made to a transaction.

MEMO

DATE: January 14, 1998

Prepare the following: <u>Credit Memo 7</u>—Sandoval, Heitz, Kaufman, and Hardin did not need 5 hours of the training billed on Invoice No. 4. Issue Credit Memo to reduce Training 2 by 5 hours.

---

*DO: Prepare the credit memo shown above:
Click **Activities** menu
Click **Create Credit Memos/Refunds**
    OR
Use QuickBooks Navigator:
    Click **Sales and Customers** tab
    Click **Refunds and Credit**

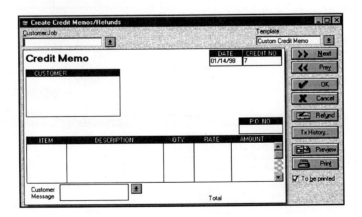

Click the down arrow for the drop-down list box next to **Customer:Job**
Click **Sandoval, Heitz, Kaufman, and Hardin**
Tab to Template
• It should say **Custom Credit Memo**.

- If not, click the drop-down list arrow and click Custom Credit Memo.

Tab to or click **Date**

Type in the date of the credit memo—**01/14/98**

The **Credit No.** field should show the number **7**

- Because credit memos are included in the numbering sequence for invoices, this number matches the number of the next blank invoice.

There is no PO No.

- Omit this field.

Tab to or click in **Item**

Click the drop-down list arrow in the Item column

Click **Training 2**

Tab to or click in **Quantity**

Type in **5**

Click the next blank line in the Description column

Type **Deduct 5 hours of additional training, which was not required. Reduce the amount due for Invoice #4.**

- This will print as a note or explanation to the customer.

Click the drop-down list arrow next to Customer Message

Click **It's been a pleasure working with you!**

Click **Print** on Create Credit Memos/Refunds

Click **Print** on Print One Credit Memo

If the Credit Memo prints without error, click **OK** in the **Did form(s) print OK?** dialog box

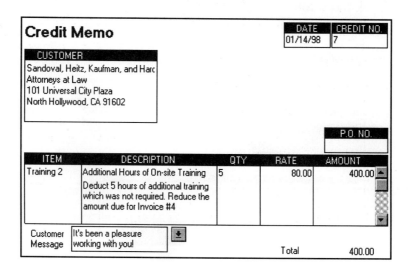

Click **OK** button on Create Credit Memos/Refunds to close credit memo

VIEW CUSTOMER BALANCE DETAIL REPORT

Periodically viewing reports allows you to verify the changes that have occurred to accounts. The Customer Balance Detail report shows all the transactions for each *credit* customer. Cash customers must be viewed through sales reports.

*DO: Click **Reports** on the menu bar
        Point to **A/R Reports**
            OR
        Use QuickBooks Navigator:
            Click **Sales and Customers** tab
            Click **Accounts Receivable** under Reports
        Click **Customer Balance Detail**
        Scroll through the report
        - Notice that the account for Sandoval, Heitz, Kaufman, and Hardin shows Credit Memo 7 for $400.00. The total amount owed was reduced by $400 and is $2,815.00.

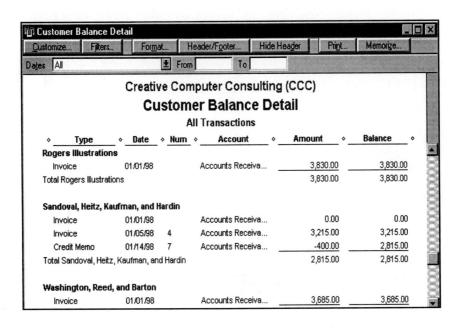

Click **Close** button to close the report without printing

ADD A NEW ACCOUNT TO THE CHART OF ACCOUNTS

Because account needs can change as a business is in operation, QuickBooks allows you to make changes to the chart of accounts at anytime. Some changes to the chart of accounts require additional changes to lists.

Roger Owens has determined that CCC has received a lot of calls from customers for assistance with hardware installation. Samuel Yee will be responsible for installing hardware for customers. As a result of this decision, you will be adding a third income account. This account will be used when revenue from hardware installation is earned. In addition to adding the account, you will also have to add two new sales items to the Item list.

 *DO: Click the **Accnt** button on the iconbar
OR
Use QuickBooks Navigator:
    Click **Company** tab
    Click **Chart of Accounts** folder

- Remember that the Chart of Accounts is also the General Ledger.

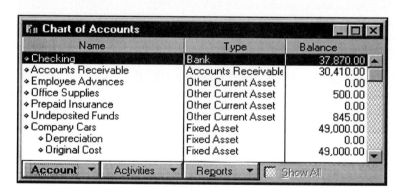

Click **Account** button at the bottom of the Chart of Accounts screen
Click **New**

Click arrow for drop-down list next to **Type**
Click **Income**

Click **Name**
Type **Installation Income**
Click the **Check box** for **Subaccount of**
Click arrow for drop-down list for Subaccount of
Click **Income**
Tab to or click **Description**
Type **Hardware Installation Income**
Click **Tax Line** drop-down list arrow. Click **Schedule C: Gross Receipts or Sales**
Click **OK** to record new account and close New Account screen

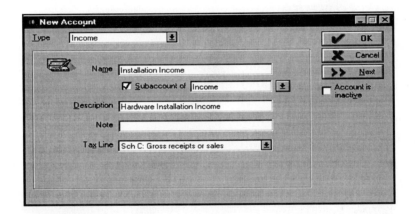

Scroll through the Chart of Accounts
• Verify that Installation Income has been added under Income.
Close **Chart of Accounts**

ADD NEW ITEMS TO LIST

In order to accommodate the changing needs of a business, all QuickBooks lists allow you to make changes at any time. The Item list stores information about the services CCC provides. In order to use the new Hardware Installation Income account, two new items need to be added to the Item list.

 *DO: Click **Item** button
　　　OR
Use QuickBooks Navigator:
　　Click **Sales and Customers** tab
　　Click **Items & Services** folder
Click **Items** button at the bottom of the **Item List** screen
Click **New**

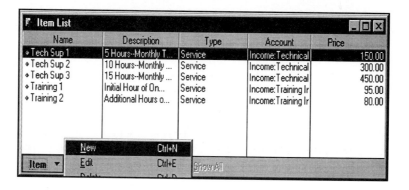

Item Type is **Service**

Tab to or click **Item Name/Number**

Type **Install 1**

Tab to or click **Description**

Type **Initial Hour of Hardware Installation**

Tab to or click **Rate**

Type in **95**

Click drop-down list arrow for **Account**

Click **Installation Income**

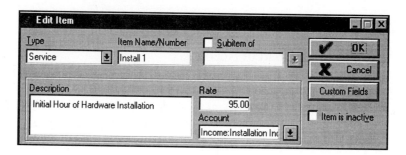

Click **>>Next** on the New Item dialog box

Repeat the steps above to add **Install 2**

The description is **Additional Hours of Hardware Installation**

The rate is **$80.00** per hour

When finished adding Install 2, click **OK** to add new items and to close New Item screen

- Whenever hardware installation is provided for customers, the first hour will be billed as Install 1, and additional hours will be billed as Install 2.
- Verify the addition of Install 1 and Install 2 on the Item List. If everything is correct, close the Item List.
    - If you find an error, click on the item with the error, click the **Item** button, click **Edit**, and make corrections as needed.

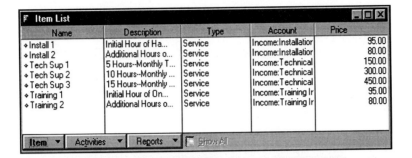

Close Item list

ADD A NEW CUSTOMER

Because customers are the life-blood of a business, QuickBooks allows customers to be added "on the fly" as you create an invoice or sales receipt. You may choose between Quick Add (used to add only a customer's name) and Set Up (used to add complete information for a customer).

MEMO

DATE: January 14, 1998

Prepare the following: <u>Invoice 8</u>—A new customer, Larry McBride, has purchased several upgrade items for his personal computer but needed assistance with the installation. Samuel Yee spent two hours installing this hardware. Bill Mr. McBride for 2 hours of hardware installation. His address is: 20985 Ventura Blvd., Woodland Hills, CA 91371. His telephone number is: 818-555-2058. He does not have a fax. His credit limit is $1,000; and the terms are Net 30.

---

*DO: Record the above sale on account to a new customer:
Click **Invoice** button
OR
Use QuickBooks Navigator:
Click **Sales and Customers** tab
Click **Invoices**
In the Customer:Job dialog box type **McBride, Larry**
Press **Tab**

- You will see a message box for **Customer:Job Not Found** with buttons for three choices:

  Quick Add (used to add only a customer's name)

  Set Up (used to add complete information for a customer)

  Cancel (used to cancel the Customer:Job Not Found message box)

Click **Set Up**

Complete the **New Customer** dialog box

- The name **McBride, Larry** is displayed in the Customer field and as the first line of Bill To in the Address section on the Address Info tab.

Complete the information for the Address Info tab:

Tab to or click the first line for Bill To

If necessary, highlight **McBride, Larry**

Type **Larry McBride**

- Entering the customer name in this manner allows for the Customer:Job list to be organized according to the last name, yet the bill will be printed with the first name then the last name.

Press **Enter** or click the second line of the billing address

Type the address **20985 Ventura Blvd.**

Press **Enter** or click the third line of the billing address

Type **Woodland Hills, CA 91371**

There is no Contact person, so leave this blank

Tab to or click **Phone**

Type the phone number **818-555-2058**

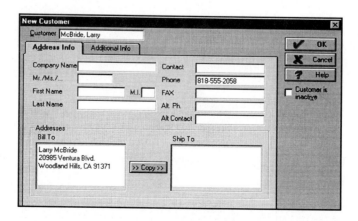

Click **Additional Info** tab
Tab to or click **Terms**
Click the drop-down list arrow
Click **Net 30**
Tab to or click **Credit Limit**
Type the amount **1000**
- Do not use a dollar sign. QuickBooks will insert the comma for you.

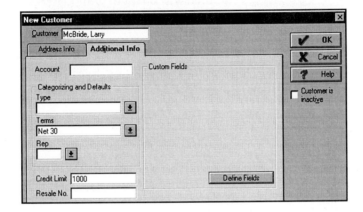

Click **OK** to return to Invoice
Enter Invoice information as previously instructed
Date of the invoice is **01/14/98**
Invoice No. is **8**
The bill is for 2 hours of hardware installation
- Remember to bill for the initial or first hour, then bill the other hour separately.
The message is **Thank you for your business.**
The invoice total should be $175.00

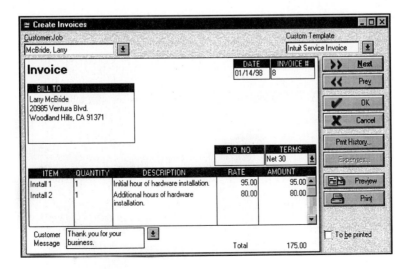

Print the invoice as previously instructed
Click **OK** to answer **Did form(s) print OK?**
Click **OK** on the invoice to record and close the transaction

MODIFY CUSTOMER RECORDS

Occasionally, information regarding a customer will change. QuickBooks allows you to modify customer accounts at any time by editing the Customer:Job list.

MEMO

DATE: January 15, 1998

Update the following account: Design Institute has changed its fax number to 310-555-5959.

DO: Edit the above account:
Access the Customer:Job list:
There are four ways to access the Customer:Job list:
- Click **Lists** on the drop-down menu, click **Customer:Job**.
- Use QuickBooks Navigator: click **Sales and Customers** tab, click **Customers** folder.
- Click **Cust** button on the iconbar.
- Use the keyboard shortcut: **Ctrl+J**.

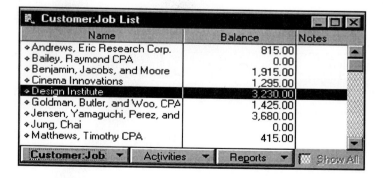

Select Design Institute and access the account in one of the following three ways:

- Click **Design Institute** on the Customer:Job List: click **Customer:Job** button, click **Edit**.
- Click **Design Institute** on the Customer:Job List: use the keyboard shortcut **Ctrl+E**
- Double-click **Design Institute** on the Customer:Job List.

Change the fax number to 310-555-5959:

Click at the end of the fax number

Backspace to delete **11**

Type **59**

Click **OK**

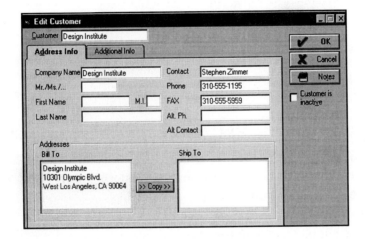

Close **Customer:Job List**

RECORD CASH SALES

Not all sales in a business are on account. In many instances payment is made at the time the service is performed. This is entered as a cash sale. When entering a cash sale, you prepare a sales receipt rather than an invoice. QuickBooks records the transaction in the Journal and places the amount of cash received in an account called "Undeposited Funds." The funds received remain in Undeposited Funds until you record a deposit to your bank account.

MEMO:

DATE: January 7, 1998

Prepare the following to record cash sales: <u>Sales Receipt 1</u>—Roger Owens provided 5 hours of on-site training to Raymond Bailey, CPA, and received Ray's Check No. 3287 for the full amount due. Prepare Sales Receipt 1 for this transaction. Use "It's been a pleasure working with you!" as the message.

---

*DO: Enter the following transaction as a cash sale:
Click **Activities** menu
Click **Enter Cash Sales**
    OR
Use QuickBooks Navigator:
    Click **Sales and Customers** tab
    Click **Cash Sales** icon
Click the drop-down list arrow next to **Customer:Job**
Click **Bailey, Raymond, CPA**
Tab to **Template**
- This should have **Custom Cash Sales** as the template. If not, click the drop-down list arrow and click Custom Cash Sales.

Tab to or click **Date**
Type **01/07/98**
Sales No. should be **1**
Tab to or click **Check No.**
Type **3287**
Click the drop-down list arrow next to **PAYMENT METH**
Click **Check**
Tab to or click beneath **Item**
Click the drop-down list arrow next to **Item**
Click **Training 1**
Tab to or click **Qty**
Type **1**
- Total is automatically calculated when you move to the next field.

Tab to or click the second line for **Item**
Click the drop-down list arrow next to **Item**
Click **Training 2**
Tab to or click **Qty**

Type **4**
- Total is automatically calculated when you go to the Customer Message.

Click **Customer Message**

Click the drop-down list arrow for Customer Message

Click **It's been a pleasure working with you!**
- Message is inserted.

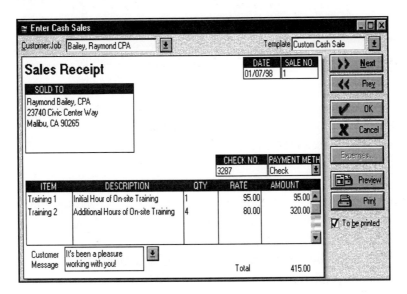

PRINT SALES RECEIPT

 *DO: Print the sales receipt immediately after entering information

Click **Print** button on the right side of the **Enter Cash Sales** screen

Check the information on the **Print One Sales Receipt Settings** tab:

Printer Name: (Should identify the type of printer you are using.)
- This may be different from the printer identified in this text.

Printer Type: Page-oriented (Single sheet)

Print on: Blank Paper
- The circle next to this should be filled. If it is not, click the circle to select.

Lines around each field check box should be blank
- If it is checked, click the box to remove the check mark.

Number of copies should be **1**
- If not, click in the box, drag to highlight the number, then type 1.

Click **Print** button
- This initiates the printing of the sales receipt through QuickBooks. However, since all classroom configurations are not the same, check with your instructor for specific printing instructions.

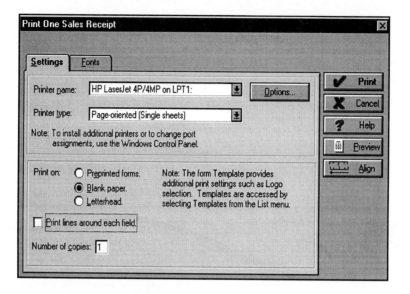

While the sales receipt is printing, you will receive a dialog box **Did form(s) print OK?**

When the form has been correctly printed, click **OK**

Click **OK** on the right side of the Enter Cash Sales screen to exit and close the sales receipt

ENTER CASH SALES TRANSACTIONS WITHOUT STEP-BY-STEP INSTRUCTIONS

MEMO:

DATE: January 9, 1998

Sales Receipt 2—Raymond Bailey needed additional on-site training to correct some error messages he received on his computer. Roger Owens provided 1 hour of on-site training for Raymond Bailey, CPA, and received Ray's Check No. 3306 for the full amount due.

Sales Receipt 3—Roger Owens provided 4 hours of on-site Internet training for Eric Andrews Research Corp. so the company could be on line. Roger received Check No. 10358 for the full amount due.

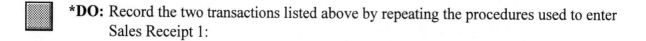   ***DO:** Record the two transactions listed above by repeating the procedures used to enter Sales Receipt 1:

- Remember, the <u>first hour for on-site training</u> is billed as <u>Training 1</u> and the <u>remaining hours</u> are billed as <u>Training 2</u>.
    - Always use the Item List to determine the appropriate sales items for billing.
    - Use "**Thank you for your business.**" as the message for these sales receipts.
    - Print each sales receipt immediately after entering the information for it.
    - If you make an error, correct it.
    - To go from one sales receipt to the next, click **>>NEXT** button on the right side of the Enter Cash Sales screen rather than **OK**.
    - Click **OK** after you have entered and printed Sales Receipt 3.

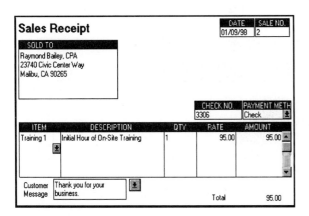
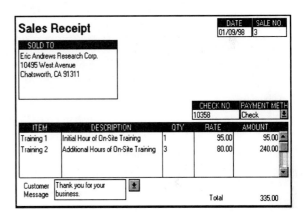

PRINT SALES BY CUSTOMER DETAIL REPORT

QuickBooks has reports available that enable you to obtain sales information about sales items or customers. To get information about the total amount of sales to each customer during a specific period, print a Sales Report by Customer Detail. The total shown represents both cash and/or credit sales.

 *DO: Click **Reports** on the menu bar

Point to **Sales Reports**

Click **By Customer Detail**

Remove the Current Date from the report:

Click **Header/Footer** button

Click **Date Prepared** check box to deselect this item

Click **OK**

Change the dates to reflect the sales period desired:

Click the drop-down list arrow next to **Dates**

Click **Custom**

Tab to **From**

Type **01/01/98**

Tab to **To**

Type **01/15/98**

Tab to generate the report

- Notice that the report information includes the type of sales to each customer, the date of the sale, the sales item(s), the quantity for each item, the sales price, the amount, and the balance.
- The report does not include information regarding opening or previous balances due.
- The scope of this report is to focus on "sales."

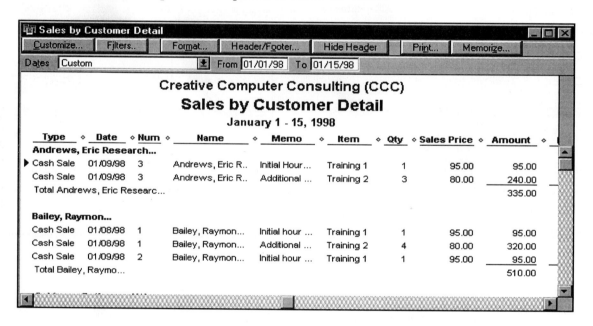

Click **Print** button on the Sales By Customer Detail

On the **Print Report** screen: Check the Settings tab to verify that

　　Print To: Printer is selected

- Verify that the Name of your printer is correct.

　　Check that the Orientation is Portrait

　　Verify Range is All

On the Print Report screen, click **Print**

- Do not select Fit report on one page wide.
- The printed report may require more than one page.

Close Sales By Customer Detail report

CORRECT A SALES RECEIPT AND PRINT THE CORRECTED FORM

QuickBooks makes correcting errors user friendly. When an error is discovered in a transaction such as a cash sale, you can simply return to the form where the transaction was recorded and correct the error. Thus, to correct a sales receipt you could click on Activities, click on Enter Cash Sales, click the Prev button until you found the appropriate sales receipt, and then correct the error. However, because cash or checks received for cash sales are held in the Undeposited Funds account until the bank deposit is made, you can access the sales receipt through the Undeposited Funds account in the Chart of Accounts. Accessing the receipt in this manner allows you to see all the transactions entered in the account for Undeposited Funds.

When a correction for a sale is made, QuickBooks not only changes the form, it also changes all journal and account entries for the transaction to reflect the correction. QuickBooks then allows a corrected sales receipt to be printed.

MEMO

DATE: January 15, 1998

After reviewing transaction information, you realize the date for the Sales Receipt No. 1 to Raymond Bailey, CPA, was entered incorrectly. Change the date to 01/08/98.

---

*DO: Correct the error indicated in the memo above and print a corrected sales receipt:
   Click **Accnt** button
   Click **Undeposited Funds**

Chart of Accounts		
Name	Type	Balance
◆ Checking	Bank	37,870.00
◆ Accounts Receivable	Accounts Receivable	30,585.00
◆ Employee Advances	Other Current Asset	0.00
◆ Office Supplies	Other Current Asset	500.00
◆ Prepaid Insurance	Other Current Asset	0.00
◆ Undeposited Funds	Other Current Asset	845.00
◆ Company Cars	Fixed Asset	49,000.00
◆ Depreciation	Fixed Asset	0.00
◆ Original Cost	Fixed Asset	49,000.00
Account ▼ Activities ▼ Reports ▼ Show All		

   Click **Activities** button
   Click **Use Register**

- The register maintains a record of all the transactions recorded within the Undeposited Funds account.

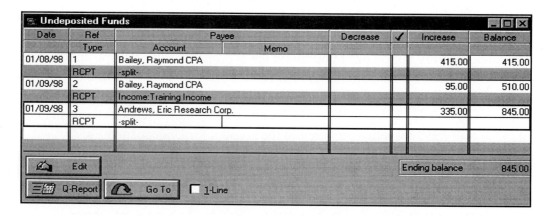

Click anywhere in the transaction for Sale No. 1 to Raymond Bailey, CPA

- Look at the Ref/Type column to see the type of transaction.
- The number in the Ref line indicates the number of the sales receipt or the customer's check number.
- Type shows RCPT for a sales receipt.

Click **Edit**

- The sales receipt appears on the screen.

Tab to or click **Date** field

Change the Date to **01/08/98**

Position insert line between 0 and 7

Press **Delete**

Type an **8**

Click **Print** button on the Enter Cash Sales screen to print a corrected sales receipt

Click **Print** on the Print One Sales Receipt screen

On the Did form(s) print OK? screen, click **OK**

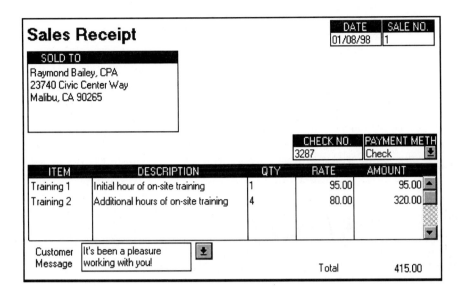

Click **OK** on the Enter Cash Sales screen to record changes, close sales receipt, and return to the Register for Undeposited Funds

Do not close the Register

VIEW A QUICKREPORT

After editing the sales receipt and returning to the register, you may get a detailed report regarding the customer's transactions by clicking the Q-Report button.

*DO: After closing the sales receipt, you returned to the register for the Undeposited Funds account

Click **Q-Report** button to display the Register QuickReport for Raymond Bailey, CPA

Creative Computer Consulting (CCC)
Register QuickReport
All Transactions

Type	Date	Num	Memo	Account	Clr	Split	Amount
Bailey, Raymond CPA							
Cash Sale	01/08/98	1		Undeposited Funds		-SPLIT-	415.00
Cash Sale	01/09/98	2		Undeposited Funds		Training Income	95.00
Total Bailey, Raymond CPA							510.00
TOTAL							**510.00**

ANALYZE THE QUICKREPORT FOR RAYMOND BAILEY

 *DO: Notice that the date for Sales Receipt 1 has been changed to **01/08/98**
- You may need to use the horizontal scroll bar to view all the columns in the report.

The account used is Undeposited Funds

The Split column contains the other accounts used in the transaction
- For Sales Receipt 2, the account used is **Income: Training**.
- For Sales Receipt 1, you see the word **Split** rather than an account name.
  - Split means that more than one account was used for this portion of the transaction.

View the accounts used for the Split by using QuickZoom to view the actual Sales Receipt

Use QuickZoom by double-clicking anywhere on the information for Sales Receipt 1
- The accounts used are Training 1 and Training 2.

Close the Sales Receipt

Close the Register QuickReport without printing

Close the Register for Undeposited Funds

Close the Chart of Accounts

ANALYZE SALES

To obtain information regarding the amount of sales by item, you can print or view sales reports. Sales reports provide information regarding cash and credit sales. When information regarding the sales according to the Sales Item is needed, a Summarized Sales Report by Item is the appropriate report to print or view. This report enables you to see how much revenue is being generated by each sales item. This provides important information for decision making and managing the business. For example, if a sales item is not generating much income, it might be wise to discontinue that sales item.

 *DO: Print a summarized list of sales by item
Click **Reports** on the menu bar
Point to **Sales Reports**
    OR
Use QuickBooks Navigator:
    Click **Sales and Customers** tab
    Under **Reports** at the bottom of the screen, click **Sales**
Click **By Item Summary**
Click **Header/Footer** button
Click **Date Prepared** to deselect this feature
Click **OK**

Click the drop-down list arrow for **Dates**
Click **Custom**
Tab to or click **From**
Enter **01/01/98**
Tab to or click **To**
Enter **01/15/98**
Tab to generate the report
Click **Print**
Click **Print** on **Print Reports** dialog box

Creative Computer Consulting (CCC)				
Summary Sales by Item				
January 1 - 15, 1998				
		Jan 1 - 15, '98		
	◇ Qty ◇	Amount ◇	% of Sales ◇	Avg Price ◇
Service				
Install 1 ▶	1 ◀	95.00	1.1%	95.00
Install 2	1	80.00	0.9%	80.00
Tech Sup 1	1	150.00	1.7%	150.00
Tech Sup 2	1	300.00	3.4%	300.00
Tech Sup 3	1	450.00	5%	450.00
Training 1	6	570.00	6.4%	95.00
Training 2	91	7,280.00	81.6%	80.00
Total Service		8,925.00	100.0%	
TOTAL		**8,925.00**	**100.0%**	

Close the report

*DO: In order to obtain information regarding which transactions apply to each sales item, view a sales report by item detail
Click **Reports** on the menu bar
Point to **Sales Reports**
    OR
Use QuickBooks Navigator:
    Click **Sales and Customers** tab
    Under **Reports** at the bottom of the screen, click **Sales**
Click **By Item Detail**
Change **Header/Footer** so **Date Prepared** does not print on the report
Click the drop-down list arrow for **Dates**
Click **Custom**
Tab to **From**

Enter **01/01/98**

Tab to **To**

Enter **01/15/98**

Tab to generate report

Scroll through the report to view the types of Sales and the transactions that occurred within each category

- Notice how many transactions occurred in each sales item.

Type	Date	Num	Name	Memo	Qty	Sale...	Amount	Balance
Service								
Install 1								
Invoice	01/14...	8	McBride, Larry	Initial h...	1	95.00	95.00	95.00
Total Install 1							95.00	95.00
Install 2								
Invoice	01/14...	8	McBride, Larry	Additio...	1	80.00	80.00	80.00
Total Install 2							80.00	80.00
Tech Sup 1								
Invoice	01/05...	6	Wensel, Ham...	5 Hour...	1	150.00	150.00	150.00
Total Tech Sup 1							150.00	150.00

Creative Computer Consulting (CCC)
Itemized Sales by Item
January 1 - 15, 1998

Partial Report

Close the report without printing

RECORD CUSTOMER PAYMENTS ON ACCOUNT

When customers pay the amount they owe, QuickBooks places the money received in an account called "Undeposited Funds." The money stays in the account until a bank deposit is made. When you start to record a payment made by a customer, you see the customer's balance, any credits made to the account, and a complete list of outstanding invoices. QuickBooks automatically applies the payment received to the oldest invoice.

MEMO

DATE: January 15, 1998

Record the following cash receipt: Received Check No. 0684 for $815 from Eric
Andrews Research Corp. as payment on account.

*DO: Record the above payment on account:
Click **Activities**
Click **Receive Payments**
   OR
Use QuickBooks Navigator:
   Click **Sales and Customers** tab
   Click **Receive Payments**

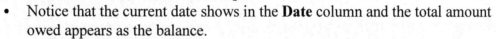

Click drop-down list arrow for **Customer:Job**
Click **Andrews, Eric Research Corp.**
• Notice that the current date shows in the **Date** column and the total amount
  owed appears as the balance.
• At the bottom of the Receive Payments screen, notice that the unpaid invoice
  for Eric Andrews Research Corp. shows under Outstanding Invoices/
  Statement Charges.
Tab to or click **Date**
• If you click, you will need to delete the date. If you tab, the date will be
  deleted when you type 01/15/98.
Type date **01/15/98**
Tab to or click **Amount**
• If you click, you will need to delete the 0.00. If you tab, it will be deleted
  when you type in the amount.
Enter **815**
• QuickBooks will enter the **.00** when you tab to or click Pmt. Method.
Click drop-down list arrow for **Pmt. Method**
• Notice that the cursor moves into the Pmt. Method text box and that the
  payment amount is entered in the Payment column for Outstanding Invoices/
  Statement Charges.
Click **Check**
Tab to or click **Check No.**
Enter **0684**
• QuickBooks automatically applies the payment to the oldest open invoice.

Click **OK**

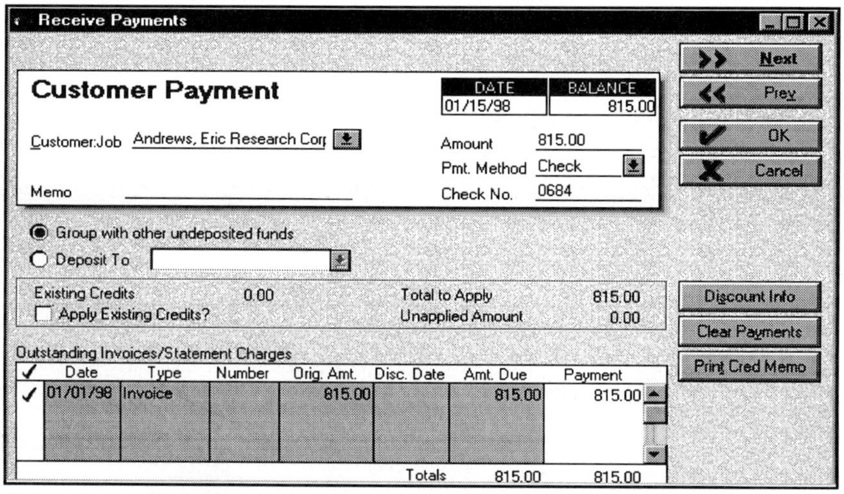

RECORD ADDITIONAL PAYMENTS ON ACCOUNT WITHOUT STEP-BY-STEP INSTRUCTIONS

MEMO

DATE: January 15, 1998

Received Check No. 1952 from Jensen, Yamaguchi, Perez, and Weissman for $3,680.

Received Check No. 8925 for $2,000 from Rogers Illustrations in partial payment of account. This receipt requires a Memo notation of Partial Payment.

Received Check No. 39251 from Timothy Matthews for $415.

Received Check No. 2051 for $2,190 from Williams Productions in partial payment of account. Record a Memo for this receipt. The memo is Partial Payment.

Received Check No. 5632 from Jose Mendoza for $150.

Received Check No. 80195 from Washington, Reed, and Barton for $3,685.

---

*DO: Refer to the previous steps listed to enter the above payments:
Click **>>NEXT** to go from one Receive Payments Screen to the next
Click the **OK** button after all payments received have been recorded

Customer Payment

	DATE	BALANCE
	01/15/98	3,680.00

Customer:Job Jensen, Yamaguchi, Perez, a

Amount 3,680.00
Pmt. Method Check
Check No. 1952

Memo

○ Group with other undeposited funds
○ Deposit To

Existing Credits	0.00	Total to Apply	3,680.00
☐ Apply Existing Credits?		Unapplied Amount	0.00

Outstanding Invoices/Statement Charges

✓	Date	Type	Number	Orig. Amt.	Disc. Date	Amt. Due	Payment
✓	01/01/98	Invoice		3,680.00		3,680.00	3,680.00
					Totals	3,680.00	3,680.00

Customer Payment

	DATE	BALANCE
	01/15/98	3,830.00

Customer:Job Rogers Illustrations

Amount 2,000.00
Pmt. Method Check
Check No. 8925

Memo Partial Payment

○ Group with other undeposited funds
○ Deposit To

Existing Credits	0.00	Total to Apply	2,000.00
☐ Apply Existing Credits?		Unapplied Amount	0.00

Outstanding Invoices/Statement Charges

✓	Date	Type	Number	Orig. Amt.	Disc. Date	Amt. Due	Payment
✓	01/01/98	Invoice		3,830.00		3,830.00	2,000.00
					Totals	3,830.00	2,000.00

Customer Payment

	DATE	BALANCE
	01/15/98	415.00

Customer:Job Matthews, Timothy CPA

Amount 415.00
Pmt. Method Check
Check No. 39251

Memo

○ Group with other undeposited funds
○ Deposit To

Existing Credits	0.00	Total to Apply	415.00
☐ Apply Existing Credits?		Unapplied Amount	0.00

Invoices paid (with this payment) and those still outstanding

✓	Date	Type	Number	Orig. Amt.	Disc. Date	Amt. Due	Payment
✓	01/01/98	Invoice		415.00		415.00	415.00
					Totals	415.00	415.00

Customer Payment

	DATE	BALANCE
	01/15/98	3,190.00

Customer:Job Williams Productions

Amount 2,190.00
Pmt. Method Check
Check No. 2051

Memo Partial Payment

○ Group with other undeposited funds
○ Deposit To

Existing Credits	0.00	Total to Apply	2,190.00
☐ Apply Existing Credits?		Unapplied Amount	0.00

Outstanding Invoices/Statement Charges

✓	Date	Type	Number	Orig. Amt.	Disc. Date	Amt. Due	Payment
✓	01/01/98	Invoice		3,190.00		3,190.00	2,190.00
					Totals	3,190.00	2,190.00

Customer Payment

	DATE	BALANCE
	01/15/98	450.00

Customer:Job Mendoza, Jose

Amount 150.00
Pmt. Method Check
Check No. 5632

Memo

○ Group with other undeposited funds
○ Deposit To

Existing Credits	0.00	Total to Apply	150.00
☐ Apply Existing Credits?		Unapplied Amount	0.00

Outstanding Invoices/Statement Charges

✓	Date	Type	Number	Orig. Amt.	Disc. Date	Amt. Due	Payment
✓	01/01/98	Invoice		150.00		150.00	150.00
	01/02/98	Invoice	1	300.00		300.00	0.00
					Totals	450.00	150.00

Customer Payment

	DATE	BALANCE
	01/15/98	3,685.00

Customer:Job Washington, Reed, and Bart

Amount 3,685.00
Pmt. Method Check
Check No. 80195

Memo

○ Group with other undeposited funds
○ Deposit To

Existing Credits	0.00	Total to Apply	3,685.00
☐ Apply Existing Credits?		Unapplied Amount	0.00

Outstanding Invoices/Statement Charges

✓	Date	Type	Number	Orig. Amt.	Disc. Date	Amt. Due	Payment
✓	01/01/98	Invoice		3,685.00		3,685.00	3,685.00
					Totals	3,685.00	3,685.00

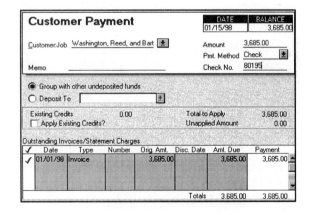

VIEW TRANSACTIONS BY CUSTOMER

In order to see the transactions for credit customers, you need to prepare a transaction report by customer. This report shows all sales, credits, and payments for each customer on account.

 *DO: Click **Reports** on the menu bar

Point to **Transaction Reports**
Click **By Customer**
    OR
Use QuickBooks Navigator:
    Click **Sales and Customers** tab
    Under the **Reports** option at the bottom of the screen, click **Sales**
    Click **Transaction by Customer**
Click **Header/Footer** button, click **Date Prepared** to deselect, click **OK**
Click the drop-down list arrow for **Dates**
Click **Custom**
Tab to or click **From**
Enter **01/01/98**
Tab to or click **To**
Enter **01/15/98**
Tab to generate the report
Scroll through the report
- Notice that information is shown for the opening balances, invoices, cash sales, credit memo, and payments made on the accounts.
- Notice that the **Num** column shows the invoice numbers, sales receipt numbers, credit memo numbers, and check numbers.

Click **Close** to exit the report

Creative Computer Consulting (CCC)
Transactions by Customer
January 1 - 15, 1998

Type	Date	Num	Memo	Account	Clr	Split	Amount
Andrews, Eric Research Corp.							
Invoice	01/01/98		Opening bal...	Accounts Receiva...		Uncategoriz...	815.00
Cash Sale	01/09/98	3		Undeposited Funds		-SPLIT-	335.00
Payment	01/15/98	0684		Undeposited Funds		Accounts R...	815.00
Bailey, Raymond CPA							
Cash Sale	01/08/98	1		Undeposited Funds		-SPLIT-	415.00
Cash Sale	01/09/98	2		Undeposited Funds		Training Inco...	95.00
Benjamin, Jacobs, and Moore							
Invoice	01/01/98		Opening bal...	Accounts Receiva...		Uncategoriz...	1,915.00

Partial Report

DEPOSIT CHECKS RECEIVED FOR CASH SALES AND PAYMENTS ON ACCOUNT

When you record cash sales and the receipt of payments on accounts, QuickBooks places the money received in the "Undeposited Funds" account. Once the deposit is recorded, the funds are transferred from "Undeposited Funds" to the account selected when preparing the deposit.

MEMO

DATE: January 15, 1998

Deposit all checks received for cash sales and payments on account.

---

*DO: Deposit checks received:
　　Click **Activities** on the menu bar
　　Click **Make Deposits**
　　　　OR
　　Use QuickBooks Navigator:
　　　　Click **Sales and Customers**
　　　　Click **Deposits**

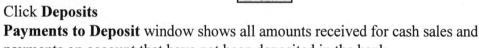

- **Payments to Deposit** window shows all amounts received for cash sales and payments on account that have not been deposited in the bank.
- Notice that the ✓ column to the left of the Date column is empty.

Click ✓✓✓**Select All** button
- Notice the check marks in the ✓ column.

Click **OK** to close Payment to Deposit screen and open Make Deposit screen

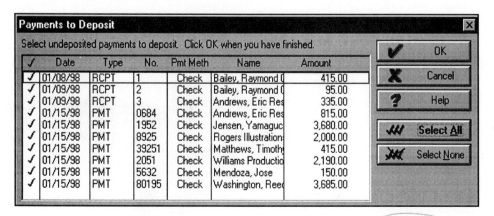

On the Make Deposits screen, **Deposit To** should be **Checking**
Date should be **01/15/98**

- Tab to date and change if not correct.

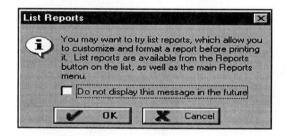

Click **Print** button to print **Deposit Summary**
If a List Reports dialog box appears, click **OK**

Click **Print** on the **Print Lists** dialog box
Check the **Settings** for **Print List**, click **Print**
When printing is finished, click **OK** on Make Deposits to record and close

PRINT JOURNAL

Even though QuickBooks displays registers and reports in a manner that focuses on the transaction—for example, entering a sale on account via an invoice—it still keeps a General Journal. The Journal records each transaction and lists the accounts and the amounts for debit and credit entries.

*DO: Print the Journal
    Click **Reports**
    Point to **Other Reports**
        OR
    Use QuickBooks Navigator:
        Click **Company** tab

        Under **Reports**, click **Other**

Click **Journal**

Change the **Header/Footer** so the **Date Prepared** is not selected, click **OK**

Click the drop-down list arrow for **Date**

Click **Custom**

Tab to **From** date

Enter **01/01/98**

Tab to **To** field

Enter **01/15/98**

Tab to generate the report

Scroll through the report to view the transactions

Click **Print** button

On the Print Reports screen, the settings will be the same used previously except:

        Click **Landscape** to select Landscape orientation

        Click on **Fit report to one page wide** to select this item

        • The printer will print the Journal using a smaller font so the report will fit across the 11-inch width.

Click **Print**

• The Journal will be several pages in length.

Close the report

Creative Computer Consulting (CCC)
Journal
January 1 - 15, 1998

Trans #	Type	Date	Num	Name	Memo	Account	Debit	Credit
1	Invoice	01/01/98		Andrews, Eric Re...	Opening b...	Accounts Rece...	815.00	
				Andrews, Eric Re...	Opening b...	Uncategorized ...		815.00
							815.00	815.00
2	Invoice	01/01/98		Benjamin, Jacobs...	Opening b...	Accounts Rece...	1,915.00	
				Benjamin, Jacobs...	Opening b...	Uncategorized ...		1,915.00
							1,915.00	1,915.00
3	Invoice	01/01/98		Cinema Innovations	Opening b...	Accounts Rece...	1,295.00	
				Cinema Innovations	Opening b...	Uncategorized ...		1,295.00
							1,295.00	1,295.00

Partial Report

PRINT THE TRIAL BALANCE

When all sales transactions have been entered, it is important to print the trial balance and verify that the total debits equal the total credits.

 *DO: Click **Reports**

        Point to **Other**

            OR

Use QuickBooks Navigator:
    Click **Company** tab
    Under **Reports**, click **Other**
Click **Trial Balance**
Change **Header/Footer** so **Date Prepared** does not print, Click **OK**
Click drop-down list arrow next to **Dates**
Click **Custom**
Tab to **From**
Enter **01/01/98**
Tab to **To**
Enter **01/15/98**
Tab to generate the report
Click **Print** button
On the Print Reports screen, click **Portrait** to select Portrait orientation
If necessary, click on **Fit report to one page wide** to deselect this item
Click **Print**

Creative Computer Consulting (CCC) Trial Balance As of January 15, 1998	Jan 15, '98 Debit	Credit
Checking	51,650.00	
Accounts Receivable	17,650.00	
Office Supplies	500.00	
Undeposited Funds	0.00	
Company Cars: Original Cost	49,000.00	
Office Equipment: Original Cost		8,050.00
Accounts Payable		850.00
Loan Payable	0.00	
Loan Payable: Company Cars Loan		35,000.00
Loan Payable: Office Equipment Loan		4,000.00
Roger Owens, Capital		31,420.00
Roger Owens, Capital: Investments		25,000.00
Income: Installation Income		175.00
Income: Technical Support Income		900.00
Income: Training Income		7,850.00
Uncategorized Income		22,505.00
Uncategorized Expenses	850.00	850.00
TOTAL	127,700.00	127,700.00

Close the report

GRAPHS IN QUICKBOOKS®

Once transactions have been entered, transaction results can be visually represented in a graphic form. QuickBooks illustrates Accounts Receivable by Aging Period as a bar chart, and it illustrates Accounts Receivable by Customer as a pie chart. For further details, double-click on an individual section of the pie chart or chart legend to create a bar chart analyzing an individual customer. QuickBooks also prepares graphs based on sales and will show the results of sales by item and by customer.

PREPARE ACCOUNTS RECEIVABLE GRAPHS

Accounts Receivable graphs illustrate account information based on the age of the account and the percentage of accounts receivable owed by each customer.

  *DO: Create graphs for accounts receivable:
      Click **Reports** on the menu bar
      Point to **Graphs** on the drop-down menu
      Click **Accounts Receivable**
        OR
      Use QuickBooks Navigator:
        Click **Sales and Customers** tab
        Under **Reports**, click **Accounts Receivable**
        Click **Accounts Receivable Graph**
      Click **Dates** button on the QuickInsight: Accounts Receivable Graphs
      On the **Change Graph Dates** change **Show Age As of** to **01/15/98**
      Click **OK**
      • QuickBooks generates a bar chart illustrating Accounts Receivable by Aging Period and a pie chart illustrating Accounts Receivable by Customer
      Click **Print**

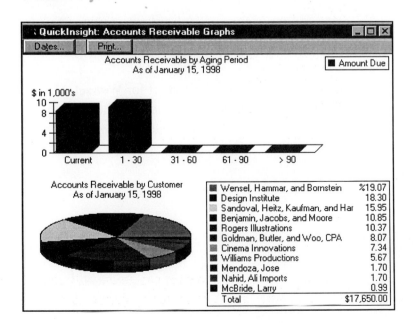

Click **Dates** button

Enter **02/01/98** for the **Show Aging As of** date

Click **OK**

• Notice the difference in the aging of accounts.

Click **Dates**

Enter **03/01/98**

Click **OK**

• Again, notice the difference in aging of accounts.

Click **Dates**

Enter **01/15/98**

Do not close the report

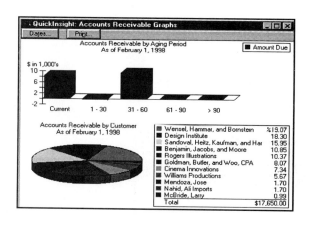
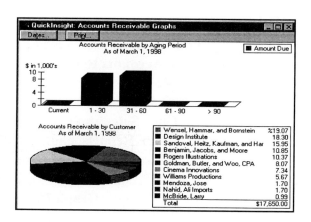

USE QUICKZOOM FEATURE TO OBTAIN INDIVIDUAL CUSTOMER DETAILS

It is possible to get detailed information regarding the aging of transactions for an individual customer by using the QuickZoom feature of QuickBooks.

*DO: Double-click on the section of the pie chart for **Wensel, Hammar, and Bornstein**

• You get a bar chart aging the transactions of the customer.

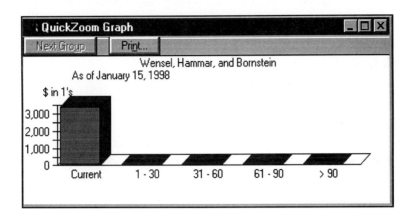

Printing is not required for this chart
- If a hard (printed) copy is desired, click **Print**.

Close the chart for Wensel, Hammar, and Bornstein

Double-click the section of the pie chart for **Cinema Innovations**
- Notice the age of the transactions for this customer.

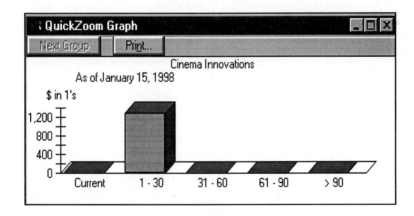

Printing is not required for this chart
- If you want a hard copy, click **Print**.

Close all charts

PREPARE SALES GRAPHS

Sales graphs illustrate the amount of cash and credit sales for a given period as well as the percentage of sales for each sales item.

 *DO: Click **Reports**
Point to **Graphs**
Click **Sales**

OR

Use QuickBooks Navigator:

> Click **Sales and Customers** tab
> Under **Reports**, click **Sales**
> Click **Sales Graph**

Click **Dates** button

Click drop-down list arrow next to **Graph Dates** button

Click **Custom**

Tab to **From**

Enter **01/01/98**

Tab to **To**

Enter **01/15/98**

Click **OK**

By Item button should be indented

- You will see a bar chart representing Sales by Month and a pie chart displaying a Sales Summary by item.

Printing is not required for this chart

- If you want a printed copy, click **Print**.

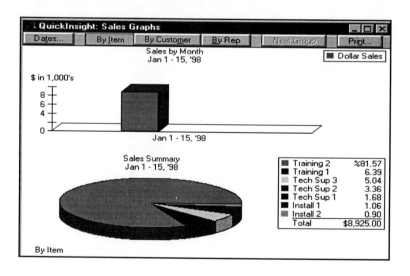

Click **By Customer** button

- Again, you will see a bar chart representing Sales by Month; however, the pie chart will display a Sales Summary by customer.

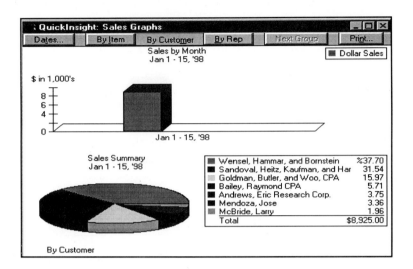

Printing is not required for this graph
- If you want a printed copy, click **Print**.

USE QUICKZOOM TO VIEW AN INDIVIDUAL ITEM OR CUSTOMER

It is possible to use QuickZoom to view details regarding an individual item's sales by month or an individual customer's sales by month.

 *DO: Sales Summary by Customer must be on the screen
In the chart legend, double-click **Larry McBride**
You will see the Sales by Month for Larry McBride

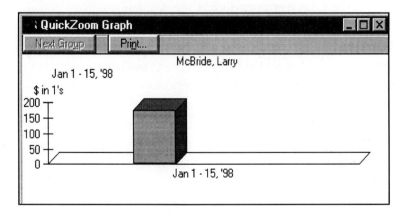

Close the QuickZoom graph for Larry McBride
Click **By Item**
You will see the Sales Summary by Item

In the chart legend, double-click **Install 1**

You will see the Sales by Month for Install 1

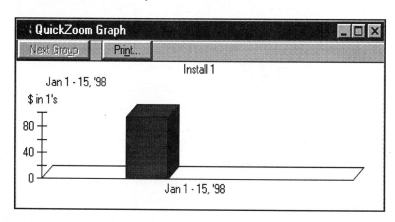

Click **Print** button to print the graph

Close Graphs

BACK UP AND CLOSE COMPANY

 *DO: Back up the company

Click **File Menu**

Click **Back Up...**

The **Back Up Company To...** dialog box appears

File name for the backup copy of the company files is **Creative.qbb**

Verify that the drive is A:\

- QuickBooks will back up the information for Creative Computer Consultants on the **Creative** data disk in the A:\ drive
- If you wish to use a separate backup disk, place the backup disk in the B:\ drive. When you see the name Creative.qbb on the Back Up Company To... screen, click drop-down list arrow next to Drives, click B:\. If you have only one disk drive, see your instructor.

Click **OK** button on the **Back Up Company To...** dialog box

- QuickBooks displays a dialog box stating that the backup was successful

Click **OK**

Click **File Menu**

Click **Close Company**

SUMMARY

In this chapter, cash and credit sales were prepared for Creative Computer Consulting, a service business, using sales receipts and invoices. Credit memos were issued. Customer accounts were added and revised. Invoices and sales receipts were edited, deleted, and voided. Cash payments were received and bank deposits were made. All the transactions entered reinforced the QuickBooks concept of using the business form to record transactions rather than enter information in journals. However, QuickBooks does not disregard traditional accounting methods. Instead, it performs this function in the background. The Journal was accessed and changes to transactions were made via the Journal. The fact that the Customer:Job list functions as the Accounts Receivable ledger and that the Chart of Accounts is the General Ledger in QuickBooks was pointed out. The importance of reports for information and decision making was illustrated. Exploration of the various sales and accounts receivable reports and graphs allowed information to be viewed from a sales standpoint and from an accounts receivable perspective. Sales reports emphasized both cash and credit sales according to the customer or according to the sales item generating the revenue. Accounts receivable reports focused on amounts owed by credit customers. The traditional trial balance emphasizing the equality of debits and credits was prepared.

END-OF-CHAPTER QUESTIONS

TRUE/FALSE

ANSWER THE FOLLOWING QUESTIONS IN THE SPACE PROVIDED BEFORE THE QUESTION NUMBER.

____T____ 1.   A new customer can be added to a company's records "on the fly."

____T____ 2.   In QuickBooks, error correction for a sale on account can be accomplished by editing the invoice.

____F____ 3.   A Sales Item list stores information about products you purchase.

____F____ 4.   Once transactions have been entered, modifications to a customer's account may be made only at the end of the fiscal year.

____F____ 5.   In QuickBooks all transactions must be entered with the traditional debit/credit method.

____T____ 6.   Checks received for cash sales are held in the undeposited funds account until the bank deposit is made.

____T____ 7.   When a correction for a transaction is made, QuickBooks not only changes the form used to record the transaction, it also changes all journal and account entries for the transaction to reflect the correction.

____T____ 8.   QuickGraphs allow information to be viewed from both a sales standpoint and from an accounts receivable perspective.

____T____ 9.   QuickZoom allows you to print a report instantly.

____F____ 10. A customer's payment on account is immediately recorded in the cash account.

MULTIPLE CHOICE

WRITE THE LETTER OF THE CORRECT ANSWER IN THE SPACE PROVIDED BEFORE THE QUESTION NUMBER.

_____ 1. To remove an invoice without a trace, it is ___.
A. voided
B. deleted
C. erased
D. reversed

_____ 2. To enter a cash sale, a(n) ___ is completed.
A. debit
B. invoice
C. sales receipt
D. bank deposit

_____ 3. Two primary types of lists used in this chapter are ___.
A. receivables and payables
B. invoices and checks
C. registers and navigator
D. customers and sales item

_____ 4. When you enter an invoice, an error may be corrected by ___.
A. backspacing or deleting
B. tabbing and typing
C. dragging and typing
D. all of the above

_____ 5. While in the Customer Balance Summary Report, it is possible to get an individual customer's information by using ___.
A. QuickReport
B. QuickZoom
C. QuickGraph
D. QuickSummary

_____ 6. Undeposited Funds represents ___.
A. cash or checks received from customers but not yet deposited in the bank
B. all cash sales
C. the balance of the accounts receivable account
D. none of the above

_____ 7.   QuickBooks uses graphs to illustrate information about ___.
           A. the chart of accounts
           B. sales
           C. the cash account
           D. supplies

_____ 8.   Changes to the chart of accounts may be made ___.
           A. at the beginning of a fiscal period
           B. before the end of the fiscal year
           C. at any time
           D. once established, the chart of accounts may not be modified

_____ 9.   To obtain information about sales by item, you can view ___.
           A. the income statement
           B. the trial balance
           C. receivables reports
           D. sales reports

_____ 10. When you add a customer using the Set Up method, you ___.
           A. add complete information for a customer
           B. add only a customer's name
           C. add the customer's name, address, and telephone number
           D. add the customer's name and telephone number

FILL-IN

IN THE SPACE PROVIDED, WRITE THE ANSWER THAT MOST APPROPRIATELY
COMPLETES THE SENTENCE.

1. The report used to view all the balances on account of each customer is the _____.

2. The form prepared to show a reduction to a transaction is a(n) _____.

3. The report that proves that debits equals credits is the _____.

4. QuickBooks generates a _____ illustrating Accounts Receivable by Aging Period.

5. To verify the company being used in QuickBooks, you check the _____.

SHORT ESSAY

Explain how the method used to enter an accounts receivable transaction in QuickBooks is different from the method used to enter a transaction in an accounting textbook.

_____

_____

_____

_____

_____

END-OF-CHAPTER PROBLEM

SUNSHINE LAWN AND POOL MAINTENANCE

Sunshine Lawn and Pool Maintenance is owned and operated by George Gordon. Sylvia and Greg Gordon also work for the company. Sylvia manages the office and keeps the books for the business. George provides lawn maintenance and supervises the lawn maintenance employees. Greg provides the pool maintenance. Sunshine is located in Santa Barbara, California.

INSTRUCTIONS

Check with your instructor to obtain a disk containing the data for Sunshine Lawn and Pool Maintenance. Copy the data file **Sunshine.QBW** to a new disk and open the company. Record the following transactions using invoices and sales receipts. Make bank deposits as indicated. Print the reports and graphs as indicated.

The invoices and sales receipts are numbered consecutively. Invoice #25 is the first invoice number used in this problem. Sales Receipt #15 is the first sales receipt number used in this problem. Each invoice recorded should contain a message. Choose the one that you feel is most appropriate for the transaction.

When recording transactions, use the following Sales Item chart to determine the item(s) billed. If the transaction does not indicate the size of the pool or property, use the first category for the item—for example, LandCom 1 or LandRes 1 would be used for standard-size landscape service. Remember that PoolCom 1 and PoolRes 1 are services for spas—not pools. The appropriate billing for a standard-size pool would be PoolCom 2 or PoolRes 2.

SUNSHINE POOL AND LAWN MAINTENANCE
SALES ITEM LIST

ITEM	DESCRIPTION	AMOUNT
LandCom 1	Commercial Landscape Maintenance (Standard Size)	$150 mo.
LandCom 2	Commercial Landscape Maintenance (Med.)	250 mo.
LandCom 3	Commercial Landscape Maintenance (Lg.)	500 mo.
LandRes 1	Residential Landscape Maintenance (Standard Size)	$100 mo.
LandRes 2	Residential Landscape Maintenance (Med.)	200 mo.
LandRes 3	Residential Landscape Maintenance (Lg.)	350 mo.
PoolCom 1	Commercial Spa Service	$100 mo.
PoolCom 2	Commercial Pool Service (All pools unless specified as Lg.)	300 mo.
PoolCom 3	Commercial Pool Service (Lg.)	500 mo.
PoolRes 1	Residential Spa Service	$ 50 mo.
PoolRes 2	Residential Pool Service (All pools unless specified as Lg.)	100 mo.
PoolRes 3	Residential Pool Service (Lg.)	150 mo.
LandTrim	Trimming and Pruning	$75 hr.
LandPlant	Planting and Cultivating	50 hr.
LandWater	Sprinklers, Timers, etc.	75 hr.
LandGrow	Fertilize, Spray for Pests	75 hr.
PoolRepair	Mechanical Maintenance and Repairs	$75 hr.
PoolWash	Acid Wash, Condition	Price by the job
PoolStart	Startup for New Pools	500.00

RECORD TRANSACTIONS

Add your name to the company name. The company name will be **Sunshine Lawn and Pool Maintenance--Student's Name**. (Type your actual name *not* the words "Student's Name.")

Print each invoice and sales receipt as it is completed.

May 1

Billed Johnson Motel for monthly landscape services and monthly pool maintenance services, Invoice #25. (Use LandCom 1 to record the monthly landscape service fee and PoolCom 2 to record the monthly pool service fee. The quantity for each item is 1.) Terms are Net 15.

Billed Dr. Robbins for monthly landscape and pool services at his home. Both the pool and landscaping are standard size. The terms are Net 30.

Billed Corner Creations for 2 hours shrub trimming. Terms are Net 30.

Received Check No. 381 for $500 from Joseph Johansen for pool startup services at his home, Sales Receipt #15.

Received Check No. 8642 from Jose Montoya for $150 for 3 hours of planting flowers. This is payment in full on the account.

May 15

Billed a new customer: Ron Glass—10824 Hope Ranch St., Santa Barbara, CA 93110, 805-555-9825, terms Net 30—for monthly service on his large pool and large residential landscape maintenance.

Received Check No. 6758 from Johnson Motel in payment of Invoice 25.

Received Check No. 987 from a new customer: Winston Chang (a neighbor of Ron Glass) for $75 for 1 hour of pool repairs. Even though this is a cash sale, do a complete customer setup: 10877 Hope Ranch St., Santa Barbara, CA 93110, 805-555-7175, fax 805-555-5717, terms Net 30.

Billed Paradise Resorts for maintenance on their large pool and large landscaping maintenance. Also bill for 5 hours planting, 3 hours trimming, and 2 hours spraying on the landscaping and for 3 hours pool repair services. Terms are Net 15.

May 30

Received Check No. 1247 for $525 as payment in full from Corner Creations.

Received Check No. 8865 from Julia Smythe for amount due.

Billed Blue Roof Resorts for large pool and large landscaping maintenance. Terms are Net 15.

Billed Andrews Arms Apartments for standard-size commercial pool service and standard-size commercial landscape maintenance. Terms are Net 30.

Deposit all cash receipts. Print Deposit Summary.

PRINT REPORTS

Customer Balance Detail Report. Portrait orientation, fit to one page wide.
Summary Sales by Item Report for 5/1/98 through 5/31/98. Portrait orientation.
Journal Reports for 5/1/98 through 5/31/98. Print in Landscape orientation, fit to one page wide.
Trial Balance. Portrait orientation.
Sales Graph for 5/1/98 through 5/31/98

PAYABLES AND PURCHASES: SERVICE BUSINESS

LEARNING OBJECTIVES

At the completion of this chapter you will be able to:

1. Understand the concepts for computerized accounting for payables.
2. Enter, edit, correct, delete, and pay bills.
3. Add new vendors and modify vendor records.
4. View accounts payable transaction history from the enter bills window.
5. View and/or print QuickReports for vendors, Accounts Payable Register, etc.
6. Use the QuickZoom feature.
7. Record and edit transactions in the Accounts Payable Register.
8. Enter vendor credits.
9. Print, edit, void, and delete checks.
10. Pay for expenses using petty cash.
11. Add new accounts.
12. Display and print Accounts Payable Aging Summary Report, an Unpaid Bills Detail Report, a Vendor Balance Summary Report, and an Accounts Payable Graph by Aging Period.

ACCOUNTING FOR PAYABLES AND PURCHASES

In a service business, most of the accounting for purchases and payables is simply paying bills for expenses incurred in the operation of the business. Purchases are for things used in the operation of the business. Some transactions will be in the form of cash purchases, and others will be purchases on account. Bills can be paid when they are received or when they are due. Rather than use cumbersome journals, QuickBooks continues to focus on recording transactions based on the business document; therefore, you use the Enter Bills and Pay Bills features of the program to record the receipt and payment of bills. QuickBooks can remind you when payments are due and can calculate and apply discounts earned for paying bills early. Payments can be made by recording payments in the pay bills window or, if using the cash basis for accounting, by writing a check. A cash purchase can be recorded by writing a check or by using petty cash. Even though QuickBooks focuses on recording transactions on the business forms used, all transactions are recorded behind the scenes in the general journal. QuickBooks uses a Vendor's list for all vendors with which the company has an account. QuickBooks does not refer to the Vendor list as the Accounts Payable ledger, yet that is exactly what it is. The total of the Vendor list/Accounts Payable ledger will match the total of the Accounts Payable account in the Chart of Accounts/General ledger.

As in Chapter 2, corrections can be made directly on the bill or within the transaction journal. New accounts and vendors may be added "on the fly" as transactions are entered. Reports illustrating vendor balances, unpaid bills, accounts payable aging, transaction history, and accounts payable registers may be viewed and printed. Graphs analyzing the amount of accounts payable by aging period provide a visual illustration of the accounts payable.

TRAINING TUTORIAL AND PROCEDURES

The following tutorial will once again work with Creative Computer Consulting (CCC). As in Chapter 2, transactions will be recorded for this fictitious company. To maximize training benefits, you should:

1. Read the entire chapter *before* beginning to enter transactions for CCC.
2. Answer the end-of-chapter questions.
3. Be aware that transactions to be entered are given within a **MEMO**.
4. Complete all the steps listed for the Creative Computer Consulting (CCC) tutorial in the chapter. The steps are indicated by: ▨ ***DO:**
5. When you have completed a step, put an **X** on the button next to ***DO:**
6. As you complete your work, proofread carefully and check for accuracy. Double-check amounts of money.
7. If you find an error while preparing a transaction, correct it. If you find the error after the transaction has been entered, follow the steps indicated in this chapter to correct, void, or delete the transaction.
8. Print as directed in the chapter.
9. You may not finish the entire chapter in one computer session. Always back up your work at the end of your work session as described in Chapter 1.
10. When you complete your computer session, always close your company.

OPEN QUICKBOOKS® AND CREATIVE COMPUTER CONSULTING—CCC

▨ ***DO:** Open QuickBooks as instructed in Chapters 1 and 2
   Open Creative Computer Consulting (CCC)
     Click **File**
     Click **Open Company**
     Click **Creative.qbw**
     Check to make sure you are using the disk in A:\

Click **Open** button
Close the Reminders screen
Check the title bar to verify that Creative Computer Consulting (CCC)--Student's
Name is the open company

BEGINNING THE TUTORIAL

In this chapter you will be entering bills incurred by the company in the operation of the business. You will also be recording the payment of bills, purchases using checks, and purchases/payments using petty cash.

The Vendor list keeps information regarding the vendors with whom you do business and is the Accounts Payable ledger. Vendor information includes the vendor names, addresses, telephone numbers, payment terms, credit limits, and account numbers. You will be using the following list for vendors with which CCC has an account:

Vendor List	
Name	**Balance**
Communication Services Telephone	0.00
Computer Professionals Magazine	0.00
Global Advertising	500.00
Joe's Garage and Auto Services	0.00
Johnson Realtors	0.00
Office Supplies Wholesale	350.00
Southern California Electric	0.00
Southern California Gas Co.	0.00
Southern California Water	0.00
XYZ Insurance Company	0.00
Zip Delivery Service	0.00
Vendor ▼ Activities ▼ Reports ▼ ☒ Show All	

All transactions are listed on memos. The transaction date will be the same date as the memo date unless otherwise specified within the transaction. Vendor names, when necessary, will be given in the transaction. Unless otherwise specified, terms are Net 30. Once a specific type of transaction has been entered in a step-by-step manner, additional transactions of the same or a similar type will made without having instructions provided. Of course, you may always refer to instructions given for previous transactions for ideas or for steps used to enter those transactions. To determine the account used in the transaction, refer to the Chart of Accounts. When you are entering account information on a bill, clicking on the drop-down list arrow will show a copy of the Chart of Accounts.

ENTER A BILL

QuickBooks provides accounts payable tracking. Entering bills as soon as they are received is an efficient way to record your liabilities. Once bills have been entered, QuickBooks will be able to provide up-to-date cash flow reports, and QuickBooks will remind you when it's time to pay your bills. A bill is divided into two sections: a vendor-related section (the upper part of the bill that looks similar to a check and has a memo text box under it) and a detail section (the area that is divided into columns for Account, Amount, and Memo). The vendor-related section of the bill is where information for the actual bill is entered, including a memo with information about the transaction. The detail section is where the expense accounts, expense account amounts, and transaction explanations are indicated.

MEMO

DATE: January 16, 1998

Record the following bill: Global Advertising prepared and placed advertisements in local business publications announcing our new hardware installation service. Received bill for $260 for this, Global's Inv. #9875, terms Net 30.

---

*DO: Record the above transaction
  Click **Bill** on the iconbar
    OR
  Use QuickBooks Navigator:
    Click **Purchases and Vendors** tab
    Click **Enter Bills**
  Complete the **Vendor-Related Section** of the bill:
    Click the drop-down list arrow next to **Vendor**
    Click **Global Advertising**
   • Name is entered as the vendor.
    Tab to **Date**
   • When you tab to the date, it will be highlighted.
   • When you type in the new date, the highlighted date will be deleted.
    Type **01/16/98** as the date
    Tab to **Ref No.**
    Type the vendor's invoice number: **9875**
    Tab to **Amount Due**
    Type **260**
   • QuickBooks will automatically insert the .00 after the amount.

Bill

Tab to **Terms**

Click the drop-down list arrow next to **Terms**

Click **Net 30**

- QuickBooks automatically changes the Bill Due date to show 30 days from the transaction date.
- At this time no change will be made to Bill Due date, and nothing will be inserted as a memo.

Complete the **Detail Section** of the bill:

Tab to or click in the column for **Account**

Click the drop-down list arrow next to **Account**

Click **Advertising Expense**

- Based on the accrual method of accounting, Advertising Expense is selected as the account used in this transaction because this expense should be matched against the revenue of the period.

The **Amount** column already shows **260.00**—no entry required

Tab to or click the first line in the column for **Memo**

Enter the transaction explanation of **Ads for Hardware Installation Services**

Do not click OK

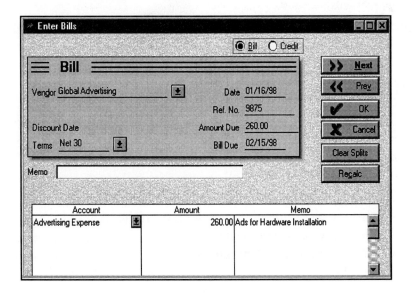

EDIT AND CORRECT ERRORS

If an error is discovered while entering invoice information, it may be corrected by positioning the cursor in the field containing the error. You may do this by tabbing to move forward through each field or pressing Shift+Tab to move back to the field containing the error. If the error is highlighted, type the correction. If the error is not highlighted, you can correct the error by pressing the backspace or the delete key as many times as necessary to remove the error, then type the correction. (Alternate method: Point to error, highlight by dragging the mouse through the error, then type the correction.)

*DO: Practice editing and making corrections to the bill for Global Advertising:
Click the drop-down list arrow for **Vendor**
Click **Communication Services Telephone Co.**
- The entire name will *not* show because only the first 28 characters in a company name are displayed on the list.

Tab to **Date**
To increase the date by one day, press **+**
- You may capitalize the **=** next to the backspace key, or you may press the **+** key on the numerical keypad.

Press **+** two more times
- The date should be **01/19/98**.

To decrease the date by one day, press **-**
- You may type a hyphen (**-**) next to the number **0**, or you may press the hyphen (**-**) key on the numerical keypad.

Press **-** two more times
- The date should be **01/16/98**.

Click between the **2** and the **6** in **Amount Due**
Press **Delete** key two times to delete the **60**
Key in **99**
- The Amount Due should be **299.00**.
- The transaction explanation has been entered in the Memo column in the detail area of the bill and shows the transaction explanation of Ads for Hardware Installation Services.
  - This memo prints on all reports that include the transaction.
- The same information should be in the Memo text box in the vendor-related area of the bill so it will appear as part of the transaction in the Accounts Payable Account as well as all reports that include the transaction.

Copy **Ads for Hardware Installation Services** from the Memo column to the Memo text box:
Click to the left of the letter **A** in Ads
Highlight the memo text—Ads for Hardware Installation Services:
Hold down the primary mouse button
While holding down the primary mouse button, drag through the memo text **Ads for Hardware Installation Services**
Click **Edit** menu
Click **Copy**

- Notice that the keyboard shortcut **Ctrl+C** is listed. This shortcut could be used rather than using the Edit menu and Copy.
- This actually copies the text and places it in a temporary storage area of Windows called the Clipboard.

Click in the **Memo** text box beneath the **Terms**

Click **Edit** menu

Click **Paste**

- Notice the keyboard shortcut **Ctrl+V**.
- This inserts a copy of the material in the Windows Clipboard into the Memo text box—**Ads for Hardware Installation Services**
  - This explanation will appear in the Memo area for the transaction in the Accounts Payable account as well as in any report that used the individual transaction information.

Click the drop-down list arrow for **Vendor**

Click **Global Advertising**

Click to the right of the last **9** in **Amount Due**

Backspace two times to delete the **99**

Key in **60**

- The **Amount Due** should once again show **260.00**

Click **Terms** drop-down list arrow

Click **Net 30**

Click **OK** button to record the bill and return to the main screen

- The **Name Information Changed** dialog box will appear. It states: "You have changed the Terms for Global Advertising. Would you like the have this new information appear next time?"

Click **NO**

PREPARE A BILL USING MORE THAN ONE EXPENSE ACCOUNT

MEMO
DATE: January 18, 1998

On the recommendation of the office manager, Carmen Mendoza, CCC is trying out several different models of fax machines on a monthly basis. Received a bill from Office Supplies Wholesale for one month's rental of a fax machine, $25, and for fax supplies, which were consumed during January, $20, Invoice # 1035A, Terms Net 10.

---

*DO: Record the transaction listed in the above memo. This transaction involves two expense accounts:

Click **Bill** on the iconbar
    Or

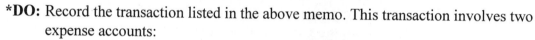

Use QuickBooks Navigator:
    Click **Purchases and Vendors** tab
    Click **Enter Bills**
Complete the **Vendor-Related Section** of the bill:
    Click the drop-down list arrow next to **Vendor**
    Click **Office Supplies Wholesale**
    Tab to or click **Date**
    •   If you click in Date, you will have to delete the current date.
    Enter **01/18/98**
    Tab to or click **Reference Number**
    Key in the vendor's invoice number: **1035A**
    Tab to or click **Amount Due**
    Enter **45**
    Tab to or click on the line for **Terms**
    Type **Net 10** on the line for Terms
    •   You will get a Terms Not Found Message Box.

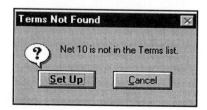

Click **Set Up** button

Complete the information required in the **New Terms** dialog box:

    Net 10 should appear as the Term

    Standard should be selected

    Net due should be **10** days

    Discount percentage should be **0**

    Discount if paid within **0** days

    Click **OK**

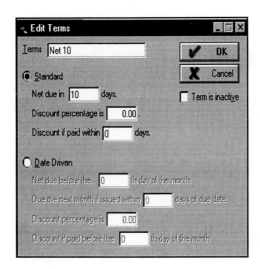

Tab to or click the Memo text box

Enter **Fax Rental and Fax Supplies for the Month** as the transaction
description

Complete the **Detail Section** of the bill:

    Tab to or click the first line for **Account**

    Click the drop-down list arrow next to **Account**

    Click **Equipment Rental**

- Because a portion of this transaction is for equipment that is being rented,
  Equipment Rental is the appropriate account to use.

Amount column shows **45.00**

Change this to reflect the actual amount of the Equipment Rental Expense

    Tab to **Amount** to highlight

    Type **25**

Tab to **Memo**

Enter **Fax Rental for the Month** as the transaction explanation

Tab to **Account**

Click the drop-down list arrow next to **Account**

Click **Office Supplies Expense**

- The transaction information indicates that the fax supplies will be used within the month of January. Using Office Supplies Expense account correctly charges the supplies expense against the period.
- If the transaction indicated that the fax supplies were purchased to have on hand, the appropriate account to use would be the asset Office Supplies.

Amount column correctly shows **20.00** as the amount

Tab to or click **Memo**

Enter **Fax Supplies for the Month** as the transaction explanation

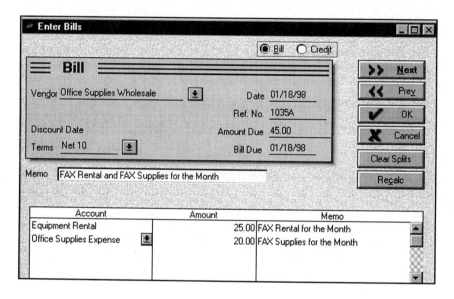

Click **OK** to close the bill

- If you get a message regarding the change of Terms for Office Supplies Wholesale, click **No**.

PRINT TRANSACTION BY VENDOR REPORT

To obtain information regarding individual transactions grouped by vendor, you prepare a transaction report by vendor. This allows you to view the vendors for which you have recorded transactions. The type of transaction is identified; for example, the word *Bill* appears when you have entered the transaction as a bill. The transaction date, any invoice numbers or memos entered when recording the transaction, the accounts used, and the transaction amount appear in the report.

 *DO: Prepare a Transaction by Vendor Report

    Click **Reports** menu

    Point to **Transaction Reports**

Click **By Vendor**
    OR
Use QuickBooks Navigator:
    Click **Purchases and Vendors** tab
    In the Report section of the Navigator screen, click **Transaction By Vendor**
Click **Header/Footer**
Click **Date Prepared** to deselect this feature
Click **OK**
Click the drop-down list arrow for **Dates**
Click **Custom**
Tab to or click **From**
Enter **01/01/98**
Tab to or click **To**
Enter **01/18/98**
Tab to generate the report
Analyze the report:
- Look at each vendor account.
- Note the type of transaction, any invoice numbers and memos.
- The **Account** column shows **Accounts Payable** as the account.
- As in any traditional accounting transaction recording a purchase on account, the Accounts Payable account is credited.
- The **Split** column shows the other accounts used in the transaction.
- If the word **-SPLIT-** appears in this column, it indicates that more than one account was used.
- The last transaction for Office Supplies Wholesale has -SPLIT- in the Split Column. This is because the transaction used two accounts: Equipment Rental and Office Supplies Expense for the debit portion of the transaction.

Click **Print** button
Complete the information on the **Print Reports Screen**:
    Print To: The selected item should be **Printer**
- The printer name should appear in the printer text box. This may be different from the printer identified in this text.
  - If the correct printer does not appear, click the drop-down list arrow, click the correct printer.

    Orientation: Click **Landscape** for this report
    Page Range: All should be selected; if it is not, click All
    Click **Fit report to one page wide** to select
    Click **Print** button on the Print Reports Screen

Creative Computer Consulting (CCC)
Transactions by Vendor
January 1 - 18, 1998

◇	Type	◇	Date	◇	Num	◇	Memo	◇	Account	◇ Clr	◇	Split	◇	Amount
Global Advertising														
	Bill		01/01/98				Opening bal...		Accounts Payable			Uncategori...		-500.00
	Bill		01/16/98		9875				Accounts Payable			Advertising...		-260.00
Office Supplies Wholesale														
	Bill		01/01/98				Opening bal...		Accounts Payable			Uncategori...		-350.00
	Bill		01/18/98		1035A		FAX Rental ...		Accounts Payable			-SPLIT-		-45.00

USE THE QUICKZOOM FEATURE

Carmen Mendoza wants more detailed information regarding the accounts used in the Split column of the report. Specifically, she wants to know what accounts were used for the transaction of 1/18/98 for Office Supplies Wholesale. In order to see these account names, Carmen will use the QuickZoom feature of QuickBooks.

   *DO: Point to the word **-SPLIT-** in the Split column
- The mouse pointer turns into a magnifying glass with a **Z** in it.
  Double-click to **Zoom** in to see the accounts used in the transaction
- This returns you to the *original bill* entered for Office Supplies Wholesale for the transaction of 1/18/98.
- The accounts used are Equipment Rental Expense and Office Supplies Expense.

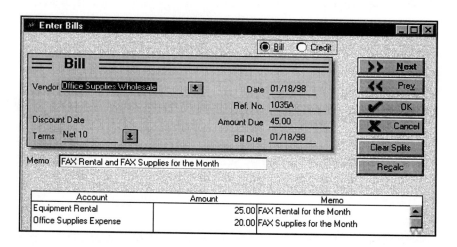

Click **Cancel** button to return to the Transaction by Vendor Report
Click **Close** button to close the report

PREPARE BILLS WITHOUT STEP-BY-STEP INSTRUCTIONS

MEMO
DATE: January 19, 1998

Received a bill from Computer Professionals Magazine for a 6-month subscription for Roger Owens, $74, Invoice Number 1579-53, Net 30 days. (Enter as an expense.)

Carmen Mendoza received office supplies from Office Supplies Wholesale, Invoice 8950S, $450, terms Net 10 days. These supplies will be used over a period of several months so enter as a prepaid expense. (Note: After you enter the vendor's name, the information from the previous bill appears on the screen. As you enter the transaction, simply delete any unnecessary information. This may be done by tabbing to the information and pressing the delete key until the information is deleted or dragging through the information to highlight, then in either method typing the new information.)

While Carolyn Masters was on her way to a training session at Sandoval, Heitz, Kaufman, and Harden, the company car broke down. It was towed to Joe's Garage and Auto Services, where it was repaired. The total bill for the towing and repair is $575, Invoice 630, Net 30 days.

Received a bill from XYZ Insurance Company for the annual auto insurance premium, $2,850, Invoice 3659, terms Net 30.

---

 *DO: Enter the four transactions in the memo above.
- Refer to the instructions given for the two previous transactions entered.
- Enter information for Memos where transaction explanation is needed for clarification.
- To go from one bill to the next, click **>>NEXT** button on the right side of the Bill.
- After entering the fourth bill, click **OK** to record and exit **ENTER BILLS** screen.

Remember that when recording bills, you will need to determine the accounts used in the transaction. The accrual method of accounting matches the expenses of a period against the revenue of the period. When you pay something in advance, it is recorded as an increase (debit) to an asset rather than an increase (debit) to an expense. At the time the prepaid asset is used, an adjusting entry is made to account for the amount used during the period. Unless otherwise instructed, use the accrual basis of accounting when recording the above entries. (Notice the exception in the first transaction.) To determine the appropriate accounts to use, refer to the Chart of Accounts/General Ledger as you record the above transactions.

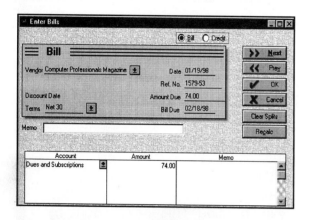
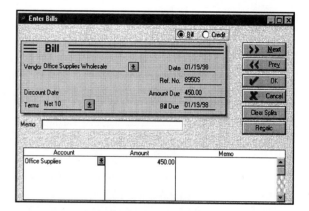
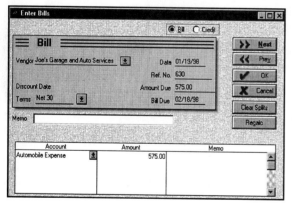
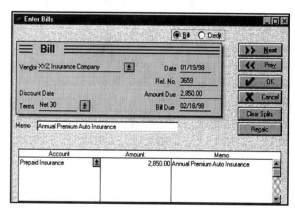

ENTER A BILL USING THE ACCOUNTS PAYABLE REGISTER

The Accounts Payable Register maintains a record of all the transactions recorded within the Accounts Payable account. Entering a bill directly into the Accounts Payable Register can be faster than filling out all of the information through Enter Bills.

MEMO

DATE: January 19, 1998

ZIP Delivery Service provides all of our delivery service for training manuals delivered to customers. Received monthly bill for January deliveries from ZIP Delivery Service, $175, Inv. No., 88764, terms Net 10.

---

*DO: Use the Accounts Payable Register to record the above transaction:
   Click the **Lists** menu, click **Chart of Accounts**
      OR
   Click the **Accnts** button on the iconbar
      OR
   Use the keyboard shortcut **Ctrl+A**
   Click **Accounts Payable**

Chart of Accounts		
Name	**Type**	**Balance**
◆ Checking	Bank	51,650.00
◆ Accounts Receivable	Accounts Receivable	17,650.00
◆ Employee Advances	Other Current Asset	0.00
◆ Office Supplies	Other Current Asset	950.00
◆ Prepaid Insurance	Other Current Asset	2,850.00
◆ Undeposited Funds	Other Current Asset	0.00
◆ Company Cars	Fixed Asset	49,000.00
◆ Depreciation	Fixed Asset	0.00
◆ Original Cost	Fixed Asset	49,000.00
◆ Office Equipment	Fixed Asset	8,050.00
◆ Depreciation	Fixed Asset	0.00
◆ Original Cost	Fixed Asset	8,050.00
◆ Accounts Payable	Accounts Payable	5,104.00
◆ Payroll Liabilities	Other Current Liability	0.00
◆ Loan Payable	Long Term Liability	39,000.00
◆ Company Cars Loan	Long Term Liability	35,000.00
◆ Office Equipment Loan	Long Term Liability	4,000.00
◆ Retained Earnings	Equity	
◆ Roger Owens, Capital	Equity	56,420.00
◆ Draws	Equity	0.00
◆ Investments	Equity	25,000.00
◆ Income	Income	

| Account ▼ | Activities ▼ | Reports ▼ | Show All |

Click **Activities** button at the bottom of the Chart of Accounts
Click **Use Register**
   OR
Use the keyboard shortcut **Ctrl+R**

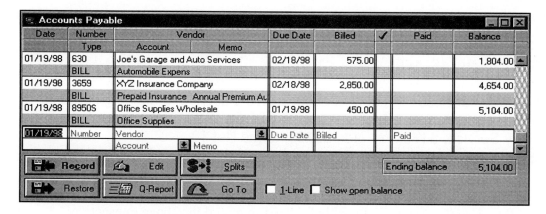

Click in the blank entry at the end of the Accounts Payable Register

The date is highlighted

Key in **01/19/98** for the transaction date

The word Number is in the next column

Tab to or click **Number**

• The word Number disappears.

Enter the Invoice Number **88764**

Tab to or click **Vendor**

Click the drop-down list arrow for Vendor

Click **Zip Delivery Service**

Tab to or click **Due Date**

Verify the due date of **01/29/98**

• If this is not the date showing, drag through the due date to highlight, then type **01/29/98**.

Tab to or click **Billed**

Enter the amount **175**

Tab to or click **Account**

Click the drop-down list arrow for **Account**

Determine the appropriate account to use for the delivery expense

• If all of the accounts do not appear in the drop-down list, scroll through the accounts until you find the one appropriate for this entry.

Click **Postage and Delivery**

Tab to or click **Memo**

For the transaction memo, key **January Delivery Expense**

Click **Record** button to record the transaction

Do not close the register

01/19/98	88764	Zip Delivery Service		01/29/98	175.00				5,279.00
	BILL	Postage and Deliv January Delivery E							

EDIT A TRANSACTION IN THE ACCOUNTS PAYABLE REGISTER

Because QuickBooks makes corrections extremely user friendly, a transaction can be edited or changed directly in the Accounts Payable Register as well as on the original bill. By eliminating the columns for Type and Memo, it is possible to change the register to show each transaction on one line. This can make the register easier to read.

MEMO
DATE: January 20, 1998

Upon examination of the invoices and the bills entered, Carmen Mendoza discovers two errors: The actual amount of the invoice for ZIP Delivery Services was $195. The amount recorded was $175. The amount of the Invoice for Computer Professionals Magazine was $79, not $74. Change the transaction amounts for these transactions.

---

*DO: Correct the above transactions in the Accounts Payable Register
   Click the check box for **1-line** to select
   • Each Accounts Payable transaction will appear on one line.
   Click between the **1** and **7** in the amount column for the invoice from ZIP Delivery Service
   Press **Delete** to delete the 7
   Type a **9**
   • The amount should be **195.00**.
   Scroll through the register until the transaction for *Computer Professionals Magazine* is visible
   Click between the **7** and the **4** in the transaction for *Computer Professionals Magazine*
   Leaving Transaction dialog box appears on the screen

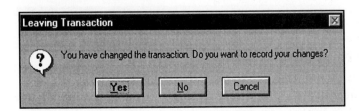

   Click **Yes** to record the changes to the Zip Delivery Service transaction

- The transaction for *Computer Professionals Magazine* will be the active transaction.

Click between the **4** and the **decimal point**

Press the **Backspace** key one time to delete the 4

Type a **9**

- The amount for the transaction should be **79.00**.

Click the **Record** button at the bottom of the Register to record the change in the transaction

Do not close the register

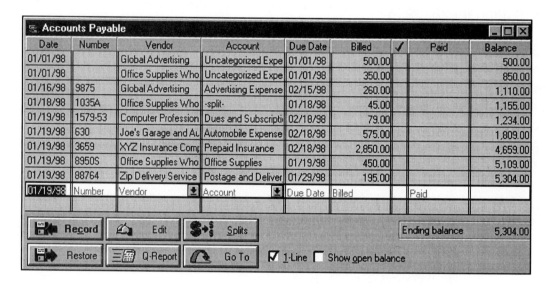

PREVIEW AND PRINT A QUICKREPORT
FROM THE ACCOUNTS PAYABLE REGISTER

After editing the transaction, you may want to view information about a specific vendor. This can be done quickly and efficiently by clicking the vendor's name within a transaction and clicking the Q-Report button at the bottom of the Register.

MEMO

DATE: January 20, 1998

Several transactions have been entered for Office Supplies Wholesale. The owner, Roger Owens, likes to view transaction information for all vendors that have several transactions within a short period of time.

*DO: Prepare a QuickReport for Office Supplies Wholesale

Click any field in any transaction for Office Supplies Wholesale

Click the **Q-Report** button at the bottom of the Register

- The Register QuickReport for All Transactions for Office Supplies Wholesale appears on the screen.

To remove the **Date Printed**, click **Header/Footer** button

Click **Date Prepared** to deselect this option

Click **OK**

Click **Print** button

Complete the information on the **Print Reports** screen:

   Print To: The selected item should be **Printer**

   - The printer name should appear in the printer text box.

   Orientation: click **Landscape** for this report

   Page Range: All should be selected; if it is not, click All

   Click **Fit report to one page wide** to select

Click **Preview** to view the report before printing

- The report appears on the screen as a full page.
- A full-page report on the screen usually cannot be read.

To read the text in the report, click **Zoom In** button at the top of the screen

Use the scroll buttons and bars to view the report columns

Click **Zoom Out** to return to a full-page view of the report

When finished viewing the report, click **Close**

- You will return to the Print Reports screen.

Click **Print** button on the Print Reports screen

Creative Computer Consulting (CCC)
Register QuickReport
All Transactions

◇ Type	◇ Date	◇ Num	◇ Memo	◇ Account	◇ Paid	◇ Open Balance	◇ Amount
Office Supplies Wholesale							
Bill	01/01/98		Opening bal...	Accounts Payable		350.00	350.00
Bill	01/18/98	1035A	FAX Rental ...	Accounts Payable		45.00	45.00
Bill	01/19/98	8950S		Accounts Payable		450.00	450.00
Total Office Supplies Wholesale						845.00	845.00
TOTAL						**845.00**	**845.00**

Click the **Close** button to close the Report

Close the Accounts Payable Register by double-clicking on the **Control-Menu Button or Icon** in the top left corner of the title bar

Click the **Close** button to close the Chart of Accounts

PREPARE UNPAID BILLS DETAIL REPORT

It is possible to get information regarding unpaid bills by simply preparing a report—no more digging through tickler files, recorded invoices, ledgers, or journals. QuickBooks prepares an Unpaid Bills Report listing each unpaid bill grouped and subtotaled by vendor.

MEMO

DATE: January 25, 1998

Even though QuickBooks shows a Reminders List when accessing the program, Carmen Mendoza prepares an Unpaid Bill Report for Roger Owens each week. Because CCC is a small business, Roger likes to have a firm control over cash flow so he determines which bills will be paid during the week.

---

*DO: Prepare and print an Unpaid Bills Report

Click **Report** on the Menu Bar, point to **A/P Reports**, click **Unpaid Bills Detail**
OR
Use QuickBooks Navigator:

Click **Purchases and Vendors** tab
In the Report section of the Navigator screen, click **Accounts Payable**
Click **Unpaid Bills Detail**

• Unpaid Bills Report shows on the screen.

Remove the current date from the report by clicking **Header/Footer**, clicking **Date Prepared** to deselect this option, and clicking **OK**

Provide report date by clicking in the text box for **Date**, dragging through the date to highlight, and typing **01/25/98**

Tab to generate report

Click **Print** button

Complete the information on the **Print Reports Screen**:

Print To: The selected item should be **Printer**
Orientation: click **Portrait** for this report
Page Range: All should be selected; if it is not, click All
If necessary, click **Fit report to one page wide** to deselect
Click **Print**

Click **Close** button to close the report

DELETE A BILL

QuickBooks makes it possible to delete any bill that has been recorded. No adjusting entries are required in order to do this. Simply access the Accounts Payable Register and delete the bill.

Creative Computer Consulting (CCC)					
Unpaid Bills by Vendor					
As of January 25, 1998					
◇ Type	◇ Date	◇ Num	◇ Due Date	◇ Aging	◇ Open Balance
Computer Professionals Magazine					
Bill	01/19/98	1579...	02/18/98		79.00
Total Computer Professionals Magazine					79.00
Global Advertising					
Bill	01/01/98		01/01/98	24	500.00
Bill	01/16/98	9875	02/15/98		260.00
Total Global Advertising					760.00
Joe's Garage and Auto Services					
Bill	01/19/98	630	02/18/98		575.00
Total Joe's Garage and Auto Services					575.00

Partial Report

> **MEMO**
> DATE: January 26, 1998
>
> After reviewing the Unpaid Bills Report, Carmen Mendoza realizes that the bill recorded for *Computer Professionals Magazine* should have been recorded for *Computer Technologies Magazine*.

*DO: Delete the bill recorded for *Computer Professionals Magazine*
   Access the Chart of Accounts:
      Use the keyboard shortcut **Ctrl+A**
         OR
      Use iconbar, click **Accnt** button
         OR
      Use menu bar, click **List**, click **Chart of Accounts**
   With the Chart of Accounts showing on the screen, click **Accounts Payable**
   Open the Accounts Payable Register:

Use keyboard shortcut **Ctrl+R**
> OR

Click Activities Button, click **Use Register**

Click on the bill for *Computer Professionals Magazine*

To delete the bill:

> Click the **Edit on the MENU BAR** (Do not click the EDIT button at the
> bottom of the Register), click **Delete Bill**

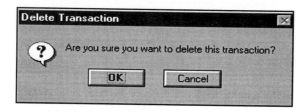

OR

Use the keyboard shortcut **Ctrl+D**

- The **Delete Transaction** dialog box appears on the screen.

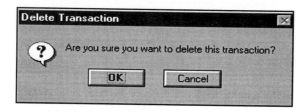

> Click **OK** to delete the bill

- Notice that the transaction no longer appears in the Accounts Payable
  Register.

Close the Accounts Payable Register

Close the Chart of Accounts

ADD A NEW VENDOR WHILE RECORDING A BILL

When entering bills, typing the first letter(s) of a vendor name enters the name on the Vendor line. If the vendor is not on the Vendor List, QuickBooks allows you to add a new vendor "on the fly" while entering a bill. If you key in the vendor name, a QuickBooks dialog box for Vendor Not Found appears with choices for a Quick Add—adding just the vendor name—or

Set Up—adding the vendor name and all vendor account information. When the new vendor information is complete, QuickBooks fills in the blanks on the bill for the vendor; and you finish entering the rest of the transaction.

MEMO

DATE: January 26, 1998

Record the bill for a 6-month subscription to *Computer Technologies Magazine*. The transaction date is 01/19/98, Invoice Number 1579-53, Terms Net 30, amount $79. This is recorded as an expense. The address and telephone for *Computer Technologies Magazine* is 12405 Menlo Park Drive, Menlo Park, CA 94025 (510) 555-3829.

 ***DO:** Record the above transaction
- Step-by-step instructions will be provided only for entering a new vendor.
- Refer to transactions previously recorded for all other steps used in entering a bill.

Access the **Enter Bill** screen
- When you key the first few letters of a vendor name, QuickBooks will automatically enter a vendor name.

On the line for Vendor, type the **C** for *Computer Technologies Magazine*
- The vendor name **Communication Services Telephone Company** appears on the vendor line and is highlighted.

Type **omp**
- The vendor name changes to **Computer Professionals Magazine**.

Finish typing **uter Technologies Magazine**

Press **Tab**

The **Vendor Not Found** dialog box appears on the screen with buttons for
- **Quick Add**—adds only the name to the vendor list.
- **Set Up**—adds the name to the vendor list and allows all account information to be entered.
- **Cancel**—cancels the addition of a new vendor.

Click **Cancel**
- The name *Computer Technologies Magazine* is still on the Vendor line and is highlighted.

Click the drop-down list arrow for Vendor

Click **<Add New>**

Enter **Computer Technologies Magazine** in the Vendor text box

Enter the information needed for the **Address Info** tab:

    Tab to or click **Company Name**

    Key **Computer Technologies Magazine**

    Tab to or click the first line for **Address**

    • Computer Technologies Magazine appears as the first line of the address.

    Press **Enter** or click the line beneath the company name (Do not tab)

    Type the address listed in the transaction

    Press **Enter** at the end of each line

    When finished with the address, tab to or click **Phone**

    Enter the telephone number

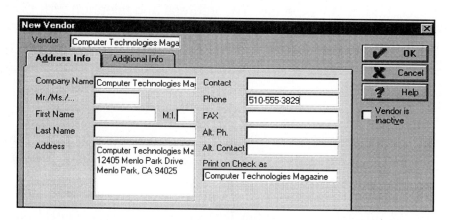

Enter the information for **Additional Info** tab

    Click **Additional Info** tab

    Click drop-down list arrow next to terms

    Click **Net 30**

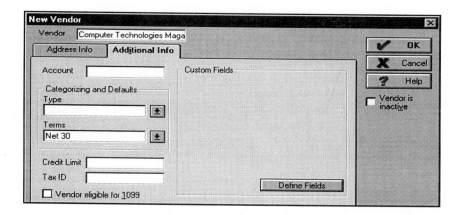

    Click **OK** button for New Vendor screen

• The information for Vendor, Terms, and the Dates is filled in on the Enter Bills screen.

If necessary, change the transaction date to **01/19/98**
Complete the bill using instructions previously provided for entering bills
When finished, click **OK** to close the bill and exit

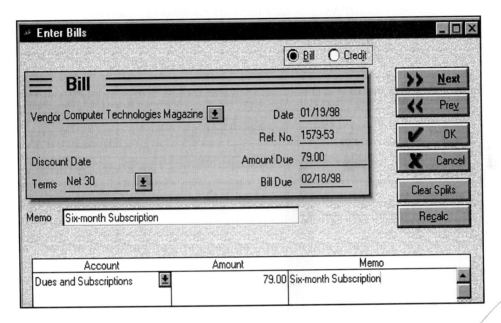

MODIFY VENDOR RECORDS

Occasionally information regarding a vendor will change. QuickBooks allows vendor accounts to be modified at anytime by editing the vendor list.

MEMO

DATE: January 26, 1998

Because Joel Chang received a promotion, the contact person for ZIP Delivery Service has been changed to Consuela Hernandez.

---

 *DO: Modify the vendor records for Zip Delivery Service
      Access the Vendor List:
          Click **Lists** menu, click **Vendor**
              OR
          Click **Vend** button on the iconbar
              OR

Use QuickBooks Navigator:
    Click **Purchases and Vendors** tab
    Click **Vendors**
Scroll through the Vendor List until **ZIP Delivery Service**
    appears
Click **ZIP Delivery Service**
Click **Vendor** button at the bottom of the list, click **Edit**
    OR
Use the keyboard shortcut **Ctrl+E**
• The Edit Vendor screen appears.
Click **Contact** text box
Drag through **Joel Chang** to highlight
Type **Consuela Hernandez**
Click **OK** to record the change
Click **Close** button on Vendor List to close

ENTER A CREDIT FROM A VENDOR

Credit memos are prepared to record a reduction to a transaction. With QuickBooks you use the Enter Bills window to record credit memos received from vendors acknowledging a return of or an allowance for a previously recorded bill and/or payment. The amount of a credit memo is deducted from the amount owed.

MEMO

DATE: January 26, 1998

Received Credit Memo 789 for $5 from Office Supplies Wholesale for a return of fax paper that was damaged.

---

*DO: Access the **Enter Bills** window and record the Credit Memo shown above
    On the Enter Bills screen, click **Credit** to select
    • Notice that the word Bill changes to Credit.
    Click the drop-down list arrow next to vendor
    Click **Office Supplies Wholesale**
    Tab to or click the **Date**
    Type **01/26/98**
    Tab to or click **Ref No.**

Type **789**
Tab to or click **Credit Amount**
Type **5**
Tab to **Memo**
Enter **Returned Fax Paper**
Tab to or click the first line of **Account**
Click drop-down list arrow
Because this was originally entered as an expense, click the account **Office Supplies Expense**
- The amount should show **5.00**; if not, enter 5.
- The **Memo** column may be left blank.

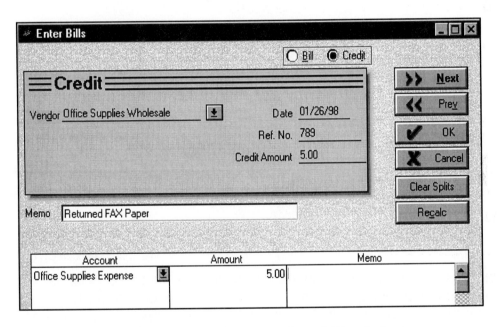

Click **OK** to record the credit and exit Enter Bills window
- QuickBooks records the credit in the Accounts Payable account and shows the transaction type as BILLCRED in the Accounts Payable Register.

VIEW CREDIT IN ACCOUNTS PAYABLE REGISTER

When recording the credit in the last transaction, QuickBooks listed the transaction type as BILLCRED in the Accounts Payable Register.

*DO: Verify the credit from Office Supplies Wholesale
Follow steps previously provided to access the Accounts Payable Register.
If a check ✔ shows in the 1-Line check box, remove it by clicking the check box

- This changes the display in the Accounts Payable Register from 1-Line to multiple lines.

Check the **Number/Type** column to verify the type **BILLCRED**

| 01/26/98 | 789 | | Office Supplies Wholesale | | | | | 5.00 | 5,299.00 |
| | BILLCRED | | Office Supplies Exp Returned FAX Pap | | | | | | |

Close the Accounts Payable Register
Close the Chart of Accounts

PAYING BILLS

When using QuickBooks, you may choose to pay your bills directly from the pay bills command and let QuickBooks write your checks for you; or you may choose to write the checks yourself. Just remember not to do both! Using the Pay Bills window enables you to determine which bills to pay, the method of payment—on-line payment, check, or credit card—and the appropriate account. When determining which bills to pay, QuickBooks allows you to display the bills by due date, discount date, vendor, or amount. All bills may be displayed, or only those bills that are due by a certain date may be displayed.

MEMO

DATE: January 26, 1998

Whenever possible, Carmen Mendoza pays the bills on a weekly basis. With the Pay Bills window showing the bills due for payment before 01/31/98, Carmen compares the bills shown with the Unpaid Bills Report previously prepared. The report has been marked by Roger Owens to indicate which bills should be paid. Carmen will select the appropriate bills for payment and record the bill payment for the week.

---

*DO: Pay the bills for the week
Access the Pay Bills window:
Click **Activities** menu, click **Pay Bills**
OR
Use QuickBooks Navigator:
Click **Purchases and Vendors** tab, click **Pay Bills**
Determine the bills to be paid:

Tab to or click **Payment Date**

Enter the Payment Date of **01/26/98**

Click **Show All Bills** to select

Sort Bills by **Due Date**

- If this is not showing, click the drop-down list arrow next to the Sort Bills text box, click **Due Date**.

Scroll through the list of bills

Click the drop-down list arrow next to Sort Bills text box

Click **Vendor**

- This shows you how much you owe each vendor.

Again, click the drop-down list arrow next to Sort Bills text box

Click **Amount Due**

- This shows you your bills from the highest amount owed to the lowest.

Click drop-down list arrow next to Sort Bills text box, click **Due Date**

- The bills will be shown according to the date due.

Click **Show bills due on or before** to select this option

Click in the text box for the date

Drag through the date to highlight, enter **01/31/98** as the date

Scroll through the list of bills due

Select the bills to be paid

- The bills shown on the screen are an exact match to the bills Roger Owens marked to be paid.

Click **Pay All Bills** button

- To pay some of the bills but not all of them, mark each bill to be paid by clicking on the individual bill or using the cursor keys to select a bill and pressing the space bar.

The **Pay All Bills** button changes to **Clear Payments** so bills can be unmarked and the bills to be paid may be selected again

In the **Pay By** section of the screen, make sure **Check** has been selected as the payment method

Make sure **To be printed** box has a check in it

If it is not checked, click in the box to insert a check (✔)

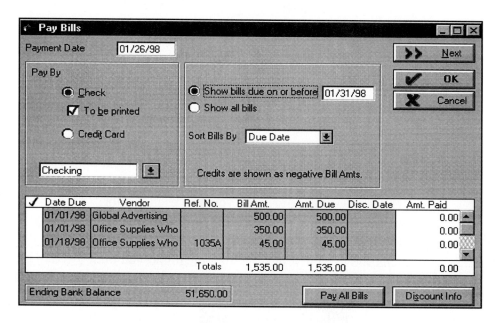

Click **OK** to record your payments and close Pay Bills window

PRINTING CHECKS FOR BILLS

Once bills have been marked and recorded as paid, you may handwrite checks to vendors, or you may have QuickBooks print the checks to vendors. If there is more than one amount due for a vendor, QuickBooks totals the amounts due to the vendor and prints one check to the vendor.

 *DO: Print the checks for the bills paid
Click **File** menu
Point to **Print Forms**
Click **Print Checks**
Bank Account should be **Checking**
•   If this is not showing, click the drop-down list arrow, click **Checking**.
Check **1** should be the check number in **First Check Number**
•   If not, delete the number showing, key **1**.
In the ✔ column the checks selected to be printed are marked with a check ✔
Click **OK** to print the checks
•   The Print Checks screen appears.
Verify and if necessary change information on the **Settings** tab
   Printer name: The name of your printer should show in the text box
   •   If the correct printer name is not showing, click the drop-down list arrow, click the correct printer name.
   Printer type: Page-oriented (Single sheets) should be in the text box

- If this does not show or if you use Continuous (Perforated Edge) checks, click the drop-down list arrow, click the appropriate sheet style to select.

Check style: Three different types of check styles may be used: Standard, Voucher, or Wallet

If it is not in the check style text box, click **Standard Checks** to insert

Print Company Name and Address: If the box does not have a check ✔, click to select

Click **Print** button to print the checks

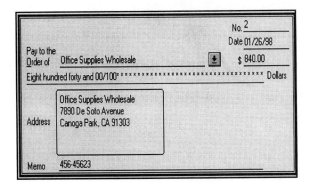   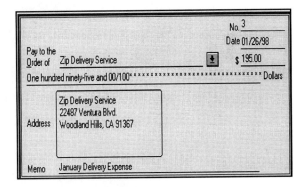

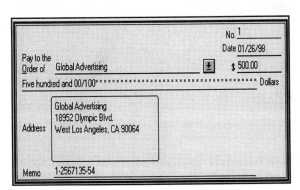

Did check(s) print OK? dialog box appears

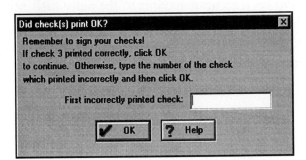

If checks printed correctly, click **OK**
- The checks have the address for Creative Computer Consulting, the name and address of the company being paid, and the amount being paid.
- The actual checks will not have a check number printed because QuickBooks is set up to work with pre-printed check forms containing check numbers.
- In the memo section of the check, any memo entered on the bill shows.
- If there was no memo entered for the bill, the vendor account number appears as the memo.

REVIEW BILLS THAT HAVE BEEN PAID

In order to avoid any confusion about payment of a bill, QuickBooks marks the Bill **PAID**. Scrolling through the recorded bills in the Enter Bills window, you will see the paid bills marked **PAID**.

 *DO: Scroll the Enter Bills window to view PAID bills
Click **Enter Bills** on QuickBooks Navigator or click the **Bill** icon on the iconbar
Click **<<Prev** button to go back through all the bills recorded
- Notice that the bills paid for Office Supplies Wholesale, ZIP Delivery Service, and Global Advertising are marked **PAID**.
Click **Cancel**

PETTY CASH

Frequently, a business will need to pay for small expenses with cash. These might include expenses such as postage, office supplies, and miscellaneous expenses. For example, rather than write a check for postage due of 75 cents, you would use money from petty cash. QuickBooks allows you to establish and use a petty cash account to track these small expenditures. Normally, a Petty Cash Voucher is prepared and, if available, the receipt for the transaction is stapled to it. It is important in a business to keep accurate records of the petty cash expenditures, and procedures for control of the Petty Cash fund need to be established to prohibit access to and unauthorized use of the cash. Periodically, the petty cash expenditures are recorded so that the records of the company accurately reflect all expenses incurred in the operation of the business.

ADD PETTY CASH ACCOUNT TO THE CHART OF ACCOUNTS

QuickBooks allows accounts to be added to the Chart of Accounts list at any time. Petty Cash is identified as a "Bank" account type so it will be placed at the top of the Chart of Accounts along with other checking and savings accounts.

 *DO: Add Petty Cash to the Chart of Accounts
Access Chart of Accounts:
    Click **Lists** menu, click **Chart of Accounts**
       OR
    Click **Accnt** button on the iconbar
       OR
    Click **Company** tab on QuickBooks Navigator, click **Chart of Accounts** icon
Access **New Account** screen:
    Click **Account** button at the bottom of the Chart of Accounts, click **New**
       OR
    Use the keyboard shortcut **Ctrl+N**
Create a new account:
    Type should be **Bank**
    • If it is not, click the drop-down list arrow next to the text box for type, then click **Bank**.
    Enter **Petty Cash** in the **Name** text box
    Leave the following items blank:
       Subaccount
       Bank No.
       Tax Line (Unassigned)
       Opening Balance
       • This is used only when setting up QuickBooks, not when adding an account.

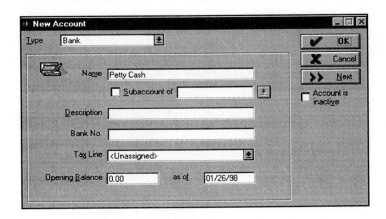

If the date of **01/26/98** is not shown for the **as of** date, enter it
Click **OK** to record the new account
Do not close the Chart of Accounts

ESTABLISH PETTY CASH FUND

Once the account has been established, the petty cash fund must have money in order to pay for small expenses. A cash withdrawal from checking must be made or a check must be written and cashed to obtain petty cash funds. This must be recorded in the Checking Register.

 *DO: Record the cash withdrawal of $100 from checking to establish petty cash:
To access the Check Register, click **Checking** account in the Chart of Accounts, click **Activities** button, click **Use Register**

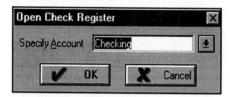

Click **OK**
- The Check Register should be on the screen.
- If the cursor is not already in the Date column, click **Date** column for a new transaction at the end of Check Register.
- The date should be highlighted; if it is not, drag through the date to highlight.
Enter **01/26/98**
Tab to or click **Number**
Enter **CASH**
Because this is a cash withdrawal, a Payee name will not be entered
Tab to or click **Payment**
Enter **100**
Tab to or click **Account**
Click the drop-down list arrow next to Account
Click **Petty Cash**
- The account shows Petty Cash and Type changed from CHK to TRANSFR.
Tab to or click **Memo**
Enter **Establish Petty Cash Fund**
Click **Record** button to record the withdrawal

01/26/98	CASH			100.00			50,015.00
	TRANSFR	Petty Cash	Establish Petty Cash Fund				

Close **Checking** Register
Do not close Chart of Accounts

RECORD PAYMENT OF AN EXPENSE USING PETTY CASH

As petty cash is used to pay for small expenses in the business, these payments must be recorded. QuickBooks makes it a simple matter to record petty cash expenditures directly into the Petty Cash Register.

MEMO

DATE: January 30, 1998

Carmen Mendoza needs to record the petty cash expenditures made during the week: postage due, 32 cents; purchased staples and paper clips, $3.59; reimbursed Carolyn Masters for gasoline purchased for company car, $13.88.

---

*DO: In the petty cash account, record a compound entry for the above expenditures:
Click **Petty Cash** on the Chart of Accounts
Access Register:
    Ctrl+R
     OR
    Click **Activities** button, click **Use Register**
Click in the Date column, highlight the date if necessary
Type **01/30/98**
- No entry is required for Number; QuickBooks inserts **1** for the number.
- No entry is required for Payee.

Tab to or click **Payment**
Enter **17.79** (you must type the decimal point)
Tab to or click in **Account** text box
Click **Splits** button at the bottom of the screen
- Split is used because the total amount of the transaction will be split among three expense accounts.

In the **Account** column showing on the screen, click the drop-down list arrow

Scroll until you see **Postage and Delivery**

Click **Postage and Delivery**

Tab to **Amount** column

• Using the tab key will highlight **17.79**.

Type **.32**

• Memo notations are not necessary because the transactions are self-explanatory.

Tab to or click the next blank line in **Account**

Repeat the steps listed above to record **3.59** for **Office Supplies Expense** and **13.88** for **Automobile Expense**

Click **Close** when all expenses have been recorded

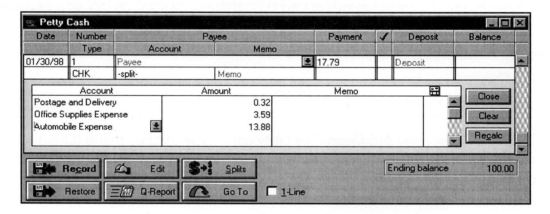

Click **Record** to record the transaction

• Notice that the word "payee," the account name, and memo are removed from the transaction. The only item indicated is **-split-**

Close **Petty Cash** and if necessary close **Chart of Accounts**

PAY BILLS BY WRITING CHECKS

Although it is more efficient to record all bills in the Enter Bills window and pay all bills through the Pay Bills window, QuickBooks also allows bills to be paid by writing a check. The check window is divided into two main areas: the check face and the detail area. The check face includes information such as the date of the check, the payee's name, the check amount, the payee's address, and a line for a memo—just like a paper check. The detail area is used to indicate transaction accounts and amounts.

MEMO

DATE: January 31, 1998

Write checks to pay the following bills:

Johnson Realtors—rent for the month, $1,500
Communication Services Telephone Co.—telephone bill for the month, $350
Southern California Electric—electric bill for the month, $250
Southern California Water—water bill for the month, $35
Southern California Gas Co.—heating bill for the month, $175

*DO: Write checks to pay the bills listed above:
Access Checking:
>Click **Activities** menu, click **Write Checks**
>>OR
>Click **Check** icon on the iconbar
>>OR
>Click **Checking and Credit Cards** tab in QuickBooks Navigator, click
>>**Checks**
>>OR
>Use the keyboard shortcut **Ctrl+W**
Tab to or click **Date**
Enter **01/31/98**
- If the screen shows **Write Checks-Petty Cash**, click the drop-down list arrow
for **Bank Account**, click **Checking**.
Click **To Be Printed** to indicate that the check needs to be printed
- If the check has been written by hand, this will be left blank.
Complete the check face:
>Click the drop-down list arrow next to **Pay to the Order of**
>Click **Johnson Realtors**
>Tab to or click **Amount**
>Enter the amount of the rent
>Tab to or click **Memo**
>Enter **Monthly Rent**
>- This memo prints on the check, not on reports.
Complete the detail area:
>Tab to or click the first line of **Account**
>Click the drop-down list arrow for Account

Click **Rent**
- The total amount of the check is shown in Amount column—no entry required.
- If you want a transaction description to appear in reports, enter the description in the memo column—no entry is required because these are standard transactions.

Click >>**Next** to record the check and advance to the next check

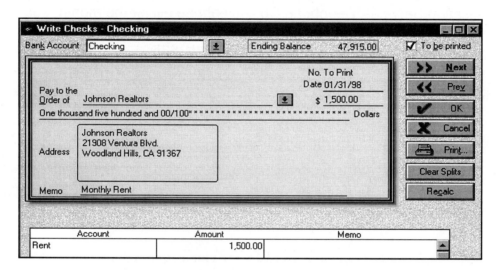

Repeat the steps indicated above to record payment of the telephone, electric, water, and gas bills
- While entering the bills, you may see a dialog box on the screen, indicating that QuickBooks allows you to do on-line banking. On-line banking will not be used at this time. Click OK to close the dialog box.

ENTER THE CHECK FOR THE ELECTRIC BILL A SECOND TIME
Click the drop-down list arrow and click Southern California Electric
- The first payment entered for the electric payment appears on the screen.

Click **OK** to record the second payment for the electric bill and exit the Write Checks window

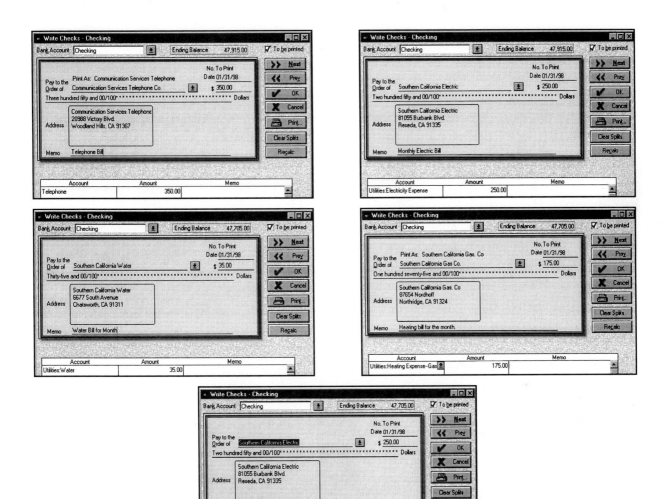

Duplicate Check

EDIT CHECKS

Mistakes can occur in business—even on a check. QuickBooks allows for checks to be edited at anytime. You may use either the Check Register or the Write Checks window to edit checks.

MEMO
DATE: January 30, 1998

Once the check for the rent had been entered, Carmen realized that it should have been for $1,600. Edit the check written to Johnson Realtors.

---

*DO: Revise the check written to pay the rent
    Use the steps given previously to access the **Check Register**
    Click anywhere in the check to **Johnson Realtors**
    Click between the **1** and the **5** in the **Amount** column
    Press **Delete** to delete the **5**
    Type a **6**
    Click **Record**
    Do not close the register for checking

01/31/98	To Print	Johnson Realtors		1,600.00			48,415.00
	CHK	Rent	Monthly Rent				

VOID CHECKS

QuickBooks allows checks to be voided. Rather than deleting the transaction, voiding a check changes the amount of the check to zero but keeps a record of the transaction.

MEMO
DATE: January 31, 1998

The telephone bill should not have been paid until the first week of February. Void the check written for the telephone expense.

---

*DO: Void the check written for the telephone expense
    Click anywhere in the check to Communication Services Telephone Co.
    Click **Edit** on the menu bar at the top of the screen—not the Edit button
    Click **Void Check**
    • The amount of the check is now 0.00 and the memo shows VOID.

Click **Record** button
Do not close the register for checking

01/31/98	Number	Communication Services Telephone Co.		0.00		✓	Deposit		48,065.00
	CHK	Telephone		VOID: Telephone Bill					

DELETE CHECKS

Deleting a check completely removes it and any transaction information for the check from QuickBooks. Make sure you definitely want to remove the check before deleting it because once it is deleted, a check cannot be recovered. It is often preferable to void a check than to delete it because a voided check is maintained in the company records, whereas no record is kept of a deleted check.

MEMO
DATE: January 31, 1998

In reviewing the register for the checking account, Carmen Mendoza discovered that two checks were written to pay the electric bill. Delete the second check.

---

*DO: Delete the second entry for the electric bill
- Notice that there are two transactions showing for Southern California Electric.

Click anywhere in the second entry to Southern California Electric
Click **Edit** on the menu bar at the top of the screen, click **Delete Check**
    OR
Use the keyboard shortcut **Ctrl+D**
Click **OK** button on the Delete Transaction dialog box

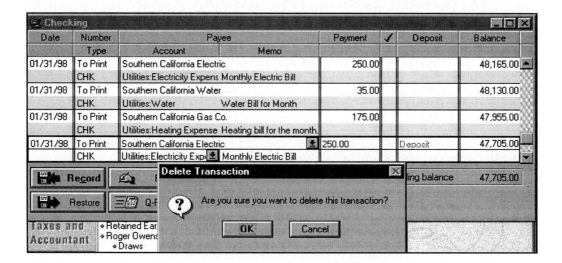

- After you have clicked the OK button, there is only one transaction in Checking for Southern California Electric.

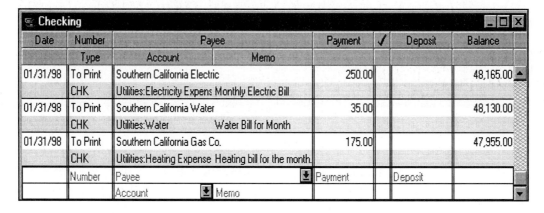

Close the Checking Register

PRINT CHECKS

Checks may be printed as they are entered, or they may be printed at a later time. When checks are to be printed, QuickBooks inserts the word To Print rather than a check number in the Check Register. The appropriate check number is indicated during printing. Because QuickBooks is so flexible, a company must institute a system for cash control. For example, if the check for rent of $1,500 had been printed, QuickBooks would allow a second check for $1,600 to be printed. As a matter of practice in a small business, the owner or a person separate from the one writing checks should sign the checks. Pre-numbered checks should be used, and any checks printed but not mailed should be submitted along with those for signature. In order to avoid any impropriety, more than one person can be designated to review checks.

MEMO

DATE: January 31, 1998

Carmen needs to print checks and obtain Roger Owens' signature so the checks can be mailed.

---

*DO: Print the checks for rent and utility bills paid by writing checks
  Click **File** menu, point to **Print Forms**, click **Print Checks**
  Bank Account should be **Checking**
  • If this is not showing, click the drop-down list arrow, click **Checking**
  Because Checks 1, 2, and 3 were printed previously, check **4** should be in **First Check Number** text box
    • If not, delete the number showing, key **4**
  • In the ✔ column the checks selected to be printed are marked with a check ✔.
    • If not, click the **Select All** button.

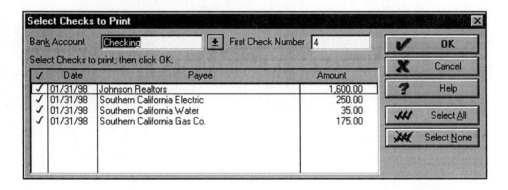

  Click **OK** to print the checks
  • The Print Checks screen appears.
  Verify and if necessary change information on the **Settings** tab
    Printer name: The name of your printer should show in the text box
    Printer type: Page-oriented (Single sheets) should be in the text box
    • If this does not show or if you use Continuous (Perforated Edge) checks, click the drop-down list arrow, click the appropriate sheet style to select.
    Check style: Three different types of check styles may be used: Standard, Voucher, or Wallet

- If it is not in the check style text box, click **Standard Checks** to insert.
  Print Company Name and Address: if the box does not have a check ✔,
  click to select
Click **Print** button to print the checks

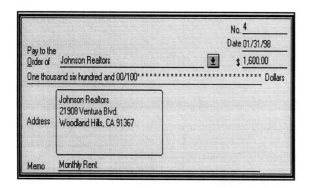

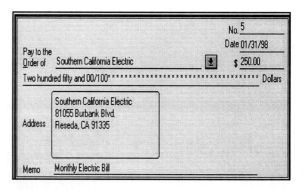

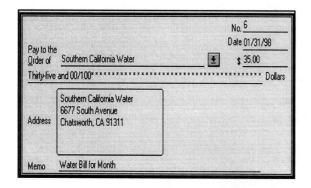

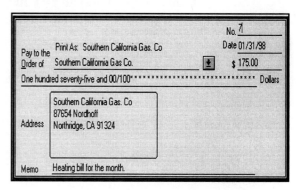

Did check(s) print OK? dialog box appears
If the checks printed correctly, click **OK**
- The checks have the address for Creative Computer Consulting, the name and
  address of the company being paid, and the amount being paid. There is no
  check number printed on the checks because QuickBooks is set up to use pre-
  numbered checks.
- In the memo section of the check, any memo entered when preparing the
  check shows. If there was no memo entered for the bill, the vendor account
  number appears as the memo.

PREPARE CHECK DETAIL REPORT

Once checks have been printed, it is important to review information about checks. The check
detail report provides detailed information regarding each check, including the checks for 0.00

amounts. Information indicates the type of transaction, the date, the check number, the payee, the account used, the original amount, and the paid amount of the check.

MEMO

DATE: January 31, 1998

Now that the checks have been printed, Carmen prints a Check Detail Report. She will give this to Roger Owens to examine when he signs the printed checks.

---

*DO: Print a Check Detail Report:
    Click **Reports** menu, point to **Other Reports**, click **Check Detail**
       OR
    Click **Other**, click **Check Detail**, on the **Checking and Credit Cards** tab of
       QuickBooks Navigator
    To remove the current date from the report, click **Header/Footer**, click **Date**
       Prepared to deselect this option, click **OK**
    Provide report period:
       Click in the text box for **From**
       Drag through the date to highlight, type **01/31/98**
       Tab to **To**
       Enter **01/31/98**
    Tab to generate report
    Click **Print** button
    Complete the information on the **Print Reports Screen**:
       Print To: The selected item should be **Printer**
       Orientation: click **Landscape** for this report
       Page Range: All should be selected; if it is not, click All
       If necessary, click **Fit report to one page wide** to deselect
       Click **Print**
    Click **Close** button to close the report

Creative Computer Consulting (CCC)
Check Detail
January 31, 1998

Type	◇	Date	◇ Num ◇	Name	◇	Item	◇	Account	◇ Original Amount	◇ Paid Amount
Check		01/31/98		Johnson Realtors				Checking	-1,600.00	
						Rent			1,600.00	-1,600.00
TOTAL									1,600.00	-1,600.00
Check		01/31/98		Communication...				Checking	0.00	
TOTAL									0.00	0.00

Partial Report

VIEW MISSING CHECK REPORT

A missing check report lists the checks written for a bank account in order by check number. If there are any gaps between numbers or duplicate check numbers, this information is provided. The report indicates the type of transaction, Check or Bill Payment-Check, check date, check number, payee name, account used for the check, checking, the split or additional accounts used, and the amount of the check.

MEMO
DATE: January 13, 1998

To see a listing of all checks printed, view a Missing Check report for all dates.

---

 *DO: View a missing check report

Click **Reports** menu, point to **Other Reports**, click **Missing Checks**
OR
Click **Other**, click **Missing Checks** on the **Checking and Credit Cards** tab of QuickBooks Navigator
If **Checking** appears on the Missing Check Report dialog box, click **OK**
- If it does not appear, click the drop-down list arrow, click **Checking**, click **OK**.

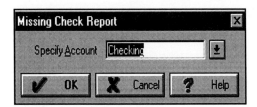

Examine the report:
- The Account in all cases is Checking.
- The Split column indicates which accounts in addition to checking have been used in the transaction.
- Look at the Type column.
  - The checks written through pay bills indicate the transaction type as Bill Pmt-Check.
  - The bills paid by actually writing the checks show Check as the transaction type.

Creative Computer Consulting (CCC)
Missing Check Report
All Transactions

Type	Date	Num	Name	Memo	Account	Split	Amount
Bill Pmt -Check	01/26/98	1	Global Advertising	1-2567135-...	Checking	Accounts P...	-500.00
Bill Pmt -Check	01/26/98	2	Office Supplies ...	456-45623	Checking	Accounts P...	-840.00
Bill Pmt -Check	01/26/98	3	Zip Delivery Ser...	January De...	Checking	Accounts P...	-195.00
Check	01/31/98	4	Johnson Realtors	Monthly Rent	Checking	Rent	-1,600.00
Check	01/31/98	5	Southern Califor...	Monthly Ele...	Checking	Electricity Ex...	-250.00
Check	01/31/98	6	Southern Califor...	Water Bill fo...	Checking	Water	-35.00
Check	01/31/98	7	Southern Califor...	Heating bill ...	Checking	Heating Exp...	-175.00

Close the report without printing

PURCHASE AN ASSET WITH A COMPANY CHECK

Not all purchases will be transactions on account. If something is purchased and paid for with a check, a check is written and the purchase recorded.

MEMO

DATE: January 31, 1998

Having tried out several fax machines from Office Supplies Wholesale on a rental basis, Carmen Mendoza and Ralph Owens decide to purchase a fax from them. Because the fax is on sale if it is purchased for cash, Ralph decides to buy it by writing a company check for the asset for $486.

---

 *DO: Record the check written for the purchase of a fax machine

Access **Write Checks-Checking** window as previously instructed
- This check was hand written by Roger Owens and does not need printing.
- If a ✔ appears in the box **To be printed**, click the box to deselect.
- The **No.** shows as **1**; do not change.

Click the drop-down list arrow for **Pay to the Order of**

Click **Office Supplies Wholesale**

Tab to or click **$0.00**
- If necessary, highlight 0.00.

Enter **$486**

Tab to or click **Memo**

Enter **Purchase Fax Machine**

Tab to or click **Account**

Click drop-down list arrow, scroll to the top of the chart of accounts, and click **Original Cost** under **Office Equipment**
- **Amount** column shows the transaction total of **486.00**. This does not need to be changed.

Click **Memo**

Enter **Purchase Fax Machine**

Click **OK** to record the check and exit Write Checks window

Duplicate Number dialog box appears on the screen indicating "Check number 1 has already been used. Continue?"

Click **No**

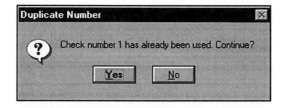

Click to the right of **1** in No.
Backspace to delete the 1
Because Checks 1 through 7 have been printed, enter **8** for the check number
Click **OK** to record the check and exit Write Checks window

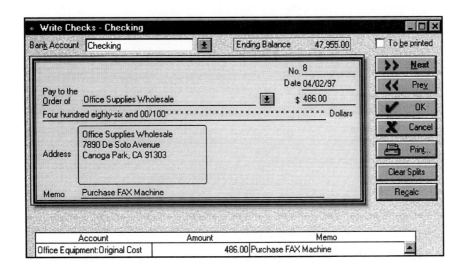

CUSTOMIZE REPORT FORMAT

The report format used in one company may not be appropriate for all companies that use QuickBooks. In order to allow program users the maximum flexibility, QuickBooks makes it very easy to customize many of the user preferences of the program. For example, you may choose to use the iconbar or to turn it off and use QuickBooks Navigator. You may customize menus, reminder screens, and reports and graphs.

 *DO: Customize the report preferences so the current date does not print on reports:
Click **File** Menu, click **Preferences**
    OR
Use QuickBooks Navigator: Click **Company** tab, click **Preferences**
Scroll through the items listed on the left side of the screen until you
    get to Reports and Graphs
Click **Reports and Graphs**

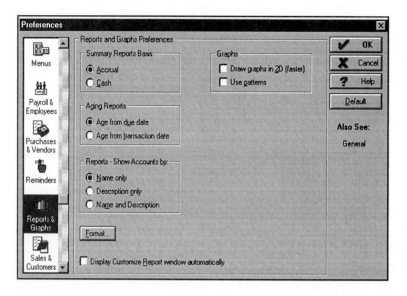

Click the **Format** button

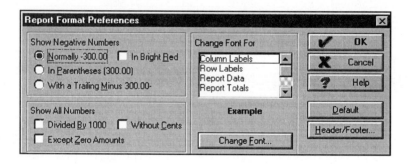

Click the **Header/Footer** button
Click **Date Prepared** to deselect

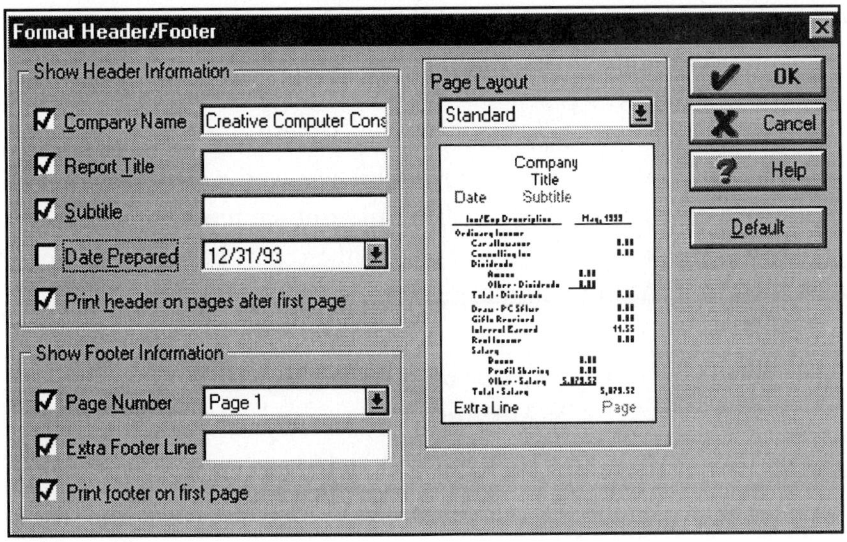

Click **OK** to save the change
Click **OK** to exit the Report Format Preferences
Click **OK** to close Preferences

PRINT ACCOUNTS PAYABLE AGING SUMMARY

It is important in a business to maintain a good credit rating and make sure that payments are made on time. In order to avoid overlooking a payment, the accounts payable aging summary lists the vendors to which the company owes money and shows how long the money has been owed.

MEMO

DATE: January 31, 1998

Prepare the Accounts Payable Aging Summary for Roger Owens.

---

*DO: Prepare an Accounts Payable Aging Summary
    Click **Reports** on the menu bar, point to **A/P Reports**, click **Aging Summary**
       OR
    On the **Purchases and Vendors** tab in QuickBooks Navigator, under **Reports**
      click **Accounts Payable**, click **Aging Summary**
- Notice that the current date does not appear as part of the heading information.

Tab to or click in the box for the **Date**
- If it is not highlighted, highlight the current date.

Enter **01/31/98**
- Tab through but leave Interval (days) as 30 and Through (days past due) as 90.
- The report will show the current bills as well as any past due bills.

Follow instructions provided earlier to print the report:

    Use **Landscape** orientation so that the report prints on one page

Close the A/P Aging Summary screen

Creative Computer Consulting (CCC)
A/P Aging Summary
As of January 31, 1998

	Current	1 - 30	31 - 60	61 - 90	> 90	TOTAL
Computer Technologies Magazine ▶	79.00 ◀	0.00	0.00	0.00	0.00	79.00
Global Advertising	260.00	0.00	0.00	0.00	0.00	260.00
Joe's Garage and Auto Services	575.00	0.00	0.00	0.00	0.00	575.00
XYZ Insurance Company	2,850.00	0.00	0.00	0.00	0.00	2,850.00
TOTAL	3,764.00	0.00	0.00	0.00	0.00	3,764.00

PRINT UNPAID BILLS DETAIL REPORT

Another important report is the unpaid bills detail report. Even though it was already printed once during the month, it is always a good idea to print the report at the end of the month.

MEMO
DATE: January 31, 1998

At the end of every month Carmen Mendoza prepares an Unpaid Bills Detail report for Roger Owens. Prepare the report.

*DO: Follow instructions provided earlier in the chapter to prepare and print an Unpaid Bills Detail Report for **01/31/98**

```
         Creative Computer Consulting (CCC)
                Unpaid Bills by Vendor
                  As of January 31, 1998
  ◇     Type      ◇   Date   ◇  Num  ◇ Due Date ◇ Aging ◇  Open Balance
  Computer Technologies Magazine
     Bill             01/19/98  1579...  02/18/98                79.00
  Total Computer Technologies Magazine                          79.00


  Global Advertising
     Bill             01/16/98  9875    02/15/98                260.00
  Total Global Advertising                                     260.00


  Joe's Garage and Auto Services
     Bill             01/19/98  630     02/18/98                575.00
  Total Joe's Garage and Auto Services                         575.00
```

Partial Report

PRINT VENDOR BALANCE SUMMARY

There are two vendor balance reports available in QuickBooks. There is a summary report that shows unpaid balances for vendors and a detail report that lists each transaction for a vendor. In order to see how much is owed to each vendor, prepare a Vendor Balance Summary report.

MEMO

DATE: January 31, 1998

Prepare a Vendor Balance Summary Report to give to Roger Owens.

---

*DO: Prepare and print a Vendor Balance Summary Report
Click **Reports** menu, point to **A/P Reports**, click **Vendor Balance Summary**
OR
Click **Purchases and Vendors** tab on QuickBooks Navigator, click **Accounts Payable** under Reports, click **Vendor Balance Summary**
- The report should show only the totals owed to each vendor on January 31, 1998.
  - If it does not, tab to or click **From**, enter **01/31/98**. Then tab to or click **To**, enter **01/31/98**.

Tab to generate the report

Creative Computer Consulting (CCC)	
Vendor Balance Summary	
All Transactions	
	◇ Jan 31, '98 ◇
Computer Technologies Magazine ▶	79.00 ◀
Global Advertising	260.00
Joe's Garage and Auto Services	575.00
XYZ Insurance Company	2,850.00
TOTAL	**3,764.00**

Follow steps listed previously to print the report in Portrait orientation
Close the Report

VIEW A QUICKREPORT FOR A VENDOR

A QuickReport for an individual vendor can be prepared by accessing the vendor's account via the vendor list, clicking on the vendor name, and clicking on the report button. This QuickReport provides information regarding the type of transaction, the transaction date, vendor's invoice number, the account and the split account(s) used, and the amount owed.

 *DO: View a QuickReport for Joe's Garage and Auto Services
Click **Vend** button on iconbar
    OR
Click **Lists**, click **Vendors** on the menu bar
    OR
Click **Purchases and Vendors** tab in QuickBooks Navigator, click **Vendor** icon
Click **Joe's Garage and Auto Services**
Click **Report** button at the bottom of the Vendor List
Click **QuickReport: Joe's Garage and Auto Services**
    OR
Use the keyboard shortcut **Ctrl+Q**
Tab to or click **From**, enter **01/01/98**
Tab to or click **To**, enter **01/31/98**
Tab to generate the report
Analyze the report

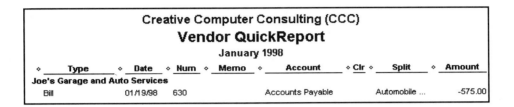

Creative Computer Consulting (CCC)
Vendor QuickReport
January 1998

◇	Type	◇	Date	◇	Num	◇	Memo	◇	Account	◇	Clr	◇	Split	◇	Amount
Joe's Garage and Auto Services															
	Bill		01/19/98		630				Accounts Payable				Automobile ...		-575.00

Close the report without printing
- If necessary, close the Vendor List.

CREATE AN ACCOUNTS PAYABLE GRAPH BY AGING PERIOD

Graphs provide a visual representation of certain aspects of the business. It is sometimes easier to interpret data in a graphical format. For example, to determine if any payments are overdue for accounts payable accounts, use an Accounts Payable graph to provide that information instantly on a bar chart. In addition, the Accounts Payable graph feature of QuickBooks also displays a pie chart showing what percentage of the total amount payable is owed to each vendor.

*DO: Prepare an Accounts Payable Graph
Click **Reports** on the menu bar, point to **Graphs**, click **Accounts Payable**
    OR
Click **Accounts Payable** in the Reports section of the **Purchases and Vendors** tab on QuickBooks Navigator, click **Accounts Payable Graph**
Click **Dates** button at the top of the report
Enter **01/31/98** for Show Aging as of in the Change Graph Dates text box

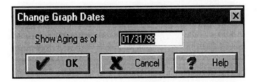

Click **OK**

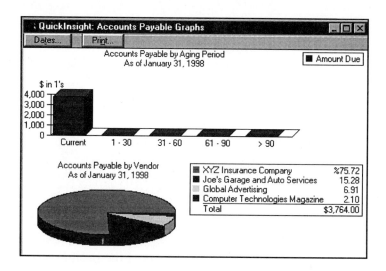

Click **Dates** button again, enter **02/28/98** for the date
Click **OK**

- Notice that the bar moved from Current to 1-30. This means at the end of February the bills will be between 1 and 30 days overdue.

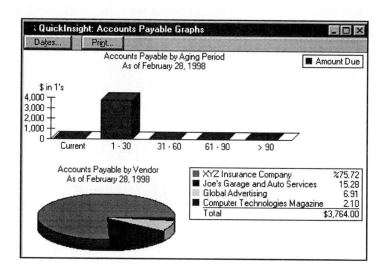

USE QUICKZOOM TO VIEW GRAPH DETAILS

To obtain detailed information from a graph, use the QuickZoom feature. For example, to see the actual number of days an individual account is overdue, double-click on a vendor in the pie chart, and this information will appear in a separate bar chart.

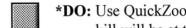

*DO: Use QuickZoom to see how many days overdue the XYZ Insurance Company's bill will be at the end of February
Point to the section of the pie chart for **XYZ Insurance Company**
Double-click

- The bar chart shows the bill will be in the 1-30 day category at the end of February.

Close the QuickZoom Graph for XYZ Insurance

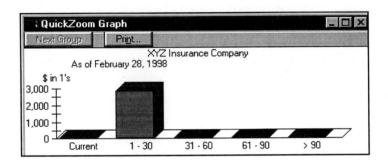

Click the **Dates** button on the QuickInsight: Accounts Payable Graphs screen
Change the date to **01/31/98**
In the legend of the pie chart, double-click on **Computer Technologies Magazine**
This payable is current as of January 31, 1998

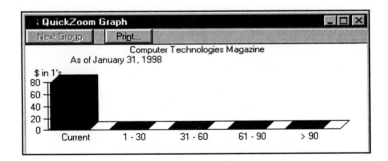

Close the QuickZoom Graph
Close the QuickInsight: Accounts Payable Graph

BACK UP CCC DATA AND CLOSE COMPANY

Whenever an important work session is complete, you should always back up your data. If your data disk is damaged or an error is discovered at a later time, the backup disk may be restored and the information used for recording transactions. As in previous chapters, you should close the company at the end of each work session.

 *DO: Follow the instructions given in Chapters 1 and 2 to back up data for Creative Computer Consultants and to close the company

SUMMARY

In this chapter, bills were recorded and paid, checks were written, and reports were prepared. The petty cash fund was established and used for payments of small expense items. Checks were voided, deleted, and corrected. Accounts were added and modified. QuickReports were accessed in various ways, and QuickZoom was used to obtain transaction detail while in various reports. Unpaid vendor reports provided information regarding bills that had not been paid. The graphing feature of QuickBooks allowed you to determine accounts payable by aging period and to see the percentage of accounts payable for each vendor.

END-OF-CHAPTER QUESTIONS

TRUE/FALSE

ANSWER THE FOLLOWING QUESTIONS IN THE SPACE PROVIDED BEFORE THE QUESTION NUMBER.

_____ 1. Credit memos are prepared to record a reduction to a transaction.

_____ 2. When you use QuickBooks, all checks must be printed by the computer.

_____ 3. QuickZoom is a QuickBooks feature that allows detailed information to be displayed.

_____ 4. A cash purchase can be recorded by writing a check or by using petty cash.

_____ 5. Once a report format has been customized as a QuickBooks preference for a company, QuickBooks will automatically use the custom format for the company.

_____ 6. A graph is a visual representation of certain aspects of a business.

_____ 7. The accrual method of accounting matches the income of the period with the cash received for sales.

_____ 8. A Missing Check report lists any duplicate check numbers or gaps between check numbers.

_____ 9. The Accounts Payable Register keeps track of all checks written in the business.

_____ 10. If a check has been edited, it cannot be printed.

MULTIPLE CHOICE

WRITE THE LETTER OF THE CORRECT ANSWER IN THE SPACE PROVIDED BEFORE THE QUESTION NUMBER.

_____ 1. When using QuickBooks graphs, information regarding the percentage of accounts payable owed to each vendor is displayed as a ___.
A. pie chart
B. bar chart
C. line chart
D. both A and B

_____ 2. A check may be entered in ___.
A. the Write Checks window
B. the Check Register
C. both A and B
D. neither A nor B

_____ 3. When you enter a bill, typing the first letter(s) of a vendor's name on the vendor line ___.
A. enters the vendor's name on the line if the name is on the Vendors list
B. displays a list of vendor names
C. displays the Address Info tab for the vendor
D. indicates that you want to type the vendor name completely

_____ 4. To erase an incorrect amount in a bill, you may ___ then key the correction.
A. drag through the amount to highlight
B. position the cursor in front of the amount and press the delete key until the amount has been erased
C. position the cursor after the amount and press the backspace key until the amount has been erased
D. all of the above

_____ 5. When a document prints sideways, it is called ___ orientation.
A. portrait
B. landscape
C. standard
D. horizontal

_____ 6. A correction to a bill that has been recorded can be made on the bill or ___.
   A. not at all
   B. on the Accounts Payable Graph
   C. in the Accounts Payable Register
   D. none of the above

_____ 7. When a bill is deleted, ___.
   A. the amount is changed to 0.00
   B. the word "deleted" appears as the Memo
   C. it is removed without a trace
   D. a bill cannot be deleted

_____ 8. To increase the date on a bill by one day, ___.
   A. press the + key
   B. press the - key
   C. tab
   D. press the # key

_____ 9. If a bill is recorded in the Enter Bills window, it is best to pay the bill by ___.
   A. writing a check
   B. using the Pay Bills window
   C. using petty cash
   D. allowing QuickBooks to generate the check automatically five days before the due date

_____ 10. When entering several bills at once on the Enter Bills screen, it is most efficient to __ go to the next blank screen.
   A. click >>Prev
   B. click >>Next
   C. click OK
   D. click Preview

FILL-IN

IN THE SPACE PROVIDED, WRITE THE ANSWER THAT MOST APPROPRIATELY COMPLETES THE SENTENCE.

1. The _____ section of a bill is used to record the information for the actual bill.

2. An Accounts Payable Graph by Aging Period shows a _____ chart detailing the amounts due by aging period and a _____ chart showing the percentage of the total amount payable owed to each vendor.

3. Three different check styles may be used in QuickBooks: _____, _____, or _____.

4. The keyboard shortcut to edit or modify a vendor's record is _____.

5. Petty Cash is identified as a _____ account type so, it will be placed at the top of the Chart of Accounts along with checking and savings accounts.

SHORT ESSAY

When viewing a Transaction by Vendor Report that shows the entry of a bill for the purchase of office supplies and office equipment, you will see the term **-split-** displayed. Explain what the term **Split** means when used as a column heading and when used within the Split column for the bill indicated.

_____

_____

_____

_____

_____

END-OF-CHAPTER PROBLEM

SUNSHINE LAWN AND POOL MAINTENANCE

Chapter 3 continues with the transactions for bills, bill payments, and purchases for Sunshine Lawn and Pool Maintenance. Even though it is a family-owned business, cash control measures have been implemented. Sylvia prints the checks and any related reports; Greg initials his approval of the checks; and George, the owner, signs the checks.

INSTRUCTIONS

Continue to use the data disk for Sunshine. Open the company—the file used is
SUNSHINE.QBW. Record the bills, bill payments, and purchases as instructed within the
chapter. Always read the transactions carefully and review the Chart of Accounts when selecting
transaction accounts. Print reports and graphs as indicated. If a bill is recorded on the Enter Bills
screen, it should be paid on the Pay Bills screen—not by writing the check yourself.

RECORD TRANSACTIONS

May 1—Use Enter Bills to record the following bills:
Received a bill from Universal Communications for cellular phone service, $485, Invoice
No. 1109, Net 10, Memo: Cellular Telephone Services for May.

Received a bill from the Office Group for supplies purchased, $275, Invoice No. 58-9826,
Net 30. (This is a prepaid expense.) No memo is necessary.

Received a bill from Larry's Motors for truck service and repairs, $519, Invoice No. 1-62,
Net 10, Memo: Truck Service and Repairs. (There is only one expense account that can be used
for this bill. We will be changing the name to something more appropriate in Chapter 4.)

Received a bill from Green Street Gasoline for gasoline for the month, $375, Invoice No. 853,
Net 10, Memo: Gasoline for Month.

Received a bill from Cooler/Heating for a repair of the office air conditioner, $150, Invoice
No. 87626, Net 30, Memo: Air Conditioner Repair. (The air conditioner is part of the building.)

May 15—Use Enter Bills to record new bills. Use Pay Bills to pay any bills previously recorded:
Add a new expense account: Disposal Expense, Description: City Dump Charges, Tax Line is
Schedule C: Other Business Expenses.

Received a bill from City Dump for disposing of lawn, tree, and shrub trimmings, $180, Invoice
No. 667, Net 30, no memo necessary.

Received a bill from California Water Company, $25, Invoice No. 098-1, Net 10, no memo.

Change the QuickBooks Preferences to customize the report format so that the Date Prepared
does not print as part of the header.

Print an Unpaid Bills Detail Report for May 1-15.

Pay all bills due on or before May 15, print checks.

Record the receipt of a bill from Quality Equipment Maintenance. Add this new vendor as you
record the transaction. Additional information needed to do a complete Set Up is: 1234 State
Street, Santa Barbara, CA 93110, 805-555-0770. The bill was for the repair of the lawn mower,
$75, Invoice No. 5-1256, Net 10, no memo necessary.

Change the telephone number for City Dump. The new number is 805-555-3798.

Print the Vendor Balance Detail Report.

May 30—When paying bills that have been entered in the Enter Bills window, use Pay Bills.

Received a $10 credit from Quality Equipment Maintenance. The repair of the lawn mower wasn't as extensive as originally estimated.

Add Petty Cash to the Chart of Accounts.

Use the Check Register to transfer $50 from Checking to Petty Cash, memo: Establish Petty Cash Fund.

Record the use of Petty Cash to pay for postage due 64 cents, and office supplies, $1.59 (this is a current expense). Memo notations are not necessary.

Write Check # 5 to Quality Equipment Maintenance to buy a lawn fertilizer spreader as a cash purchase of equipment, $349, memo: Purchase of Lawn Fertilizer Spreader. Print the check. (If you get a dialog box indicating that you currently owe money to Quality Equipment Maintenance, click the button that will allow you to continue writing the check.)

Print an Unpaid Bills Report for May 30.

Pay all bills due on or before May 30; print the checks. (Note: There may some bills that were due after May 15 but before May 30. Be sure to pay these bills now.)

Prepare and print an Accounts Payable Graph as of 5/30/98.

Prepare and print a QuickZoom Graph for City Dump as of 5/30/98.

Back up your data and close company.

GENERAL ACCOUNTING AND END-OF-PERIOD PROCEDURES: SERVICE BUSINESS

LEARNING OBJECTIVES

At the completion of this chapter, you will be able to use QuickBooks to:

1. Complete the end-of-period procedures.
2. Change account names, delete accounts, and make accounts inactive.
3. View an account name change and its effect on subaccounts.
4. Record depreciation, adjustment to Uncategorized Income, and adjustment to Uncategorized Expenses.
5. Enter the adjusting entries required for accrual basis accounting.
6. Record owner's equity transactions for a sole proprietor including capital investment and owner withdrawals.
7. Reconcile the bank statement, record bank service charges, and mark cleared transactions.
8. Print Trial Balance, Profit and Loss Statement, and Balance Sheet.
9. Perform end-of-period backup and assign end-of-period password.

GENERAL ACCOUNTING AND END-OF-PERIOD PROCEDURES

As previously stated, QuickBooks operates from the standpoint of the business document rather than an accounting form, journal, or ledger. While QuickBooks does incorporate all of these items into the program, in many instances they operate behind the scenes. QuickBooks does not require special closing procedures at the end of a period. At the end of the fiscal year, QuickBooks transfers the net income into the Retained Earnings account and allows you to protect the data for the year by assigning a password to the period. All of the transaction detail is maintained and viewable, but it cannot be changed unless accessed by using the assigned password.

Even though a formal "closing" does not have to be performed within QuickBooks, when you use accrual basis accounting, several transactions must be recorded to reflect all expenses and income for the period. For example, bank statements must be reconciled and any charges or bank collections need to be recorded. During the business period, the CPA for the company will review things such as account names, adjusting entries, depreciation schedules, owner's equity adjustments, and so on. Sometimes the changes and adjustments will be made by the accountant on a separate disk called the Accountant's Copy of the business files. This disk is then merged with the company files that are used to record day-to-day business transactions, and all adjustments made by the CPA are added to the current company files. There are certain restrictions to the types of transactions that may be made on an Accountant's Copy of the business files. In some instances, the accountant will make adjustments on a backup copy of the company data because there are no restrictions on the types of entries that may be made. However, transactions entered by the accountant on backup company files must also be entered in the active company files because a backup disk cannot be merged with the active data files.

Once necessary adjustments have been made, reports reflecting the end-of-period results of operations should be prepared. For archive purposes at the end of the fiscal year an additional backup disk is prepared and stored.

TRAINING TUTORIAL AND PROCEDURES

The following tutorial will once again work with Creative Computer Consulting (CCC). As in Chapters 2 and 3, transactions will be recorded for this fictitious company. To maximize training benefits, you should:

1. Read the entire chapter *before* beginning to enter transactions for CCC.
2. Answer the end-of-chapter questions.
3. Be aware that transactions to be entered are given within a **MEMO**.
4. Complete all the steps listed for the Creative Computer Consulting tutorial in the chapter. The steps are indicated by: ▨***DO:**
5. When you have completed a step, put an **X** on the button next to ***DO:**
6. As you complete your work, proofread carefully and check for accuracy. Double-check amounts of money.
7. If you find an error while preparing a transaction, correct it. If you find the error after the transaction has been entered, follow the steps indicated in this chapter to correct, void, or delete the transaction.
8. Print as directed in the chapter.
9. You may not finish the entire chapter in one computer session. Always back up your work at the end of your work session as described in Chapter 1.
10. When you complete your computer session, always close your company.

OPEN QUICKBOOKS® AND CREATIVE COMPUTER CONSULTING

▨   ***DO:** Open QuickBooks as instructed in Chapters 1 and 2
       Open Creative Computer Consulting (CCC)

- To close an open company and open your copy of CCC, click **File**, click **Open Company**, click **Creative.qbw**, check to make sure you are using the disk in **A:**, click **Open** button.

Close the Reminders screen

Check the title bar to verify that CCC is the open company

BEGINNING THE TUTORIAL

In this chapter you will be recording end-of-period adjustments, reconciling bank statements, changing account names, and preparing traditional end-of-period reports. Because QuickBooks does not perform a traditional "closing" of the books, you will learn how to password protect transactions and data recorded during previous accounting periods.

All transactions are listed on memos. The transaction date will be the same as the memo date unless otherwise specified within the transaction. Once a specific type of transaction has been entered in a step-by-step manner, additional transactions of the same or a similar type will be made without instructions being provided. Of course, you may always refer to instructions given for previous transactions for ideas or for steps used to enter those transactions. To determine the account used in the transaction, refer to the Chart of Accounts, which is also the General Ledger.

CHANGE THE NAME OF EXISTING ACCOUNTS IN THE CHART OF ACCOUNTS

Even though transactions have been recorded during the month of January, QuickBooks makes it a simple matter to change the name of an existing account. Once the name of an account has been changed, all transactions using the "old" name are updated and show the "new" account name.

MEMO
DATE: January 31, 1998

Upon the recommendation from the company's CPA, Roger Owens decided to change the account named Company Cars to Business Vehicles.

---

*DO: Change the account name of Company Cars

Access the Chart of Accounts:

Click **Lists**, click **Chart of Accounts** on the menu bar

OR

> Click **Accnt** button on the iconbar
> > OR
>
> Click **Company** tab, click **Chart of Accounts** on QuickBooks Navigator
> > OR
>
> Use the keyboard shortcut **Ctrl+A**

Scroll through accounts until you see Company Cars, click **Company Cars**

Click **Account** Button at the bottom of the chart, click **Edit**
> OR

Use the keyboard shortcut **Ctrl+E**

On the **Edit Account** screen highlight **Company Cars**

Enter the new name **Business Vehicles**

- At the bottom of the Edit Account screen you will see 0.00 for the amount, **DO NOT CHANGE THIS**.
- The balances of any subaccounts of business vehicles will be reflected in the account total on the chart of accounts and in reports.

Click **OK** to record the name change and to close the Edit Account screen

- Notice that the name of the account appears as Business Vehicles in the Chart of Accounts and that the balance of $49,000 shows.

Follow the steps above to change the names of:
> **Company Cars Loan** to **Business Vehicles Loan**
>
> **Automobile Expense** to **Business Vehicles Expense**
> - Delete the Description Automobile Expense.
>
> **Auto Insurance Expense** to **Business Vehicle Insurance**
>
> **Office Equipment** to **Office Furniture and Equipment**
>
> **Loan Interest** to **Interest on Loans**

Do not close the Chart of Accounts

Name	Type	Balance
◆ Business Vehicles	Fixed Asset	49,000.00
◆ Depreciation	Fixed Asset	0.00
◆ Original Cost	Fixed Asset	49,000.00
◆ Office Furniture and Equipm	Fixed Asset	8,536.00
◆ Depreciation	Fixed Asset	0.00
◆ Original Cost	Fixed Asset	8,536.00
◆ Loan Payable	Long Term Liability	39,000.00
◆ Business Vehicles Loan	Long Term Liability	35,000.00
◆ Office Equipment Loan	Long Term Liability	4,000.00
◆ Business Vehicle Expense	Expense	
◆ Insurance	Expense	
◆ Business Vehicle Insuranc	Expense	
◆ Disability Insurance	Expense	
◆ Liability Insurance	Expense	
◆ Work Comp	Expense	
◆ Interest Expense	Expense	
◆ Finance Charge	Expense	
◆ Interest on Loans	Expense	

Chart of Accounts

EFFECT OF AN ACCOUNT NAME CHANGE ON SUBACCOUNTS

Any account that uses Company Car as part of the account name needs to be changed. However, when the account name of Company Car was changed to Business Vehicles, the subaccounts of Company Car automatically became subaccounts of Business Vehicles.

 *DO: Examine the Depreciation and Original Cost accounts for Business Vehicles
　　　Click **Depreciation** under Business Vehicles
　　　Click **Account** button at the bottom of the chart, click **Edit**
　　　　OR
　　　Use the keyboard shortcut **Ctrl+E**
　　　Notice that the text box for **Subaccount of** shows as **Business Vehicles**

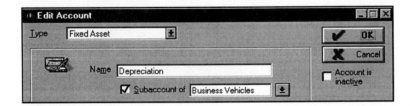

　　　Click **Cancel**
- Repeat the above steps to examine the **Original Cost** account.
- Examine **Office Furniture and Equipment** and the subaccounts of **Depreciation** and **Original Cost**.

　　　Do not close the Chart of Accounts

MAKE AN ACCOUNT INACTIVE

If you are not using an account and do not have plans to use it in the near future, the account may be made inactive. The account remains available for use, yet it does not appear on your chart of accounts unless you check the Show All check box.

MEMO
DATE: January 31, 1998

At present CCC does not plan to purchase its own building. The accounts **Interest Expense: Mortgage** and **Taxes: Property** should be made inactive.

---

*DO: Make the accounts listed above inactive

Click **Mortgage** under Interest Expense

Click **Account** button at the bottom of Chart of Accounts, click **Make Inactive** OR

Use Keyboard Shortcut **Ctrl+E** to edit the account, click the check box **Account is inactive** to insert a ✔ in the box, click **OK** to close Edit Account window

- The account no longer appears in the Chart of Accounts.
- If you wish to view all accounts including the inactive ones, click **Show All** check box at the bottom of the Chart of Accounts and all accounts will be displayed.
- Notice the icon next to Mortgage. It marks the account as inactive.

⬥ Interest Expense	Expense
⬥ Finance Charge	Expense
⬥ Interest on Loans	Expense
⬥ Mortgage	Expense

Repeat the above to make **Taxes: Property** inactive

⬥ Taxes	Expense
⬥ Federal	Expense
⬥ Local	Expense
⬥ Property	Expense

DELETE AN EXISTING ACCOUNT FROM THE CHART OF ACCOUNTS

If you do not want to make an account inactive because you have not used it and do not plan to use it at all, QuickBooks allows the account to be deleted at anytime. However, as a safeguard QuickBooks does prevent the deletion of an account once it has been used even if it simply contains an opening or an existing balance.

MEMO

DATE: January 31, 1998

In addition to previous changes to account names, Roger Owens finds that he does not use nor will he use the expense account: Contributions. Delete this account from the Chart of Accounts. In addition, Roger wants you to delete the Dues and Subscriptions account.

*DO: Delete the Contributions expense account
　　　Scroll through accounts until you see Contributions, click **Contributions**
　　　Click **Account** button at the bottom of the chart, click **Delete**
　　　　OR
　　　Use the keyboard shortcut **Ctrl+D**

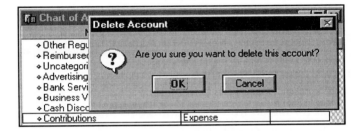

Click **OK** on the **Delete Accounts** dialog box
- The account has now been deleted.

Repeat the above steps for the deletion of **Dues and Subscriptions**
- As soon as you try to delete Dues and Subscriptions a **Warning** appears stating, "This account has a balance or is used in a transaction, an invoice item, or your payroll setup. It cannot be deleted."

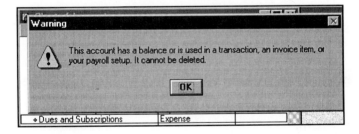

Click **OK**
- The account remains in the Chart of Accounts.

Close the Chart of Accounts

ADJUSTMENTS FOR ACCRUAL BASIS ACCOUNTING

As previously stated, the accrual basis for accounting matches the income from a period and the expenses of a period in order to arrive at an accurate figure for net income. Thus, the revenue is earned at the time the service is performed or the sale is made no matter when the actual cash is received. The cash basis of accounting records income or revenue at the time cash is received no matter when the sale was made or the service performed. The same holds true when a business buys things or pays bills. In the accrual basis of accounting the expense is recorded at the time the bill is received or the purchase is made regardless of the actual payment date. In the cash basis the expense is not recorded until it is paid.

There are several internal transactions that must be recorded when using the accrual basis of accounting. These entries are called adjusting entries. For example, equipment does wear out and will eventually need to be replaced. Rather than wait until replacement to record the use of the equipment, one makes an adjusting entry to allocate the use of equipment as an expense for a period. This is called depreciation. Certain items used in a business are paid for in advance. As these are used, they become expenses of the business. For example, insurance for the entire year would be used up month by month and should, therefore, be a monthly expense. Commonly, the insurance is billed and paid for the entire year. Until the insurance is used, it is an asset. Each month the portion of the insurance used becomes an expense for the month.

UNCATEGORIZED EXPENSES AND UNCATEGORIZED INCOME ADJUSTMENTS

When the records for CCC were set up, QuickBooks stored the amounts of the opening balances for customers in an account called Uncategorized Income and the amounts of the opening balances for vendors in an account called Uncategorized Expenses. This was done because a business using the accrual basis for accounting would have already recorded the amounts in the opening balances as income or expenses. These opening balances need to be cleared from Uncategorized Expenses and Uncategorized Income accounts. This is done by recording an adjusting entry.

MEMO
DATE: January 31, 1998

The CPA noted that the adjusting entries for Uncategorized Income and Uncategorized Expenses had not been made at the completion of the company setup.

---

*DO: Make adjustments for Uncategorized Income and Uncategorized Expenses
Open Chart of Accounts as previously instructed
Click on the account **Uncategorized Income**
Click **Reports** button at the bottom of the screen
Click **QuickReport: Uncategorized Income**
    OR
Use keyboard shortcut **Ctrl+Q**

Enter the **From** date as **01/01/98**
Enter **To** date as **01/31/98**
Tab to generate the report
Scroll to the bottom of the report
- Check the total of the Opening Balances—**22,505**.

Type	Date	Num	Name	Memo	Split	Amount
\multicolumn{7}{l}{Creative Computer Consulting (CCC)}						

Creative Computer Consulting (CCC)
Account QuickReport
January 1998

Type	Date	Num	Name	Memo	Split	Amount
Invoice	01/01/98		Goldman, Butler, a...	Opening ba...	Accounts R...	0.00
Invoice	01/01/98		Jensen, Yamaguc...	Opening ba...	Accounts R...	3,680.00
Invoice	01/01/98		Jung, Chai	Opening ba...	Accounts R...	0.00
Invoice	01/01/98		Matthews, Timoth...	Opening ba...	Accounts R...	415.00
Invoice	01/01/98		Mendoza, Jose	Opening ba...	Accounts R...	150.00
Invoice	01/01/98		Nahid, Ali Imports	Opening ba...	Accounts R...	300.00
Invoice	01/01/98		Rogers Illustrations	Opening ba...	Accounts R...	3,830.00
Invoice	01/01/98		Sandoval, Heitz, K...	Opening ba...	Accounts R...	0.00
Invoice	01/01/98		Washington, Reed...	Opening ba...	Accounts R...	3,685.00
Invoice	01/01/98		Wensel, Hammar,...	Opening ba...	Accounts R...	0.00
Invoice	01/01/98		Williams Productio...	Opening ba...	Accounts R...	3,190.00
Total Uncategorized Income						22,505.00

Close the QuickReport for Uncategorized Income
Repeat the steps to determine the amount for Uncategorized Expenses
- The total of Uncategorized Expenses should be **850**.

Creative Computer Consulting (CCC)
Account QuickReport
January 1998

Type	Date	Num	Name	Memo	Split	Amount
Uncategorized Expenses						
Bill	01/01/98		Global Advertising	Opening bal...	Accounts Pa...	500.00
Bill	01/01/98		Office Supplies W...	Opening bal...	Accounts Pa...	350.00
Total Uncategorized Expenses						850.00
TOTAL						**850.00**

Close the QuickReport for Uncategorized Expenses
Enter the adjustments to Roger Owens, Capital:
  In the Chart of Accounts, click **Roger Owens, Capital**
  Click the **Activities** button, click **Use Register**
     OR
  Use the keyboard shortcut **Ctrl+R**

Enter the adjustment for Uncategorized Income:

Position the cursor in the empty transaction at the bottom of the Register for Roger Owens, Capital

The **Date** is the start date of **01/01/98**

Tab to or click **Account**

Click the drop-down list arrow, click **Uncategorized Income**

Tab to or click **Increase** field

Enter **22505**

Click **Record**

Enter the adjustment for Uncategorized Expenses:

Position the cursor in the next empty transaction at the bottom of the register

Enter the start date of **01/01/98** in the **Date** column

Tab to or click **Account**

Click the drop-down list arrow, click **Uncategorized Expenses**

Tab to or click **Decrease** field

Enter **850**

Click **Record**

- The balance of Roger Owens, Capital account is $53,075 after recording Uncategorized Expenses. The Ending Balance beneath the Balance column shows $78,075.00. The difference between the balance after Uncategorized Expenses and the Ending Balance is due to a Transfer into the checking account of the owner's investment of $25,000. QuickBooks puts a GENJRNL entry before a TRANSFER.

Date	Number	Payee		Increase	✓	Decrease	Balance
	Type	Account	Memo				
01/01/98						4,000.00	31,420.00
	GENJRNL	Loan Payable:Office Equ Account Opening Balanc					
01/01/98				22,505.00			53,925.00
	GENJRNL	Uncategorized Income					
01/01/98						850.00	53,075.00
	GENJRNL	Uncategorized Expenses					
01/01/98				25,000.00			78,075.00
	TRANSFR	Checking					

Record   Edit   Splits   Ending balance   78,075.00

Restore   Q-Report   Go To   ☐ 1-Line

Close the Register for Roger Owens, Capital

Close the Chart of Accounts

ADJUSTING ENTRIES—PREPAID EXPENSES

During the operation of a business, companies purchase supplies to have on hand for use in the operation of the business. In accrual basis accounting, the supplies are considered to be prepaid assets (something the business owns) until they are used in the operation of the business. As the supplies are used, the amount used becomes an expense for the period. The same system applies to other things paid for in advance such as insurance. At the end of the period an adjusting entry must be made to allocate the amount of prepaid assets used to expenses.

The transactions for these adjustments may be recorded in the register for the account by clicking on the prepaid asset in the Chart of Accounts, or they may be made in the General Journal.

MEMO
DATE: January 31, 1998

NOTE *from Roger*—
Carmen, remember to record the monthly adjustment for Prepaid Insurance. The $2,850 is the amount we paid for the year. Also, we used $350 worth of supplies this month. Please adjust accordingly.

---

*DO: Record the adjusting entries for office supplies expense and business vehicle insurance expense in the General Journal.
Access the General Journal:
Click **Activities** on the menu bar, click **Make Journal Entry**
OR
Open **Chart of Accounts** as previously instructed, click **Activities** button, click **Make Journal Entry**
OR
Click **Taxes and Accountant** tab in QuickBooks Navigator, click **Make Journal Entry**
Record the adjusting entry for Prepaid Insurance
Enter **01/31/98** as the **Date**
- **Entry No.** is left blank unless you wish to record a specific number.
  - Because all transactions entered for the month have been entered in the Journal as well as on an invoice or a bill, all transactions automatically have a Journal entry number.
Tab to or click **Account** column

Click the drop-down list arrow for Account, click **Business Vehicle Insurance**
Tab to or click **Debit**
- The $2,850 given in the memo is the amount for the year; calculate the amount of the adjustment for the month:
  Click **Activities**, point to **Other Activities**, click **Use Calculator**
  Enter **2850** by:
    Using the mouse to click the numbers
      OR
    Typing the numbers at the top of the keyboard
      OR
    Keying the numbers on the **10-key pad** (preferred)
    - Be sure Num Lock is on. There should be a light by Num Lock on/or above the 10-key pad. If not, press Num Lock to activate.
  Press / for division
  Key **12**
  Press = or **Enter**
  Click the **Close** button to close the calculator
  - For additional calculator instructions refer to Chapter 1.
Enter the amount of the adjustment **237.5** in the Debit column
Tab to or click the **Memo** column
Type **Adjusting Entry, Insurance**
Tab to or click **Account**
Click the drop-down list arrow for Account
Click **Prepaid Insurance**
- The amount for the Credit column was entered automatically. There are several reasons why an amount may not appear in the credit column; if 237.50 does not appear, type it in the credit column.
Tab to or click the **Memo** column
Type **Adjusting Entry, Insurance**

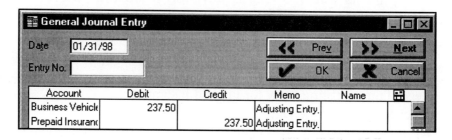

Click **>>NEXT** to record the adjustment and advance to the next General Journal Entry screen
Repeat the above procedures to record the adjustment for the office supplies used

- The amount given in the memo is the actual amount of the supplies used in January.

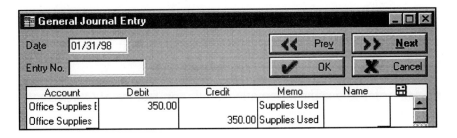

Click **OK**

ADJUSTING ENTRIES—DEPRECIATION

Using the accrual basis of accounting requires companies to record an expense for the amount of equipment used in the operation of the business. Unlike supplies—where you can actually see , for example, the paper supply diminishing—it is very difficult to see how much of a computer has been "used up" during the month. To account for the fact that machines do wear out and need to be replaced, an adjustment is made for depreciation. This adjustment correctly matches the expenses of the period against the revenue of the period.

The adjusting entry for depreciation can be made in the account register for Depreciation, or it can be made in the General Journal.

MEMO

DATE: January 31, 1998

Having received the necessary depreciation schedules, Carmen records the adjusting entry for depreciation: Business Vehicles, $583 per month; Equipment, $142 per month.

---

*DO: Record a compound adjusting entry for depreciation of the equipment and the business vehicles in the General Journal:

Access the General Journal:

Access the **Chart of Accounts**, click **Activities** button, click **Make Journal Entry**

OR

Click **Activities** on the menu bar, click **Make Journal Entry**
OR
Click **Taxes and Accountant** tab in QuickBooks Navigator, click **Make Journal Entry**

Enter **01/31/98** as the **Date**

Entry No. is left blank

- In order to use the automatic calculation feature of QuickBooks, you will enter the credit entries first.

Tab to or click **Account** column

Click the drop-down list arrow for Account, click **Depreciation** under **Business Vehicles**

Tab to or click **Credit**, enter **583**

Tab to or click **Memo**

Enter **Adjusting Entry January**

Tab to or click **Account** column

- The amount of the 583 credit shows in the debit column temporarily.

Click the drop-down list arrow for Account, click **Depreciation** under **Office Furniture and Equipment**

Tab to or click **Credit**

Enter **142**

- The 583 in the debit column disappears when you tab to or click Memo.

Tab to or click **Memo**

Enter **Adjusting Entry January**

Tab to or click **Account** column

Click the drop-down list arrow for Account

Click **Depreciation Expense**

Debit column should automatically show **725**

- If 725 does not appear, enter it in the debit column.

Tab to or click **Memo**, enter **Adjusting Entry January**

Click **OK** to record the adjustment and close the General Journal

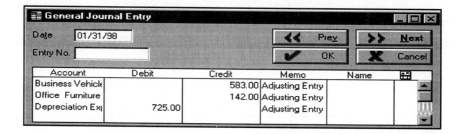

Close Chart of Accounts, if necessary

VIEW GENERAL JOURNAL

Once transactions have been entered in the General Journal, it is important to view them. QuickBooks also refers to the General Journal as the Journal and allows it to be viewed or printed at any time. Even with the special ways in which transactions are entered in QuickBooks through invoices, bills, checks, and account registers, the Journal is still the book of original entry. All transactions recorded for the company may be viewed in the Journal even if they were entered elsewhere.

 *DO: View the Journal for January

Click **Reports** on the menu bar, point to **Other Reports**, click **Journal**
   OR
Click **Taxes and Accountant** tab on QuickBooks Navigator, click **Other** on the
   Reports section, click **Journal**
Tab to or click **From**
- If necessary, delete existing date.
Enter **01/01/98**
Tab to or click **To**
Enter **01/31/98**
Tab to generate the report
- Notice that the transactions do not begin with the adjustments entered directly into the Journal.
- The first transaction shows the opening balance entry for Andrews, Eric Research.

Creative Computer Consulting (CCC)
Journal
January 1998

Type	Date	Num	Name	Memo	Account	Debit	Credit
Invoice	01/01/98		Andrews, Eric Res...	Opening ba...	Accounts Receiva...	815.00	
			Andrews, Eric Res...	Opening ba...	Uncategorized Inc...		815.00
						815.00	815.00
Invoice	01/01/98		Benjamin, Jacobs,...	Opening ba...	Accounts Receiva...	1,915.00	
			Benjamin, Jacobs,...	Opening ba...	Uncategorized Inc...		1,915.00
						1,915.00	1,915.00
Invoice	01/01/98		Cinema Innovations	Opening ba...	Accounts Receiva...	1,295.00	
			Cinema Innovations	Opening ba...	Uncategorized Inc...		1,295.00
						1,295.00	1,295.00

Partial Report

Scroll through the report to view all transactions recorded in the Journal
Close the report without printing

OWNER WITHDRAWALS

In a sole proprietorship an owner cannot receive a paycheck because he or she owns the business. An owner withdrawing money from a business—even to pay personal expenses—is similar to withdrawing money from a savings account. A withdrawal simply decreases the owner's capital. QuickBooks allows you to establish a separate account for owner withdrawals. If a separate account is not established, owner withdrawals may be subtracted directly from the owner's capital or investment account.

MEMO

DATE: January 31, 1998

Because Roger Owens works in his business full time, he does not earn a paycheck. Prepare his check for his monthly withdrawal, $2,500.

---

*DO: Write Check No. 9 to Roger Owens for $2,500 withdrawal
Open the **Write Checks - Checking** window:
>   Click **Activities** on the menu bar, click **Write Checks**
>   OR
>   Click **Check** icon on the iconbar
>   OR
>   Click **Checking and Credit Card** tab on QuickBooks Navigator, click **Checks**
>   OR
>   Use the keyboard shortcut **Ctrl+W**
Click the check box **To be printed**
>   The Check No. should be **To Print**
Date should be **01/31/98**
Enter **Roger Owens** on the **Pay to the Order of** line
Press **Tab** key
- Because Roger's name was not added to any list when the company was created, the **Name Not Found** dialog box appears on the screen.
Click **Quick Add** button to add Roger's name to a list

Select Name Type dialog box appears
Click **Other**
Click **OK**

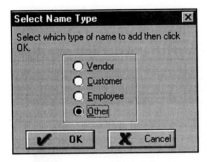

*   Roger's name is added to a list of "Other" names, which are used for owners, partners, and other miscellaneous names.
Tab to or click in the area for the amount of the check
*   If necessary, delete any numbers showing for the amount (0.00).
Enter **2500**
Tab to or click **Memo**
Enter **Owner Withdrawal for January**
Tab to or click in the Account column at the bottom of the check
Click the drop-down list arrow, click the Equity account **Draws**
*   The amount 2,500.00 should appear in the Amount column.
*   If it does not, tab to or click in the Amount column and enter 2500.
Click **Print** to print the check
Print Check dialog box appears
Printed Check Number should be **9**
*   If necessary, change the number to 9.
Once the check has printed successfully, click **OK** to close **Did check(s) print OK?** dialog box
Click **OK** to record the check

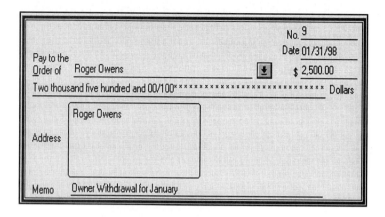

ADDITIONAL CASH INVESTMENT BY OWNER

An owner may decide to invest more of his or her personal cash in the business at any time. The new investment is entered into the owner's investment account and into cash. The investment may be recorded in the account register for checking or in the register for the owner's investment account. It may also be recorded in the Journal.

MEMO

DATE: January 31, 1998

Roger Owens received money from a Certificate of Deposit. Rather than reinvest in another Certificate of Deposit, he decided to invest an additional $5,000 in CCC.

---

*DO: Record the additional cash investment by Roger Owens in the Journal
Access the Journal as previously instructed
The **Date** should be **01/31/98**
- Nothing is needed for Entry No.
Debit **Checking, $5,000**
Credit **Roger Owens, Investments, $5,000**
The memo for both entries should be **Cash Investment, Roger Owens**

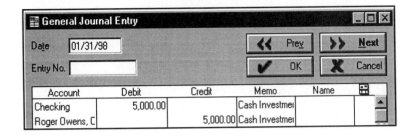

Click **OK** to record and exit

NONCASH INVESTMENT BY OWNER

Investments in a business may be made at any time by an owner. The investment may be cash; but it may also be something such as reference books, equipment, tools, buildings, and so on. Additional investments by an owner or owners is added to owner's equity. In the case of a sole proprietor, the investment is added to the Capital account.

MEMO

DATE: January 31, 1998

Originally, Roger Owens planned to have an office in his home as well as in the company and purchased new office furniture for his home. He decided the business environment would appear more professional if the new furniture were in the office rather than his home. Roger gave the new office furniture to CCC as an additional owner investment. The value of the investment is $3,000.

---

*DO: Record the additional investment by Roger Owens in the Journal
Access the Journal as previously instructed
The **Date** should be **01/31/98**
Nothing is needed for Entry No.
Debit **Office Furniture and Equipment: Original Cost, $3,000**
Credit **Roger Owens, Investment, $3,000**
The memo for both entries should be **Investment of Furniture by Roger Owens**

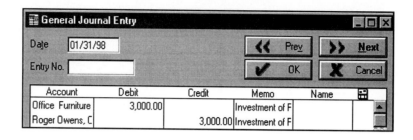

Click **OK** to record and exit

VIEW BALANCE SHEET

Prior to the owner's making an additional investment in the business, there had been no withdrawals, and the drawing account balance was zero. Once the owner makes a withdrawal, that amount is carried forward in the owner's drawing account. Subsequent withdrawals are added to this account. When you view the balance sheet, notice the balance of the Drawing account after the check for withdrawal was written. Also notice the Net Income account that appears in the equity section of the balance sheet. This account is automatically added by QuickBooks to track the net income for the year.

    *DO: View a Standard Balance Sheet:

      Click **Reports** on the menu bar, point to **Balance Sheet**, click **Standard**
        OR
      Click **Taxes and Accountant** tab on QuickBooks Navigator, click **Balance Sheet**, click **Standard**
      Tab to or click **As Of**
      • If necessary, delete existing date.
      Enter **01/31/98**
      Tab to generate the report
      Scroll through the report
      • Notice the Equity section, especially Retained Earnings and Net Income.
      Close the report

```
┌─────────────────────────────────────────────────────────┐
│        Creative Computer Consulting (CCC)--Your Name       │
│                     Balance Sheet                          │
│                  As of January 31, 1998                    │
│                                    ◇   Jan 31, '98   ◇      │
│       Total Liabilities                    42,764.00       │
│                                                            │
│       Equity                                               │
│         Net Income                          4,385.71       │
│         Roger Owens, Capital                               │
│           Draws                      -2,500.00             │
│           Investments                33,000.00             │
│           Roger Owens, Capital - Other  53,075.00          │
│         Total Roger Owens, Capital          83,575.00      │
│                                                            │
│       Total Equity                          87,960.71      │
└─────────────────────────────────────────────────────────┘
```

BANK RECONCILIATION

Each month the checking account should be reconciled with the bank statement to make sure that the balances agree. The bank statement will rarely have an ending balance that matches the balance of the checking account. This is due to several factors: outstanding checks (written by the business but not paid by the bank), deposits in transit (deposits that were made too late to be included on the bank statement), bank service charges, interest earned on checking accounts, collections made by the bank, and errors made in recording checks and/or deposits by the company or by the bank.

In order to have an accurate amount listed as the balance in the checking account, it is important that the differences between the bank statement and the checking account be reconciled. If something such as a service charge or a collection made by the bank appears on the bank statement, it needs to be recorded in the checking account.

Reconciling a bank statement is an appropriate time to find any errors that may have been recorded in the checking account. The reconciliation may be out of balance because a transposition was made (recording $94 rather than $49), a transaction was recorded backwards, a transaction was recorded twice, or a transaction was not recorded at all. If a transposition was made, the error may be found by dividing the difference by 9. For example, if $94 was recorded and the actual transaction amount was $49, you would subtract 49 from 94 to get 45. The number 45 can be divided by 9, so your error was a transposition. If the error can be evenly divided by 2, the transaction may have been entered backwards. For example, if you were out of balance $200, look to see if you had any $100 transactions. Perhaps you recorded a $100 debit, and it should have been a credit (or vice versa).

OPEN RECONCILE - CHECKING

To begin the reconciliation, you need to open the Reconcile - Checking window. Verify the information shown for the checking account. The Opening Balance should match the amount of the final balance on the last reconciliation, or it should match the starting account balance.

MEMO

DATE: January 31, 1998

Received the bank statement from Southern California Bank. The bank statement is dated January 30, 1998. Carmen Mendoza needs to reconcile the bank statement and print a Reconciliation Report for Roger Owens.

---

*DO: Reconcile the bank statement for January

Open the **Reconcile - Checking** window and enter preliminary information

Open **Chart of Accounts** as previously instructed, click **Checking**, click

　　Activities button, click **Reconcile**

　　OR

Click **Checking and Credit Cards** on QuickBooks Navigator, click **Reconcile**

The **Account To Reconcile** should be **Checking**

　　If not, click the drop-down list arrow, click **Checking**

Opening Balance should be **12,870**

- This is the same amount as the checking account starting balance.

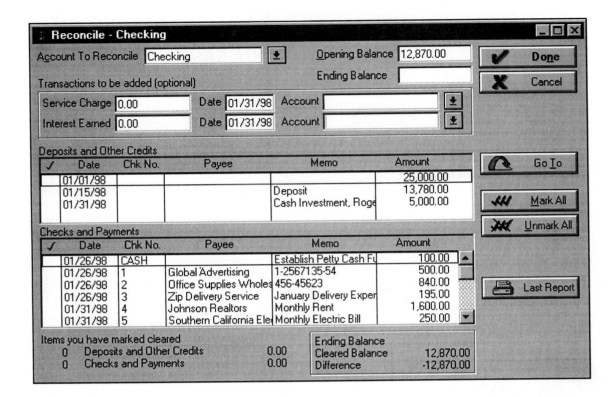

ENTER BANK STATEMENT INFORMATION

Information appearing on the bank statement is entered into **Reconcile - Checking** as the next step. This information includes bank service charges and interest earned. Remember, the dates shown for the checks on the bank statement are the dates the checks were processed by the bank, not the dates the checks were written.

SOUTHERN CALIFORNIA BANK

12345 West Colorado Avenue
Woodland Hills, CA 91377
(818) 555-3880

BANK STATEMENT FOR:

Creative Computer Consulting
2895 West Avenue
Woodland Hills, CA 91367

Acct. # 123-456-7890   January, 1998

Beginning Balance 1/1/98			$12,870.00
1/1/98 Deposit	25,000.00		37,870.00
1/15/98 Deposit	13,780.00		51,650.00
1/26/98 Cash Transfer		110.00	51,540.00
1/28/98 Check 1		500.00	51,040.00
1/28/98 Check 2		840.00	50,200.00
1/29/98 Check 3		195.00	50,005.00
1/30/98 Vehicle Loan Pmt.: $467.19 Principal, $255.22 Interest		722.41	49,282.59
1/30/98 Office Equip. Loan Pmt.: $29.17 Principal, $53.39 Interest		82.56	49,200.03
1/30/98 Service Chg.		8.00	49,192.03
1/30/98 Interest	66.43		49,258.46
Ending Balance 1/30/98			49,258.46

*DO: Continue to reconcile the bank statement above with the checking account
- Note: The date next to the check on the bank statement is the date the check cleared the bank, not the date the check was written.

Enter the **Ending Balance** from the Bank Statement, **49,258.46**
Tab to or click **Service Charge**
Enter the **Service Charge, 8.00**
Tab to or click Service Charge **Date**, change to **01/30/98**
Tab to or click **Account**

Click the drop-down list arrow for **Account**
Click **Bank Service Charges**
Tab to or click **Interest Earned**, enter **66.43**
Tab to or click Interest Earned **Date**, change to **01/30/98**
Tab to or click **Account**
Click the drop-down list arrow for **Account**
Click **Interest Income**

MARK CLEARED TRANSACTIONS FOR BANK RECONCILIATION

Once bank statement information for service charges and interest has been entered, compare the checks and deposits listed on the statement with the transactions for the checking account. If a deposit or a check is listed correctly on the bank statement and in the Reconcile - Checking window, it has cleared and should be marked. An item may be marked individually by positioning the cursor on the deposit or the check and clicking the primary mouse button. If all deposits and checks match, click the Mark All button. To remove all the checks, click the Unmark All button. To unmark an individual item, click the item to remove the check mark.

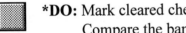 ***DO:** Mark cleared checks and deposits
Compare the bank statement with the Reconcile - Checking window
Click the items that appear on both statements
- Include Petty Cash transaction on 1/26/98 even though the bank statement shows 110 and the check register shows 100.
Look at the Bottom of the Reconcile - Checking window
You have marked cleared:
3 Deposits and Other Credits for 38,846.46
- This includes interest earned.
5 Checks and Payments for 1,643.00
- This includes the $100 for petty cash and the $8 service charge.
The Ending Balance is 49,258.43
The Cleared Balance is 50,073.43
There is a Difference of -814.97

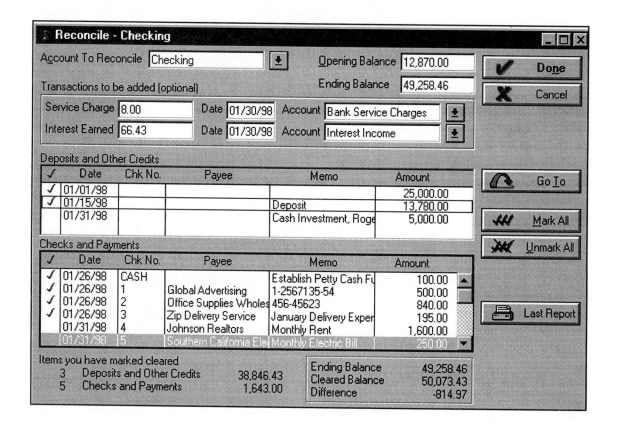

ADJUSTING AND CORRECTING ENTRIES—BANK RECONCILIATION

As you complete the reconciliation, you may find errors that need to be corrected or transactions that need to be recorded. Anything entered as a service charge or interest earned will be entered automatically when the reconciliation is complete and the **Done** button is clicked. To correct an error such as a transposition, click on the entry, then click the **Go To** button. The original entry will appear on the screen. The correction can be made and will show in the **Reconcile - Checking** window. If there is a transaction, such as an automatic loan payment to the bank, access the register for the account used in the transaction and enter the payment.

*DO: Correct the error on the transfer into Petty Cash and enter the automatic loan payments shown on the bank statement.

Correct the entry for the transfer of cash into Petty Cash:

In the section of the reconciliation for **Checks and Payments**, click the entry for **CASH** with a Memo of **Establish Petty Cash Fund**

Click **Go To** button

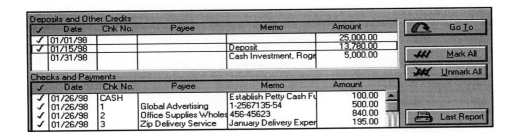

Change the amount on Transfer Funds Between Accounts from 100 to **110**

Click **OK**
- Notice that the amount for the Petty Cash transaction now shows 110.
- You may need to click the Petty Cash transaction to mark it.

With the Reconcile - Checking window still showing, enter the automatic loan payments:

Click **Register** button on the iconbar

    OR

Click **Activities** on the menu bar, click **Use Register**

    OR

Use the keyboard shortcut **Ctrl+R**

In the blank transaction at the bottom of the register enter the **Date, 01/30/98**

Tab to or click **Number**

Enter **TRANSFER**

Tab to or click **Payee**

Enter **Southern California Bank**

Tab to or click the **Payment** column
- Because Southern California Bank does not appear on any list, you will get a Name Not Found dialog box when you move to another field.

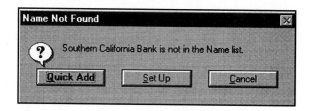

Click **Quick Add** button to add the name of the bank to the Name list
Click **Other**

Click **OK**
- Once the name of the bank has been added to the Other list, the cursor will be positioned in the **Payment** column.

Enter **722.41** in the **Payment** column
Click **Account** column
Click **Splits** button at the bottom of the register
Click drop-down list arrow for **Account**
Click **Interest on Loans** under Interest Expense
Tab to or click **Amount**, delete the amount 722.41 shown
Enter **255.22** as the amount of interest
Tab to or click **Memo**
Enter **Interest Business Vehicles Loan**
Tab to or click **Account**
Click drop-down list arrow for **Account**
Click **Business Vehicles Loan** under Loan Payable
- The correct amount of principal, 467.19, should be showing for the amount.

Tab to or click **Memo**
Enter **Payment Business Vehicles Loan**

Account	Amount	Memo		
Interest Expense:Interest on Loan	255.22	Interest Business Vehicles Loan		Close
Loan Payable:Business Vehicles	467.19	Payment Business Vehicles Loan		Clear
				Recalc

Click **Close**
- This closes the window for the information regarding the way the transaction is to be "split" between accounts.

For the **Memo** in the Checking register, record **Loan Pmt., Business Vehicles**

Click the **Record** button to record the transaction
- Because the Register organizes transactions according to date, you will notice that the loan payment will not appear as the last transaction in the Register.

01/30/98	TRANSFE	Southern California Bank	722.41		49,282.59
	CHK	-split- Loan Pmt. Business Vehi			

Repeat the procedures to record the loan payment for office equipment
- When you enter the Payee as Southern California Bank, the amount for the previous transaction (722.41) appears in amount.

Enter the new amount **82.56**

Click **Splits** button

Click the appropriate accounts and enter the correct amount for each item
- Refer to the bank statement for details regarding the amount of the payment for interest and the amount of the payment applied to principal.
- Note: The amounts for the previous loan payment automatically appear. You will need to enter the amounts for both accounts in this transaction.

Account	Amount	Memo		
Interest Expense:Interest on Loan	53.39	Interest on Office Equipment Loan		Close
Loan Payable:Office Equipment L	29.17	Payment on Office Equipment Loan		Clear

Click **Close** button to close the window for the information regarding the "split" between accounts

Enter the transaction Memo

Click **Record** button to record the loan payment

01/30/98	TRANSFE	Southern California Bank	82.56		49,200.03
	CHK	-split- Loan Pmt. Office Equipm			

Close the **Checking** register
- You should return to **Reconcile - Checking**

Scroll to the top of Check and Payments
- Notice the two entries for the payments in Checks and Payments.

Mark the two entries
- At this point the Ending Balance and Cleared Balance should be equal—$49,258.46 with a difference of 0.00.

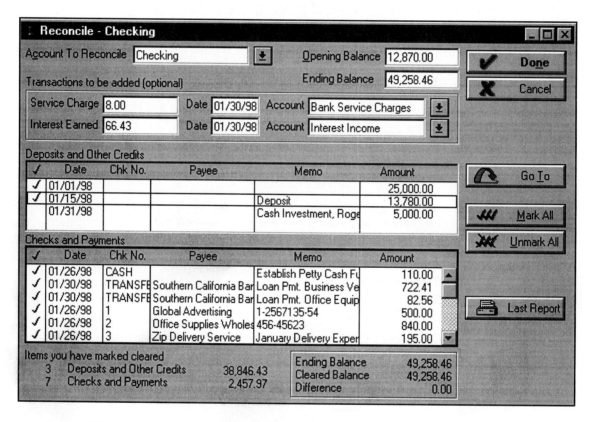

If your entries agree with the above, click **Done** to finish the reconciliation
- If your reconciliation is not in agreement, do not click **Done** until the errors are corrected.
- Once you click Done, you may not return to this Reconciliation - Checking window.

PRINT A RECONCILIATION REPORT

As soon as the Ending Balance and the Cleared Balance are equal or when you finish marking and click Done, a screen appears allowing you to select the level of Reconciliation report you would like to print. You may select **None** and get no report, **Summary** and get a report that lists totals only, or **Full** and get totals and transaction detail for cleared, uncleared, and new transactions. You may print the report at the time you have finished reconciling the account or you may print the report later by returning to the Reconciliation window. QuickBooks keeps your last two reconciliation reports in memory. If you think you may want to print the report again in the future, print the report to a file to save it permanently.

 *DO: Print a Full Reconciliation Report
On the **Reconciliation Complete** screen, click **Full**
Enter **Statement Closing Date** of **01/30/98**

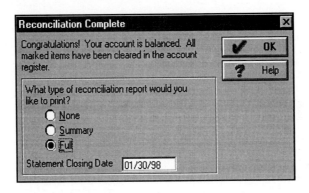

Click **OK** to print
Print as previously instructed:
Printer should be default printer
Orientation is Portrait
Page Range is All
When the report finishes printing, click **Yes**

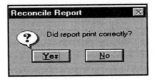

VIEW THE CHECKING ACCOUNT REGISTER

Once the bank reconciliation has been completed, it is wise to scroll through the Check register to view the effect of the reconciliation on the account. You will notice that the check column shows ✔ for all items that were marked as cleared during the reconciliation. This check mark may not be removed. However, if at a later date an error is discovered, the transaction may be changed and the correction will be reflected in the Beginning Balance on the reconciliation.

*DO: View the register for the Checking account

Access the register as previously instructed

To display more of the register, click the check box for **1-Line**

Scroll through the register

- Notice that the transactions are listed in chronological order.
  - Even though the bank reconciliation transactions were recorded after the checks written on January 31, the bank reconciliation transactions appear before the checks because they were recorded with the date of January 30.

Checking

Date	Number	Payee	Account	Payment	✓	Deposit	Balance
01/26/98	2	Office Supplies Wholesal	Accounts Payable	840.00	✓		50,310.00
01/26/98	3	Zip Delivery Service	Accounts Payable	195.00	✓		50,115.00
01/26/98	CASH	Payee	Petty Cash	110.00	✓	Deposit	50,005.00
01/30/98			Interest Income		✓	66.43	50,071.43
01/30/98			Bank Service Charges	8.00	✓		50,063.43
01/30/98	TRANSFE	Southern California Bank	-split-	722.41	✓		49,341.02
01/30/98	TRANSFE	Southern California Bank	-split-	82.56	✓		49,258.46
01/31/98		Communication Services	Telephone	0.00	✓		49,258.46
01/31/98	4	Johnson Realtors	Rent	1,600.00			47,658.46
01/31/98	5	Southern California Elect	Utilities:Electricity Expens	250.00			47,408.46
01/31/98	6	Southern California Wate	Utilities:Water	35.00			47,373.46
01/31/98	7	Southern California Gas (	Utilities:Heating Expense	175.00			47,198.46
01/31/98	8	Office Supplies Wholesal	Office Furniture and Equ	486.00			46,712.46
01/31/98	9	Roger Owens	Roger Owens, Capital:Dr	2,500.00			44,212.46
01/31/98			Roger Owens, Capital:In			5,000.00	49,212.46

Record   Edit   Splits   Ending balance   49,212.46

Restore   Q-Report   GoTo   ☑ 1-Line

EDIT CLEARED TRANSACTIONS

 *DO: Edit transactions that were marked and cleared during the bank reconciliation:

Try to delete one of the check marks on one of the cleared transactions:

Position the cursor over a check mark

- When you try to position the cursor in the ✔ column, the cursor turns into a ✔.

Edit the Petty Cash transaction:

Click in the entry for the transfer of funds to **Petty Cash** on January 26

Change the **Payment** amount to **100**

Click **Record**

01/26/98	CASH	Payee	⬇ Petty Cash	⬇ 100.00	✓	Deposit	50,005.00
01/30/98						3	50,071.43

Transaction Cleared ✕

❓ You have changed a transaction that has already been cleared. Do you want to record your changes?

[Yes]   [No]

01/30/98					50,063.43
01/30/98	TRANSF				49,341.02
01/30/98	TRANSF				49,258.46
01/31/98					49,258.46
01/31/98	4				47,658.46
01/31/98	5				47,408.46
01/31/98	6				47,373.46

Click **Yes** on the Transaction Cleared dialog box
- The transaction amount has been changed.

View the effects of the change to the Petty Cash transaction in the Reconcile - Checking window:

Display the Reconcile - Checking window by:

Accessing the Chart of Accounts

Clicking **Checking**, clicking **Activities**, clicking **Reconcile**

- Notice that the Opening Balance has been increased by $10 and shows $49,268.46.

Click **Cancel** button on the **Reconcile - Checking** screen

Close the Chart of Accounts
- The Checking account register should be on the screen.

Change the amount for the **Petty Cash** transaction back to **110**

Click **Record** to record the change

On the Transaction Cleared dialog box, click **Yes**

01/26/98	3	Zip Delivery Service	Accounts Payable	195.00	✓		50,115.00
01/26/98	CASH	Payee	⬇ Petty Cash	⬇ 110.00	✓	Deposit	50,005.00
01/30/98			Interest Income		✓	66.43	50,071.43
01/30/98			Bank Service Charges	8.00	✓		50,063.43

Close the Checking register

VIEW THE JOURNAL

After entering several transactions, it is helpful to view the Journal. In the Journal all transactions regardless of the method of entry are shown in traditional debit/credit format.

> ***DO:** View the Journal for January
> > Click **Reports** on the menu bar, point to **Other Reports**, click **Journal**
> > > OR
> > Click **Taxes and Accountant** tab on QuickBooks Navigator, click **Other** on the Reports section, click **Journal**
> > Tab to or click **From**
> > - If necessary, delete existing date.
> > Enter **01/01/98**
> > Tab to or click **To**
> > Enter **01/31/98**
> > Tab to generate the report
> > Close the Journal without printing

PREPARE TRIAL BALANCE

After all adjustments have been recorded and the bank reconciliation has been completed, it is wise to prepare the trial balance. As in traditional accounting, the QuickBooks trial balance proves that debits equal credits.

MEMO

DATE: January 31, 1998

Because adjustments have been entered, prepare a trial balance.

> ***DO:** Prepare a trial balance
> > Click **Reports** on the menu bar, point to **Other Reports**, click **Trial Balance**
> > > OR
> > Click **Taxes and Accountant** or **Company** tab on QuickBooks Navigator, click **Other** in the Reports section, click **Trial Balance**
> > Tab to or click **From**
> > - If necessary, highlight or delete the existing date.
> > Enter the date **01/01/98**

Tab to or click **To**
- If necessary, highlight or delete the existing date.

Enter the date **01/31/98**

Tab to generate the report

Scroll through the report and study the amounts shown
- Notice that the final totals of debits and credits are equal: $138,059.07.

USE QUICKZOOM IN TRIAL BALANCE

QuickZoom is a QuickBooks features that allows you to make a closer observation of transactions, amounts, and other entries. With QuickZoom you may zoom in on an item when the mouse pointer turns into a magnifying glass with a Z inside. If you point to an item and you do not get a magnifying glass with a Z inside, you cannot zoom in on the item. For example, if you point to Interest Expense, you will see the magnifying glass with the Z inside. If your Trial Balance had Retained Earnings and you pointed to the account, the mouse pointer would not change from the arrow. This means that you can see transaction details for Interest Expense but not for Retained Earnings.

 *DO: Use QuickZoom to view the details of Interest Expense:

Scroll through the Trial Balance until you see Interest Expense

Position the mouse pointer over the amount of Interest Expense: Interest on Loans, **308.61**
- Notice that the mouse pointer changes to a magnifying glass with a Z.

Double-click the primary mouse button
- A Transactions by Account report appears on the screen showing the two transactions entered for payment of loan interest.

Scroll through the report

Close the report without printing

PRINT THE TRIAL BALANCE

Once the trial balance has been prepared, it may be printed.

*DO: Print the Trial Balance

Click the **Print** button at the top of the Trial Balance

Click **Preview** button to view a miniature copy of the report
- This helps determine the orientation and whether you need to select the feature to print one page wide.

Click **Close**

Verify the **Settings**
>   **Printer** should be selected
>   **Orientation** is **Portrait**
>   **Page Range** is **All**
>   Do not use "Fit report to one page wide"
Click **Print**
Close the Trial Balance

SELECT ACCRUAL BASIS REPORTING PREFERENCE

QuickBooks allows a business to customize the program and select certain preferences for reports, displays, graphs, accounts, and so on. There are two report preferences available in QuickBooks: Cash and Accrual. You need to choose the preference you prefer. If you select **Cash** as the report preference, income on reports will be shown as of the date payment is received and expenses will be shown as of the date you pay the bill. If **Accrual** is selected, QuickBooks shows the income on the report as of the date of the invoice and expenses as of the bill date. Prior to printing end-of-period reports, it is advisable to verify which reporting basis is selected. If cash has been selected and you are using the accrual method, it is imperative that you change your report basis.

MEMO

DATE: January 31, 1998

Prior to printing reports, check the report preference selected for CCC. If necessary, choose Accrual. After the selection has been made, print a Standard Profit and Loss and a Standard Balance Sheet for Roger Owens.

---

*DO: Select Accrual as the Summary Report Basis
>   Click **File** on the menu bar, click **Preferences**
>   OR
>   Click **Company** tab on QuickBooks Navigator, click
>   **Preferences** icon
>   Scroll through the Preferences list until you see **Reports**
>   **& Graphs**
>   Click **Reports & Graphs**
>   If necessary, click **Accrual** to select the Summary Reports Basis
>   Click **OK** to close the Preferences window

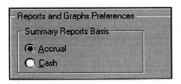

PREPARE AND PRINT CASH FLOW FORECAST

In planning for the cash needs of a business, QuickBooks can prepare a Cash Flow Forecast. This report is useful when determining the expected income and disbursement of cash. It is important to know if your company will have enough cash on hand to meet its obligations. A company with too little cash on hand may have to borrow money to pay its bills, while another company with excess cash may miss out on investment, expansion, or dividend opportunities. QuickBooks Cash Flow Forecast does not analyze investments. It simply projects the amount you will be receiving if all those who owe you money pay on time and the amounts you will be spending to pay your accounts payable on time.

MEMO
DATE: January 31, 1998

Prepare Cash Flow Forecast for January 1-31, 1998, and February 1-28, 1998.

DO: Prepare Cash Flow Forecast for January and February
Click **Reports**, point to **Other Reports**, click **Cash Flow Forecast**
   OR
Click **Company** tab on QuickBooks Navigator, click **Other** in the Reports
   section, click **Cash Flow Forecast**
Enter the **From** date of **01/01/98** and the **To** date of **01/31/98**
Tab to generate the report
- Notice that Periods show Week. Use Week, but click the drop-down list arrow to see the periods available for the report.
- Analyze the report for January: The Beginning Balance for Accounts Receivable and Accounts Payable show the past due amounts as of 12/31/97.
- The amounts for A/R and A/P for the future weeks are for the customer payments you expect to receive and the bills you expect to pay. This information is based on the due dates for invoices and bills.
- The bank account amount for future weeks is based on deposits made or deposits that need to be made.

- Net Inflows summarizes the amounts that should be received and the amounts that should be paid to get a net inflow of cash.
- The projected balance is the total in all bank accounts if all customer and bill payments are made on time.

Creative Computer Consulting (CCC)--Your Name
Cash Flow Forecast
January 1998

	◇ Accnts Rece...	◇ Accnts Paya...	◇ Bank Accnts	◇ Net Inflows	◇ Proj Balance ◇
Beginning Balance	0.00	0.00	0.00		0.00
Jan 1 - 3, '98	▶ 9,570.00	◀ 0.00	37,870.00	47,440.00	47,440.00
Week of Jan 4, '98	0.00	0.00	845.00	845.00	48,285.00
Week of Jan 11, '98	-400.00	0.00	12,935.00	12,535.00	60,820.00
Week of Jan 18, '98	0.00	0.00	0.00	0.00	60,820.00
Week of Jan 25, '98	0.00	0.00	-2,345.33	-2,345.33	58,474.67
Jan '98	9,170.00	0.00	49,304.67	58,474.67	
Ending Balance	**9,170.00**	**0.00**	**49,304.67**		**58,474.67**

Change the dates: **From** is **02/01/98** and **To** is **02/28/98**
Tab to generate the report

Creative Computer Consulting (CCC)--Your Name
Cash Flow Forecast
February 1998

	◇ Accnts Recei...	◇ Accnts Payable	◇ Bank Accnts	◇ Net Inflows	◇ Proj Balance
Beginning Balance	9,170.00	0.00	49,304.67		58,474.67
Week of Feb 1, '98	▶ 8,305.00	◀ 0.00	0.00	8,305.00	66,779.67
Week of Feb 8, '98	175.00	0.00	0.00	175.00	66,954.67
Week of Feb 15, '98	0.00	3,764.00	0.00	-3,764.00	63,190.67
Week of Feb 22, '98	0.00	0.00	0.00	0.00	63,190.67
Feb '98	8,480.00	3,764.00	0.00	4,716.00	
Ending Balance	**17,650.00**	**3,764.00**	**49,304.67**		**63,190.67**

- Compare the differences between the two reports.
  Use Preview to determine if it is necessary to use print Fit report to one page wide
  Print the report for February in Landscape, then close the report

PRINT STANDARD PROFIT AND LOSS STATEMENT

Because all income, expenses, and adjustments have been made for the period, a Profit and Loss Statement can be prepared. This statement is also known as the Income Statement. QuickBooks has several different types of Profit and Loss statements available: Standard—summarizes income and expenses; YTD Comparison—like the Standard Profit and Loss but contains columns for this year to date, $ change, and % change; <u>Prev Year Comparison</u>—like standard statement but contains one column for this month to date and a second column for this year to date; and <u>Itemized</u>—shows year-to-date transactions instead of totals for each income and expense account.

 *DO: Print a Standard Profit and Loss report
Click **Reports** on the menu bar, point to **Profit & Loss**, click **Standard**
  OR
Click **Company** tab on QuickBooks Navigator, click **Profit & Loss** in the
  Reports section, click **Standard**
Tab to or click **From**, enter **01/01/98**
Tab to or click **To**, enter **01/31/98**
Tab to generate the report
Scroll through the report to view the income and expenses listed
Print the report in Portrait orientation
Close the Profit and Loss report

Partial Report

Business Vehicle Insurance	237.50
Total Insurance	237.50
Interest Expense	
Interest on Loans	308.61
Total Interest Expense	308.61
Office Supplies Expense	368.59
Postage and Delivery	195.32
Rent	1,600.00
Telephone	0.00
Uncategorized Expenses	0.00
Utilities	
Electricity Expense	250.00
Heating Expense--Gas	175.00
Water	35.00
Total Utilities	460.00
Total Expense	4,855.90
Net Ordinary Income	4,069.10
Other Income/Expense	
Other Income	
Interest Income	66.43
Total Other Income	66.43
Net Other Income	66.43
Net Income	**4,135.53**

PRINT STANDARD BALANCE SHEET

The Balance Sheet proves the fundamental accounting equation: Assets = Liabilities + Owner's Equity. When all transactions and adjustments for the period have been recorded, a balance sheet should be prepared. QuickBooks has several different types of Balance Sheet statements available: <u>Standard</u>—shows as of today the balance in each balance sheet account with subtotals provided for assets, liabilities, and equity; <u>Comparison</u>—has columns for a year ago today, $ change, and % change; <u>Summary</u>—shows amounts for each account type but not for individual accounts; and <u>Itemized</u>—shows balances as of last month, shows balances as of today, and shows transactions for each account for this month.

     *DO: Print a Standard Balance Sheet report

Click **Reports** on the menu bar, point to **Balance Sheet**, click **Standard**
    OR
Click **Company** tab on QuickBooks Navigator, click **Balance Sheet** in the
    Reports section, click **Standard**
Tab to or click **As of**, enter **01/31/98**, tab to generate the report
Scroll through the report to view the assets, liabilities, and equities listed
Print the report in Portrait orientation
Close the Standard Balance Sheet

- Notice the Net Income account listed in the Equity section of the report. This is the same amount of Net Income shown on the Profit and Loss Statement.

Assets

Current Assets	
Checking/Savings	
Checking	49,212.46
Petty Cash	92.21
Total Checking/Savings	49,304.67
Accounts Receivable	
Accounts Receivable	17,650.00
Total Accounts Receivable	17,650.00
Other Current Assets	
Office Supplies	600.00
Prepaid Insurance	2,612.50
Total Other Current Assets	3,212.50
Total Current Assets	70,167.17
Fixed Assets	
Business Vehicles	
Depreciation	-583.00
Original Cost	49,000.00
Total Business Vehicles	48,417.00
Office Furniture and Equipment	
Depreciation	-142.00
Original Cost	11,536.00
Total Office Furniture and Equipment	11,394.00
Total Fixed Assets	59,811.00
TOTAL ASSETS	**129,978.17**

Liabilities & Equity

LIABILITIES & EQUITY	
Liabilities	
Current Liabilities	
Accounts Payable	
Accounts Payable	3,764.00
Total Accounts Payable	3,764.00
Total Current Liabilities	3,764.00
Long Term Liabilities	
Loan Payable	
Business Vehicles Loan	34,532.81
Office Equipment Loan	3,970.83
Total Loan Payable	38,503.64
Total Long Term Liabilities	38,503.64
Total Liabilities	42,267.64
Equity	
Net Income	4,135.53
Roger Owens, Capital	
Draws	-2,500.00
Investments	33,000.00
Roger Owens, Capital - Other	53,075.00
Total Roger Owens, Capital	83,575.00
Total Equity	87,710.53
TOTAL LIABILITIES & EQUITY	**129,978.17**

ADJUSTMENT TO TRANSFER NET INCOME/RETAINED EARNINGS INTO ROGER OWENS, CAPITAL

Because Creative Computer Consulting is a sole proprietorship, the amount of net income should appear as part of Roger Owens' capital account rather than set aside in Retained Earnings. In many instances, this is the type of adjustment the CPA makes on the accountant's copy of the

QuickBooks company files. The adjustment may be made before the closing date for the fiscal year, or it may be made after the closing has been performed. Because QuickBooks automatically transfers Net Income into Retained Earnings, the closing entry will transfer the net income into the owner's capital account. This adjustment is made by debiting Retained Earnings and crediting the Owner's Capital account. When you view a report before the end of the year, you will see an amount in Net Income and the same amount as a negative in Retained Earnings. If you view a report after the end of the year, you will not see any information regarding Retained Earnings or Net Income because the adjustment correctly transferred the amount to the Owner's Capital account.

If you prefer to use the power of the program and not make the adjustment, QuickBooks simply carries the amount of Retained Earnings forward. Each year net income is added to retained earnings. On the Balance Sheet Retained Earnings and/or Net Income appears as part of the equity section. The owner's drawing and investment accounts are kept separate from Retained Earnings at all times. If Creative Computer Consulting had used a traditional QuickBooks set up for the Equity section of the Balance Sheet, it would appear as:

```
Equity
        Retained Earnings
        Net Income

        Owner's Equity
                Owner's Draw
                Owner's Investment
                Total Owner's Equity

    Total Equity
```

*DO: Transfer the net income into Roger Owens, Capital account after year end:
Open the General Journal as previously instructed
Enter the date of **01/31/98**
The first account used is **Retained Earnings**
Debit **Retained Earnings, 4,135.53**
For the Memo record, **Transfer Net Income into Capital**
The other account used is **Roger Owens, Capital**
4,135.53 should appear as the credit amount for **Roger Owens, Capital**

Enter the same Memo

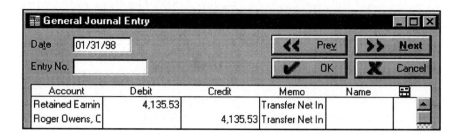

Click **OK** to record and close the General Journal

PRINT STANDARD BALANCE SHEET

Once the adjustment for Net Income/Retained Earnings has been performed, viewing or printing the Balance Sheet will show you the status of the Owner's Equity.

    *DO: Print a Standard Balance Sheet for January 1998

Prepare a Standard Balance Sheet as previously instructed

Tab to or click **As Of**, enter **01/31/98**, tab to generate the report

Scroll through the report

• Notice the Equity section, especially Retained Earnings and Net Income.

Print the **Balance Sheet** for January 1998 in Portrait orientation

• The Balance Sheet shows on the screen after printing is complete.

Creative Computer Consulting (CCC)--Your Name	
Balance Sheet	
As of January 31, 1998	
	◇ **Jan 31, '98** ◇
Equity	
Retained Earnings	-4,135.53
Net Income	4,135.53
Roger Owens, Capital	
Draws	-2,500.00
Investments	33,000.00
Roger Owens, Capital - Other	57,210.53
Total Roger Owens, Capital	87,710.53
Total Equity	87,710.53
TOTAL LIABILITIES & EQUITY	**129,978.17**

Partial Report After Adjusting Entry

Change the **As Of** date to **01/31/99**
- Notice the Equity section.
- Nothing is shown for Retained Earnings or Net Income.
- The Net Income has been added to the account Roger Owens, Capital - Other.
- Verify this by adding the net income of 4,153.53 to 53,075.00, the balance of the Roger Owens, Capital - Other account on the Balance Sheet printed before the adjusting entry was made. The total should equal 57,210.53, which is the amount of Roger Owens, Capital - Other on the 1999 Balance Sheet.

Print the **Balance Sheet** for January 1999

Close the Balance Sheet

Creative Computer Consulting (CCC)--Your Name	
Balance Sheet	
As of January 31, 1999	
	Jan 31, '99
Total Liabilities	42,267.64
Equity	
Roger Owens, Capital	
Draws	-2,500.00
Investments	33,000.00
Roger Owens, Capital - Other	57,210.53
Total Roger Owens, Capital	87,710.53
Total Equity	87,710.53
TOTAL LIABILITIES & EQUITY	**129,978.17**

Partial Report 1999

PRINT JOURNAL

It is always wise to have a printed or "hard copy" of the data on disk. After all entries and adjustments for the month have been made, print the Journal for January. This copy should be kept on file as an additional backup to the data stored on your disk. If something happens to your disk to damage it, you will still have the paper copy of your transactions available for re-entry into the system.

*DO: Print the Journal for January
Click **Reports** on the menu bar, point to **Other Reports**, click **Journal**
   OR
Click **Taxes and Accountant** tab on QuickBooks Navigator, click **Other** on the Reports section, click **Journal**
Tab to or click **From**, enter **01/01/98**
Tab to or click **To**, enter **01/31/98**, tab to generate the report

Print in Landscape orientation, select Fit report to one page wide
Close the Journal

END-OF-PERIOD BACKUP

Once all end-of-period procedures have been completed, a regular backup and a second backup of the company data should be made and filed as an archive copy. Preferably this copy will be located someplace other than on the business premises. The archive or file copy is set aside in case of emergency or in case damage occurs to the original and current backup copies of the company data.

*DO: Back up company data and prepare an archive copy of the company data
Your **Creative** disk should be in **A:**
Insert your backup disk in the **B:** drive
Click **File** on the menu bar, click **Back Up**
    OR
Click **Company** tab on QuickBooks Navigator, click **Back Up**
On the **Back Up Company to** screen, click **Drives** drop-down arrow list, click **B:**
- If you do not have a B: drive, see your instructor for the procedures to follow to back up your data.
In the **File Name** text box enter **1-31-98.qbb** as the name for the backup
Click **OK**

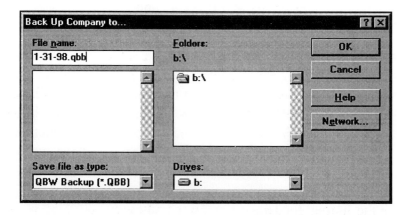

Click **OK** on the QuickBooks Information dialog box to acknowledge the successful backup

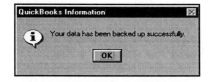

Remove the backup from **B:**
The label for this disk should be **Back Up**
Insert a second backup disk in **B:**
Repeat the procedures listed above
Label this disk **Archive, 1-31-98**

PASSWORDS

Not every employee of a business should have access to all the financial records for the company. In some companies only the owner will have complete access. In others, one or two key employees will have full access while other employees are provided limited access based on the jobs they perform. Passwords are secret words used to control access to data. QuickBooks has several options available to assign passwords:

Owner Password—allows unrestricted access to all QuickBooks functions.

Payroll Password—allows entry and editing of new transactions including payroll transactions; disallows editing of previous transactions and the use of reports, graphs, and registers.

Data Entry Password—allows entry and editing of new transactions; disallows entry and editing of payroll transactions and use of reports, graphs, and registers and editing of previous transactions.

Transaction Password—allows editing of transactions of a prior period.

A password should be kept secret at all times. It should be something that is easy for the individual to remember yet difficult for someone else to guess. Birthdays, names, initials, and similar devices are not good passwords because the information is too readily available. Never write down your password where it can be easily found or seen by someone else.

ASSIGN OWNER PASSWORD

QuickBooks requires an owner password before it will allow any other passwords to be assigned. Before it will open a company file, QuickBooks will ask you for the password for the company.

MEMO

DATE: January 31, 1998

Carmen, assign **QB** as the owner password.

---

*DO: Assign **QB** as the owner password:
Click **File** on the menu bar, click **Passwords**
Click **Set Password** for **Owner Password**

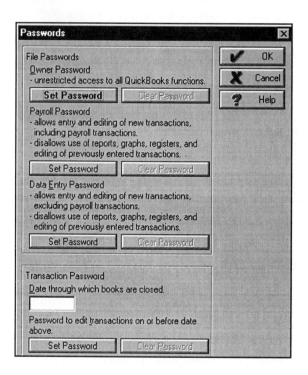

Enter **QB** as the **New Password** on the **Set Owner Password** dialog box
- Notice the password is entered as ******.
- This is to prevent someone from reading the password while it is being established.

Enter **qb** in the **Confirm Password** text box
- Again, you see ******.

Click **OK** to assign the password

- You made an error and the two passwords typed do not match.
- The error can be typographical, not entering the same information, or not capitalizing the same way.
- A Warning dialog box appears: "The new password you entered does not match the confirmation."

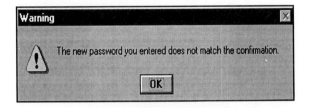

Click **OK,** repeat the procedure to assign the password
Enter **QB** as the **New Password** on the **Set Owner Password** dialog box
Enter **QB** in the **Confirm Password** text box
Click **OK** to assign the password
Do not close Passwords screen

ASSIGN END-OF-PERIOD PASSWORD

A password assigned to transactions for a period prevents change to data from the period. This is helpful to discourage casual changes or transaction deletions to a period that has been closed. QuickBooks does allow changes to be made to a prior period if you know the password.

*DO: Assign the password **January** to the transactions for the period ending 1/31/98
In the Transaction Password text box at the bottom of the Passwords screen, enter
01/31/98 as the date through which the books are closed

Click **Set Password** button for **Transaction Password**
Enter **January** as the **New Password** on the **Set Transaction Password** dialog
box
• Notice that the password is entered as *******.
• This is to prevent someone from reading the password while it is being
established.
Enter **January** in the **Confirm Password** text box
• Again, you see *******.
Click **OK** to assign the password

• If you make an error and the two passwords typed do not match, you get a
Warning: "The new password you entered does not match the confirmation."
Click **OK,** repeat the procedure to assign the password.

Click **OK** to exit Passwords

ACCESS COMPANY INFORMATION USING OWNER PASSWORD

Once an owner password is assigned, company information may not be accessed unless the appropriate password is entered.

 *DO: Test the owner password
Close CCC, close QuickBooks, reopen QuickBooks
QuickBooks dialog box appears requesting the password for CREATIVE

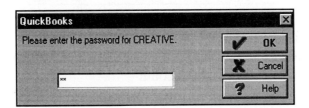

Enter *your* FIRST NAME in the text box, click **OK**
A **Warning** dialog box appears, click **OK**

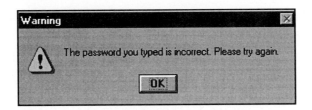

Type the correct password **QB**
Click **OK**

ACCESS TRANSACTION FOR PREVIOUS PERIOD

Even though the month of January has been "closed," transactions still appear in the account registers, the journal, and so on. The transactions shown may not be changed unless the appropriate password is provided.

 *DO: Try to change Prepaid Insurance to 2,500 without providing a transaction
password
Access Chart of Accounts as previously instructed
Click **Prepaid Insurance**
Click **Activities** button at the bottom of the Chart of Accounts, click **Use Register**
OR
Use the keyboard shortcut, **Ctrl+R**

Click the **Increase** column showing **2,850** paid to XYZ Insurance Co.
Highlight 2,850, enter **2,500**
Click **Record** button
QuickBooks dialog box requiring the password appears

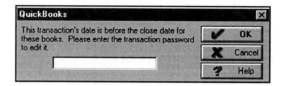

Click **Cancel** to cancel the password request
Click **Restore** button to restore the transaction to the original 2,850
Close the Prepaid Insurance account
Do not close the Chart of Accounts

EDIT TRANSACTION FROM PREVIOUS PERIOD

If it is determined that an error was made in a previous period, QuickBooks does allow the correction. Before it will record any changes for previous periods, QuickBooks requires the correct transaction password for each change. The adjusting entry used to transfer retained earnings/net income into the owner's capital account also needs to be adjusted as a result of any changes to transactions. Increasing the amount of supplies on hand by $25 will decrease the amount of expense incurred and will result in a $25 increase in net income/retained earnings.

MEMO

DATE: February 1, 1998

After reviewing the journal and reports printed at the end of January, Roger Owens finds that the amount of supplies used was $325, not $350. Make the correction to the adjusting entry of January 31.

---

*DO: Change Office Supplies adjusting entry to $325 from $350
    Click **Office Supplies** account
    Use the keyboard shortcut **Ctrl+R** to use the register
       OR
    Click **Activities** button at the bottom of the Chart of Accounts
    Click **Use Register**

Click the **Decrease** column for the Adjusting Entry recorded to the account on 01/31/98

Change 350 to **325**

Click **Record** button

On the **QuickBooks** dialog box, enter **January** as the password

Click **OK**

- The change to the transaction has been made.
- Notice that the Balance for the Office Supplies account now shows 625 instead of 600.

01/31/98				325.00			625.00
	GENJRNL	Office Supplies Expense Supplies Used					

Close the Register for Office Supplies

Click **Roger Owens, Capital**

Click **Activities** button at the bottom of the Chart of Accounts

Click **Make Journal Entry**

Click **<<Prev** button until you find the entry adjusting Retained Earnings

Change the Debit to Retained Earnings from 4135.53 to **4160.53**

Change the Credit to Roger Owens, Capital from 4135.53 to **4160.53**

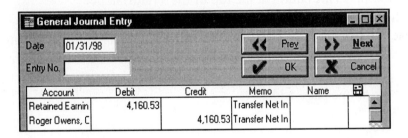

Click **OK**

Enter **January** as the Transaction Password

Click **OK** on the QuickBooks dialog box for the transaction password

Close the Chart of Accounts

PRINT POST-CLOSING TRIAL BALANCE

After "closing" has been completed, it is helpful to print a post-closing trial balance. This proves that debits still equal credits.

MEMO

DATE: February 1, 1998

Print a Post-Closing Trial Balance, a Post-Closing Profit and Loss Statement, and a Post-Closing Balance Sheet for Roger Owens. The dates should be as of or for 02/01/98.

---

*DO: Print a post-closing trial balance to prove debits still equal credits

Click **Reports** on the menu bar, point to **Other Reports**, click **Trial Balance**

OR

Click **Company** or **Taxes and Accountant** tab on QuickBooks Navigator, click **Other** in the Reports section, click **Trial Balance**

Tab to or click **From**, enter the date **02/01/98**

Tab to or click **To**, enter the date **02/01/98**

Tab to generate the report

Scroll through the report and study the amounts shown

- Notice that the final totals of debits and credits are equal.

Click the **Print** button at the top of the Trial Balance

Click **Preview** button to view a miniature copy of the report

- Notice that the report appears in Landscape orientation. Using Preview helps determine if you should still use Landscape orientation or change to Portrait.
- Preview also helps you determine whether you need to select the feature to print one page wide.

Click **Close**

Print the report in Portrait orientation

Close the Trial Balance

Partial Trial Balance: February 1, 1998

Loan Payable	0.00	
Loan Payable:Business Vehicles Loan		34,532.81
Loan Payable:Office Equipment Loan		3,970.83
Retained Earnings	4,160.53	
Roger Owens, Capital		57,235.53
Roger Owens, Capital:Draws	2,500.00	
Roger Owens, Capital:Investments		33,000.00
Income:Installation Income		175.00
Income:Technical Support Income		900.00
Income:Training Income		7,850.00
Uncategorized Income	0.00	
Advertising Expense	260.00	
Bank Service Charges	8.00	
Business Vehicles Expense	588.88	
Depreciation Expense	725.00	
Dues and Subscriptions	79.00	
Equipment Rental	25.00	
Insurance:Business Vehicle Insurance	237.50	
Interest Expense:Interest on Loans	308.61	
Office Supplies Expense	343.59	
Postage and Delivery	195.32	
Rent	1,600.00	
Telephone	0.00	
Uncategorized Expenses	0.00	
Utilities:Electricity Expense	250.00	
Utilities:Heating Expense--Gas	175.00	
Utilities:Water	35.00	
Interest Income		66.43
TOTAL	142,219.60	142,219.60

PRINT POST-CLOSING PROFIT AND LOSS STATEMENT

Because February 1 is after the closing date of January 31, 1998, the Profit and Loss Statement for February 1 is the Post-Closing Profit and Loss Statement. To verify the closing, print a Profit and Loss statement for February 1.

*DO: Print a Standard Profit and Loss report for February

Click **Reports** on the menu bar, point to **Profit & Loss**, click **Standard**

OR

Click **Company** or **Taxes and Accountant** tab on QuickBooks Navigator, click **Profit & Loss** in the **Reports** section, click **Standard**

Tab to or click **From**, enter **02/01/98**

Tab to or click **To**, enter **02/01/98**

Tab to generate the report

Print the report in Portrait orientation

Close the Profit and Loss report

- The Net Income is 0.00.

```
┌──────────────────────────────────────────────┐
│      Creative Computer Consulting (CCC)        │
│              Profit and Loss                   │
│             February 1, 1998                   │
│              ◇ Feb 1, '98 ◇                    │
│         Net Income ▶    0.00  ◀                │
└──────────────────────────────────────────────┘
```

PRINT POST-CLOSING BALANCE SHEET

Proof that assets are equal to liabilities and owner's equity needs to be displayed in a Post-Closing Balance Sheet. The Balance Sheet for February 1 is considered to be a Post-Closing Balance Sheet because it is prepared after the closing of the period. Most of the adjustments were for the month of January 1998. Because this report is for a month, the adjustment to Retained Earnings and Net Income will result in both accounts being included on the Balance Sheet. If, however, this report were prepared for the year, neither account would appear.

*DO: Print a Standard Balance Sheet report for February 1, 1998, and February 1, 1999
Prepare a Standard Balance Sheet as previously instructed
Tab to or click **As of**, enter **02/01/98**
Tab to generate the report
Scroll through the report to view the assets, liabilities, and equities listed
- Because this report is for a one-month period, both Retained Earnings and Net Income are included on this report.
Print the report in Portrait orientation

```
┌──────────────────────────────────────────────────┐
│   Creative Computer Consulting (CCC)--Your Name    │
│              Balance Sheet                         │
│           As of February 1, 1998                   │
│                       ◇   Feb 1, '98   ◇           │
│   Equity                                           │
│     Retained Earnings              -4,160.53       │
│     Net Income                      4,160.53       │
│     Roger Owens, Capital                           │
│       Draws               -2,500.00                │
│       Investments         33,000.00                │
│       Roger Owens, Capital - Other  57,235.53      │
│     Total Roger Owens, Capital      87,735.53      │
│                                                    │
│   Total Equity                      87,735.53      │
│                                                    │
│   TOTAL LIABILITIES & EQUITY       130,003.17      │
└──────────────────────────────────────────────────┘
```

Partial Report

Change the date to **02/01/99**, tab to generate the report

Scroll through the report to view the assets, liabilities, and equities listed
- Because this report is prepared after the end of the fiscal year, neither Retained Earnings nor Net Income is included on this report.

Print the report

Close the Balance Sheet

Creative Computer Consulting (CCC)--Your Name		
Balance Sheet		
As of February 1, 1999		
	◇ Feb 1, '99 ◇	
Total Liabilities		42,267.64
Equity		
Roger Owens, Capital		
Draws	-2,500.00	
Investments	33,000.00	
Roger Owens, Capital - Other	57,235.53	
Total Roger Owens, Capital		87,735.53
Total Equity		87,735.53
TOTAL LIABILITIES & EQUITY		130,003.17

Partial Report

END-OF-CHAPTER BACKUP AND CLOSE COMPANY

As in previous chapters, you should back up your company and close the company.

 *DO: Follow instructions previously provided to back up company files and close CCC

SUMMARY

In this chapter, end-of-period adjustments were made, a bank reconciliation was performed, backup and archive disks were prepared, and passwords were assigned. The use of Net Income and Retained Earnings accounts were explored and interpreted for a sole proprietorship. Owner passwords and passwords for a prior "closed" period were assigned. Account name changes were made, and the effect on subaccounts was examined. Even though QuickBooks focuses on entering transactions on business forms, a Journal recording each transaction is kept by QuickBooks. This chapter presented transaction entry directly into the Journal. The differences between accrual basis and cash basis accounting were discussed. Company preferences were established for reporting preferences. Owner withdrawals and additional owner investments were made. Many of the different report options available in QuickBooks were examined. A variety of reports was printed. Correction of errors was explored, and changes to transactions in "closed" periods were made. The fact that QuickBooks does not require an actual closing entry at the end of the period was examined.

END-OF-CHAPTER QUESTIONS

TRUE/FALSE

ANSWER THE FOLLOWING QUESTIONS IN THE SPACE PROVIDED BEFORE THE QUESTION NUMBER.

_____ 1. Accrual basis accounting matches the income from the period and the expenses for the period in order to determine the net income or net loss for the period.

_____ 2. In QuickBooks the Journal is called the book of final entry.

_____ 3. An account may be deleted at any time.

_____ 4. In a sole proprietorship an owner's name is added to the vendor list for recording withdrawals.

_____ 5. Additional investments made by an owner may be cash or noncash items.

_____ 6. QuickBooks keeps a Journal of every transaction recorded.

_____ 7. QuickBooks keeps the last two Bank Reconciliation reports in memory.

_____ 8. Once an account has been used in a transaction, no changes may be made to the account name.

_____ 9. Anything entered as a service charge or as interest earned during a bank reconciliation will be entered automatically when the reconciliation is complete.

_____ 10. A balance sheet is prepared to prove the equality of debits and credits.

MULTIPLE CHOICE

WRITE THE LETTER OF THE CORRECT ANSWER IN THE SPACE PROVIDED BEFORE THE QUESTION NUMBER.

_____ 1. To assign an end-of-period password, you must also assign a(n) ___.
A. transaction password
B. owner password
C. entry password
D. opening password

_____ 2. When an account name such as "cars" is changed to "automobiles," all related subaccounts such as car "depreciation" ___.
A. need to be changed to "automobile depreciation"
B. are automatically changed to "automobile depreciation"
C. cannot be changed
D. must be deleted and re-entered

_____ 3. The report that proves assets = liabilities + owner's equity is the ___.
A. Trial Balance
B. Income Statement
C. Profit and Loss Statement
D. Balance Sheet

_____ 4. If the adjusting entry to transfer net income/retained earnings into the owner's capital account is made prior to the end of the year, the Balance Sheet shows ___.
A. Retained Earnings
B. Net Income
C. both Net Income and Retained Earnings
D. none of the above because the income/earnings has been transferred into capital

_____ 5. The type of profit and loss report showing year-to-date transactions instead of totals for each income and expense account is a(n) ___ Profit and Loss Report.
A. Standardized
B. YTD Comparison
C. Prev Year Comparison
D. Itemized

_____ 6. A bank statement may ___.
    A. show services charges or interest not yet recorded
    B. be missing deposits in transit or outstanding checks
    C. both of the above
    D. none of the above

_____ 7. The Journal shows ___.
    A. all transactions no matter where they were recorded
    B. only those transactions recorded in the journal
    C. only transactions recorded in account registers
    D. only those transactions that have been edited

_____ 8. A backup disk ___.
    A. is a duplicate of the company data
    B. is prepared in case of emergencies or errors on current disks
    C. must be restored before information can be used
    D. all of the above

_____ 9. An error known as a transposition can be found by ___ during reconciliation.
    A. dividing the amount out of balance by 9
    B. dividing the amount out of balance by 2
    C. multiplying the difference by 9, then dividing by 2
    D. dividing the amount out of balance by 5

_____ 10. The type of Balance Sheet report showing information for today and a year ago is a(n) ___ Balance Sheet.
    A. Standard
    B. Summary
    C. Comparison
    D. Itemized

FILL-IN

IN THE SPACE PROVIDED, WRITE THE ANSWER THAT MOST APPROPRIATELY COMPLETES THE SENTENCE.

1. Bank reconciliations should be performed on a(n) _____ basis.

2. A _____ password allows changes to be made to transactions within a period that has been closed.

3. An owner's paycheck is considered a(n) _____.

4. The two types of reporting are _____ basis and _____ basis.

5. The Cash Flow Forecast _____ column shows the total in all bank accounts if all customer and bill payments are made on time.

SHORT ESSAY

Describe the four types of Balance Sheet reports available in QuickBooks.

_____

_____

_____

_____

_____

END-OF-CHAPTER PROBLEM

SUNSHINE LAWN AND POOL MAINTENANCE

Chapter 4 continues with the end-of-period adjustments, bank reconciliation, archive disks, and password protection for a prior "closed" period for Sunshine Lawn and Pool Maintenance. The company does use a certified professional accountant for guidance and assistance with appropriate accounting procedures. The CPA has provided information for Sylvia to use for adjusting entries and so on.

INSTRUCTIONS

Continue to use the student data disk for Sunshine. Open the company—the file used is **SUNSHINE.QBW**. Record the adjustments and other transactions as you were instructed in the chapter. Always read the transaction carefully and review the Chart of Accounts when selecting transaction accounts. Print the reports and journals as indicated.

RECORD TRANSACTIONS

May 30—Enter the following:

Change the name of the following accounts:

Automobile Expense to **Business Trucks Expense**

Auto Insurance Expense to **Business Trucks Insurance**

Make the following accounts inactive:

Recruiting

Travel & Ent

   Travel & Ent: Entertainment

   Travel & Ent: Meals

   Travel & Ent: Travel

Delete the following accounts:

Sales

Services

Amortization Expenses

Contributions

Interest: Mortgage

Taxes: Property

Print the Chart of Accounts

[handwritten: 1450   330]

May 31—Enter the following:

Owner adjustments to the capital account:

   Transfer Uncategorized Income and Uncategorized Expenses to George Gordon, Capital

Enter adjusting entries in the Journal for:

   Office Supplies Used, $185. Memo: Office Supplies Used for May *[handwritten: ✓]*

   Depreciation for the month:

      Business Trucks, $950   *[handwritten: Dep. exp 1156.25]*

      Equipment, $206.25   *[handwritten: Business Trucks; acc. dep. 950 Equip. acc. dep 206.25 ✓]*

      Memo for all accounts used: Depreciation Expense May

   The amount of insurance remaining in the Insurance Expense account is for three months of insurance on the business trucks. Record the business trucks insurance expense for the month, $250. Memo: Insurance Expense May *[handwritten: ✓]*

Enter transactions for Owner's Equity:

   Owner withdrawal $1,000. Memo: Withdrawal for May

   Additional cash investment by George Gordon, $2,000. Memo: Additional Investment: Cash

   Additional noncash investment by owner, $1,500 of lawn equipment. Memo: Additional Investment: Equipment *[handwritten: ✓]*

Prepare Bank Reconciliation and Enter Adjustments for the Reconciliation:

• Be sure to enter automatic payments as in the chapter.

SANTA BARBARA COASTAL BANK
1234 Coast Highway
Santa Barbara, CA 93100
(805) 555-9310

BANK STATEMENT FOR:

Sunshine Lawn and Pool Maintenance
18527 State Street
Santa Barbara, CA 93103

Acct. # 987-352-9152   May, 1998

Beginning Balance, May 1, 1998			$23,850.00
5/18/98, Check 1		180.00	23,670.00
5/18/98, Check 2		375.00	23,295.00
5/18/98, Check 3		669.00	22,626.00
5/18/98, Check 4		485.00	22,141.00
5/31/98, Service Chg.		10.00	22,131.00
5/31/98, Business Trucks Loan Pmt.: 795.54 Interest, 160.64 Principal		956.18	21,174.82
5/31/98, Interest	59.63		21,234.45
Ending Balance, 5/31/98			21,234.45

Print a Full Reconciliation Report

Change Preferences:

     Verify or change reporting preferences to accrual basis

     Change report format to eliminate the current date as part of the header

Print:

     Chart of Accounts

     Trial Balance

     Standard Profit & Loss Statement

     Standard Balance Sheet

Transfer Net Income/Retained Earnings into Capital Account

Print a Standard Balance Sheet

Assign Owner Password and End-of-period Password:

     Owner password is **QB**

     End-of-period or Transaction Password is **May**

Edit a Transaction from a closed period:

Discovered an error in the amount of office supplies used. The amount used should be **$175**, not $185. (Don't forget to adjust Retained Earnings and Capital.)

June 1, 1998—Print the following:

Journal (Landscape orientation, Fit report to one page wide)

Trial Balance, June 1, 1998

Cash Flow Forecast for June 1-30, 1998

Standard Profit & Loss Statement, June 1, 1998

Standard Balance Sheet, June 1, 1998

June 1, 1999—Print the following:

Standard Balance Sheet

END OF SECTION 1—
HELPING HANDS PRACTICE SET:
SERVICE BUSINESS

The following is a comprehensive practice set combining all the elements of QuickBooks studied in the first section of the text. In this practice set you will keep the books for a company for one month. Entries will be made to record invoices, receipt of payments on invoices, cash sales, receipt and payment of bills, and credit memos for invoices and bills. Account names will be added, changed, deleted, and made inactive. Customer, vendor, and owner names will be added to the appropriate lists. Reports will be prepared to analyze sales, bills, and receipts. Formal reports including the trial balance, profit and loss statement, and balance sheet will be prepared. Adjusting entries for depreciation, supplies used, and insurance expense will be recorded. A bank reconciliation will be prepared. Passwords will be assigned for the end of period.

HELPING HANDS

Located in Beverly Hills, California, Helping Hands is a service business providing assistance with errands, shopping, home repairs, simple household chores, and transportation for children and others who do not drive. Rates are on a per hour basis and differ according to the service performed.

Helping Hands is a sole proprietorship owned and operated by Helena Cervantes. Helena has one assistant, Carmen Hsing, helping her with errands, scheduling of duties, and doing the bookkeeping for Helping Hands. In addition, a part-time employee, Greta Gunderssen, works weekends for Helping Hands.

INSTRUCTIONS

To work with transactions for Helping Hands, obtain a disk from your instructor and make a copy of the file **Helping.QBW** onto a new disk. Label the disk **Helping**.

The following lists are used for all sales items, customers, and vendors. You will be adding additional customers and vendors as the company is in operation. When entering transactions, you are responsible for any memos you wish to include in transactions. Unless otherwise specified, the terms for each sale or bill will be the terms specified on the Customer or Vendor list. (Choose edit for the individual customers or vendors, and select the Additional Info tab to see the terms for each customer or vendor.)

Customers:

Customer:Job List		
Name	Balance	Notes
◆ Aaron, Gregg Dr.	275.00	
◆ Andrews, Matthew	750.00	
◆ Beverly, Colleen	150.00	
◆ Childers, Cristie	0.00	
◆ Cohn, Randall	250.00	
◆ Cranston, Bernadette	600.00	
◆ deMarco, Raphael	450.00	
◆ Egkan, Bryce	50.00	
◆ Johnson, MaryBeth	200.00	
◆ Mahmud, Mohammed	1,000.00	
◆ Susman, Richard Dr.	500.00	

Vendors:

Vendor List	
Name	Balance
Beverly Hills Auto Repairs	500.00
BH Stationers	350.00
Boulevard Flowers	25.00
Corner Gasoline	250.00

Sales Items:

Helping Hands
Item Detail
September 1, 1998

Item	Description	Type	Price	Cost	Taxable
Errands	Household Errands	Service	25.00	0	No
Household	Household Chores	Service	15.00	0	No
Party	Party Planning and Supervision	Service	50.00	0	No
Pets	Pet Sitting	Service	25.00	0	No
Repairs	Repair Service	Service	50.00	0	No
Shopping	Client Shopping	Service	25.00	0	No
Transport	Transportation	Service	25.00	0	No

Each Item is priced per hour. Unless otherwise specified within the transactions, a minimum of one hour is charged for any service provided.

RECORD TRANSACTIONS

Enter the transactions for Helping Hands and print as indicated:

HELPING HANDS PRACTICE SET: SERVICE BUSINESS   S 1-3

Week 1: September 1-6, 1998:

Add your name to the company name. The company name will be **Helping Hands--Student's Name**. (Type your actual name, *not* the words "Student's Name.")

Change Report Preferences: Report Header/Footer should *not* include the Date Prepared

Find all accounts with the name **Automobile** as part of the account name. Change every occurrence of Automobile to **Business Vehicle**.

Find all accounts with the name **Office Equipment** as part of the account name. Change every occurrence of Office Equipment to **Office Furniture/Equipment**.

Make the following inactive: **Interest Expense: Mortgage, Taxes: Property, Travel & Ent**

Delete the following accounts: **Sales, Recruiting, Contributions, Amortization Expenses**

Add **Petty Cash** to the Chart of Accounts.

Print the Chart of Accounts.

Prior to recording any transactions, print a Trial Balance as of September 1, 1998.

9/1/98

Transfer $100 from checking to Petty Cash to fund the account.

Transfer Uncategorized Income and Uncategorized Expenses to Helena Cervantes, Capital.

Cristie Childers is having a party in two weeks. Bill Cristie Childers for 3 hours of party planning. Refer to the Item Detail list for the appropriate sales item. Invoice #35, terms, Net 30.

Dr. Susman has arranged for you to feed and walk his dogs every day. Bill Dr. Susman for pet sitting, 1 hour per day for 7 days.

We were out of paper, ink cartridges for the laser printer, computer disks, and various other office supplies that we need to have on hand. Received a bill—Invoice #1806-1—from BH Stationers for $350 for the office supplies we received today.

Every week we put fresh flowers in the office in order to provide a welcoming environment for any customers who happen to come to the office. Received a bill—Invoice #887—from Boulevard Flowers for $25 for office flowers for the week. (Miscellaneous Expense)

9/2/98

Dr. Aaron almost forgot his wife's birthday. He called Helping Hands with an emergency request for help. The store will bill the doctor for the actual gift purchased. Bill Dr. Gregg Aaron, 3 hours of shopping for his wife's birthday gift.

Colleen Beverly needed to have her shelves relined. You did part of the house this week and will return next week to continue the work. Bill her for 5 hours of household chores.

9/3/98

Raphael's mother has several doctor appointments. Mr. deMarco has asked Helping Hands to take her to these appointments. Bill Raphael deMarco for 3 hours of transportation.

Auto exp. ?

9/4/98

Received a bill—Invoice #81056—from Corner Gasoline, $125 for the weekly gasoline charge.

Received checks from the following customers on account: Dr. Gregg Aaron, Check # 713 for $275; Randall Cohn, Check # 3381 for $250; Raphael deMarco, Check # 6179 for $450; Mohammed Mahmud, Check # 38142 for $1000.

9/5/98

Fionna Johnson has a birthday party to attend on Saturday. Her mother, MaryBeth, has hired Helping Hands to take her to the party and stay with her while she is there. Bill MaryBeth Johnson 3 hours of transportation for the birthday party (This transportation charge also includes the time at the party.)

9/6/98

Prepare Sales Receipt #22 to record a cash sale. Received Check #2894 for 1 hour of errands for a new customer: Claudia Richards, 18062A Camden Drive, Beverly Hills, CA 90210, 310-555-7206, terms Net 10 days.

Prepare Unpaid Bills Report. Print the report.

Pay bills for the amount owed on September 1: Check 1—Corner Gasoline and Check 2—Boulevard Flowers. (Refer to the Vendor list on Page 2 to determine the amounts for the checks.)

Print all invoices, sales receipts, and checks.

Make bank deposit for all checks received during the week. The date of the deposit is 9/6/98. Print a Deposit Summary.

Print Trial Balance.

Week 2: September 7-13, 1998

9/7/98

Cristie Childers is having a party September 19. Bill Cristie Childers for 4 hours of party planning.

Raphael's mother has several additional doctor appointments. Mr. deMarco has asked Helping Hands to take her to these appointments. Bill Raphael deMarco for 4 hours of transportation.

Dr. Susman was pleased with Helping Hands' service and has arranged to have Helping Hands feed and walk his dogs every day on a permanent basis. Bill Dr. Susman for pet sitting, 1 hour per day for 7 days.

9/8/98

Bernadette Cranston really likes the floral arrangements in the office of Helping Hands. She has asked that flowers be brought to her home and arranged throughout the house. When Helena completes the placement of the flowers in the house, Bernadette gives her Check # 387 for 1 hour of errands and 1 hour of household chores, $40.

9/9/98

Received checks from the following customers: Dr. Susman, #7891, $500; Ms. Johnson, #97452, $200; Ms. Cranston, #395, $600; Mr. Egkan, #178, $50; Mr. Andrews, #3916, $750.

Received a bill—Invoice #943—from Boulevard Flowers for $25 for office flowers for the week.

Received a bill—Invoice #81085—from Corner Gasoline, $100 for the weekly gasoline charge.

9/10/98

Mohammed Mahmud has arranged for Helping Hands to supervise and coordinate the installation of new tile in his master bathroom. Bill Mr. Mahmud for 4 hours of repair service for hiring the subcontractor, scheduling the installation for 9/15 and 9/16, and contract preparation.

9/11/98

Colleen Beverly needed to have her shelves relined. Helena did part of the house last week and completed the work today. Bill Ms. Beverly for 5 hours of household chores.

Returned faulty printer cartridge. Received Credit Memo #5 from BH Stationers, $75.

9/13/98

Pay all bills for the amounts due on or before September 13. (Hint: There should be three checks.)

Print all invoices, sales receipts, and checks.

Correct the invoice issued to Colleen Beverly on 9/11/98. The number of hours billed should be 7 instead of 5. Print the corrected invoice.

Deposit checks received for the week. Print Deposit Summary

After depositing checks, print A/R Aging Detail Report as of 9/13/98.

Week 3: September 14-20, 1998
9/14/98

Cristie Childers is having a party Saturday. Bill Cristie Childers for 2 hours of party planning.

9/15/98

Pay postage due 64 cents. Use petty cash.

Print Petty Cash QuickReport. Fit report to one page wide.

Bernadette Cranston was really pleased with the floral arrangements Helena did last week. She has asked that flowers be brought to her home and arranged throughout the house on a weekly basis. This week when Helena completes the placement of the flowers in the house, Bernadette gives her Check # 421 for 1 hour of errands and 1 hour of household chores.

9/17/98

Received a bill—Invoice #81109—from Corner Gasoline, $150 for the weekly gasoline charge.

Received a bill—Invoice #979—from Boulevard Flowers for $25 for office flowers for the week.

The bathroom tile was installed on 9/15 and 9/16. The installation was completed to Mr. Mahmud's satisfaction. Bill him for 16 hours of repair service.

9/18/98

Bernadette Cranston's neighbor, Dr. Gustav Gunther, really liked the flowers in Bernadette's house and asked Helena to bring flowers to his home and office. This week he gave her Check #90-163 for 1 hour of errands and 1 hour of household chores. Add him to the customer list: Dr. Gustav Gunther, 236 West Canon Drive, Beverly Hills, CA 90210, 310-555-0918, Net 10.

9/19/98

Tonight is Cristie's big party. She has arranged for both Helena and Greta to supervise the party from 3 p.m. until 1 a.m. Bill Cristie for 20 hours of party planning and supervision.

Print invoices and sales receipts.

Print Vendor Balance Detail report.

9/20/98

Record the checks received from customers for the week: Mr. deMarco, #9165, $175; Ms. Beverly, #7-303, $150; Dr. Susman, #89162, $175; Ms. Johnson, #5291, $75.

Deposit checks received for the week. Print Deposit Summary.

Week 4: September 21-27, 1998
9/22/98

Bernadette Cranston gave Helena Check # 439 for 1 hour of errands and 1 hour of household chores in payment for the flowers that were brought to her home and arranged throughout the house this week.

9/23/98

Use petty cash to pay for a box of staples, $4.23.

Print a Petty Cash QuickReport. Fit the report on one page wide.

The party went so smoothly Saturday that Helena went home at 11 p.m. rather than 1 a.m. Issue a credit memo to Cristie Childers for 2 hours of party planning and supervision.

Bryce Egkan arranged to have his pets cared for by Helping Hands during the past 7 days. Bill him for 1 hour of pet sitting each day.

9/24/98

Helena arranged for theater tickets and dinner reservations for Dr. Aaron. Bill him for 1 hour of errands.

Received a bill—Invoice #81116—from Corner Gasoline, $110 for the weekly gasoline charge.

Received a bill—Invoice #1002—from Boulevard Flowers for $25 for office flowers for the week.

9/25/98

Write a check to BH Stationers for the purchase of a new printer for the office, $500. (If you get a warning to use Pay Bills because we owe the company money, disregard the warning.)

9/27/98

Dr. Susman has arranged for Helping Hands to feed and walk his dogs every day. Bill Dr. Susman for pet sitting, 1 hour per day for the past two weeks.

Write checks to pay bills for rent and utilities. The utility companies and the rental agent will need to be added to the Vendor list. Vendor information is provided in each transaction:

Monthly telephone bill: $192, California Telephone, 2015 Wilshire Boulevard, Beverly Hills, CA 90210, 310-555-8888, Net 30 days.

Monthly rent for office space: $1,500, Robertson Rentals, 3016 Robertson Boulevard, Beverly Hills, CA 90210, 310-555-1636, Net 30 days.

Monthly water bill: $153, Beverly Hills Water, 9916 Sunset Boulevard, Beverly Hills, CA 90210, 310-555-1961, Net 30 days.

Monthly gas and electric bill: $296, California Power, 10196 Olympic Boulevard, West Los Angeles, CA 90016, 310-555-9012, Net 30 days.

Prepare and print an Unpaid Bills by Vendor Report. Fit report to one page wide.

Pay bills for all amounts due on or before September 27.

Prepare a Check Detail Report from 9/1/98 to 9/27/98. Fit report to one page wide.

Print all invoices, sales receipts, credit memos, and checks.

Record payments received from customers: Ms. Childers, # 4692, $150; Dr. Susman, # 7942, $175; Mr. Egkan, #235, $175; Dr. Aaron, # 601, $75; Ms. Beverly, #923-10, $75.

Make deposits for the week. Print Deposit Summary.

Print Customer Balance Detail Report. Fit report to one page wide.

Record adjusting entries for:

    Business Vehicle Insurance, $200

    Office Supplies Used, $150

    Depreciation:

        Business Vehicles, $500

        Office Furniture and Equipment, $92

Write a check for a withdrawal by Helena Cervantes, $1,000.

Because a fax is a business necessity, Helena decided to give her new fax machine to Helping Hands. Record this additional $350 investment of equipment by Helena Cervantes.

Robertson Rentals decreased the amount of rent to $1,000 per month. Correct and reprint the check for rent.

End of the Month: September 30, 1998

Prepare bank reconciliation using the following bank statement. Record any adjustments necessary as a result of the bank statement. Print a Reconciliation report.

Beverly Hills Bank, 1234 Rodeo Drive, Beverly Hills, CA 90210

Helping Hands, 27800 Beverly Boulevard, Beverly Hills, CA 90210

Beginning Balance, 9/1/98			$15,350.00
9/1/98, Transfer		100.00	15,250.00
9/6/98, Deposit	2,000.00		17,250.00
9/7/98, Check 1		250.00	17,000.00
9/7/98, Check 2		25.00	16,975.00
9/13/98, Check 5		25.00	16,950.00
9/13/98, Deposit	2,140.00		19,090.00
9/15/98, Check 3		500.00	18,590.00
9/15/98, Check 4		275.00	18,315.00
9/20/98, Deposit	655.00		18,970.00
9/28/98, Check 6		500.00	18,470.00
9/29/98, Check 12		1,000.00	17,470.00
9/30/98, Payment: Business Vehicle Loan: interest $445.15; principal $86.06		531.21	16,938.79
9/30/98, Payment: Office Equipment Loan: interest $53.42; principal $10.33		63.75	16,875.04
9/30/98, Service Charge		15.00	16,860.04
9/30/98, Interest	42.50		16,902.54
9/30/98, Ending Balance			16,902.54

Print the following reports as of 9/30/98: Journal from 9/1/98 through 9/30/98 in Landscape orientation and Fit to one page wide. Print the remaining reports in Portrait orientation: Trial Balance from 9/1/98 through 9/30/98, Cash Flow Forecast, Standard Profit and Loss Statement from 9/1/98 through 9/30/98, Standard Balance Sheet for 9/30/98.

Transfer the net income/retained earnings to owner's capital account.

Print a Standard Balance Sheet as of 9/30/98.

SALES AND RECEIVABLES: MERCHANDISING BUSINESS

LEARNING OBJECTIVES

At the completion of this chapter, you will be able to use QuickBooks to:

1. Enter sales transactions for a retail business.
2. Prepare invoices that use sales tax, have sales discounts, and exceed a customer's credit limit.
3. Prepare transactions for cash sales with sales tax.
4. Add new accounts to the Chart of Accounts and new sales items to the Item list.
5. Add new customers and modify existing customer records.
6. Delete and void invoices.
7. Prepare credit memos with and without refunds.
8. Record customer payments on account with and without discounts.
9. Deposit checks and credit card receipts for sales and customer payments.
10. Customize report preferences and prepare and print customer balance detail reports, open invoice reports, and sales reports.
11. View a QuickReport and use the QuickZoom feature.
12. Prepare and print accounts receivable and sales graphs.

ACCOUNTING FOR SALES AND RECEIVABLES IN A MERCHANDISING BUSINESS

Rather than use a traditional Sales Journal to record transactions using debits and credits and special columns, QuickBooks uses an invoice to record sales transactions for accounts receivable in the Accounts Receivable Register. Because cash sales do not involve accounts receivable, a Sales Receipt is prepared and QuickBooks puts the money from a cash sale into the Undeposited Funds account until a deposit to a bank account is made. Instead of being recorded within special journals, cash receipt transactions are entered as activities. However, all transactions regardless of the activity are placed in the general journal behind the scenes. A new account, sales item, or customer can be added "on the fly" as transactions are entered. Customer information may be changed by editing the Customer list.

For a retail business QuickBooks tracks inventory, maintains information on reorder limits, tracks the quantity of merchandise on hand, maintains information on the value of the inventory, and can inform you of the percentage of sales for each inventory item. Discounts to certain types of customers can be given as well as early-payment discounts.

Unlike many computerized accounting programs, QuickBooks makes error correction easy. A sales form may be edited, voided, or deleted in the same window where it was created or via an account register. If a sales form has been printed prior to correction, it may be reprinted after the correction has been made.

A multitude of reports are available when using QuickBooks. Accounts receivable reports include Customer Balance Summary or Balance Detail reports. Sales reports provide information regarding the amount of sales by item. Transaction Reports by Customer are available as well as the traditional accounting reports such as Trial Balance, Profit and Loss, and Balance Sheet. QuickBooks also has graphing capabilities so that you can see and evaluate your accounts receivable and sales at the click of a button.

TRAINING TUTORIAL

The following tutorial is a step-by-step guide to recording receivables (both cash and credit) for a fictitious company with fictitious employees. This company is called Mountain Adventure Ski Shoppe. In addition to recording transactions using QuickBooks, you will prepare several reports and graphs for Mountain Adventure Ski Shoppe. The tutorial for Mountain Adventure Ski Shoppe will continue in Chapters 6 and 7 when accounting for payables, bank reconciliations, financial statement preparation, and closing an accounting period for a merchandising business will be completed.

COMPANY PROFILE: MOUNTAIN ADVENTURE SKI SHOPPE

Mountain Adventure Ski Shoppe is a sporting goods store located in Mammoth Lakes, California. Mountain Adventure Ski Shoppe specializes in equipment, clothing, and accessories for skiing and snowboarding and is open only in the winter. The company is a partnership between Eric Boyd and Matt Wayne. Each partner has a 50 percent share of the business, and both devote all of their efforts to Mountain Adventure Ski Shoppe. They have several part-time employees who work in the evenings and on the weekends during ski season. There is a full-time bookkeeper and manager, Renee Squires, who oversees purchases, maintains the inventory, and keeps the books for the company.

Need to be finished 5-3 ~ 5-75

OPEN A COMPANY—MOUNTAIN ADVENTURE SKI SHOPPE

As in previous chapters, obtain a disk from your instructor containing the data for Mountain Adventure Ski Shoppe. Make a duplicate of **Mountain.QBW** to a new disk labeled **Mountain**, access QuickBooks, and open the company.

*DO: Start the computer
　　　Insert your Mountain data disk in **A:**
　　　Access QuickBooks
　　　Open a company Mountain Adventure Ski Shoppe

VERIFYING AN OPEN COMPANY

*DO: Verify the title bar heading:

Mountain Adventure Ski Shoppe - QuickBooks

CLOSE OPENING MESSAGES

As in earlier chapters, QuickBooks may prompt you with a message box regarding Navigator, Inside Tips, Qcards, and a Reminders screen. These items should be closed before beginning work in Mountain Adventure Ski Shoppe.

*DO: Close all opening screens

ADD YOUR NAME TO THE COMPANY NAME

As with Creative Computer Consulting, each student in the course will be working for the same company and printing the same documents. Personalizing the company name to include your name will help identify many of the documents you print during your training.

*DO: Add your name to the company name
　　　Click **File** menu
　　　　OR
　　　Click **Company** tab on QuickBooks Navigator
　　　Click **Company Info**
　　　Click to the right of **Mountain Adventure Ski Shoppe**

Type **--Your Name**
- Type your real name, *not* the words "Your Name." For example, Donna O'Dell would type **--Donna O'Dell**.

Click **OK**
- The title bar now shows Mountain Adventure Ski Shoppe--Student's Name.

BEGINNING THE TUTORIAL

In this chapter you will be entering both accounts receivable transactions and cash sales transactions for a retail company that charges its customers sales tax. Much of the organization of QuickBooks is dependent upon lists. The two primary types of lists you will use in the tutorial for receivables are a Customer list and a Sales Item list.

The names, addresses, telephone numbers, credit terms, credit limits, balances, and tax terms for all established credit customers are contained in the Customer list. The Customer list is also the Accounts Receivable ledger. You will be using the following Customer list for established credit customers:

Customer:Job List	
Name	**Balance**
Chin, Melinda	53.63
Clancy, Cheryl	455.00
David, Ellen	1,136.00
Donaldson, Fran	650.00
Finley, Viv Dr.	417.00
Jones, Richard	1,085.00
Mammoth Schools	0.00
Moreno, Jose Dr.	95.45
Pitcher, Sara	408.48
Travis, Carrie	670.31
Tyler, Tim	911.63
Vernon, Melvin	975.00
Wilson, Roger	85.00

Sales are often made up of various types of income. In Mountain Adventure Ski Shoppe there are several income accounts. In addition, there are sales categories within an income account. For example, each sales item represents an inventory item and is a subaccount of an income account—Ski Boots is a sales item and is a subaccount of Equipment Income. QuickBooks uses lists to organize sales items. Using lists for sales items allows for flexibility in billing and a more accurate representation of the way in which income is earned. If the company charges a standard price for an item, the price of the item will be included on the list. In Mountain Adventure Ski Shoppe all items sell at different prices, so the price given for each item is listed at 0.00. In a retail business with an inventory, the number of units on hand can be tracked; and, when the amount on hand gets to a predetermined limit, an order can be placed. The following Item list for the various types of merchandise and sales categories will be used for Mountain Adventure Ski Shoppe:

Name	Description	Type	Account	On Hand	Price
◆ Accessories	Sunglasses, Ski W	Inventory Part	Clothing & Acce	800	0.00
◆ Bindings-Skis	Ski Bindings	Inventory Part	Equipment Sale	50	0.00
◆ Bindings-Snow	Snowboard Bindin	Inventory Part	Equipment Sale	50	0.00
◆ Boots	After Ski Boots an.	Inventory Part	Clothing & Acce	20	0.00
◆ Boots-Ski	Ski Boots	Inventory Part	Equipment Sale	15	0.00
◆ Boots-Snowbrd	Snowboard Boots	Inventory Part	Equipment Sale	12	0.00
◆ Gloves	Gloves	Inventory Part	Clothing & Acce	22	0.00
◆ Hats	Hats and Scarves	Inventory Part	Clothing & Acce	30	0.00
◆ Pants	Ski Pants	Inventory Part	Clothing & Acce	50	0.00
◆ Pants-Ski	Ski Pants	Inventory Part	Clothing & Acce	95	0.00
◆ Parkas	Parkas and Jacke	Inventory Part	Clothing & Acce	75	0.00
◆ Poles-Ski	Ski Poles	Inventory Part	Equipment Sale	18	0.00
◆ Skis	Snow Skis	Inventory Part	Equipment Sale	50	0.00
◆ Snowboard	Snowboard	Inventory Part	Equipment Sale	30	0.00
◆ Socks	Ski Socks	Inventory Part	Clothing & Acce	75	0.00
◆ Sweaters	Sweaters & Shirts	Inventory Part	Clothing & Acce	75	0.00
◆ Underwear	Long Underwear	Inventory Part	Clothing & Acce	33	0.00
◆ CA Sales Tax	CA Sales Tax	Sales Tax Item	Sales Tax Paya		7.25%

As in previous chapters, all transactions are listed on memos. The transaction date will be the same date as the memo date unless otherwise specified within the transaction. Customer names, when necessary, will be given in the transaction. Unless otherwise specified, all terms for customers on account are Net 30 days. If a memo contains more than one transaction, there will be a horizontal line separating the transactions.

Even when you are instructed how to enter a transaction step by step, you should always refer to the memo for transaction details. Once a specific type of transaction has been entered in a step-by-step manner, additional transactions will be made without having instructions provided. Of course, you may always refer to instructions given for previous transactions for ideas or for steps used to enter those transactions.

CUSTOMIZE REPORT FORMAT

The report format used in one company may not be appropriate for all companies that use QuickBooks. The preferences selected in QuickBooks are only for the current company. In Section 1 of the text, report preferences were changed for Creative Computer Consulting, but those changes have no effect on Mountain Adventure Ski Shoppe. The header/footer for reports in Mountain Adventure Ski Shoppe must be customized to eliminate the printing of the current date as part of a report heading.

MEMO

DATE: January 1, 1998

Before recording any transactions or preparing any reports, customize the report format by removing the current date from report headings.

---

*DO: Customize the report preferences so the current date does not print on reports:
Click **File** Menu, click **Preferences**
>   OR
Use QuickBooks Navigator: Click **Company** tab, click **Preferences**
Scroll through the items listed on the left side of the screen until you
>   get to Reports and Graphs
Click **Reports and Graphs**
Click the **Format** button
Click the **Header/Footer** button
Click **Date Prepared** to deselect

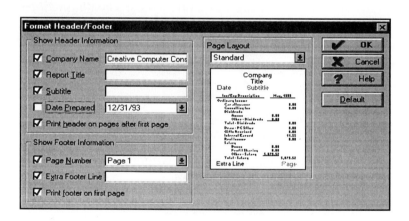

>   Click **OK** to save the change
>   Click **OK** to exit the Report Format Preferences
>   Click **OK** to close Preferences

ENTER SALES ON ACCOUNT

Because QuickBooks operates on a business form premise, a sale on account is entered via an invoice. You prepare an invoice including sales tax and payment terms information, and

QuickBooks records the transaction in the Journal and updates the customer's account automatically.

MEMO

DATE: January 2, 1998

Bill the following: Invoice 1—An established customer, Roger Wilson, purchased a pair of after-ski boots for $75.00 on account. Terms are Net 15.

---

*DO: Record the sale on account shown in the invoice above. This invoice is used to bill a customer for a sale using one sales item:
Click **Invoice** button on the iconbar
   OR
Use **QuickBooks Navigator**, click **Sales and Customers** tab, click **Invoice** icon
- A blank invoice will show on the screen.

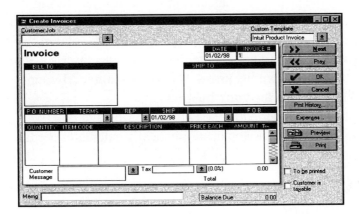

Click the drop-down list arrow next to **Customer:Job**
Click **Wilson, Roger**
- Name is entered as Customer:Job and Bill To: information is completed automatically.
Tab to **Custom Template**
- Intuit Product Invoice should be showing. If it is not, click the drop-down arrow beneath Custom Template. Click Intuit Product Invoice.
Tab to **Date**
- When you tab to the date, it will be highlighted. When you type in the new date, the highlighted date will be deleted.

Type **01/02/98** as the date

Invoice No. 1 should be showing in the **Invoice No.** box

- The Invoice No. should not have to be changed.

There is no PO No. to record

Terms should be indicated as **Net 15**

- If not, click the drop-down list arrow next to **Terms** and click **Net 15**

Tab to or click **Quantity**

Type **1**

- The quantity is one because you are billing for one pair of after-ski boots.

Tab to or click the first line beneath **Item Code**

Click the drop-down list arrow next to **Item Code**

- Refer to the memo above and the Item list for appropriate billing information.

Click **Boots** to bill for one pair of after-ski boots

- The **Description "After Ski Boots and Shoes"** is automatically inserted.

Tab to or click **Price Each**

- If necessary, highlight the 0.00 amount shown by holding down the primary mouse button and dragging through the amount. Press the Delete key.

Type in the amount of the after-ski boots **75**

- Because the price on ski boots differs with each style, QuickBooks cannot be given the price in advance. It must be inserted during the invoice preparation.

Click in the box for **Customer Message**

- QuickBooks will automatically calculate the total in the **Amount** column.
- Because this is a taxable item, QuickBooks inserts a **T** in the **Tax** column.

Click the drop-down list arrow next to **Customer Message**

Click **Thank you for your business.**

- Message is inserted in the Customer Message box.
- Notice that QuickBooks automatically calculates the tax for the invoice and adds it to the invoice total.

EDIT AND CORRECT ERRORS

If an error is discovered while entering invoice information, position the cursor in the field containing the error. As in previous chapters, you may do this by tabbing to move forward through each field or pressing Shift+Tab to move back to the field containing the error. If the error is highlighted, type the correction. If the error is not highlighted, you can correct the error by pressing the backspace or the delete key as many times as necessary to remove the error, then typing the correction. (Alternate method: Point to error, highlight by dragging the mouse through the error, then type the correction.)

 *DO: If you are not comfortable correcting errors, do the following on Invoice 1:

Click the drop-down list arrow next to **Customer:Job**

Click **Chin, Melinda**

- Name is changed in Customer:Job and Bill To: information is also changed.

Click to the left of the first number in the **Date**—this is **0**

Hold down primary mouse button and drag through the date to highlight.

Type **11/19/99** as the date

- This removes the 01/02/98 date originally entered.

Click to the right of the **1** in **Quantity**

Backspace and type a **2**

To eliminate the changes made to Invoice 1, click the drop-down list arrow next
   to **Customer:Job**

Click **Wilson, Roger**

Click the cursor so it is in front of the **1** in the **Date**

Press the **Delete** until the date is removed

Type **01/02/98**

Click to the right of the **2** in **Quantity**

Backspace and type a **1**

Press Tab key

- This will cause QuickBooks to calculate the amount and the total for the
  invoice and will move the cursor to Description field.
- Invoice 1 has been returned to the correct customer, date, and quantity.
  Compare the information you entered with the information provided in the
  memo and on the following:

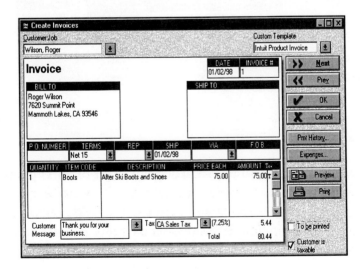

PRINT AN INVOICE

*DO: With Invoice 1 on the screen, print the invoice immediately after entering the corrected information

Click **Print** button on the **Create Invoice** screen

Check the information on the **"Print One Invoice" Settings** tab:

    Printer Name: (Should identify the type of printer you are using)

    Printer Type: Page-oriented (Single sheet)

    Print On: Blank Paper

    Print Lines Around Each Field check box: click the box to enter a check mark

- If there is a check in the box, lines will print around each field.
- If a check is not in the box, lines will not print around each field.

    Number of Copies should be 1

- If a number other than 1 shows, click in the box, drag to highlight the number shown, type **1**.

Click **Print** button

- This initiates the printing of the invoice through QuickBooks. However, because not all classroom configurations are the same, check with your instructor for specific printing instructions.

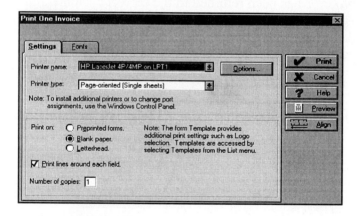

While the invoice is printing, a dialog box **"Did form(s) print OK?"** will appear on the screen

When the form has been correctly printed, click **OK** button on the dialog box

Click **OK** button on the right side of the **Create Invoice** screen to record and close the invoice

ENTER TRANSACTIONS USING MORE THAN ONE SALES ITEM AND SALES TAX

Frequently, sales to customers will be for more than one item. For example, new bindings are usually purchased along with a new pair of skis. Invoices can be prepared to bill a customer for several items at once.

MEMO

DATE: January 3, 1998

Bill the following: <u>Invoice 2</u>—Every year Dr. Jose Moreno gets new ski equipment. Bill him for his equipment purchase for this year: skis, $425; bindings, $175; ski boots, $250; and ski poles, $75.

---

*DO: Record a transaction on account for a sale involving several taxable sales items:
Click **Invoice** button on the iconbar
   OR
Use **QuickBooks Navigator**, click **Sales and Customers** tab, click **Invoice** icon
Click the drop-down list arrow next to **Customer:Job**
Click **Moreno, Jose Dr.**
- Name is entered as Customer:Job and Bill To: information is completed automatically.
Tab to or click **Date**
Delete the current date, if showing
- Refer to instructions for Invoice 1 or to editing practice if necessary.
Type **01/03/98** as the date
Make sure the Invoice No. 2 is showing in the **Invoice No.** box
- The Invoice No. should not have to be changed.
There is no PO No. to record
Terms should be indicated as **2% 10 Net 30**
Tab to or click **Quantity**
Type **1**
Tab to or click the first line beneath **Item Code**
- Refer to memo and Item list for appropriate billing information.
Click the drop-down list arrow next to **Item Code**
Click **Skis**
- Skis is inserted as the item code.
- **Snow Skis** is inserted as the **Description**.
Tab to or click **Price Each**

Delete **0.00**

Enter **425**

- Total is automatically calculated when you go to the next line. Notice that the amount is $425.00.
- Notice that the **Customer is taxable** check box in the lower-right corner of the Create Invoices screen contains a ✔. This means that the customer is taxable.
- Because Dr. Moreno is a taxable customer, sales tax is indicated by a **T** in the **Tax** column.

Tab to or click the second line for **Quantity**

Type **1**

Tab to or click the second line for **Item Code**

Click the drop-down list arrow next to **Item Code**

Click **Bindings-Skis**

- **Ski Bindings** is inserted as the **Description**.

Tab to or click **Price Each**

Delete **0.00**

Enter **175**

- Total is automatically calculated when you go to the next line. Notice that the amount is $175.00.
- Notice that sales tax is indicated by a **T** in the **Tax** column.

Repeat the above steps to enter the information for the ski boots and the ski poles

Click the drop-down list arrow next to **Customer Message**

Click **Thank you for your business.**

- Message is inserted in the Customer Message box.
- Notice that QuickBooks automatically calculates the tax for the invoice and adds it to the invoice total.

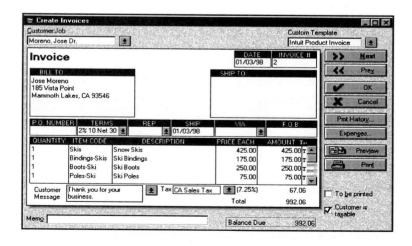

PRINT AN INVOICE

 *DO: With Invoice No. 2 on the screen, print the invoice immediately after entering invoice information by following the instructions provided for Invoice No. 1

PREPARE INVOICES WITHOUT STEP-BY-STEP INSTRUCTIONS

MEMO
DATE: January 3

Bill the following: Invoice 3—We give Mammoth Schools a special rate on equipment and clothing for the ski team. This year the school purchases 5 pairs of skis, $299 each; 5 pairs of bindings, $100 each; and 5 sets of ski poles, $29 each. Terms are 2/10 Net 30.

Invoice 4—Sara Pitcher purchased a new ski outfit: 1 parka, $249; a hat, $25; a sweater, $125; 1 pair of ski pants, $129; long underwear, $68; ski gloves, $79; ski socks, $15.95; sunglasses, $89.95; and a matching ski boot carrier, $2.95. Terms Net 15.

Invoice 5—Tim Tyler broke his snowboard when he was going down his favorite run, "Dragon's Back." He purchased a new one without bindings for $499.95, terms 1/10 Net 30.

Invoice 6—Roger Wilson decided to buy some new powder skis and bindings. Bill him for skis, $599, and bindings, $179. The terms are Net 15.

---

*DO: Enter the four transactions in the memo above. Refer to instructions given for the two previous transactions entered.
- Always use the Item list to determine the appropriate sales items for billing.
- Use "Thank you for your business." as the message for these invoices.
- If you make an error, correct it.
- Print each invoice immediately after you enter the information for it, and print lines around each field.
- To go from one invoice to the next, click **>>NEXT** button on the right side of the Create Invoice screen rather than **OK**.
- Click **OK** after Invoice 6 has been entered and printed.

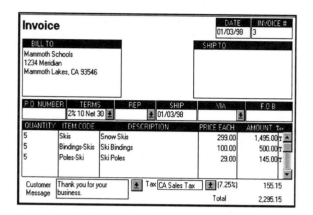

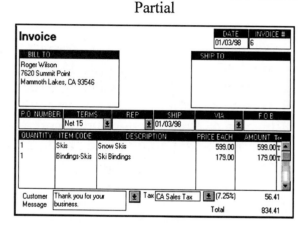

Partial

ENTER A TRANSACTION EXCEEDING A CUSTOMER'S CREDIT LIMIT

When a customer is added to the customer list and a complete setup is performed, the file tab for Additional Info will appear. Additional Info contains a dialog box in which a credit limit can be established for a customer. QuickBooks does allow transactions for a customer to exceed the established credit limit, but a dialog box appears with information regarding the transaction amount and the credit limit for a customer.

MEMO

DATE: January 5, 1998

Bill the following: <u>Invoice 7</u>—Melinda Chin decided to get a new snowboard, $489.95; bindings, $159.99; snowboard boots, $249; and a special case to carry her boots, $49.95. Terms are Net 30.

---

*DO: Prepare and print Invoice 7 as instructed previously
- Always use the Item list to determine the appropriate sales items for billing.
- Use "Thank you for your business." as the message for the invoice.
- If you make an error, correct it.
- Print the invoice immediately after you enter the information for it.
- Print lines around each field.

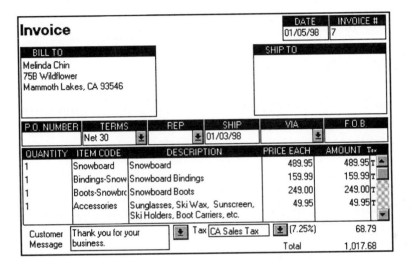

Click **OK** after Invoice 7 has been entered and printed.

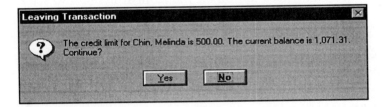

- If you click **No**, you are returned to the invoice in order to make changes.
- If you click **Yes**, the transaction is recorded.

Click **Yes** to record the transaction

ACCOUNTS RECEIVABLE REPORTS

A variety of reports are available regarding accounts receivable. Data regarding customers may be displayed on the basis of account aging, open invoices, collections reports, or customer balances, or they may be itemized according to the sales by customer. Many reports may be printed in a summarized form while other reports provide detailed information.

PREPARE CUSTOMER BALANCE DETAIL REPORT

The Customer Balance Detail report lists information regarding each customer. The information provided for each customer includes all invoices on which there is a balance, the date of the invoice, the invoice number, the account used to record the invoice, the amount of each invoice, the balance after each invoice, and the total balance due from each customer.

MEMO

DATE: January 5, 1998

Prepare and print a Customer Balance Detail report so that the owners can see exactly how much each customer owes to Mountain Adventure Ski Shoppe.

---

*DO: Prepare a Customer Balance Detail report for all customers for all transactions:
Click **Reports** on the menu bar, point to **A/R Reports**, click **Customer Balance Detail**
OR
Use **QuickBooks Navigator**:
Click **Sales and Customers** side tab
- You may need to turn off the iconbar in order to see Reports at the bottom of the screen. Click Company tab, click Preferences, click iconbar, click Don't show iconbar.
Click **Accounts Receivable** in Reports section, click **Customer Balance Detail**
Dates should be **All**
- If not, click the drop-down list arrow next to the Dates text box, click All.
- Scroll through the report. See how much each customer owes for each invoice.
- Notice that the amount owed by Melinda Chin for Invoice 7 is $1,017.68 and that her total balance is $1,071.31.
Do not close Customer Balance Detail Report

USE THE QUICKZOOM FEATURE

QuickZoom is a feature of QuickBooks that allows you to view additional information within a report. For example, an invoice may be viewed when the Customer Balance Detail report is on the screen simply by using the QuickZoom feature.

MEMO

DATE: January 5, 1998

The bookkeeper, Renee Squires, could not remember if Invoice 7 was for ski equipment or snowboard equipment. With the Customer Balance Detail report on the screen, use QuickZoom to view Invoice 7.

*DO: Use QuickZoom to view Invoice 7

Position the cursor over any part of the report showing information about Invoice 7
- The cursor will turn into a magnifying glass with a letter **Z** inside.

Double-click
- Invoice 7 appears on the screen.
- Check to make sure the four items on the invoice are: Snowboard, Bindings-Snowbrd, Boots-Snowbrd, and Accessories.

With Invoice 7 on the screen, proceed to the next section.

CORRECT AN INVOICE AND PRINT THE CORRECTED FORM

QuickBooks allows corrections and revisions to an invoice even if the invoice has been printed. The invoice may be corrected by going directly to the original invoice or by accessing the original invoice via the Accounts Receivable register. An invoice can be on view in QuickZoom and still be corrected.

MEMO

DATE: January 5, 1998

While viewing Invoice 7 for Melinda Chin in QuickZoom, the bookkeeper, Renee Squires, realizes that the snowboard should be $499.95, not the $489.95 that is on the original invoice. Make the correction and reprint the invoice.

*DO: Correct Invoice 7 while showing on the screen in QuickZoom

Click in the **Price Each** column

Position the cursor between the **4** and **8** in 489.95

Press **Delete** to delete the **8**

Type a **9**

Tab twice to have the **Amount** calculated for the Snowboard

Print the corrected Invoice 7

Click **OK** button on the right side of the **Create Invoice** screen to record and close the invoice

Leaving Transaction message box appears on the screen regarding the credit limit of $500 for Melinda Chin

Click **Yes** to accept the current balance of $1,082.04

- This closes the invoice and returns you to the Customer Balance Detail report.
- Notice that the total amount for Invoice 7 is $1,028.41 and that Melinda Chin's total balance is $1,082.04

Click **Print** button at the top of the Customer Balance Detail Report

Complete the information on the **Print Report Settings** tab:

Print To: The selected item should be **Printer**

Orientation: Click **Portrait** to select Portrait orientation for this report

Page Range: **All** should be selected; if it is not, click **All**

Click the check box for **Fit report to one page wide** to select this item

- When selected, the printer will print the report using a smaller font so that the report will be one page in width.

Click **Print** on the **Print Reports** screen

After the report is printed, click **Close** button to close **Customer Balance Detail Report**

Mountain Adventure Ski Shoppe--Student's Name					
Customer Balance Detail					
All Transactions					
◇ **Type**	◇ **Date**	◇ **Num** ◇	**Account** ◇	**Amount** ◇	**Balance**
Chin, Melinda					
Invoice	01/01/98		1200 · Accounts R...	53.63	53.63
Invoice	01/05/98	7	1200 · Accounts R...	1,028.41	1,082.04
Total Chin, Melinda				1,082.04	1,082.04
Clancy, Cheryl					
Invoice	01/01/98		1200 · Accounts R...	455.00	455.00
Total Clancy, Cheryl				455.00	455.00
David, Ellen					
Invoice	01/01/98		1200 · Accounts R...	1,136.00	1,136.00
Total David, Ellen				1,136.00	1,136.00

ADDING NEW ACCOUNTS TO THE CHART OF ACCOUNTS

Because account needs can change as a business is in operation, QuickBooks allows you to make changes to the Chart of Accounts at any time. Some changes to the Chart of Accounts require additional changes to other lists, such as the Item list. An account may be added by accessing the Chart of Accounts. It is also possible to add an account to the Chart of Accounts while adding an item to another list.

ADD NEW ITEMS TO LIST

In order to accommodate the changing needs of a business, all QuickBooks lists allow you to make changes at any time. New items may be added to the list via the Item list or "on the fly" while entering invoice information. The Item list stores information about the items Mountain Adventure Ski Shoppe sells. Because the store sells to the school district, it would be appropriate to have an item allowing for sales discounts. Having a discount item allows discounts to be recorded on the sales form. A discount can be a fixed amount or a percentage. A discount is calculated only on the line above it on the sales form. To allow the entire amount of the invoice to receive the discount, an item for a subtotal will also need to be added. When you complete the sales form, the subtotal item will appear before the discount item.

MEMO
DATE: January 5, 1998

Add an item for Sales Discounts and a Subtotal Item. Add a new account, Discount Expense, to the Chart of Accounts.

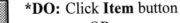 ***DO:** Click **Item** button
                OR
        Use QuickBooks Navigator:
            Click **Sales and Customers** tab
            Click **Items & Services** folder
        Click **Items** button at the bottom of the **Item(s) List** screen
        Click **New**
        Item Type is **Discount**
        Tab to or click **Item Name/Number**
        Type **Nonproft Disc**

- Note that Nonprofit is spelled without the "i"—Nonproft.

Tab to or click **Description**

Type **10% Discount to Nonprofit Agencies**

Tab to or click **Amount or %**

Type in **10%**

- The "%" must be included in order to differentiate between a $10 discount and a 10% discount.

Click drop-down list arrow for **Account**

Type **Sales Discount**

- QuickBooks does not have Sales Discount in the Chart of Accounts for Mountain Adventures Ski Shoppe. It does have account 4030 Sales Discounts. If account 4030 Sales Discounts appears, you may need to delete **4030** and the **s** at the end of Discounts from the Account text box and click **OK**.

- **Account Not Found** dialog box appears on the screen.

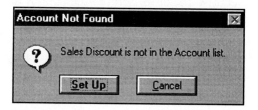

Click **Set Up** on the **Account Not Found** dialog box

Complete the information for a New Account:

   Type should be **Expense**

   - If not, click the drop-down list arrow next to the text box for Type.
   - Click **Expense**.

   Number shows **Sales D**

   Delete **Sales D**

   Enter the Account Number **6130**

   Tab to or click **Name**

   Type **Sales Discount**

   Tab to or click **Description**

   Enter **Discount on Sales**

   Click **OK** to add the Sales Discount account and close the New Account
      dialog box

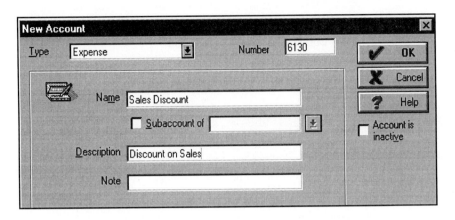

If a ✓ does not appear in the check box for **Apply discount before sales tax** on
New Item, click the check box

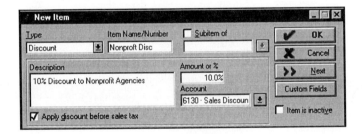

Click >>**Next** on the New Item dialog box
- A discount is calculated only on the line above it on the sales form. To allow
  the entire amount of the invoice to receive the discount, an item for a subtotal
  will also need to be added.

Repeat the steps for adding a New Item to add **Subtotal**

Type should be **Subtotal**

Item Name/Number is **Subtotal**

The description is **Subtotal**

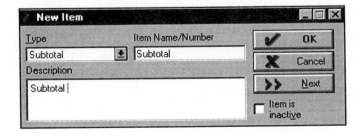

Click **OK** to add the new items and to close New Item screen

- Verify the addition of Nonproft Discount and Subtotal on the Item list. If everything is correct, close the Item list.
- If you find an error, click on the item with the error, click the **Item** button, click **Edit**, make corrections as needed.

Name	Description	Type	Account	On Hand	Price
Accessories	Sunglasses, Ski W	Inventory Part	4011 · Clothing	798	0.00
Bindings-Skis	Ski Bindings	Inventory Part	4012 · Equipm	43	0.00
Bindings-Snow	Snowboard Bindir	Inventory Part	4012 · Equipm	49	0.00
Boots	After Ski Boots an	Inventory Part	4011 · Clothing	20	0.00
Boots-Ski	Ski Boots	Inventory Part	4012 · Equipm	14	0.00
Boots-Snowbrd	Snowboard Boots	Inventory Part	4012 · Equipm	11	0.00
Gloves	Gloves	Inventory Part	4011 · Clothing	21	0.00
Hats	Hats and Scarves	Inventory Part	4011 · Clothing	29	0.00
Pants-Ski	Ski Pants	Inventory Part	4011 · Clothing	94	0.00
Pants-Snowbrd	Snowboard Pants	Inventory Part	4011 · Clothing	50	0.00
Parkas	Parkas and Jacke	Inventory Part	4011 · Clothing	74	0.00
Poles-Ski	Ski Poles	Inventory Part	4012 · Equipm	12	0.00
Skis	Snow Skis	Inventory Part	4012 · Equipm	43	0.00
Snowboard	Snowboard	Inventory Part	4012 · Equipm	29	0.00
Socks	Ski and Snowboa	Inventory Part	4011 · Clothing	74	0.00
Sweaters	Sweaters & Shirts	Inventory Part	4011 · Clothing	74	0.00
Underwear	Long Underwear	Inventory Part	4011 · Clothing	32	0.00
Subtotal	Subtotal	Subtotal			
Nonproft Disc	10% Discount to N	Discount	6130 · Sales D		-10.0%
CA Sales Tax	CA Sales Tax	Sales Tax Item	2200 · Sales T		7.25%

Item ▼   Activities ▼   Reports ▼   ☒ Show All

Close Item list

CORRECT AN INVOICE TO INCLUDE SALES DISCOUNT

MEMO

DATE: January 6, 1998

Now that the appropriate accounts for sales discounts have been created, correct the invoice to Mammoth Schools to give the schools a 10% discount as a nonprofit organization.

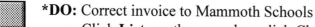 ***DO:** Correct invoice to Mammoth Schools
Click **Lists** on the menu bar, click Chart of Accounts
  OR
Click the **Accnt** button on the iconbar
  OR
Use QuickBooks Navigator:

Click **Company** side tab
Click **Chart of Accounts**
In the Chart of Accounts click **Accounts Receivable**

Name	Type	Balance
◆1100 · Checking	Bank	25,943.00
◆1200 · Accounts Receivable	Accounts Receivable	12,879.64
◆1120 · Inventory Asset	Other Current Asset	31,614.35
◆1310 · Supplies	Other Current Asset	1,425.00
◆1311 · Office Supplies	Other Current Asset	850.00
◆1312 · Sales Supplies	Other Current Asset	575.00
◆1340 · Prepaid Insurance	Other Current Asset	250.00
◆1510 · Office Equipment	Fixed Asset	5,000.00
◆1511 · Original Cost	Fixed Asset	5,000.00

Account ▼   Activities ▼   Reports ▼   ☐ Show All

Click **Activities** button
Click **Use Register**

- The Accounts Receivable Register appears on the screen with information regarding each transaction entered into the account.

1200 · Accounts Receivable

Date	Number	Customer	Item	Qty	Rate	Amt Chrg	Amt Paid
	Type	Description				Billed Date	Due Date
01/03/98	2	Moreno, Jose Dr.				992.06	
	INV						02/02/98
01/03/98	3	Mammoth Schools				2,295.15	
	INV						02/02/98
01/03/98	4	Pitcher, Sara				840.68	
	INV						01/18/98
01/03/98	6	Wilson, Roger				834.41	
	INV						01/18/98

Ending balance   12,879.64

Record   Edit   Restore   Q-Report   Go To   ☐ 1-Line ☐ Show open balance

If necessary, scroll through the register until the transaction for **Invoice No. 3** is on the screen

- Look at the **Number/Type** column to identify the number of the invoice and the type of transaction.
    - On the <u>Number line</u> you will see a <u>check number</u> or the <u>invoice number</u>.
    - On the <u>Type line</u> <u>PMT</u> indicates a payment was received on account, and <u>INV</u> indicates a sale on account.

Click anywhere in the transaction for Invoice No. 3 to Mammoth Schools
Click **Edit** at the bottom of the register
- Invoice No. 3 appears on the screen.
Click in **Item Code** beneath the last Item Poles-Ski
Click the drop-down list arrow for **Item Code**
Click **Subtotal**
- You may need to scroll through the Item list until you find Subtotal.
- Remember that QuickBooks must subtotal the items on the invoice in order to calculate a discount on all items on the invoice.
Tab to or click the next blank line in **Item Code**
Click **Nonproft Disc**
- You may need to scroll through the Item list until you find Nonproft Disc.
Click **Print** button on the **Create Invoice** screen to print a corrected invoice

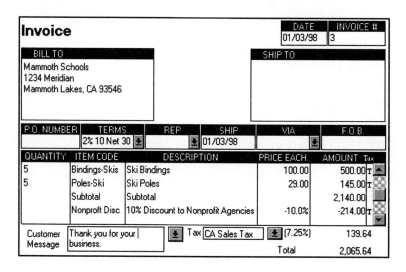

- Notice the subtotal of $2,140.00, the discount of $214, and the new invoice total of $2,065.64.
Click **OK** on the **Create Invoices** screen to save the corrected invoice and return to the Accounts Receivable Register
- Notice the new Amt Chg of $2,065.64 for Invoice 3 in the register.
Do not close the Accounts Receivable register

VIEW A QUICKREPORT

After editing the invoice and returning to the register, you may get a detailed report regarding the customer's transactions by clicking the Q-Report button.

*DO: With the cursor in Invoice 3, click **Q-Report** button to view the **Mammoth Schools** account
Verify the account balance of $2,065.64

ANALYZE THE QUICKREPORT FOR MAMMOTH SCHOOLS

 *DO: Notice that the total of Invoice 3 is $2,065.64

Mountain Adventure Ski Shoppe
Register QuickReport
All Transactions

Type	Date	Num	Memo	Account	Paid	Open Balance	Amount
Mammoth Schools							
Invoice	01/03/98	3		1200 · Accounts R...		2,065.64	2,065.64
Total Mammoth Schools						2,065.64	2,065.64
TOTAL						2,065.64	2,065.64

Close the QuickReport without printing
Close Accounts Receivable register
Close Chart of Accounts

ADD A NEW CUSTOMER

QuickBooks allows customers to be added at any time. They may be added to the company records through the Customer list, or they may be added "on the fly" as you create an invoice or sales receipt. When adding "on the fly," you may choose between Quick Add (used to add only a customer's name) and Set Up (used to add complete information for a customer).

MEMO
DATE: January 10, 1998

Renee was instructed to add a new customer. The information provided for the new customer is: Mammoth Recreation Center, 985 Old Mammoth Road, Mammoth Lakes, CA 93546, Contact: Melanie Clark, Phone: 619-555-2951, Fax: 619-555-1592, Terms: 1%10 Net 30, Credit Limit: 5,000, Taxable, Tax Item: CA Sales Tax, as of 01/09/98 there is a 0.00 opening balance for the customer.

---

*DO: Add a new customer using the Customer:Job list
        Click **List** menu, click **Customer:Jobs**
            OR
        Click the **Cust** button on the iconbar
            OR
        Use QuickBooks Navigator:
            Click **Sales and Customers** tab, click **Customers** icon
        With the Customer list showing on the screen
            Use the keyboard shortcut **Ctrl+N** to create a new customer
                OR
            Click **Customer:Job** button at the bottom of the list, click **New**
        In the **Customer** text box enter **Mammoth Recreation Center**
        Tab to or click **Company Name**
        Enter **Mammoth Recreation Center**
        Tab to or click the second line in **Bill To**
        Enter the address listed above
        Tab to or click **Contact**
        Enter the name of the person to contact
        Tab to or click **Phone**, enter the telephone number
        Tab to or click **FAX**, enter the fax number

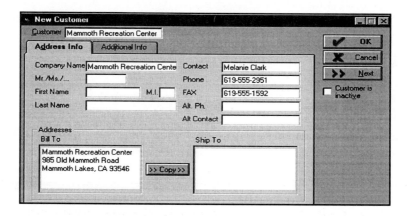

Click **Additional Info** tab
Enter the required information for Additional Info

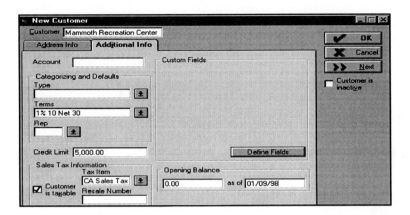

Click **OK** to complete the addition of Mammoth Recreation Center as a customer
- Verify the addition of Mammoth Recreation Center to the Customer:Job list.

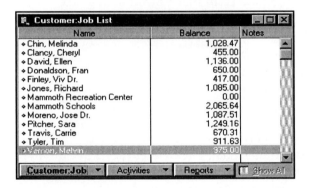

Close the Customer:Job list

RECORD A SALE TO A NEW CUSTOMER

Once a customer has been added, sales may be recorded for a customer.

MEMO

DATE: January 9, 1998

Record a sale of 5 sleds at $119.99 each and 5 toboggans at $229.95 each to Mammoth Recreation Center. Because the sale is to a nonprofit organization, include a nonprofit discount.

---

*DO: Record the above sale on account to a new customer:
Click **Invoice** button
  OR
Use QuickBooks Navigator:
  Click **Sales and Customers** tab, click **Invoices**
Enter invoice information for **Mammoth Recreation Center** as previously
  instructed
Date of the invoice is **01/09/98**
Invoice No. is **8**
Tab to or click **Quantity**
Enter **5**
Tab to or click **Item Code**
Because sleds is not on the item list, type **Sleds** for the **Item Code**, press **Enter**
Click **Set Up** on the **Item Not Found** dialog box

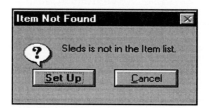

On the **New Item** screen, click **Inventory Part** for **Type**
• If necessary, click the drop-down list menu to get a list of choices for **Type**.
Item Name/Number should be **Sleds**
• If not, tab to or click in the text box for Item Name/Number, type **Sleds**.
Complete **Purchase Information**:
• This section provides information to be used for orders of sleds for Mountain
  Adventure Ski Shoppe.
  Description on Purchase Transactions: enter **Sleds**
  Cost: 0.00
  • Because different styles and models of sleds are purchased at different
    prices, leave this amount at 0.00.
  COGS Account: 5000 Cost of Goods Sold
  • If this account is not in the COGS Account text box, click the drop-down
    list arrow, click 5000 Cost of Goods Sold.
  Preferred Vendor: leave blank
Complete **Sales Information**:
• This section provides the information used when Mountain Adventure Ski
  Shoppe sells sleds to customers.
  Description on Sales Transactions: should be **Sleds**

- If Sleds was not inserted at the same time as the Purchase Information Description, enter **Sleds** for the description.

Sales Price: leave 0.00

- Because different styles and models of sleds are sold at different prices, leave this amount at 0.00.

Taxable: there should be a ✓ in the check box

- If not, click the check box to insert a ✓.

Click the drop-down list arrow for **Income Account**

Click **4012 Equipment Sales**

Complete the **Inventory Information**:

- QuickBooks uses this information to track the amount of inventory on hand and to provide reorder information.

  Asset Account: should be **1120 Inventory Asset**

  - If this account is not in the COGS Account text box, click the drop-down list arrow, click 1120 Inventory Asset.

Tab to or click **Reorder Point**

Enter **5**

Tab to or click **Qty on Hand**

Enter **10**

Tab to or click **Total Value**

- Five of the ten sleds were purchased by Mountain Adventure Ski Shoppe for $75 each. The other five sleds were purchased for $60 each.

Enter **675** for the Total Value

Tab to or click **As of**

Enter the As of date of **01/09/98**

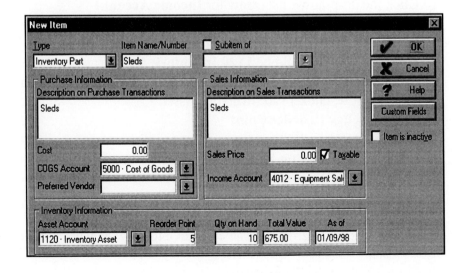

Click **OK** to add Sleds as a sales item

On the invoice, tab to or click **Price Each**
Enter **119.99**
Tab to or click the second line in **Quantity**
Enter **5**
Tab to or click **Item Code**
Click the drop-down list arrow for Item Code
- There is no item listed for Toboggans.
Click **<Add New>** at the top of the Item list
Complete the information for **New Item**
On the **New Item** screen, click **Inventory Part** for **Type**
- If necessary, click the drop-down list menu to get a list of choices for **Type**.
Tab to or click **Item Name/Number**
Enter **Toboggans**
Complete **Purchase Information**:
    Description on Purchase Transactions: enter **Toboggans**
    Cost: 0.00
    COGS Account: 5000 Cost of Goods Sold
    Preferred Vendor: leave blank
Complete **Sales Information**:
    Description on Sales Transactions: should be **Toboggans**
    - If Toboggans was not inserted at the same time as the Purchase
      Information Description, enter **Toboggans** for the description.
    Sales Price: leave **0.00**
    Taxable: there should be a ✓ in the check box
    - If not, click the check box to insert a ✓.
    Click the drop-down list arrow for **Income Account**
    Click **4012 Equipment Sales**
Complete the **Inventory Information**:
    Asset Account: should be **1120 Inventory Asset**
    - If this account is not in the COGS Account text box, click the drop-down
      list arrow, click 1120 Inventory Asset.
    Tab to or click **Reorder Point**
    Enter **5**
    Tab to or click **Qty on Hand**
    Enter **10**
    Tab to or click **Total Value**
    - Five of the ten toboggans were purchased by Mountain Adventure Ski
      Shoppe for $125 each. The other five toboggans were purchased for $150
      each.
    Enter **1375** for the Total Value
    Tab to or click **As of**

Enter the As of date of **01/09/98**

Click **OK** to add Toboggans as a sales item

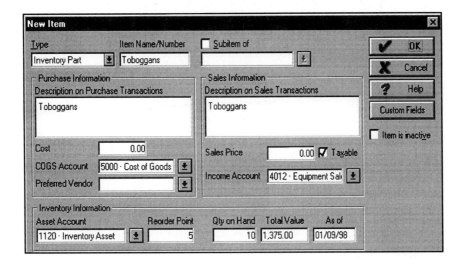

Complete the invoice
- Remember that Mammoth Recreation Center is a nonprofit organization.

The message is **Thank you for your business.**

Print the invoice as previously instructed

Click **OK** to answer "Did Form(s) Print OK?"

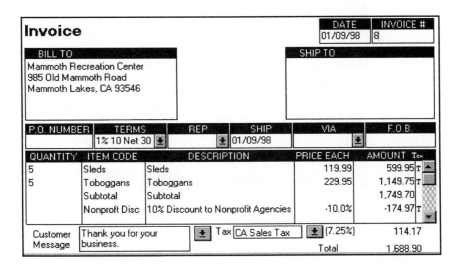

Click **OK** on the invoice to record and close the transaction

MODIFY CUSTOMER RECORDS

Occasionally information regarding a customer will change. QuickBooks allows customer accounts to be modified at anytime by editing the customer list.

MEMO

DATE: January 15, 1998

In order to update Melinda Chin's account, change her credit limit to $2,500.00.

DO: To edit the above account, access the Customer list
There are four ways to access the Customer list:
- Click **Lists** on the drop-down menu, click **Customer:Job**.
- Use QuickBooks Navigator: Click **Sales and Customers** tab, click **Customers** folder.
- Click **Cust** button on the iconbar.
- Use the keyboard shortcut: **Ctrl+J**.

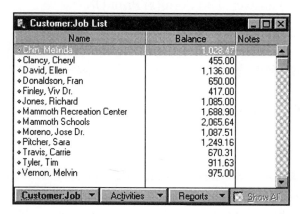

Access Melinda Chin's account in one of the following three ways:
- Click **Chin, Melinda** on the Customer:Job list, click **Customer:Job** button, click **Edit**.
- Click **Chin, Melinda** on the Customer:Job list, use the keyboard shortcut **Ctrl+E**.
- Double-click **Chin, Melinda** on the Customer:Job list.
Click the **Additional Info** tab
Tab to or click **Credit Limit**

Enter **2500** for the amount
- You may have to delete the existing credit limit of 500.00.
- You do not have to enter a comma between the 2 and the 5. You do not need to enter a decimal point and the two zeros. QuickBooks will format the number for you automatically.

Click **OK** to record the change and exit the information for Melinda Chin
Close **Customer:Job list**

VOID AND DELETE SALES FORMS

Deleting an invoice or sales receipt permanently removes it from QuickBooks without leaving a trace. If you want to correct financial records for the invoice that you no longer want, it is more appropriate to void the invoice. When an invoice is voided, it remains in the QuickBooks system, but QuickBooks doesn't count it. Voiding an invoice should be used only if there have been no payments made on the invoice. If any payment has been received, a Credit Memo would be appropriate for recording a return.

Void an Invoice

MEMO

DATE: January 6, 1998

Roger Wilson returned the after-ski boots he purchased for $80.44 including tax on January 2. He had not made any payments on this purchase. Void the invoice.

---

 *DO: Void the above transaction using FIND to locate the invoice:
- Find is useful when you have a large number of invoices and want to locate an invoice for a particular customer.
- Using Find will locate the invoice without requiring you to scroll through all the invoices for the company. For example, if customer Sanderson's transaction was on Invoice 7 and the invoice on the screen was 784, you would not have to scroll through 777 invoices because Find would locate Invoice 7 instantly.

To use Find:
    Click **Edit** menu, click **Find**
        OR
    Click **Find** button

In the list displayed under **Filter**, click **Name**

In the **Name** dialog box, click the drop-down list arrow, click **Wilson, Roger**

Click the **FIND** button on the FIND dialog box

- QuickBooks will find all transactions recorded for Roger Wilson.

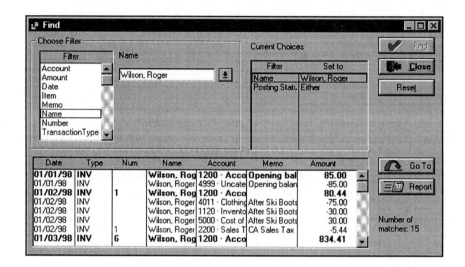

- Because there are several invoices, another filter would need to be defined in order to find the invoice with the exact amount of 80.44.

This would be done by selecting a second filter:

Click **Amount** under **Filter**

Click the Select box in front of the = sign

Key in **80.44** in the text box

Press **Tab**

- Notice that the Current Choices Box shows "Filter: Amount" and "Set to: 80.44": followed by "Filter: Name" and "Set to: Wilson, Roger."

Click the **FIND** button on the FIND dialog box

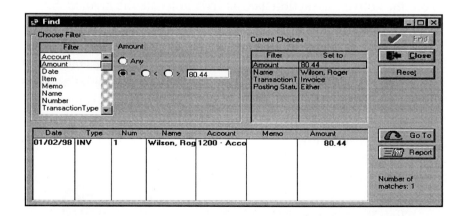

Click the line for **Invoice 1**

Click **Go To** button

• Invoice No. 1 appears on the screen.

With the invoice on the screen, click **Edit** menu, click **Void Invoice**

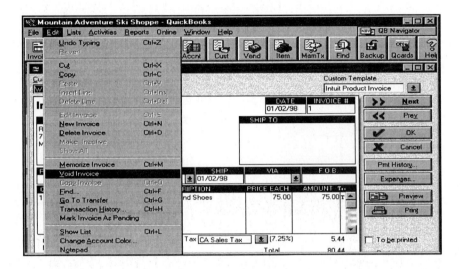

• Notice that the amount and the total for Invoice 1 are no longer 80.44. Both are **0.00**.

Click **OK** button on the **Create Invoices** screen to close invoice

• Notice that Invoice 1 no longer shows on Find.

Click **Close** button to close Find

Delete an Invoice

MEMO

DATE: January 6, 1998

Tim Tyler lost his part-time job. He decided to repair his old snowboard and return the new one he purchased from Mountain Adventure Ski Shoppe. Delete Invoice 5.

---

*DO: Delete Invoice 5 by going directly to the original invoice

Click **Invoice** button on the iconbar

    OR

Use **QuickBooks Navigator**:

    Click **Sales and Customers** tab, click **Invoice** icon

- You may also access the invoice via the register for Accounts Receivable.
Click **<<Prev** button until you get to Invoice 5
With Invoice 5 on the screen, click **Edit** menu
Click **Delete Invoice**

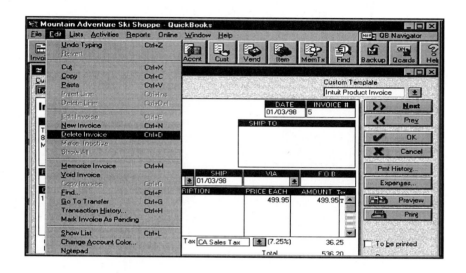

Click **OK** in the **Delete Transaction** dialog box

- Notice that the cursor is now positioned on Invoice 6.
Click **<<Prev** button
- Notice that the cursor is positioned on Invoice 4.
Click **OK** button on the **Create Invoices** screen to close invoice
View the Customer Balance Detail report
Click **Reports**, point to **A/R Reports**, click **Customer Balance Detail**
Scroll through the report
- Look at Tim Tyler's account.
- Notice that Invoice No. 5 doesn't show up in the account listing. When an invoice is deleted, there is no record of it anywhere in the report.
- Notice that the Customer Balance Detail report does not include the information telling you which amounts are opening balances.
- The report does give information regarding the amount owed on each transaction plus the total amount owed by each customer.

- Look at Roger Wilson's account.
- Notice that the amount for Invoice 1 shows as **0.00**.

Mountain Adventure Ski Shoppe
Customer Balance Detail

Type	Date	Num	Account	Amount	Balance
Tyler, Tim					
Invoice	01/01/98		1200 · Accounts R...	911.63	911.63
Total Tyler, Tim				911.63	911.63
Vernon, Melvin					
Invoice	01/01/98		1200 · Accounts R...	975.00	975.00
Total Vernon, Melvin				975.00	975.00
Wilson, Roger					
Invoice	01/01/98		1200 · Accounts R...	85.00	85.00
Invoice	01/02/98	1	1200 · Accounts R...	0.00	85.00
Invoice	01/03/98	6	1200 · Accounts R...	834.41	919.41
Total Wilson, Roger				919.41	919.41

Close the report without printing

PREPARE CREDIT MEMOS

Credit memos are prepared to show a reduction to a transaction. If the invoice has already been sent to the customer, it is more appropriate and less confusing to make a change to a transaction by issuing a credit memo rather than voiding the invoice and issuing a new invoice. A credit memo notifies a customer that a change has been made to a transaction.

MEMO
DATE: January 9, 1998

Prepare <u>Credit Memo 9</u> for Melinda Chin to show a reduction to her account for the return of the boot carrying case purchased for $49.95 on Invoice 7.

---

*DO: Prepare the credit memo shown above
Click **Activities** menu, click **Create Credit Memos/Refunds**
OR
Use QuickBooks Navigator

Click **Sales and Customers** tab, click **Refunds and Credit**

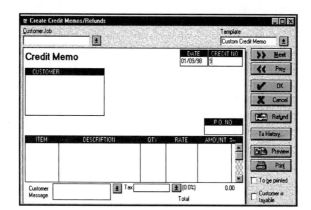

Click the down arrow for the drop-down list box next to **Customer:Job**
Click **Chin, Melinda**
Tab to Template
- It should say **Custom Credit Memo**.
- If not, click the drop-down list arrow and click Custom Credit Memo.
Tab to or click **Date**
Type in the date of the credit memo—**01/09/98**
The **Credit No.** field should show the number **9**
- Because credit memos are included in the numbering sequence for invoices, this number matches the number of the next blank invoice.
There is no PO No.
Tab to or click in **Item**
Click the drop-down list arrow next to Item, click **Accessories**
Tab to or click in **Quantity**, type in **1**
Tab to or click **Rate**, enter **49.95**
Press tab to enter 49.95 in the Amount column
Click the drop-down list arrow next to Customer Message
Click **Thank you for your business.**
Click **Print** on Create Credit Memo/Refunds
Click **Print** on Print One Credit Memo
If the Credit Memo prints without error, click **OK** in the **"Did form(s) print OK?"** dialog box

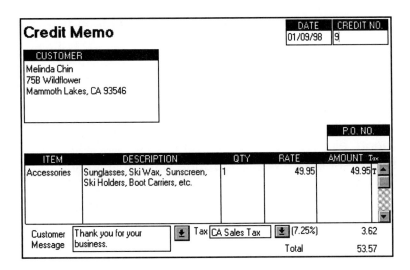

Click **OK** button on Create Credit Memo/Refunds to close credit memo

PRINT OPEN INVOICES BY CUSTOMER REPORT

To determine which invoices are still open—they have not been paid—QuickBooks allows you to print a report titled Open Invoices by Customer. This report shows information regarding the type of transaction (invoice or credit memo), the transaction date, the invoice or credit memo number, a purchase order number (if there is one), terms of the sale, due date, aging, and the amount of the open balance. The total amount due from each customer for all open invoices less credit memos is also listed.

When you view and print reports, each column of information is separated by a ◊ between the column headings. These diamonds may be used to change the size/width of a column. This is useful if the report is too wide to view on screen, if a column is taking up too much room, or a column does not contain any information.

MEMO

DATE: January 10, 1998

Renee needs to prepare and print an Open Invoices by Customer report to give to the owners, Eric and Matt, so they can see which invoices are open. When preparing the report, eliminate the column for P.O. # and adjust the width of the columns. The report should be one page wide without selecting the print option "Fit report to one page wide."

*DO: Prepare and print an Open Invoices by Customer Report

Click **Reports** menu, point to **A/R Reports**, click **Open Invoices**

OR

On the **Sales and Customers** tab of QuickBooks Navigator, click **Accounts Receivable** in the Reports section, click **Open Invoices**

Tab to or click the text box for the date, enter **011098** or **01/10/98**

Press Tab to generate the report

Click **Print**

- Be sure that "Fit report to one page wide" is not selected.

Click **Preview**

Click **Next Page** to see all of the pages in the report

- Page 3 contains one column of information.

Click **Zoom In** to see what information is contained on page 3

Click **Close** to close the Preview

Click **Cancel** to close Print Reports

Hide columns or resize the width of the columns so the report will fit on one page wide

- The column for P.O. # does not contain any information.

To hide the column from view, position the cursor on the diamond ◊ between **P.O. #** and **Terms**

- The cursor turns into a plus with arrows pointing left and right.

Hold down the primary mouse button

Drag the cursor from the ◊ between **P.O. #** and **Terms** to the ◊ between **P.O. #** and **Num**

- You will see a dotted vertical line while you are dragging the mouse and holding down the primary mouse button.
- When you release the primary mouse button, the column for **P.O. #** will not show on the screen.

Click **Print**

- Verify that **Fit report to one page wide** is not selected.
- If it is selected, click the check box to remove the check mark.

Click **Preview**

- The report will now fit on one page wide.
- The report may be two pages in length.

Click **Close** to close the Preview

Click **Print**

Mountain Adventure Ski Shoppe

Open Invoices by Customer

As of January 10, 1998

Type	Date	Num	Terms	Due Date	Aging	Open Balance
Chin, Melinda						
Invoice	01/01/98			01/01/98	9	53.63
Credit Memo	01/09/98	9		01/09/98	1	-53.57
Invoice	01/03/98	7	Net 30	02/02/98		1,028.41
Total Chin, Melinda						1,028.47
Clancy, Cheryl						
Invoice	01/01/98			01/01/98	9	455.00
Total Clancy, Cheryl						455.00
David, Ellen						
Invoice	01/01/98			01/01/98	9	1,136.00

Partial Report

Close the Open Invoices by Customer report

RECORD CASH SALES WITH SALES TAX

Not all sales in a business are on account. In many instances, payment is made at the time the merchandise is purchased. This is entered as a cash sale. Sales with cash, credit cards, or checks as the payment method are entered as cash sales. When entering a cash sale, you prepare a sales receipt rather than an invoice. QuickBooks records the transaction in the Journal and places the amount of cash received in an account called "Undeposited Funds." The funds received remain in Undeposited Funds until you record a deposit to your bank account.

MEMO:

DATE: January 11, 1998

Record the following cash sale: <u>Sales Receipt 1</u>—Received cash from a customer who purchased a pair of sunglasses, $29.95; a boot carrier, $2.99; and some lip balm, $1.19. Use "Thank you for your business." as the message.

*DO: Enter the above transaction as a cash sale to a cash customer
Click **Activities** menu, click **Enter Cash Sales**
    OR
Use QuickBooks Navigator
    Click **Sales and Customers** tab, click **Cash Sales** icon
Click the drop-down list arrow next to **Customer:Job**
Enter **Cash Customer**
Tab to **Template**

- Because Mountain Adventure Ski Shoppe does not have a customer named Cash Customer, a Customer:Job Not Found dialog box appears on the screen.

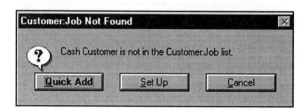

Click **Quick Add** to add the customer name Cash Customer to the Customer list
- Details regarding Cash Customer are not required, so Quick Add is the appropriate method to use to add the name to the list.
- Now that the customer name has been added to the Customer:Job list, the cursor moves to the Template field.
Template should be **Custom Cash Sales**
- If not, click the drop-down list arrow and click Custom Cash Sales.
Tab to or click **Date**, type **01/11/98**
Sales No. should be **1**
Click the drop-down list arrow next to **PAYMENT METH**, click **Cash**
Tab to or click beneath **Item**
Click the drop-down list arrow next to **Item**, click **Accessories**
Tab to or click **Qty**, type **1**

Tab to or click **Rate**, enter **29.95**
- When you move to the next field, the total for **Amount** is calculated automatically.

Tab to or click the next line in **Item**

Click the drop-down list arrow next to **Item**, click **Accessories**

Tab to or click **Qty**, type **1**

Tab to or click **Rate**, enter **2.99**
- The Total for **Amount** is calculated when you move to the next field.

Repeat the steps above to enter $1.19 for the lip balm
- Total for **Amount** is calculated when you go to the Customer Message.

Click **Customer Message**

Click the drop-down list arrow for Customer Message, click **Thank you for your business.**
- Message is inserted.

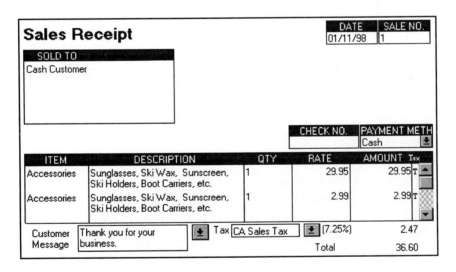

PRINT SALES RECEIPT

*DO: Print the sales receipt immediately after entering information

Click **Print** button on the right side of the **Enter Cash Sales** screen

To print with Lines around each Field, the check box should have a ✓
- If it is not checked, click the box to insert the check mark.

While the sales receipt is printing, a dialog box **"Did form(s) print OK?"** will appear on the screen

When the form has been correctly printed, click **OK**

Click **OK** on the right side of the Enter Cash Sales screen to exit and close the sales receipt

ENTERING A CREDIT CARD SALE

A credit card sale is treated exactly like a cash sale. When you prepare the sales receipt, the payment method selected is credit card. The credit cards available on the payment method list are American Express, Discover, MasterCard, and Visa. Except for American Express, the credit card deposits are made into the checking or bank account, and bank fees for the charge cards are deducted directly from the bank account. Because American Express is not a "bank" charge card, charge receipts are sent to American Express, and American Express sends a check to the company for the amount of the charge, less American Express fees.

MEMO

DATE: January 11, 1998

Enter a sale to a customer using a Visa card. Identify the customer as Cash Customer. The sale was for a sled, $199.95. Use "Thank you for your business." as the message.

---

*DO: Record the credit card sale
Click **Activities** menu, click **Enter Cash Sales**
    OR
Use QuickBooks Navigator:
    Click **Sales and Customers** tab, click **Cash Sales** icon
Click the drop-down list arrow next to **Customer:Job**, click **Cash Customer**
Tab to **Template**, template should be **Custom Cash Sales**
• If not, click the drop-down list arrow and click Custom Cash Sales.
Tab to or click **Date**, type **01/11/98**
Sales No. should be **2**
Click the drop-down list arrow next to **PAYMENT METH**, click **VISA**
Tab to or click beneath **Item**
Click the drop-down list arrow next to **Item**, click **Sleds**
Tab to or click **Qty**, type **1**
Tab to or click **Rate**, enter **199.95**
• The total for **Amount** is calculated when you go to the Customer Message.
Click **Customer Message**
Click the drop-down list arrow for Customer Message, click **Thank you for your business.**
• Message is inserted.

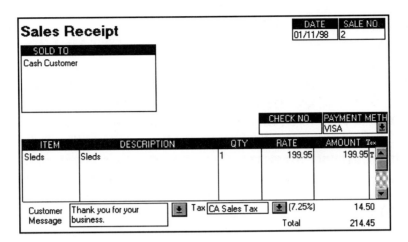

Print the sales receipt immediately after entering information

Click >>**Next** to go to Sales Receipt 3

RECORD SALES PAID BY CHECK

A sale paid for with a check is considered a cash sale. A sales receipt is prepared to record the sale.

MEMO

DATE: January 11, 1998

We do take checks for sales even if a customer is from out of town. Record the sale of 2 pairs of socks at $15.99 each to a cash customer using check number 5589. The message for the sales receipt is "Thank you for your business."

---

 *DO: With Sales Receipt 3 on the screen, enter the information for the above transaction

Click the drop-down list arrow next to **Customer:Job**, click **Cash Customer**

Tab to **Template**

- This should have **Custom Cash Sales** as the template. If not, click the drop-down list arrow and click Custom Cash Sales.

Tab to or click **Date**, type **01/11/98**

Sales No. should be **3**

Tab to or click **Check No.**, type **5589**

Click the drop-down list arrow next to **PAYMENT METH**, click **Check**

Tab to or click beneath **Item**

Click the drop-down list arrow next to **Item**, click **Socks**

Tab to or click **Qty**, type **2**

Tab to or click **Rate**, enter **15.99**

• Total is automatically calculated when you go to the Customer Message.

Click **Customer Message**

Click the drop-down list arrow for Customer Message, click **Thank you for your business.**

Print Sales Receipt 3

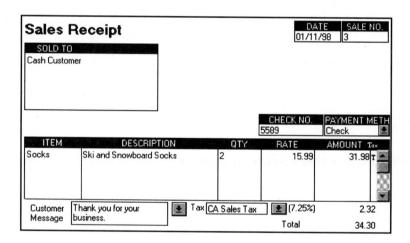

Click **>>Next** button to go to Sales Receipt 4

ENTER CASH SALES TRANSACTIONS WITHOUT STEP-BY-STEP INSTRUCTIONS

MEMO

DATE: January 12, 1998

After a record snowfall, the store is really busy. Use Cash Customer as the customer name for the transactions. Record the following cash, check, and credit card sales:

Sales Receipt 4—A cash customer used Check #196 to purchase a ski parka, $249.95; ski pants, $129.95; and a ski sweater, $89.95.

Sales Receipt 5—A cash customer used a MasterCard to purchase a snowboard, $389.95; snowboard boots, $229.95; and snowboard bindings, $189.95.

Sales Receipt 6—A cash customer purchased gloves for $89.95.

*DO: Repeat the procedures used to enter Sales Receipts 1, 2, and 3 to record the additional transactions listed above:
- Always use the Item list to determine the appropriate sales items for billing.
- Use **Thank you for your business.** as the message for these sales receipts.
- Print each sales receipt immediately after entering the information for it.
- If you make an error, correct it.
- To go from one sales receipt to the next, click >>**NEXT** button on the right side of the Enter Cash Sales screen rather than **OK**.
- Click **OK** after you have entered and printed Sales Receipt 6.

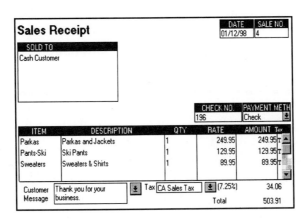

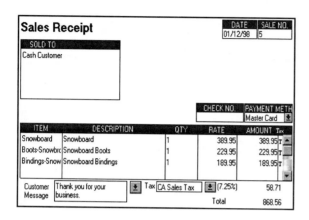
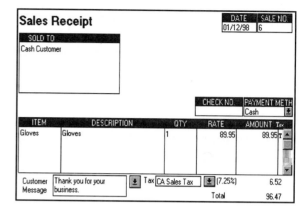

PRINT SUMMARY SALES BY ITEM REPORT

The Summary Sales by Item report analyzes the quantity of merchandise on hand by item, gives the amount or value of the merchandise, gives the percentage of the total sales of each item, and calculates the average price per item, the cost of goods sold for each item, the average cost of goods sold for each item, the gross margin for each item, and the percentage of gross margin for each item. Information regarding the total inventory is also provided. This includes the value of the total inventory, the cost of goods sold for the inventory, and the gross margin for the inventory of merchandise.

MEMO

DATE: January 15, 1998

At the middle of the month, Renee prepares a Summary Sales by Item report to obtain information about sales, inventory, and merchandise costs. Prepare this report in landscape form for 1/1/98–1/15/98. Adjust the widths of the column so the report prints on one page without selecting the print option "Fit report to one page wide."

---

*DO: Prepare the above report

Click **Reports** on the menu bar, point to **Sales Reports**, click **By Item Summary**
OR
Click **Sales and Customers** tab on QuickBooks Navigator, click **Sales** in the **Reports** section, click **By Item Summary**
Tab to or click **From**, enter **010198**

- The "/" between the elements of the date is optional.

Tab to or click **To**, enter **011598**

Tab to generate the report

Scroll through the report

Click **Print**

Click **Landscape** to select **Orientation: Landscape**

Click **Preview**

Click **Next Page**

- Notice that the report does not fit on one page wide.

Click **Close**

Click **Cancel** to return to the report

Position the cursor on the ◇ between columns

Drag to resize the columns

- The names of the column headings should appear in full.
- The column headings should not have **...** as part of the heading.

If you get a **Resize Columns** dialog box wanting to know if all columns should be the same size, click **No**

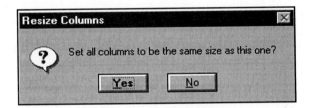

When the columns have been resized, click **Print** and **Preview**

When the report fits on one page wide, print the report

Mountain Adventure Ski Shoppe
Summary Sales by Item
January 1 - 15, 1998

| | Jan 1 - 15, '98 | | | |
	◇ Avg Price ◇	COGS ◇	Avg COGS ◇	Gross Margin ◇	Gross Margin % ◇
Parkas	249.48	116.66	58.33	382.29	76.6%
Poles-Ski	36.67	180.00	30.00	40.00	18.2%
Skis	359.86	700.00	100.00	1,819.00	72.2%
Sleds	133.32	405.00	67.50	394.90	49.4%
Snowboard	444.95	200.00	100.00	689.90	77.5%
Socks	15.98	9.00	3.00	38.93	81.2%
Sweaters	107.48	50.00	25.00	164.95	76.7%
Toboggans	229.95	687.50	137.50	462.25	40.2%
Underwear	68.00	8.00	8.00	60.00	88.2%
Total Inventory		3,372.46		5,548.74	62.2%

Partial Report

CORRECT A SALES RECEIPT AND PRINT THE CORRECTED FORM

QuickBooks makes correcting errors "user friendly." When an error is discovered in a transaction such as a cash sale, you can simply return to the form where the transaction was recorded and correct the error. Thus, to correct a sales receipt, you could click on Activities, click on Enter Cash Sales, click the Prev button until you found the appropriate sales receipt, and then correct the error. However, because cash or checks received for cash sales are held in the Undeposited Funds account until the bank deposit is made, a sales receipt can be accessed through the Undeposited Funds account in the Chart of Accounts. Accessing the receipt in this manner allows you to see all the transactions entered in the account for Undeposited Funds.

When a correction for a sale is made, QuickBooks not only changes the form, it also changes all journal and account entries for the transaction to reflect the correction. QuickBooks then allows a corrected sales receipt to be printed.

MEMO

DATE: January 15, 1998

After reviewing transaction information, you realize that the date for Sales Receipt No. 1 was entered incorrectly. Change the date to 01/08/98.

---

*DO: Correct the error indicated in the memo above, and print a corrected sales receipt
Open the Chart of Accounts:
Click **Accnt** button
OR

Click **Lists** menu, click **Chart of Accounts**
OR
Use the keyboard shortcut **Ctrl+A**
Click **Undeposited Funds**

Chart of Accounts		
Name	Type	Balance
◆ 1100 · Checking	Bank	25,943.00
◆ 1200 · Accounts Receivable	Accounts Receivable	14,339.03
◆ 1120 · Inventory Asset	Other Current Asset	32,176.54
◆ 1310 · Supplies	Other Current Asset	1,425.00
◆ 1311 · Office Supplies	Other Current Asset	850.00
◆ 1312 · Sales Supplies	Other Current Asset	575.00
◆ 1340 · Prepaid Insurance	Other Current Asset	250.00
◆ 1499 · Undeposited Funds	Other Current Asset	1,754.29
◆ 1510 · Office Equipment	Fixed Asset	5,000.00

Account ▼ Activities ▼ Reports ▼ Show All

Click **Activities** button
Click **Use Register**
- The register maintains a record of all the transactions recorded within the Undeposited Funds account.

Date	Ref	Payee		Decrease	✓	Increase	Balance
	Type	Account	Memo				
01/11/98	1	Cash Customer				36.60	36.60
	RCPT	-split-					
01/11/98	2	Cash Customer				214.45	251.05
	RCPT	-split-					
01/11/98	3	Cash Customer				34.30	285.35
	RCPT	-split-					
01/12/98	4	Cash Customer				503.91	789.26
	RCPT	-split-					

1499 · Undeposited Funds

Edit

Q-Report   Go To   ☐ 1-Line

Ending balance   1,754.29

Click anywhere in the transaction for Sale No. 1
- Look at the Ref/Type column to see the type of transaction.
- The number in the Ref line indicates the number of the sales receipt or the customer's check number.
- Type shows RCPT for a sales receipt.
Click **Edit**
- The sales receipt appears on the screen.
Tab to or click **Date** field
Change the Date to **01/08/98**: position insert line between 01/ and 11/98, press **Delete** two times to delete the 11, type **08**
Click **Print** button on the Enter Cash Sales screen to print a corrected sales receipt
Click **Print** on the Print "One Sales Receipt" screen
On the **"Did form(s) print OK?"** screen, click **OK**

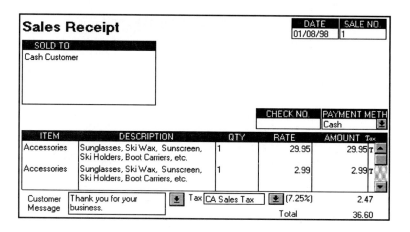

> Click **OK** on the Enter Cash Sales screen to record changes, close Sales Receipt, and return to the Register for Undeposited Funds
> Do not close the Register

VIEW A QUICKREPORT

After editing the sales receipt and returning to the register, you may get a detailed report regarding the customer's transactions by clicking the Q-Report button. If you use Cash Customer for all cash sales, a Q-Report will be for all the transactions of Cash Customer.

 *DO: After closing the sales receipt, you returned to the register for the Undeposited Funds account

Click **Q-Report** button to display the Register QuickReport for **Cash Customer**

Because there are no entries in the Memo and Clr columns, drag the ◊ between columns to eliminate the columns for **Memo** and **Clr**

Widen the column with the account name **Undeposited Funds** until the account name appears in full

Mountain Adventure Ski Shoppe
Register QuickReport
All Transactions

◊ Type	◊ Date	◊ Num	◊ Account	◊ Split	◊ Amount
Cash Customer					
Cash Sale	01/08/98	1	1499 · Undeposited Funds	-SPLIT-	36.60
Cash Sale	01/11/98	2	1499 · Undeposited Funds	-SPLIT-	214.45
Cash Sale	01/11/98	3	1499 · Undeposited Funds	-SPLIT-	34.30
Cash Sale	01/12/98	4	1499 · Undeposited Funds	-SPLIT-	503.91
Cash Sale	01/12/98	5	1499 · Undeposited Funds	-SPLIT-	868.56
Cash Sale	01/12/98	6	1499 · Undeposited Funds	-SPLIT-	96.47
Total Cash Customer					1,754.29
TOTAL					**1,754.29**

ANALYZE THE QUICKREPORT FOR CASH CUSTOMER

 *DO: All transactions for Cash Customer appear in the report
- Notice that the date for Sales Receipt 1 has been changed to **01/08/98**.
The account used is Undeposited Funds
The Split column contains the other accounts used in the transactions
- For all the transactions you see the word **-Split-** rather than an account name.
  - Split means that more than one account was used for this portion of the transaction.
  - In addition to a variety of sales items, sales tax was charged on all sales, so each transaction will show **-Split-** even if only one item was sold as in Sales Receipt 2.
View the accounts used for the Split by using QuickZoom to view the actual Sales Receipt
Use QuickZoom by double clicking anywhere on the information for Sales Receipt 2
- The accounts used are Sleds and Sales Tax.
Close the Sales Receipt
Close the report without printing
Close the Register for Undeposited Funds
Do not close the Chart of Accounts

VIEW SALES TAX PAYABLE REGISTER

The sales tax payable register shows a detailed listing of all transactions with sales tax. The option of 1-Line may be selected in order to view each transaction on one line rather than the standard two lines. The account register provides information regarding the vendor and the account used for the transaction.

 *DO: View the register for the Sales Tax Payable account
Click **Sales Tax Payable** in the Chart of Accounts
Click **Activities** button at the bottom of the Chart of Accounts, click **Use Register**

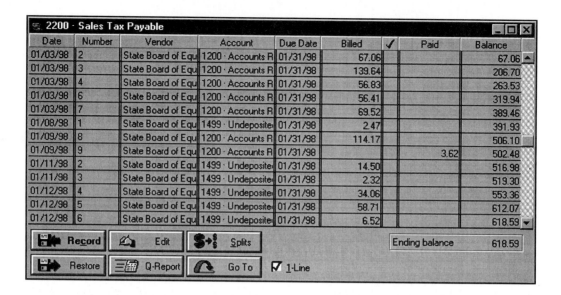

Once the register is displayed on the screen, click **1-Line** to view the transactions
on single lines
Close the Register for Sales Tax Payable, and close the Chart of Accounts

RECORD CUSTOMER PAYMENTS ON ACCOUNT

When customers pay the amount they owe, QuickBooks places the money received in an account
called "Undeposited Funds." The money stays in the account until a bank deposit is made. When
you start to record a payment made by a customer, you see the customer's balance, any credits
made to the account, and a complete list of outstanding invoices. QuickBooks automatically
applies the payment received to the oldest invoice.

MEMO

DATE: January 15, 1998

Record the following cash receipt of check no. 765 for $975 from Melvin Vernon as
payment in full.

---

*DO: Record the above payment on account:
Click **Activities**, click **Receive Payments**
OR

Use QuickBooks Navigator:

 Click **Sales and Customers** tab, click **Receive Payments**

Click drop-down list for **Customer:Job**, click **Vernon, Melvin**

- Notice that the current date shows in the **Date** column and that the total amount owed appears as the balance.
- At the bottom of the Receive Payments screen, notice that the unpaid invoice for Melvin Vernon shows under Outstanding Invoices/Statement Charges.

Tab to or click **Date**, type date **01/15/98**

Tab to or click **Amount**, enter **975**

- QuickBooks will enter the **.00** when you tab to or click Pmt. Method.

Click drop-down list arrow for **Pmt. Method**

- Notice that the cursor moves into the Pmt. Method text box and that the payment amount is entered in the Payment column for Outstanding Invoices/Statement Charges.

Click **Check**

Tab to or click **Check No.**, enter **765**

- QuickBooks automatically applies the payment to the oldest open invoice.

Click **>>Next** to record this payment and advance to the next **Receive Payments** screen

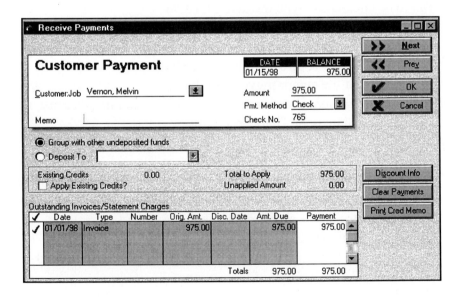

RECORD CUSTOMER PAYMENT ON ACCOUNT AND APPLY CREDIT

If there are any existing credits (such as a Credit Memo) on an account that have not been applied to the account, they may be applied to a customer's account when a payment is made.

MEMO

DATE: January 18, 1998

Melinda Chin sent Check Number 1026 for $1,028.47 to pay her account in full. Apply existing credits to the Outstanding Invoices/Statement Charges.

---

*DO: Record the payment by Melinda Chin and apply existing credits to her outstanding invoices and statement charges

Click drop-down list for **Customer:Job**, click **Chin, Melinda**

- Notice that the current date shows in the **Date** column and that the total amount owed appears as the balance.
- At the bottom of the Receive Payments screen, notice that the unpaid invoices for Melinda Chin show under Outstanding Invoices/Statement Charges.
- In the center of the Receive Payments window is information regarding existing credits. Melinda has $53.57 in existing credits that may be applied to her account.

Tab to or click **Date**, type the date **01/18/98**

Tab to or click **Amount**, enter **1028.47**

- Notice that this amount is different from the balance of $1,082.04.

Click drop-down list arrow for **Pmt. Method**

- Notice that the cursor moves into the Pmt. Method text box and that the payment amount is entered in the Payment column for Outstanding Invoices/Statement Charges.

Click **Check**

Tab to or click **Check No.**, enter **1026**

- QuickBooks automatically applies payments to the oldest invoice first.
- On the Outstanding Invoices/Statement Charges the original invoice is paid in full, and Invoice 7 shows a payment of $974.84.

Complete the information to Apply Existing Credits:

- Notice that the Existing Credits are $53.57 and that the Total to Apply is $1,028.47—the amount of the payment.

Click the check box for **Apply Existing Credits** to insert a ✓ and to select
  - The Total to Apply is now $1,082.04.
  - Outstanding Invoices/Statement Charges shows Invoice 7 receiving a payment of $1,028.41, and the Total for Payments matches the amount shown as **Balance**.

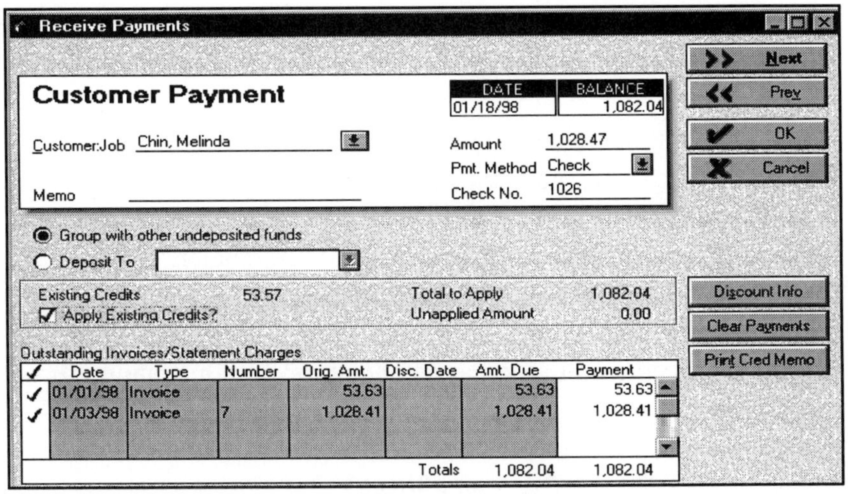

Click >>**Next** to record this payment and to advance to the next **Receive Payments** screen

RECORD PAYMENT ON ACCOUNT FROM A CUSTOMER QUALIFYING FOR AN EARLY-PAYMENT DISCOUNT

Each customer may be assigned terms as part of the customer information. When terms such as 1% 10 Net 30 or 2% 10 Net 30 are given, customers whose payments are received within ten days of the invoice date are eligible to deduct 1% or 2% from the amount owed when making their payments.

MEMO
DATE: January 18, 1998

Received payment from Mammoth Recreation Center for Invoice 8. Check No. 981-13 was for $1672.01 as full payment. Record the payment and the 1% discount for early payment under the invoice terms of 1% 10 Net 30.

---

*DO: Record the receipt of the check and apply the discount to the above transaction
Click drop-down list for **Customer:Job**
Click **Mammoth Recreation Center**
- Notice that the current date shows in the **Date** column and that the total amount owed, $1,688.90, appears as the balance.

- At the bottom of the Receive Payments screen, notice that the unpaid invoice for Mammoth Recreation Center shows under Outstanding Invoices/Statement Charges.
- Notice that the column for Disc. Date shows the date of 01/19/98.

Tab to or click **Date**, type date **01/18/98**

Tab to or click **Amount**, enter **1672.01**

- Notice that this amount is different from the balance of $1,688.90.

Click drop-down list arrow for **Pmt. Method**

- Notice that the cursor moves into the Pmt. Method text box and the payment amount is entered in the Payment column for Outstanding Invoices/Statement Charges.

Click **Check**

Tab to or click **Check No.**, enter **981-13**

Tab to or click **Memo**, type **Includes Early Payment Discount**

Click the button for **Discount Info**

Click the drop-down list arrow for **Discount Account**, click **6130 Sales Discount**

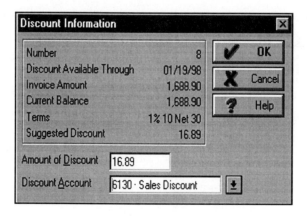

Click **OK** to apply the discount of $16.89

- Notice that the Amount Due on Invoice 8 changes to $1,672.01 because the discount has been subtracted from the total amount due.

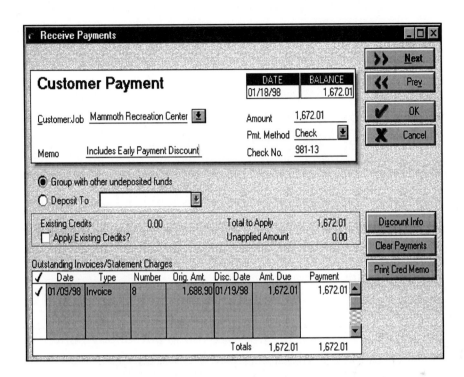

- If you make an error in applying the discount, click Cancel and re-enter the transaction.

Click **>>Next** to record this payment and to advance to the next **Receive Payments** screen

MEMO

DATE: January 18, 1998

Received Check No. 152 from Roger Wilson for $919.41
Received Check No. 8252 dated January 11 and postmarked 1/12 for $2024.33 from Mammoth Schools. Even though the date we are recording the payment is after the discount date, the check was postmarked within the discount period. Apply the discount for early payment to this transaction. This receipt requires an item as a Memo. The memo is: Includes Early Payment Discount.
Received Check No. 3951 from Dr. Jose Moreno for $1,087.51.
Received Check No. 1051 for $500 from Ellen David in partial payment of account. Record the memo: Partial Payment.
Received Check No. 563 from Sara Pitcher for $408.48 in payment of the January 1 balance.
Received Check No. 819 from Tim Tyler for $100 in partial payment of his account.

   *DO: Refer to the previous steps listed to enter the above payments:

Click **>>NEXT** to go from one Receive Payments screen to the next

- Any discounts or partial payments should be noted as a Memo on the Customer Payment slip.

Click the **OK** button after all payments received have been recorded

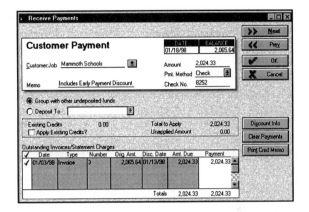

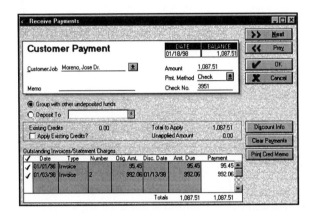

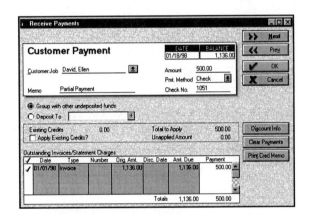

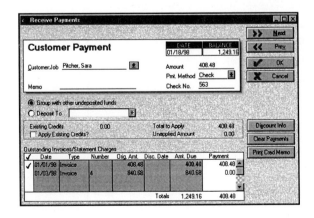

VIEW TRANSACTIONS BY CUSTOMER REPORT

In order to see the transactions for customers, you need to prepare a Transaction Report by Customer. This report shows all sales, credits, and payments for each customer on account and for the customer named Cash Customer. The report does not show the balance remaining on account for the individual customers.

 *DO: Click **Reports** on the menu bar
Point to **Transaction Reports**
Click **By Customer**
    OR
Use QuickBooks Navigator:
    Click **Sales and Customers** tab
    Click **Sales** under the **Reports** option at the bottom of the screen
    Click **Transaction by Customer**
Click the drop-down list arrow for **Dates**, click **Custom**
Tab to or click **From**, enter **01/01/98**
Tab to or click **To**, enter **01/18/98**
Tab to generate the report
Scroll through the report

- Notice that information is shown for the opening balances, invoices, cash sales, credit memo, and payments made on the accounts.
- Notice that the **Num** column shows the invoice numbers, sales receipt numbers, credit memo number, and check numbers.

Click **Close** to exit the report

Mountain Adventure Ski Shoppe
Transactions by Customer
January 1 - 18, 1998

Type	◇ Date	◇ Num ◇	Memo	◇ Account	◇ Clr ◇	Split	◇ Amount
Cash Custo...							
Cash Sale	01/08/98	1		1499 · Undeposite...		-SPLIT-	36.60
Cash Sale	01/11/98	2		1499 · Undeposite...		-SPLIT-	214.45
Cash Sale	01/11/98	3		1499 · Undeposite...		-SPLIT-	34.30
Cash Sale	01/12/98	4		1499 · Undeposite...		-SPLIT-	503.91
Cash Sale	01/12/98	5		1499 · Undeposite...		-SPLIT-	868.56
Cash Sale	01/12/98	6		1499 · Undeposite...		-SPLIT-	96.47
Chin, Me...							
Invoice	01/01/98		Opening bal...	1200 · Accounts R...		4999 · Unca...	53.63
Invoice	01/03/98	7		1200 · Accounts R...		-SPLIT-	1,028.41
Credit Memo	01/09/98	9		1200 · Accounts R...		-SPLIT-	-53.57
Payment	01/18/98	1026		1499 · Undeposite...		1200 · Acco...	1,028.47

Partial Report

PRINT CUSTOMER BALANCE SUMMARY

A report that will show you the balance owed by each customer is the Customer Balance Summary. The report presents the total balance owed by each customer as of a certain date.

MEMO

DATE: January 18, 1998

The owners, Eric and Matt, want to see how much each customer owes to Mountain Adventure Ski Shoppe. Print a Customer Balance Summary report.

---

*DO: Click **Reports** on the menu bar
        Point to **A/R Reports**
        Click **Customer Balance Summary**
            OR
        Use QuickBooks Navigator:
            Click **Sales and Customers** tab
            Under the **Reports** option at the bottom of the screen, click **Accounts Receivable**
            Click **Customer Balance Summary**
        Print the report using **Portrait Orientation**

Mountain Adventure Ski Shoppe
Customer Balance Summary
All Transactions

	◇ Jan 18, '98 ◇
Clancy, Cheryl ▶	455.00 ◀
David, Ellen	636.00
Donaldson, Fran	650.00
Finley, Viv Dr.	417.00
Jones, Richard	1,085.00
Pitcher, Sara	840.68
Travis, Carrie	670.31
Tyler, Tim	811.63
TOTAL	**5,565.62**

Close the report

DEPOSIT CHECKS AND CREDIT CARD RECEIPTS
FOR CASH SALES AND PAYMENTS ON ACCOUNT

When cash sales are made and payments on accounts are received, QuickBooks places the money received in the "Undeposited Funds" account. Once the deposit is recorded, the funds are transferred from "Undeposited Funds" to the account selected when preparing the deposit.

MEMO

DATE: January 18, 1998

Deposit all checks and credit card receipts for cash sales and payments on account.

---

*DO: Deposit checks and credit card receipts

Click **Activities** on the menu bar, click **Make Deposits**
   OR
Use QuickBooks Navigator:
   Click **Sales and Customers**, click **Deposits**
- **Payments to Deposit** window shows all amounts received for cash sales and payments on account that have not been deposited in the bank.
- Notice the ✓ column to the left of the Date column is empty.
Click ✓✓✓**Select All** button
- Notice the check marks in the ✓ column.

✓	Date	Type	No.	Pmt Meth	Name	Amount
✓	01/18/98	PMT	1026	Check	Chin, Melinda	1,028.47
✓	01/18/98	PMT	981-13	Check	Mammoth Recreat	1,672.01
✓	01/18/98	PMT	152	Check	Wilson, Roger	919.41
✓	01/18/98	PMT	8252	Check	Mammoth Schools	2,024.33
✓	01/18/98	PMT	3951	Check	Moreno, Jose Dr.	1,087.51
✓	01/18/98	PMT	1051	Check	David, Ellen	500.00
✓	01/18/98	PMT	563	Check	Pitcher, Sara	408.48
✓	01/18/98	PMT	819	Check	Tyler, Tim	100.00
✓	01/12/98	RCPT	5	Master Card	Cash Customer	868.56
✓	01/11/98	RCPT	2	VISA	Cash Customer	214.45

Payments to Deposit — Select undeposited payments to deposit. Click OK when you have finished. Buttons: OK, Cancel, Help, Select All, Select None

Partial List

Click **OK** to close Payments to Deposit screen and open Make Deposits screen

On the Make Deposits screen, **Deposit To** should be **1100 Checking**
Date should be **01/18/98**
- Tab to date and change if not correct.

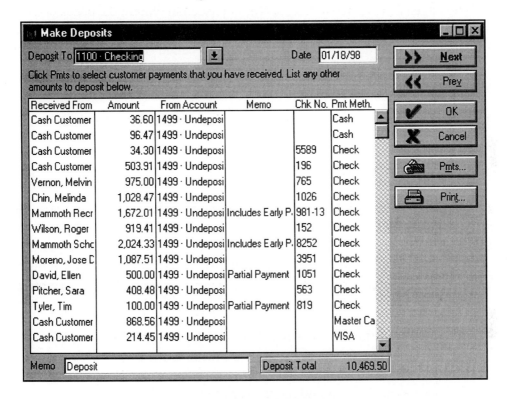

Click **Print** button to print **Deposit Summary**
If a List Reports dialog box appears, click **OK**

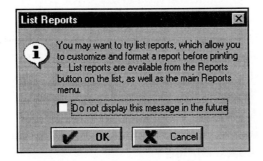

Click **Print** on the **Print Lists** dialog box
When printing is finished, click **OK** on Make Deposits to record and close

RECORD THE RETURN OF A CHECK BECAUSE OF NONSUFFICIENT FUNDS

If a customer pays you with a check and the check bounces, the amount of the check and the associated bank charges need to be subtracted from the account where the check was deposited; and the Accounts Receivable account needs to be updated to show the amount the customer owes you for the check that bounced. This type of check is also called "nonsufficient funds" or NSF. In order to track the amount of a bad check and to charge a customer for the bank charges and any penalties you impose, Other Charge items may need to be created.

MEMO

DATE: January 20, 1998

The bank returned Tim Tyler's Check No. 819 for $100 marked NSF. The bank imposed a $10 service charge for the NSF check. Mountain Adventure Ski Shoppe charges a $15 fee for NSF checks. Record the NSF and related charges on an invoice to Tim Tyler. Add any necessary items for Other Charges to the Items list.

---

 *DO: Prepare an invoice to record the NSF check and related charges indicated above
- The invoice is prepared to increase the amount that Tim Tyler owes. That amount will include the bad check and the fees for the bad check.

Access Invoice 10 as previously instructed

Click the drop-down list arrow for **Customer:Job**, click **Tyler, Tim**

Tab to or click **Date**, enter **012098**

Click drop-down list arrow for **Terms**, click **Due on receipt**

Click the drop-down list arrow for **Item Code**
- You need to add an item that will identify the transaction as a bad check. Because you are preparing an invoice to record the NSF check, using this item will keep the bad check from being incorrectly identified as a sale.

Click **<Add New>**

Click **Other Charge**

Enter **Bad Check** as the **Item Name/Number**

Tab to or click **Description**

Enter **Check returned by bank.**

Price should be **0.00**

Remove the ✓ by clicking the check box next to **Taxable**

Click the drop-down list arrow for **Account**

Click **1100 Checking**

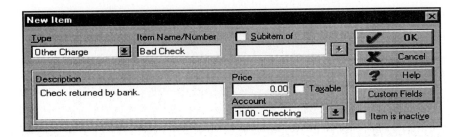

Click **OK**

Click or tab to **Price Each**

Enter **100**

- This is the amount of Tim's bad check.
- QuickBooks will insert the decimal point and two zeros.

Tab to or click the next line for **Item Code**, click the drop-down list arrow for
Item Code

- Another item needs be added in order to identify the amount that Tim owes
for the NSF charges from the bank and from Mountain Adventure Ski Shoppe.

Click **<Add New>**

- The list for **Type** automatically appears.

Click **Other Charge** for **Type**

Tab to or click **Item Name/Number**

Enter **Bad Ck Chrg**

Tab to or click **Description**

Enter **Bank service and other charges for returned check.**

Price should be **0.00**

Remove the ✓ by clicking the check box next to **Taxable**

Click the drop-down list arrow for **Account**

Scroll through the list of accounts

- There are no appropriate accounts for this item.

Add a new account to the Chart of Accounts by clicking **<Add New>** at the top of
the list for the Accounts

Type of account is **Income**

Enter **4040** for the **Number**

Tab to or click **Name**

Enter **Returned Check Service Charges**

Click **OK** to record the new account in the Chart of Accounts

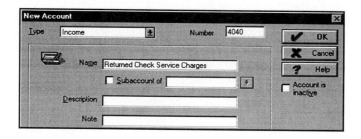

Account 4040 is inserted as the **Account** for the **New Item**

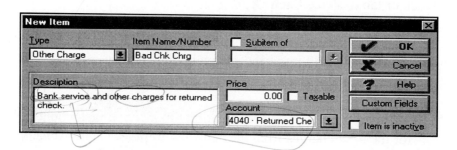

Click **OK** to add Bad Chk Chrg to item list

Tab to or click **Price Each**

Enter **25**

- This is the total amount of the charges Tim has incurred for the NSF check.

Click drop-down list arrow for **Customer Message**, click **Please remit to above address.**

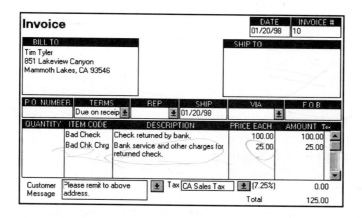

Print the Invoice

Click **OK** to save and exit Create Invoices

- You may get a message box regarding the change in terms for Tim Tyler.

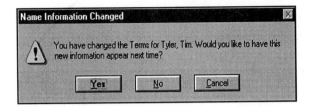

Click **No**

ISSUE A CREDIT MEMO AND A REFUND CHECK

If merchandise is returned and the invoice has been paid in full or the sale was for cash, a refund check may be issued at the same time as the credit memo is prepared. Simply clicking a Refund button instructs QuickBooks to prepare the refund check for you.

MEMO

DATE: January 20, 1998

Dr. Jose Moreno returned the ski poles he purchased for $75 January 3 on Invoice 2. He has already paid his bill in full. Record the return and issue a check refunding the $75 plus tax.

---

*DO: Prepare Credit Memo to record the return of the ski poles and issue a refund check
Issue a credit memo as previously instructed
Use the Customer Message **Thank you for your business.**

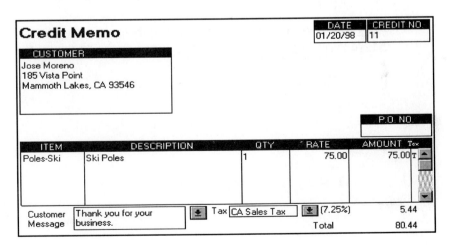

Once the Credit Memo is complete, click **Refund** button
The completed check appears on the screen

- Note: You may have to change the date on the check.
- If so, follow the usual procedures to highlight the existing day, delete the date, and enter 01/20/98.

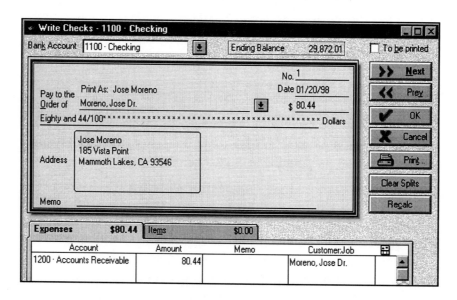

Click **Print** button to print the check
Click **OK** button on **Print Check** dialog box to print check number 1

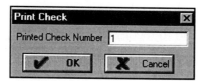

Click **Print** on the **Print Checks** dialog box
- Make sure Standard Checks are selected as the check style.

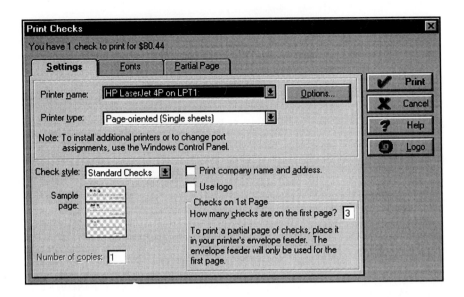

When finished printing the check, click **OK** for **Did check(s) print OK?**
Click **OK** on the **Write Checks** screen
Click **Print** on the Credit Memo to print Credit Memo 11
•   Print on blank paper with lines around each field.
Click **OK** to answer **Did form(s) print OK?**
Click **OK** to record the credit memo and exit

PRINT JOURNAL

Even though QuickBooks displays registers and reports in a manner that focuses on the
transaction—that is, entering a sale on account via an invoice rather than a Sales Journal or a
General Journal—it still keeps a General Journal. The Journal records each transaction and lists
the accounts and the amounts for debit and credit entries.

*DO: Print the Journal
Click **Reports**, point to **Other Reports**, click **Journal**
     OR
Use QuickBooks Navigator: Click **Company** tab, click **Other** under **Reports**,
     click **Journal**
Tab to **From** date, enter **01/01/98**
Tab to **To** field, enter **01/20/98**
Tab to generate the report
Scroll through the report to view the transactions
Click **Print** button

On the Print Reports screen, the settings will be the same as those used previously except:
Click **Landscape** to select Landscape orientation
Click on **Fit report to one page wide** to select this item
Click **Print**

		Mountain Adventure Ski Shoppe						

Journal

January 1 - 20, 1998

Trans # ◇	Type ◇	Date ◇	Num ◇	Name ◇	Memo ◇	Account ◇	Debit ◇	Credit
1	Inventory Adjust	01/01/98			Pants O...	3010 · Boyd & W...		1,750.00
					Pants O...	1120 · Inventory...	1,750.00	
							1,750.00	1,750.00
2	Inventory Adjust	01/01/98			Access...	3010 · Boyd & W...		2,925.00
					Access...	1120 · Inventory...	2,925.00	
							2,925.00	2,925.00
3	Inventory Adjust	01/01/98			Bindings...	3010 · Boyd & W...		3,750.00
					Bindings...	1120 · Inventory...	3,750.00	
							3,750.00	3,750.00
4	Inventory Adjust	01/01/98			Bindings...	3010 · Boyd & W...		3,750.00
					Bindings...	1120 · Inventory...	3,750.00	

Partial Report

Close the report

PRINT THE TRIAL BALANCE

When all sales transactions have been entered, it is important to print the trial balance and verify that the total debits equal the total credits.

 *DO: Click **Reports**, point to **Other**, click **Trial Balance**
OR
Use QuickBooks Navigator: Click **Company** tab, click **Other** under **Reports**, click **Trial Balance**
The report dates are **From 01/01/98 To 01/20/98**
Tab to generate the report
Print the Trial Balance in **Portrait** orientation
Click on **Fit report to one page wide** to deselect this item
Click **Print**

Mountain Adventure Ski Shoppe
Trial Balance
As of January 20, 1998

	Jan 20, '98	
	Debit	Credit
2510 · Office Equipment Loan		3,000.00
2520 · Store Fixtures Loan		2,500.00
3010 · Boyd & Wayne Capital		26,777.00
3011 · Eric Boyd, Investment		20,000.00
3012 · Matthew Wayne, Investment		20,000.00
4011 · Clothing & Accessory Sales		1,409.76
4012 · Equipment Sales		7,436.44
4040 · Returned Check Service Charges		25.00
4999 · Uncategorized Income		6,942.50
5000 · Cost of Goods Sold	3,342.46	
6130 · Sales Discount	447.17	
6999 · Uncategorized Expenses	8,500.00	
TOTAL	97,353.85	97,353.85

Partial Report

Close the report

GRAPHS IN QUICKBOOKS®

Once transactions have been entered, transaction results can be visually represented in a graphic form. QuickBooks illustrates Accounts Receivable by Aging Period as a bar chart, and it illustrates Accounts Receivable by Customer as a pie chart. For further details, double-click on an individual section of the pie chart or chart legend to create a bar chart analyzing an individual customer. QuickBooks also prepares graphs based on sales and will show the results of sales by item and by customer.

PREPARE ACCOUNTS RECEIVABLE GRAPHS

Accounts Receivable graphs illustrate account information based on the age of the account and the percentage of accounts receivable owed by each customer.

*DO: Prepare an accounts receivable graph
Click **Reports** on the menu bar, point to **Graphs**, click **Accounts Receivable**
OR
Use QuickBooks Navigator: Click **Sales and Customers** tab, click **Accounts Receivable** under **Reports**

Click **Accounts Receivable Graph**
Click **Dates** button on the QuickInsight: Accounts Receivable Graphs
On the **Change Graph Dates** change **Show Aging As of** to **01/20/98**
Click **OK**
- QuickBooks generates a bar chart illustrating Accounts Receivable by Aging Period and a pie chart illustrating Accounts Receivable by Customer.

Click **Print**

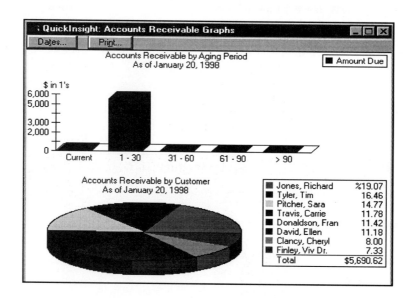

Click **Dates** button
Enter **02/01/98** for the **Show Aging As of** date
Click **OK**
- Notice the difference in the aging of accounts.

Click **Dates**, enter **03/01/98**
Click **OK**
- Again, notice the difference in aging of accounts.

Click **Dates**, enter **01/20/98**
Close the graph

PREPARE SALES GRAPHS

Sales graphs illustrate the amount of cash and credit sales for a given period as well as the percentage of sales for each sales item.

*DO: Click **Reports**, point to **Graphs**, click **Sales**
        OR

Use QuickBooks Navigator: Click **Sales and Customers** tab, click **Sales** under
    Reports

Click **Sales Graph**

Click **Dates** button

Click drop-down list arrow next to **Graph Dates** button

Click **Custom**

Tab to **From**, enter **01/01/98**

Tab to **To**, enter **01/20/98**

Click **OK**

By Item button should be indented

* You will see a bar chart representing Sales by Month and a pie chart
  displaying a Sales Summary by item.

Printing is not required for this chart

* If you want a printed copy, click **Print**.

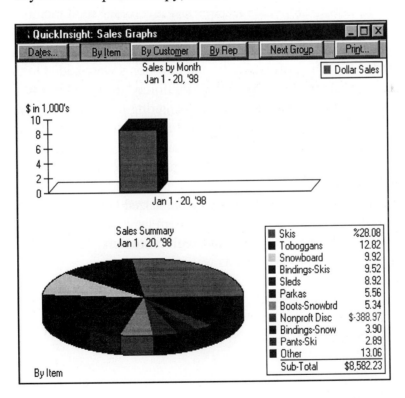

Close the graph

BACK UP MOUNTAIN ADVENTURE SKI SHOPPE DATA

Whenever an important work session is complete, you should always back up your data. If your data disk is damaged or an error is discovered at a later time, the backup disk may be restored and the information used for recording transactions. No matter what type of business, the backup procedure remains the same.

 *DO: Follow the instructions given in Chapters 1 and 2 to back up data for Mountain Adventure Ski Shoppe

SUMMARY

In this chapter, cash, bank charge card, and credit sales were prepared for Mountain Adventure Ski Shoppe, a retail business, using sales receipts and invoices. Credit memos and refund checks were issued, and customer accounts were added and revised. Invoices and sales receipts were edited, deleted, and voided. Cash payments were received, and bank deposits were made. New accounts were added to the Chart of Accounts, and new items were added to the Item list while entering transactions. All the transactions entered reinforced the QuickBooks concept of using the business form to record transactions rather than entering information in journals. However, QuickBooks does not disregard traditional accounting methods. Instead, it performs this function in the background. The Journal was accessed and printed. The importance of reports for information and decision making was illustrated. Exploration of the various sales and accounts receivable reports and graphs allowed information to be viewed from a sales standpoint and from an accounts receivable perspective. Sales reports emphasized both cash and credit sales according to the customer or according to the sales item generating the revenue. Accounts receivable reports focused on amounts owed by credit customers. The traditional trial balance emphasizing the equality of debits and credits was prepared.

END-OF-CHAPTER QUESTIONS

TRUE/FALSE

ANSWER THE FOLLOWING QUESTIONS IN THE SPACE PROVIDED BEFORE THE QUESTION NUMBER.

_____ 1. If an invoice has been paid in full, a refund check is issued along with a credit memo.

_____ 2. QuickBooks automatically applies payment received to the most current invoice.

_____ 3. Sales tax will be calculated automatically on an invoice if a customer is marked taxable.

_____ 4. A new sales item may be added only at the beginning of a period.

_____ 5. A new customer may be added "on the fly."

_____ 6. Report formats may be customized.

_____ 7. The Discount Info button on the Receive Payments window allows discounts to be applied to invoices being paid by clicking Cancel.

_____ 8. Cash sales are recorded on invoices and marked paid.

_____ 9. If a customer issues a check that is returned marked NSF, you may charge the customer the amount of the bank charges and any penalty charges you impose.

_____ 10. Sales tax must be calculated manually and added to sales receipts.

MULTIPLE CHOICE

WRITE THE LETTER OF THE CORRECT ANSWER IN THE SPACE PROVIDED BEFORE
THE QUESTION NUMBER.

_____ 1. Information regarding details of a customer's balance may be obtained by viewing __.
   A. the trial balance
   B. the customer's balance summary report
   C. the customer's balance detail report
   D. an invoice for the customer

_____ 2. Even though transactions are entered via business documents such as invoices and
   sales receipts, QuickBooks keeps track of all transactions __.
   A. in a chart
   B. in the register
   C. on a graph
   D. in the Journal

_____ 3. If a transaction is __, it will not show up in the Customer Balance Detail Report.
   A. voided
   B. deleted
   C. corrected
   D. canceled

_____ 4. A credit card sale is treated exactly like a __.
   A. cash sale
   B. sale on account until reimbursement is received from a bank
   C. sale on account
   D. bank deposit

_____ 5. If the word -Split- appears in the Split column of a report rather than an account
   name, it means that the transaction is split between two or more __.
   A. accounts or items
   B. customers
   C. journals
   D. reports

_____ 6. When adding a customer "on the fly," you may choose to add just the customer's name by selecting ___.
A. Quick Add
B. Set Up
C. Condensed
D. none of the above—a customer cannot be added "on the fly"

_____ 7. The Item list stores information about ___.
A. each item that is out of stock
B. each item in stock
C. each customer with an account
D. each item a company sells

_____ 8. A report prepared to obtain information about sales, inventory, and merchandise costs is a ___.
A. Stock Report
B. Income Statement
C. Summary Sales by Vendor Report
D. Summary Sales by Item Report

_____ 9. If a customer has a balance for an amount owed and a return is made, a credit memo is prepared and ___.
A. a refund check is issued
B. the amount of the return may be applied to the balance owed at the time the invoice is paid
C. the customer determines whether to apply the amount to the balance owed or to get a refund check
D. all of the above

_____ 10. Purchase information regarding an item sold by the company is entered ___.
A. in the invoice register
B. when adding a sales item
C. only when creating the company
D. when the last item in stock is sold

FILL-IN

IN THE SPACE PROVIDED, WRITE THE ANSWER THAT MOST APPROPRIATELY COMPLETES THE SENTENCE.

1. A report showing all sales, credits, and payments for each customer on account but not the remaining balance on the account is the _____ report.

2. When you make a bank deposit, the _____ window shows all amounts received for cash sales and payments on account that have not been deposited in the bank.

3. If the Quantity and Price Each are entered on an invoice, pressing the _____ key will cause QuickBooks to calculate and enter the correct information in the Amount column of the invoice.

4. QuickBooks allows you to view additional information within a report by using the _____ feature.

5. When you receive payments from customers, QuickBooks places the amount received in an account called _____.

SHORT ESSAY

Describe the use of Find. Based on chapter information, what is used to instruct Find to limit its search?

_____

_____

_____

_____

_____

END-OF-CHAPTER PROBLEM

HAWAII SUN CLOTHING CO.

Hawaii Sun Clothing Co. is a men's and women's clothing store located in San Luis Obispo, California, specializing in resort wear. The store is owned and operated by Nalani Kalaniki and Maile Kahala. Maile keeps the books and runs the office for the store, and Nalani is responsible for buying merchandise and managing the store. Both partners sell merchandise in the store, and they have some college students working part time during the evenings and on the weekends.

INSTRUCTIONS

As in previous chapters, obtain a disk from your instructor containing the data for Hawaii Sun Clothing Co. Copy **Hawaii.QBW** to a new disk. Open the company, and record the following transactions using invoices and sales receipts. Hawaii Sun accepts cash, checks, and credit cards for "cash" sales. Make bank deposits as instructed. Print the reports and graphs as indicated. Add new accounts, items, and customers where appropriate.

When recording transactions, use the Item list to determine the item(s) sold. All transactions are taxable unless otherwise indicated. Terms for sales on account are the standard terms assigned to each customer individually. If a customer exceeds his or her credit limit, accept the transaction. When receiving payment for sales on account, always check to see if a discount should be given. A customer's beginning balance is not eligible for a discount. The date of the sale begins the discount period. A check should be received or postmarked within ten days of the invoice in order to qualify for a discount. If the customer has any credits to the account because of a return, apply the credits when payments are received. If the customer makes a return and does not have a balance on account, prepare a refund check for the customer. Invoices begin with number 15, are numbered consecutively, and have lines printed around each field. Sales Receipts begin with number 25, are also numbered consecutively, and have lines printed around each field. Each invoice should contain a message. Use the one you feel is most appropriate.

If you write any checks, keep track of the check numbers used. QuickBooks does not always display the check number you are expecting to see. Remember that QuickBooks does not print check numbers on checks because most businesses use checks with the check numbers pre-printed.

LISTS

Item List

Name	Description	Type	Account	On Hand	Price
◆ Access-Belts	Belts	Inventory Part	4010 · Sales:4(	40	0.00
◆ Access-Shades	Sunglasses	Inventory Part	4010 · Sales:4(	50	0.00
◆ Access-Ties	Ties and Scarves	Inventory Part	4010 · Sales:4(	100	0.00
◆ Men-Pants	Men's Pants and S	Inventory Part	4010 · Sales:4(	100	0.00
◆ Men-Shirts	Men's Shirts	Inventory Part	4010 · Sales:4(	100	0.00
◆ Men-Shoes	Men's Shoes	Inventory Part	4010 · Sales:4(	100	0.00
◆ Women-Pants	Women's Pants ar	Inventory Part	4010 · Sales:4(	30	0.00
◆ Women-Shirts	Women's Shirts ar	Inventory Part	4010 · Sales:4(	100	0.00
◆ Women-Shoes	Women's Shoes	Inventory Part	4010 · Sales:4(	100	0.00
◆ CA Sales Tax	CA Sales Tax	Sales Tax Item	2200 · Sales T<		7.25%
◆ Out of State	Out-of-state sale.	Sales Tax Item	2200 · Sales T<		0.0%

Customer:Job List

Name	Balance	Notes
◆ Afaf, Minzara	1,359.00	
◆ Collins, Caren	325.00	
◆ Elmani, Elizar	598.00	
◆ Keith, Robyn	785.00	
◆ Lai, Lee Yung	1,065.00	
◆ Lomeli, Timothy	0.00	
◆ Lopez, Arturo	750.00	
◆ Lyons, Richard	950.00	
◆ Maruchican, Elham	0.00	
◆ Peters, Gloria	1,254.00	
◆ Retig, Teri	945.00	
◆ Salazar, Jose	75.00	
◆ Thomsen, Robert	450.00	
◆ Watts, Andrew	835.00	
◆ Wilson, Marie	375.00	

RECORD TRANSACTIONS

January 3, 1998:

Add your name to the company name. The company name will be **Hawaii Sun Clothing Co.--Student's Name**. (Type your actual name, *not* the words "Student's Name.")

Change the company preferences so that the current date does not print as part of the heading on reports.

Prepare Invoice #15 to record the sale on account for 1 belt for $29.95, 1 pair of shorts for $39.95, and a shirt for $39.95 to Timothy Lomeli.

Received Check No. 3305 from Caren Collins for $325 in payment of her bill in full.

Record the sale on account of 1 pair of sunglasses for $89.95 to Robert Thomsen.

Record the sale of a dress to Gloria Peters for $79.95. (Add a new sales item: Women-Dress, Women's Dresses, preferred vendor is Aloha Clothes, Income Account is 4011 Women's Clothing, Reorder Point is 20, Qty on Hand 25, Total Value $750, as of 01/01/98.)

Add a new customer: San Luis Recreation Center, 451 Marsh Street, San Luis Obispo, CA 93407, Contact person is Katie Gregg, 805-555-2241, Credit Terms are 2% 10 Net 30, Credit Limit $1,000, they are taxable for CA Sales Tax.

Sold 5 men's Hawaiian shirts to San Luis Recreation Center for $29.95 each, 5 pair of men's shorts for $29.95 each. Because San Luis Recreation Center is a nonprofit organization, include a subtotal for the sale and apply a 10% sales discount for a nonprofit organization. (Create any new sales items necessary by following the instructions given in the chapter. If you need to add a Sales Discount account to the Chart of Accounts, assign account number 6130.)

Sold 1 women's blouse for $59.95 to Jerri Gardener. Received Check No. 378 for the full amount including tax. Record sale as a cash customer. (If necessary, refer to steps provided within the chapter for instructions on creating a cash customer.) Issued Sales Receipt 25.

Received a belt returned by Andrew Watts. The original price of the belt was $49.95. Prepare a credit memo.

Sold a dress to a customer for $99.95. The customer paid with her VISA. Record the sale.

Sold a scarf for $19.95 plus tax for cash. Record the sale.

January 5:

Received payments from the following customers:
Elizar Elmani, $598.00, Check No. 145
Marie Wilson, $375, Check No. 4015
Arturo Lopez, $750, Check No. 8915-02
Andrew Watts, $781.43, Check No. 6726

January 15:

Received a NSF notice from the bank for the check for $325 from Caren Collins. Enter the necessary transaction for this nonsufficient funds check. The bank's charges are $15, and Hawaii Sun charges $15 for all NSF checks. (If necessary, refer to steps provided within the chapter for instructions on adding accounts or items necessary to record this transaction.)

Arturo Lopez returned a shirt he had purchased for $54.99 plus tax. Record the return. Check the balance of his account. If there is no balance, issue a refund check.

Sold 3 men's shirts to Richard Ralph, a cash customer, for $39.95 each plus tax. Richard used his MasterCard for payment. *cash sale*

Sold on account 1 dress for $99.99, 1 pair of sandals for $79.95, and a belt for $39.95 to Robyn Keith.

Sold 1 pair of women's shorts for $34.95 to a cash customer. Accepted Check No. 8160 for payment.

Received a partial payment on account from Lee Yung Lai, $250, Check No. 2395.

use invoice

Received payment in full from Jose Salazar, Check No. 9802.

Received $1,338.03 from Gloria Peters as payment in full on account, Check No. 2311. The payment was postmarked 1/11/98. (Because the beginning balance—Outstanding Invoices/Statement Charges shows this as 01/01/98 Invoice for 1,254—and Invoice 17 are being paid with this check, the payment will be applied to both. In order to apply the discount to Invoice 17, you may have to click both the beginning balance and Invoice 17 to deselect; then click Invoice 17; click Discount Info; apply the discount; and, finally, click the beginning balance.)

Sold 3 pairs of men's pants for $75.00 each, 3 men's shirts for $50.00 each, 3 belts for $39.99 each, 2 pairs of men's shoes for $90.00 each, 2 ties for $55.00 each, and 1 pair of sunglasses for $75.00 to Teri Retig. (If the amount of the sale exceeds Teri's credit limit, accept the sale anyway.)

Sold 1 pair of sunglasses for $95.00, 2 dresses for $99.95 each, and 2 pairs of women's shoes for $65.00 to Marie Wilson.

Print Customer Balance Detail Report. Adjust column widths so the report is one page wide without selecting Fit report to one page wide. The report length may be longer than one page.

Print an Itemized Sales by Item Report for 01/01/98 to 01/15/98 in Landscape orientation. Adjust column widths so the report fits on one page wide. Do not select Fit report to one page wide.

Deposit all payments, check, and charges received from customers. Print the Deposit Summary.

Print a Trial Balance for 01/01/98 to 01/15/98.

Prepare and print a Sales Graph by Item for 01/01/98 to 01/15/98.

PAYABLES AND PURCHASES: MERCHANDISING BUSINESS

LEARNING OBJECTIVES

At the completion of this chapter you will be able to:

1. Understand the concepts for computerized accounting for payables in a merchandising business.
2. Prepare, view, and print purchase orders and checks.
3. Enter items received against purchase orders.
4. Enter bills, enter vendor credits, and pay bills.
5. Edit and correct errors in bills and purchase orders.
6. Add new vendors, modify vendor records, and add new accounts.
7. View accounts payable transaction history from the enter bills window.
8. View, use the QuickZoom feature, and/or print QuickReports for vendors, accounts payable register, and so on.
9. Record and edit transactions in the Accounts Payable Register.
10. Edit, void, and delete bills, purchase orders, and checks.
11. Display and print a Sales Tax Liability report, an Accounts Payable Aging Summary report, an Unpaid Bills Detail report, and a Vendor Balance Summary Report.
12. Display and print Accounts Payable Graph by Aging Period.

ACCOUNTING FOR PAYABLES AND PURCHASES

In a merchandising business, much of the accounting for purchases and payables consists of ordering merchandise for resale and paying bills for expenses incurred in the operation of the business. Purchases are for things used in the operation of the business. Some transactions will be in the form of cash purchases; others will be purchases on account. Bills can be paid when they are received or when they are due. Merchandise received must be checked against purchase orders, and completed purchase orders must be closed. Rather than use cumbersome journals, QuickBooks continues to focus on recording transactions based on the business document; therefore, you use the Enter Bills and Pay Bills features of the program to record the receipt and payment of bills. While QuickBooks does not refer to it as such, the Vendor list is the same as the Accounts Payable Subsidiary Ledger.

QuickBooks can remind you when inventory needs to be ordered and when payments are due. Purchase orders are prepared when ordering merchandise. The program automatically tracks inventory and uses the average cost method to value the inventory. QuickBooks can calculate and apply discounts earned for paying bills early. Payments can be made by recording payments in the pay bills window or, if using the cash basis for accounting, by writing a check. Merchandise purchased may be paid for at the same time the items and the bill are received, or it may be paid for at a later date. A cash purchase can be recorded by writing a check, by using a credit card, or by using petty cash. Even though QuickBooks focuses on recording transactions on the business forms used, all transactions are recorded behind the scenes in the general journal.

As in previous chapters, corrections can be made directly on the bill or within the transaction journal. New accounts and vendors may be added "on the fly" as transactions are entered. Purchase orders, bills, or checks may be voided or deleted. Reports illustrating vendor balances, unpaid bills, accounts payable aging, sales tax liability, transaction history, and accounts payable registers may be viewed and printed. Graphs analyzing the amount of accounts payable by aging period provide a visual illustration of the accounts payable.

TRAINING TUTORIAL AND PROCEDURES

The following tutorial will once again work with Mountain Adventure Ski Shoppe. As in Chapter 5, transactions will be recorded for this fictitious company. Refer to procedures given in Chapter 5 to maximize training benefits.

OPEN QUICKBOOKS® AND MOUNTAIN ADVENTURE SKI SHOPPE

*DO: Open QuickBooks as instructed in previous chapters
Open Mountain Adventure Ski Shoppe
- There should not be a company open. If a company is open, close it, then open **Mountain.qbw**.
Close Reminders
- Check the title bar to verify that Mountain Adventure Ski Shoppe is the open company and that your name shows.

Mountain Adventure Ski Shoppe--Student's Name - QuickBooks

BEGINNING THE TUTORIAL

In this chapter you will be entering purchases of merchandise for resale in the business and entering bills incurred by the company in the operation of the business. You will also be recording the payment of bills and purchases using checks and credit cards.

The Vendor list keeps information regarding the vendors with which you do business. This information includes the vendor names, addresses, telephone numbers, payment terms, credit limits, and account numbers. You will be using the following list for vendors with which Mountain Adventure Ski Shoppe has an account:

Name	Balance
ABC Accessories	350.00
Bindings Abound	2,000.00
Mammoth Power Company	0.00
Mammoth Telephone Company	0.00
Mammoth Water Company	0.00
Office Supply Company	750.00
Rent, Inc.	0.00
Shoe Supply	400.00
Ski Supply	5,000.00
SkiWear, Inc.	0.00
Sports Boots	0.00
State Board of Equalization	613.15

All transactions are listed on memos. The transaction date will be the same date as the memo date unless otherwise specified within the transaction. Vendor names, when necessary, will be given in the transaction. Unless otherwise specified, terms are 2% 10 Net 30. Once a specific type of transaction has been entered in a step-by-step manner, additional transactions of the same or a similar type will be made without having instructions provided. Of course, you may always refer to instructions given for previous transactions for ideas or for steps used to enter those transactions. To determine the account used in the transaction, refer to the Chart of Accounts. When entering account information on a bill, clicking on the drop-down list arrow will show a copy of the Chart of Accounts.

VIEW THE REMINDERS LIST TO DETERMINE MERCHANDISE TO ORDER

QuickBooks has a Reminders list that is used to remind you of things that need to be completed. The company preferences can be set so that the Reminders list automatically appears whenever you start QuickBooks. Even if the list is not visible on the screen when you wish to view it, simply click the List menu and click Reminders on the Other List menu. Information on the Reminders list may be displayed in summary form or in detailed form.

MEMO

DATE: January 15, 1998

Display the Reminders list to determine which items need to be ordered.

---

*DO: Display the Reminders list
Click **List** menu, point to **Other Lists**, click **Reminders**
OR
Use QuickBooks Navigator:
Click **Company** tab, click **Reminders** icon

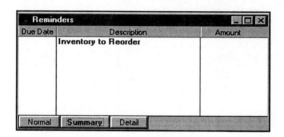

- Reminders list appears on the screen in Summary form.

To obtain more information, click **Detail** button at the bottom of the list

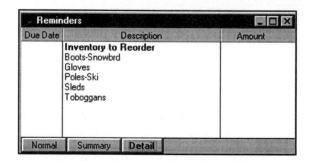

Do not close the Reminders list

PRINT THE REMINDERS LIST

To use the Reminders list as an aid in reordering merchandise, it is helpful to have it available in printed form. As with all other lists, QuickBooks allows the Reminders list to be printed.

*DO: With the Reminders list on the screen, print the list
Click **File** on the menu bar, click **Print List**
     OR
Use the keyboard shortcut **Ctrl+P**
- You may get a dialog box indicating that this list could be printed through Reports.

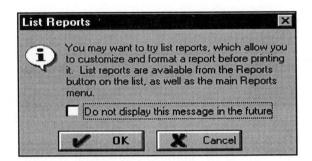

Click **OK** to close the dialog box
- Verify that the printer, Portrait orientation, and print all pages are all selected on the Print list dialog box.
Click **Print** button
When printing is complete, close Reminders

PURCHASE ORDERS

Using QuickBooks Purchase Order feature helps you track your inventory. Information regarding the items on order or the items received may be obtained at any time. Once merchandise has been received, QuickBooks marks the purchase order "Received in full." The Purchase order feature must be selected as a Preference when setting up the company, or it may be selected prior to processing your first purchase order. QuickBooks will automatically set up an account called Purchase Orders in the Chart of Accounts. The account does not affect the balance sheet or the profit and loss statement of the company. As with other business forms, QuickBooks allows you to customize your purchase orders to fit the needs of your individual company or to use the purchase order format that comes with the program.

VERIFY PURCHASE ORDERS ACTIVE AS A COMPANY PREFERENCE

Verify that the purchase order feature of QuickBooks is active by checking the company preferences.

MEMO

DATE: January 15, 1998

Prior to completing the first purchase order, verify that Purchase Orders are active.

---

*DO: Verify that Purchase Orders are active by accessing the Company Preferences
Click **File** menu, click **Preferences**
   OR
Click **Company** tab on QuickBooks Navigator, click **Preferences**
Scroll through Preference list until you see **Purchases & Vendors**
Click **Purchases & Vendors**
- Make sure there is a ✓ in the check box for Inventory. If Inventory is selected, purchase orders are active.
- If not, click the check box to select.

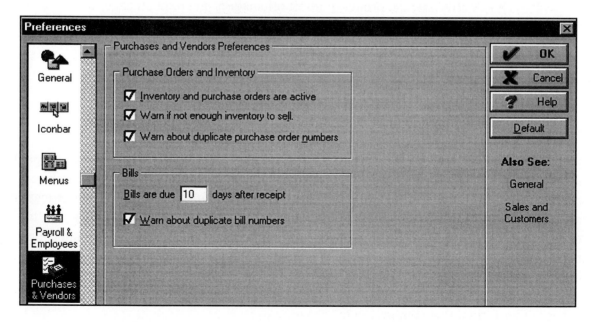

Click **OK** to accept and close

PREPARE PURCHASE ORDERS TO ORDER MERCHANDISE

Once the purchase order feature is selected, purchase orders may be prepared. Primarily, purchase orders are prepared to order merchandise; but they may also be used to order non-inventory items like supplies or services.

MEMO

DATE: January 15, 1998

With only 10 pairs of snowboard boots in stock in the middle of January, Eric and Matt decide to order an additional 25 pairs of boots in assorted sizes from Sports Boots for $75 per pair. Prepare Purchase Order 1.

---

 *DO: Prepare Purchase Order 1 for 25 pairs of snowboard boots

Click **Activities** menu, click **Create Purchase Orders**
> OR

Click **Purchases and Vendors** tab on QuickBooks Navigator, click **Purchase Orders**
> OR

Click **PO** button on iconbar

Click drop-down list arrow for Vendor, click **Sports Boots**

Tab to or click **Date**, enter **01/15/98**
- P.O. No. should be 1.
- If not, enter 1 as the P.O. No.

Tab to or click **Item**, click **Boots-Snowbrd**

Tab to or click **Qty**, enter **25**
- Rate should appear as **75.00**

Tab to generate Amount

Click **Print** to print the Purchase Order

Check printer settings:
- Make sure the appropriate printer is selected.
- Printer Type is Page-oriented (Single sheets).
- Print on Blank forms.
- Print lines around each field.

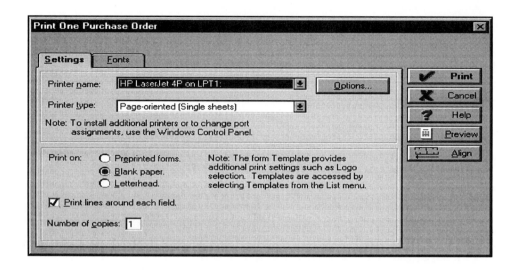

Click **Print**
Click **OK** on **Did form(s) print OK?** dialog box

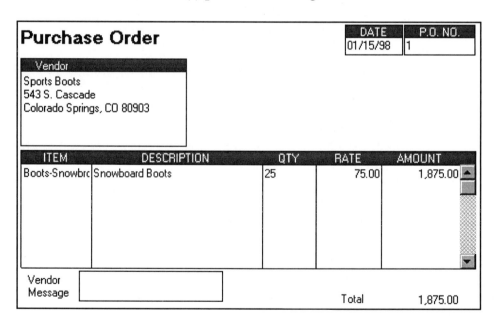

Click >>**Next** to go to the next Purchase Order

PREPARE A PURCHASE ORDER FOR MORE THAN ONE ITEM

If more than one item is purchased from a vendor, all items purchased can be included on the same purchase order.

MEMO
DATE: January 15, 1998

Prepare a purchase order for 3 sleds @ $50 each, and 2 toboggans @ $110 each from a new vendor: Flying Snow, Inc., 7105 Camino del Rio, Durango, CO 81302, Contact: Lyle Jenkins, Phone: 303-555-7765, Fax: 303-555-5677, Terms: 2% 10 Net 30, Credit Limit: $2000.

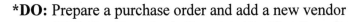

*DO: Prepare a purchase order and add a new vendor

Click the drop-down list arrow for **Vendor**, click **< Add New >**

Enter **Flying Snow, Inc.** for the **Vendor** name and the **Company** name

Click the second line of the address, enter **7105 Camino del Rio**

Click the third line of the address, enter **Durango, CO 81302**

Tab to or click **Contact**, enter **Lyle Jenkins**

Tab to or click **Phone**, enter **303-555-7765**

Tab to or click **FAX**, enter **303-555-5677**

Click **Additional Info** tab, click the drop-down list arrow for **Terms**, click **2% 10 Net 30**

Tab to or click **Credit Limit**, enter **2000**

Click **OK** to add Vendor

- The Date should be 01/15/98. If it is not, delete the date shown and enter 01/15/98.
- P.O. No. should be 2. If it is not, enter 2.

Tab to or click the first line in the column for **Item**

Click drop-down list arrow for **Item**, click **Sleds**

Tab to or click **Qty**, enter **3**

Tab to or click **Rate**, enter **50**

Tab to generate the total for Amount

Repeat steps necessary to enter the information to order 2 toboggans at $110 each

Print Purchase Order 2

Click **OK** button on **Did form(s) print OK?** dialog box

Click **>>Next** to save Purchase Order 2 and go to the next purchase order

Purchase Order

	DATE	P.O. NO.
	01/15/98	2

Vendor
Flying Snow, Inc.
7105 Camino del Rio
Durango, CO 81302

ITEM	DESCRIPTION	QTY	RATE	AMOUNT
Sleds	Sleds	3	50.00	150.00
Toboggans	Toboggans	2	110.00	220.00

Vendor Message

	Total	370.00

ENTER PURCHASE ORDERS WITHOUT STEP-BY-STEP INSTRUCTIONS

MEMO

DATE: January 15, 1998

Prepare purchase orders for the following:
25 pairs of gloves @ 15.00 each from SkiWear, Inc.
12 sets of ski poles @ 30.00 each from Ski Supply.

*DO: Prepare and print the purchase orders indicated above.
Compare your completed purchase orders with the ones below:

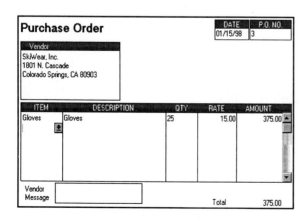

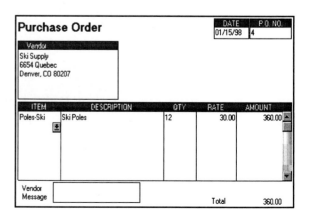

VIEW PURCHASE ORDERS LIST

To see a list of purchase orders, select Purchase Orders from the Lists menu. When viewing the list in this fashion, you may choose to see all the purchase orders for the company or to see only the open purchase orders for the company. Another way in which you can see a list of purchase orders is to select Chart of Accounts from the Lists menu, select Purchase Orders, and choose QuickReport from the Reports menu button.

MEMO
DATE: January 15, 1998

Eric and Matt need to see which purchase orders are open. View the Purchase Orders list.

---

 *DO: View the open purchase orders for Mountain Adventure Ski Shoppe
Click **Lists** menu, click **Purchase Orders**
    OR
Click **Purchases and Vendors** tab in QuickBooks Navigator, click **PO List**
• The list shows all open purchase orders, the date of the purchase order, and the number of the purchase order.

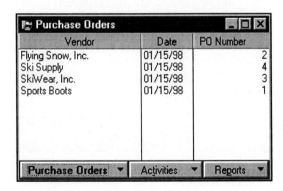

Close the Purchase Order list

CHANGE MINIMUM REORDER LIMITS FOR AN ITEM

Any time that you determine your reorder limits are too low or too high, you can change the Reorder Point by editing the Item on the Item list.

MEMO

DATE: January 15, 1998

View the Item list to see the amount on hand for each item. In viewing the list, Eric and Matt determine that they should have a minimum of 35 sets of long underwear on hand at all times. Currently, there are 32 sets of long underwear in stock. Change the reorder point for long underwear to 35.

---

     *DO: View the Item list

         Click **Lists** menu, click **Items**

            OR

         Click **Purchases and Vendors** tab on QuickBooks Navigator, click

            Items & Services icon

            OR

         Click **Item** button on iconbar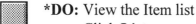

         Scroll through Item list, click **Underwear**

         Click **Item** button at the bottom of the Item list, click **Edit**

         Click in **Reorder Point**

         Change 30 to **35**

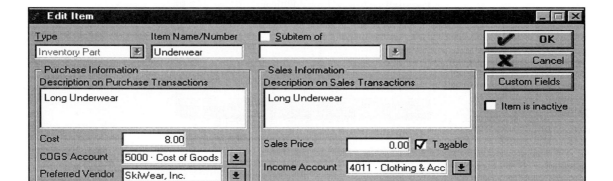

Click **OK** to save and exit
Close the Item list

VIEW EFFECT OF REORDER POINT ON REMINDERS LIST

Once the reorder point has been changed and the quantity on hand is equal to or falls below the new minimum, the item will be added to the Reminders list so you will be reminded to order it.

MEMO

DATE: January 20, 1998

View the Reminders list to see what items need to be ordered.

---

    *DO: View the Reminders list
Click **Lists**, point to **Other Lists**, click **Reminders**
• The Reminders list will appear and show **Inventory to Reorder**.
Click **Detail** button to see what items need to be reordered

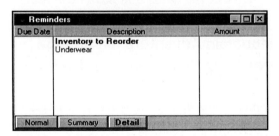

Close Reminders list

VIEW STOCK STATUS BY ITEM INVENTORY REPORT

Several inventory reports are available for viewing and/or printing. One report is the Stock Status by Item report. This report provides information regarding the stock on hand, the stock on order, and the stock that needs to be reordered.

MEMO

DATE: January 15, 1998

More detailed information regarding the stock on hand, stock ordered, and stock needed to be ordered needs to be provided. View the inventory report for stock status by item.

---

 *DO: View the inventory report for stock status by item
Click **Lists**, click **Purchase Orders**
Click the **Report** button at the bottom of the Purchase Order list, point to
   Inventory Reports, click **Stock Status by Item**
Tab to or click **From**, delete the date shown, and enter **01/01/98**
Tab to or click **To**, delete the date shown, and enter **01/15/98**
Tab to generate the report
Scroll through the report
- Notice the items in stock.
- Notice the reorder point for items.
- Find the items marked as needing to be ordered.
- Notice the dates of the items that have been ordered.

Mountain Adventure Ski Shoppe
Inventory Stock Status by Item
January 1 - 15, 1998

	◇ Item Description	◇ Pref Vend...	◇ Reorder Pt	◇ On Hand	◇ On Order	◇ Next De...	◇ Order
Pants-Ski	Ski Pants	SkiWear, Inc.	10	93	0		
Pants-Snow...	Snowboard Pants	SkiWear, Inc.	10	50	0		
Parkas	Parkas and Jack...	SkiWear, Inc.	25	73	0		
Poles-Ski	Ski Poles	Ski Supply	15	12	12	01/15/98	
Skis	Snow Skis	Ski Supply	15	43	0		
Sleds	Sleds		5	4	3	01/15/98	
Snowboard	Snowboard	Ski Supply	15	28	0		
Socks	Ski and Snowbo...	Sports Boots	25	72	0		
Sweaters	Sweaters & Shirts	SkiWear, Inc.	25	73	0		
Toboggans	Toboggans		5	5	2	01/15/98	
Underwear	Long Underwear	SkiWear, Inc.	35	32	0		✓

Partial Report

Close the report without printing
Close the Purchase Order list

PRINT A PURCHASE ORDER QUICKREPORT

It is possible to prepare a QuickReport providing information about purchase orders. The QuickReport can be prepared by accessing Purchase Orders through the Chart of Accounts.

MEMO
DATE: January 15, 1998

Prepare and print a QuickReport of purchase orders as of January 15.

---

*DO: Prepare a QuickReport of Purchase Orders
Access Chart of Accounts as instructed in other chapters
Scroll through the Chart of Accounts until you find **Purchase Orders**
• Purchase Orders is the last item in the Chart of Accounts.
Click **Purchase Orders**
Click **Reports** button at the bottom of the Chart of Accounts
Click **QuickReport: 2-Purchase Orders**
    OR
Use the keyboard shortcut **Ctrl+Q**
Insert the appropriate dates:
    From 01/01/98
    To 01/15/98
Tab to generate the report
Resize the columns as previously instructed to:
    Eliminate the **Memo** column
    Be able to view the account name in full in the **Split** column
    Be able to print in Portrait orientation on one page without using "Fit to one
        page wide"
Click Print to print the report

Mountain Adventure Ski Shoppe
Account QuickReport
As of January 15, 1998

Type	Date	Num	Name	Split	Amount
2 · Purchase Orders					
Purchase Order	01/15/98	1	Sports Boots	1120 · Inventory Asset	-1,875.00
Purchase Order	01/15/98	2	Flying Snow, Inc.	-SPLIT-	-370.00
Purchase Order	01/15/98	3	SkiWear, Inc.	1120 · Inventory Asset	-375.00
Purchase Order	01/15/98	4	Ski Supply	1120 · Inventory Asset	-360.00
Total 2 · Purchase Orders					-2,980.00
TOTAL					**-2,980.00**

> Close the report
> Close the Chart of Accounts

RECEIVING ITEMS ORDERED

The QuickBooks form used to record the receipt of items depends on the way in which the ordered items are received. Items received may be recorded in three ways. If the items are received without a bill and you pay later, record the receipt on an item receipt. If the items are received at the same time as the bill, record the item receipt on a bill. If the items are received and paid for at the same time, record the receipt of items on a check or a credit card.

RECORD RECEIPT OF ITEMS NOT ACCOMPANIED BY A BILL

The ability to record inventory items prior to the arrival of the bill keeps quantities on hand, quantities on order, and the inventory up to date. Items ordered on a purchase order that arrive before the bill is received are recorded on an item receipt. At the time the bill arrives, it is recorded.

MEMO

DATE: January 18, 1998

The sleds and toboggans ordered from Flying Snow, Inc., arrive without a bill.
Record the receipt of the 3 sleds and 2 toboggans.

---

*DO: Record the receipt of the items above

Click **Activities** menu, point to **Inventory**, click **Receive Items**
   OR

Use QuickBooks Navigator:
   Click **Purchases and Vendors** tab, click **Receive Items** icon
      OR
   Click **PO List** icon on **Purchases and Vendors** tab, click
      Activities, click **Receive Items**

Click drop-down list arrow for **Vendor**, click **Flying Snow, Inc.**

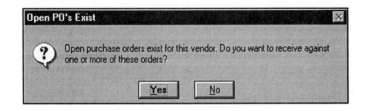

Click **Yes** on the **Open PO's Exist** message box
- An **Open Purchase Orders** dialog box appears showing all open purchase
  orders for the vendor, Flying Snow, Inc.

Point to any part of the line for P.O. No. 2
Click to select the purchase order
Click **OK**

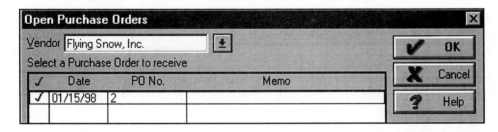

- Notice the completed information for Items tab indicating how many sleds
  and toboggans were received.
- Notice the Memo box beneath the Item Receipt. It states "Received items (bill
  to follow)."
- If necessary change the date to **01/18/98**.

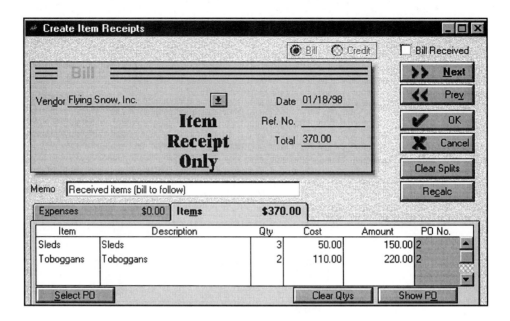

Click **OK**
If necessary, close Purchase Order list

VERIFY THAT PURCHASE ORDER IS MARKED RECEIVED IN FULL

Once items have been marked as received, QuickBooks stamps the Purchase Order "Received in Full" and marks each item received in full as "Clsd."

MEMO

DATE: January 18, 1998

View the original Purchase Order 2 to verify that it has been stamped Received in Full and each item received is marked Clsd.

---

*DO: Verify that Purchase Order 2 is marked Received in Full and all items received are Closed
Access Purchase Orders as previously instructed
Click **<<Prev** until you get to Purchase Order 2
- The Purchase Order should be stamped RECEIVED IN FULL.
- Next to the Amount column, you will see two new columns: RCVD and Clsd.
  - RCVD indicates the number of the items received.

- Clsd indicates that the number of items were received in full so the Purchase Order has been closed for that Item.

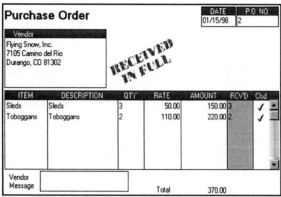

Close Create Purchase order window and Purchase Order list

ENTER RECEIPT OF A BILL FOR ITEMS ALREADY RECEIVED

For items that have been received prior to the bill, the receipt of items is recorded as soon as the items arrive. When the bill is received, it must be recorded. To do this, indicate that the bill is for items received and mark the receive items list as bill received. When completing a bill for items already received, QuickBooks fills in all essential information on the bill. A bill is divided into two sections: a vendor-related section (the upper part of the bill that looks similar to a check and has a memo text box under it) and a detail section (the area that has two tabs marked Items and Expenses). The vendor-related section of the bill is where information for the actual bill is entered, including a memo with information about the transaction. The detail section is where the information regarding the items ordered, the quantity ordered and received, and the amounts due for the items received is indicated.

MEMO

DATE: January 20, 1998

Record the bill for the sleds and toboggans already received from Flying Snow, Inc. Vendor's Invoice No. 97 dated 01/18/98, Terms 2% 10 Net 30.

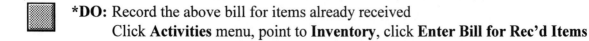

*DO: Record the above bill for items already received
Click **Activities** menu, point to **Inventory**, click **Enter Bill for Rec'd Items**

OR

Use QuickBooks Navigator:

   Click **Purchases and Vendors** tab, click **Receive Bill**

      OR

   Click **PO List**, click **Activities** button, click **Enter Bill**

      for Received Items

On the **Select Item Receipt**, click the drop-down arrow for **Vendor**, click **Flying Snow, Inc.**

- Name is entered as the vendor.

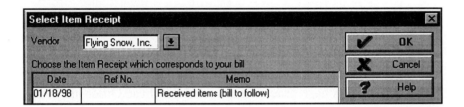

Click anywhere on the line **01/18/98 Received items (bill to follow)**

Click **OK**

- QuickBooks displays the **Enter Bills** screen and the completed bill for Flying Snow, Inc.
- The date shown is the date the items were received **01/18/98**.

Tab to or click **Ref No.**, type the vendor's invoice number **97**

- Notice that the **Amount Due** of **370** has been inserted.
- Terms of **2% 10 Net 30** and the due date are shown.
- The discount date does not always appear on the bill. If you change the date on the bill and press tab, the discount date may appear. With terms of 2% 10 Net 30, the discount date, if it appears, will be ten days from the date of the invoice or 01/28/98.

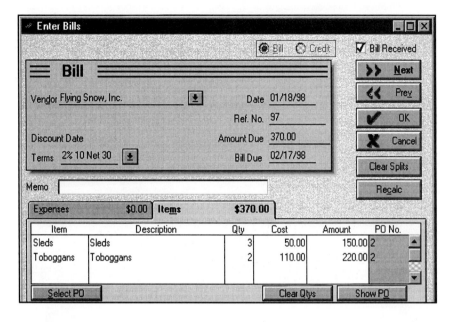

Click **OK**

RECORD RECEIPT OF ITEMS AND A BILL

When ordered items are received and accompanied by a bill, the receipt of the items is recorded while entering the bill.

MEMO

DATE: January 20, 1998

Received 25 pairs of snowboard boots and a bill from Sports Boots. Record the bill dated 01/18/98 and the receipt of the items.

---

*DO: Record the receipt of the items and the bill
 Click **Receive Items with Bill** on QuickBooks Navigator, click **Purchases and Vendors** tab
  OR
 Click **PO List** on QuickBooks Navigator **Purchases and Vendors** tab, click **Activities**, click **Receive Items & Enter Bill**
  OR
 Click **Activities** menu, point to **Inventory**, click **Receive Items and Enter Bill**

OR

Click **Item** button on the iconbar, click **Activities** button at the bottom of the list,
   click **Receive Items & Enter Bill**
Click drop-down list for **Vendor**, click **Sports Boots**
Click **Yes** button on the **Open PO's Exist** message box

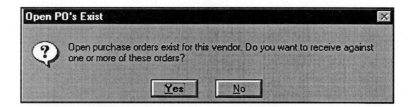

Click anywhere in P.O. No. 1 line to select

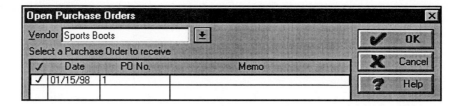

Click **OK**
- The bill appears on the screen and is complete.
- Because no invoice number was given in the transaction, leave the Ref. No.
  blank.

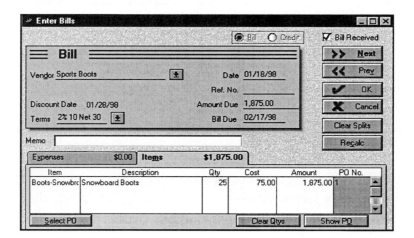

Click **OK**
- If necessary, close any open Item list or Purchase Orders list.

EDIT A PURCHASE ORDER

As with any other form, purchase orders may be edited once they have been prepared. Purchase orders may be accessed by clicking on the Purchase Order icon in QuickBooks Navigator, the PO button on the iconbar, or by displaying the Purchase Order list and clicking the Activities button and Edit.

MEMO
DATE: January 20, 1998

Renee realized that Purchase Order Number 4 should be for 15 pairs of ski poles. Change the purchase order and reprint.

---

  *DO: Change Purchase Order 4

      Access Purchase Order 4:

            Click the **Purchase Order** icon in QuickBooks Navigator, click **<<Prev** until you see P.O. 4
            OR
            Click the **PO** button on the iconbar, click **<<Prev** until you get to P.O. 4
            OR
            Click the **PO List** icon on QuickBooks Navigator, click **Ski Supply**, click the **Purchase Order** button, click **Edit**
            Click in **Qty**, change the number from 12 to **15**
            Tab to recalculate the amount due for the purchase order
            Click **OK** to record the changes and exit
           • If it is open, close the Purchase Order list.

RECORD A PARTIAL RECEIPT OF MERCHANDISE ORDERED

Sometimes when items on order are received, they are not received in full. The remaining items may be delivered as back-ordered items. This will usually occur if an item is out of stock, and you must wait for delivery until more items are manufactured and/or received by the vendor. With QuickBooks you record the number of items you actually receive, and the bill is recorded for that amount.

> ## MEMO
> DATE: January 20, 1998
>
> Record the bill and the receipt of 20 pairs of gloves ordered on Purchase Order 3.
> On the purchase order, 25 pairs of gloves were ordered. SkiWear, Inc., will no
> longer be carrying these gloves, so the remaining 5 pairs of gloves on order will not
> be shipped. Manually close the purchase order. The date of the bill is 01/18/98.

*DO: Record the receipt of and the bill for 20 pairs of gloves from SkiWear, Inc.

   Access **Receive Items with Bill** or **Receive Items & Enter Bill** as previously
      instructed

   If necessary, change the Date of the bill to **01/18/98**

   Click the drop-down list arrow for **Vendor**, click **SkiWear, Inc.**

   Click **Yes** on **Open PO's Exist** dialog box

   Click anywhere in the line for **P.O. 3** on **Open Purchase Orders** dialog box

   Click **OK**

   Click the **Qty** column on the Items tab at the bottom of the Enter Bills window

   Change the quantity to **20**

   Tab to change **Amount** to **300**

   •   Notice the Amount Due on the bill also changes.

   Click **OK** to record the items received and the bill

CLOSE PURCHASE ORDER MANUALLY

If you have issued a purchase order and it is determined that you will not be receiving the items
on order, a purchase order can be closed manually.

*DO: Close Purchase Order 3

   Use **Find** to locate Purchase Order 3

   Click **Find** button on the iconbar

   Scroll through **Choose Filter**

   •   Filter helps to narrow the search for locating something.

   Click **Transaction Type**, click the drop-down list arrow for **Transaction Type**,
      click **Purchase Order**

   Click **Find**

   •   A list of all purchase orders shows on the screen.

   Click Purchase Order 3 for SkiWear, Inc.

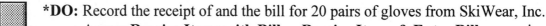

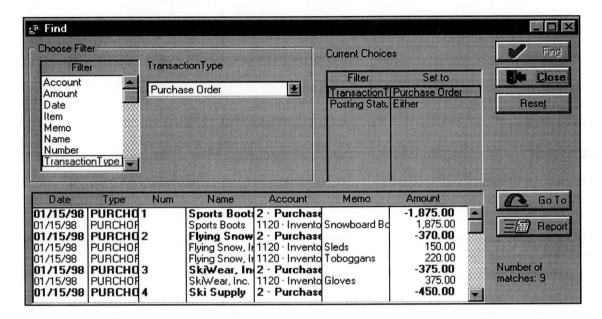

Click **Go To**

Click the **Clsd** column to mark and close the purchase order

- Notice that the ordered Qty is 25 and RCVD is 20.

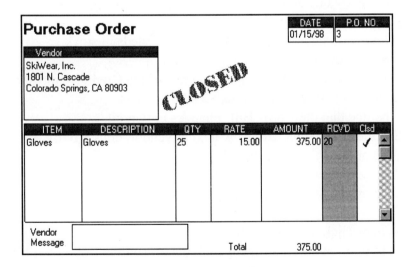

Click **OK** button to close the purchase order

Close Find

ENTER A CREDIT FROM A VENDOR

Credit memos are prepared to record a reduction to a transaction. With QuickBooks you use the Enter Bills window to record credit memos received from vendors acknowledging a return of or an allowance for a previously recorded bill and/or payment. The amount of a credit memo can be applied to the amount owed to a vendor when paying bills.

MEMO

DATE: January 23, 1998

Upon further inspection of merchandise received, Renee Squires found that one of the sleds received from Flying Snow, Inc., was cracked. The sled was returned. Received Credit Memo 9912 from Flying Snow, Inc., for $50, the full amount on the return of 1 sled.

---

*DO: Prior to recording the above return, check the Items list to verify how many sleds are currently on hand

Access Items list as previously instructed
- Look at Sleds to verify that there are 7 sleds in stock.

Close the Item list

Access the **Enter Bills** window and record the Credit Memo shown above

On the Enter Bills screen, click **Credit** to select
- Notice that the word "Bill" changes to "Credit."

Click the drop-down list arrow next to vendor, click **Flying Snow, Inc.**

Tab to or click the **Date**, type **01/23/98**

Tab to or click **Ref No.**, type **9912**

Tab to or click **Credit Amount**, type **50**

Tab to **Memo**, enter **Returned 1 Sled**

Tab to or click the **Items** tab

Tab to or click the first line in **Item** column, click drop-down list arrow, click **Sleds**

Tab to or click **Qty**, enter **1**

Tab to or click **Cost**, enter **50**

Tab to enter the **50** for **Amount**

Click **OK** to record the credit and exit Enter Bills window
- QuickBooks decreases the quantity of sleds on hand and creates a credit with the vendor that can be applied when paying the bill. The Credit Memo also appears in the Accounts Payable account in the **Paid** column, which decreases

the amount owed and shows the transaction type as BILLCRED in the Accounts Payable register.

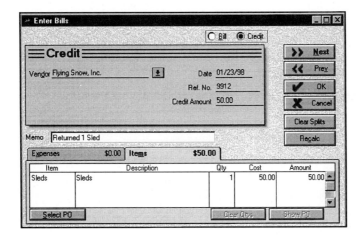

Access **Item list**
• Verify that there are 6 Sleds in stock after the return.
Close the list
Access the **Chart of Accounts** as previously instructed, click **Accounts Payable**
Click **Activities** button, click **Use Register**
Scroll through the register until you see the BILLCRED for Flying Snow, Inc.

01/23/98	9912	Flying Snow, Inc.				50.00	10,995.00
	BILLCRED	1120 · Inventory A:	Returned 1 Sled				

Close the Accounts Payable register
Close the Chart of Accounts

MAKE A PURCHASE USING A CREDIT CARD

Some businesses use credit cards as an integral part of their finances. Many companies have a credit card used primarily for gasoline purchases for company vehicles. Other companies use credit cards as a means of paying for expenses or purchasing merchandise or other necessary items for use in the business.

MEMO

DATE: January 23, 1998

Renee discovered that she was out of paper. She purchased a box of paper to be used for copies, for the laser printer, and for the fax machine from Office Supply Company for $21.98. Rather than add to the existing balance owed to the company, Eric and Matt decided to have Renee pay for the office supplies using the company's Visa card.

---

*DO: Purchase the above office supplies using the company's Visa card
>   Click **Activities** menu, click **Enter Credit Card Charges**
>   OR
>   Click QuickBooks Navigator **Checking and Credit Cards** tab, click **Credit Card**
>   **Credit Card** should indicate **2100 Visa**
>   Click drop-down list arrow for **Purchased From**, click **Office Supply Company**
>   Click **OK** on the **Warning** screen

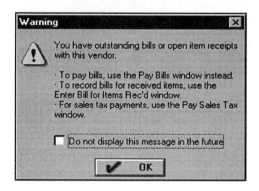

>   **Date** should be **01/23/98**
>   **Ref No.** is blank
>   Tab to or click **AMOUNT**, enter **21.98**
>   Tab to or click **Memo**, enter **Purchase Paper**
>   Tab to or click the **Account** column on the **Expense** tab, click the drop-down list arrow for Account, click **1311 Office Supplies**

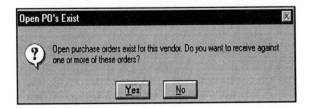

Click >>**Next** to record the charge and go to the next credit card entry

PAY FOR INVENTORY ITEMS ON ORDER USING A CREDIT CARD

It is possible to pay for inventory items using a credit card. The payment may be made using the Pay Bills window, or it may be made by recording an entry for Credit Card Charges. If you are purchasing something that is on order, you may record the receipt of merchandise on order first, or you may record the receipt of merchandise and the credit card payment at the same time.

MEMO

DATE: January 23, 1998

Note from Eric: Renee, record the receipt of 10 ski poles from Ski Supply. Pay for the ski poles using the company's Visa.

---

*DO: Pay for the ski poles received using the Visa
    Click the drop-down list for **Vendor**, click **Ski Supply**
    Click **OK** on the **Warning** regarding outstanding bills or open item receipts with the vendor
    Click **Yes** button on the **Open PO's Exist** message box

To select P.O. No. 4, click the line containing information regarding P.O. No. 4 on the **Open Purchase Orders** dialog box

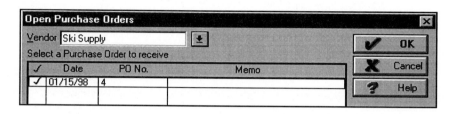

Click **OK**

Click **Clear Qtys** button on the bottom of the screen to clear 15 from the Qty column

Tab to or click **Qty**, enter **10**

Click **OK** to record and close the transaction

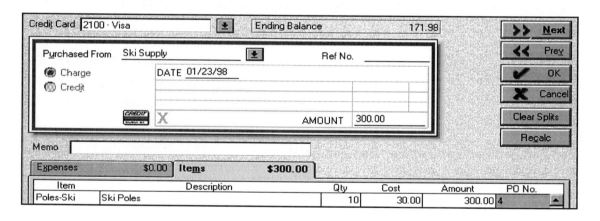

CONFIRM THE RECORDING OF THE SKI POLES RECEIVED ON PURCHASE ORDER 4

MEMO

DATE: January 23, 1998

View P.O. No. 4 to determine whether or not the amount of ski poles received was recorded.

---

*DO: Access Purchase Order 4 as previously instructed
- The **RCVD** column should show **10**.

- Notice that the **QTY** column shows **15** and **Clsd** is not marked. This indicates that 5 sets of ski poles are still on order.

Click **Cancel** button to close Purchase Order 4

ENTER BILLS

Whether the bill is to pay for expenses incurred in the operation of a business or to pay for merchandise to sell in the business, QuickBooks provides accounts payable tracking for all vendors to which the company owes money. Entering bills as soon as they are received is an efficient way to record your liabilities. Once bills have been entered, QuickBooks will be able to provide up-to-date cash flow reports, and QuickBooks will remind you when it's time to pay your bills. As previously stated, a bill is divided into two sections: a vendor-related section (the upper part of the bill that looks similar to a check and has a memo text box under it) and a detail section (the area that is divided into columns for Account, Amount, and Memo). The vendor-related section of the bill is where information for the actual bill is entered, including a memo with information about the transaction. If the bill is for paying an expense, the Expenses tab is used for the detail section. Using this tab allows you to indicate the expense accounts for the transaction, to enter the amounts for the various expense accounts, and to provide transaction explanations. If the bill is for merchandise, the Items tab will be used to record the receipt of items ordered.

MEMO

DATE: January 23, 1998

Took out an ad in the *Mammoth News* announcing our February sale. Received a bill for $95.00 from *Mammoth News*, terms Net 30, Invoice #381-22. The newspaper is a new vendor. The address is 1450 Main Street, Mammoth Lakes, CA 93546, Contact: Frieda Gustaf, Phone: 619-555-2525, FAX: 619-555-5252.

---

*DO: Record the receipt of the bill from *Mammoth News* and add the newspaper as a new vendor

Click **Bill** on the iconbar

Or

Use QuickBooks Navigator:

Click **Purchases and Vendors** tab, click **Enter Bills**

Complete the **Vendor-Related Section** of the bill:

Click the drop-down list arrow next to **Vendor**, click **<Add New>**

Enter the **Vendor** name as **Mammoth News**

Tab to or click **Company Name**, enter Mammoth News

Tab to or click the second line in the **Address**, enter **1450 Main Street**, press **Enter**

Key in **Mammoth Lakes, CA 93546**

Tab to or click **Contact**, key in **Frieda Gustaf**

Tab to or click **Phone**, enter **619-555-2525**

Tab to or click **FAX**, enter **619-555-5252**

Click **OK** to exit and add the name to the Vendor list

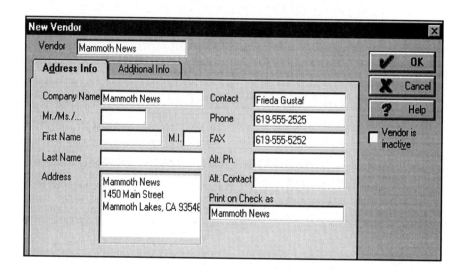

- Name is entered as the vendor on the bill.

Tab to **Date**, type **01/23/98** as the date

Tab to **Ref No.**, type the vendor's invoice number **381-22**

Tab to **Amount Due**, type **95**

- QuickBooks will automatically insert the .00 after the amount.

Tab to **Terms**, click the drop-down list arrow next to **Terms**, click **Net 30**

- QuickBooks automatically changes the Bill Due date to show 30 days from the transaction date.
- At this time no change will be made to Bill Due date, and nothing will be inserted as a memo.

Complete the **Detail Section** of the bill:

Tab to or click in the column for **Account**, click the drop-down list arrow next to **Account**, scroll through the list to find **Advertising Expense**

Because the account does not appear, click **<Add New>**

- **Type** of account should show **Expense**. If not, click drop-down list arrow and click Expense.

Enter **6140** as the account number in **Number**

Tab to or click **Name**, enter **Advertising Expense**
Click **OK**

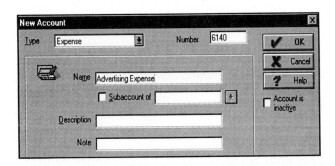

6140 Advertising Expense shows as the Account
- Based on the accrual method of accounting, Advertising Expense is selected as the account for this transaction because this expense should be matched against the revenue of the period.
- The **Amount** column already shows **95.00**—no entry required

Tab to or click the first line in the column for **Memo**
Enter the transaction explanation of:

    Ad for February Sale

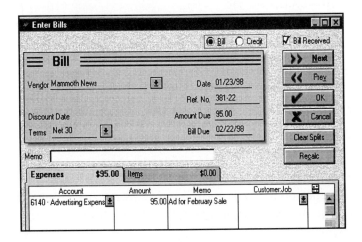

Click **OK**
- If you get a dialog box for **Name Information Changed**, click **No**.

CHANGE EXISTING VENDORS' TERMS

Once a vendor has been established, changes can be made to the vendor's account information. The changes will take effect immediately and will be reflected in any transactions recorded for the vendor.

MEMO

DATE: January 25, 1998

Renee Squires realizes that no terms were recorded for Mammoth Power Company, Mammoth Water Company, and Mammoth Telephone Company when vendor accounts were established. Change the terms for the three companies to Net 30.

---

*DO: Change the terms for all of the vendors listed above
Access Vendor list as previously instructed
Click **Mammoth Power Co.**, click **Vendor** button, click **Edit**
Click **Additional Info** tab
Click drop-down list arrow for terms, click **Net 30**
Click **OK**
Repeat for the other vendors indicated in the memo above
Close Vendor list when all changes have been made

PREPARE BILLS WITHOUT STEP-BY-STEP INSTRUCTIONS

It is more efficient to record bills in a group or "batch" than it is to record them one at a time. If an error is made while preparing the bill, correct it. Mountain Adventure Ski Shoppe uses the accrual basis of accounting. In the accrual method of accounting the expenses of a period are matched against the revenue of the period. Unless otherwise instructed, use the accrual basis of accounting when recording entries.

MEMO

DATE: January 25, 1998

Record the receipt of the following bills:

| Mammoth Power Company electrical power for January, $359.00, Invoice 3510-1023, Net 30. |
| Mammoth Telephone Company telephone service for January, $156.40, Invoice 7815-21, Net 30. |
| Mammoth Water Company water for January, $35.00, Invoice 3105, Net 30. |

---

 *DO: Enter the three transactions in the memo above.

- Refer to the instructions given for previous transactions.
- Remember, when recording bills, you will need to determine the accounts used in the transaction. To determine the appropriate accounts to use, refer to the Chart of Accounts as you record the transactions.
- Enter information for Memos where transaction explanation is needed for clarification.
- To go from one bill to the next, click **>>NEXT** button on the right side of the bill.
- After entering the last bill, click **OK** to record and exit **ENTER BILLS** screen.

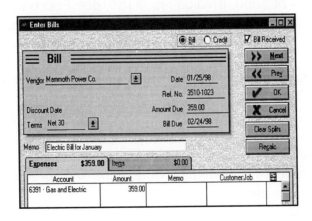

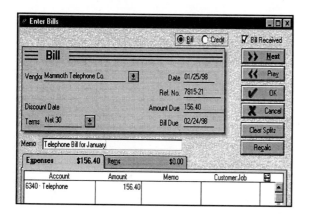 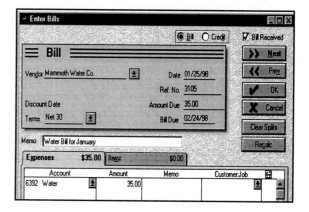

ENTER A BILL USING THE ACCOUNTS PAYABLE REGISTER

The Accounts Payable register maintains a record of all the transactions recorded within the Accounts Payable account. Not only is it possible to view all of the account activities through the account's register, it is also possible to enter a bill directly into the Accounts Payable register. This can be faster than filling out all of the information through Enter Bills.

MEMO

DATE: January 25, 1998

Received a bill for the rent from Rent, Inc. Use the Accounts Payable register and record the bill for rent of $950, Invoice No. 7164, due February 4, 1998.

---

*DO: Use the Accounts Payable Register to record the above transaction:
Click the **Lists** menu, click **Chart of Accounts**
    OR
Click the **Accnts** button on the iconbar
Click **Accounts Payable**
Click **Activities** button at the bottom of the Chart of Accounts
Click **Use Register**
    OR
Use the keyboard shortcut **Ctrl+R**
Click in the blank entry at the end of the register
The date is highlighted, key in **01/25/98** for the transaction date
The word "Number" is in the next column

Tab to or click **Number**
- The word "Number" disappears.

Enter the Invoice Number **7164**

Tab to or click **Vendor**, click the drop-down list arrow for the Vendor, click
    Rent, Inc.

Tab to or click **Due Date**, enter the due date **02/04/98**

Tab to or click **Billed**, enter the amount **950**

Tab to or click **Account**, click the drop-down list arrow for **Account**

Determine the appropriate account to use for rent
- If all of the accounts do not appear in the drop-down list, scroll through the
  accounts until you find the one appropriate for this entry.

Click **6300 Rent**

Tab to or click Memo, key **Rent**

Click **Record** button to record the transaction

01/25/98	7164	Rent, Inc.		02/04/98	950.00		Paid	12,590.40
	BILL	6300 · Rent	Rent					

Do not close the register

EDIT A TRANSACTION IN THE ACCOUNTS PAYABLE REGISTER

Because QuickBooks makes corrections extremely user friendly, a transaction can be edited or changed directly in the Accounts Payable register as well as on the original bill. By eliminating the columns for Type and Memo, it is possible to change the register to show each transaction on one line. This can make the register easier to read.

MEMO

DATE: January 25, 1998

Upon examination of the invoices and the bills entered, Renee discovers an error: The actual amount of the bill from the water company was **$85**, not $35. Change the transaction amount for this bill.

---

*DO: Correct the above transaction in the Accounts Payable Register
    Click the check box for **1-line** to select
- Each Accounts Payable transaction will appear on one line.

Change the amount of the transaction from $35.00 to **$85.00**

Click the **Record** button at the bottom of the register to record the change in the transaction

Date	Number	Vendor	Account	Due Date	Billed	✓	Paid	Balance
01/18/98		Flying Snow, Inc.	-split-	02/17/98	370.00			8,870.00
01/18/98		Sports Boots	1120 · Inventory A:	02/17/98	1,875.00			10,745.00
01/18/98		SkiWear, Inc.	1120 · Inventory A:	02/17/98	300.00			11,045.00
01/23/98	381-22	Mammoth News	6140 · Advertising	02/22/98	95.00			11,140.00
01/23/98	9912	Flying Snow, Inc.	1120 · Inventory A:	Paid			50.00	11,090.00
01/25/98	7815-21	Mammoth Telepho	6340 · Telephone	02/24/98	156.40			11,246.40
01/25/98	3510-102	Mammoth Power C	6391 · Gas and Ele	02/24/98	359.00			11,605.40
01/25/98	3105	Mammoth Wate	6392 · Water	02/24/98	85.00		Paid	11,690.40
01/25/98	7164	Rent, Inc.	6300 · Rent	02/04/98	950.00			12,640.40

Record | Edit | Splits | | | Ending balance | 11,890.40

Restore | Q-Report | Go To | ☑ 1-Line ☐ Show open balance

Do not close the register

PREVIEW AND PRINT A QUICKREPORT
FROM THE ACCOUNTS PAYABLE REGISTER

After editing the transaction, you may want to view information about a specific vendor. This can be done quickly and efficiently by clicking the vendor's name within a transaction and clicking the Q-Report button at the bottom of the Register.

MEMO

DATE: January 25, 1998

More than one transaction has been entered for Flying Snow, Inc. The owners, Eric and Matt, like to view transaction information for all vendors that have several transactions within a short period of time.

---

*DO: Prepare a QuickReport for Flying Snow, Inc.

Click any field in any transaction for Flying Snow, Inc.

Click the **Q-Report** button at the bottom of the Register

- The Register QuickReport for All Transactions for Flying Snow, Inc., appears on the screen.

Click **Print** button

Complete the information on the **Print Reports Screen**:
    Print To: Printer
    Orientation: Landscape
    Page Range: All
Click **Preview** to view the report before printing
- The report appears on the screen as a full page.
- A full-page report usually cannot be read on the screen.

To read the text in the report, click the **Zoom In** button at the top of the screen
Use the scroll buttons and bars to view the report columns
Click the **Zoom Out** button to return to a full-page view of the report
When finished viewing the report, click **Close**
- You will return to the Print Report Screen.

Click **Print** button on the Print Reports Screen

Mountain Adventure Ski Shoppe
Register QuickReport
All Transactions

◇	Type	◇	Date	◇	Num	◇	Memo	◇	Account	◇	Paid	◇	Open Balance	◇	Amount
Flying Snow, Inc.															
	Bill		01/18/98						2000 · Accounts P...				320.00		370.00
	Credit		01/23/98		9912		Returned 1 S...		2000 · Accounts P...		X				-50.00
Total Flying Snow, Inc.													320.00		320.00
TOTAL													320.00		320.00

Click the **Close** button to close the Report
Close the Accounts Payable register by double-clicking on the **Control Menu Button or Icon** in the top left corner of the title bar
Click the **Close** button to close the Chart of Accounts

PREPARE AND PRINT UNPAID BILLS REPORT

It is possible to get information regarding unpaid bills by simply preparing a report. No more digging through tickler files, recorded invoices, ledgers, or journals. QuickBooks prepares an Unpaid Bills Report listing each unpaid bill grouped and subtotaled by vendor.

MEMO

DATE: January 25, 1998

Renee Squires prepares an Unpaid Bill Report for Eric and Matt each week. Because Mountain Adventure Ski Shoppe is a small business, the owners like to have a firm control over cash flow so they can determine which bills will be paid during the week.

---

*DO: Prepare and print an Unpaid Bills Report

Click **Report** on the menu bar, point to **A/P Reports**, click **Unpaid Bills Detail**
OR

Use QuickBooks Navigator: click **Purchases and Vendors** tab, click **Accounts Payable** in the Report section of the Navigator screen, click **Unpaid Bills Detail**

- Unpaid Bills Report shows on the screen.

Enter the date of **01/25/98** as the report date

Tab to generate report

Click **Print** button, use Portrait Orientation

	Mountain Adventure Ski Shoppe				
	Unpaid Bills by Vendor				
	As of January 25, 1998				
◇ **Type**	◇ **Date**	◇ **Num**	◇ **Due Date**	◇ **Aging**	◇ **Open Balance** ◇
Ski Supply					
Bill	01/01/98		01/01/98	24	5,000.00
Total Ski Supply					5,000.00
SkiWear, Inc.					
Bill	01/18/98		02/17/98		300.00
Total SkiWear, Inc.					300.00
Sports Boots					
Bill	01/18/98		02/17/98		1,875.00
Total Sports Boots					1,875.00

Partial Report

Click **Close** button to close the report

PAYING BILLS

When using QuickBooks, you may choose to pay your bills directly from the pay bills command and let QuickBooks write your checks for you, or you may choose to write the checks yourself. Just remember not to do both! Using the Pay Bills window enables you to determine which bills to pay, the method of payment—on-line payment, check, or credit card—and the appropriate account. When you are determining which bills to pay, QuickBooks allows you to display the bills by due date, discount date, vendor, or amount. All bills may be displayed, or only those bills that are due by a certain date may be displayed.

MEMO
DATE: January 25, 1998

Whenever possible, Renee Squires pays the bills on a weekly basis. Show all the bills in the Pay Bills window. Select the bills, except the bill for Flying Snow, Inc., with discounts dates of 1/28/98 for payment.

---

*DO: Pay the bills that are eligible for a discount
Access the Pay Bills window:
> Click **Activities** menu, click **Pay Bills**
> > OR
> Use QuickBooks Navigator: Click **Purchases and Vendors** tab, click **Pay Bills**

Determine the bills to be paid:
> Tab to or click **Payment Date**, enter the Payment Date of **01/25/98**
> Click **Show All Bills** to select
> - Verify that **Pay By** has **Check** selected and **To be printed** is marked by a ✓.
> Sort Bills by **Due Date**
> - If this is not showing, click the drop-down list arrow next to the Sort Bills text box, click **Due Date**.
> Scroll through the list of bills
> - The bills will be shown according to the date due.

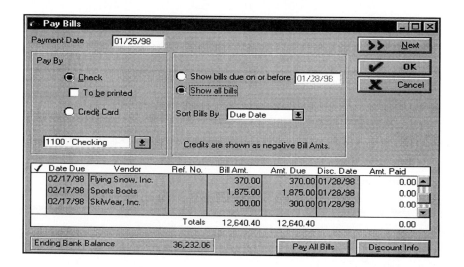

Select the bills to be paid and apply the discounts:

Click in the ✔column for the transaction for Sports Boots with a due date of 2/17/98

Click **Discount Info** button

- Verify the amount of the discount.
- If necessary, select account 4030 Purchases Discounts as the discount account. Notice that the discount account is an income account. QuickBooks considers discounts earned by early payment a type of income and lists purchases discounts as income and not as part of cost of goods sold.

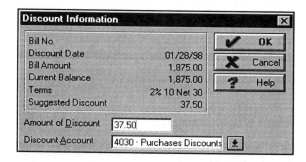

Click **OK** to record the discount

Repeat the steps for the other transaction eligible for a discount

- Remember to skip the transaction for Flying Snow, Inc.

✔	Date Due	Vendor	Ref. No.	Bill Amt.	Amt. Due	Disc. Date	Amt. Paid
✔	02/17/98	Sports Boots		1,875.00	1,837.50	01/28/98	1,837.50
✔	02/17/98	SkiWear, Inc.		300.00	294.00	01/28/98	294.00

- Once you click OK to accept the discount, the amount due and amount paid amounts change to reflect the amount of the discount taken.
Click >>**Next** button to record the payments and go to the next Pay Bills screen

PAY A BILL QUALIFYING FOR A PURCHASE DISCOUNT AND APPLY CREDIT AS PART OF PAYMENT

When paying bills, it is a good idea to apply credits received for returned or damaged merchandise to the accounts as payment is made.

MEMO

DATE: January 25, 1998

As she is getting ready to pay bills, Renee looks for any credits that may be applied to the bill as part of the payment. In addition, Renee looks for bills that qualify for an early-payment discount. Apply the credit received from Flying Snow, Inc., as part of the payment for the bill, then apply the discount, and pay bill within the discount period.

---

*DO: Apply the credit received from Flying Snow, Inc., as part of the payment for the bill and pay bill within the discount period
Verify **Payment Date** of **01/25/98**
Verify **Pay By** is **Check** and **To be printed** is marked
Verify **1100 Checking** is the account for **Pay By**
Select **Show all bills**
Click drop-down list for **Sort Bills By**, click **Vendor**
Scroll through transactions until you see two transactions for Flying Snow, Inc.
Click the transaction indicating the $50 credit to select
- This must be completed before applying the discount to the bill for $370.
Click the second transaction with a Bill Amt. of 370 to select
Click **Discount Info** button, click **OK** to accept the discount

✓	Date Due	Vendor	Ref. No.	Bill Amt.	Amt. Due	Disc. Date	Amt. Paid
✓		Flying Snow, Inc.	9912	-50.00	-50.00		-50.00
✓	02/17/98	Flying Snow, Inc.		370.00	362.60	01/28/98	362.60

- The credit will be applied once OK is clicked and the payment is recorded. Click **OK** to record the payment

PRINT CHECKS TO PAY BILLS

Once bills have been selected for payment and any discounts taken or credit applied, the checks should be printed, signed, and mailed. QuickBooks has two methods which may be used to print checks. Checks may be accessed and printed one at a time. This allows you to view the Bill Payment Information for each check. A more efficient way to print checks is to click the file menu and select checks from the print forms menu. This method will print all checks that are marked "To be printed," but will not allow you to view the bill payment information for any of the checks.

MEMO

DATE: January 25, 1998

Renee needs to print the checks for bills that have been paid. She decides to print checks individually so she can view bill payment information for each check while printing. When she finishes with the checks, she will give them to Eric for his approval and signature.

---

 *DO: Print the checks for bills that have been paid

> To access checks, click the **Activities** menu, click **Write Checks**
> > OR
> Click **Checking and Credit Cards** tab in QuickBooks Navigator, click **Checks**
> > OR
> Click the **Check** icon on the iconbar
> > OR
> Use the keyboard shortcut **Ctrl+W**
> - A blank check will show on the screen.
> Click **<<Prev** button until you get to the check for **Sports Boots**
> Click **Print** to print the check
> Click **OK** on the Print Check screen to select Check Number 2
> - Check 1 was issued in Chapter 5 to Dr. Jose Moreno for a return. If Check Number 2 is not on the Print Check screen, change the screen so that the check number is 2.

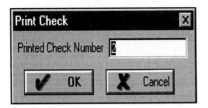

- On the Print Checks screen, verify the printer name, printer type, and check style.
- Make sure the Print Company Name and Address check box is selected.

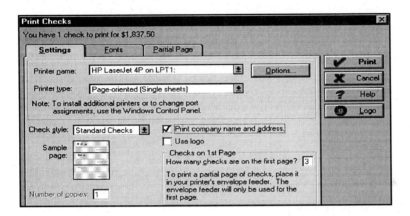

Click **Print** to print the check
Click **OK** on **Did check(s) print OK?**

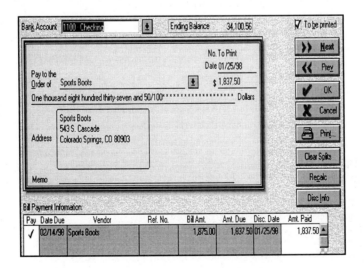

Repeat the steps to print Check Number 3 for SkiWear, Inc., and Check Number 4 Flying Snow, Inc.

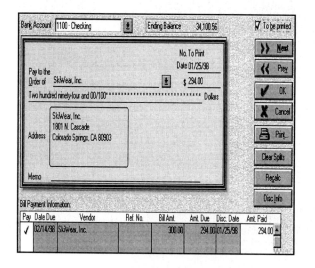 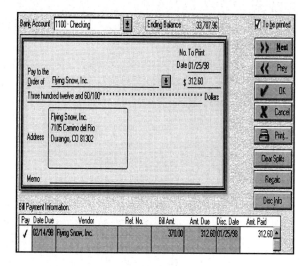

- Notice that the amount of the check to Flying Snow, Inc., is $312.60. This allows for the original bill of $370 less the return of $50 and the discount of $7.40.
- If necessary, click **OK** to close Write Checks window.

PAY BILLS USING A CREDIT CARD

Rather than a check, a credit card may be used to pay a bill. Use the Pay Bills feature, but select Pay By Credit Card rather than Pay By Check.

MEMO

DATE: January 25, 1998

In viewing the bills due, Eric and Matt direct Renee to pay the bills to ABC Accessories and Shoe Supply using the Visa credit card.

---

*DO: Pay the above bills with a credit card
Access Pay Bills as previously instructed
Payment Date should be **01/25/98**
In **Pay By** click **Credit Card** to select
- In the text box beneath Credit Card account 2100 Visa should show. If it does not, click the drop-down list arrow and click on 2100 Visa.
Select **Show all bills**

Scroll through the list of bills and select **ABC Accessories** and **Shoe Supply** by clicking in the ✓ column

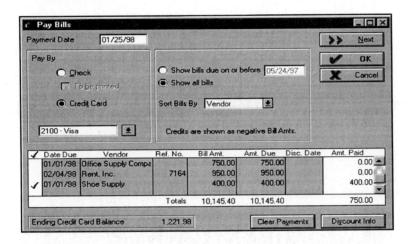

Click **OK** to record the payment

VERIFY THE CREDIT CARD PAYMENT OF BILLS

Paying bills with a credit card in Pay Bills automatically creates a Credit Card transaction in QuickBooks. This can be verified through the Visa account register in the Chart of Accounts and through Enter Credit Card Charges.

MEMO

DATE: January 25, 1998

Verify the credit card charges for ABC Accessories and Shoe Supply.

---

*DO: Verify the credit card charges
Access the Visa account register in the Chart of Accounts
Scroll through the register to see the charges for ABC Accessories and Shoe Supply

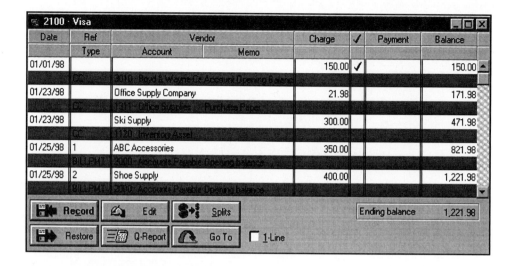

Close the Register and the Chart of Accounts

SALES TAX

When the company is set up in QuickBooks, a Sales Tax Payable liability account is automatically created if the company indicates that it charges sales tax on sales. The Sales Tax Payable account keeps track of as many tax agencies as the company needs. As invoices are written, QuickBooks records the tax liability in the Sales Tax Payable account. To determine the sales tax owed, a Sales Tax Liability Report is prepared.

PRINT SALES TAX LIABILITY REPORT

The Sales Tax Liability report shows your total taxable sales, the total nontaxable sales, and the amount of sales tax owed to each tax agency.

MEMO

DATE: January 25, 1998

Prior to paying the sales tax, Renee prepares the Sales Tax Liability report.

---

*DO: Prepare the Sales Tax Liability report

Click **Reports** menu, point to **A/P Reports**, click **Sales Tax Liability Report**
The Report Dates are **From 01/01/98 To 01/25/98**
Print in Landscape orientation
- If necessary, adjust the column width so the report will fit on one page.
- If you get a message box asking if all columns should be the same size as the one being adjusted, click **No**.

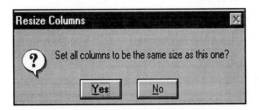

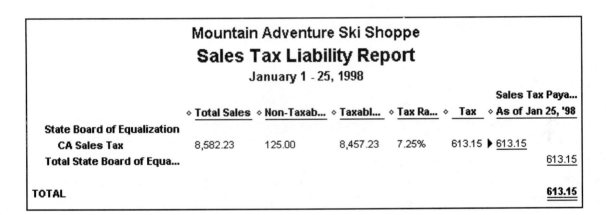

Close the report

PAYING SALES TAX

Use Pay Sales Tax window to determine how much sales tax you owe and to write a check to the tax agency. QuickBooks will update the sales tax account with payment information.

MEMO

DATE: January 25, 1998

Note from Matt: Renee, pay the sales taxes owed.

---

*DO: Pay the sales taxes owed

    Click **Activities** menu, click **Pay Sales Tax**

        OR

    Click **Taxes and Accountants** tab on QuickBooks Navigator,
        click **Pay Sales Tax** icon

    Pay From Account is **1100 Checking**

    Check Date is **01/25/98**

    •   **To be printed** should be selected with a ✓ in the check box.

    Show sales tax due through is **01/25/98**

    Click **Pay All Tax** button

Pay Sales Tax

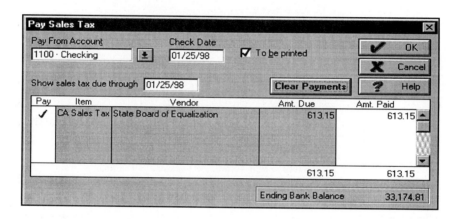

•   Once Pay All Tax has been clicked and the item selected, the Ending Bank
     Balance changes to reflect the amount in checking after the tax has been paid.

Click **OK**

Print Check 5:

    Click **File** menu, point to Print Forms, click **Print Checks**

    •   Verify Bank Account 1100 Checking, First Check #5, ✔ in front of State
        Board of Equalization. Make any changes needed.

    Click **OK**, click **Print**, click **OK** to answer "Did check(s) print Ok?"

VOIDING AND DELETING PURCHASE ORDERS, BILLS, CHECKS, AND CREDIT CARD PAYMENTS

QuickBooks is so user friendly it allows any business form to be deleted. Some accounting programs do not allow error corrections, except as adjusting entries, once an entry has been made. QuickBooks, however, allows a purchase order, a bill, a credit card payment, or a check to be voided or deleted. If a business form is voided, the form remains as a transaction. The transaction shows as a zero amount. This is useful when you want a record to show that an entry was made. If the form is deleted, all trace of the form is deleted. QuickBooks allows a company to keep an "audit trail" if it wants a complete record of all transactions entered. The audit trail includes information regarding deleted transactions as well as transactions that appear on business forms, in the Journal, and in reports. An audit trail helps to eliminate misconduct such as printing a check and then deleting the check from the company records.

The procedures for voiding and deleting business forms are the same whether the business is a retail business or a service business. For actual assignments and practice in voiding and deleting business forms, refer to Chapters 2, 3, and 5.

CREATE AN ACCOUNTS PAYABLE GRAPH BY AGING PERIOD

Graphs provide a visual representation of certain aspects of the business. It is sometimes easier to interpret data in a graphical format. For example, to determine if any payments are overdue for accounts payable accounts, an Accounts Payable graph will provide that information instantly on a bar chart. In addition, the Accounts Payable graph feature of QuickBooks also displays a pie chart showing what percentage of the total amount payable is owed to each vendor.

DO: Prepare an Accounts Payable Graph

Click **Reports** on the menu bar, point to **Graphs**, click **Accounts Payable**
    OR
Click **Accounts Payable** in the **Reports** section of the **Purchases and Vendors** tab on QuickBooks Navigator, click **Accounts Payable Graph**
Click **Dates** button at the top of the report, enter **01/25/98** for Show Aging as of text box

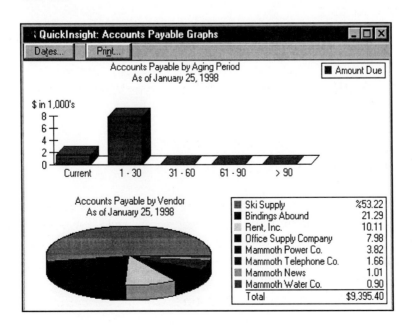

Click **OK**

Close without printing

BACK UP MOUNTAIN ADVENTURE SKI SHOPPE DATA

Whenever an important work session is complete, you should always back up your data. If your data disk is damaged or an error is discovered at a later time, the backup disk may be restored and the information used for recording transactions.

 ***DO:** Follow the instructions given in previous chapters to back up data for Mountain Adventure Ski Shoppe

SUMMARY

In this chapter purchase orders were completed, inventory items were received and bills were recorded. Payments for purchases and bills were made by cash and by credit card. Sales taxes were paid. Vendors, inventory items, and accounts were added while transactions were being recorded. Various reports and graphs were prepared to determine the unpaid bills, the sales tax liability, and the aging of accounts payable accounts.

END-OF-CHAPTER QUESTIONS

TRUE/FALSE

ANSWER THE FOLLOWING QUESTIONS IN THE SPACE PROVIDED BEFORE THE QUESTION NUMBER.

_____ 1. Receipt of purchase order items is never recorded before the bill arrives.

_____ 2. A bill can be paid by check or credit card.

_____ 3. A purchase order can be entered via the Reminders list.

_____ 4. Voiding a purchase order removes all trace of the purchase order from the company records.

_____ 5. QuickBooks can prepare a bar chart illustrating the overdue accounts payable accounts.

_____ 6. A single purchase order can be prepared and sent to several vendors.

_____ 7. A sales tax account is automatically created if a company indicates that it charges sales tax on sales.

_____ 8. A credit received from a vendor for the return of merchandise can be applied to a payment to the vendor.

_____ 9. A new vendor cannot be added while recording a transaction.

_____ 10. A purchase order is closed automatically when a partial receipt of merchandise is recorded.

MULTIPLE CHOICE

WRITE THE LETTER OF THE CORRECT ANSWER IN THE SPACE PROVIDED BEFORE THE QUESTION NUMBER.

_____ 1. If you change the minimum quantity for an item, it becomes effective ___.
A. immediately
B. the beginning of next month
C. as soon as outstanding purchase orders are received
D. the beginning of the next fiscal year

_____ 2. If an order is received with a bill but is incomplete, QuickBooks will ___.
A. record the bill for the full amount ordered
B. record the bill only for the amount received
C. not allow the bill to be prepared until all the merchandise is received
D. close the purchase order

_____ 3. The Purchase Order feature must be selected as a preference ___.
A. when setting up the company
B. prior to recording the first purchase order
C. is automatically set when first the purchase order is prepared
D. both A and B

_____ 4. A faster method of entering bills can be entering the bills ___.
A. while writing the checks for payment
B. in the Pay Bills window
C. in the Accounts Payable register
D. none of the above

_____ 5. When items ordered are received with a bill, you record the receipt ___.
A. on an item receipt form
B. on the bill
C. on the original purchase order
D. in the Journal

_____ 6. Sales tax is paid by using the ___ window.
A. pay bills
B. pay sales tax
C. write check
D. credit card

_____ 7. An individual vendor's percentage of the total amount for accounts payable is displayed in a ___.
A. pie chart
B. bar chart
C. line graph
D. 3-dimensional line graph

_____ 8. Checks to pay bills may be printed ___.
A. individually
B. all at once
C. as the checks are written
D. all of the above

_____ 9. When recording a bill for merchandise received, you click the ___ tab on the vendor section of the bill.
A. Memo
B. Expenses
C. Items
D. Purchase Order

_____ 10. The ___ matches income for the period against expenses for the period.
A. cash basis of accounting
B. credit basis of accounting
C. accrual basis of accounting
D. debit/credit basis of accounting

FILL-IN

IN THE SPACE PROVIDED, WRITE THE ANSWER THAT MOST APPROPRIATELY COMPLETES THE SENTENCE.

1. Orders are prepared using the QuickBooks _____ form.

2. Information on the Reminders list may be displayed in _____ or _____ form.

3. The _____ report shows the total taxable sales and the amount of sales tax owed.

4. A purchase order can be closed _____ or _____.

5. To see the bill payment information, checks must be printed _____.

SHORT ESSAY

Describe the cycle of obtaining merchandise. Include the process from ordering the merchandise through paying for it. Include information regarding the QuickBooks forms prepared for each phase of the cycle, the possible ways in which an item may be received, and the ways in which payment may be made.

_____

_____

_____

_____

_____

_____

END-OF-CHAPTER PROBLEM

HAWAII SUN CLOTHING CO.

Chapter 6 continues with the transactions for purchase orders, merchandise receipts, bills, bill payments, and sales tax payments. Maile prints the checks, purchase orders, and any related reports; and Nalani signs the checks. This procedure establishes cash control procedures and lets both owners know about the checks being processed.

INSTRUCTIONS

Continue to use the copy of HAWAII you used in Chapter 5. Open the company—the file used is **Hawaii.QBW**. Record the purchase orders, bills, payments, and other purchases as instructed within the chapter. Always read the transactions carefully and review the Chart of Accounts when selecting transaction accounts. Print reports and graphs as indicated. Add new vendors and minimum quantities where indicated. Print all purchase orders and checks issued. The first purchase order used is Purchase Order 1. When paying bills, always check for credits that may be applied to the bill, and always check for discounts.

In addition to the Item list indicating sales items and the Chart of Accounts, you will need to use the Vendor list when ordering merchandise and paying bills.

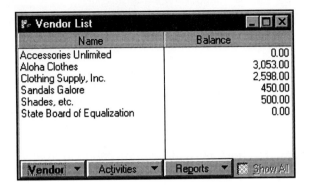

RECORD TRANSACTIONS

January 5, 1998:

Change the reorder point for dresses from 20 to 25.

Change the reorder point for women's pants to 30.

Display and print a detailed Reminders list.

Prepare and print a Stock Status by Item Inventory report for January 1-5 in Landscape orientation.

Prepare Purchase Orders for all items marked Order on the Stock Status by Item Inventory report. Refer to the Stock Status by Item report for vendor information. The quantity for each item ordered is 10. The rate is $35 for dresses and $20 for pants. Print purchase orders with lines around each field.

Order an additional 10 dresses from a new vendor: The Clothes House, 9382 Grand Avenue, San Luis Obispo, CA 93407, contact person is Marshall Rowland, 805-555-5512, fax is 805-555-2155, credit terms are 2% 10 Net 30, credit limit is $2000. The rate for the dresses is $25.

Print a Purchase Order QuickReport in Landscape orientation for January 1-5.

January 8, 1998:

Received pants ordered without the bill. Enter the receipt of merchandise. The transaction date is 01/08/98.

Received dresses from Aloha with the bill. Enter the receipt of the merchandise and the bill.

Received 8 dresses from The Clothes House. Enter the receipt of the merchandise and the bill.

After recording the receipt of merchandise, view the three purchase orders. Notice which ones are marked Received in Full and Clsd.

January 9, 1998:

Received bill for pants. The bill was dated 01/08/98.

Pay for the dresses from The Clothes House with a credit card. (Take a purchase discount if the transaction qualifies for one. Use 4030 Purchases Discount Income account for any discounts.)

January 10, 1998:
Discovered unstitched seams in two pairs of pants. Return the pants for credit.

January 15, 1998:
Record bill for rent of $1150. (Vendor is Real Estate Rental Company, 301 Marsh St., San Luis Obispo, CA 93407, contact person is Marsha Roberts, 805-555-4100, fax 805-555-0014, terms Net 30.)

Record bill for telephone service of $79.85. (Vendor is SLO Telephone Service Company, 8851 Hwy. 58, San Luis Obispo, CA 93407, 805-555-1029. No terms or credit limits have been given.)

January 18, 1998:
Pay all bills that are eligible for a discount. Take any discounts for which you are eligible. If there are any credits to an account, apply the credit prior to paying the bill. Pay the bill(s) by check.

Print Checks 2 and 3 for the bills that were paid.

January 25, 1998:
Purchase office supplies for $250 with a credit card from Office Inventory Masters, 8330 Grand Avenue, Arroyo Grande, CA 93420, contact person is Larry Thomas, 805-555-9915, fax 805-555-5199, terms Net 30, credit limit $500.

Print Unpaid Bills report in Portrait orientation.

Pay bills for rent and telephone. Use Print Forms to print the checks prepared for these bills on one page.

January 30, 1998:
Prepare Sales Tax Liability report from 01/01/98 to 01/30/98. Print the report in Landscape orientation. Change columns widths, if necessary, so the report will fit on one page.

Pay Sales Tax and print the check.

Prepare a Vendor Balance Detail report as of 01/30/98. Print in Portrait orientation. Adjust column widths so the report will print on one page without selecting Fit report on one page wide.

Prepare and print an Accounts Payable Graph as of 01/30/98.

Print a Trial Balance for 01/01/98 to 01/30/98.

GENERAL ACCOUNTING AND END-OF-PERIOD PROCEDURES: MERCHANDISING BUSINESS

LEARNING OBJECTIVES

At the completion of this chapter, you will be able to use QuickBooks to:

1. Complete the end-of-period procedures.
2. Change the name of existing accounts in the Chart of Accounts, view the account name change, and view the effect of an account name change on subaccounts.
3. Delete an existing account from the Chart of Accounts.
4. Enter the adjusting entries required for accrual basis accounting.
5. Record depreciation, adjustments to Uncategorized Income and Uncategorized Expenses, and an adjustment for Purchases Discounts.
6. Understand how to record owners' equity transactions for a partnership.
7. Enter a transaction for owner withdrawals, and transfer owner withdrawals and net income to the owners' capital accounts.
8. Reconcile the bank statement, record bank service charges, and mark cleared transactions.
9. Reconcile a credit card statement.
10. Print the journal.
11. Print reports such as trial balance, profit and loss statement, and balance sheet.
12. Perform end-of-period backup, assign end-of-period password, and record transactions in a "closed" period.

GENERAL ACCOUNTING AND END-OF-PERIOD PROCEDURES

As stated in previous chapters, QuickBooks operates from the standpoint of the business document rather than an accounting form, journal, or ledger. While QuickBooks does incorporate all of these items into the program, in many instances they operate behind the scenes. Many other accounting programs require special closing procedures at the end of a period. QuickBooks does not require special closing procedures at the end of a period. At the end of the fiscal year, QuickBooks transfers the net income into the Retained Earnings account and allows you to protect the data for the year by assigning a password to the period. All of the transaction detail is maintained and viewable, but it cannot be changed unless it is accessed by using the assigned password.

Even though a formal "closing" does not have to be performed within QuickBooks, when using accrual basis accounting, several transactions must be recorded in order to reflect all expenses and income for the period accurately. For example, bank statements and credit cards must be reconciled; and any charges or bank collections need to be recorded. An adjustment to transfer purchase discounts from income to cost of goods sold needs to be made. Other adjusting entries such as depreciation, office supplies used, and so on will also need to be made. These adjustments may be recorded by the CPA or by the company's accounting personnel. At the end of the year, net income for the year and the owner withdrawals for the year should be transferred to the owners' capital accounts.

As in a service business, the CPA for the company will review things such as account names, adjusting entries, depreciation schedules, owner's equity adjustments, etc. If the CPA makes the changes and adjustments, they may be made on the Accountant's Copy of the business files. This disk is then merged with the company files that are used to record day-to-day business transactions. All adjustments made by the CPA are added to the current company files. There are certain restrictions to the types of transactions that may be made on an accountant's copy of the business files. In some instances, the accountant will make adjustments on a backup copy of the company data. This method may be used because there are no restrictions on the types of entries that may be made. If the backup is used, the transactions entered by the accountant on backup company files will also need to be entered in the company files used to record day-to-day transactions. The two sets of company files cannot be merged.

Once necessary adjustments have been made, reports reflecting the end-of-period results of operations should be prepared. For archive purposes, at the end of the fiscal year an additional backup disk is prepared and stored.

TRAINING TUTORIAL AND PROCEDURES

The following tutorial will once again work with Mountain Adventure Ski Shoppe. As in Chapters 5 and 6, transactions will be recorded for this fictitious company. Refer to procedures given in Chapter 5 to maximize training benefits.

OPEN QUICKBOOKS® AND MOUNTAIN ADVENTURE SKI SHOPPE

*DO: Open QuickBooks as instructed in previous chapters
Open Mountain Adventure Ski Shoppe
Close Reminders
- Check the title bar to verify that Mountain Adventure Ski Shoppe is the open company.

 Mountain Adventure Ski Shoppe--Student's Name - QuickBooks

BEGINNING THE TUTORIAL

In this chapter you will be recording end-of-period adjustments, reconciling bank and credit card statements, changing account names, and preparing traditional end-of-period reports. Because QuickBooks does not perform a traditional "closing" of the books, you will learn how to password protect transactions and data recorded during previous accounting periods.

All transactions are listed on memos. The transaction date will be the same as the memo date unless otherwise specified within the transaction. Once a specific type of transaction has been entered in a step-by-step manner, additional transactions of the same or a similar type will be made without having instructions provided. Of course, you may always refer to instructions given for previous transactions for ideas or for steps used to enter those transactions. To determine the account used in the transaction, refer to the Chart of Accounts.

CHANGE THE NAME OF EXISTING ACCOUNTS IN THE CHART OF ACCOUNTS

Even though transactions have been recorded during the month of January, QuickBooks makes it a simple matter to change the name of an existing account. Once the name of an account has been changed, all transactions using the old name are updated and show the new account name.

MEMO

DATE: January 31, 1998

On the recommendation of the company's CPA, Eric and Matt decided to change the account named Freight Income to Delivery Income.

---

*DO: Change the account name of Freight Income
Access the Chart of Accounts:
    Click **Lists**, click **Chart of Accounts** on the menu bar
        OR
    Click **Acent** button on the iconbar
        OR
    Click **Company** tab, click **Chart of Accounts** on QuickBooks Navigator
        OR
    Use the keyboard shortcut **Ctrl+A**
Scroll through accounts until you see Freight Income, click **Freight Income**
Click **Account** Button at the bottom of the chart, click **Edit**

OR

Use the keyboard shortcut **Ctrl+E**

On the **Edit Account** screen highlight **Freight Income**

Enter the new name **Delivery Income**

Change the description from Freight Income to Delivery Income

Click **OK** to record the name change and to close the Edit Account screen

- Notice that the name of the account appears as Delivery Income in the Chart of Accounts.

Name	Type
Chart of Accounts	
◆ 4010 · Sales	Income
◆ 4011 · Clothing & Accessory Sales	Income
◆ 4012 · Equipment Sales	Income
◆ 4020 · Delivery Income	Income
◆ 4030 · Purchases Discounts	Income
◆ 4040 · Returned Check Service Charges	Income
◆ 4999 · Uncategorized Income	Income
◆ 5000 · Cost of Goods Sold	Cost of Goods Sold
◆ 6110 · Automobile Expense	Expense
◆ 6120 · Bank Service Charges	Expense
◆ 6130 · Sales Discount	Expense
◆ 6140 · Advertising Expense	Expense
◆ 6150 · Depreciation Expense	Expense
◆ 6160 · Dues and Subscriptions	Expense
◆ 6170 · Equipment Rental	Expense
◆ 6180 · Insurance	Expense
◆ 6181 · Liability Insurance	Expense
◆ 6182 · Disability Insurance	Expense
◆ 6210 · Interest Expense	Expense
◆ 6211 · Finance Charge	Expense
◆ 6212 · Loan Interest	Expense
◆ 6213 · Mortgage	Expense

Do not close the Chart of Accounts

MAKE AN ACCOUNT INACTIVE

If you are not using an account and do not have plans to do so in the near future, the account may be made inactive. The account remains available for use, yet it does not appear on your Chart of Accounts unless you check the Show All check box.

MEMO

DATE: January 31, 1998

Mountain Adventure Ski Shoppe does not plan to rent any equipment. The account Equipment Rental should be made inactive. In addition, Eric and Matt do not plan to use Disability Insurance. Make this account inactive.

---

 *DO: Make the accounts listed above inactive

Click **Equipment Rental**

Click **Account** button at the bottom of the Chart of Accounts, click **Make Inactive**

OR

Use Keyboard Shortcut **Ctrl+E** to edit the account, click the check box **Account is inactive** to insert a ✔ in the box, click **OK** to close Edit Account window

• The account no longer appears in the Chart of Accounts.

Repeat the procedures indicated and make **Disability Insurance** inactive

• If you wish to view all accounts including the inactive ones, click the **Show All** check box at the bottom of the Chart of Accounts, and all accounts will be displayed.

• Notice the icons that mark Equipment Rental and Disability Insurance as inactive accounts.

🗀 ♦ 6170 · Equipment Rental	Expense
♦ 6180 · Insurance	Expense
♦ 6181 · Liability Insurance	Expense
🗀 ♦ 6182 · Disability Insurance	Expense

Do not close the Chart of Accounts

DELETE AN EXISTING ACCOUNT FROM THE CHART OF ACCOUNTS

If you do not want to make an account inactive because you have not used it and do not plan to use it at all, QuickBooks allows the account to be deleted at anytime. However, as a safeguard QuickBooks does prevent the deletion of an account once it has been used even if it simply contains an opening or an existing balance.

MEMO

DATE: January 31, 1998

In addition to previous changes to account names, Eric and Matt find that they do not use nor will they use the expense accounts: Interest Expense: Mortgage, Taxes: Property, and Travel & Ent. Delete these accounts from the Chart of Accounts.

*DO: Delete the account Interest Expense: Mortgage

Access the Chart of Accounts as previously instructed

Scroll through accounts until you see Interest Expense: Mortgage, click **Interest Expense: Mortgage**

Click **Account** button at the bottom of the chart, click **Delete**
OR

Use the keyboard shortcut **Ctrl+D**

Click **OK** on the **Delete Accounts** dialog box

- The account has now been deleted.

Repeat the above steps to delete **Taxes: Property**

Also follow the same procedures to delete the subaccounts of **Travel & Ent.**

- Note whenever an account has subaccounts, the subaccounts must be deleted before QuickBooks will let you delete the main account. This is what you must do before you can delete Travel & Ent. A subaccount is deleted the same as any other account. In fact, Taxes: Property is a subaccount of Taxes.

When the subaccounts of Travel & Ent. have been deleted, delete **Travel & Ent.**

Close the Chart of Accounts

ADJUSTMENTS FOR ACCRUAL BASIS ACCOUNTING

In accrual basis accounting, the income from a period is matched against the expenses of a period in order to arrive at an accurate figure for net income. Thus, the revenue is earned at the time the service is performed or the sale is made regardless of when the cash is actually received. The same holds true when a business buys things or pays bills. In the accrual basis of accounting, the expense is recorded at the time the bill is received or the purchase is made regardless of the actual payment date. The cash basis of accounting records income or revenue at the time cash is received regardless of when the sale was made or the service performed. In cash basis accounting, the expense is not recorded until it is paid.

There are several internal transactions that must be recorded when using the accrual basis of accounting. These entries are called adjusting entries. For example, equipment does wear out and will eventually need to be replaced. Rather than wait until replacement to record the use of the equipment, an adjusting entry is made to allocate the use of equipment as an expense for a period. This is called depreciation. Certain items used in a business are paid for in advance. As these are used, they become expenses of the business. For example, insurance for the entire year would be used up month by month and should, therefore, be a monthly expense. Commonly, the insurance is billed and paid for the entire year. Until the insurance is used, it is an asset. Each month the portion of the insurance used becomes an expense for the month.

UNCATEGORIZED INCOME AND UNCATEGORIZED EXPENSES ADJUSTMENTS

When the records for Mountain Adventure Ski Shoppe were set up, QuickBooks stored the amounts of the opening balances for customers in an account called Uncategorized Income and the amounts of the opening balances for vendors in an account called Uncategorized Expenses. This was done because a business using the accrual basis for accounting would have already recorded the amounts in the opening balances as income or expenses. These opening balances need to be cleared from Uncategorized Expenses and Uncategorized Income accounts. This is done by recording an adjusting entry.

MEMO

DATE: January 31, 1998

The CPA pointed out that after the company setup was performed, the adjusting entry for Uncategorized Income and Uncategorized Expenses had not been made.

---

   *DO: Make adjustments for Uncategorized Income and Uncategorized Expenses
         Open Chart of Accounts as previously instructed
         Click on the account **Uncategorized Income**
         Click **Reports** button at the bottom of the screen
         Click **QuickReport: Uncategorized Income**
              OR
         Use keyboard shortcut **Ctrl+Q**
         Enter the **From** date as **01/01/98**
         Enter **To** date as **01/31/98**
         Tab to generate the report
         Scroll to the bottom of the report

- Check the total of the Opening Balance—**6,942.50**.
Close the QuickReport for Uncategorized Income

Mountain Adventure Ski Shoppe
Account QuickReport
January 1998

Type	Date	Num	Name	Memo	Split	Amount
Invoice	01/01/98		Vernon, Melvin	Opening bal...	1200 · Accou...	975.00
Invoice	01/01/98		Donaldson, Fran	Opening bal...	1200 · Accou...	650.00
Invoice	01/01/98		David, Ellen	Opening bal...	1200 · Accou...	1,136.00
Invoice	01/01/98		Wilson, Roger	Opening bal...	1200 · Accou...	85.00
Invoice	01/01/98		Finley, Viv Dr.	Opening bal...	1200 · Accou...	417.00
Invoice	01/01/98		Clancy, Cheryl	Opening bal...	1200 · Accou...	455.00
Invoice	01/01/98		Chin, Melinda	Opening bal...	1200 · Accou...	53.63
Invoice	01/01/98		Travis, Carrie	Opening bal...	1200 · Accou...	670.31
Invoice	01/01/98		Tyler, Tim	Opening bal...	1200 · Accou...	911.63
Invoice	01/01/98		Pitcher, Sara	Opening bal...	1200 · Accou...	408.48
Invoice	01/01/98		Moreno, Jose Dr.	Opening bal...	1200 · Accou...	95.45
Total 4999 · Uncategorized Income						6,942.50

Partial Report

Repeat the steps to determine the amount for Uncategorized Expenses
- The total of Uncategorized Expenses should be **8,500**.

Mountain Adventure Ski Shoppe
Account QuickReport
January 1998

Type	Date	Num	Name	Memo	Split	Amount
6999 · Uncategorized Expenses						
Bill	01/01/98		Office Supply Com...	Opening bal...	2000 · Accou...	750.00
Bill	01/01/98		ABC Accessories	Opening bal...	2000 · Accou...	350.00
Bill	01/01/98		Bindings Abound	Opening bal...	2000 · Accou...	2,000.00
Bill	01/01/98		Shoe Supply	Opening bal...	2000 · Accou...	400.00
Bill	01/01/98		Ski Supply	Opening bal...	2000 · Accou...	5,000.00
Total 6999 · Uncategorized Expenses						8,500.00
TOTAL						**8,500.00**

Close the QuickReport for Uncategorized Expenses
Enter the adjustments to Boyd & Wayne, Capital:
    In the Chart of Accounts, click **Boyd & Wayne, Capital**
    Click the **Activities** button, click **Use Register**

OR

Use the keyboard shortcut **Ctrl+R**

In the empty transaction at the bottom of the Register for Boyd & Wayne,
>   Capital, enter the adjustment for Uncategorized Income:
>>   The **Date** is the start date of **01/01/98**
>>   Tab to or click **Account**, click the drop-down list arrow, click
>>>   **Uncategorized Income**
>>   Tab to or click **Increase** field, enter **6942.50**
>>   Click **Record**
>   Enter the adjustment for Uncategorized Expenses:
>>   Position the cursor in the next empty transaction at the bottom of the
>>>   register
>>   Enter the start date of **01/01/98** in the **Date** column
>>   Tab to or click **Account**, click the drop-down list arrow, click
>>>   **Uncategorized Expenses**
>>   Tab to or click **Decrease** field, enter **8500**
>>   Click **Record**
- The balance of Boyd & Wayne, Capital account is $65,459.50.

01/01/98				6,942.50			-1,349.50
	GENJRNL	4999 · Uncategorized Inc					
01/01/98						8,500.00	-9,849.50
	GENJRNL	6999 · Uncategorized Ex					
Record		Edit		Splits		Ending balance	65,459.50

Close the Register for Boyd & Wayne, Capital
Close the Chart of Accounts

ADJUSTING ENTRIES—PREPAID EXPENSES

During the operation of a business, companies purchase supplies to have on hand for use in the operation of the business. In accrual basis accounting, the supplies are considered to be prepaid assets (something the business owns) until they are used in the operation of the business. As the supplies are used, the amount used becomes an expense for the period. The same rationale applies to other things paid for in advance, such as insurance. At the end of the period an adjusting entry must be made to allocate correctly the amount of prepaid assets to expenses.

The transactions for these adjustments may be recorded in the register for the account by clicking on the prepaid asset in the Chart of Accounts, or they may be made in the General Journal.

MEMO

DATE: January 31, 1998

NOTE from Matt: Renee, remember to record the monthly adjustment for Prepaid Insurance. The $250 is the amount we paid for two months of liability insurance coverage. Also, we have a balance of $521.98 in office supplies and a balance of $400 in sales supplies. Please adjust accordingly.

---

*DO: Record the adjusting entries for insurance expense, office supplies expense, and sales supplies expense in the General Journal.

Access the General Journal:

Click **Activities** on the menu bar, click **Make Journal Entry**
   OR
Open **Chart of Accounts** as previously instructed
Click **Prepaid Insurance**, click **Activities** button, click **Make Journal Entry**
   OR
Click **Taxes and Accountant** tab in QuickBooks Navigator, click **Make Journal Entry**

Record the adjusting entry for Prepaid Insurance

Enter **01/31/98** as the **Date**

- **Entry No.** is left blank unless you wish to record a specific number.
- Because all transactions entered for the month have been entered in the Journal as well as on an invoice or a bill, all transactions automatically have a Journal entry number.

Tab to or click **Account** column, click the drop-down list arrow for Account, click **6181 Liability Insurance Expense**

Tab to or click **Debit**

- The $250 given in the memo is the amount for two months.

Calculate the amount of the adjustment for the month:

Click **Activities** on the menu bar, point to **Other Activities**, click **Use Calculator**

Enter **250** by:

Using the mouse to click the numbers
   OR
Typing the numbers at the top of the keyboard
   OR
Keying the numbers on the **10-key pad** (preferred)

Press **/** for division

Key **2**

Press **=**, or **Enter**

Click the **Close** button to close the calculator

• For additional calculator instructions refer to Chapter 1.

Enter the amount of the adjustment **125** in the Debit column

Tab to or click the **Memo** column, type **Adjusting Entry, Insurance**

Tab to or click **Account**, click the drop-down list arrow for Account, click **1340 Prepaid Insurance**

• The amount for the Credit column should have been entered automatically. If not, enter **125**.

Tab to or click the **Memo** column, type **Adjusting Entry, Insurance**

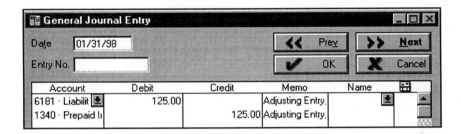

Click **>>NEXT** to record the adjustment and to advance to the next General Journal Entry screen

Repeat the above procedures to record the adjustment for the office supplies used

• The amount given in the memo is the balance of the account after the supplies have been used.

• The actual amount of the supplies used in January must be calculated.

• Follow the instructions above for use of the calculator to determine the amount of the transaction.

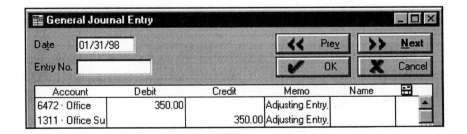

Click **>>Next**

Repeat the above procedures to record the adjustment for the sales supplies used

- The amount given in the memo is the balance of the account after the supplies have been used. The actual amount of the supplies used in January must be calculated.

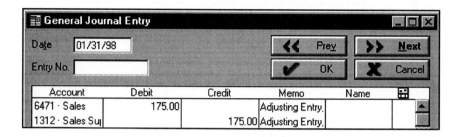

Click **OK**

If necessary, close Chart of Accounts and General Journal

ADJUSTING ENTRIES—DEPRECIATION

Using the accrual basis of accounting requires companies to record an expense for the amount of equipment used in the operation of the business. Unlike supplies, where you can actually see the paper supply diminishing, it is very difficult to see how much of a cash register has been used up during the month. To account for the fact that machines do wear out and need to be replaced, an adjustment is made for depreciation. This adjustment correctly matches the expenses of the period against the revenue of the period.

The adjusting entry for depreciation can be made in the depreciation account register, or it can be made in the General Journal.

MEMO

DATE: January 31, 1998

Having received the necessary depreciation schedules, Renee records the adjusting entry for depreciation:

Office Equipment, $85 per month
Store Fixtures, $75 per month

---

*DO: Record a compound adjusting entry for depreciation of the office equipment and the store supplies in the General Journal:

Access the General Journal as previously instructed

Enter **01/31/98** as the **Date**

Entry No. is left blank

- In order to use the automatic calculation feature of QuickBooks, the credit entries will be entered first.

Tab to or click **Account** column, click the drop-down list arrow for Account, click **1512 Depreciation** under **Office Equipment**

Tab to or click **Credit**, enter **85**

Tab to or click **Memo**, enter **Adjusting Entry, January**

Tab to or click **Account** column, click the drop-down list arrow for Account, click **1522 Depreciation** under **Store Fixtures**

Tab to or click **Credit**, enter **75**

Tab to or click **Memo**, enter **Adjusting Entry, January**

Tab to or click **Account** column, click the drop-down list arrow for Account, click **6150 Depreciation Expense**

Debit column should automatically show **160**

Tab to or click **Memo**, enter **Adjusting Entry, January**

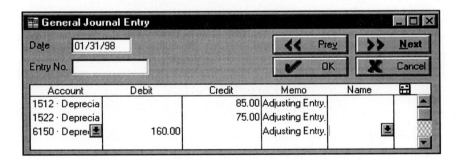

Click **OK** to record the adjustment and close the General Journal

Close Chart of Accounts, if necessary

VIEW PROFIT AND LOSS STATEMENT TO DETERMINE NEED FOR AN ADJUSTMENT TO PURCHASE DISCOUNTS

QuickBooks records purchase discounts as a form of income. Because paying for merchandise within the discount period reduces the amount you pay for an item, the amount of income is increased. However, income is taxed in many areas and to leave the purchase discounts as an income item would make it subject to tax.

*DO: View Profit and Loss Statement to see how Purchase Discounts are shown as income
Click **Reports** menu, click **Profit & Loss**, click **Standard**
Enter the Dates: **From 01/01/98** and **To 01/31/98**
Tab to generate the report

Mountain Adventure Ski Shoppe
Profit and Loss
January 1998

	Jan '98
Income	
4010 · Sales	
4011 · Clothing & Accessory Sales	▶ 1,409.76 ◀
4012 · Equipment Sales	7,436.44
Total 4010 · Sales	8,846.20
4030 · Purchases Discounts	50.90
4040 · Returned Check Service Charges	25.00
4999 · Uncategorized Income	0.00
Total Income	8,922.10
Cost of Goods Sold	
5000 · Cost of Goods Sold	3,352.46
Total COGS	3,352.46

Partial Report

- Notice that 4030 Purchases Discounts is shown as a form of income and not as a reduction to the cost of goods sold.

ADJUSTING ENTRY TO TRANSFER PURCHASES DISCOUNTS INCOME TO COST OF GOODS SOLD

To conform to generally accepted accounting procedures, purchase discounts should be shown as a reduction to the cost of goods sold. It is necessary to prepare an adjusting entry to transfer the income account 4030 Purchases Discounts to a cost of goods sold Purchases Discounts account. This adjustment places the discount where it belongs—as a reduction to the cost of merchandise rather than income.

MEMO

DATE: January 31, 1998

Note from Eric: Renee, create a cost of goods sold account 5100 Purchases Discounts. Transfer the amount of Purchases Discounts from income account 4030 to cost of goods sold account 5100.

*DO: Create new account 5100 Purchases Discounts as a subaccount of cost of goods sold

Open Chart of Accounts as previously instructed

Click **Account** button, click **New**
    OR
Use keyboard shortcut **Ctrl+N**

Click drop-down list arrow for **Type**, click **Cost of Goods Sold**

Tab to or click **Number**, enter **5100**

Tab to or click **Name**, enter **Purchases Discounts**

Click **Subaccount of** to select, click drop-down list arrow for Subaccount, click **5000 Cost of Goods Sold**

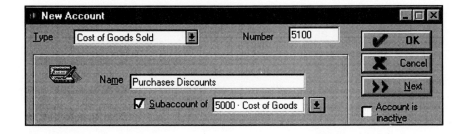

Click **OK**

With the Chart of Accounts still showing on the screen, click **Activities** button

Click **Make Journal Entry**

• Verify that the date is **01/31/98**. If not, change the date to 01/31/98.

Click the drop-down list arrow for **Account**, click **4030 Purchases Discounts**

Tab to or click the **Debit** column, enter the amount of Purchases Discounts **50.90**

Tab to or click **Memo**, enter **Transfer to CoGS** as the Memo

Click the drop-down list arrow for **Account**, click **5100 Purchases Discounts**

• The credit amount of 50.90 is already entered.

Tab to or click **Memo**, enter **Transfer to CoGS** as the Memo

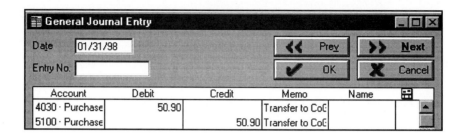

Click **OK**

Close the Chart of Accounts

PREPARE PROFIT AND LOSS STATEMENT

MEMO

DATE: January 31, 1998

Print a Profit and Loss Statement for January 1-31, 1998.

---

*DO: To view the effect of the adjustment, print a Profit and Loss Statement for January 1-31, 1998

Prepare the report as previously instructed

- Notice that the amount of 4030 Purchases Discounts is 0.00.
- The amount of 5100 Purchases Discounts is -50.90.
- The amount of Cost of Goods Sold is now $3,301.56 rather than $3,352.46.
- The Total Income is $8,871.20 rather than $8,922.10.

```
┌─────────────────────────────────────────────────────────┐
│              Mountain Adventure Ski Shoppe                │
│                   Profit and Loss                        │
│                    January 1998                          │
│                                          ◇  Jan '98   ◇  │
│          Total 4010 · Sales                    8,846.20  │
│                                                          │
│          4030 · Purchases Discounts                0.00  │
│          4040 · Returned Check Service Charges    25.00  │
│          4999 · Uncategorized Income               0.00  │
│       Total Income                             8,871.20  │
│                                                          │
│       Cost of Goods Sold                                 │
│          5000 · Cost of Goods Sold                       │
│             5100 · Purchases Discounts      -50.90       │
│             5000 · Cost of Goods Sold - Other 3,352.46   │
│          Total 5000 · Cost of Goods Sold       3,301.56  │
│                                                          │
│       Total COGS                               3,301.56  │
└─────────────────────────────────────────────────────────┘
```

Partial Report

Print the report in Portrait orientation
Close the report

VIEW GENERAL JOURNAL

Once transactions have been entered in the General Journal, it is important to view them. QuickBooks also refers to the General Journal as the Journal and allows it to be viewed or printed at any time. Even with the special ways in which transactions are entered in QuickBooks through invoices, bills, checks, and account registers, the Journal is still the book of original entry. All transactions recorded for the company may be viewed in the Journal even if they were entered elsewhere.

*DO: View the Journal for January
> Click **Reports** on the menu bar, point to **Other Reports**, click **Journal**
> > OR
> Click **Taxes and Accountant** tab on QuickBooks Navigator, click **Other** on the
> > Reports section, click **Journal**
> Tab to or click **From**
> • If necessary, delete existing date.
> Enter **01/01/98**

Tab to or click **To**, enter **01/31/98**

Tab to generate the report

- Notice that the transactions do not begin with the adjustments entered directly into the Journal.
- The first transaction shows the Inventory Adjustment/Opening Balance for Pants.

Mountain Adventure Ski Shoppe
Journal
January 1998

Trans #	Type	Date	Memo	Account	Debit	Credit
1	Inventory Adjust	01/01/98	Pants Openi...	3010 · Boyd & W...		1,750.00
			Pants Openi...	1120 · Inventory ...	1,750.00	
					1,750.00	1,750.00
2	Inventory Adjust	01/01/98	Accessories...	3010 · Boyd & W...		2,925.00
			Accessories...	1120 · Inventory ...	2,925.00	
					2,925.00	2,925.00
3	Inventory Adjust	01/01/98	Bindings-Sk...	3010 · Boyd & W...		3,750.00
			Bindings-Sk...	1120 · Inventory ...	3,750.00	
					3,750.00	3,750.00

Partial Report

Scroll through the report to view all transactions recorded in the Journal

Close the report without printing

DEFINITION OF A PARTNERSHIP

A partnership is a business owned by two or more individuals. Because it is unincorporated, each partner owns a share of all the assets and liabilities. Each partner receives a portion of the profits based on the percentage of his or her investment in the business or according to any partnership agreement drawn up at the time the business was created. Because the business is owned by the partners, they do not receive a salary. Any funds obtained by the partners are in the form of withdrawals against their share of the profits. QuickBooks makes it easy to set up a partnership and create separate accounts, if desired, for each partner's equity, investment, and withdrawals.

OWNER WITHDRAWALS

In a partnership, owners cannot receive a paycheck because they own the business. An owner withdrawing money from a business—even to pay personal expenses—is similar to an owner withdrawing money from a savings account. A withdrawal simply decreases the owners' capital. QuickBooks allows you to establish a separate account for owner withdrawals for each owner. If a separate account is not established, owner withdrawals may be subtracted directly from each owner's capital or investment account.

MEMO

DATE: January 31, 1998

Because Eric Boyd and Matthew Wayne work in the business full time, they do not earn a paycheck. Prepare checks for Eric's monthly withdrawal of $1,000 and Matt's monthly withdrawal of $1,000.

---

*DO: Write Check No. 6 to Eric Boyd for $1,000 withdrawal

Open the **Write Checks - Checking** window:

Click **Activities** on the menu bar, click **Write Checks**
    OR
Click **Check** icon on the iconbar
    OR
Click **Checking and Credit Card** tab on QuickBooks Navigator, click **Checks**
    OR
Use the keyboard shortcut **Ctrl+W**

Click the check box **To be printed**, the Check No. should be **To Print**

Date should be **01/31/98**

Enter **Eric Boyd** on the **Pay to the Order of** line, press **Tab** key

- Because Eric's name was not added to any list when the company was created, the **Name Not Found** dialog box appears on the screen.

Click **Quick Add** button to add Eric's name to a list

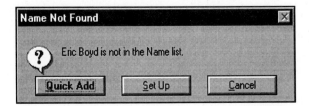

Select Name Type dialog box appears
Click **Other**, click **OK**

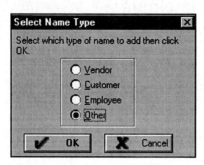

- Eric's name is added to a list of "Other" names, which is used for owners, partners, and other miscellaneous names.

Tab to or click in the area for the amount of the check
- If necessary, delete any numbers showing for the amount (0.00).

Enter **1000**

Tab to or click **Memo**, enter **Owner Withdrawal for January**

Tab to or click in the Account column at the bottom of the check, click the drop-down list arrow, click the Equity account **3013 Eric Boyd, Drawing**
- The amount 1,000.00 should appear in the Amount column.
- If it does not, tab to or click in the Amount column and enter 1000.

Click **Print** to print the check

Print Check dialog box appears

Printed Check Number should be **6**
- If necessary, change the number to 6.

Once the check has printed successfully, click **OK** to close **Did check(s) print OK?** dialog box

Click **>>Next** to record the check and advance to the next check

Repeat the above procedures to prepare and print Check No. 7 to Matthew Wayne for $1,000 withdrawal

Click **OK** to record the check

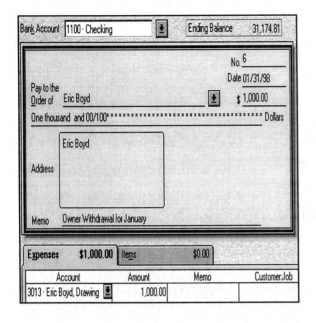
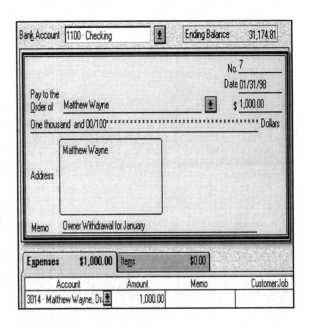

PREPARE BALANCE SHEET

A balance sheet proves that assets equal liabilities plus owners' equity; however, the owners' equity in a partnership may be organized in a manner that is more meaningful than is currently shown.

 *DO: View the Balance Sheet for January 31, 1998

        Click **Reports** on the menu bar, point to **Balance Sheet**, click **Standard**
           OR
        Click **Taxes and Accountant** tab on QuickBooks Navigator, click **Balance Sheet**
           on the Reports section, click **Standard**
        Tab to or click **As Of**
- If necessary, delete existing date.

        Enter **01/31/98**
        Tab to generate the report
        Scroll through the report
- Notice the Equity section, especially the Investment and Drawing accounts for each owner.
- Also notice the Boyd & Wayne Capital account balance. When the capital for both owners is combined into one account, the report does not indicate how much of the capital is for each owner.

Mountain Adventure Ski Shoppe
Balance Sheet
As of January 31, 1998

	Jan 31, '98
Equity	
Net Income	2,667.07
3010 · Boyd & Wayne Capital	
3011 · Eric Boyd, Investment	20,000.00
3012 · Matthew Wayne, Investment	20,000.00
3013 · Eric Boyd, Drawing	-1,000.00
3014 · Matthew Wayne, Drawing	-1,000.00
3010 · Boyd & Wayne Capital - Other	25,219.50
Total 3010 · Boyd & Wayne Capital	63,219.50
Total Equity	65,886.57

Partial Report

Do not close the report

TRANSFER COMBINED CAPITAL INTO AN INDIVIDUAL CAPITAL ACCOUNT FOR EACH OWNER:

A better display of owners' equity would be to show all equity accounts for each owner grouped together by owner. In addition, each owner should have an individual capital account.

MEMO
DATE: January 31, 1998

Change the account number of Boyd & Wayne, Capital to 3100. Create separate capital accounts for Eric Boyd and Matthew Wayne. Name the accounts 3110 Eric Boyd, Capital and 3120 Matthew Wayne, Capital. In addition, renumber Eric's Investment account to 3111 and his Drawing account to 3112. Make these subaccounts of his capital account. Do the same for Matt's accounts: 3121 Investment and 3122 Drawing.

---

 *DO: Create separate capital accounts and change subaccounts for existing owners' equity accounts

Access the **Chart of Accounts** as previously instructed

    Click **3010 Boyd & Wayne, Capital**

    Click **Account** button at the bottom of the Chart of Accounts, click **Edit**
        OR

    Use the keyboard shortcut **Ctrl+E**

    Change the account number to **3100**

    Click **OK**

    Click **Account** button at the bottom of the Chart of Accounts, click **New**
        OR

    Use the keyboard shortcut **Ctrl+N**

    Click the drop-down list arrow for Type, click **Equity**

    Tab to or click **Number**, enter **3110**

    Tab to or click **Name**, enter **Eric Boyd, Capital**

    Click **Subaccount**, click the drop-down list arrow next to subaccount, click **3100
        Boyd & Wayne, Capital**

    Click **OK**

    Click **Eric Boyd, Investment**

    Edit the account following steps previously listed

    Change the account number to **3111**

    Make this a subaccount of **3110 Eric Boyd, Capital**

    Click **OK** when the changes have been made

    Make the following changes to **Eric Boyd, Drawing**: Account number is **3112**,
        Subaccount of **3110**

    Create the equity account **3120 Matthew Wayne, Capital**, Account 3120 is a
        subaccount of **3100**

    Change **3012 Matthew Wayne, Investment** to **3121**, Account 3121 is a
        subaccount of **3120**

    Change **3014 Matthew Wayne, Drawing** to **3122**, Account 3122 is a subaccount
        of **3120**

◆ 3100 · Boyd & Wayne Capital	Equity	63,459.50
◆ 3110 · Eric Boyd, Capital	Equity	19,000.00
◆ 3111 · Eric Boyd, Investment	Equity	20,000.00
◆ 3112 · Eric Boyd, Drawing	Equity	-1,000.00
◆ 3120 · Matthew Wayne, Capital	Equity	19,000.00
◆ 3121 · Matthew Wayne, Investme	Equity	20,000.00
◆ 3122 · Matthew Wayne, Drawing	Equity	-1,000.00

Close the Chart of Accounts

- Since the Balance Sheet is still on the screen, the changes made to the capital accounts will be shown in the report.
- Notice the change in the Equity section of the Balance Sheet.

Mountain Adventure Ski Shoppe
Balance Sheet
As of January 31, 1998

	Jan 31, '98
3100 · Boyd & Wayne Capital	
3110 · Eric Boyd, Capital	
3111 · Eric Boyd, Investment	20,000.00
3112 · Eric Boyd, Drawing	-1,000.00
Total 3110 · Eric Boyd, Capital	19,000.00
3120 · Matthew Wayne, Capital	
3121 · Matthew Wayne, Investment	20,000.00
3122 · Matthew Wayne, Drawing	-1,000.00
Total 3120 · Matthew Wayne, Capital	19,000.00
3100 · Boyd & Wayne Capital - Other	25,219.50
Total 3100 · Boyd & Wayne Capital	63,219.50

Partial Report

DISTRIBUTE CAPITAL TO EACH OWNER

As you view the Balance Sheet, you will notice that the balance for Boyd & Wayne, Capital is $25,219.50. Because Boyd & Wayne Capital is a combined capital account, the report does not indicate how much of the capital should be distributed to each partner. In order to clarify this section of the report, the capital should be distributed between the two owners. Each owner has contributed an equal amount as an investment in the business, so the capital should be divided equally between Eric and Matt.

*DO: Make an adjusting entry to distribute capital between the two owners

Access **General Journal Entry** screen as previously instructed

Close account **3100 Boyd & Wayne, Capital** by debiting the account **25219.50**
- If the Journal disappears from the screen, simply open the General Journal again and continue with the entry.

Memo for all entries in the transaction is **Transfer Capital to Individual Accounts**

Transfer one-half of the amount debited to **3110 Eric Boyd, Capital** by crediting this account
- To determine one-half the amount, you may use the calculator as previously instructed.

Credit **3120 Matthew Wayne, Capital** for the other one-half of the amount

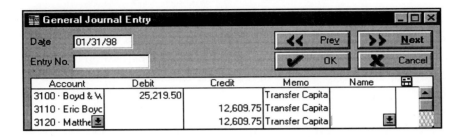

Click **OK** to record
- Notice the change in the equity section of the balance sheet.
- Total of 3100 Boyd & Wayne Capital is still 63,219.50; however, accounts 3110 and 3120 each show 12,609.75, which is the amount of capital for each owner.

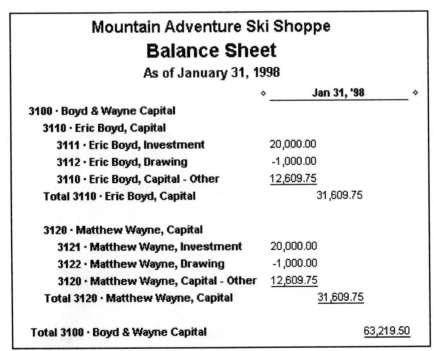

Partial Report

Close the report

BANK RECONCILIATION

Each month the Checking account should be reconciled with the bank statement to make sure both balances agree. The bank statement will rarely have an ending balance that matches the balance of the Checking account. This is due to several factors: outstanding checks (written by the business but not paid by the bank), deposits in transit (deposits that were made too late to be included on the bank statement), bank service charges, interest earned on checking accounts, collections made by the bank, errors made in recording checks and/or deposits by the company or by the bank, etc.

In order to have an accurate amount listed as the balance in the Checking account, it is important that the differences between the bank statement and the Checking account be reconciled. If something such as a service charge or a collection made by the bank appears on the bank statement, it needs to be recorded in the Checking account.

Reconciling a bank statement is an appropriate time to find any errors that may have been recorded in the Checking account. The reconciliation may be out of balance because a transposition was made (recording $45 rather than $54), a transaction was recorded backwards, a transaction was recorded twice, or a transaction was not recorded at all.

OPEN RECONCILE - CHECKING

To begin the reconciliation, the Reconcile - Checking window needs to be opened. Verify the information shown for the Checking account. The Opening Balance should match the amount of the final balance on the last reconciliation, or it should match the starting account balance.

MEMO

DATE: January 31, 1998

Received the bank statement from Mountain Bank. The bank statement is dated January 30, 1998. Renee needs to reconcile the bank statement and print a Reconciliation Report for Eric and Matt.

---

*DO: Reconcile the bank statement for January
    Open the **Reconcile - Checking** window and enter preliminary information
    Open **Chart of Accounts** as previously instructed, click **Checking**, click
        Activities button, click **Reconcile**
        OR
    Click **Checking and Credit Cards** on QuickBooks Navigator, click **Reconcile**
    The **Account To Reconcile** should be **1100 Checking**
    • If not, click the drop-down list arrow, click **Checking**.

Opening Balance should be **25,943.00**

- This is the same amount as the Checking account starting balance.

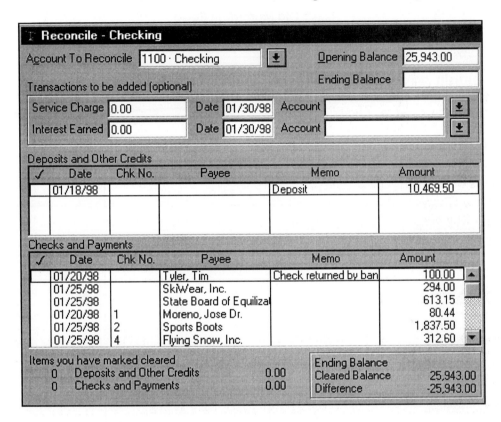

ENTER BANK STATEMENT INFORMATION

Information appearing on the bank statement is entered into **Reconcile - Checking** as the next step. This information includes bank service charges and interest earned.

MOUNTAIN BANK
12345 Old Mammoth Road
Mammoth Lakes, CA 93546
(619) 555-3880

Mountain Adventure Ski Shoppe
875 Mountain Road
Mammoth Lakes, CA 93546

Acct. # 123-456-7890   **January, 1998**

Beginning Balance 1/1/98	25,943.00		$25,943.00
1/18/98 Deposit	10,469.50		36,412.50
1/20/98 NSF Returned Check		100.00	36,312.50
1/20/98 Check 1		80.44	36,232.06
1/25/98 Check 2		1,837.50	34,394.56
1/25/98 Check 3		294.00	34,100.56
1/25/98 Check 4		312.60	33,787.96
1/25/98 Check 5		613.15	33,174.81
1/30/98 Office Equip. Loan Pmt.: $10.33 Principal, $53.42 Interest		63.75	33,111.06
1/30/98 Store Fixtures Loan Pmt.: $8.61 Principal, $44.51 Interest		53.12	33,057.94
1/30/98 Service Chg.		8.00	33,049.94
1/30/98 NSF Charge		10.00	33,039.94
1/30/98 Interest	54.05		33,093.99
Ending Balance 1/30/98			33,093.99

*DO: Continue to reconcile the bank statement above with the Checking account
Enter the **Ending Balance** from the bank statement, **33,093.99**
Tab to or click **Service Charge**, enter the **Service Charge, 18.00**
- Note that this includes both the service charge of $8.00 and the $10.00 charge for Tim Tyler's NSF check in Chapter 5.
Tab to or click Service Charge **Date**, change to **01/30/98**
Tab to or click **Account**, click the drop-down list arrow for **Account**, click **6120 Bank Service Charges**

Tab to or click **Interest Earned**, enter **54.05**
Tab to or click Interest Earned **Date**, change to **01/30/98**
Tab to or click **Account**, click the drop-down list arrow for **Account**, click **7010 Interest Income**

MARK CLEARED TRANSACTIONS FOR BANK RECONCILIATION

Once bank statement information for service charges and interest has been entered, compare the checks and deposits listed on the statement with the transactions for the Checking account. If a deposit or a check is listed correctly on the bank statement and in the Reconcile - Checking window, it has cleared and should be marked. An item may be marked individually by positioning the cursor on the deposit or the check and clicking the primary mouse button. If all deposits and checks match, click the Mark All button to mark all the deposits and checks at once. To remove all the checks, click the Unmark All button. To unmark an individual item, click the item to remove the check mark.

 *DO: Mark cleared checks and deposits
Compare the bank statement with the Reconcile - Checking window
Click the items that appear on both statements
Look at the bottom of the Reconcile - Checking window
You have marked cleared:
2 Deposits and Other Credits for 10,523.55
- This includes interest earned.
7 Checks and Payments for 3,255.69
- This includes the $100 NSF check returned, the $10 charge for the return of the NSF check, and the $8 service charge.
The Ending Balance is 33,093.99
The Cleared Balance is 33,210.86
There is a Difference of -116.87

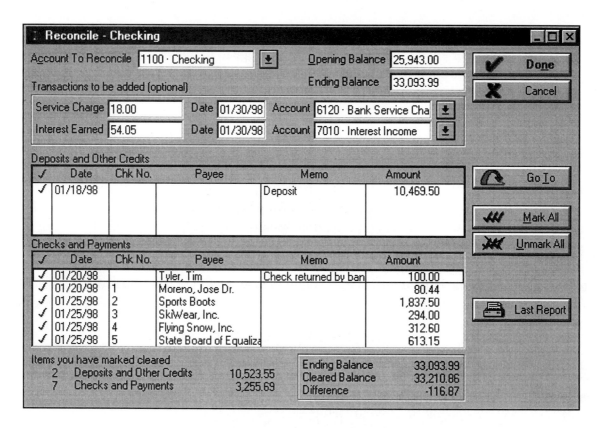

Leave the bank statement on the screen while you complete the next section

ADJUSTING AND CORRECTING ENTRIES—BANK RECONCILIATION

As you complete the reconciliation, you may find errors that need to be corrected or transactions that need to be recorded. Anything entered as a service charge or interest earned will be entered automatically when the reconciliation is complete and the **Done** button is clicked. To correct an error such as a transposition, click on the entry then click the **Go To** button. The original entry will appear on the screen. The correction can be made and will show in the **Reconcile - Checking** window. If there is a transaction, such as an automatic loan payment to the bank, access the register for the account used in the transaction and enter the payment.

        *DO: Enter the automatic loan payments shown on the bank statement
                Open the Register for the **1100 Checking** account:
                        Click **Register** button on the iconbar
                            OR
                        Click **Activities** on the menu bar, click **Use Register**
                            OR
                        Use the keyboard shortcut **Ctrl+R**

In the blank transaction at the bottom of the register enter the **Date, 01/30/98**
Tab to or click **Number**, enter **TRANSFER**
Tab to or click **Payee**, enter **Mountain Bank**
Tab to or click the **Payment** column
- Because Mountain Bank does not appear on any list, you will get a Name Not Found dialog box when you move to another field.

Click **Quick Add** button to add the name of the bank to the Name list
Click **Other**

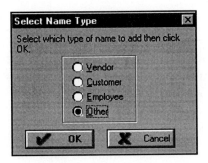

Click **OK**
- Once the name of the bank has been added to the Other list, the cursor will be positioned in the **Payment** column.

Enter **63.75** in the **Payment** column
Click **Account** column
Click **Splits** button at the bottom of the register
Click drop-down list arrow for **Account**, click **6212 Loan Interest**
Tab to or click **Amount**, delete the amount 63.75 shown
Enter **53.42** as the amount of interest
Tab to or click **Memo**, enter **Interest Office Equipment Loan**
Tab to or click **Account**, click drop-down list arrow for **Account**, click
    2510 Office Equipment Loan
- The correct amount of principal, 10.33, should be shown as the amount.

Tab to or click **Memo**, enter **Payment Office Equipment Loan**

Account	Amount	Memo
6212 · Loan Interest	53.42	Interest Office Equipmen
2510 · Office Equipment Loan	10.33	Payment Office Equipme

Click **Close**
• This closes the window for the information regarding the way the transaction is to be "split" between accounts.
For the **Memo** in the Checking register, record **Loan Pmt., Office Equipment**
Click the **Record** button to record the transaction
• Because the Register organizes transactions according to date, you will notice that the loan payment will not appear as the last transaction in the Register.

01/30/98	TRANSFE	Mountain Bank		63.75		33,111.06
	CHK	-split- Loan Payment Office Equ				

Repeat the procedures to record the loan payment for store fixtures
• When you enter the Payee as Mountain Bank, the amount for the previous transaction (63.75) appears in amount.
Enter the new amount **53.12**
Click **Splits** button
Click the appropriate accounts and enter the correct amount for each item
• Refer to the bank statement for details regarding the amount of the payment for interest and the amount of the payment applied to principal.

Account	Amount	Memo
6212 · Loan Interest	44.51	Interest Store Fixtures Lo
2520 · Store Fixtures Loan	8.61	Payment Store Fixtures L

Click **Close** button to close the window for the information regarding the "split" between accounts
Enter the transaction Memo
Click **Record** button to record the loan payment

01/30/98	TRANSFE	Mountain Bank		53.12		33,057.94
	CHK	-split- Loan Payment Store Fixtu				

Close the **Checking** register
• You should return to **Reconcile - Checking**.

Scroll to the top of Check and Payments
- Notice the two entries for the payments in Checks and Payments.

Mark the two entries
- At this point the Ending Balance and Cleared Balance should be equal—$33,093.99 with a difference of 0.00.

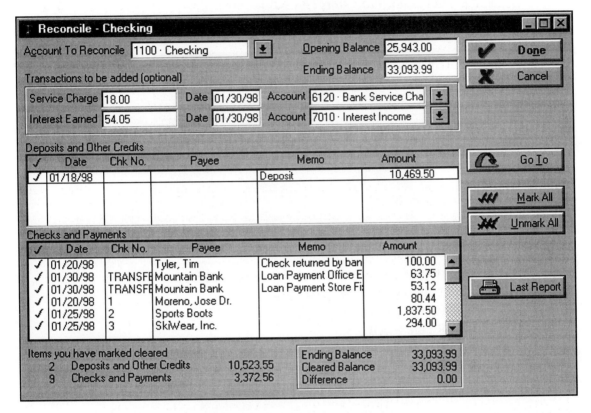

If your entries agree with the above, click **Done** to finish the reconciliation
- If your reconciliation is not in agreement, do not click **Done** until the errors are corrected.
- Once you click **Done**, you may not return to this Reconciliation - Checking window.

PRINT A RECONCILIATION REPORT

As soon as the Ending Balance and the Cleared Balance are equal or when you finish marking and click Done, a screen appears allowing you to select the level of Reconciliation report you would like to print. You may select **None** and get no report, **Summary** and get a report that lists totals only, or **Full** and get totals and transaction detail for cleared, uncleared, and new transactions. You may print the report at the time you have finished reconciling the account, or you may print the report later by returning to the Reconciliation window. QuickBooks keeps your last two Reconciliation reports in memory. If you think you may want to print the report again in the future, print the report to a file to save it permanently.

 *DO: Print a Full Reconciliation report
On the **Reconciliation Complete** screen, click **Full**
Enter **Statement Closing Date** of **01/30/98**

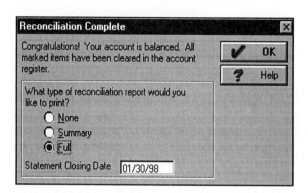

Click **OK** to print
Print as previously instructed:
    Printer should be **default printer**
    Orientation is **Portrait**
    Page Range is **All**
When the report finishes printing, click **Yes**

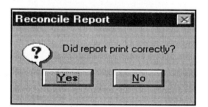

VIEW THE CHECKING ACCOUNT REGISTER

Once the bank reconciliation has been completed, it is wise to scroll through the Check register to view the effect of the reconciliation on the account. You will notice that the check column shows ✔ for all items that were marked as cleared during the reconciliation. This check mark may not be removed. However, if at a later date an error is discovered, the transaction may be changed, and the correction will be reflected in the Beginning Balance on the reconciliation.

 *DO: View the register for the Checking account

Access the register as previously instructed
To display more of the register, click the check box for **1-Line**
Scroll through the register
- Notice that the transactions are listed in chronological order.
    - Even though the bank reconciliation transactions were recorded after the checks written on January 31, the bank reconciliation transactions appear before the checks because they were recorded with the date of January 30.

1100 · Checking

Date	Number	Payee	Account	Payment	✓	Deposit	Balance
12/31/97			3100 · Boyd & Wayne Ca		✓	25,943.00	25,943.00
01/18/98			-split-		✓	10,469.50	36,412.50
01/20/98		Tyler, Tim	1200 · Accounts Receiv.	100.00	✓		36,312.50
01/20/98	1	Moreno, Jose Dr.	1200 · Accounts Receiv.	80.44	✓		36,232.06
01/25/98	2	Sports Boots	-split-	1,837.50	✓		34,394.56
01/25/98	3	SkiWear, Inc.	-split-	294.00	✓		34,100.56
01/25/98	4	Flying Snow, Inc.	-split-	312.60	✓		33,787.96
01/25/98	5	State Board of Equalizati	2200 · Sales Tax Payabl	613.15	✓		33,174.81
01/30/98			7010 · Interest Income		✓	54.05	33,228.86
01/30/98			6120 · Bank Service Cha	18.00	✓		33,210.86
01/30/98	TRANSFE	Mountain Bank	-split-	63.75	✓		33,147.11
01/30/98	TRANSFE	Mountain Bank	-split-	53.12	✓		33,093.99
01/31/98	6	Eric Boyd	3112 · Eric Boyd, Drawin	1,000.00			32,093.99
01/31/98	7	Matthew Wayne	3122 · Matthew Wayne,	1,000.00			31,093.99

- Notice that the Cleared Balance on the Reconciliation Report shows $33,093.99.
Compare the cleared balance with the balance of the account after the last transaction of 1/30/98
- Notice that the final balance of the account is $31,093.99. This is because the two owner withdrawals of $1,000 each were recorded 1/31/98.
Compare the final account balance with the Ending Account Balance on the Reconciliation Report. Both amounts should be $31,093.99
Close the register

CREDIT CARD RECONCILIATION

Any account used in QuickBooks may be reconciled. As with a checking account, it is a good practice to reconcile the credit card account each month. When the credit card statement is received, the transactions entered in QuickBooks should agree with the transactions shown on the credit card statement. A reconciliation of the credit card should be completed on a monthly basis.

MEMO

DATE: January 31, 1998

The monthly bill for the Visa has arrived and is to be paid. Prior to paying the monthly credit card bill, reconcile the credit card account.

---

*DO: Reconcile and pay the credit card bill
   On the menu bar click **Activities**, click **Reconcile**
      OR
   Click **Checking and Credit Cards** on the QuickBooks Navigator menu, click **Reconcile**
   Click the drop-down list arrow for **Account to Reconcile**, click **2100 Visa**
   The Opening Balance should be **150.00**

MOUNTAIN BANK
VISA
12345 Old Mammoth Road
Mammoth Lakes, CA 93546
(619) 555-3880

Mountain Adventure Ski Shoppe
875 Mountain Road
Mammoth Lakes, CA 93546   Acct. # 098-776-4321

Beginning Balance 1/1/98		150.00	$150.00
1/23/98 Office Supply Company		21.98	171.98
1/23/98 Ski Supply		300.00	471.98
1/25/98 ABC Accessories		350.00	821.98
1/25/98 Shoe Supply		400.00	1,221.98
Ending Balance 1/25/98			1,221.98

Minimum Payment Due: $50.00   Payment Due Date: February 5, 1998

Compare the credit card statement with the Reconcile Credit Card - Visa
Enter the **Ending Balance** of **1,221.98**
Mark each item that appears on both the statement and in the reconciliation

Verify that all items are marked and that the Ending and Cleared Balances are 1,221.98 and the Difference is 0.00

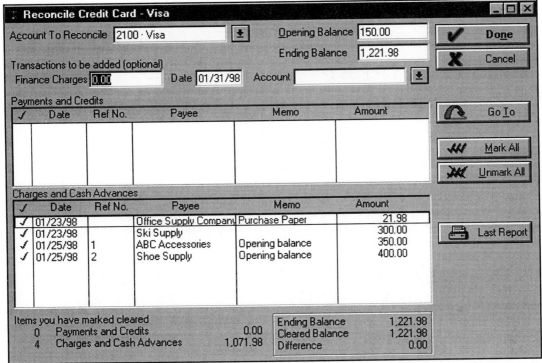

If all is in agreement, click **Done**
- If there are any discrepancies, make any necessary corrections *before* clicking Done.

A **Make Payment** dialog box appears on the screen

Make sure **Write a check for payment now** is selected, click **OK**
- If it is not selected, click on Write a check for payment now to select, then click OK.

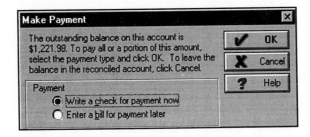

Check Number 8 should appear on the screen
- If the check number is not 8, change the number to 8.

The **Date** of the check should be **01/31/98**

Click the drop-down list next to **Pay to the Order of**, click **Mountain Bank**

• If you get a dialog box for Auto Recall, click **No**.

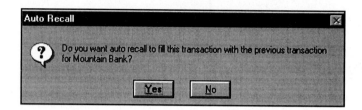

Tab to or click **Memo**

Enter **January Visa Payment** as the memo

Print the check as previously instructed

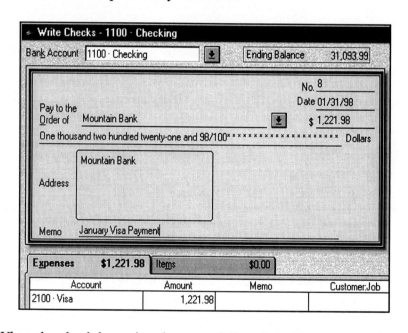

When the check has printed successfully, click **OK** to record and exit Write
Checks

VIEW THE JOURNAL

After entering several transactions, it is helpful to view the Journal. In the Journal all transactions
regardless of the method of entry are shown in traditional debit/credit format.

*DO: View the Journal for January

Click **Reports** on the menu bar, point to **Other Reports**, click **Journal**

OR

Click **Taxes and Accountant** tab on QuickBooks Navigator, click **Other** on the Reports section, click **Journal**

Tab to or click **From**

- If necessary, delete existing date.

Enter **01/01/98**

Tab to or click **To**, enter **01/31/98**

Tab to generate the report

Scroll through the Journal and view all the transactions that have been made

Close the Journal without printing

PREPARE TRIAL BALANCE

After all adjustments have been recorded and the bank reconciliation has been completed, it is wise to prepare the trial balance. As in traditional accounting, the QuickBooks trial balance proves that debits equal credits.

MEMO

DATE: January 31, 1998

Because adjustments have been entered, prepare a trial balance.

---

*DO: Prepare a trial balance

Click **Reports** on the menu bar, point to **Other Reports**, click **Trial Balance**
OR
Click **Taxes and Accountant** or **Company** tab on QuickBooks Navigator, click **Other** in the Reports section, click **Trial Balance**

Tab to or click **From**, enter the date **01/01/98**

Tab to or click **To**, enter the date **01/31/98**

Tab to generate the report

Scroll through the report and study the amounts shown

- Notice that the final totals of debits and credits are equal: $89,232.11.

Do not close the report

USE QUICKZOOM IN TRIAL BALANCE

QuickZoom is a QuickBooks feature that allows you to make a closer observation of transactions, amounts, etc. With QuickZoom you may zoom in on an item when the mouse pointer turns into a magnifying glass with a Z inside. If you point to an item and you do not get a magnifying glass with a Z inside, you cannot zoom in on the item. For example, if you point to Store Fixtures Loan, you will see the magnifying glass with the Z inside.

 *DO: Use QuickZoom to view the details of Store Fixtures Loan:
Scroll through the Trial Balance until you see 2520 Store Fixtures Loan
Position the mouse pointer over the amount of Store Fixtures Loan, **2,491.39**
- Notice that the mouse pointer changes to a magnifying glass with a Z.

Double-click the primary mouse button
- A Transactions by Account report appears on the screen showing the two transactions entered for the store fixtures loan.

Scroll through the report

Mountain Adventure Ski Shoppe
Transactions by Account
As of January 31, 1998

Type	Date	Num	Name	Memo	Clr	Split	Amount	Balance
2520 · Store Fixtures Loan								0.00
General Jo...	01/01/98			Account O...	✓	3100 · Boyd...	2,500.00	2,500.00
Check	01/30/98	TRA...	Mountain Bank	Payment S...		1100 · Chec...	-8.61	2,491.39
Total 2520 · Store Fixtures Loan							2,491.39	2,491.39
TOTAL							**2,491.39**	**2,491.39**

Close the report

PRINT THE TRIAL BALANCE

Once the trial balance has been prepared, it may be printed.

 *DO: Print the Trial Balance
Click the **Print** button at the top of the Trial Balance
Click **Preview** button to view a miniature copy of the report
- This helps determine the orientation, whether you need to select the feature to print one page wide, or whether you need to adjust the column widths.

Click **Close**

Use **Portrait** orientation
Click **Print**
Close the Trial Balance

SELECT ACCRUAL BASIS REPORTING PREFERENCE

QuickBooks allows a business to customize the program and select certain preferences for reports, displays, graphs, accounts, and so on. There are two report preferences available in QuickBooks: Cash and Accrual. You need to choose the preference you prefer. If you select Cash as the report preference, income on reports will be shown as of the date payment is received, and expenses will be shown as of the date you pay the bill. If Accrual is selected, QuickBooks shows the income on the report as of the date of the invoice and expenses as of the bill date. Prior to printing end-of-period reports, it is advisable to verify which reporting basis is selected. If cash has been selected and you are using the accrual method, it is imperative that you change your report basis.

MEMO

DATE: January 31, 1998

Prior to printing the Balance Sheet, Profit and Loss or Income Statement, or any other reports, check the report preference. If necessary, choose Accrual. After the selection has been made, print a Standard Profit and Loss, and a Standard Balance Sheet for Mountain Adventure Ski Shoppe.

---

*DO: Select Accrual as the Summary Report Basis
  Click **File** on the menu bar, click **Preferences**
    OR
  Click **Company** tab on QuickBooks Navigator, click
  Preferences icon
  Scroll through the Preferences list until you see **Reports &**
    Graphs
  Click **Reports & Graphs**
  If necessary, click **Accrual** to select the Summary Reports Basis
  Click **OK** to close the Preferences window

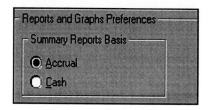

PRINT STANDARD PROFIT AND LOSS STATEMENT

Because all income, expenses, and adjustments have been made for the period, a Profit and Loss Statement can be prepared. This statement is also known as the Income Statement. QuickBooks has several different types of Profit and Loss statements available: <u>Standard</u>—summarizes income and expenses; <u>YTD Comparison</u>—like the Standard Profit and Loss but containing columns for this year to date, $ change, and % change; <u>Prev Year Comparison</u>—like the Standard statement but containing one column for this month to date and a second column for this year to date; and <u>Itemized</u>—shows year-to-date transactions instead of totals for each income and expense account.

 *DO: Print a Standard Profit and Loss report

Click **Reports** on the menu bar, point to **Profit & Loss**, click **Standard**
 OR
Click **Company** tab on QuickBooks Navigator, click **Profit & Loss** in the
 Reports section, click **Standard**
Tab to or click **From**
• If necessary, highlight or delete existing date.
Enter **01/01/98**
Tab to or click **To**
• If necessary, highlight or delete existing date.
Enter **01/31/98**
Tab to generate the report
Scroll through the report to view the income and expenses listed
Print the report
Use **Portrait** orientation
Close the Profit and Loss report

```
                    Mountain Adventure Ski Shoppe
                           Profit and Loss
                             January 1998

                                              ◇    Jan '98    ◇
           6999 · Uncategorized Expenses                0.00
        Total Expense                                 3,018.50

     Net Ordinary Income                               2,551.14

     Other Income/Expense
        Other Income
           7010 · Interest Income                       54.05
        Total Other Income                              54.05

     Net Other Income                                   54.05

     Net Income                                       2,605.19
```

Partial Report

PRINT STANDARD BALANCE SHEET

The Balance Sheet proves the fundamental accounting equation: Assets = Liabilities + Owners' Equity. When all transactions and adjustments for the period have been recorded, a Balance Sheet should be prepared. QuickBooks has several different types of Balance Sheet statements available: Standard—shows the balance in each balance sheet account as of today with subtotals provided for assets, liabilities, and equity; Comparison—has columns for today a year ago, $ change, and % change; Summary—shows amounts for each account type but not for individual accounts; and Itemized—shows balances as of last month, shows balances as of today, and shows transactions for each account for this month.

*DO: Print a Standard Balance Sheet report
   Click **Reports** on the menu bar, point to **Balance Sheet**, click **Standard**
      OR
   Click **Company** tab on QuickBooks Navigator, click **Balance Sheet** in the
      Reports section, click **Standard**
   Tab to or click **As of**
   • If necessary, highlight or delete existing date.
   Enter **01/31/98**
   Tab to generate the report
   Scroll through the report to view the assets, liabilities, and equities listed
   Print the report in **Portrait** orientation
   Close the Standard Balance Sheet

- Notice the Net Income account listed in the Equity section of the report. This is the same amount of Net Income shown on the Profit and Loss Statement.

Mountain Adventure Ski Shoppe
Balance Sheet
As of January 31, 1998

	Jan 31, '98
Net Income	2,605.19
3100 · Boyd & Wayne Capital	
3110 · Eric Boyd, Capital	
3111 · Eric Boyd, Investment	20,000.00
3112 · Eric Boyd, Drawing	-1,000.00
3110 · Eric Boyd, Capital - Other	12,609.75
Total 3110 · Eric Boyd, Capital	31,609.75
3120 · Matthew Wayne, Capital	
3121 · Matthew Wayne, Investment	20,000.00
3122 · Matthew Wayne, Drawing	-1,000.00
3120 · Matthew Wayne, Capital - Other	12,609.75
Total 3120 · Matthew Wayne, Capital	31,609.75
Total 3100 · Boyd & Wayne Capital	63,219.50

Partial Report

Do not close the report

ADJUSTMENT TO TRANSFER NET INCOME/RETAINED EARNINGS INTO ERIC BOYD, CAPITAL, AND MATTHEW WAYNE, CAPITAL

Because Mountain Adventure Ski Shoppe is a partnership, the amount of net income should appear as part of each owner's capital account rather than be set aside in Retained Earnings. In many instances, this is the type of adjustment the CPA makes on the accountant's copy of the QuickBooks company files. The adjustment may be made before the closing date for the fiscal year, or it may be made after the closing has been performed. Because QuickBooks automatically transfers the amount in the Net Income account into Retained Earnings, the closing entry for a partnership will transfer the net income into each owner's capital account. This adjustment is made by debiting Retained Earnings and crediting the owners' individual capital accounts. When you view a report before the end of the year, you will see an amount in Net Income and the same amount as a negative in Retained Earnings. If you view a report after the end of the year, you will not see any information regarding Retained Earnings or Net Income because the adjustment correctly transferred the amount to the owners' capital accounts.

If you prefer to use the power of the program and not make the adjustment, QuickBooks simply carries the amount of Retained Earnings forward. Each year the amount of net income is added to

Retained Earnings. On the Balance Sheet, Retained Earnings and/or Net Income appear as part of the equity section. The owners' drawing and investment accounts are kept separate from Retained Earnings at all times. If Mountain Adventure Ski Shoppe had used a traditional QuickBooks setup for the Equity section of the Balance Sheet, it would appear as:

Equity
> **Retained Earnings**
> **Net Income**
>
> **Owners' Equity**
> > **Owners' Draw**
> > **Owners' Investment**
> > **Total Owners' Equity**

Total Equity

*DO: Evenly divide and transfer the net income into Eric Boyd, Capital, and Matthew Wayne, Capital, accounts after year end:
Open the General Journal as previously instructed
The **Date** is **01/31/98**
The first account used is **3000 Retained Earnings**
Debit **3000 Retained Earnings, 2,605.19**
- If the Journal disappears from the screen, simply open the General Journal again and continue with the entry.

For the Memo record **Transfer Net Income into Capital**
The other accounts used are **3110 Eric Boyd, Capital** and **3120 Matthew Wayne, Capital**
1,302.60 should be entered as the credit amount for **3110 Eric Boyd, Capital**
- QuickBooks enters **1,302.59** as the credit amount for **3120 Matthew Wayne, Capital**.
- Note that because QuickBooks accepts only two numbers after a decimal point, the cents must be rounded. Thus, there is a 1¢ difference in the distribution between the two owners. If there is an uneven amount in the future, Matthew will receive the extra amount.

Enter the same Memo as entered for Retained Earnings

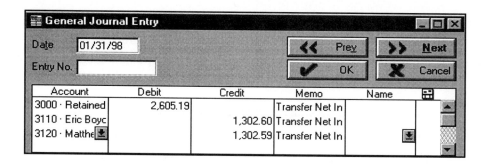

Click **OK** to record and close the General Journal

- Since you did not close the report, the Balance Sheet should still be on the screen.
- Notice the change in the Equity section of the Balance Sheet.
- Not all companies have a profit each month. If your business has a negative amount for net income, the appropriate adjustment would be to debit each owner's individual capital account and to credit Retained Earnings. For example, if Net Income was -500.00, you would record the following: 3110 Eric Boyd, Capital—debit 250; 3120 Matthew Wayne, Capital—debit 250; and 3000 Retained Earnings—credit 500.

Mountain Adventure Ski Shoppe
Balance Sheet
As of January 31, 1998

	Jan 31, '98
3000 · Retained Earnings	-2,605.19
Net Income	2,605.19
3100 · Boyd & Wayne Capital	
3110 · Eric Boyd, Capital	
3111 · Eric Boyd, Investment	20,000.00
3112 · Eric Boyd, Drawing	-1,000.00
3110 · Eric Boyd, Capital - Other	13,912.35
Total 3110 · Eric Boyd, Capital	32,912.35
3120 · Matthew Wayne, Capital	
3121 · Matthew Wayne, Investment	20,000.00
3122 · Matthew Wayne, Drawing	-1,000.00
3120 · Matthew Wayne, Capital - Other	13,912.34
Total 3120 · Matthew Wayne, Capital	32,912.34

Partial Report after Adjusting Entry

Do not close the report

PRINT STANDARD BALANCE SHEET

Once the adjustment for Net Income/Retained Earnings has been performed, viewing or printing the Balance Sheet will show you the status of the Owners' Equity.

 *DO: Print a Standard Balance Sheet for January 1998
Click **Print** button
- The Balance Sheet still appears on the screen after printing is complete.
Change the **As Of** date to **01/31/99**
- Notice the Equity section.
- Nothing is shown for Retained Earnings or Net Income.
- The net income has been added to the owners' capital accounts.

Mountain Adventure Ski Shoppe
Balance Sheet
As of January 31, 1999

	Jan 31, '99	
3100 · Boyd & Wayne Capital		
3110 · Eric Boyd, Capital		
3111 · Eric Boyd, Investment	20,000.00	
3112 · Eric Boyd, Drawing	-1,000.00	
3110 · Eric Boyd, Capital - Other	13,912.35	
Total 3110 · Eric Boyd, Capital		32,912.35
3120 · Matthew Wayne, Capital		
3121 · Matthew Wayne, Investment	20,000.00	
3122 · Matthew Wayne, Drawing	-1,000.00	
3120 · Matthew Wayne, Capital - Other	13,912.34	
Total 3120 · Matthew Wayne, Capital		32,912.34
Total 3100 · Boyd & Wayne Capital		65,824.69

Print the **Balance Sheet** for January, 1999
Do not close the report
Change the **As of** date for the Balance Sheet to **01/31/98**

CLOSE DRAWING AND TRANSFER INTO OWNERS' CAPITAL ACCOUNTS

In traditional accrual basis accounting, there are four entries that need to be made at the end of a fiscal year. These entries close income, expenses, and the drawing accounts and transfer the net income into owners' equity. When preparing reports during the next fiscal year, QuickBooks will not show any amounts in the income and expense accounts for the previous year. However, QuickBooks does not close the owners' drawing accounts, nor does it transfer the net income into the owners' capital accounts. If you prefer to use the power of the program and omit the last two closing entries, QuickBooks will keep a running account of the owner withdrawals, and it will put net income into a Retained Earnings account. However, transferring the net income and drawing into the owners' capital accounts provides a clearer picture of the value of the owners' equity.

The entry transferring the net income into the owners' capital accounts has already been made. While this is not the actual end of the fiscal year for Mountain Adventure Ski Shoppe, the closing entry for the drawing accounts will be entered at this time so that you will have experience in recording this closing entry.

MEMO

DATE: January 31, 1998

Record the closing entry to close 3112 Eric Boyd, Drawing, and 3122 Matthew Wayne, Drawing, into each owner's capital account.

---

 *DO: Record the closing entry for each owner's drawing account
Access the General Journal as previously instructed
Debit **3110 Eric Boyd, Capital** for the amount of the drawing account **1,000**
- If the Journal disappears from the screen, simply open the General Journal again and continue with the entry.
The Memo for the transaction is **Close Drawing**
Credit **3112 Eric Boyd, Drawing** for **1,000**
Use the same memo for this portion of the transaction
Click >>**Next**

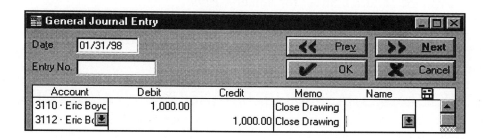

Repeat the above steps to close **3122 Matthew Wayne, Drawing**

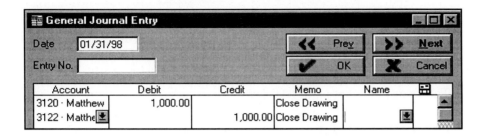

Click **OK**

- Notice the change in the Equity section of the balance sheet.

Mountain Adventure Ski Shoppe
Balance Sheet
As of January 31, 1998

	Jan 31, '98
3000 · Retained Earnings	-2,605.19
Net Income	2,605.19
3100 · Boyd & Wayne Capital	
3110 · Eric Boyd, Capital	
3111 · Eric Boyd, Investment	20,000.00
3110 · Eric Boyd, Capital - Other	12,912.35
Total 3110 · Eric Boyd, Capital	32,912.35
3120 · Matthew Wayne, Capital	
3121 · Matthew Wayne, Investment	20,000.00
3120 · Matthew Wayne, Capital - Other	12,912.34
Total 3120 · Matthew Wayne, Capital	32,912.34
Total 3100 · Boyd & Wayne Capital	65,824.69

Print the Balance Sheet
Close the report

PRINT JOURNAL

It is always wise to have a printed or "hard copy" of the data on disk. After all entries and adjustments for the month have been made, print the Journal for January. This copy should be kept on file as an additional backup to the data stored on your disk. If something happens to your disk to damage it, you will still have the paper copy of your transactions available for re-entry into the system.

 *DO: Print the Journal for January
Click **Reports** on the menu bar, point to **Other Reports**, click **Journal**

OR

Click **Taxes and Accountant** tab on QuickBooks Navigator, click **Other** on the
Reports section, click **Journal**
Tab to or click **From**, enter **01/01/98**
Tab to or click **To**, enter **01/31/98**
Tab to generate the report
Print the report in Landscape orientation
Close the Journal

END-OF-PERIOD BACKUP

Once all end-of-period procedures have been completed, in addition to a regular backup copy of
company data, a second backup of the company data should be made and filed as an archive
copy. Preferably this copy will be located someplace other than on the business premises. The
archive or file copy is set aside in case of emergency or in case damage occurs to the original and
current backup copies of the company data.

*DO: Back up company data and prepare an archive copy of the company data
Insert your Backup disk in the **B:** drive
- Your working copy of the company data should be in A:\.
- If you do not have two disk drives on your computer, see your professor for
  instructions.
Click **File** on the menu bar, click **Back Up**
OR
Click **Company** tab on QuickBooks Navigator, click **Back Up**
On the **Back Up Company to** screen, click **Drives** drop-down arrow list, click **B:**
In the **File Name** text box enter **1-31-98.qbb** as the name for the backup

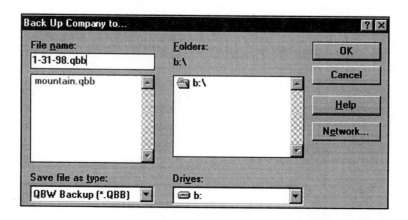

Click **OK**

Click **OK** on the QuickBooks Information dialog box to acknowledge the
successful backup
Remove the backup disk from B:\
The label for this disk should be **Backup**
Insert a second backup disk in **B:**
Repeat the procedures listed above
Label this disk **Archive, 1-31-98**

PASSWORDS

Not every employee of a business should have access to all the financial records. In some
companies only the owner(s) will have complete access. In others, one or two key employees
will have full access while other employees are provided limited access based on the jobs they
perform. Passwords are secret words used to control access to data. QuickBooks has several
options available to assign passwords:

Owner Password—allows unrestricted access to all QuickBooks functions.

Payroll Password—allows entry and editing of new transactions including payroll transactions;
disallows editing of previous transactions and use of reports, graphs, and registers.

Data Entry Password—allows entry and editing of new transactions; disallows entry and editing
of payroll transactions, editing of previous transactions, and use of reports, graphs, and registers.

Transaction Password—allows editing of transactions of a prior period.

A password should be kept secret at all times. It should be something that is easy for the
individual to remember yet difficult for someone else to guess. Birthdays, names, initials, and
other similar devices are not good passwords because the information is too readily available.
Never write down your password where it can be easily found or seen by someone else.

ASSIGN OWNER PASSWORD

QuickBooks requires an owner password before it will allow any other passwords to be assigned.
Once an owner password has been assigned, QuickBooks will ask you for the password before it
will open a company file.

MEMO

DATE: January 31, 1998

Renee, in preparation for assigning password protection to the data for January, assign **QB** as the owner password.

---

*DO: Assign **QB** as the owner password:

Click **File** on the menu bar, click **Passwords**, click **Set Password** for **Owner Password**

Enter **QB** as the **New Password** on the **Set Owner Password** dialog box

- In an actual business, QB would not be an appropriate or recommended password because it would be too easy for someone to guess. Nor would the password be written down as it is in the menu above.
- Notice that the password is entered as ******.
- This is to prevent someone from reading the password while it is being established.

Enter **qb** in the **Confirm Password** text box

- Again, you see ******.

Click **OK** to assign the password

- You made an error and the two passwords typed do not match.
- The error can be typographical, not entering the same information, or not capitalizing the same way.
- A warning dialog box appears: "The new password you entered does not match the confirmation."

Click **OK,** repeat the procedure to assign the password

Enter **QB** as the **New Password** on the **Set Owner Password** dialog box

Enter **QB** in the **Confirm Password** text box

Click **OK** to assign the password

Do not close Passwords screen

ASSIGN END-OF-PERIOD PASSWORD

A password assigned to transactions for a period prevents change to data from the period. This is helpful to discourage casual changes or transaction deletions to a period that has been closed. QuickBooks does allow changes to be made to a prior period if you know the password.

MEMO

DATE: January 31, 1998

Now that the closing transactions have been performed, protect the data by
assigning the password "January" to the period ending 1/31/98.

---

 *DO: Assign the password **January** to the transactions for the period ending 1/31/98
In the Transaction Password text box at the bottom of the Passwords screen, enter
01/31/98 as the date through which the books are closed
Click **Set Password** button for **Transaction Password**
Enter **January** as the **New Password** on the **Set Transaction Password** dialog
box
- Notice that the password is entered as ***********.
- This is to prevent someone from reading the password while it is being
established.
Enter **January** in the **Confirm Password** text box
- Again, you see ***********.
Click **OK** to assign the password
- If you make an error and the two passwords typed do not match, you get a
warning: "The new password you entered does not match the confirmation";
click **OK,** repeat the procedure to assign the password.
Click **OK** to exit Passwords

ACCESS COMPANY INFORMATION USING OWNER PASSWORD

Once an owner password is assigned, company information may not be accessed unless the
appropriate password is entered.

 *DO: Test the owner password
Close the Company
Close QuickBooks
Reopen QuickBooks
Reopen Mountain.qbw
QuickBooks dialog box appears requesting the password for MOUNTAIN
Enter *your* first name in the text box, click **OK**
A **Warning** dialog box appears, click **OK**
Type the correct password QB, click **OK**

ACCESS TRANSACTION FOR PREVIOUS PERIOD

Even though the month of January has been "closed," transactions still appear in the account registers, the Journal, etc. The transactions shown may not be changed unless the appropriate password can be provided.

 *DO: Try to change Prepaid Insurance to 2,500 without providing a transaction password

Access Chart of Accounts as previously instructed, click **Prepaid Insurance**

Click **Activities** button at the bottom of the Chart of Accounts, click **Use Register**
  OR
Use the keyboard shortcut, **Ctrl+R**
Click the **Increase** column showing **250**
Highlight 250, enter **2,500**
Click **Record** button
QuickBooks dialog box requiring the password appears

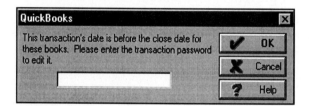

Click **Cancel** to cancel the password request
Click **Restore** button to restore the transaction to the original 250
Close the Prepaid Insurance account
Do not close the Chart of Accounts

EDIT TRANSACTION FROM PREVIOUS PERIOD

If it is determined that an error was made in a previous period, QuickBooks does allow the correction. Before it will record any changes for previous periods, QuickBooks requires a correct transaction password for each change.

MEMO

DATE: February 1, 1998

After reviewing the Journal and reports printed at the end of January, Renee finds that the $25 of the amount of Office Supplies should have been recorded as Sales Supplies. Record an entry in the Journal to transfer $25 from Office Supplies to Sales Supplies.

*DO: Transfer $25 from Office Supplies to Sales Supplies
Access the **General Journal** as previously instructed
Enter the date of **01/31/98**
Tab to or click drop-down list arrow for Account
In the **QuickBooks** dialog box, enter **January** as the password
Click **OK**

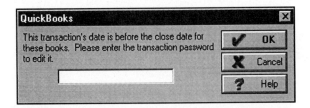

Tab to or click Account, click the drop-down list arrow for Account, click
   1312 Sales Supplies
Enter the debit of **25.00**
Enter the Memo **Correcting Entry**
Tab to or click Account, click the drop-down list arrow for Account, click
   1311 Office Supplies
•   A credit amount of 25.00 should already be in the credit column. If not, enter the amount.
Enter the Memo **Correcting Entry**

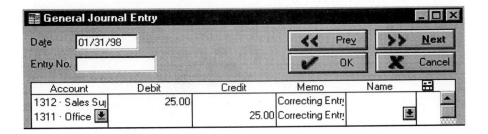

Click **OK**

The transaction password dialog appears again

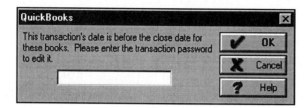

Enter the password **January**

Click **OK**

- The transaction has been entered.

VERIFY THE CORRECTION TO OFFICE AND SALES SUPPLIES

Once the correction has been made, it is important to view the change in the accounts. The transfer of an amount of one asset into another will have no direct effect on the total assets in your reports. The account balances for Office Supplies and Sales Supplies will be changed. To view the change in the account, open the Chart of Accounts and look at the balance of each account. You may also use the account register to view the correcting entry as it was recorded in each account.

MEMO

DATE: January 31, 1998

Access the Chart of Accounts and view the change in the account balances and the correcting entry in each account's register.

---

  *DO: View the correcting entry in each account

Open the **Chart of Accounts** as previously instructed

- Notice that the balance for Office Supplies has been changed from 521.98 to 496.98.
- Notice that the balance for Sales Supplies has been changed from 400.00 to 425.00.

◆1310 · Supplies	Other Current Asset	921.98
◆1311 · Office Supplies	Other Current Asset	496.98
◆1312 · Sales Supplies	Other Current Asset	425.00

Click **Office Supplies**
Click **Activities** button, click **Use Register**
- Notice that the correcting entry was recorded for Office Supplies.

1311 · Office Supplies						_ □ ✕
Date	Ref	Payee	Decrease	✓	Increase	Balance
	Type	Account	Memo			
01/31/98			25.00			496.98
	GENJRNL	1312 · Sales Supplies	Correcting Entry			

Close the Office Supplies register
Repeat the steps to view the correcting entry in Sales Supplies

1312 · Sales Supplies						_ □ ✕
Date	Ref	Payee	Decrease	✓	Increase	Balance
	Type	Account	Memo			
01/31/98					25.00	425.00
	GENJRNL	1311 · Office Supplies	Correcting Entry			

Close the Sales Supplies register
Close the Chart of Accounts

PRINT POST-CLOSING TRIAL BALANCE

After "closing" has been completed, it is helpful to print a post-closing trial balance. This proves that debits still equal credits.

MEMO

DATE: February 1, 1998

Print a Post-Closing Trial Balance, a Post-Closing Profit and Loss Statement, and a Post-Closing Balance Sheet for Mountain Adventure Ski Shoppe. The dates should be as of or for 02/01/98.

---

*DO: Print a Post-Closing Trial Balance to prove debits still equal credits
Click **Reports** on the menu bar, point to **Other Reports**, click **Trial Balance**
OR

Click **Company** or **Taxes and Accountant** tab on QuickBooks Navigator, click
    Other in the Reports section, click **Trial Balance**

Tab to or click **From**, enter the date **02/01/98**

Tab to or click **To**, enter the date **02/01/98**

Tab to generate the report

Scroll through the report and study the amounts shown

- Notice that the final totals of debits and credits are equal.

Click the **Print** button at the top of the Trial Balance

Click **Preview** button to view a miniature copy of the report

- This helps determine the orientation, whether you need to select the feature to
  print one page wide, or whether you need to adjust column widths.

Click **Close**

Print in Portrait orientation

Close the Trial Balance

Mountain Adventure Ski Shoppe
Trial Balance
As of February 1, 1998

	Feb 1, '98	
	Debit	Credit
6130 · Sales Discount	447.17	
6140 · Advertising Expense	95.00	
6150 · Depreciation Expense	160.00	
6181 · Liability Insurance	125.00	
6212 · Loan Interest	97.93	
6300 · Rent	950.00	
6340 · Telephone	156.40	
6391 · Gas and Electric	359.00	
6392 · Water	85.00	
6471 · Sales	175.00	
6472 · Office	350.00	
6999 · Uncategorized Expenses	0.00	
7010 · Interest Income		54.05
TOTAL	**89,837.30**	**89,837.30**

Partial Report

PRINT POST-CLOSING PROFIT AND LOSS STATEMENT

Because February 1 is after the closing date of January 31, 1998, the Profit and Loss Statement
for February 1 is the Post-Closing Profit and Loss Statement. To verify the closing, print a Profit
and Loss Statement for February 1.

*DO: Print a Standard Profit and Loss report for February
Click **Reports** on the menu bar, point to **Profit & Loss**, click **Standard**
    OR
Click **Company** or **Taxes and Accountant** tab on QuickBooks Navigator, click
    Profit & Loss in the **Reports** section, click **Standard**
Tab to or click **From**, enter **02/01/98**
Tab to or click **To**, enter **02/01/98**
Tab to generate the report
• The Net Income is 0.00.
Print the report in Portrait orientation

> ### Mountain Adventure Ski Shoppe
> ## Profit and Loss
> #### February 1, 1998
> ◇ Feb 1, '98 ◇
> Net Income ▶   **0.00** ◀

Close the Profit and Loss report

PRINT POST-CLOSING BALANCE SHEET

The proof that assets equal liabilities and owners' equity after the closing entries have been made needs to be displayed in a Post-Closing Balance Sheet. The Balance Sheet for February 1 is considered to be a Post-Closing Balance Sheet because it is prepared after the closing of the period. Most of the adjustments were for the month of January 1998. Because this report is for a month, the adjustment to Retained Earnings and Net Income will result in both of the accounts being included on the Balance Sheet. If, however, this report were prepared for the year, neither account would appear.

*DO: Print a Standard Balance Sheet report for February 1, 1998, and February 1, 1999
Click **Reports** on the menu bar, point to **Balance Sheet**, click **Standard**
    OR
Click **Company** or **Taxes and Accountant** tab on QuickBooks Navigator, click
    Balance Sheet in the **Reports** section, click **Standard**
Tab to or click **As of**, enter **02/01/98**
Tab to generate the report
Scroll through the report to view the assets, liabilities, and equities listed

- Because this report is for a one-month period, both Retained Earnings and Net Income are included on this report.

Print the report, orientation is **Portrait**

Mountain Adventure Ski Shoppe
Balance Sheet
As of February 1, 1998

	Feb 1, '98
3000 · Retained Earnings	-2,605.19
Net Income	2,605.19
3100 · Boyd & Wayne Capital	
3110 · Eric Boyd, Capital	
3111 · Eric Boyd, Investment	20,000.00
3110 · Eric Boyd, Capital - Other	12,912.35
Total 3110 · Eric Boyd, Capital	32,912.35
3120 · Matthew Wayne, Capital	
3121 · Matthew Wayne, Investment	20,000.00
3120 · Matthew Wayne, Capital - Other	12,912.34
Total 3120 · Matthew Wayne, Capital	32,912.34
Total 3100 · Boyd & Wayne Capital	65,824.69

Partial Report

Change the date to **02/01/99**

Tab to generate the report

Scroll through the report to view the assets, liabilities, and equities listed

- Because this report is prepared after the end of the fiscal year, neither Retained Earnings nor Net Income is included on this report.

Print the report

Mountain Adventure Ski Shoppe
Balance Sheet
As of February 1, 1999

	Feb 1, '99
3100 · Boyd & Wayne Capital	
3110 · Eric Boyd, Capital	
3111 · Eric Boyd, Investment	20,000.00
3110 · Eric Boyd, Capital - Other	12,912.35
Total 3110 · Eric Boyd, Capital	32,912.35
3120 · Matthew Wayne, Capital	
3121 · Matthew Wayne, Investment	20,000.00
3120 · Matthew Wayne, Capital - Other	12,912.34
Total 3120 · Matthew Wayne, Capital	32,912.34
Total 3100 · Boyd & Wayne Capital	65,824.69
Total Equity	65,824.69

Partial Report

Close the Balance Sheet

SUMMARY

In this chapter, end-of-period adjustments were made, a bank reconciliation and a credit card reconciliation were performed, backup and archive disks were prepared, and adjusting entries were made. The use of Drawing, Net Income, and Retained Earnings accounts were explored and interpreted for a partnership. Owner passwords and passwords for a prior "closed" period were assigned. Account names were changed, and new accounts were created. Even though QuickBooks focuses on entering transactions on business forms, a Journal recording each transaction is kept by QuickBooks. This chapter presented transaction entry directly into the Journal. The difference between accrual basis and cash basis accounting was discussed. Company preferences were established for accrual basis reporting preferences. Owner withdrawals and distribution of capital to partners were examined. Many of the different report options available in QuickBooks were explored. A variety of reports were printed. Correction of errors was analyzed, and corrections were made after the period was "closed." The fact that QuickBooks does not require an actual closing entry at the end of the period was addressed.

END-OF-CHAPTER QUESTIONS

TRUE/FALSE

ANSWER THE FOLLOWING QUESTIONS IN THE SPACE PROVIDED BEFORE THE QUESTION NUMBER.

_____ 1. The owner's drawing account should be transferred to capital each month.

_____ 2. Even if entered elsewhere, all transactions are recorded in the Journal.

_____ 3. You must assign an owner password before assigning an end-of-period password.

_____ 4. If Show All is selected, inactive accounts will not appear in the Chart of Accounts.

_____ 5. When you reconcile a bank statement, anything entered as a service charge will automatically be entered as a transaction when the reconciliation is complete.

_____ 6. Once an account has been used, the name cannot be changed.

_____ 7. The adjusting entry for depreciation may be made in the depreciation account register.

_____ 8. At the end of the year, QuickBooks transfers the net income into retained earnings.

_____ 9. A withdrawal by an owner in a partnership reduces the owner's capital.

_____ 10. As with other accounting programs, QuickBooks requires that a formal closing be performed at the end of each year.

MULTIPLE CHOICE

WRITE THE LETTER OF THE CORRECT ANSWER IN THE SPACE PROVIDED BEFORE
THE QUESTION NUMBER.

_____ 1. To print a reconciliation report that lists only totals select ___.
   A. none
   B. summary
   C. full
   D. complete

_____ 2. The report that proves debits equal credits is the ___.
   A. sales graph
   B. balance sheet
   C. profit and loss statement
   D. trial balance

_____ 3. If reports are prepared as of January 31, net income will appear in the ___.
   A. Profit and Loss Statement
   B. Balance Sheet
   C. Both A and B
   D. Neither A nor B

_____ 4. The balances of Uncategorized Income and Uncategorized Expenses are transferred to
       ___.
   A. the Retained Earnings account
   B. the Capital account
   C. the Investment account
   D. none of the above

_____ 5. QuickBooks automatically records Purchases Discount as ___.
   A. income
   B. a decrease to cost of goods sold
   C. an expense
   D. an asset

_____ 6. If a transaction is recorded in the Journal, it may be viewed ___.
   A. in the Journal
   B. in the register for each account used in the transaction
   C. by using QuickZoom in a report
   D. both A and B

_____ 7. Entries for bank collections ___.
   A. are automatically recorded at the completion of the bank reconciliation
   B. must be recorded after the bank reconciliation is complete
   C. should be recorded while one is reconciling the bank statement
   D. should be recorded on the first of the month

_____ 8. The accounts that may be reconciled are ___.
   A. checking
   B. credit card
   C. all accounts
   D. both A and B

_____ 9. The closing entry for drawing transfers the balance of an owner's drawing account into the ___ account.
   A. Retained Earnings
   B. Net Income
   C. Capital
   D. Investment

_____ 10. The type of password that allows only the entry and editing of new transactions is a(n) ___.
   A. transaction password
   B. data entry password
   C. payroll password
   D. owner password

FILL-IN

IN THE SPACE PROVIDED, WRITE THE ANSWER THAT MOST APPROPRIATELY COMPLETES THE SENTENCE.

1. _____ basis accounting matches income and expenses against a period and _____ basis accounting records income when the money is received and expenses when the purchase is made or the bill is paid.

2. The _____ proves that assets = liabilities + owners' equity.

3. When the records for a company are created, the opening balances for vendors are placed in an account called _____, and the opening balances for customers are placed in an account called _____.

4. The _____ password is the first password that must be assigned.

5. No matter where transactions are recorded, they all appear in the _____.

SHORT ESSAY

Describe the adjustment required for Purchase Discounts, and explain why this adjustment should be made.

_____
_____
_____
_____
_____

END-OF-CHAPTER PROBLEM

HAWAII SUN CLOTHING CO.

Chapter 7 continues with the end-of-period adjustments, bank and credit card reconciliations, archive disks, and password protection for a prior "closed" period for Hawaii Sun Clothing Co. The company does use a certified professional accountant for guidance and assistance with appropriate accounting procedures. The CPA has provided information for Maile to use for adjusting entries, etc.

INSTRUCTIONS

Continue to use the copy of HAWAII you used in the previous chapters. Open the company—the file used is **Hawaii.QBW**. Record the adjustments and other transactions as you were instructed in the chapter. Always read the transaction carefully and review the Chart of Accounts when selecting transaction accounts. Print the reports and journals as indicated.

RECORD TRANSACTIONS

January 31—Enter the following:

Change the names of the following accounts:

6260 Printing and Reproduction to **6260 Printing and Duplication**

6350 Travel & Ent to **6350 Travel**

3010 Kalaniki & Kahala Capital to **3100 Kalaniki & Kahala, Capital**

(Note: Check the description for each account to see if it needs to be changed as well.)

Add the following accounts:

Cost of Goods Sold account **5010 Purchases Discounts** (subaccount of **5000**)

Equity account **3110 Nalani Kalaniki, Capital** (subaccount of **3100**)

Equity account **3120 Maile Kahala, Capital** (subaccount of **3100**)

Change the following accounts:

3011 Nalani Kalaniki, Investment to **3111 Nalani Kalaniki, Investment** (subaccount of **3110**)

3013 Nalani Kalaniki, Drawing to **3112 Nalani Kalaniki, Drawing** (subaccount of **3110**)

3012 Maile Kahala, Investment to **3121 Maile Kahala, Investment** (subaccount of **3120**)

3014 Maile Kahala, Drawing to **3122 Maile Kahala, Drawing** (subaccount of **3120**)

Make the following accounts inactive:

6291 Building Repairs

6351 Entertainment

Delete the following accounts:

6182 Disability Insurance

6213 Mortgage

6823 Property

Print the Chart of Accounts (Do *not* show inactive accounts)

Enter the following adjustment:

Transfer the amount of purchases discounts from Income: 4030 Purchases Discounts to Cost of Goods Sold: 5010 Purchases Discounts (Memo: Transfer to CoGS)

Enter owner adjustments to the capital account:

Transfer Uncategorized Income and Uncategorized Expenses to 3100 Kalaniki & Kahala, Capital (Memo: Transfer to Capital)

Enter adjusting entries in the Journal for:

Office Supplies Used, the amount used is $35. (Memo: Office Supplies Used for January)

Sales Supplies Used, account balance at the end of the month is $1,400 (Memo: Sales Supplies Used for January)

Record a compound entry for depreciation for the month: Office Equipment, $66.67 and Store Fixtures, $79.17 (Memo for all accounts used: Depreciation Expense January)

The amount of insurance remaining in the Prepaid Insurance account is for six months of liability insurance. Record the liability insurance expense for the month. (Memo: Insurance Expense January)

Enter transactions for Owners' Equity:

Each owner withdrew $500. (Memo: Withdrawal for January) Print Checks 7 and 8 for the owners' withdrawals.

Distribute capital to each owner: divide the balance of 3100 Kalaniki & Kahala, Capital equally between the two partners. Record an entry to transfer each owner's portion of capital to her individual capital account. (Memo: Transfer Capital to Individual Accounts)

Prepare Bank Reconciliation and Enter Adjustments for the Reconciliation:

(Refer to the chapter for appropriate memo notations)

SAN LUIS OBISPO CENTRAL COAST BANK
1234 Coast Highway
San Luis Obispo, CA 93407
(805) 555-9300

Hawaii Sun Clothing Co.
784 Marsh Street
San Luis Obispo, CA 93407

Acct. # 987-352-9152   January, 1998

Beginning Balance, January 1, 1998			$32,589.00
1/15/98, Deposit	4,851.38		37,440.38
1/15/98, NSF Returned Check		325.00	37,115.38
1/15/98, Check 1		58.98	37,056.40
1/18/98, Check 2		156.00	36,900.40
1/18/98, Check 3		343.00	36,557.40
1/25/98, Check 4		1,150.00	35,407.40
1/25/98, Check 5		79.85	35,327.55
1/31/98, Service Charge		10.00	35,317.55
1/31/98, NSF Charge		15.00	35,302.55
1/31/98, Office Equipment Loan Pmt.: $44.51 Interest, $8.61 Principal		53.12	35,249.43
1/31/98, Store Fixtures Loan Pmt.: $53.42 Interest, $10.33 Principal		63.75	35,185.68
1/31/98, Interest	73.30		35,258.98
Ending Balance, 1/31/98			35,258.98

Print a Full Reconciliation Report

Reconcile the Visa account

SAN LUIS OBISPO CENTRAL COAST BANK
VISA DEPARTMENT
1234 Coast Highway
San Luis Obispo, CA 93407
(805) 555-9300

Hawaii Sun Clothing Co.
784 Marsh Street
San Luis Obispo, CA 93407

VISA Acct. # 9187-52-9152   January, 1998

Beginning Balance, January 1, 1998			0.00
1/9/98, The Clothes House		196.00	196.00
1/18/98, Office Inventory Masters		250.00	446.00
Ending Balance, 1/20/98			446.00

Minimum Payment Due: $50.00   Payment Due Date: February 5, 1998

Pay the Visa bill using Check No. 9. Print Check 9

Verify or change reporting preferences to accrual basis

Print the following for January 1-31, 1998, or as of January 31, 1998:
   Trial Balance
   Standard Profit and Loss Statement
   Standard Balance Sheet

Divide in half and transfer Net Income/Retained Earnings into owners' individual capital
   accounts.

Close drawing accounts into owner's individual capital accounts.

Print a Standard Balance Sheet

Assign Owner Password and End-of-period Password:
   Owner password is **QB**
   End-of-period is 01/31/98 and the Transaction Password is **January**

Edit a Transaction from a closed period:

Discovered an error in the amount of Office Supplies and Sales Supplies: Transfer $40 from
   Office Supplies to Sales Supplies on 01/31/98.

February 1, 1998—Print the following:
Journal for 01/01/98-02/01/98 (Landscape orientation, Fit on one page wide)
Trial Balance, February 1, 1998
Standard Profit and Loss Statement, February 1, 1998
Standard Balance Sheet, February 1, 1998

February 1, 1999—Print the following:
Standard Balance Sheet

END OF SECTION 2—
GOLF WORLD PRACTICE SET:
MERCHANDISING BUSINESS

The following is a comprehensive practice set combining all the elements of QuickBooks studied in the second section of the text. In this practice set you will keep the books for a company for the month of January 1998. Entries will be made to record invoices, receipt of payments on invoices, cash sales, credit card sales, receipt and payment of bills, orders and receipt of merchandise, credit memos for invoices and bills, sales tax payments, and credit card payments. Account names will be added, changed, deleted, and made inactive. Customer, vendor, and owner names will be added to the appropriate lists. Reports will be prepared to analyze sales, bills, receipts, and items ordered. Formal reports including the Trial Balance, Profit and Loss Statement, and Balance Sheet will be prepared. Adjusting entries for depreciation, supplies used, insurance expense, and automatic payments will be recorded. Both bank and credit card reconciliations will be prepared. Entries to transfer purchase discounts to from income to cost of goods sold will be made. Entries to display partnership equity for each partner will be made. The owners' drawing accounts will be closed. Passwords will be assigned for the end of the period.

GOLF WORLD

Located in Palm Springs, California, Golf World is a full-service golf shop that sells golf equipment and golf clothing. Golf World is a partnership owned and operated by Larry Summers and Ann Winters. Each partner contributed an equal amount to the partnership. Larry buys the equipment and manages the store. Ann buys the clothing and accessory items and keeps the books for Golf World. There are several part-time employees working for Golf World selling merchandise.

INSTRUCTIONS

Check with your instructor to obtain a disk containing the data for Golf World. Copy the file **Golf.QBW** to a new disk and open the company. The following lists are used for all sales items, customers, and vendors. You will be adding additional customers and vendors as the company is in operation. When entering transactions, you are responsible for any memos you wish to include in transactions. Unless otherwise specified, the terms for each sale or bill will be the term specified on the Customer or Vendor list. (Chose edit for the individual customers or vendors and select the Additional Info tab to see the terms for each customer or vendor.) Customer Message is usually "Thank you for your business." However, any other message that is appropriate may be used. If a customer's order exceeds the established credit limit, accept the order and process it. If the terms allow a discount for a customer, make sure to apply the discount if payment is made within the discount period. Use 6130 Sales Discounts as the discount account. If a customer has a credit and has a balance on the account, apply the credit to payments received for the customer. If there is no balance for a customer and a return is made, issue a credit memo and a refund check. Always pay bills in time to take advantage of purchase discounts. Remember that the discount due date will be ten days from the date of the bill.

Invoices, purchase orders, and other business forms should be printed with lines around each field. Most reports will be printed in Portrait orientation; however, if the report (such as the Journal) will fit across the page using Landscape, use Landscape orientation. Whenever possible, adjust the column widths so that reports fit on one page wide *without* selecting "Fit report to one page wide."

Customers:

Customer:Job List	
Name	Balance
⬧ Alhama, Eli	1,575.00
⬧ Basil, Dennis	1,850.00
⬧ Chung, Chiang	1,700.00
⬧ Clark, Marilyn	0.00
⬧ Donald, Mel	850.00
⬧ Harrison, Frank	0.00
⬧ Lopez, Julie	375.00
⬧ Morgan, Jerri	550.00
⬧ Norton, Joe	450.00
⬧ O'Dell, Donna	850.00
⬧ Phillips, Richard	1,200.00
⬧ Raymond, Ron	750.00
⬧ Samuels, Steve	950.00
⬧ Scott, Lois	75.00
⬧ Sepulveda, Sanchez	1,200.00
⬧ Stein, Stanley	150.00
⬧ Towne, Darla	350.00
⬧ Wayama, June	0.00

Vendors:

Vendor List	
Name	Balance
Golf Clothes, Inc.	5,000.00
Golf Club Distribution	15,000.00
Golf Supplies	500.00
Shoe Supply	500.00
State Board of Equalization	0.00

Sales Items:

Name	Description	Type	Account	On Hand	Price
◆ Bags	Golf Bags	Inventory Part	4000 · Sales:4I	15	0.00
◆ Clubs-Irons	Golf Clubs: Irons	Inventory Part	4000 · Sales:4I	150	0.00
◆ Clubs-Sets	Golf Clubs: Sets	Inventory Part	4000 · Sales:4I	50	0.00
◆ Clubs-Woods	Golf Clubs: Wood:	Inventory Part	4000 · Sales:4I	150	0.00
◆ Gift Sets	Golf Gift Sets	Inventory Part	4000 · Sales:4I	10	0.00
◆ Gloves	Golf Gloves	Inventory Part	4000 · Sales:4I	35	0.00
◆ Golf Balls	Golf Balls	Inventory Part	4000 · Sales:4I	60	0.00
◆ Hats	Golf Hats	Inventory Part	4000 · Sales:4I	20	0.00
◆ Men's Jackets	Men's Jackets	Inventory Part	4000 · Sales:4I	12	0.00
◆ Men's Pants	Men's Pants	Inventory Part	4000 · Sales:4I	15	0.00
◆ Men's Shirts	Men's Shirts	Inventory Part	4000 · Sales:4I	15	0.00
◆ Men's Shoes	Men's Shoes	Inventory Part	4000 · Sales:4I	18	0.00
◆ Men's Shorts	Men's Shorts	Inventory Part	4000 · Sales:4I	12	0.00
◆ Tees	Golf Tees	Inventory Part	4000 · Sales:4I	30	0.00
◆ Towels	Golf Towels	Inventory Part	4000 · Sales:4I	10	0.00
◆ Women's Pants	Women's Pants	Inventory Part	4000 · Sales:4I	12	0.00
◆ Women's Shirt	Women's Shirts	Inventory Part	4000 · Sales:4I	12	0.00
◆ Women's Shoes	Women's Shoes	Inventory Part	4000 · Sales:4I	20	0.00
◆ Women's Short	Women's Shorts	Inventory Part	4000 · Sales:4I	15	0.00
◆ Women'sJacket	Women's Jackets	Inventory Part	4000 · Sales:4I	12	0.00
◆ CA Sales Tax	CA Sales Tax	Sales Tax Item	2200 · Sales T		7.25%

RECORD TRANSACTIONS:

Enter the transactions for Golf World and print as indicated.

Week 1—January 2-8, 1998:
Add your name to the company name. The company name will be **Golf World--Student's Name**. (Type your actual name *not* the words "Student's Name.")

Change the Report Preferences: Report Header/Footer should *not* include the Date Prepared.

Change the names and, if necessary, the descriptions of the following accounts:

    4200 Sales Discounts to **4200 Purchases Discounts**

    6130 Cash Discounts to **6130 Sales Discounts**

    6350 Travel & Ent to **6350 Travel**

    6381 Marketing to **6381 Sales** (this is a subaccount of 6380 Supplies Expense)

Delete the following accounts:

    4050 Reimbursed Expenses

    4070 Resale Discounts

    4090 Resale Income

    4100 Freight Income

    6140 Contributions

    6182 Disability Insurance

    6213 Mortgage

6265 Filing Fees
6285 Franchise Fees
6351 Entertainment

Make the following accounts inactive:

6311 Building Repairs
6413 Property

Add the following accounts:

Equity account: **3010 Larry Summers, Capital** (Subaccount of **3000**)
Equity account: **3020 Ann Winters, Capital** (Subaccount of **3000**)
Cost of Goods Sold account: **5010 Purchases Discounts** (Subaccount of **5000**)

Change the following accounts:

Larry Summers, Investment to **3011 Larry Summers, Investment** (Subaccount of **3010**)
Larry Summers, Drawing to **3012 Larry Summers, Drawing** (Subaccount of **3010**)
Ann Winters, Investment to **3021 Ann Winters, Investment** (Subaccount of **3020**)
Ann Winters, Drawing to **3022 Ann Winters, Drawing** (Subaccount of **3020**)

Print the Chart of Accounts. Do *not* show inactive accounts.

Prior to recording any transactions, print a Trial Balance as of January 1, 1998.

Print invoices, checks, and other items as they are entered in the transactions.

1/2/98

Transfer Uncategorized Income and Uncategorized Expenses to 3000 Summers & Winters, Capital.

Sold 2 pairs of women's shorts @ $64.99 each, 2 women's shirts @ $59.99 each, 1 women's jacket @ $129.99, and 1 pair of women's shoes @ $179.99 to June Wayama. (Remember: Print the invoice when the transaction is entered.)

Having achieved her goal of a handicap under 30, Marilyn treated herself to the new clubs she had been wanting. Sold 1 set of graphite clubs for $750, 1 golf bag for $129.95, and 5 sleeves (packages) of golf balls @ $6.95 each to Marilyn Clark.

Frank heard that titanium would give him extra yardage with each shot. Sold 4 titanium woods to Frank Harrison @ $459.00 each.

Sold 5 golf bags @ $59.99 each and 5 sets of starter clubs @ $159.99 each to Palm Springs Schools for the high school golf team. Palm Springs Schools located at 99-4058 South Palm Canyon Drive, Palm Springs, CA 92262 is a nonprofit organization. The telephone number is 619-555-4455, and the contact person is Claudia Colby. The terms are Net 30 and the credit limit is $1500. Even though this is a nonprofit organization, it does pay California Sales Tax on all purchases. Include a subtotal for the sale and apply a 10% sales discount for a nonprofit organization. (Create any new sales items necessary.)

Correct the invoice to Marilyn Clark. The price of the golf bag should be $179.95. Reprint the invoice.

Received Check No. 2285 from Eli Alhama in full payment of his account.

Received Check No. 102-33 from Sanchez Sepulveda, $600, in partial payment of his account.

1/3/98

Sold 3 gift sets @ $14.99 each and 3 sleeves (packages) of golf balls @ $8.95 each to Lois Scott to be given away as door prizes at an upcoming ladies' club tournament.

Sold 2 pairs of men's shorts @ $49.95 each, 2 men's shirts @ $59.99 each, and 1 pair of golf shoes @ $119.99 to Stanley Stein.

Received Check No. 815 from Mel Donald for $850 in full payment of his account.

Sold 2 golf towels @ $9.95 each to a cash customer.

Sold 1 pair of women's golf shoes @ $149.95 to a new customer: Chris Laymon, 45-2215 PGA Drive, Rancho Mirage, CA 92270, 619-555-3322, terms 1% 10 Net 30, credit limit $1,000, taxable customer for California Sales Tax.

Received Check No. 2233 for $950 from Richard Phillips in partial payment of his account.

Sold a golf bag for $99.95 to a cash customer using a Visa card.

1/5/98

Check Reminders list to see if any merchandise needs to be ordered. Display the list in detail. Print the list.

Prepare and print a Stock Status by Item Inventory Report for January 1-5 in Landscape orientation.

Prepare Purchase Orders for all items marked Order on the Stock Status by Item Inventory Report. Place all orders with the preferred vendors. Only prepare one purchase order per vendor. For all items ordered, the Qty on Hand should exceed the Reorder Point by 10 when the new merchandise is received. The cost of golf bags are $40 each, gift sets are $3 each, men's shorts are $20 each, towels are $2 each, and women's shirts are $20 each.

Order 5 Women's Hats @ $10.00 each from a new vendor: Hats Galore, 45980 West Los Angeles Street, Los Angeles, CA 90025, Contact Krista Ruiz, Phone 310-555-8787, FAX 310-555-7878, Terms 2% 10 Net 30, Credit Limit $500. Add a new sales item: Women's Hats with Hats Galore as the preferred vendor. The purchase and sales description is Women's Golf Hats. The COGS account is 5000. Leave the sales price at 0.00. The hats are taxable. The Income account is 4000-Sales: 4010-Accessory Sales. The Asset account is 1120-Inventory Asset. The reorder point is 10. Quantity on Hand is 0 as of 01/05/98.

Change the current sales item Hats from Item Name: Hats to **Men's Hats**. The purchase and sales descriptions should be **Men's Golf Hats**. Change the reorder point from 15 to 12.

Print a Purchase Order QuickReport in Landscape orientation for January 1-5.

1/8/98

Received Check No. 1822 for a cash sale of 2 men's golf hats @ $49.95 each.

Deposit all checks received for the week. Print the Deposit Detail report for January 1-8, 1998.

Week 2—January 9-15:
1/10/98

Received the order from Hats Galore without the bill.

Received the orders from Golf Supplies and Golf Clothes, Inc., along with the bills for the merchandise received. All items were received in full except the golf bags. Of the 12 bags ordered, only 8 were received. Use 01/10/98 for the bill date for both transactions.

Lois Scott returned 1 of the gift sets purchased on January 3. Issue a credit memo.

Mel Donald returned 1 pair of men's golf shorts that had been purchased for $59.95. (The shorts had been purchased previously and were part of his $850 opening balance.) Issue the appropriate items.

Sold 1 complete set of golf clubs on account to Joe Norton for $1,600.00.

Sold a graphite sand wedge and a graphite gap wedge @ $119.95 each to a customer using a Visa card. (Both clubs are classified as irons.)

1/12/98

Received the telephone bill for the month, $85.15 from Desert Telephone Co., 11-092 Highway 111, Palm Springs, CA 92262, 619-555-9285. The bill is due January 25.

Purchased $175 of office supplies to have on hand from Desert Office Supply, 3950 46th Avenue, Indio, CA 92201, Contact Cheryl Lockwood, Phone 619-555-1535, FAX 619-555-5351. Used the company Visa card for the purchase.   p. 6-28

1/14/98

Received the bill for the order from Hats Galore. Use 01/14/98 for the bill date.

Received a bill from the Desert Electric Co., 995 Date Palm Drive, Cathedral City, CA 92234, 619-555-4646 for the monthly electric bill. The bill is for $275.00 and is due January 30.

Received the monthly water bill for $65 from Desert Water, 84-985 Jackson Street, Indio, CA 92202, 619-555-5653. The bill is due January 30.

Sold a set of golf clubs on account to Chris Laymon for $895.00.

Received Check No. 3801 for $1,949.42 from Frank Harrison in full payment of his bill. *acct.* 6()°

Received Check No. 783 for $594.53 from June Wayama in full payment of her bill.

Deposit all checks and credit card receipts for the week. Print Deposit Summary.

Week 3—January 16-22:

1/16/98

Received Check No. 1822 back from the bank. This check was for $107.14 from a cash customer: Wilson Johnson, 8013 Desert Drive, Desert Hot Springs, CA 92270, 619-555-0100. Payment is due on receipt. Charge Wilson the bank charge of $15 plus Golf World's own NSF charge of $15. Add any necessary customers, items and/or accounts. (Returned Check Service Charges should be income account 4040.)

Received Check No. 67-086 for $135.95 from Lois Scott in full payment of her account.   *apply credit*

Received the remaining 4 golf bags and the bill from Golf Supplies on earlier purchase order. The date of the bill is 01/16/98.

1/18/98

Pay all bills that are eligible to receive a discount if paid between January 18 and 22. Use account 4200 Purchases Discounts as the Discount Account.

Sold 1 golf bag @ $199.95, 1 set of graphite golf clubs @ $1,200, 1 putter @ $129.95 (record the putter as Golf Clubs: Irons), and 3 sleeves of golf balls @ $9.95 each to Lois Scott.   *$1672.83*

Returned 2 men's shirts that had poorly stitched seams at a cost of $20 each to Golf Clothes, Inc. Received a credit memo from the company.   *$40 credit*

company credit: Enter Bill, credit
customer credit: Create credit memos

1/20/98

Sold 1 men's golf hat @ $49.95 and 1 men's golf jacket at $89.95 to a customer using a MasterCard.   *$150.04*

Sold 1 towel @ $9.95, 2 packages of golf tees @ $1.95 each, and 1 sleeve of golf balls at $5.95 to a customer for cash.   *$21.24*

Received Check No. 1256 in full payment of account from Chiang Chung.   *$1700*

Richard Phillips bought a starter set of golf clubs for his son @ $250.00 and a new titanium driver for himself @ $549.95 (a driver is categorized as Golf Club: Woods).   *$857.95*

A businessman in town with his wife bought them each a set of golf clubs @ $1495.00 per set and a new golf bag for each of them @ $249.95 per bag. He purchased a men's jacket for $179.95. His wife purchased a pair of golf shoes for $189.99 and a women's jacket for $149.99. He used his Visa to pay for the purchases.   *$4300.54*

Prepare Purchase Orders to order any inventory items indicated on a Stock Status by Item report for January 1-20. As with earlier orders, use the preferred vendor, issue only one purchase order per vendor, and order enough to have 10 more than the minimum quantity of the ordered items on hand. (Golf balls cost $3.50 per sleeve, men's and women's jackets cost $20 each, and women's hats cost $10 each.)   *$42 $400*

Deposit the checks and credit card receipts for the week.

Week 4—January 23-30:

1/23/98

Pay all bills eligible to receive a discount if paid between January 23 and 30. Pay the telephone bill in full.   *$85.15 1/23/98*

Lois Scott was declared Club Champion and won a prize of $500. She brought in the $500 cash as a payment to be applied to the amount she owes on her account.   *$500*

Received the bill and all the items ordered from Golf Clothes, Inc., and Golf Supplies. The date of the bill is 01/23/98.   *$400 Dis 2/2 $42 Dis. 2/2*

Sold Lois Scott 5 Women's Golf Hats @ $25.99 each to give away as prizes at her next ladies' club tournament.   *$139.37*

Received Check No. 5216 from Dennis Basil as payment in full on his account.   *$1850*

Received Check No. 1205 from Marilyn Clark as payment in full on her account.

Received a letter of apology for the NSF check and a new check for $137.14 from Wilson Johnson to pay his account in full. The new check is Check No. 9015.   *$137.14*

1/25/98

Received the bill and all the hats ordered from Hats Galore. The date of the bill is 01/23/98.

Received the bill for $3,000 rent from Desert Rentals, 11-2951 Palm Canyon Drive, Palm Springs, CA 92262, Contact Tammi Moreno, Phone 619-555-8368, FAX 619-555-8638. The rent is due February 1.

Purchased sales supplies for $150 from Desert Office Supply. Used the company Visa for the purchase.

Prepare an Unpaid Bills Report by Vendor for January 25, 1998. Print the report.

Pay $1,000 to Golf Clothes, Inc., for the amount due 01/01/98; pay $5,000 to Golf Club Distribution toward the amount due 01/01/98; pay $500 to Golf Supplies to pay the amount due 01/01/98; pay $500 to Shoe Supply to pay the amount due 01/01/98. Also pay the rent, the electric bill, and the water bill. (NOTE: Apply the credit you have from Golf Clothes, Inc., because of returned merchandise and click NEXT before you record any of the above payments. If you do not apply the credit and click NEXT, the amount of the credit will be included as part of the payment and less cash will be deducted from checking. You want to pay $1,000 plus use the $40 credit and reduce the amount owed by $1,040 *not* $960. If you are not paying the full amount owed, simply click in Amt. Paid column and enter the amount you are paying.)

1/26/98

Prepare and print an Unpaid Bills Report by Vendor for January 26, 1998. (NOTE: check Golf Clothes, Inc., the amount owed should be $4,360. If your report does not show this, check to see how you applied the credit when you paid bills. If necessary, QuickBooks does allow you to delete the previous bill payment and redo it. If this is the case, be sure to apply the credit, click NEXT, then pay the $1,000 for the 01/01/98 bill.)

Received $1,000 from Joe Norton, Check No. 3716, in partial payment of his account.

Received payment in full from Sanchez Sepulveda, Check No. 102-157.

Sold 15 sleeves of golf balls @ $5.95 each to a cash customer to use as prizes in a retirement golf tournament for an employee of his company. Paid with Check No. 2237.

1/30/98

Deposit all checks and credit card receipts for the week.

Prepare Sales Tax Liability report from January 1-30, 1998. Adjust the column widths and print the report in Landscape orientation. The report should fit on one page.

Pay Sales Tax and print the check.

Print a Sales by Item Summary report for January 1-30. Use Landscape orientation and, if necessary, adjust column widths so the reports fits on one page wide.

Prepare and print a Sales by Item graph for January 1-30.

Prepare and print a Sales by Customer graph for January 1-30.

Print a Trial Balance for January 1-30 in Portrait orientation.

Transfer the amount of purchases discounts from Income: 4200 Purchases Discounts to Cost of Goods Sold: 5010 Purchases Discounts.

Enter the following adjusting entries:
   Office Supplies Used for the month is $125.
   The balance of the Sales Supplies is $650 on January 30.
   The amount of Prepaid Insurance represents the liability insurance for 12 months. Record the
      adjusting entry for the month of January.
   Depreciation for the month is: Office Equipment, $83.33, and Store Fixtures, $100.

Record the transactions for owner's equity:
   Each owners' withdrawal for the month of January is $2,000.
   Divide the amount in account 3000-Summers & Winters, Capital and transfer one-half the
      amount into each owner's individual capital account. Prepare a Standard Balance Sheet
      for January 30 to determine the amount to divide.

01/31/98
Use the following bank statement to prepare a bank reconciliation. Enter any adjustments. Print a
Full Reconciliation report.

DESERT BANK
1234-110 Highway 111
Palm Springs, CA 92270

(619) 555-3300

Golf World
55-100 PGA Boulevard
Palm Springs, CA 92270   Acct. # 9857-32-922

January, 1998

Beginning Balance, January 1, 1998			$35,275.14
1/8/98, Deposit	4,210.68		39,485.82
1/10/98, Check 1		64.30	39,421.52
1/14/98, Deposit	2,801.24		42,222.76
1/16/98, NSF Check		107.14	42,115.62
1/18/98, Check 2		392.00	41,723.62
1/25/98, Check 3		365.54	41,358.08
1/25/98, Check 4		85.15	41,272.93
1/23/98, Check 5		156.80	41,116.13
1/23/98, Check 6		49.00	41,067.13
1/25/98, Deposit	6,307.77		47,374.90
1/25/98, Check 7		275.00	47,099.90
1/25/98, Check 8		3,000.00	44,099.90
1/25/98, Check 9		65.00	44,034.90
1/25/98, Check 10		1,000.00	43,034.90
1/25/98, Check 11		5,000.00	38,034.90
1/25/98, Check 12		500.00	37,534.90
1/25/98, Check 13		500.00	37,034.90
1/30/98, Service Charge,$15, and NSF Charge, $15		30.00	37,004.90
1/31/98, Store Fixtures Loan Pmt.: $89.03 Interest, $17.21 Principal		106.24	36,898.66
1/31/98, Office Equipment Loan Pmt.: $53.42 Interest, $10.33 Principal		63.75	36,834.91
1/31/98, Interest	76.73		36,911.64
Ending Balance, 1/31/98			$36,911.64

Received the Visa bill. Prepare a credit card reconciliation and pay the Visa bill. Print the check.

DESERT BANK
VISA DEPARTMENT
1234-110 Highway 111
Palm Springs, CA 92270   (619) 555-3300

Golf World
55-100 PGA Boulevard
Palm Springs, CA 92270
VISA Acct. # 9287-52-952   January, 1998

Beginning Balance, January 1, 1998			0.00
1/12/98, Desert Office Supply		175.00	175.00
1/25/98, Desert Office Supply		150.00	325.00
Ending Balance, 1/25/98			325.00

Minimum Payment Due: $50.00   Payment Due Date: February 7, 1998

Make sure the reporting preference is for accrual basis.

Print the following reports for January 1-31, 1998, or as of January 31, 1998: Trial Balance, Standard Profit & Loss Statement, Standard Balance Sheet

Divide the Net Income/Retained Earnings in half and transfer one-half into each owner's individual capital account.

Close the drawing account for each owner into the owner's individual capital account.

Print a Standard Balance Sheet for January 31, 1998.

Assign an Owner Password and End-of-Period Password:
Owner Password is **QB**
End of Period is 01/31/98 and the Transaction Password is **January**

Edit a transaction from the closed period: Discovered an error in the Supplies accounts. Transfer $50 from 1320-Sales Supplies to 1310-Office Supplies.

2/1/98
Print the following: Journal (Landscape orientation, Fit on one page wide) for January 1, 1998-February 1, 1998; Trial Balance, February 1, 1998; Standard Profit and Loss Statement, February 1, 1998; Standard Balance Sheet, February 1, 1998

2/1/99
Print a Standard Balance Sheet for February 1, 1999

PAYROLL

LEARNING OBJECTIVES

At the completion of this chapter, you will be able to use QuickBooks to:

1. Create, preview, and print payroll checks.
2. Adjust pay stub information.
3. Correct, void, and delete paychecks.
4. Change employee information and add a new employee.
5. Print a Payroll Summary by Employee report.
6. View an Employee Journal report.
7. Pay Taxes and Other Liabilities.
8. Prepare and print Forms 941 and 940.
9. Prepare and preview W-2 forms.

PAYROLL

Many times a company begins the process of computerizing simply to be able to do the payroll using the computer. It is much faster and easier to let QuickBooks look at the tax tables and determine how much withholding should be deducted for each employee than to have an individual perform this task. In addition, QuickBooks will also print paychecks and help prepare W-2s and Quarterly Federal Tax Returns. In this chapter paychecks will be created, printed, corrected, and voided. Tax reports, tax payments, and tax forms will be prepared.

NOTE: The tax table used when writing this text was 9701. As QuickBooks has new releases or the tax tables change, new tax tables may be issued. If you are using a version of QuickBooks that does not have 9701 as the tax table, your answers may be different from those given in the text. As long as you show amounts for withholding, Social Security, Medicare, and so on, it is acceptable if your answers are not an exact match. Because the tax tables used in this problem are 9701, the year used in the examples is 1997; however, in order to avoid confusion during training, the year will be shown as 19**. Check with your instructor to determine the year to use for training. If the tax table year and the year used in your work are not the same, you will get error messages on the screen.

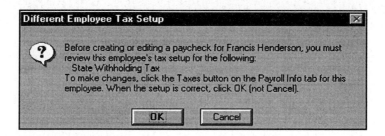

When you try to process a paycheck, you will get these error messages:

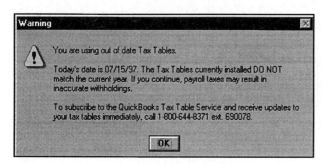
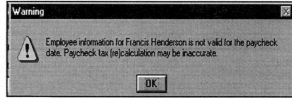

TRAINING TUTORIAL

The Barnes Company is a medical clinic located in Long Beach, California, that is owned and operated by Dr. Greg Barnes and Dr. Richard Drew. Dr. Barnes and Dr. Drew operate the clinic as a partnership. They have a thriving practice and currently employ six people. Francis Henderson is the office manager and is responsible for the smooth operation of the medical clinic and for all the employees. Currently, his salary is $33,500 per year. Wilson Ahmed is also a salaried employee at $29,500 per year. Wilson is responsible for the bookkeeping and the insurance billing. The company is advertising for a part-time billing clerk so that the insurance claims can be processed a little faster. The other employees are the nurse, Julie Meredith; the medical assistant, Tran Ng; the receptionist, Jessica Ruiz; and the lab technician, Heidi Thom. These employees are paid on an hourly basis, and any hours in excess of 80 for the pay period will be paid as overtime. Paychecks for all employees are issued on a semi-monthly basis.

 *DO: Obtain a copy of the data for the Barnes Co. from your instructor
Make a copy of **Barnes.QBW** to a new disk
Back up your work periodically
Change --Your Name in the company name to your actual name
Change report headers so the current date is not printed

CREATE PAYCHECKS

Clicking on the QuickBooks Navigator icon, the payroll icon, or the activities menu to create paychecks allows you to select which employees will be receiving paychecks. You may enter hours and preview the checks before creating them, or you may create the checks without previewing. Once the payroll has been processed, checks may be printed.

MEMO
DATE: March 15, 19**

Create and print the checks for March 15, 19**. Use the above date as the pay period ending date and the check date. Pay all employees as follows:

Francis Henderson worked 80 hours; Heidi Thom worked 80 hours plus 5 hours overtime; Jessica Ruiz worked 40 hours; Julie Meredith worked 40 hours and used 40 vacation hours; Tran Ng worked 75 hours and used 5 sick hours; and Wilson Ahmed worked 20 hours, used 40 vacation hours, and 20 sick hours.

DO: Create checks for the above employees
Click **Payroll** icon on the iconbar
   OR
Click **Payroll & Employees** on the QuickBooks Navigator, click **Create Paychecks**
   OR
Click **Activities** menu, point to **Payroll**, click **Pay Employees**
Click **To be printed**
- Verify the Bank Account is Payroll Checking. If not, click the drop-down list for Bank Account and select Payroll Checking.
Select **Enter hours and preview check**
Check Date is **03/15/**** and the **Pay Period Ends 03/15/****
Click **Mark All** to select all employees to be paid
- Notice the check mark in front of each employee name.
Click **Create**

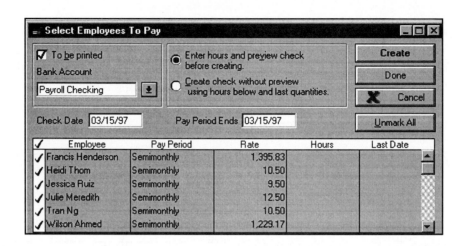

- The Preview Paycheck screen for Francis Henderson appears.
  Tab to or click **Hours**, enter **80**, click **Create**

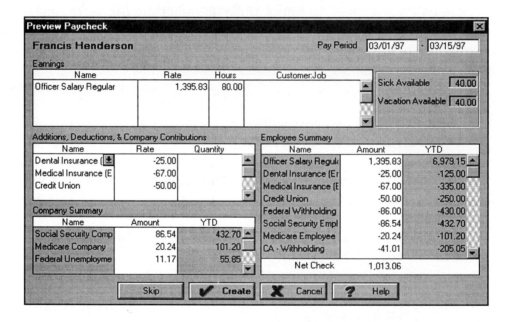

Tab to or click the **Hours** column next to **Hourly Regular Rate** for **Heidi Thom**,
   enter **80**
Tab to or click the **Hours** column next to **Overtime Hourly Rate 1**, enter **5**
Click **Create**

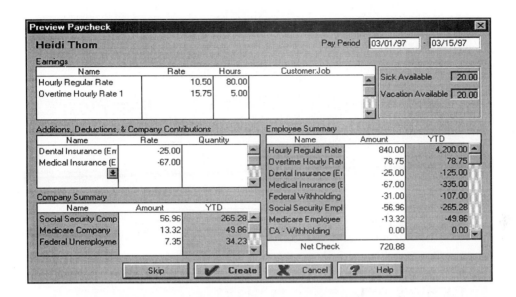

- Notice that the amount of overtime pay in the Employee Summary.

Pay **Jessica Ruiz** for **40** hours of **Hourly Regular Rate** following the steps previously indicated

Pay **Julie Meredith**

- Notice that the number of Vacation Hours listed in **Vacation Available** is 40.00.

Tab to or click the **Hours** column for **Hourly Regular Rate**, enter **40**

In the **Name** column under **Earnings**, click on the blank line beneath Overtime Hourly Rate 1, click the drop-down list arrow that appears, click **Vacation Hourly Rate**, tab to or click the **Hours** column, enter **40**, click **Create**

- Notice that the number of Vacation Hours in **Vacation Available** is 0.00.

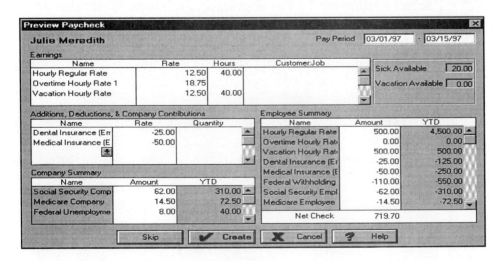

Process the paycheck for **Tran Ng**

- Follow the procedures indicated when paying Julie Meredith except click **Sick Hourly Rate** rather than Vacation Hourly Rate and enter 5 hours of sick time. Remember to reduce her regular hours by 5.

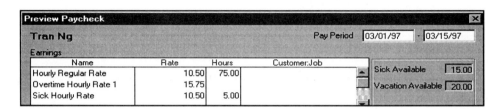

Process the paycheck for Wilson Ahmed, select Payroll items for Officer Salary Regular, Officer Vac Salary, and Officer Sick Salary

- Do not make any changes to the amounts listed in the Rate column.

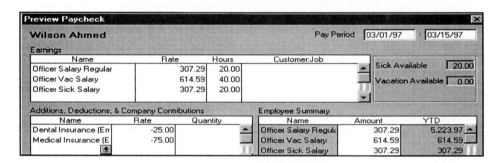

- Notice how QuickBooks reallocates the salary from Officer Salary Regular to Officer Salary Regular, Officer Sick Salary, and Officer Vac Salary.

Click **Create** for Wilson Ahmed

- **Select Employees To Pay** appears on the screen. Notice that the check marks have been removed, the Hours column has the hours for each employee, and the Last Date shows 03/15/97 for all employees.

Click **Done** when finished reviewing Select Employees To Pay screen

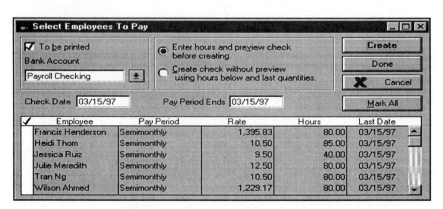

- You may get a **Leaving Pay Employees** message box that states "You have marked employee(s) to pay. Do you wish to record the paychecks now?" Click Yes.

PRINT PAYCHECKS

Paychecks may be printed one at a time or all at once; however, they must be printed separately from other checks. You may use the same printer setup as your other checks in QuickBooks, or you may print using a different printer setup. If you use a voucher check, the pay stub is printed as part of the check. If you do not use a voucher check, you may print the pay stub separately. The pay stub information includes the employee's name, address, Social Security number, the pay period start and end dates, pay rate, the hours, the amount of pay, all deductions, sick and vacation time used and available, net pay, and year-to-date amounts.

MEMO
DATE: March 15, 19**

Print the paychecks for all employees using a voucher-style check with 2 parts.
Print the company name on the checks.

 DO: Print the March 15 paychecks
Click **File** menu, point to **Print Forms**, click **Print Paychecks**
Bank Account should be **Payroll Checking**; if it is not, click the drop-down list
for Bank Account, click Payroll Checking.
Select All employees, **First Check Number** is **1**; if it is not change it to 1

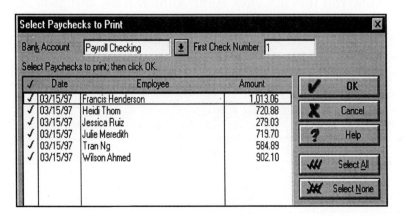

Click **OK**
- Printer Name and Printer Type will be the same as in the earlier chapters.

Click the drop-down list arrow for **Check Style**, click **Voucher Checks**
- If necessary, click **Print company name and address** to select. There should not be a check mark in Use logo. **Number of copies** should be **1**.

Click **Print**, click **OK** for **Did checks print OK?**
- Note: The pay stub information may be printed on the check two times. This is acceptable.

CHANGE EMPLOYEE INFORMATION

Whenever a change occurs for an employee, it may be entered at any time.

MEMO

DATE: March 16, 19**

Effective today, Francis Henderson will receive a pay raise to $35,000 annually.

DO: Change the salary for Francis
Click the **Employees** icon on the **Payroll & Employees** screen of QuickBooks Navigator
OR
Click **Lists** menu, click **Employees**
Click **Francis Henderson**
Ctrl+E OR click **Employee** button, click **Edit**
Click **Payroll Info** tab, click **Hour/Annual Rate**, change to **35,000**, click **OK**

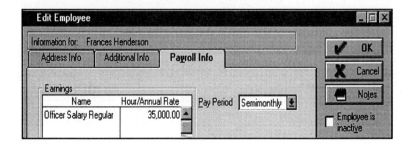

Do *not* close the Employee list

ADD A NEW EMPLOYEE

As new employees are hired, they should be added.

MEMO

DATE: March 24, 19**

Hired a part-time employee to help process insurance claims. Ms. Elizabeth Hall, 102 Bayshore Drive, Long Beach, CA 90713, 562-555-9874, SS No. 100-55-6936. Paid hourly rate of $7.00. Federal and state withholding: Single, 0 Allowances. No local taxes, dental insurance, medical insurance, sick time, or vacation time.

DO: Add Elizabeth Hall
  Ctrl+N OR click **Employee**, click **New**
  Tab to or click **Mr./Ms./...**, enter **Ms.**
  Tab to or click in each field on **Address Info** and enter the information provided in the memo
  • Leave Alt. Ph. and Released blank.

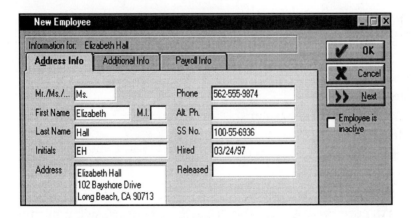

  Click **Payroll Info** tab
  Click **Name** column under **Earnings**, click drop-down list arrow that appears, click **Hourly Regular Rate**
  Tab to or click **Hour/Annual Rate**, enter the hourly rate she will be paid

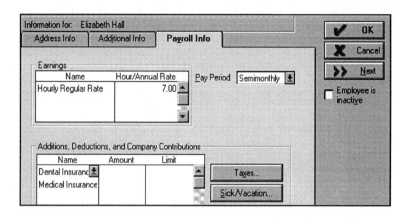

Click **Taxes** button
- **Federal** taxes should show **Filing Status: Single, Allowances: 0, Extra Withholding: 0.00, Subject to:** all items should be selected.

Click **State** tab
- Information on the State tab should show **State Unemployment Filing State: CA, State Disability Filing State: CA, State Withholding Filing State: CA, Filing Status: Single, Allowances: 0, Extra Withholding: 0.00; Estimated Deductions: 0**.

Click **OK**

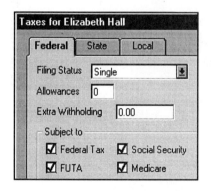

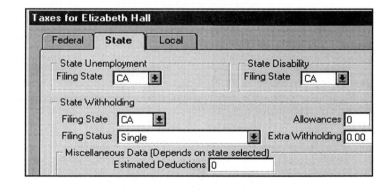

Click **OK** to add employee
- An error message appears because local taxes, sick time, and vacation time were not accessed.

Click **Leave As Is** button

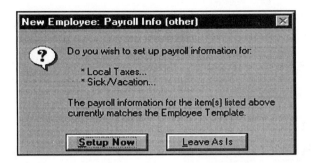

New Employee: Payroll Info (other)   ☒

? Do you wish to set up payroll information for:

         * Local Taxes...
         * Sick/Vacation...

The payroll information for the item(s) listed above
currently matches the Employee Template.

            Setup Now   Leave As Is

        Close the Employee List

CREATE PAYCHECKS WITH AND WITHOUT PREVIEWING

Paychecks may be created automatically without previewing. This is used if hours, and other details from the previous pay period have not changed.

MEMO

DATE: March 31, 19**

Enter the payroll for 03/31/**. All employees worked 80 hours except Elizabeth Hall, who worked 20 hours. No one worked overtime or used sick or vacation time. Preview the checks for the hourly employees. For the salaried employees, create the checks without preview.

DO: Process the payroll for March 31
    Access **Create Paychecks** as previously instructed
    Click in the ✔ column next to each hourly employee, click **Create**
    Enter **80** hours for **Hourly Regular Rate** for each hourly employee except
        Elizabeth Hall, enter **20** hours for Elizabeth
    Highlight and delete any overtime, sick, or vacation hours listed
    Click **Create** for each hourly employee
    Click in the ✔ column next to Francis Henderson and Wilson Ahmed
    Click **Create check without preview using hours below and last quantities.** to
        select
    Click **Create**, click **Done**

VIEW CHECKS, MAKE CORRECTIONS, AND PRINT CHECKS INDIVIDUALLY

As in earlier chapters, checks may be viewed individually and printed one at a time. A paycheck differs from a regular check. Rather than list accounts and amounts, it provides a Payroll Summary and an option to view Paycheck Detail at the bottom of the screen. When you are viewing the paycheck detail, corrections may be made and will be calculated for the check.

MEMO

DATE: March 31, 19**

Print each paycheck separately. Francis Henderson used two hours of sick time during this pay period. The sick time was not entered when the paycheck was calculated. When viewing the check for Francis Henderson, correct the paycheck.

DO: View, correct, and print the paychecks as indicated

To view the paychecks, use the keyboard shortcut **Ctrl+W**

Click **Prev** until you get to the check for **Elizabeth Hall** for **03/31/**

Click **Paycheck Detail** button to view the withholding details, click **OK**

Click **Print, Printed Check Number** should be **7**; if it is not, change the number to 7, click **OK** on Print Paycheck

Repeat the above, print checks for all employees except Francis Henderson

Click **Paycheck Detail** on Francis Henderson's paycheck

Change the Officer Salary Regular Hours to **78**

Tab to or click in the **Name** column for **Earnings**, click the drop-down list arrow, click **Officer Sick Salary**

Tab to or click in the **Hours** column, enter **2**, click **OK**

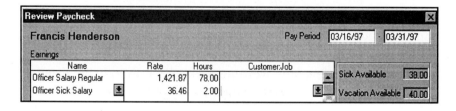

Print the check

VOIDING AND DELETING CHECKS

As with regular checks, paychecks may be voided or deleted. A voided check still remains as a check, but it has an amount of 0.00 and a memo that says void. If a check is deleted, it is completely removed from the company records. The only way to have a record of the deleted check would be if an audit trail had been selected as a company preference. If you have pre-numbered checks and the original check is misprinted, lost, or stolen, you should void the check. If an employee's check is lost or stolen and needs to be replaced and you are not using pre-numbered checks, it may be deleted and reissued. For security reasons, it is better to void a check than to delete it.

MEMO

DATE: March 31, 19**

Jessica Ruiz lost her paycheck for the March 15 pay period. Void the check, issue, and print a new one. Remember that she worked 40 hours.

DO: Void Jessica's March 15 paycheck and issue a new one
Click **Prev** until Jessica's paycheck appears on the screen, click **Edit** menu, click **Void Paycheck**
Click **OK** to the question **Are you sure you want to void this paycheck?**
- Notice that the amount is 0.00 and that the Memo is VOID.

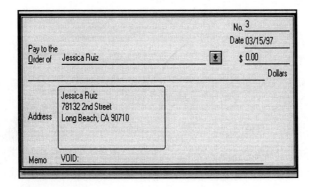

Print Check No. 3 again
Click **OK** to close Paycheck-Payroll Checking
Issue Jessica's replacement check as previously instructed:
Click **Create Paychecks** on the **Payroll & Employees** section of QuickBooks Navigator

The Bank Account is Payroll Checking
Select: To be printed and Enter hours and preview check before creating
The Check Date is 03/31/** and the Pay Period Ends 03/15/**
Select **Jessica Ruiz**, click **Create**
Pay Period is **03/01/** - **03/15/****
Jessica worked **40** hours at the Hourly Regular Rate
Click **Create**, click **Done**, click **Yes** on Preview Paycheck

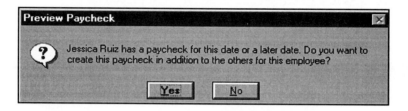

Print the replacement check as Check Number **14**

PAYROLL SUMMARY BY EMPLOYEE REPORT

The Payroll Summary by Employee report shows gross pay, sick and vacation hours and pay, deductions from gross pay, adjusted gross pay, taxes withheld, deductions from net pay, net pay, and employer-paid taxes and contributions for each employee individually and for the company.

MEMO
DATE: March 31, 19**

Dr. Drew and Dr. Barnes have Wilson print a Payroll Summary by Employee report at the end of every month.

DO: Print the Payroll Summary by Employee report for March
Click **Reports** menu, point to **Payroll**, click **Summary by Employee**
Enter the dates from **03/01/**** to **03/31/**** as the report dates
Remove the current date from the header as instructed in previous chapters
• View the information listed for each employee and for the company.
Print the report in Landscape orientation
• If you adjust the width of the Hours, Rate, and Mar '97 columns for each employee, it may be possible to have the report fit on three pages.
Close the report

VIEW THE EMPLOYEE JOURNAL REPORT

The Employee Journal report lists the same information as the Summary by Employee report above. The information is simply presented in a different layout.

MEMO
DATE: March 31, 19**

View the Employee Journal report.

 DO: View the above report
Refer to the instructions in the preceding section to prepare the report, click **Employee Journal** rather than Summary by Employee
Use the same dates as the Summary by Employee report
Scroll through the report
Close without printing

LIABILITIES BY PAYROLL ITEM REPORT

The third payroll report is the Liabilities by Payroll Item report. This report lists the company's payroll liabilities that are unpaid as of the report date.

MEMO
DATE: March 31, 19**

Prior to paying taxes, the doctors have Wilson print the Liabilities by Payroll Item report.

 DO: Print the above report
Refer to the instructions in the Payroll Summary by Employee report section to prepare the report, use the same dates as the previous reports, click **Liabilities by Item** rather than Summary by Employee, and print in Portrait orientation

```
┌─────────────────────────────────────────────┐
│         Barnes Co. (Your Name)              │
│       Liabilities by Payroll Item           │
│          As of March 31, 1997               │
│                                             │
│                        ◇ Mar 31, '97 ◇      │
│   Social Security Employee      2,250.06    │
│   Federal Unemployment            275.83    │
│   Medicare Company                518.03    │
│   Social Security Company       2,250.06    │
│   CA - Withholding                529.60    │
│   CA - Disability Employee        181.48    │
│   CA - Unemployment Company     1,379.15    │
│   Credit Union                    300.00    │
│   Dental Insurance (Emp)          900.00    │
│   Medical Insurance (Emp)       2,034.00    │
│   Total Payroll Liabilities    14,019.24    │
└─────────────────────────────────────────────┘
```

Partial Report

Close the report

PAY TAXES AND OTHER LIABILITIES

QuickBooks keeps track of the payroll taxes and other payroll liabilities that you owe. When it is time to make your payments, QuickBooks allows you to choose to pay all liabilities or to select individual liabilities for payment. When the liabilities to be paid have been selected, QuickBooks will consolidate all the amounts for one vendor and prepare one check for that vendor.

MEMO

DATE: March 31, 19**

Based on the information in the Liabilities by Item report, Wilson has been instructed to pay all the payroll liabilities.

DO: Pay all the payroll liabilities
Access **Pay Liabilities**: click **Activities** menu, point to **Payroll**, click **Pay Liabilities/Taxes**
OR
Click **Pay Liabilities** icon in QuickBooks Navigator **Payroll &Employees**

- Checking Account should be Payroll Checking; if it is not, select it from the drop-down list.

Payment Date is **03/31/****

If necessary, select **To be printed**

Show liabilities as of **03/31/****, sort by **Payable To**

- Other sort options are alphabetically by payroll item or in descending order by amount.

Click **Mark All** to select all the liabilities for payment

- Notice the check marks next to each item once you click Mark All.

Create liability check without previewing should be selected

- If you wanted to preview the check in order to enter any other expenses or penalties, you would select Preview liability check to enter expenses/penalties.

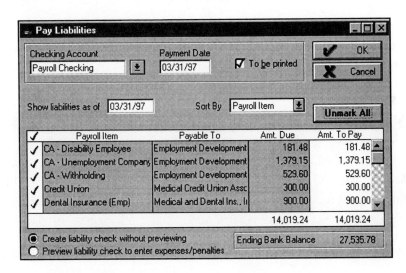

Click **OK**

Print the checks as previously instructed

FILING PAYROLL TAX FORMS

QuickBooks creates and prints your Form 941—Employer's Quarterly Federal Tax Return and your Form 940—Employer's Annual Federal Unemployment Tax Return. These forms are accurate and updated with each release of QuickBooks. You may also create a custom tax form that may be submitted in conjunction with any state taxes paid. Because each state has different reporting requirements, we will not create a customized state form in this chapter.

PREPARE AND PRINT FORM 941

Form 941 for the Employer's Federal Tax Return is prepared to report federal income tax withheld, Social Security tax, and Medicare tax. The taxes are based on the total wages paid. QuickBooks guides you through the completion of the form step by step.

MEMO

DATE: March 31, 19**

Because March 31 is the end of the first quarter, prepare and print Form 941.

DO: Prepare and print Form 941 for the first quarter
Access **Process Form 941** from QuickBooks Navigator or Activities menu
CA is the state in which the deposit is made
03/31/** is the date the quarter ended

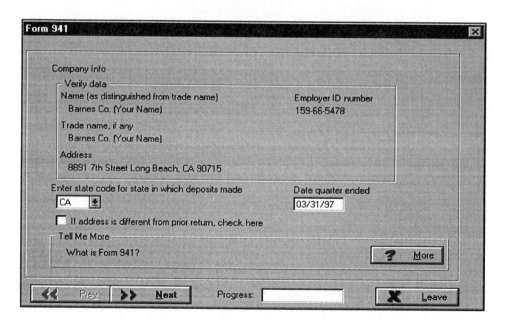

Click **Next** to continue
Because nothing needs to be selected on the following screen, click **Next**

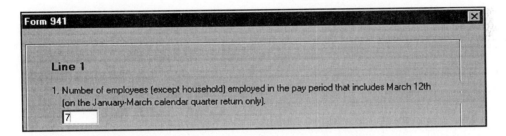

Enter **7** as the number of employees paid during the first quarter

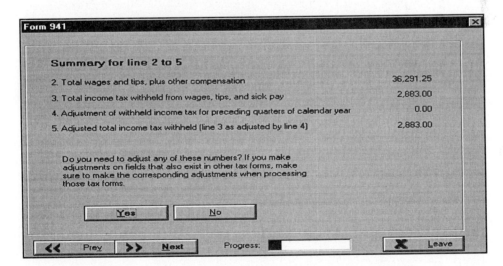

There are no adjustments to be made, click **No**

The summary for lines 6-10 is correct, click **No**

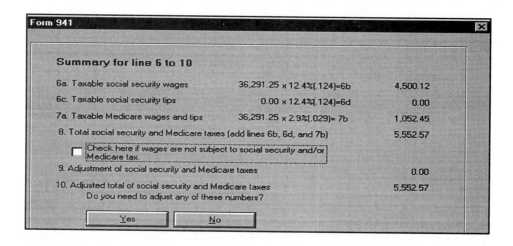

As with the earlier summaries, lines 11 to 14 are correct, click **No**

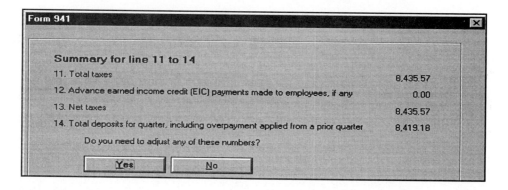

There are no changes to make to lines 15 and 16, click **Next** to continue

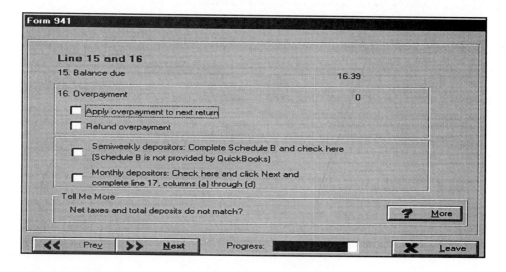

There are no adjustments to be made to liabilities and taxes in line 17, click **Next**

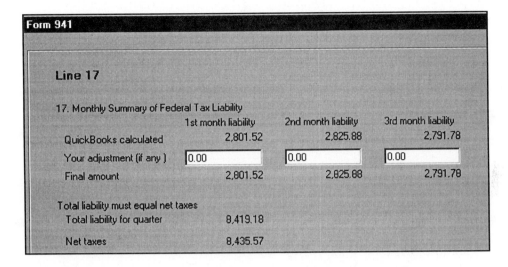

The form is now complete, click **Print Form 941** to print the form
• The printed form is a government-approved form printed on blank paper.
Check to be sure printer selected is correct, print range is all, press OK

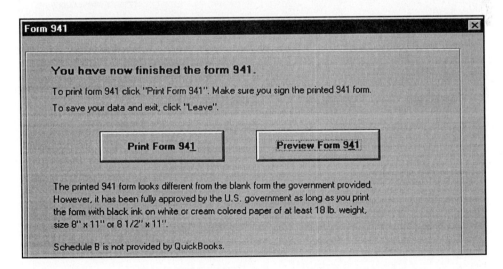

Click **Leave** to exit Form 941

PREPARE AND PRINT FORM 940

The preparation of Form 940 for the Employer's Annual Federal Unemployment Tax Return (FUTA) is similar to the preparation of Form 941. The progress bar at the bottom of the screen provides a graphic representation of the amount of the form completed.

MEMO

DATE: March 31, 19**

Even though Form 940 for FUTA is filed as an annual tax return, Wilson prepares this form at the end of each quarter.

     DO: Prepare and print Form 940
Calendar year is **
Click >>**Next**

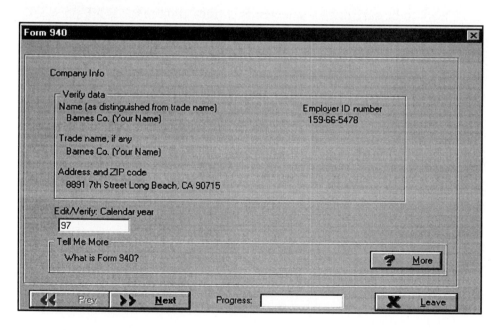

Click **Yes** for Questions A, B, and C
Click >>**Next**

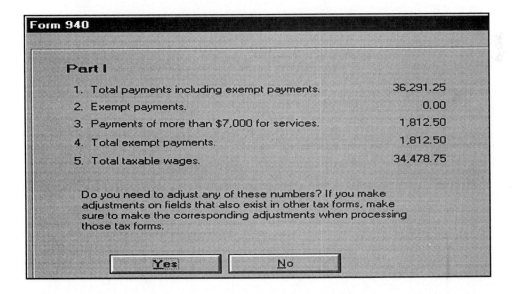

Form 940

940 Filing Information

A) Are you required to pay unemployment contributions to only one state?   ☑ Yes ☐ No
   (if no, skip questions B and C)
   (This form can be used to replace the need to file form 940-EZ)

B) Did you pay all state unemployment contributions by January 31, 1997?   ☑ Yes ☐ No
   (if a 0% experience rate is granted, check "Yes.")
   (If no, skip question C.)

C) Were all wages that were taxable for FUTA tax also taxable for your state's   ☑ Yes ☐ No
   unemployment tax?

☐ If you will not have to file returns in the future, check here.

☐ If this is an Amended Return, check here.

No adjustments are required for Part I, click **No**

Form 940

Part I

1. Total payments including exempt payments.   36,291.25
2. Exempt payments.   0.00
3. Payments of more than $7,000 for services.   1,812.50
4. Total exempt payments.   1,812.50
5. Total taxable wages.   34,478.75

Do you need to adjust any of these numbers? If you make
adjustments on fields that also exist in other tax forms, make
sure to make the corresponding adjustments when processing
those tax forms.

[**Yes**]   [**No**]

The Part II Summary is correct, click **No**

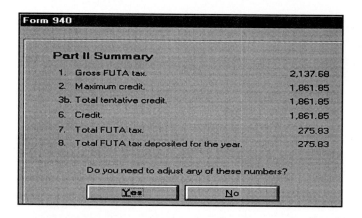

Nothing is due, click **Next**

No adjustment is necessary in Part III, click **Next**

Print all pages of the Form 940, click **Leave** to exit

PREPARE AND PREVIEW EMPLOYEES' W-2 FORMS

The W-2 form is prepared at the end of the year, mailed to each employee, and mailed to the Social Security Administration. The wages earned and taxes withheld for the individual employee for the year are shown on the form. A W-3 form is a summary of all the W-2 forms you are submitting to the federal government. QuickBooks is set up to fill in this information on blank W-2 and W-3 forms. Electronic filing of W-2s for companies employing 250 or more is required. QuickBooks does not support electronic filing of W-2s.

MEMO

DATE: March 31, 19**

W-2s and the corresponding W-3 are prepared at the end of the year. However, for experience with this procedure, you will prepare and review the W-2s for each employee. Because the W-3 cannot be viewed and cannot be printed unless all W-2s have been printed, we will not prepare this form.

 DO: Prepare and review the W-2s for Barnes Co.
Access **Process W-2s** using the Activities menu or QuickBooks Navigator
The year should be **, click **Mark All**
Click **Review W-2**, click **Next** to continue to the next W-2, repeat for all
employees
- You may have to turn off the iconbar in order to see the Next button.

Employee W-2

b Employer's identification number	1 Wages, tips, other comp.	2 Federal income tax withheld
159-66-5478	7,375.02	708.00

c Employer's name, address, and ZIP code	3 Social security wages	4 Social security tax withheld
Barnes Co. (Your Name) 8891 7th Street Long Beach, CA 90715	7,375.02	457.26

	5 Medicare wages and tips	6 Medicare tax withheld
	7,375.02	110.92

	7 Social security tips	8 Allocated tips

d Employee's social security number	9 Advance EIC payment	10 Dependent care benefits
100-55-6042		

e Employee's name (first, middle initial, last)	11 Nonqualified plans	12 Benefits included in box 1
Wilson Ahmed		

5690 7th Street	13 See Instrs. for box 13	14 Other
Long Beach, CA 90712		SDI 36.90

☐ Statutory Emp. ☐ Pension Plan ☐ Hshld. Emp. ☐ Deferred Comp.
☐ Deceased ☐ Legal Rep. ☐ Subtotal

16 State Employer's state I.D.	17 State wages	18 State tax	19 Locality	20 Local wages	21 Local tax
CA	7,375.02	45.34			

Click **OK**

- QuickBooks will mark each employee with a ✔ in the Reviewed column once the W-2 has been reviewed. W-2s may not be printed until all have been reviewed.

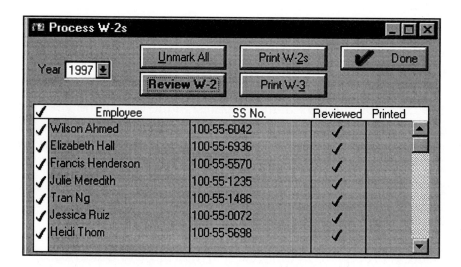

Do *not* print the forms; when all W-2s have been reviewed, click **Done**

BACK UP

Follow the instructions provided in previous chapters to make a backup copy of Barnes Co.

SUMMARY

In this chapter, paychecks were generated for employees who worked their standard number of hours, who took vacation time, who took sick time, and who were just hired. Changes to employee information were made, and a new employee was added. Payroll reports were printed and/or viewed, payroll liabilities were paid, and 941, 940, and W-2 forms were prepared.

END-OF-CHAPTER QUESTIONS

TRUE/FALSE

ANSWER THE FOLLOWING QUESTIONS IN THE SPACE PROVIDED BEFORE THE QUESTION NUMBER.

_____ 1. The tax table year and the calendar year must agree, or you get error messages.

_____ 2. Once a paycheck has been printed, you may not edit it.

_____ 3. Paychecks and regular checks may be printed at the same time.

_____ 4. A W-3 is printed and mailed to all employees at the end of the year.

_____ 5. Checks may be created and previewed or created without previewing.

_____ 6. QuickBooks includes an accurate and up-to-date Form 941 and Form 940.

_____ 7. If several taxes are owed to a single agency, QuickBooks generates a separate check to the agency for each tax liability item.

_____ 8. If a salaried employee uses vacation pay, QuickBooks will automatically distribute the correct amount of earnings to Officer Vac Salary once the number of vacation hours has been entered.

_____ 9. Processing the Liabilities by Payroll Item report also generates the checks for payment of the liabilities.

_____ 10. All W-2s must be printed before a W-3 can be printed.

MULTIPLE CHOICE

WRITE THE LETTER OF THE CORRECT ANSWER IN THE SPACE PROVIDED BEFORE THE QUESTION NUMBER.

_____ 1. To create a paycheck without previewing, ___.
   A. you must provide the information about hours worked
   B. QuickBooks will use the same hours as the last paycheck
   C. QuickBooks will always use 80 hours to process a paycheck
   D. you must preview all checks

_____ 2. The form sent to the government as a summary of the forms sent to all the individual employees of the company is the ___ form.
   A. W-2
   B. 940
   C. W-3
   D. 941

_____ 3. When paying tax liabilities, you ___.
   A. may pay all liabilities at one time
   B. may select individual tax liabilities and pay them one at a time
   C. may pay all the tax liabilities owed to a vendor
   D. all of the above

_____ 4. A new employee may be added ___.
   A. at any time
   B. only at the end of the week
   C. only at the end of the pay period
   D. only when current paychecks have been printed

_____ 5. Pay stub information may be printed ___.
   A. as part of a voucher check
   B. separate from the paycheck
   C. only as an individual employee report
   D. both A and B

_____ 6. It is best to create checks without preview for ___.
   A. employees who have the same hours as the last paycheck
   B. employees who have a total of 80 hours
   C. employees who have overtime
   D. none of the above

_____ 7. A voided check ___.
   A. shows an amount of 0.00
   B. has a memo of VOID
   C. remains as part of the company records
   D. all of the above

_____ 8. When liabilities to be paid have been selected, QuickBooks will ___.
   A. create a separate check for each liability
   B. consolidate liabilities paid and create one check for each vendor
   C. automatically process a Liabilities by Payroll Item report
   D. prepare any tax return forms necessary

_____ 9. You must purchase blank ___ forms, and QuickBooks will fill them in when printing.
   A. 940
   B. 941
   C. state tax
   D. W-2

_____ 10. Changes made to an employee's pay rate will become effective ___.
   A. immediately
   B. at the end of the next payroll period
   C. at the end of the quarter
   D. after a W-2 has been prepared for the employee

FILL-IN

IN THE SPACE PROVIDED, WRITE THE ANSWER THAT MOST APPROPRIATELY COMPLETES THE SENTENCE.

1. The form created for the Employer's Quarterly Federal Tax Return is Form _____.

2. On the iconbar, click the _____ icon to create paychecks.

3. The reports that show an employee's gross pay, sick and vacation hours and pay, deductions, taxes, and other details are _____ and _____.

4. When the Employee list is on the screen, the keyboard shortcut used to add a new employee is _____.

5. The report listing the company's unpaid payroll liabilities as of the report date is the
    _____ report.

SHORT ESSAY

What is the difference between voiding a paycheck and deleting a paycheck? Why should a
business prefer to void paychecks rather than delete them?

_____

_____

_____

_____

_____

END-OF-CHAPTER PROBLEM

SKI MFG.

Ski Mfg. is a water ski manufacturing company located in Newport Beach, California. The
company is owned and operated by equal partners, Keith Bermudez and Greg Kasper. Keith and
Greg handle all the sales and marketing for the company. Business is booming, and Ski Mfg.
currently has several advertisements for factory workers in the local newspapers.

Molly Anderson is the office manager and is responsible for the smooth operation of the
company and for all the employees. Molly's salary is $37,500 per year. The assistant manager is
responsible for the bookkeeping, ordering, delivery schedules, and so on. Ling Le is the assistant
manager and earns $32,500 per year. Justin Moore is the lead line person and supervisor in the
factory and earns $15.00 per hour. The senior line assistant is Helga Thomsen. She earns $12.50
per hour. Regular line personnel earn $9.50 per hour. Currently, Jennifer Ramon and Tien
Nguyen are regular line personnel. The employees typically work 80 hours within a semi-
monthly pay period. Any hourly employee working more than 80 hours should be paid overtime
for those hours.

INSTRUCTIONS

As in previous chapters, obtain a copy of a disk containing the data for Ski Mfg. Make a copy of
Ski.QBW to a new disk and open the company.

RECORD TRANSACTIONS:

March 15, 19**

Open **Ski.QBW** and add your name to the company name. The title bar for the company name will be **Ski Mfg.--Student's Name**. If your entire name will not fit, use your last name or your first initial and your last name.

Remove the current date from the header on reports.

Prepare and print checks for the semi-monthly pay period from March 1-March 15, 19**: Molly Anderson worked 80 hours, Ling Le used 40 hours vacation time and worked 40 hours, Justin Moore worked a total of 100 hours, Helga Thomsen worked 75 hours and used 5 hours sick time, Jennifer Ramon worked 80 hours, and Tien Nguyen worked a total of 88 hours. Print the company name and address on the voucher checks. Checks begin with number 1.

Molly hired two new employees as line trainees at $6.50 per hour and time-and-a-half overtime at $9.75 per hour: Russ Timothy; 230 Coast Way, Newport Beach, CA 92660; 714-555-2323; Social Security # 100-55-2145; Federal and State withholding: Single, 0; no dental, medical, sick, or vacation time. Victor Strauss; 7821 Laguna Canyon Drive, Newport Beach, CA 92660; 714-555-3257; Social Security # 100-55-8487; Federal and State withholding: Married (one income), 2; no dental, medical, sick, or vacation time.

Change Justin's check to a total of 105 hours and reprint Check 3.

March 24, 19**:

Hired an additional person to work in the office taking orders and answering telephones: Leo S. Lyons; $7.50 per hour and time-and-a-half overtime (calculate); 890 Cove Lane, Newport Beach, CA 92660; 714-555-2233; Social Security # 100-55-1147; Federal and State withholding: Head of Household, 1; dental $25; medical $25; no sick or vacation time.

Justin Moore received a raise to $16.00 per hour for his regular hourly rate. Enter the new rate. Calculate the new rate for time-and-a-half overtime and enter as Overtime Hourly Rate 1.

Helga's telephone number changed to 714-555-5111.

March 31, 19**:

Prepare and print checks for the semi-monthly pay period from March 16-March 31, 19**: Molly Anderson worked 60 hours and used 20 vacation hours, Ling Le worked 80 hours, Justin Moore worked a total of 90 hours, Helga Thomsen worked 65 hours and used 15 hours sick time, Jennifer Ramon worked 80 hours, Tien Nguyen worked a total of 78 hours and used 2 hours vacation time, both new line employees worked 80 hours, Leo Lyons worked 40 hours.

Victor spilled coffee on his check. Void his check for March 31, print the voided check, reissue the paycheck, and print it using Check Number 16.

Victor and Russ have completed their first two weeks of training. Because both are doing well, change their regular pay to $7.00 per hour. In addition, calculate and enter their time-and-a-half Overtime Hourly Rate 1.

Print the Employee List.

Prepare and print the Payroll Summary by Employee report for March in Landscape orientation.

Prepare and print the Liabilities by Payroll Item report for March in Portrait orientation.

Pay all the taxes and other liabilities for March and print the checks.

Prepare and print Forms 941 and 940.

COMPUTERIZING A MANUAL
ACCOUNTING SYSTEM

LEARNING OBJECTIVES

At the completion of this chapter, you will be able to use QuickBooks to:

1. Set up a company using the "EasyStep Interview."
2. Establish a chart of accounts for a company.
3. Create lists for receivables, payables, items, customers, vendors, and others.
4. Add payroll items.
5. Create an employee template and add employees to an employee list.
6. Specify a company logo.
7. Customize reports and company preferences.

COMPUTERIZING A MANUAL SYSTEM

In previous chapters QuickBooks was used to record transactions for businesses that were already set up for use in QuickBooks. In this chapter you will actually set up a business, create a chart of accounts, create various lists, add names to lists, and delete unnecessary accounts. QuickBooks makes setting up the records for a business user friendly by going through the process using the EasyStep Interview. Once the basic accounts, items, lists, and other items are established via the EasyStep Interview, you will make some refinements to accounts, add detail information regarding customers and vendors, customize report and company preferences, and create a company logo for use on business forms.

TRAINING TUTORIAL

The following tutorial is a step-by-step guide to setting up the fictitious company VideoLand. Company information, accounts, items, lists, and other items must be provided before transactions may be recorded in QuickBooks. The EasyStep Interview will be used to set up company information. Once the basic company information has been entered via the EasyStep Interview, changes and modifications to the company data will be made. As in earlier chapters, information for the company setup will be provided in memos. Information may also be shown in lists or within the step-by-step instructions provided.

Tax Table Version 9701 was used to write the text. Because the tax table is for 1997, the work for VideoLand will be completed as of 1997 and dates in screen examples will show 1997. If the year of the tax table and the year for your company are not the same, you will get error messages when you set up your payroll information. Because the year of the tax table you use may not be 1997, this chapter gives the year as **19**** in all instructions. Check with your instructor to find out what year you will be using for your training.

COMPANY PROFILE: VIDEOLAND

VideoLand is a fictitious company that sells and rents videos. In addition, VideoLand has a service department that cleans, conditions, and repairs VCRs. VideoLand is located in San Diego, California, and is a sole proprietorship owned by Daniel Lee. Mr. Lee is involved in all aspects of the business. VideoLand has two full-time employees who are paid a salary: Mark Canfield, who manages the store and is responsible for the all the employees; and Carrie Bernstein, whose duties include all the ordering, managing the office, and keeping the books. There are two full-time hourly employees: Jimmy Hernandez, who works in the service department, and Sally Richards, who works in the store selling and renting videos. There will be other employees who work part time selling and renting videos and who are paid an hourly rate.

CREATE A NEW COMPANY

Since VideoLand is a new company, it does not appear as a company file if you select Open Company on the File menu. A new company may be created by clicking New Company on the File menu or by clicking the File menu and clicking EasyStep Interview.

MEMO

DATE: July 1, 19**

Because this is the beginning of the fiscal year for VideoLand, it is an appropriate time to set up the company information in QuickBooks. Use the EasyStep Interview in QuickBooks.

DO: Open QuickBooks as previously instructed
   If a company is open, click **File** menu, click **Close Company**
   • If you do not close an open company, QuickBooks will close it as soon as you begin to create a new company.

Insert a formatted blank disk in the **A:** drive
Click **File** menu, click **EasyStep Interview**
    OR
Click **File** menu, click **New Company**

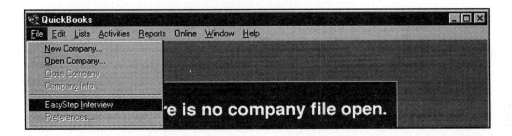

- The first screen of the EasyStep Interview will appear on the screen.

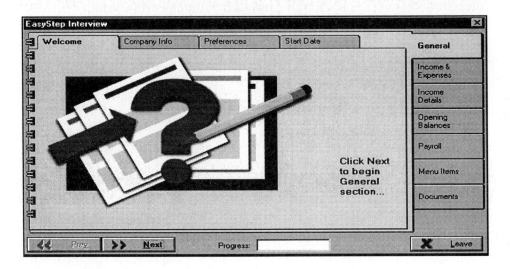

THE EASYSTEP INTERVIEW

The EasyStep Interview is a step-by-step guide to entering your company information as of a single date called a start date. It also provides tips regarding a chart of accounts, standard industry practices, and other items for the type of company indicated. The Interview is divided into seven different sections. The sections appear as tabs along the right side of the EasyStep Interview screen. The General section is used to enter general company information, select a preset Chart of Accounts, indicate preferences such as payroll and inventory, and select a start date. The Income & Expenses section allows you to add additional income and expense accounts to the Chart of Accounts, which is also the General Ledger for the company. Income Details is used to indicate and set up items to track the services and products your company sells and/or provides. It is also used to set up inventory items. The Opening Balances section allows you to input opening balances of customers, vendors, and accounts. The Payroll section is used to enter payroll items to be used on paychecks, to enter payroll information for each employee, and to enter any year-to-date amounts for employees accrued prior to using QuickBooks. Menu Items allows you to configure the lists and activities menus so they display things in a more customized manner. The Documents section recommends documents for you to display and print.

Each section is divided into topics, which are shown as tabs at the top of the screen. For example, the first screen in the General section is the Welcome screen. Once a screen has been read and any required items have been filled in or questions answered, the >>Next button is clicked to tell QuickBooks to advance to the next screen. If you need to return to a previous screen, click <<Prev or use the keyboard shortcut Alt+V.

When a topic or section is complete, QuickBooks places a large check mark on the section and/or topic tab. QuickBooks also keeps track of the amount of the interview topic completed in the Progress bar at the bottom of the screen. If you need to stop the Interview before completing everything, you may exit by clicking the Leave button in the bottom right corner of the screen or by clicking the close button at the top right corner of the EasyStep Interview screen. It is best to complete an entire topic before exiting.

GENERAL SECTION OF THE INTERVIEW

The General section of the EasyStep Interview has several tasks to be performed. The most important task is to provide a start date and to set up a chart of accounts. In order to complete the General section of the Interview you need complete company data regarding the name and address of the company, the federal tax ID number, first month of the income tax year and the first month of the fiscal year, the type of business, a chart of accounts if you have one, and the start date you plan to use.

WELCOME TOPIC

The Welcome topic of the EasyStep Interview introduces you to the procedures followed during the Interview. It also allows you to tell QuickBooks whether or not you are upgrading from another Intuit product.

MEMO

DATE: July 1, 19**

In preparation for setting up VideoLand company records, the following information is provided to Carrie by Mr. Lee:

Company: VideoLand (Your Name)
Address: 8795 Mission Bay Drive, San Diego, CA 92109
Federal Tax ID: 159-88-8654; First Month in Tax and Fiscal Year: July; Income
Tax form: None; Type of Business: Retail; Inventory: Yes; File Name: VIDEO.QBW

DO: Complete Welcome and Company Information section of the EasyStep Interview
Click >>**Next** button on the EasyStep Interview
If it is not already selected, select **NO** to answer "Will you be upgrading from another Intuit product?"

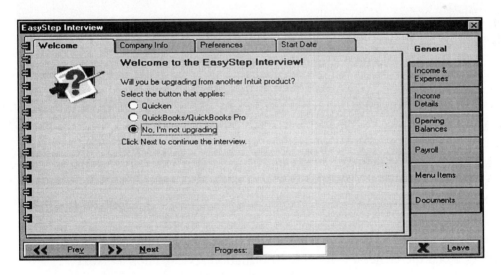

Click >>**Next** to continue
Read the screens:
    Setting up a new QuickBooks company
- Notice the Skip Interview button. This allows you to set up the company without going through the EasyStep Interview. This is a procedure that may be used if you are familiar with setting up a company in QuickBooks, have an established Chart of Accounts, and know which preferences you want to select within the QuickBooks program. Do *not* click this button.

Navigating around the interview
Sections and topics
Feel free to change your answers!
Welcome completed!
Click **>>Next** to go from one screen to the next
- When the Welcome section is complete, notice the check mark on the
  Welcome tab and the completed Progress bar at the bottom of the Interview
  screen.

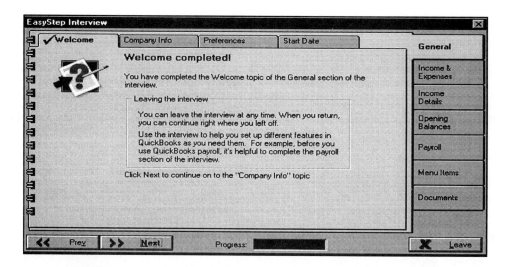

COMPANY INFO TOPIC

The Company Info topic sets up the company file, creates a Chart of Accounts designed for your specific type of business, and establishes the beginning of a company's fiscal year and income tax year.

       DO: Complete the Company Info topic
Read the General Company Information screen, click **>>Next**
Enter the Company Name **VideoLand--Your Name**, press tab
- VideoLand--Your Name is entered as the Legal name when the tab key is
  pressed. Do not actually enter the words "Your Name" as part of the company
  name. Instead, type your own name. For example, Mary Hernandez would
  show **VideoLand--Mary Hernandez**. This makes it easier for you to identify
  your work when you print.

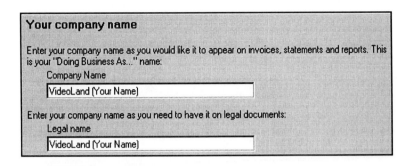

Click >>**Next**

Enter the Company Address information in the spaces provided, tab or click in the blank to move from item to item

- Note: For the state, California, type C and QuickBooks will fill in the rest or click the drop-down list arrow for State.
- The country is automatically filled in as US.

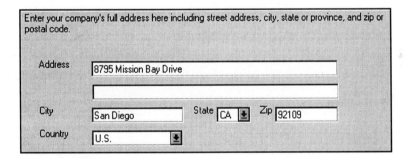

Click >>**Next**

Complete the next screen:

    Click **More** button to see information regarding federal tax ID numbers, income tax year, and fiscal year

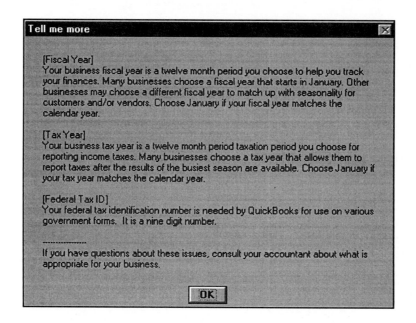

Click **OK**

Tab to or click **Tax ID number**, enter **159-88-8654**

Tab to or click **income tax year**, click the drop-down list arrow, click **July**

Tab to or click **fiscal year**, click the drop-down list arrow, click **July**

Other company information

Enter the federal tax ID number that you use on your federal income tax returns: |159-88-8654|

Enter the first month of your income tax year: |July ▾|

Enter the first month in your fiscal year: |July ▾|

Click **>>Next**

Leave the **company income tax form** as **<Other/None>**

Your company income tax form

What income tax form does your company use?

|<Other/None> ▾|

Click **>>Next**

A **Tax Form** message box appears on the screen, click **OK**

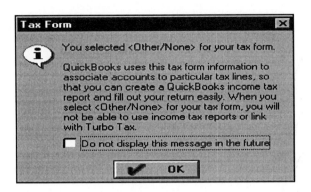

Scroll through the list of the types of businesses
Click **Retail**

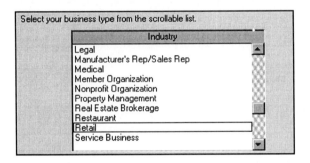

Click **>>Next**
Click **Yes** for maintaining inventory

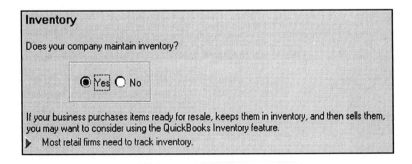

- Notice the green triangle indicating information regarding retail businesses.

Click **>>Next**

Click **More** button to get additional information on how QuickBooks can help
    with inventory

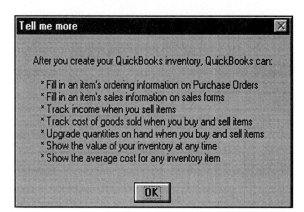

Click **OK**

Click the **Show Help** button to use QuickBooks Help feature regarding Inventory

Scroll through the Help window and read the information about inventory

- Notice the Help section with the question regarding other considerations on using QuickBooks inventory feature. In this section it states that QuickBooks does not and cannot use LIFO (last in first out) or FIFO (first in first out) inventory valuation methods. It can use only the average cost method of inventory valuation.

Close Help by clicking the **close** button in the upper right corner of the help screen

Click **>>Next**

Click **Yes** to use the QuickBooks Inventory feature

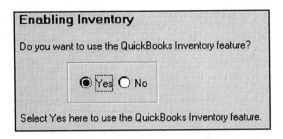

Click **>>Next**

Click **View Now** to get industry information for Retail with QuickBooks
    Inventory

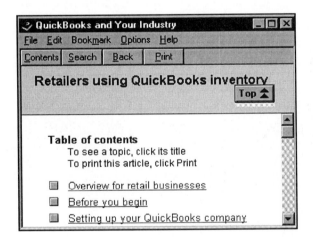

Scroll through the QuickBooks and Your Industry document to read all the
    information, or click on individual topics to read only those items of specific
    interest

Close the screen when finished

Click **Next** until you get to create the company file

Click the drop-down list arrow for **Drives**, click **a:**

For the file name, change **VideoLan.QBW** to **Video.QBW**

Click **OK**

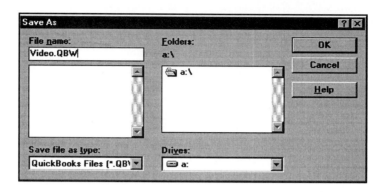

Since we are using QuickBooks to assist us with our company configuration, click **Yes** to use the income and expense accounts chosen by QuickBooks

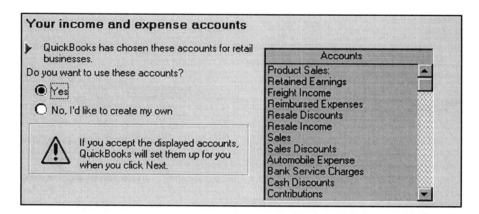

- Some accounts will not be appropriate for use by VideoLand. These will be deleted and/or changed after the EasyStep Interview is complete.

Click **Next**

Company Information is complete, click **Next**

PREFERENCES TOPIC

The Preferences topic allows you to tell QuickBooks whether or not you want to use certain features of the QuickBooks program. If you answer a question one way and then decide to change, you can always reset your preferences after you exit the Interview. Preferences include whether or not to use QuickBooks inventory feature, whether or not you collect sales tax, selection of an invoice format, the number of employees on the payroll, whether or not you use classes as an additional way of categorizing transactions, whether you want to enter bills first and pay them later, and whether or not you want the Reminders list to display automatically when you start the program.

MEMO

DATE: July 1, 19**

The information necessary to complete the Preferences topic is: Collect sales tax: Yes, at a single rate for a single tax agency; Sales tax name and description: CA Sales Tax; Tax rate: 7.25%; Government agency: State Board of Equalization; Invoice format: Custom; Employees: 4; Payroll feature: Yes; Estimates: No; Track time: No; Track reimbursable expenses: No; Classes: No; Enter bills first and payments later; Reminders list: At start up.

DO: Complete the Preferences topic
Click **Next** until you get to Sales Tax screen
Click **Yes** for collecting Sales tax

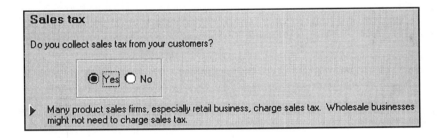

Click **Next**
* From this point on click **Next** whenever you want to move from one screen to the next. The step-by-step instructions will no longer remind you to click Next each time.

Select: **I collect single tax rate paid to a single tax agency**

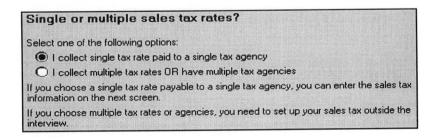

Complete the screen for Sales Tax Information:

Tab to or click the box for Reports and Lists name, enter **CA Sales Tax**
Enter the same information for the description for Invoices
Tab to or click the box for the sales tax rate, enter **7.25%**
Tab to or click the box for the government agency, enter **State Board of Equalization**

Sales tax information

Enter a short name for the sales tax. This name will be used in QuickBooks reports and pick lists:	CA Sales Tax
Enter a sales tax description to be printed on invoices:	CA Sales Tax
Enter your sales tax rate here as a percentage (e.g., "5.2%"):	7.25%
Enter the name of the government agency to which you pay sales tax:	State Board of Equalization

Click **Custom** for the Invoice format

Your invoice format

QuickBooks has several invoice formats to fit different types of businesses. Select the format you prefer to use:

- ○ Product
- ○ Professional
- ○ Service
- ◉ Custom

You can change this format at any time.

- Note: A custom invoice will be created later in the chapter.

Enter **4** as the number of employees on the payroll

Employees

How many employees do you have on your payroll?

4

Click **Yes** to use the QuickBooks payroll feature

Using QuickBooks for Payroll

Do you want to use the QuickBooks Payroll feature?

     ● Yes   ○ No

The Payroll feature is currently designed for U.S. and Puerto Rico use only.
You'll complete specific payroll setup information in the Payroll section of the interview.

If you get a Tax Table Update message, click **OK**

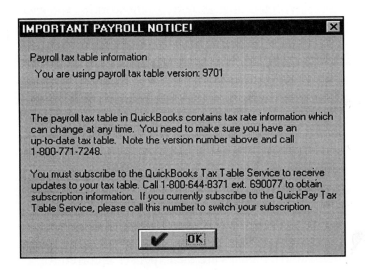

Click **No** for written or verbal estimates

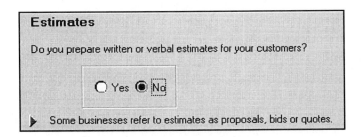

Click **No** for time tracking

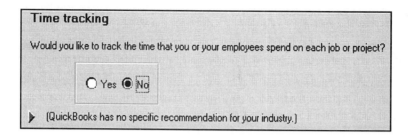

- Time tracking would be useful in a business where a particular job or client is billed based on the time actually spent working the specific job or working for a specific client. Examples would include a construction job or the hours an attorney spends on an individual client's case.

Click **No** for tracking reimbursable expenses

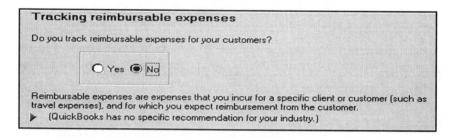

- Reimbursable expenses are the expenses incurred for a client or customer. For example, if you paid the freight on an item for a customer, you could bill the customer for the amount of freight you paid.

Click **No** for Classes

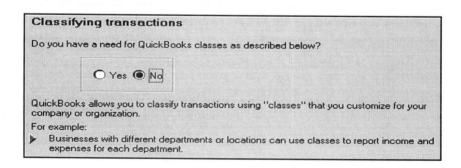

- Classes are used to categorize information into department or store locations.

To select the bill-paying method, click **Enter bills first and then enter the payments later**

Two ways to handle bills and payments

Choose one of the two following ways to track your bills and payments.
- ○ Enter the checks directly.
- ● Enter the bills first and then enter the payments later.

The first option is simple since it only involves one step.

The second option is a two step process. QuickBooks reminds you when your bills are due, so that you can pay at the last possible moment or in time to get early payment discounts.

- By selecting to enter the bills first and then entering the payments later, you are actually choosing to use QuickBooks' accounts payable feature. In addition, this is the appropriate choice when using accrual basis accounting. If you don't record an expense or a bill until the check is written, it may not be recorded within the period in which it occurred.

Click **At Start Up** to display the Reminders list

Reminders list

The reminders window is a list of all things that are due or that you need to act on. It includes such things as bills to pay, overdue invoices, checks to print, and your To Do items.

How often would you like to see your Reminders List?

- ● At start up ○ When I ask for it ○ Rarely

START DATE

The start date is the date you select to give QuickBooks the financial information for your company. Once a start date is entered, historical information will need to be entered in order to record transactions that occurred between your start date through the current date to make all records accurate. Otherwise, you will not receive correct data when preparing reports, paying taxes, and so on. For example, if the start date entered is May 1 and it is now July 1, two months of transactions (May and June) will need to be entered into QuickBooks. This could be a tremendous task if you have a busy company with many transactions to record. If you did not enter the two months of transactions, then all reports and accounts would not show income, expenses, changes in assets, changes in liabilities, or changes in owner's equity for May and June. If you enter the start date and it is also the beginning of your fiscal year, you will not have to enter any previous transactions, and all reports and accounts will be accurate for the entire year. Some companies choose to begin using QuickBooks at the beginning of their fiscal year to avoid having to enter all the transaction history; however, it is possible to begin using QuickBooks at any time of the year.

MEMO
DATE: July 1, 19**

Carrie: Use the memo date as the start date for the company. Because this is the first day of the fiscal year, historical data will not need to be entered.

DO: Enter the start date
Read each screen carefully as you advance through the screens for Start Date
At **Enter your company start date here** enter **07/01/**
   • Remember to check with your instructor to find out the year to use.

Choose your QuickBooks start date
Enter your company start date here: `07/01/97`

The General section of the EasyStep Interview is complete. Notice the check marks on each of the topic tabs and on the General tab.

INCOME & EXPENSES SECTION

In the General section a basic Chart of Accounts or General Ledger was established by QuickBooks. Because this Chart of Accounts is based on a representation of the accounts most frequently used within an industry, it will not have all the accounts that are used by an individual company. Using the preset Chart of Accounts is helpful in providing a general setup. In the Income & Expenses section of the Interview, new income and expense accounts are added.

Any accounts created by QuickBooks that are not appropriate for your individual company will be deleted after the setup procedure and EasyStep Interview are completed. QuickBooks accounts can have both account names and account numbers. The EasyStep Interview displays only account names. If account numbers are used, the numbers are added outside the Interview. In addition, changing account names, changing subaccounts, and making accounts inactive will be completed after the Interview.

INCOME ACCOUNTS TOPIC

MEMO

DATE: July 1, 19**

Because VideoLand sells videos, rents videos, and repairs VCRs, income accounts need to be established for all three types of revenue. Because QuickBooks has established a Sales account, accounts for Rental Income and Repair Income need to be added.

 DO: Add income accounts for Rental Income and Repair Income
- QuickBooks has established a Sales account that will be used for the sale of videos. It has not established accounts for rental and repair income.

Click **Yes** to add another income account

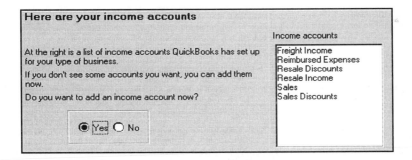

Click **Next**

Enter **Rental Income** as the account name

Adding an income account.	
Account Name	Enter the name for this income account.
Rental Income	
Tax Line (optional)	Choose the federal income tax form line to associate with this account.
<Unassigned>	

- Tax lines will not be assigned at this time.

Click **Next**

Repeat the procedures to add Repair Income

Because you do not want to add any more income accounts, click **No** after Repair Income has been added

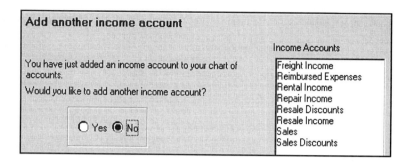

EXPENSE ACCOUNTS TOPIC

QuickBooks has created some expense accounts in the Chart of Accounts already. This topic allows you to add additional expense accounts to the Chart of Accounts. Expense accounts may be categorized further by making an expense a subaccount of another account. For example, rather than lump all insurance together in one insurance expense account, the insurance expenses will be listed separately in individual accounts, such as Disability Insurance, Liability Insurance, and so on. These accounts will be grouped together as subaccounts under Insurance Expense.

MEMO

DATE: July 1, 19**

Add the following expense accounts: Fire Insurance (subaccount of Insurance), Sales Supplies (subaccount of Supplies).

   DO: Add the accounts as indicated above
Click **More Details** and read the screens to get additional information about accounts and subaccounts

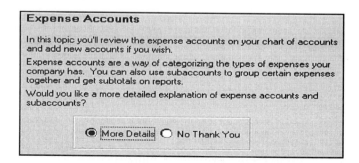

- One of the screens shows how subaccounts are displayed on reports. This shows how creating subaccounts can provide more detailed information about expenses.

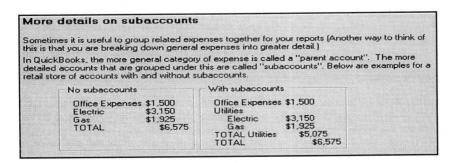

Scroll through the list of accounts created by QuickBooks
- Notice that there is not an account for Fire Insurance, nor is there an account for Sales Supplies.

Enter **Fire Insurance** as the account name

Click **This is a subaccount**

Click the drop-down list arrow next to Parent account

Click **Insurance**

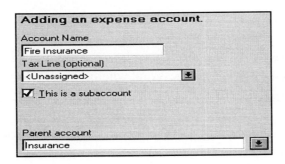

Repeat the procedures indicated to add Sales Supplies

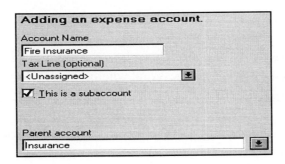

Scroll through the Chart of Accounts
Verify the addition of the two new accounts

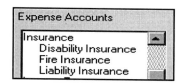   

Click **No** to add expense accounts
- Income & Expenses section is complete. Notice the check marks on the topic and section tabs.

INCOME DETAILS SECTION

The Income Details section of the EasyStep Interview allows you to track the sources of the company's income from the services and products it sells. This section also allows you to identify the service, product, and inventory items used in the various income accounts of the company. Accounts receivable features that will be used are identified in this section as well.

INTRODUCTION TOPIC

This topic tells QuickBooks the information it needs to determine which parts of the Accounts Receivable features it will use for the business and whether or not you will be using invoices for each transaction or monthly statements.

  DO: Complete the Introduction of the Income Details Section
For Receipt of payment, click **Sometimes**

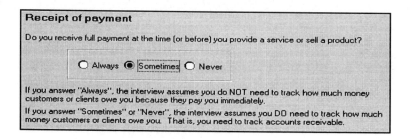

Click **No** for Statement Charges

- Note: Statement Charges allow you to enter all transactions for an individual customer into the customer's account and send one statement at the end of the month rather than complete an invoice for each transaction.

ITEMS TOPIC

The Income Details: Items topic is the section of the Interview where Items to track services performed and products sold for income are created. The Items list is used in conjunction with the income accounts previously created.

MEMO

DATE: July 1, 19**

The following service and product items are used by VideoLand (Information is listed in the order of Item Name, Sales Description, Sales Price, Taxable Item, Income Account):

Video Rental, Video Rental, 3.00, Yes, Rental Income
VCR Repair, VCR Repair, 0.00, No, Repair Income
VCR Service, VCR Service, 19.95, No, Repair Income

DO: Add the three service items above to the Items list
Click **More** on the Income Details: Items screen to get additional information about items and income accounts

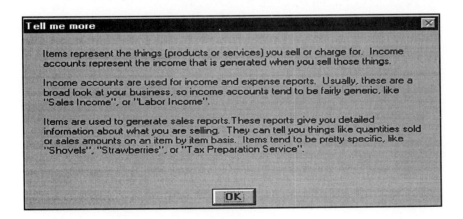

Click **OK** on Tell me more screen

Click **Yes** on Service Items screen
Enter Item Name **Video Rental**
Tab to or click Sales Description, enter **Video Rental**
Tab to or click Sales Price, enter **0.00**
Click **Taxable Item** to select

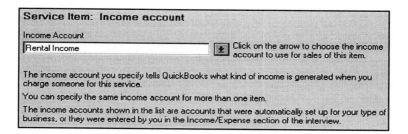

On the next screen, click drop-down list arrow for Income Account
Click **Rental Income**

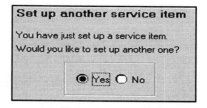

Repeat for the other two items listed in the memo above

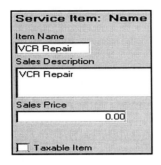 

When all Items have been entered, click **No** on Set up another service item

Click **No** for Non-Inventory parts

- Non-inventory parts are parts that are purchased and then immediately sold or installed. They are not kept as an in-stock item.

Click **No** for Other Charges

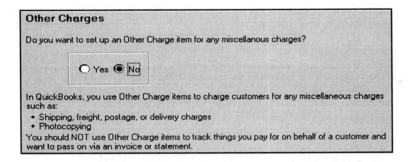

- As indicated, Other Charges are charges that you want to pass on to customers, not expenses you have paid for on behalf of customers. In VideoLand there doesn't appear to be a need for an account for other charges. If it is determined that the account is needed, it can be added at a later date.
- Items topic is complete.

INVENTORY TOPIC

The Inventory topic is completed in order to set up your inventory part items. Inventory part items are the things you purchase, hold in inventory, and then sell.

MEMO
DATE: July 1, 19**

Enter the following Inventory items (Information is listed in the order of Item Name, Sales Description, Sales Price, Taxable Item, Income Account, Purchase Description, Cost, Reorder Point, Quantity on Hand, Value):

Action, Action Video, 0.00, Yes, Sales Income, Action Video, 0.00, 100, 550, 5,500
Children, Children's Video, 0.00, Yes, Sales Income, Children's Video, 0.00, 100, 250, 2,500
Comedy, Comedy Video, 0.00, Yes, Sales Income, Comedy Video, 0.00, 100, 500, 5,000
Drama, Drama Video, 0.00, Yes, Sales Income, Drama Video, 0.00, 100, 450, 4,500

 DO: Add the Inventory Items indicated above
Click **Yes**, if necessary, to begin adding inventory items

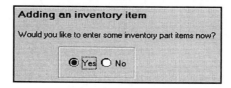

Enter **Action** as the Item Name
Tab to or click Sales Description, enter **Action Video**
• Because videos are sold for different amounts, Sales Price remains 0.00.
Click **Taxable Item**
Click the drop-down list arrow next to Income Account, click **Sales**
Enter **Action Video** as the Purchases Description
• Because videos are sold for different amounts, Sales Price remains 0.00.
Enter **100** for the **Reorder Point**
Tab to or click **Qty on Hand**, enter **550**
Tab to or click Total value as of **07/01/****, enter **5500**

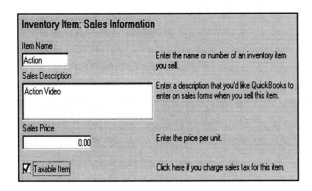

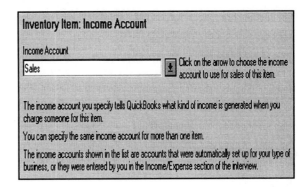

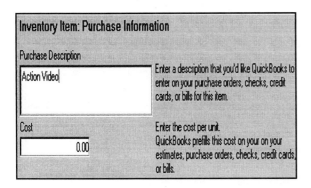

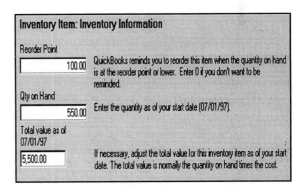

Repeat for the other three items listed in the memo above

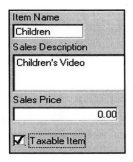

- Only the first screen of the three additional inventory items are shown above. Click **No** when all inventory items have been entered
- The Inventory topic and the Income Details section are now complete.

OPENING BALANCES SECTION

As the name implies, the Opening Balances section is the section of the EasyStep Interview where opening balances for customers, vendors, and certain General Ledger accounts are entered as of the start date previously indicated. Detail information such as the address, the credit limit, and so on regarding individual customers and vendors will be entered as a separate procedure after the Interview is complete.

When setting up your company, you should have the current bank statement, value of your assets, liabilities, credit cards, and other balance sheet accounts as of the start date, the customer names and amounts owed as of the start date, and the vendor names and the amount you owe as of the start date.

 DO: Read the screens and complete the Introduction

CUSTOMERS TOPIC

MEMO

DATE: July 1, 19**

Add the following customers and the balances they owe to VideoLand:

Goldman, Barney—$50   Mirovich, Randolph—$550
Robinson, Yolanda—$350   Thatcher, Rafael—$75

 DO: Add the customers and the amount they owe to VideoLand
Click **Yes**, if necessary, to Enter customers
Click **No**, if necessary, to Customer job tracking
Enter **Goldman, Barney** in Customer Name
Tab to or click **Balance due on start date**, enter **50**

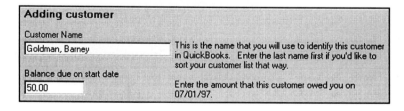

Repeat the steps above to add the remaining customers and their balances.

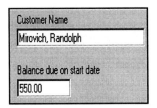

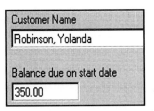

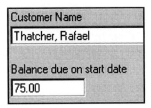

When all the customers and their balances have been added, compare your Customer:Jobs list with the following QuickBooks list

- Notice that the balances are not shown on the list.
- The customers' names were added last name, first name so that QuickBooks could alphabetize the customers by their last names. If customers are added first name then last name, the customers will be alphabetized by their first names.

Click **No** to end adding customers

VENDORS TOPIC

As with the customer topic, the Vendor topic is used to set up a list of vendors and the balances owed to the vendors. If there are vendors with which you usually do business but that do not have an existing balance, they may be set up within the Interview or they may be added at a later date. This topic simply adds a vendor's name and the balance due. It does not allow you to enter information regarding credit terms, credit limits, vendor addresses, and so forth. That information must be entered after you leave the interview.

MEMO
DATE: July 1, 19**

Carrie: Add the following vendors and the balances owed: Video Supplies, $3,000; Movies Galore, $4,000; The Rental Company, $0.00.

 DO: Add the vendors and the balances listed above

Click **Yes** to **Add Vendors with open balances**

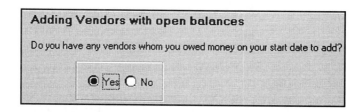

Enter **Video Supplies** as the Vendor Name
Tab to or click **Balance due on start date**, enter **3,000**

Repeat the steps above to add the other two vendors

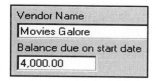   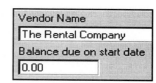

Click **No** for **Adding another vendor**
• If a person's name was part of a vendor name, you would enter the name last name, first name.
• The Vendors topic is complete.

ACCOUNTS TOPIC

In this section of the Interview, balances will be entered for balance sheet accounts. Balance sheet accounts are the assets (things owned), liabilities (things owed), and the owner's equity (owner's capital, investment, and drawing accounts).

MEMO
DATE: July 1, 19**

Set up the following balance sheet accounts and balances:

MasterCard, Statement date: 6/30/**, $500
Store Equipment Loan, $3,000, Long-term liability
Store Fixtures Loan, $3,500, Long-term liability
Checking, Statement date: 6/30/**, $16,586
Prepaid Insurance, Other Current Asset, $1,200
Office Supplies, Other Current Asset, $350
Sales Supplies, Other Current Asset, $500
Store Equipment, Fixed Asset, Depreciation: Yes, Original Cost: $8,000,
    Depreciation as of 07/01/**: $800
Store Fixtures, Fixed Asset, Depreciation: Yes, Original Cost: $15,000,
    Depreciation as of 07/01/**: $1500

DO: Add the accounts and balances listed above
Click **More**, read the information about Balance Sheet accounts, click **OK**

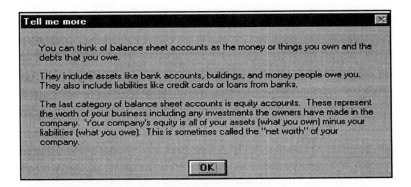

Tell me more

You can think of balance sheet accounts as the money or things you own and the debts that you owe.

They include assets like bank accounts, buildings, and money people owe you. They also include liabilities like credit cards or loans from banks.

The last category of balance sheet accounts is equity accounts. These represent the worth of your business including any investments the owners have made in the company. Your company's equity is all of your assets (what you own) minus your liabilities (what you owe). This is sometimes called the "net worth" of your company.

OK

Click **Yes** to set up a credit card account

Credit card accounts

Would you like to set up a credit card account? Note that you should NOT set up an account for a personal credit card which you sometimes use for business.

⦿ Yes ○ No

You must set up one QuickBooks credit card account for each credit card account you have.

Enter **MasterCard** as the **name**

Adding a credit card

Name

MasterCard — Enter the name of your credit card. For example, "company card", or "Quicken Visa".

Enter **0630**** as the Statement Ending Date
Tab to or click **Statement Ending Balance**, enter **500**

Last statement date and balance

Statement Ending Date

06/30/97 — Enter the date of the last credit card statement you received whose ending date was ON OR BEFORE 07/01/97 (the date you chose as your starting date).

Statement Ending Balance

500.00 — Enter the ending balance from the credit card statement.

Because there are no additional credit cards to be added, click **No**

Adding another credit card

Credit Card Accounts

You have just added a credit card account. To the right is your current list of credit card accounts.

MasterCard

Do you want to add another credit card account?

○ Yes ● No

Click **No** for **Adding lines of credit**

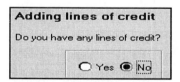

Adding lines of credit

Do you have any lines of credit?

○ Yes ● No

Because there are loans for store fixtures and store equipment, click **Yes** to add

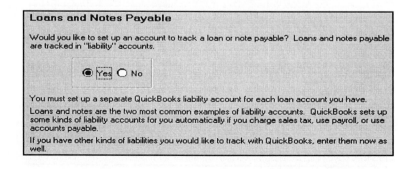

Loans and Notes Payable

Would you like to set up an account to track a loan or note payable? Loans and notes payable are tracked in "liability" accounts.

● Yes ○ No

You must set up a separate QuickBooks liability account for each loan account you have.

Loans and notes are the two most common examples of liability accounts. QuickBooks sets up some kinds of liability accounts for you automatically if you charge sales tax, use payroll, or use accounts payable.

If you have other kinds of liabilities you would like to track with QuickBooks, enter them now as well.

Enter **Store Equipment Loan** as the Name
Tab to or click **Unpaid Balance on 07/01/****, enter **3000**
Since the store equipment loan is longer than one year, click **Long-term liability**

Adding a loan (liability) account

Name
Store Equipment Loan

Enter the name of your loan.

Unpaid Balance on 07/01/97
3,000.00

Enter the amount of the loan on your start date (NOT the original amount of the loan). This is the balance of the loan as of your start date. If you got this loan after your start date, just enter 0 for the balance of the loan.

☑ Long Term Liability

Click here if this loan will not be paid off in a year. See Tell Me More below for further explanation.

Click **Yes** to add the remaining **Loan and Notes Payable** account

Name
Store Fixtures Loan
Unpaid Balance on 07/01/97
3,500.00

☑ Long Term Liability

- Does your list of liabilities match the following?

Adding another loan

You have just added a liability account. To the right is your current list of loan accounts.
Would you like to add a liability account for another loan or note payable?

○ Yes ⦿ No

Loan Accounts
Payroll Liabilities
Sales Tax Payable
Store Equipment
Store Fixtures

Click **No** to Adding another loan
Click **Yes** to Add a bank account

Bank accounts

Would you like to set up a bank account?

⦿ Yes ○ No

QuickBooks classifies all checking, savings, and money market accounts as bank accounts. We also recommend that you set up your petty cash accounts as bank accounts for ease of use in entering withdrawals and additions.

Enter **Checking** as the name of the account

Adding a bank account

Name
Checking

Enter the name of your bank account, (for example "checking", "savings", "State National Bank", etc). For petty cash accounts, you can use "Petty Cash" or "Cash Drawer".

Enter **0630**** as the Statement Ending Date
Tab to or click **Statement Ending Balance**, enter **16586**

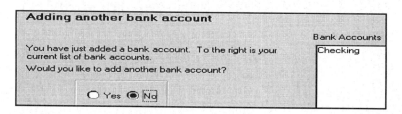

Click **No** for Adding another bank account

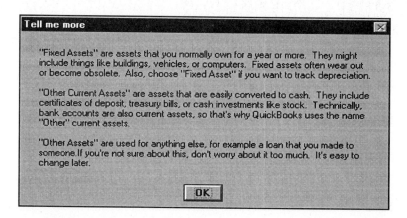

Read the screen for Introduction to assets
Click **Yes** to set up Asset accounts
Enter **Prepaid Insurance** as the Name
Click **More** to get additional information regarding fixed, current, and other assets

Tell me more

"Fixed Assets" are assets that you normally own for a year or more. They might include things like buildings, vehicles, or computers. Fixed assets often wear out or become obsolete. Also, choose "Fixed Asset" if you want to track depreciation.

"Other Current Assets" are assets that are easily converted to cash. They include certificates of deposit, treasury bills, or cash investments like stock. Technically, bank accounts are also current assets, so that's why QuickBooks uses the name "Other" current assets.

"Other Assets" are used for anything else, for example a loan that you made to someone. If you're not sure about this, don't worry about it too much. It's easy to change later.

OK

Click the drop-down list arrow for **Type**, click **Other Current Asset**
Enter **1200** as the Asset value on 07/01/**

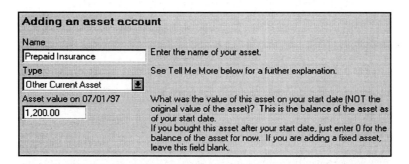

Add the additional Other Current Asset accounts listed in the memo

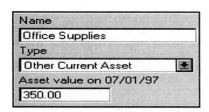
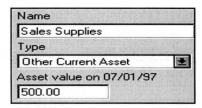

Add the Fixed Asset accounts listed in the memo

Enter **Store Equipment** as the Name

Click the drop-down list arrow for **Type**, click **Fixed Asset**

- Notice that the Asset Value section becomes a gray color and cannot be accessed.

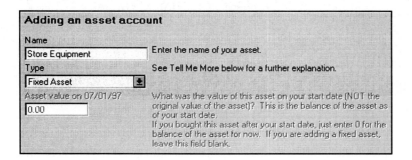

Click **Yes** to track **Depreciation**

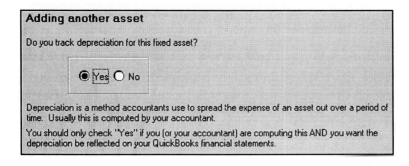

Enter **8000** as the Original Cost
Tab to or click **Depreciation as of 07/01/****, enter **800**

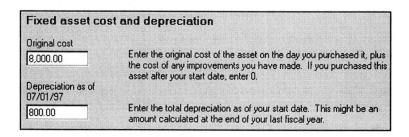

Add the other fixed asset

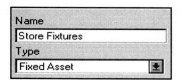 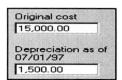

Click **No** when all assets have been added
Compare your list of assets to those shown below:

 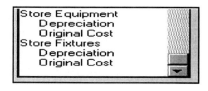

Read the **Introduction to Equity Accounts**
• Notice that QuickBooks has automatically set up two equity accounts:
  Opening Balance Equity (this is actually the owner's capital account) and
  Retained Earnings (where QuickBooks accumulates the Net Income for the
  business year after year unless an adjustment is made).

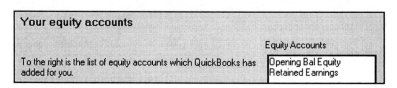

• The Opening Balance section and Accounts topic are complete.

PAYROLL SECTION

The Payroll section is used to create payroll items, such as payroll taxes, types of wages, and salary deductions. It is also used to give QuickBooks information for each employee you pay. Summaries for the current year from January 1 through the QuickBooks start date are also entered in this portion of the EasyStep Interview. **Note: The tax table used in this text is 9701.**

INTRODUCTION TOPIC

This topic gives QuickBooks some basic information about your payroll, including the frequency of the company pay period, the company filing state, and the employer ID number for the state.

MEMO
DATE: July 1, 19**

The pay period for VideoLand is semi-monthly (twice a month), and the filing state is CA. Enter this information in the Payroll Introduction.

DO: Complete the Payroll introduction
Read the Payroll Introduction screen
Click **Semi-monthly** to select as the pay period

Pay period

How frequently do you pay your employees? Click (to mark) the checkbox for all pay periods that your company uses.

- ☐ Daily (or on demand)
- ☐ Weekly
- ☐ Bi-weekly (every two weeks)
- ☑ Semi-monthly (twice a month)
- ☐ Monthly
- ☐ Quarterly
- ☐ Yearly

Type **C**
OR
Click the drop-down list arrow for **Filing State**, click **CA**

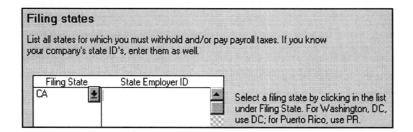

- Up to five states may be selected under Filing State. Each state in which at least one employee lives or works must be selected.
- The State Employer ID is optional. Do not complete.
- The Introduction topic is complete.

PAYROLL ITEMS TOPIC

As with other items that QuickBooks uses, payroll items are used to identify and/or track the various amounts that affect a paycheck. There are items for salaries and wages, each kind of tax, each type of other deduction, commissions, and company-paid benefits. QuickBooks automatically sets up the payroll items for salaries, federal taxes, and state taxes.

MEMO
DATE: July 1, 19**

Add the following payroll items:

The State Unemployment Tax rate for VideoLand is 4% paid by the employer. The employee pays 0%. The company pays a reduced FUTA rate of 0.8%. Employees can be hourly or on salary. Hourly wages are paid at a Regular Hourly Rate, and hourly overtime is paid at Overtime Hourly Rate 1. For employees receiving a salary, Office Salary Regular, Officer Sick Salary, and Officer Vac Salary will be used. Employees may participate in employee-paid medical and dental plans. There are no company-paid contributions.

DO: Complete the Payroll items topic
Read the screens regarding payroll items and the information needed for payroll items

For the State Unemployment Tax Rate enter **4** as the % Paid By Company, leave the % Paid By Employee at **0%**

- Note: The amount of State Unemployment Tax, if any, can change depending on the state and the company rating. Companies that fire or lay off very few employees can be granted a reduction in their State Unemployment Tax rates.
- The requirements for state taxes are different from one state to the next. In actual practice you would consult your tax adviser or the state tax agency to get information regarding the requirements for the state(s) in which your business pays and/or withholds taxes.

State Unemployment Tax Rate(s)

Enter your state unemployment tax rate(s), below:

	% Paid By Company	% Paid By Employee
CA	4.0%	0

- Once the information regarding the State Unemployment Tax Rate has been provided, QuickBooks automatically sets up state payroll tax items.

Your state tax payroll items are set up.

QuickBooks has set up the following state tax payroll items for you, based on tax table data for the state or states in which you file.

Payroll Item	Type
CA - Withholding	State Withholding Tax
CA - Disability Employee	State Disability Tax
CA - Unemployment Company	State Unemployment Tax

If it is not selected, click **Yes (company pays a reduced FUTA rate)**

Federal unemployment tax (FUTA) credit

Does your company qualify for the FUTA credit?

- ⦿ Yes (company pays a reduced FUTA rate, such as 0.8%)
- ○ No (company pays the full FUTA rate of 6.2%)
- ○ Company is exempt from FUTA tax

If you are not sure, consult your accountant or the Internal Revenue Service.

Click **Employees can be paid hourly** and **Employees can be paid on salary** for **Compensation**

Compensation

How do you pay your employees (check all that apply)?

- ☑ Employees can be paid hourly
- ☑ Employees can be paid on salary
- ☐ Employees can receive commissions

Click **Hourly Regular Rate** and **Overtime Hourly Rate 1** to indicate your
   Hourly wage types

Select your hourly wage types

Click the first column of the list below to place a check mark next to every type of hourly wage you
need to track.

+	Payroll Item	Notes
✓	Hourly Regular Rate	Standard hourly wage
✓	Overtime Hourly Rate 1	Overtime wage
	Overtime Hourly Rate 2	Overtime wage (customize and rename for your use)
	Other Hourly Rate 1	Hourly wage (customize and rename for your use)

Indicate your **Salary wage types** by clicking **Officer Salary Regular**, **Officer
   Sick Salary**, and **Officer Vac Salary**

Select your salary wage types

Click the first column of the list below to place a check mark next to every type of salary wage you
need to track.

+	Payroll Item	Notes
✓	Officer Salary Regular	Officer salary wage
✓	Officer Sick Salary	Officer sick salary
✓	Officer Vac Salary	Officer vacation salary

Click **Dental Insurance (Emp)** and **Medical Insurance (Emp)** to select
   employee-paid dental and medical insurance deductions

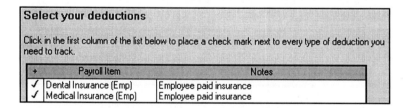

Select your deductions

Click in the first column of the list below to place a check mark next to every type of deduction you
need to track.

+	Payroll Item	Notes
✓	Dental Insurance (Emp)	Employee paid insurance
✓	Medical Insurance (Emp)	Employee paid insurance

- There are no payroll additions such as mileage.
- There are no company-paid contributions.
- Payroll Items setup is complete.

EMPLOYEES TOPIC

Employees of the company will be added in this topic. Initially, you will specify which payroll items apply to all or most of the employees of the company. This creates an Employee template, which you can use to automatically fill in information when you set up individual employees. Once the Employee template has been created, it will be used to add employees.

MEMO
DATE: July 1, 19**

Set up the information for the Employee template:

Select **none** of the Payroll Items listed for earnings. Select both of the standard payroll items, all federal taxes, and CA state taxes. Track sick time and vacation time. Give sick time and vacation time at beginning of the year: give 40 hours for the accrual period to sick and vacation time and a maximum of 120 hours per employee for sick and vacation time. Do not reset sick or vacation time each year.

DO: Create the Employee template and add the current employee information
Do not click any of the items shown in the list of payroll items to indicate the type of Earnings of employees
- The template is created so that information common to *all* employees may be entered. Because some of VideoLand's employees are paid on an hourly basis and others are paid a salary, there are no payroll earnings items common to *all* or even most of the employees.

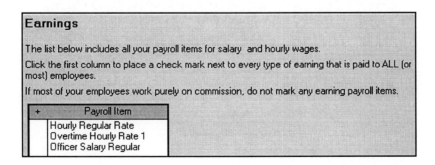

Because *all* employees may elect to participate in the **Dental Insurance (Emp)** and **Medical Insurance (Emp)**, click both items to select for use on the template

Standard payroll items

The list below shows payroll items you have set up previously in the interview.

Select those payroll items that will apply to ALL (or most) employee paychecks (you don't need to mark infrequently used payroll items.)

+	Payroll Item	Type
✓	Dental Insurance (Emp)	Deduction
✓	Medical Insurance (Emp)	Deduction

If necessary, click **Yes** for all the taxes listed

Federal taxes

What federal taxes are ALL (or most) of your employees subject to?

Federal income tax withholding?	● Yes ○ No
Social security?	● Yes ○ No
Medicare?	● Yes ○ No
Federal unemployment tax (FUTA)?	● Yes ○ No

State taxes should be CA; if not, click the drop-down list arrow, click **CA**

State taxes

In what state do you file payroll taxes for ALL (or most) of your employees?

CA ⏷

Payroll taxes include: state withholding, state disability state unemployment.

Click **Yes** to track **Sick Time**

Sick time

QuickBooks can track sick time:
* allocated as a single, lump sum at the beginning of the year, or
* as a fixed amount allocated every pay period
QuickBooks does not support allocation by actual hours worked.

Do you want to use QuickBooks to track employee sick time?

● Yes ○ No

Use the information in the memo to complete the Employee Sick Time Accrual

Employee sick time accrual

How often do you give sick time to ALL (or most) of your employees (this is the accrual period)?
- ● Beginning of year
- ○ Every pay period

How many hours do you give ALL (or most) employees per accrual period? `40.00`

What is the maximum number of hours an employee can have? `120`

QuickBooks can reset the sick time available to zero at the beginning of the year, and then add new hours for the year or pay period. ☐ Reset hours each new year?

Use the information in the memo to complete the Employee Vacation Time Accrual

Employee vacation time accrual

How often do you give vacation time to ALL (or most) of your employees (this is the accrual period)?
- ● Beginning of year
- ○ Every pay period

How many hours do you give ALL (or most) employees per accrual period? `40.00`

What is the maximum number of hours an employee can have? `120`

QuickBooks can reset the vacation time available to zero at the beginning of the year, and then add new hours for the year or pay period. ☐ Reset hours each new year?

- Information for the Employee Template is complete.

ADD EMPLOYEES USING EMPLOYEE TEMPLATE

Once the necessary information for the Employee template has been provided, the employees may be added. Even in the EasyStep Interview the Employee template is used and, unlike customers and vendors where names and balances are the only things that can be entered, complete employee information is entered at this time.

MEMO
DATE: July 1, 19**

Add individual employee information (only the information that needs to be entered is given below; if information is not provided, it is 0):

Mr. Mark Canfield: 1077 Columbia Street, San Diego, CA 92101; 619-555-1232; Social Security No. 100-55-2525; Hired 03/17/95; Birthday 12/28/49; Officer Salary Regular $35,000; Dental $35; Medical $75; Federal: Head of Household, 4 Allowances; State: Head of Household 4 Allowances; Sick 40 hrs; Vacation 40 hrs

Ms. Carrie Bernstein: 751 7th Street, San Diego, CA 92101; 619-555-3654; Social Security No. 100-55-3274, Hired 04/23/96; Birthday 05/23/57; Officer Salary Regular $26,000; Dental $25; Medical $50; Federal: Single, 0 Allowances; State: Single, 0 Allowances; Sick 20 hrs; Vacation 20 hrs

Mr. Jimmy Hernandez, 2985 A Street, San Diego, CA 92101; 619-555-9874; Social Security No. 100-55-6961; Hired 06/30/96; Birthday 04/23/73; Hourly Regular Rate $22.50; Dental $20; Medical $40; Federal: Married, 2 Allowances; State: Married (2 incomes), 2 Allowances; Sick 50 hrs; Vacation 40 hrs

Ms. Sally Richards, 159 Kettner Street, San Diego, CA 92101; 619-555-8591; Social Security No. 100-55-8723; Hired 05/02/96; Birthday 07/27/75; Hourly Regular Rate $10; Federal: Married, 1 Allowance; State: Married (1 income), 1 Allowance

---

DO: Add the employees and the information listed above
Click **Add Employee** button

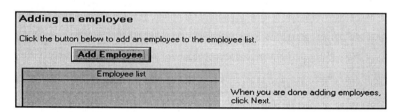

Use the information in the memo to complete the Address Info tab for Mark Canfield

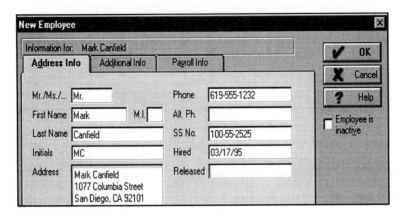

Click **Additional Info** tab
- This tab allows custom fields to be created. Custom fields contain information such as a birthday, name of spouse, and so on. Custom fields may be created and used for additional information for employees, customers, and vendors.

Click **Define Fields** button

Enter **Birthday** as the first label, click the check box under **Employees** to use for employees, click **OK**

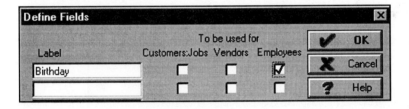

Enter **12/28/49** as Mark's birthday

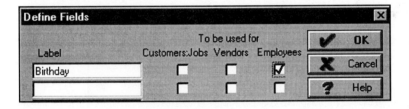

Click **Payroll Info** tab

Click in the **Name** column

Click the drop-down list arrow for **Name**, click **Officer Salary Regular**

Tab to or click **Hour/Annual Rate**, enter **35000**
- Pay Period should be Semi-monthly; if it is not, click drop-down list arrow, click **Semimonthly**

Click in the **Amount** column next to Dental Insurance, enter **35**

Tab to or click the **Amount** column next to Medical Insurance, enter **75**

Tab to or click the **Amount** column next to Medical Insurance, enter **75**

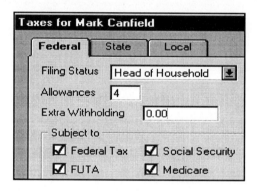

Click the **Taxes** button

Complete the federal tax information:

> Click the drop-down list for **Filing Status**, click **Head of Household**
> Tab to or click **Allowances**, enter **4**
> Extra Withholding is **0.00**

> • All taxes should be selected under Subject to; if not, click to select.

Click **State** tab

• The Filing State for State Unemployment, State Disability, and State Withholding should be CA; if it is not, click the drop-down list, click **CA**.

Tab to or click **Allowances**, enter **4**

Tab to or click **Filing Status**, click the drop-down list arrow, click **Head of Household**

• Extra Withholding is **0.00** and Estimated Deductions are **0**.

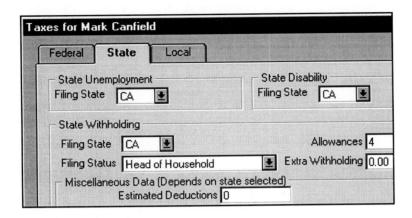

- There are no local taxes.

Click **OK**

Click **Sick/Vacation** button

Enter **40** as the Sick Hours available as of 07/01/**

- Accrual period should be Beginning of year, Hours accrued per accrual period should be 40.00, Maximum number of hours should be 120.00, Reset hours each new year? should *not* be selected.

Tab to or click **Vacation Hours available as of 07/01/****, enter **40**

- Accrual period should be Beginning of year, Hours accrued per accrual period should be 40.00, Maximum number of hours should be 120.00, Reset hours each new year? should *not* be selected.

    Click **OK**

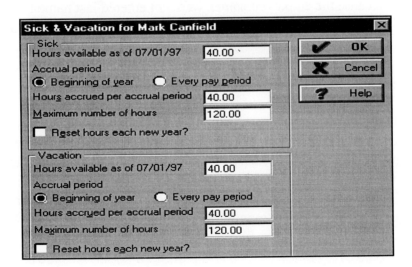

Click **OK** to add Mark Canfield

Click **Leave As Is** on the New Employee: Payroll Info (other)

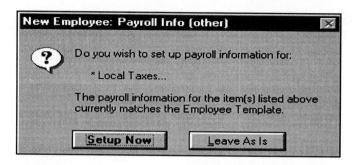

- Because the Local Taxes tab was not accessed, the New Employee: Payroll Info (other) dialog box appears. To avoid this dialog box when adding employees, click Local Taxes tab, then click OK.

Repeat the above procedures to add the other employees listed in the memo

- When complete, the employees list will show all four employees.

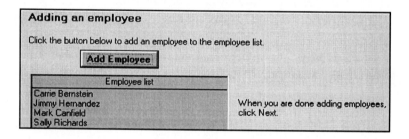

- Because the employee names were not entered last name then first name, the employee names are alphabetized by the first name.

ADD YEAR-TO-DATE AMOUNTS

The year-to-date amounts are summaries of employee paychecks, the liabilities, and the deductions for the year to date. Year-to-date amounts may be entered as an amount for the year to date, for each quarter to date, or for each month to date. Entering the amounts for the year is the fastest way to enter this historical information. Entering the amounts by the quarter allows each quarter to be summarized and allows quarterly reports to be created. Entering the information for each month will allow monthly payroll reports for each month from January 1.

MEMO
DATE: July 1, 19**

Enter the payroll summaries for each employee for 1/1/** through 6/30/**. Use the information provided in the following Employee Summary Table.

DO: Enter the year-to-date summary information for each employee

EMPLOYEE SUMMARY TABLE AS OF 06/30/**				
	Carrie Bernstein	**Jimmy Hernandez**	**Mark Canfield**	**Sally Richards**
Item Name	Officer Salary Regular	Hourly Regular Rate	Officer Salary Regular	Hourly Regular Rate
Period Amount	12,999.96	21,600.00	17,499.96	9,600.00
Hours for Period	960	960	960	960
Dental Insurance Employee	300.00	240.00	420.00	0
Medical Insurance Employee	600.00	480.00	900.00	0
Federal Withholding	1,752.00	2,364.00	1,632.00	756.00
Social Security Company	806.04	1,339.20	1,085.04	595.20
Social Security Employee	806.04	1,339.20	1,085.04	595.20
Medicare Company	188.52	313.20	253.80	139.20
Medicare Employee	188.52	313.20	253.80	139.20
Federal Unemployment	56.00	56.00	56.00	56.00
CA Withholding	379.80	1,035.72	183.24	84.12
CA Disability Employee	65.04	108.00	87.48	48.00
CA Unemployment Company	280.00	280.00	280.00	280.00

Select **Yes** for Have you already paid employees this year?

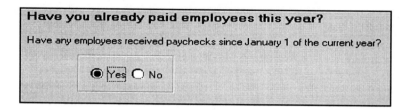

Click **Year to date** for the Employee YTD summary period

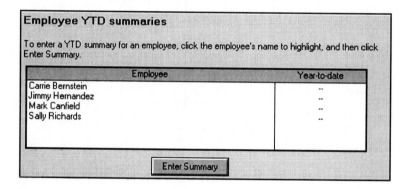

Carrie Bernstein should be selected, click **Enter Summary**
- Notice that the employees are listed in alphabetical order by first name.
- Notice that the column indicates Year-to-date.

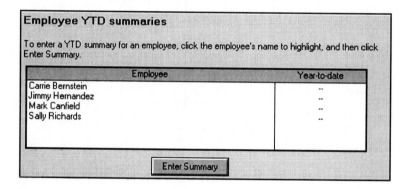

Enter the amounts listed in the table for Carrie
Year to Date is **06/30/**
Tab to or click **Period Amount**, enter **12999.96**
Tab to or click **Hours for Period**, enter **960**
Tab to or click **Period Amount** for **Dental Insurance (Emp)**, enter **300**
Continue the procedure until all the amounts are entered for Carrie

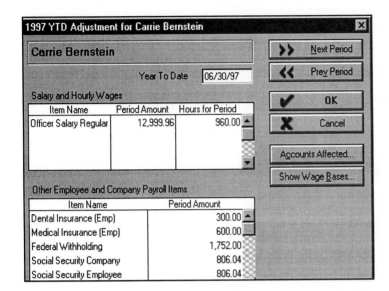

Click **OK** to record the Year-to-Date
Select **Do not affect accounts**, click **OK**

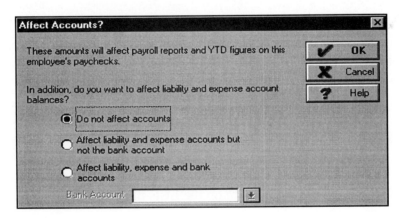

- Because VideoLand account balances have just been entered and are correct, the year-to-date balances should not affect any accounts. The other two choices are made if accounts are not in balance. For further details, click Help on the Affect Accounts screen.
- This is the only the time the Affect Accounts screen will appear.

Employee YTD summaries

To enter a YTD summary for an employee, click the employee's name to highlight, and then click Enter Summary.

Employee	Year-to-date
Carrie Bernstein	✓
Jimmy Hernandez	--
Mark Canfield	--
Sally Richards	--

[Enter Summary]

- Notice the ✔ in the Year-to-date column for Carrie.

Repeat the above procedures and enter the Year-to-Date summaries for the other employees

Select **No** for Have you paid any payroll taxes this year?

Select **No** for Liability Carryover

- YTD topic and Payroll Section are complete.

MENU SECTION

This section customizes the Lists menu and the Activities menu so that certain frequently used items will be displayed as a menu selection while other infrequently used items will be displayed as a subitem on the Other menu.

LISTS MENU TOPIC

This topic customizes the Lists menu. Infrequently used items will be placed as a subitem on the Other menu rather than as an individual item on the Lists menu.

MEMO

DATE: July 1, 19**

Customize the Lists menu. Select Yes for the To Do list.

DO: Customize List menu as indicated in the memo
        Click **Yes** for To Do list

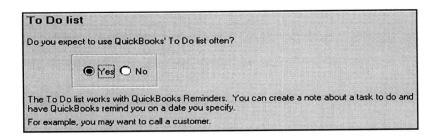

- The List menu topic is complete.

ACTIVITIES MENU TOPIC

This topic organizes items on the Activities menu so that unneeded items are placed out of the way. Infrequently used items are placed on the Other menu at the end of the Activities menu.

MEMO
DATE: July 1, 19**

We do not charge customers finance charges nor do we wish to use QuickBooks for budgeting at this time.

DO: Indicate that finance charges and budgeting items will not be used frequently
Click **No** for Finance Charges and click **No** for Budgets

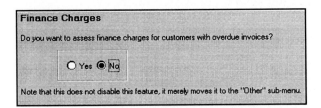

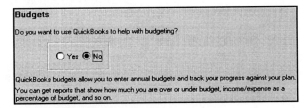

- Access Finance Charges and Set Up Budgets items will be placed on the Activities Other menu.
- Activities Menu topic and Menu Items section are now complete.

DOCUMENTS SECTION

The Documents Sections actually contains five documents designed to provide additional information about entering historical transactions, handling petty cash, combining personal and business expenses, using QuickBooks for contract management, and ordering QuickBooks supplies. It is suggested that each document be read and/or printed.

Documents

We have created some Help documents that explain how to handle some common situations that occur when using QuickBooks. The following documents are available:
- Entering historical transactions (highly recommended)
- Handling petty cash
- Combining personal and business expenses
- Using QuickBooks for contact management
- Ordering QuickBooks supplies

In this section, you will be given a chance to view each document. You may also print them out if you like.

MEMO

DATE: July 1, 19**

None of the items listed applies to VideoLand at this time. Complete the EasyStep Interview.

DO: Go through each screen in the Documents section, view each document
Read the screen for Finishing Up the QuickBooks EasyStep Interview

Finishing Up

This is the end of the EasyStep Interview.

You have still not completed all of the topics of the interview. To finish up, click on any unchecked tabs on the right hand side of the interview and then finish the unchecked topics in that section. If you would like to leave the interview at this time and come back later to finish it click Leave.

Click **Leave** to exit the EasyStep Interview

PREFERENCES

Many preferences for the use of QuickBooks are selected during the EasyStep Interview. However, there may be some preferences you would like to select in addition to those marked during the interview. The Preferences section has 12 areas that may be customized: accounting, checking, finance charge, general, iconbar, menus, purchases and vendors, reminders, reports and graphs, sales and customers, sales tax, and tax: 1099. Not all the possible changes will be discussed during this chapter; however, some of the choices will be explored.

MEMO

DATE: July 1, 19**

Open the Preferences screen and explore the choices available for each of the 12 areas.

 DO: In the following sections, click on the icons for the category and explore the choices available, but do not make any changes

ACCOUNTING PREFERENCES

 This screen is accessed to select the use of account numbers. Selecting Use Account Numbers provides an area for each account to be given a number during editing. Use audit trail is an important choice if you want QuickBooks to track all transactions (including any and all changes made to transactions). This allows an owner to see everything that has been entered, including deleted transactions, error corrections, etc. This is an important choice if there is a possibility of an employee's making unauthorized changes.

CHECKING PREFERENCES

 The preferences listed for checking allows QuickBooks to print names and addresses on check vouchers, warn of duplicate check numbers, change the check date when a check is printed, and start with the payee field on a check.

FINANCE CHARGE PREFERENCES

 This preference allows you to provide information about finance charges if they are collected. You can even tell QuickBooks if you want to collect finance charges. The information you may provide includes the annual interest rate, the minimum finance charge, the grace period, the finance charge account, and whether to calculate finance charges from the due date or from the invoice/billed date.

GENERAL PREFERENCES

 General preferences is used to indicate when to save the desktop, to set the time format, to indicate decimal point placement, to set warning screens and beeps, to turn on messages, and to hide Qcards.

ICONBAR PREFERENCES

 This preference allows you to choose whether or not to use the iconbar. If you use the iconbar, it may be customized to add icons, delete icons, and edit icons. You may also select whether or not to show the icons and text, the icons without text, or text only.

MENUS PREFERENCES

 Menus preferences allow you to select the items you want to move to the "Other" menu on the Activities Menu and the Lists Menu. These choices were also made at the end of the EasyStep Interview. If you decide to make a change, simply access this preference and make your selection.

PAYROLL & EMPLOYEES PREFERENCES

 Payroll preferences include selecting the payroll features, if any, you wish to use. Items for printing on checks and vouchers are selected. You may choose the method by which employees are sorted. The Employee template may be accessed from this screen. Once accessed, the Employee template may be changed and/or modified.

PURCHASES & VENDORS PREFERENCES

This section allows you to activate the inventory and purchase orders feature of the program. Warnings if there is not enough inventory to sell, warnings regarding duplicate purchases orders, and warnings for duplicate bill numbers are set on this screen. The number of days for bill due dates is also selected in the Purchases and Vendors preferences.

REMINDERS PREFERENCES

Items to include on the Reminders list are selected in the Reminders preferences. In this section you may also select whether or not to have the Reminders list appear when the QuickBooks program is started.

REPORTS & GRAPHS PREFERENCES

Accrual or cash reporting is selected on this screen. Preferences for report aging and account display within reports are selected in this section. Drawing graphs in 2D or using patterns is an available option. In addition, report formats may be customized on this screen. In previous chapters we have changed the report format to remove the current date by accessing this preference.

SALES & CUSTOMERS PREFERENCES

Shipping methods, markup percentages, and usual FOB (free on board) preferences may be indicated on this screen. In addition, selections to automatically apply payments, to track reimbursed expenses as income, and to warn about duplicate invoice numbers are made in this section.

SALES TAX PREFERENCES

The Sales Tax preferences indicate whether or not you charge sales tax. If you do collect sales tax, when you need to pay the sales tax, when sales tax is owed, the most common sales tax, and whether or not to mark taxable amounts with a "T" are selected on this screen.

TAX: 1099

 This preference is used to indicate whether or not you file 1099-MISC forms. If you do file 1099s, you are given categories; and you may select accounts and thresholds for the categories on this screen.

CHART OF ACCOUNTS

Using the EasyStep Interview to set up a company is a user-friendly way to establish the basic structure of the company. However, the Chart of Accounts created by QuickBooks may not be the exact Chart of Accounts you wish to use in your business. The Chart of Accounts is not only a listing of the account names and balances but also the General Ledger used by the business. As in textbook accounting, the General Ledger/Chart of Accounts is the book of final entry. In earlier chapters instructions directed you to view the Register for an account. This is actually a procedure used to view all of the transaction details listed for one General Ledger account.

In many of the earlier chapters, account names were changed, accounts were deleted, and accounts were made inactive. This was done to give you experience in customizing a QuickBooks Chart of Accounts/General Ledger. In QuickBooks your General Ledger accounts may or may not have account numbers. If your company uses account numbers, they must be added after the EasyStep Interview is complete. To add account numbers, each account must be edited individually.

MEMO

DATE: July 1, 19**

Since VideoLand does not use account numbers, they do not need to be added. However, the Chart of Accounts/General Ledger should be customized by:

<u>Deleting</u>: Freight Income, Reimbursed Expenses, Resale Discounts, Resale Income, Automobile Expense, Franchise Fees, Mortgage Interest Expense, Property Taxes, Travel & Ent.

<u>Changing the name</u>: Opening Bal Equity to **Daniel Lee, Capital** (Type: Income) Sales Discounts to (Type: Income) **Purchases Discounts**

<u>Making inactive</u>: Cash Discounts, Contributions

<u>Adding</u>: (Type: Equity) **Daniel Lee, Investment** (Balance of $5,000), Subaccount of Daniel Lee, Capital

(Type: Equity) **Daniel Lee, Drawing**, Subaccount of Daniel Lee, Capital (Balance $0.00)

(Type: Cost of Goods Sold) **Purchases Discounts**, Subaccount of **Cost of Goods Sold**

(Type: Expense) **Hourly Wages**, Subaccount of **Payroll Expenses**

DO: Make the changes indicated above

Open the Chart of Accounts as instructed in previous chapters

Position the cursor on **Freight Income**, **Ctrl+D**, click **OK** to delete

Repeat to delete the other accounts listed in the memo

Position the cursor on **Opening Bal Equity**, click **Account** button, click **Edit**, enter **Daniel Lee, Capital** as the account name, click **OK**

Repeat basic procedures to rename the other accounts listed in the memo

Position the cursor on **Cash Discounts**, click **Account** button, click **Make Inactive**

Repeat basic procedures to make the other account listed in the memo inactive

Click **Account** button, click **New**, click drop-down list arrow next to **Type**, click **Equity**, Tab to or click **Name**, enter **Daniel Lee, Investment**, click **Subaccount**, click **Daniel Lee, Capital**, tab to or click **Balance**, enter **5000**, (if necessary, enter **07/01/98** as the date), click **OK**

Repeat basic procedures to add the other accounts listed in the memo

When all changes have been made, print the Chart of Accounts

CUSTOMER INFORMATION

When customers were added during the EasyStep Interview, only the customer names and balances were entered. QuickBooks actually keeps much more detailed information regarding customers. This includes a customer's name, address, telephone and fax numbers, credit terms, credit limits, and sales tax information. This detailed information must be added after the EasyStep Interview is completed. The Customer list is also known as the Accounts Receivable Subsidiary Ledger. Whenever a transaction is entered for a customer, it is automatically posted to the General Ledger account and the Accounts Receivable Subsidiary Ledger account.

MEMO

DATE: July 1, 19**

Add information for the customers (all terms are Net 30, all customers are taxable, and pay CA Sales Tax):

Goldman, Barney: 1980 A Street, San Diego, CA 92101; 619-555-3694; credit limit $500.

Mirovich, Randolph: 719 4th Avenue, San Diego, CA 92101; 619-555-5478; credit limit $1000.

Robinson, Yolanda: 37601 State Street, San Diego, CA 92101; 619-555-2235; credit limit $750.

Thatcher, Rafael: 2210 Columbia Street, San Diego, CA 92101; 619-555-7632; credit limit $300.

DO: Add the customer information to each customer's account
Open Customer list as described in previous chapters
Click **Goldman, Barney**, **Ctrl+E** to edit, tab to or click in the fields where information is to be entered on the Address Info and Additional Info tabs, enter the appropriate information for each tab, click OK when finished
Repeat for each customer
Print the Customer:Job list, click **Customer:Job** button, click **Print List**, click **Print**

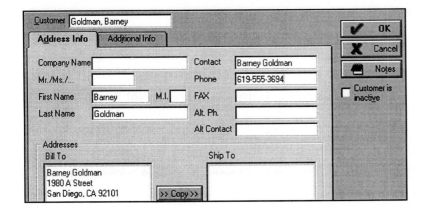

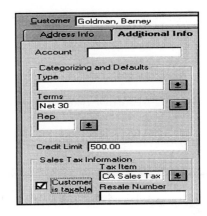

VENDOR INFORMATION

When vendors were added during the EasyStep Interview, only the vendor names and balances were entered. QuickBooks actually keeps much more detailed information regarding vendors. This includes the vendor's name, address, contact person, telephone and fax numbers, credit terms, and credit limits. This detailed information must be added after the EasyStep Interview is completed. The Vendor list is also known as the Accounts Payable Subsidiary Ledger. Whenever a transaction is entered for a vendor, it is automatically posted to the General Ledger account and the Accounts Payable Ledger account.

MEMO

DATE: July 1, 19**

Add the information for the individual vendors (all terms are 2% 10 Net 30):

Movies Galore: 7758 Broadway Avenue, San Diego, CA 92101; Contact Dori Kwan; 619-555-4489; 619-555-9844; $10,000

The Rental Company: 2687 University Avenue, San Diego, CA 92110; Contact Valerie Green; 619-555-2589; 619-555-9852; $5,000

Video Supplies: 10855 Western Avenue, Los Angeles, CA 90012; Contact Dennis Gonzalez; 310-555-6971; 310-555-1796; $15,000

The vendors who receive tax and withholding payments need to be added. There are no terms and no credit limits:

Employment Development Department; 10327 Wilshire Boulevard, Los Angeles, CA 90007; 310-555-8877

State Bank; 302 Second Street, San Diego, CA 92114; 619-555-9889

Medical and Dental Ins., Inc.; 20865 Wilshire Boulevard, Santa Monica, CA 90321; 310-555-4646

DO: Add the information for the vendors listed above
Open the Vendor list as described in previous chapters
Click **Movies Galore**, **Ctrl+E** to edit, tab to, or click in the fields where
     information is to be entered on the Address Info and the Additional Info tabs,
     enter the appropriate information for each field, click **OK** when finished

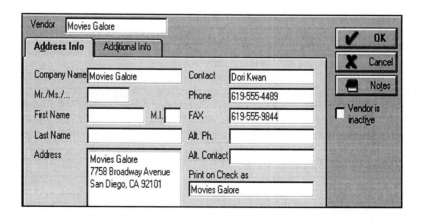

Repeat for each vendor
Print the **Vendor list**, click **Vendor:Job** button, click **Print List**, click **Print**

EMPLOYEES

As with customers and vendors, employees may be added, deleted, or made inactive at any time. When you use the Employee list to add a new employee, the Employee template appears on the screen, and you fill in the blanks just as you did during the EasyStep Interview.

MEMO
DATE: July 1, 19**

A new part-time employee was hired today. Rosa Jenkins will work on the weekends and will be paid an hourly rate of $6.00. Her address is: 151 B Street, San Diego, CA 92101; Phone 619-555-3611; Social Security No. 100-55-2151. Because she is a part-time employee, she will not be eligible for dental insurance or medical insurance nor will she accumulate any vacation hours or sick hours. Both her federal and state withholding are for Single with 0 Allowances. Her birthday is 12/07/79.

DO: Add the new employee, Rosa Jenkins
Click **List** menu **Employees**, or click **Employees** on the QuickBooks Navigator **Payroll and Employees** tab
Click **Employee** button at the bottom of the Employee list
Click **New**

Complete the information for Rosa on the Address Info, Additional Info, and
Payroll Tabs following the steps provided in the EasyStep Interview and using
the information provided in the above memo
Click **Employees** button at the bottom of the Employee list, click **Print List**

PAYROLL ITEMS

Payroll tax liabilities and payroll withholding items need to be associated with a vendor. When
payroll liabilities are paid, QuickBooks will automatically prepare one check for each vendor.
For example, all of the federal tax items will be consolidated into one check made payable to one
vendor. Federal tax liabilities are usually paid through a local bank so the check for VideoLand's
federal tax liabilities will be made to State Bank.

MEMO
DATE: July 1, 19**

Associate Payroll Items with the appropriate vendors:

Medical Insurance and Dental Insurance with Medical and Dental Ins., Inc.
Federal Unemployment, Federal Withholding, Medicare Company, Medicare
Employee, Social Security Company, Social Security Employee with State Bank
CA Withholding, CA Disability Employee, and CA Unemployment Company with
Employment Development Department.

DO: Associate Payroll Items and Vendors
Click **Lists**, click **Payroll Items**
Double-click **Dental Insurance**, click drop-down list arrow next to **Payable To**,
click Medical and Dental Ins., Inc., click **OK**

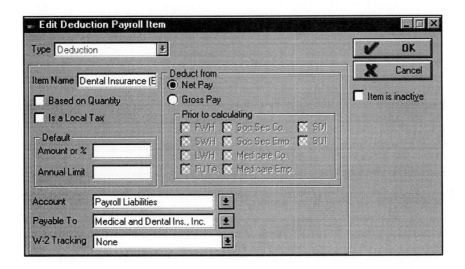

Repeat for all the other Payroll Items
- Note the screens for the Federal and State taxes will be different from the above. The Federal Unemployment and Medicare screens are shown below:

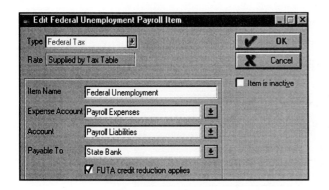 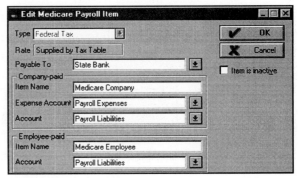

Print the **Payroll Item list**, close the **list**

ADJUSTING ENTRIES

In Chapters 4 and 7, adjusting entries were made to transfer the balances of the Uncategorized Income and Uncategorized Expenses accounts into the owner's capital account (original account name: Opening Balance Equity account). When the EasyStep Interview is completed, all existing balances are placed into the Uncategorized Income and Uncategorized Expenses accounts so that the amounts listed will not be interpreted as income or expenses for the current period. This adjustment transfers the amount of income and expenses recorded prior to the current period into the owner's capital account. In actual practice this adjustment would be made at the completion of the EasyStep Interview.

MEMO
DATE: July 1, 19**

Carrie: Make the adjusting entry to transfer Uncategorized Income and Uncategorized Expenses to Daniel Lee's capital account.

DO: Transfer the Uncategorized Income and Expenses as indicated above

Open the Chart of Accounts, double-click on the account **Uncategorized Income**, enter the to and from dates as **07/01/****, tab to generate the report, note the amount of Uncategorized Income **$1,025.00**, close the report

Repeat to determine the balance of the Uncategorized Expenses account

Click **Activities** button at the bottom of the Chart of Accounts, click **Make Journal Entry**

Enter the date **07/01/****

Tab to or click **Account**, click the drop-down list arrow, click **Uncategorized Income**, tab to or click **Debit** enter **1025**, tab to or click **Account**, click the drop-down list arrow, click **Daniel Lee, Capital**, click **>>Next**

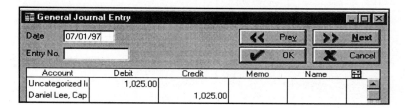

Use the above transaction and the information presented in Chapters 4 and 7 as a guide to enter the adjustment to transfer the amount of **Uncategorized Expenses** to **Daniel Lee, Capital**, click **OK**

• Remember, you will debit the capital account and credit the uncategorized expenses account.

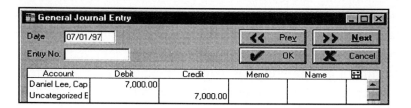

SPECIFYING A COMPANY LOGO:

If you have a special symbol or logo for your company, QuickBooks allows this logo to be printed on checks, paychecks, sales, and purchase forms. The logo must be a bitmap file (the filename has an extension of .bmp) and is added to the desired forms and checks via the printer setup or by customizing a business form.

MEMO

       DATE: July 1, 19**

 Add VideoLand's name, address, and logo to checks, paychecks, invoice and purchase order.

DO: Add the VideoLand logo to the above items
- Before completing this portion of the chapter, you should have a copy of the file **VL_Logo.bmp** on the data disk you are using to create the company. The **VL_Logo.bmp** file is located on the master data disk that you obtain from your instructor. Instructions for copying the file in Windows 95 using the Explorer are: The disk containing **Video.qbw** is in **A:**, insert the master data disk that you obtain from your instructor in **B:**, open Windows 95 Explorer, click **3½ Floppy (B:)** on the left side of the window, click **VL_Logo.bmp** on the right side of the window, right-click **VL_Logo.bmp**, click **Send To**, click **3½ Floppy (A)**, close Explorer. If you do not have two disk drives or you have a different configuration in your classroom, check with your instructor for specific instructions to copy the logo file.

Click **File** menu, click **Printer Setup**, click **Check/Paycheck**, click **Print company name and address**, click **Use Logo**

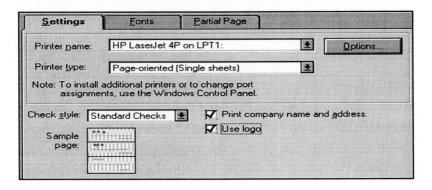

Click **File** button on **Select Logo** screen

Click **a:** for the drive location, if **vl_logo.bmp** is not shown in **File Name**, click
   vl_logo.bmp, click **OK**

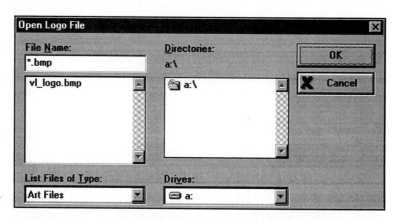

• When you return to the Logo screen, the logo will be displayed as Selected
Logo.

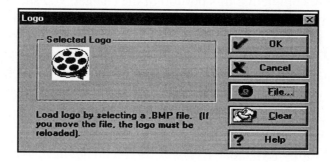

Click **OK** on Logo screen, click **OK** on Printer Setup

Add the Logo to an Invoice:
   Open Invoice, click the drop-down list arrow next to **Customized Invoice**,
   click **Customize...**, Customized Invoice should be selected (click to select if
   necessary), click **Edit**

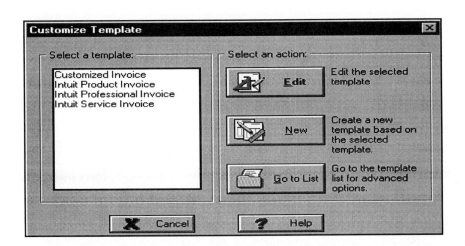

Click **Options** tab, click **Print Company Name**, click **Print Company Address**, click **Use Logo** (if necessary, click **Specify** button), repeat the procedures used to add the logo to the checks/paychecks to select vl_logo.bmp for the logo

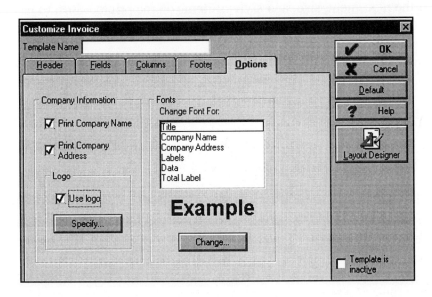

Click **OK**, click **Preview** button on the invoice to view the invoice with the logo, click **Zoom In** to get a close-up view of the logo, click **Close** to close the blank invoice, click **Cancel**

Follow the procedures used for the invoice to add the name, address, and logo to a purchase order

• If your name makes the company name longer than one line, use only your last name as part of the company name.

Invoice Logo

Purchase Order Logo

CUSTOMIZE FORMS

In addition to adding a logo, forms used by QuickBooks may be customized to change the fields (information areas) used, heading information, columns arrangement, footer information (something appearing at the bottom of the form), and the print size and style (font). The Layout Designer allows the placement, size, and style of items on the printed form to be changed and customized.

QuickBooks allows you to design your own forms for use by creating a custom form template for your business.

MEMO

DATE: July 1, 19**

Customize the Invoice by changing the word Invoice in the header to **INVOICE**, deselect the PROJECT field for printing, change the font for the company name to Arial 16. Use Layout Designer to change the width of the RATE column on the printed Invoice form.

DO: Customize the Invoice as indicated above

Open an Invoice, click the drop-down list arrow next to **Customized Invoice**, click **Customize...**, Customized Invoice should be selected (click to select if necessary), click **Edit** button

Delete the title **Invoice** on the **Header** tab, enter **INVOICE** as the title

Click **Fields** tab, click the **Print** box for **PROJECT** to deselect

Click **Options** tab, click **Company Name** in Change Font For, click **Change** button

Use the scroll bar and scroll to **Arial**, click **Arial** as the font
- Note: The font governs the shape and form of the letter. The default print style is Times Roman. Not all printers will support all print styles. If your printer does not have Times New Roman or Arial, select a different font for the company name.

Look at the **Sample** box to see the change in the letter shape and form as you change from Times Roman to Arial

Click 16 as the **Size** of the font

Click **OK** on **Example**

Click **Layout Designer** button

Scroll through the Invoice, click in the **Rate** column, position the cursor on the line on the left side of the column, hold down the primary mouse button (the cursor will turn into a large ◄╫► line with arrows on the left and right side), drag the column line to the right until it matches the vertical line for P.O. No., release the mouse, click **OK**

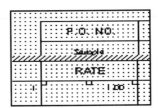

Click **OK** on Customize Invoice
- Notice the change in INVOICE on the Create Invoice screen.

Click **Preview** to view the Invoice, click **Zoom In** to enlarge the Invoice
- Notice the larger size print and the different print style on the company name.

Invoice Heading

Click **Close** to close the preview, click **Print** to print a blank custom invoice
- If you find that the company name prints on more than one line, just use your last name. You will need to change the company name via Company Info.

CUSTOMIZING REPORTS

As with the business forms, reports may also be customized to better reflect the information or a format required by a business. In earlier chapters, report formats were customized when the current date was no longer printed as part of the header.

MEMO

DATE: July 1, 19**

Customize Report formats by deselecting the current date from the header and by enlarging the Company Name to Arial 16.

DO: Make the changes indicated in the memo
Select Report & Graph Preferences as instructed previously
Verify the reporting preference of **Accrual**
Click **Format** button
Scroll through **Change Font For**, click **Company Name**, click **Change Font** button

Font should be **Arial** (if not, scroll through fonts, click Arial), click **16** for **Size**, click **OK**

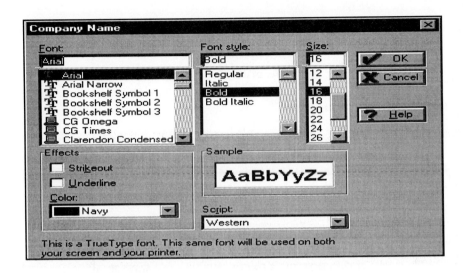

- Notice the TT symbol next to Arial in the Font selections. The TT stands for a TrueType font. This means that the font will appear the same on the printed copy as it does on the computer screen.

Click **Yes** to Change all related fonts

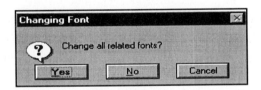

Click **Header/Footer** button on Report Format Preferences, click **Date Prepared** to deselect, click **OK** on Format Header/Footer, click **OK** on Report Format Preferences, click **OK** on Preferences

Print a Standard Balance Sheet for **07/01/****

VideoLand (Your Name)
Balance Sheet
As of July 1, 1997

	Jul 1, '97
Total Liabilities	14,000.00
Equity	
Daniel Lee, Capital	
Daniel Lee, Investment	5,000.00
Daniel Lee, Capital - Other	38,861.00
Total Daniel Lee, Capital	43,861.00
Total Equity	43,861.00
TOTAL LIABILITIES & EQUITY	**57,861.00**

Partial Report

BACKUP

As in previous chapters, a backup of the data file for Video.qbw should be made.

DO: Back up **Video.qbw** to **Video.qbb** as instructed in earlier chapters

SUMMARY

In this chapter a company was created using the EasyStep Interview provided by QuickBooks. Once the interview was complete, the company Chart of Accounts/General Ledger was customized. Detailed information was given for customers and vendors. An Employee template was created, and employees were added. Employee year-to-date payroll and earnings figures were entered. Adjusting entries were made. A logo was added to forms. An Invoice was customized, and reports were customized.

END-OF-CHAPTER QUESTIONS

TRUE/FALSE

ANSWER THE FOLLOWING QUESTIONS IN THE SPACE PROVIDED BEFORE THE QUESTION NUMBER.

_____ 1. You must return to the EasyStep Interview to add additional employees, customers, and vendors.

_____ 2. A company may be created without using the EasyStep Interview.

_____ 3. The TT symbol next to a font means that the font will appear the same on the printed copy as it does on the computer screen.

_____ 4. A company logo is a group of alphabetic symbols representing the company name.

_____ 5. The start date is the date you select to give QuickBooks the financial information for your company.

_____ 6. The EasyStep Interview allows you to include the balances for all asset accounts.

_____ 7. When selecting company preferences from the Preferences menu, select Sales & Customers Preferences to indicate whether or not you charge sales tax.

_____ 8. When using the EasyStep Interview to set up income and expenses, you must type in the name of every income and expense account you use.

_____ 9. The Additional Info tab for an employee is where custom fields may be created and is used for information such as an employee's birthday.

_____ 10. Customer addresses, credit terms, and credit limits are entered during the EasyStep Interview.

MULTIPLE CHOICE

WRITE THE LETTER OF THE CORRECT ANSWER IN THE SPACE PROVIDED BEFORE THE QUESTION NUMBER.

_____ 1. To use account numbers, select ___ Preferences from the list of preferences.
A. General
B. Accounting
C. Menus
D. Iconbar

_____ 2. The Start Date is provided in the ___ section of the EasyStep Interview.
A. Preferences
B. Menu
C. General
D. Details

_____ 3. When adding a new employee, you use the ___.
A. Employee Template
B. Employee File
C. Employee Roster
D. Employee Menu

_____ 4. The EasyStep Interview is accessed on the ___.
A. File Menu
B. QuickBooks Navigator Company Preferences screen
C. Activities Menu
D. All of the above

_____ 5. The number of employees and the use of the payroll feature are indicated in the ___ of the EasyStep Interview.
A. Payroll section
B. Preferences topic
C. Documents section
D. Menu Items topic

_____ 6. In the EasyStep Interview, section tabs are located on the ___ of the screen and topic tabs are located on the ___ of the screen.
A. left side, bottom
B. top, right side
C. left side, top
D. right side, top

_____ 7. Select the use of a(n) ___ to keep track of all transactions—including those that have been deleted.
A. General Journal
B. summary report
C. audit trail
D. unedited transaction list

_____ 8. A company logo for checks and paychecks is selected on the ___.
A. File menu, Printer Setup
B. Customized check form, Customize button
C. both of the above
D. none of the above

_____ 9. Items for the Reminders list may be selected ___.
A. during the EasyStep Interview
B. on the Reminders Preferences after the interview
C. by clicking the Reminders button at the bottom of the list
D. all of the above

_____ 10. Accounts that are listed individually but are grouped together under a main account are called ___.
A. dependent accounts
B. secondary accounts
C. mini-accounts
D. subaccounts

FILL-IN

IN THE SPACE PROVIDED, WRITE THE ANSWER THAT MOST APPROPRIATELY COMPLETES THE SENTENCE.

1. When the EasyStep Interview is completed, all existing balances are placed into the _____ and the _____ accounts.

2. Year-to-date payroll summaries may be added for _____, _____, or the _____.

3. When you complete the Opening Balances section of the EasyStep Interview, opening balances are given for _____, _____, and _____ accounts.

4. The Menu section allows you to customize the _____ menu and the _____ menu.

5. Another name for the Chart of Accounts is the _____.

SHORT ESSAY

List the seven sections in the EasyStep Interview and describe the portion of the company setup completed in each section.

_____

_____

_____

_____

_____

_____

END-OF-CHAPTER PROBLEM

THE SWEET SHOP

The Sweet Shop is a fictitious company that sells candy, pastries, and coffee. The Sweet Shop is located in San Francisco, California, and is a sole proprietorship owned by Angela Sloan. Ms. Sloan is involved in all aspects of the business. The Sweet Shop has a full-time employee who is paid a salary—Mr. Alan Tremain, who manages the store, is responsible for the all the employees, and keeps the books. There is one full-time hourly employee, who works in the shop, Margo Lewis.

CREATE A NEW COMPANY

Use the EasyStep Interview to create a new company.

The Sweet Shop--Your Name is used for both the Company Name and the Legal Name Address: 550 Geary Street, San Francisco, CA 94102. Tax ID 456-22-1346, tax year and fiscal year both begin in July, Other/None is the tax form used.

The following includes information that will help you answer some of the EasyStep Interview questions: The Sweet Shop is a retail business. It does have an inventory. The file for the company should be **Sweet.QBW**. Use the disk in **A:**. It does collect sales tax for California at the rate of 7.25%. The California sales tax is payable to the State Board of Equalization. The Sweet Shop uses a Custom invoice. As previously stated, there are two employees. QuickBooks payroll feature will be used. No estimates, time tracking, reimbursable expenses, or classes will be given or used. Bills will be entered first and paid later. The Reminders list should show on startup. The company start date is 07/01/**. (Remember to check with your instructor to determine the tax table year used. The tax table year will be the same year you will use in this problem.) The Sweet Shop does not have any service items, non-inventory part items, or other charge items. There are no lines of credit. The To Do list will be used often. The Sweet Shop will not charge finance charges and does not want to use QuickBooks for budgeting.

CHART OF ACCOUNTS

Use the following Chart of Accounts and balances as you answer the EasyStep Interview questions. (Type abbreviations: C.A.=Current Asset, F.A.=Fixed Asset, C.L.=Current Liability, COGS=Cost of Goods Sold. ***Balance is generated by QuickBooks. Only Balance Sheet accounts have balances. Accounts that are indented are subaccounts of the preceding account that is not indented—for example, Loan Interest is a subaccount of Interest Expense.) This chart will appear on two pages. You will need to look at the end of the first column on the second page of the chart before using the second column. Liability Insurance at the top of the second column is a subaccount of Insurance near the bottom of the first column.

THE SWEET SHOP CHART OF ACCOUNTS				
ACCOUNT	**TYPE**	**BALANCE**	**ACCOUNT**	**TYPE**
Checking	Bank	25,875.15	Liability Insurance	Expense
Accounts Receivable	Accts. Rec.	***	Interest Expense	Expense
Inventory Asset	Other C.A	***	Finance Charge	Expense
Office Supplies	Other C.A.	500.00	Loan Interest	Expense
Prepaid Insurance	Other C.A.	600.00	Licenses and Permits	Expense
Sales Supplies	Other C.A.	1,000.00	Miscellaneous	Expense
Store Equipment	F.A.	6,000.00	Payroll Expenses	Expense
Store Equipment: Depreciation	F.A.	0.00	Hourly Wages	Expense
Store Equipment: Original Cost	F.A.	6,000.00	Officer Salary	Expense
Store Fixtures	F.A.	10,000.00	Postage and Delivery	Expense
Store Fixtures: Depreciation	F.A.	0.00	Printing and Reproduction	Expense
Store Fixtures: Original Cost	F.A.	10,000.00	Professional Fees	Expense
Accounts Payable	Acct. Pay.	***	Accounting	Expense
MasterCard (6/30/97)	Credit Card	250.00	Legal Fees	Expense
Payroll Liabilities	Other C.L.	0.00	Rent	Expense
Sales Tax Payable	Other C.L.	0.00	Repairs	Expense
Store Equipment Loan	Long Term L.	1,000.00	Building Repairs	Expense
Store Fixtures Loan	Long Term L.	4,000.00	Computer Repairs	Expense
Angela Sloan, Capital	Equity	***	Equipment Repairs	Expense
Angela Sloan, Drawing	Equity	0.00	Storage	Expense
Angela Sloan, Investment	Equity	5,000.00	Supplies	Expense
Retained Earnings	Equity	***	Marketing	Expense
Purchases Discounts	Income		Office	Expense
Candy Sales	Income		Sales Supplies	Expense
Coffee Sales	Income		Taxes	Expense
Pastry Sales	Income		Federal	Expense
Uncategorized Income	Income		Local	Expense
Cost of Goods Sold	COGS		State	Expense
Purchases Discounts	COGS		Telephone	Expense

Bank Service Charges	Expense		Uncategorized Expenses	Expense	
Depreciation Expense	Expense		Utilities	Expense	
Dues and Subscriptions	Expense		Gas and Electric	Expense	
Equipment Rental	Expense		Water	Expense	
Filing Fees	Expense		Interest Income	Other Income	
Insurance	Expense		Other Income	Other Income	
Disability Insurance	Expense		Other Expenses	Other Expense	
Fire Insurance	Expense				

ITEMS LIST

Use the following Inventory Items list and balances as you answer the EasyStep Interview questions.

INVENTORY ITEMS			
Item Name	**Candy**	**Coffee**	**Pastries**
Sales Description	Candy Sales	Coffee Sales	Pastry Sales
Sales Price	0.00	0.00	0.00
Taxable Item	Yes	Yes	Yes
Income Account	Candy Sales	Coffee Sales	Pastry Sales
Purchase Description	Candy	Coffee	Pastries
Cost	5.00	5.00	0.50
Reorder Point	100	100	100
Quantity on Hand	2,000	2,000	500
Value	10,000	10,000	250

CUSTOMER LIST

Use the following Customer list and balances as you answer the EasyStep Interview questions.

Ralston, Inc., 785 Nob Hill, San Francisco, CA 94102, Contact Sally James, Phone 415-555-8762, Fax 415-555-2678, Net 30, Credit Limit $1,500, Balance $1,350, Taxable.

Maurice Walker, 253 Mason Street, San Francisco, CA 94102, Phone 415-555-2264, Net 30, Credit Limit $350, Balance $350, Taxable. (Enter his last name, first name for Customer:Job. Enter his first name then last name for Bill To address.)

VENDOR LIST

Use the following Vendor list and balances as you answer the EasyStep Interview questions.

Cranston Coffee Importers, 559 7th Street, San Francisco, CA 94104, Contact Alexis Sams, Phone 415-555-2788, Fax 415-555-8872, 2% 10 Net 30, Credit Limit $15,000, Balance $1,000

Pastry Perfection, 785 Market Street, San Francisco, CA 94103, Contact Colleen Jones, Phone 415-555-3184, Fax 415-555-4813, 2% 10 Net 30, Credit Limit $5,000, Balance $500

Confections, Inc. 1095 8th Street, San Francisco, CA 94104, Contact Ron Raymond, Phone 415-555-5759, Fax 415-555-9575, 2% 10 Net 30, Credit Limit $15,000, Balance $800

Employment Development Department; 10327 Washington Street, San Francisco, CA 94107; Phone 415-555-8877 (Used for California Taxes and Withholding)

State Bank; 302 Second Street, San Francisco, CA 94104; Phone 415-555-9889 (Used for all Federal Taxes and Withholding)

Medical and Dental Ins., Inc.; 20865 Oak Street, San Francisco, CA 94101; Phone 415-555-4646 (Used for Medical and Dental Insurance deductions)

EMPLOYEE LIST

Use the following information, Employee list and year-to-date balances as you answer the EasyStep Interview questions.

Only the information that needs to be entered is given below. If information is not provided, it is 0. Filing State is California, State Unemployment Tax Rate is 4%, FUTA is 0.8%. Employees are paid hourly and salary. The Sweet Shop does want to track Hourly Regular Rate, Overtime Hourly Rate 1, Officer Salary Regular, Officer Sick Regular, Officer Vac Regular. There is employee paid medical. Select *all* the federal taxes for employees. Track vacation and sick time. Hours are given at the beginning of the year, 40 hours per accrual period, maximum number of hours are 80. Hours are not reset at the beginning of the year. Employees are paid semi-monthly.

Mr. Alan Tremain, 177 Post Street, San Francisco, CA 94101; Phone 415-555-1222; Social Security No. 100-55-5259; Hired 02/17/95; Birthday 11/28/49; Officer Salary Regular $24,000; Medical $30; Federal: Single, 1 Allowance; State: Single, 1 Allowance; Sick 40 hrs; Vacation 40 hrs

Mrs. Margo Lewis, 833 Pine Street, San Francisco, CA 94102; Phone 415-555-7862; Social Security No. 100-55-6456; Hired 04/03/96; Birthday 12/07/70; Hourly Regular Rate $10 per hour; Medical $20; Federal: Married, 3 Allowances; State: Married (two incomes), 3 Allowances

EMPLOYEE SUMMARY TABLE AS OF 06/30/**		
	Alan Tremain	**Margo Lewis**
Item Name	Officer Salary Regular	Hourly Regular Rate
Period Amount	12,000.00	9,600.00
Hours for Period	960	960
Medical Insurance Employee	360.00	240.00
Federal Withholding	1,404.00	360.00
Social Security Company	744.00	595.20
Social Security Employee	744.00	595.20
Medicare Company	174.00	139.20
Medicare Employee	174.00	139.20
Federal Unemployment	56.00	56.00
CA Withholding	286.32	92.16
CA Disability Employee	60.00	48.00
CA Unemployment Company	280.00	280.00

MAKE ADJUSTMENTS

Change the accounts for The Sweet Shop as necessary so they are identical to the Chart of Accounts provided. Print a Chart of Accounts.

Add customer and vendor information. Print a Customer list and a Vendor list.

Associate Payroll Items with Vendors as indicated in the vendor table. Print a Payroll Item list.

Add a new part-time hourly employee: Jason Alexander, 1177 Front Street, San Francisco, CA 94101; Phone 415-555-7766; Social Security No. 100-55-3625; Hired 07/01/**; Birthday 12/21/76; Hourly Regular Rate $6.50; Federal: Single, 1 Allowance; State: Single, 1 Allowance. Print an Employee list.

Customize the report format so that the current date does not print as part of the header and the Company Name will print in Arial 16 point font on all reports.

Transfer the Uncategorized Income and Uncategorized Expenses to the owner's capital account. Print a Balance Sheet as of July 1, 19**.

Select Print the Company Name and Print Company Address. Change the font for the Company Name to Times Roman 16 point. Add a logo to an invoice (use the SS_Logo.bmp obtained from your instructor). Print a blank invoice with lines around each field.

END OF SECTION 3—
COLLEGE TOWN BOOK STORE
PRACTICE SET:
COMPREHENSIVE PROBLEM

The following is a comprehensive practice set combining all the elements of QuickBooks studied throughout the text. In this practice set you will set up a company and keep the books for March, 19**. You will use the EasyStep Interview to create College Town Book Store. Once the company has been created, detailed information will be provided for customers, vendors, and employees. Adjustments will be made to accounts and various items, and transactions will be recorded.

During the month, new customers, vendors, and employees will be added. When entering transactions, you are responsible for any memos you wish to include in transactions. Unless otherwise specified, the terms for each sale or bill will be the term specified on the Customer or Vendor list. The Customer Message is usually "Thank you for your business." However, any other message that is appropriate may be used. If a customer's order exceeds the established credit limit, accept the order and process it. If the terms allow a discount for a customer, make sure to apply the discount if payment is received in time for the customer to take the discount. Remember, the discount period starts with the date of the invoice. If an invoice or bill date is not provided, use the transaction date to begin the discount period. Use Sales Discounts as the discount account. If a customer has a credit and has a balance on the account, apply the credit to payments received for the customer. If there is no balance for a customer and a return is made, issue a credit memo and a refund check. Always pay bills in time to take advantage of purchase discounts.

Invoices, purchase orders, and other similar items should be printed with lines around each field. Most reports will be printed in Portrait orientation; however, if the report (such as the Journal) will fit across the page using Landscape orientation, use Landscape. Whenever possible, adjust the column widths so that reports fit on one-page wide without selecting "Fit report to one page wide."

COLLEGE TOWN BOOK STORE

The College Town Book Store is a fictitious company that sells books, sells educational supplies, and provides a typing service. College Town Book Store is located in Sacramento, California, and is a sole proprietorship owned by Ullman LeFevre. Mr. LeFevre does all the purchasing and is involved in all aspects of the business. College Town Book Store has a full-time employee who is paid a salary, Ms. Evelyn Neuman, who manages the store, is responsible for the all the employees, and keeps the books. Linda Egkan is a full-time hourly employee who works in the shop. The store is currently advertising for a part-time employee who will provide word processing/typing services.

CREATE A NEW COMPANY

Use the EasyStep Interview to create a new company.
College Town Book Store--Your Name is used for both the Company Name and the Legal Name. Address: 1055 Front Street, Sacramento, CA 95814. Tax ID 466-52-1446, tax year and fiscal year both begin in January, Other/None is the tax form used.

The following includes information that will help you answer some of the EasyStep Interview questions: College Town Book Store is a retail business. It does have an inventory. The file for the company should be **College.QBW**. Use the disk in **A:**. It does collect sales tax for California at the rate of 7.25%. The California sales tax is payable to the State Board of Equalization. College Town uses a Custom invoice. As previously stated, there are two employees. QuickBooks' payroll feature will be used. No estimates, time tracking, reimbursable expenses, or classes will be given or used. Bills will be entered first and paid later. The Reminders list should show on startup. The company start date is 03/01/**. (Remember to check with your instructor to determine the tax table year used. The tax table year will be the same year you will use in this problem.) College Town Book Store does have service items; it does not have any non-inventory part items or other charge items. There are no lines of credit. In the company setup, indicate that the To Do list will be used often. College Town will not charge finance charges and does not want to use QuickBooks for budgeting.

CHART OF ACCOUNTS

Use the following chart of accounts and balances as you answer the EasyStep Interview questions. (Type abbreviations: C.A.=Current Asset, F.A.=Fixed Asset, C.L.=Current Liability, COGS=Cost of Goods Sold. ***Balance is generated by QuickBooks. Only Balance Sheet accounts have balances. Accounts that are indented are subaccounts of the preceding account that is not indented—for example, Loan Interest is a subaccount of Interest Expense.) The chart of accounts will appear on three pages. Be sure to look at the end of the column on the left before adding accounts at the top of the column on the right.

COLLEGE TOWN BOOK STORE CHART OF ACCOUNTS				
ACCOUNT	**TYPE**	**BALANCE**	**ACCOUNT**	**TYPE**
Checking (02/28/**)	Bank	35,870.25	Liability Insurance	Expense
Accounts Receivable	Accts. Rec.	***	Interest Expense	Expense
Inventory Asset	Other C.A	***	Finance Charge	Expense

Office Supplies	Other C.A.	450.00	Loan Interest	Expense
Prepaid Insurance	Other C.A.	1,200.00	Licenses and Permits	Expense
Sales Supplies	Other C.A.	900.00	Miscellaneous	Expense
Store Equipment	F.A.	6,000.00	Payroll Expenses	Expense
Store Equipment: Depreciation	F.A.	0.00	Hourly Wages	Expense
Store Equipment: Original Cost	F.A.	6,000.00	Officer Salary	Expense
Store Fixtures	F.A.	10,000.00	Postage and Delivery	Expense
Store Fixtures: Depreciation	F.A.	0.00	Printing and Reproduction	Expense
Store Fixtures: Original Cost	F.A.	10,000.00	Professional Fees	Expense
Accounts Payable	Acct. Pay.	***	Accounting	Expense
MasterCard (02/28/**)	Credit Card	50.00	Legal Fees	Expense
Payroll Liabilities	Other C.L.	0.00	Rent	Expense
Sales Tax Payable	Other C.L.	0.00	Repairs	Expense
Store Equipment Loan	Long Term L.	1,500.00	Building Repairs	Expense
Store Fixtures Loan	Long Term L.	4,500.00	Computer Repairs	Expense
Ullman LeFevre, Capital	Equity	***	Equipment Repairs	Expense
Ullman LeFevre, Drawing	Equity	0.00	Sales Discounts	Expense
Ullman LeFevre, Investment	Equity	10,000.00	Storage	Expense
Retained Earnings	Equity	***	Supplies	Expense
Purchases Discounts	Income		Marketing	Expense
Book Sales	Income		Office	Expense
Supplies Sales	Income		Sales	Expense
Word Processing/Typing Service	Income		Taxes	Expense
Uncategorized Income	Income		Federal	Expense
Cost of Goods Sold	COGS		Local	Expense
Purchases Discounts	COGS		State	Expense
Bank Service Charges	Expense		Telephone	Expense
Depreciation Expense	Expense		Uncategorized Expenses	Expense
Dues and Subscriptions	Expense		Utilities	Expense
Equipment Rental	Expense		Gas and Electric	Expense
Filing Fees	Expense		Water	Expense
Insurance	Expense		Interest Income	Other Income

| Disability Insurance | Expense | | Other Income | Other Income |
| Fire Insurance | Expense | | Other Expenses | Other Expense |

ITEMS LIST

The is only one service item for College Town Book Store—Name: WP/Typing, Sales Description: Word Processing/Typing Service, Price: 0.00, Income Account: Word Processing/Typing Service Income

Use the following inventory items list and balances as you answer the EasyStep Interview questions.

INVENTORY ITEMS					
Item Name	**Textbooks**	**Paperback Books**	**Paper**	**Stationery**	**Pens, etc.**
Sales Description	Textbooks	Paperback Books	Paper Supplies	Stationery	Pens, etc.
Sales Price	0.00	0.00	0.00	0.00	0.00
Taxable Item	Yes	Yes	Yes	Yes	Yes
Income Account	Book Sales	Book Sales	Supplies Sales	Supplies Sales	Supplies Sales
Purchase Description	Textbooks	Paperback Books	Paper Supplies	Stationery	Pens, etc.
Cost	0.00	0.00	0.00	0.00	0.00
Preferred Vendor	Texts and Books Suppliers	Texts and Books Suppliers	Supplies Emporium	Supplies Emporium	Pens Galore
COGS Account	Cost of Goods Sold	Cost of Goods Sold	Cost of Goods Sold	Cost of Goods Sold	Cost of Goods Sold
Asset Account	Inventory Asset	Inventory Asset	Inventory Asset	Inventory Asset	Inventory Asset
Reorder Point	100	30	100	25	50
Quantity on Hand	2,000	45	200	30	50
Value	10,000	180	3,000	150	100

CUSTOMER LIST

Use the following Customer list and balances as you answer the EasyStep Interview questions. During the Interview, enter customers who are individuals last name first for Customer:Job but first name then last name on the Bill to address.

Ridgeway Training, Inc., 785 Harvard Street, Sacramento, CA 95814, Contact Susan Jones, 916-555-8762, Fax 916-555-2678, Net 30, Credit Limit $1,500, Balance $1,450, Taxable.

Maurice Walker, 253 Mason Street, Sacramento, CA 95814, 916-555-2264, Net 30, Credit Limit $350, Balance $350, Taxable.

Loreen Nelson, 8025 Richmond Avenue, Sacramento, CA 95814, 916-555-8961, 2% 10 Net 30, Credit Limit $500, Balance $100, Taxable.

Sacramento School, 1085 2nd Street, Sacramento, CA 95814, Contact Alicia Vincent, 916-555-1235, 2% 10 Net 30, Credit Limit $5,000, Balance $1,000, Taxable.

Dr. George Stein, 158 16th Street, Sacramento, CA 95814, 916-555-3693, Net 30, Credit Limit $100, Balance $0.00, Taxable.

Victoria Norton, 6784 Front Street, Sacramento, CA 95814, 916-555-6487, Net 30, Credit Limit $100, Balance $0.00, Taxable.

VENDOR LIST

Use the following Vendor list and balances as you answer the EasyStep Interview questions.

Texts and Books Suppliers, 559 4th Street, Sacramento, CA 95814, Contact Al Daruty, 916-555-2788, Fax 916-555-8872, 2% 10 Net 30, Credit Limit $15,000, Balance $1,000

Pens Galore 2785 Market Street, San Francisco, CA 94103, Contact Dennis Johnson, 415-555-3224, Fax 415-555-4223, 2% 10 Net 30, Credit Limit $5,000, Balance $500

Supplies Emporium, 95 8th Street, Sacramento, CA 95814, Contact Raymond Ahrens, 916-555-5759, Fax 916-555-9575, 2% 10 Net 30, Credit Limit $15,000, Balance $800

Employment Development Department; 1037 California Street, Sacramento, CA 95814; 916-555-8877 (Used for California Taxes and Withholding)

State Bank; 102 8th Street, Sacramento, CA 95814; 916-555-9889 (Used for all Federal Taxes and Withholding)

Medical Ins., Inc.; 20865 Oak Street, San Francisco, CA 94101; 415-555-4646 (Used for Medical Insurance deductions)

EMPLOYEE LIST

Use the following information, Employee list, and year-to-date balances as you answer the EasyStep Interview questions.

Only the information that needs to be entered is given below. If information is not provided, it is 0. Filing State is California, State Unemployment Tax Rate is 4%, FUTA is 0.8%. Employees are paid on a semi-monthly basis and receive both hourly wages and salary. College Town Book Store does want to track Hourly Regular Rate, Overtime Hourly Rate 1, Officer Salary Regular, Officer Sick Regular, Officer Vac Regular. There is employee-paid medical. Select *All* the federal taxes for employees. Track vacation and sick time. Sick and vacation hours are given at the beginning of the year, 40 hours per accrual period, maximum number of hours are 80 and are not reset each year.

Ms. Evelyn Neuman, 1777 Watt Avenue, Sacramento, CA 95814; 916-555-1222; Social Security No. 100-55-5244; Hired 02/17/95; Birthday 11/28/49; Officer Salary Regular $26,000; Medical $30; Federal and State: Single, 0 Allowance; Sick 40 hrs; Vacation 40 hrs

Mrs. Linda Egkan, 833 Oak Avenue, Sacramento, CA 95814; 916-555-7862; Social Security No. 100-55-6886; Hired 04/03/96; Birthday 12/07/70; Hourly Regular Rate $10 per hour; Overtime Hourly Rate $15 per hour; Medical $20; Federal and State: Married (one income), 1 Allowance; Sick 40 hrs; Vacation 40 hrs

EMPLOYEE YEAR-TO-DATE SUMMARY TABLE AS OF 02/28/**		
	Evelyn Neuman	**Linda Egkan**
Item Name	Officer Salary Regular	Hourly Regular Rate
Period Amount	4,333.34	3,200.00
Hours for Period	320	320
Medical Insurance Employee	60.00	40.00
Federal Withholding	584.00	252.00
Social Security Company	268.68	195.06
Social Security Employee	268.68	195.06
Medicare Company	62.84	46.40
Medicare Employee	62.84	46.40
Federal Unemployment	18.66	18.66

CA Withholding	126.60	28.04
CA Disability Employee	20.00	16
CA Unemployment Company	93.34	93.34

MAKE ADJUSTMENTS

Add, delete, and change the accounts for College Town Book Store as necessary so they are identical to the Chart of Accounts provided. Print a Chart of Accounts.

Add customer and vendor information. Print a Customer list and a Vendor list.

Associate Sales Items with Vendors. Print an Item list in Landscape orientation.

Associate Payroll Items with Vendors as indicated in the Vendor table. Print a Payroll Item list.

Add a new part-time hourly employee: Kristen Kriton, 1177 Florin Road, Sacramento, CA 95814; 916-555-7766; Social Security No. 100-55-3699; Hired 03/01/**; Birthday 1/3/76; Hourly Regular Rate $6.50; Federal and State: Single, 1 Allowance. Print an Employee list.

Customize the report format so the current date does not print as part of the header and the Company Name will print in Arial 16 point font on all reports.

Transfer the Uncategorized Income and Uncategorized Expenses to the owner's capital account. Print a Balance Sheet as of March 1, 19**.

Customize the Invoice: Select Print the Company Name and Print Company Address. Add a logo to an invoice (copy the CT_Logo.bmp to your data disk and use for the logo). Change the Title Invoice to INVOICE. Change the font for the Company Name to Arial Narrow, bold, 12 point; if your name does not print on the same line as College Town Book Store, use Layout Designer and make the area for the company name wide enough for your name. Use Layout Designer to make P.O. No. and Qty the same width, Terms and Rate the same width, and Project and Amount the same width. Print a blank invoice with lines around each field. Do the same for Credit Memos, Sales Receipts, and Purchase Orders. Do not print these additional forms.

ENTER TRANSACTIONS

Print invoices, sales receipts, purchase orders, checks, and other items as they are entered in the transactions. Create new items, accounts, customers, vendors, etc., as necessary. Refer to information given at the beginning of the problem for additional transaction details and information.

Prepare an Inventory Stock Status by Item report every five days as the last transaction of the day to see if anything needs to be ordered. If anything is indicated, order enough so you will have 10 more than the minimum number of items. (For example, if you needed to order textbooks and the minimum number on hand is 100, you would order enough books to have 110 on hand.) For this problem, the price per book ordered is $15 per textbook and $5 per paperback; pens are $2.50 each, paper is $2.00 per ream, and stationery is $4.00 per box.

Full-time employees usually work 80 hours during a payroll period. Hourly employees working in excess of 80 hours in a pay period are paid overtime. Normally, there is a separate Payroll Checking account used when paying employees; however, this problem uses the regular checking account to pay employees.

Check every five days to see if any bills are due and eligible for a discount. If any bills can be paid and a discount received, pay the bills; otherwise, wait for instructions to pay bills.

March 1:

Cash sale of one $40 textbook.

Ridgeway Training purchased 30 copies of *Computerized Accounting with QuickBooks® 5.0* for $40 each.

Sold three paperback books at $6.99 each to a cash customer.

Received Check #1096 from Loreen Nelson for $100 as payment in full on her account.

Sold 25 pens at $8.99 each to Sacramento School for awards to students.

Sold five textbooks at $39.99 each for the new quarter to a student using a Visa.

Prepare an Inventory Stock Status by Item report to see if anything needs to be ordered. Prepare Purchase Orders for any merchandise that needs to be ordered.

Check bills for discount eligibility between March 1-4. Pay any bills that qualify for a discount.

March 3:

Received Check #915 for $350 from Maurice Walker for the full amount due on his account.

Sold five pens at $12.99 each to Loreen Nelson.

Received payment of $1,450 from Ridgeway, Check #7824.

March 4:

Kristen typed a five-page paper for a student at the rate of $5 per page. Received Check #2951 for $25 as full payment.

Sold two textbooks at $40 each to a new customer: Ben Schultz, 478 Front Street, Sacramento, CA 95814, 916-555-6841, Terms Net 10, Credit Limit $100, Taxable.

March 5:

Received the pens ordered from Pens Galore with the bill.

Sold five boxes of stationery at $10.99 per box to Victoria Norton.

Sold five reams of paper at $4.99 per ream to Sacramento School.

Prepare Stock Status by Inventory Report. Order any items indicated. Check bills for discount eligibility. Pay any bills that qualify for a discount between March 5-9.

Deposit all cash, checks, and credit card payments received.

March 7:

The nonprofit organization State School bought a classroom set of 30 computer training books for $40.00 each. Add the new customer: State School, 451 State Street, Sacramento, CA 95814, Contact Allison Hernandez, 916-555-8787, Fax 619-555-7878, Terms Net 30, Credit Limit $2000, Taxable. Include a subtotal for the sale and apply a 10% sales discount for a nonprofit organization. (Create any new sales items necessary.)

Add a new sales item for Gift Ware, Sales Description: Gift Ware, Sales Price: 0.00, Taxable: Yes, Income Account: Supplies Sales, Purchase Description: Gift Ware, Cost: 0.00, COGS Account: Cost of Goods Sold; Reorder Point: 15, Quantity on Hand: 0, Value: 0.00, Preferred Vendor: Gift Gallery, 125 Oak Street, Sacramento, CA 95814, Contact: Mary Ellen Morrison, 916-555-5384, Fax 916-555-4835, Terms Net 30, Credit Limit $500.

Order 15 gift items at $5.00 each from the Gift Gallery.

March 8:

Sold ten reams of paper to George Stein at $3.99 per ream.

Received Check #10525 from Ridgeway Training, Inc., $1,000 as partial payment on account.

Loreen Nelson returned two pens purchased on March 3. She did not like the color.

Paid Texts and Books Suppliers full amount owed on account. Print using Standard Checks.

March 10:

Sold three pens at $14.95 each, two sets of stationery at $9.99 each, and three paperback books at $6.99 each to a cash customer.

Kristen typed a 15-page report at $5.00 per page for Victoria Norton.

Sold eight additional computer textbooks to Sacramento School at $40 each.

Received Check #825 as payment from Sacramento School for the 3/1 transaction for $236.22, the full amount due, less discount.

Deposit all cash, checks, and credit card receipts.

Prepare Stock Status by Inventory Report. Order any items indicated. Check bills for discount eligibility. Pay any bills that qualify for a discount between March 10-14.

March 11:

Sold ten paperback books at $6.99 each and two pens at $5.99 each to a customer using a Visa.

Sold ten reams of paper to a cash customer at $4.99 each. Received Check #8106.

March 12:

Received gift ware ordered from Gift Gallery. A bill was not included with the order.

Sold one pen at $8.99 and a box of stationery at $9.99 to a cash customer.

Kristen typed a one-page letter with an envelope for Maurice Walker, $8.00. (Qty is 1.)

March 13:

Received Check #1265 from Loreen Nelson in payment for full amount due, $40.41. (Be sure to apply any credits to her account first, then check for and apply any discounts.)

Received a notice from the bank that Check #915 from Maurice Walker was marked NSF and returned. Record the NSF check and charge Maurice the bank's $25 fee for the bad check plus College Town's fee of $15. Payment is due on receipt. Add any necessary items and/or accounts. Record charges for returned checks in an account called Returned Check Service Charges.

March 14:

Received Check #870 from Sacramento School for $26.22 as payment in full for Invoice 6.

Received Check #10-283 for $85.80 from Ben Schultz in payment of Invoice 4.

March 15:

Received all but three boxes of stationery ordered. The bill was included with the stationery and the three missing boxes are on back order. (Did you order 10 boxes?)

Received Maurice Walker's new Check #304 for payment in full of his account including all NSF charges.

Sold five paperback books to a customer using a Visa. The books were $6.99 each.

Deposit all cash, checks, and credit card receipts.

Check to see if any bills qualify for a discount between March 15-19. If any qualify, pay them.

Prepare and print a Stock Status by Item Inventory Report for March 1-15 in Landscape orientation. Prepare Purchase Orders for all items marked Order on the Stock Status by Item Inventory Report. Place all orders with preferred vendors.

Pay the payroll: Evelyn worked 80 hours, Linda worked 64 hours and took 16 hours of vacation time, and Kristen worked 40 hours during the pay period. Print using Voucher Checks.

March 17:

Sold eight textbooks at $50 each to State School, which is a nonprofit organization.

Ben Schultz returned one textbook he had purchased for $40.

March 18:

Received a Credit Memo 721 from Supplies Emporium for the return of ten reams of paper. (Be sure to apply the credit when you pay your bill.)

Print a Stock Status by Item report after recording the return of the paper. Print in Landscape.

Sold three paperback books to Maurice Walker at $8.99 each.

March 20:

Received the bill and the three boxes of stationery that were on back order with Supplies Emporium.

A cash customer purchased four textbooks at $59.99 each using Check #289.

Received Check #891 from Sacramento School for $336.34 in payment of Invoice 11.

Prepare Stock Status by Inventory Report. Order any items indicated. Check to see if any bills qualify for a discount between March 20-24. If any qualify, pay them.

March 21:

Sold one textbook for $89.95. Customer used a VISA card to pay for the purchase.

Kristen typed an eight-page exam for a professor at $5 per page. Add Professor John Smith, 1052 Florin Avenue, Sacramento, CA 95814, 916-555-8741, Terms Net 30, Credit Limit $100.

Deposit all cash, checks , and credit card receipts.

March 22:

Sold one gift item at $15.99 to a cash customer. Received Check #105.

Sold five gift items at $9.99 each to Loreen Nelson.

March 24:

Sold three pens at $8.99 to Ben Schultz.

Received Check #127 for $42.79 as payment in full from George Stein.

March 25:

Prepare Stock Status by Inventory Report. Order any items indicated. Check to see if any bills qualify for a discount between March 25-29. If any qualify, pay them. Are there any credits to apply to any bill payments?

Deposit all cash, checks, and credit card receipts.

March 27:

Received the bill and all of the paperback books ordered from Texts and Books Suppliers.

March 29:

Received Check #4325 for $133.93 from Victoria Norton.

March 30:

Received Bill #1092-5 and pens on order from Pens Galore.

Sold 60 textbooks to Ridgeway Training, Inc., for $59.95 each.

Sold 45 textbooks to Sacramento School for $49.99 each.

Prepare Stock Status by Inventory Report. Order any items indicated.

March 31:

Deposit all checks, cash, and credit card receipts.

Pay all bills eligible for a discount between March 31 and April 4.

Pay balance due to Supplies Emporium.

Pay $900 rent for April to the Rental Agency, 1234 Front Street, Sacramento, CA 95814, Contact: Gail Ruiz, 916-555-1234, Fax 916-555-4321, Terms Net 30.

Pay gas and electricity bill of $257 to California Utilities, 8905 Richmond, Sacramento, CA 95814, 916-555-8523, Terms Net 30.

Pay the telephone bill of $189 to Telephone Company, 3899 Oak Avenue, Sacramento, CA 95814, 916-555-8741, Terms Net 30.

Pay the payroll: Evelyn took 2 hours sick time during the pay period, Linda worked 3 hours overtime, and Kristen worked a total of 40 hours during the pay period.

Prepare and print the Payroll Summary by Employee report for March in Portrait orientation. (The report should fit on two pages. The information for Evelyn and Kristen should be on page 1. Information for Linda and the Totals should be on page 2. Adjust column widths to do this.)

Prepare and print the Liabilities by Payroll Item report for March in Portrait orientation.

Pay all the payroll taxes and other payroll liabilities for March. Print the checks.

Prepare and print Forms 941 and 940.

Prepare Sales Tax Liability report for March 1-31, 19**. Print in Landscape orientation. Adjust column widths so the report fits on one page, maintains the same font, and has column headings shown in full.

Pay Sales Tax and print the check.

Print a Sales by Item Summary report for March in Landscape orientation. Adjust column widths so report fits on one-page wide.

Print a Trial Balance for March 1-31 in Portrait orientation.

Transfer amount of purchases discounts from Income: Purchases Discounts to Cost of Goods Sold: Purchases Discounts.

Enter adjusting entries: Depreciation—Store Equipment $100, Store Fixtures $166.66. Supplies used—Office Supplies $150, Sales Supplies $250. Insurance a total of $100—$50 Fire Insurance, $50 Liability Insurance. (Use a compound entry to record insurance adjustment.)

Record the owner withdrawal for the month $1,500.

Prepare a bank reconciliation and record any adjustments. Print a Full Reconciliation report. Use the bank statement on the next page.

CONTINUE WITH PROBLEM

Print a Standard Profit and Loss Statement and a Standard Balance Sheet for March.

Transfer the Net Income/Retained Earnings into the capital account.

Print the following for March or as of March 31: Journal (Landscape, adjust column width to fit on one-page wide with the standard font) Trial Balance, Standard Balance Sheet.

Print Cash Flow Forecast for April in Landscape orientation.

STATE BANK
102 8th Street
Sacramento, CA 95814
(916) 555-9889

BANK STATEMENT FOR:

College Town Book Store
1055 Front Street
Sacramento, CA 95814   Acct. # 97-1132-07922   March, 19**

Beginning Balance, March 1, 19**			$35,870.25
3/5/**Deposit	2,204.84		38,075.09
3/9/**, Check 1		1,000.00	37,075.09
3/10/**, Deposit	1,328.24		38,403.33
3/13/**, NSF Check		350.00	38,053.33
3/15/**, Deposit	749.61		38,802.94
3/16/**, Check 2		85.75	38,717.19
3/16/**, Check 3		787.38	37,929.81
3/17/**, Check 4		232.81	37,697.00
3/17/**, Check 5		644.79	37,052.21
3/18/**, Check 6		42.90	37,009.31
3/21/**, Check 7		19.20	36,990.11
3/21/**, Deposit	690.17		37,680.28
3/25/**, Deposit	59.94		37,740.22
3/31/**, Service Charge,$15, and NSF Charge, $25		40.00	37,700.22
3/31/**, Store Fixtures Loan Pmt.: $80.12 Interest, $15.49 Principal		95.61	37,604.61
3/31/**, Store Equipment Loan Pmt.: $26.71 Interest, $5.16 Principal		31.87	37,572.74
3/31/**, Interest	94.03		37,666.77
Ending Balance, 3/31/**			$37,666.77

(Reminder: Print the Full Reconciliation Report. Return to previous page to complete the problem.)

IMPORTING AND EXPORTING DATA

QuickBooks makes it simple to import data from a program into QuickBooks or to export data from QuickBooks to another program. There are some limitations on what data can and cannot be imported/exported into and from QuickBooks.

File Importing and Exporting is accomplished from the File menu in QuickBooks. Importing a file brings information into QuickBooks from another program, and file exporting exports information from QuickBooks to another program. Actual transactions may not be imported or exported; however, QuickBooks does allow the import/export of certain lists and the export of certain reports. In addition to importing/exporting data from QuickBooks to another program, QuickBooks also allows you to import or export templates from one QuickBooks company to another.

EXPORTING

It is possible to export information from QuickBooks to another program in two ways. A report or a list may be printed to a file rather than printed on paper. When you print to a file, QuickBooks stores the information in a format that may be read or used by a word processing or a spreadsheet program. Whenever you export a file by printing to disk, it will need to be formatted within the word processing and/or spreadsheet program. For example, when printing a report in QuickBooks, it will look similar to the following:

VideoLand (Your Name)
Item Detail

Item	Description	Type	Quantity On Hand
VCR Repair	VCR Repair	Service	0
VCR Service	VCR Service	Service	0
Video Rental	Video Rental	Service	0
Video Sale	Video Sale	Service	0
Action	Action Video	Inventory Part	550
Children	Children's Video	Inventory Part	250
Comedy	Comedy Video	Inventory Part	500
Drama	Drama Video	Inventory Part	450
CA Sales T...	CA Sales Tax	Sales Tax Item	0
Out of State	Out-of-state sale, exempt from sales tax	Sales Tax Item	0

Yet, when opened within a word processing program, a partial report will appear similar to the following:

VideoLand (Your Name)
Item Detail

Item	Description	Type
VCR R...	VCR Repair	Service
VCR S...	VCR Service	Service
Video...	Video Rental	Service

Page 1

VideoLand (Your Name)
Item Detail

Quantity ...	Price	Cost	Ta...	Quantity O...
0	0.00	0	No	0
0	19.95	0	No	0
0	3.00	0	Yes	0

Page 2

VideoLand (Your Name)
Item Detail

Reorder...	Preferred Vendor

Page 3

The same report would appear as follows in a spreadsheet program:

,"Item","Description","Type","Quantity On Hand","Price","Cost","Taxable","Quantity On Order","Reorder Point","Preferred Vendor"
,"VCR Repair","VCR Repair","Service",0,0.00,0,"No",0,"",
,"VCR Service","VCR Service","Service",0,19.95,0,"No",0,"",
,"Video Rental","Video Rental","Service",0,3.00,0,"Yes",0,"",
,"Video Sale","Video Sale","Service",0,0.00,0,"Yes",0,"",
,"Action","Action Video","Inventory Part",550,0.00,0.00,"Yes",0,100.00,
,"Children","Children's Video","Inventory Part",250,0.00,0.00,"Yes",0,100.00,
,"Comedy","Comedy Video","Inventory Part",500,0.00,0.00,"Yes",0,100.00,
,"Drama","Drama Video","Inventory Part",450,0.00,0.00,"Yes",0,100.00,
,"CA Sales Tax","CA Sales Tax","Sales Tax Item",0,7.25%,0,"No",0,"",
,"Out of State","Out-of-state sale, exempt from sales tax","Sales Tax Item",0,0%,0,"No",0,"",

The basic information is provided for either program, but it will require formatting to make the report look as nice as it does in QuickBooks. The following is an example of a partial report formatted very simply within a word processing program:

VideoLand (Your Name)

Item	Description	Type	Quantity On Hand	Price	Cost	Taxable
VCR Repair	VCR Repair	Service	0	0	0	No
VCR Service	VCR Service	Service	0	19.95	0	No
Video Rental	Video Rental	Service	0	3	0	Yes
Video Sale	Video Sale	Service	0	0	0	Yes
Action	Action Video	Inventory Part	550	0	0	Yes
Children	Children's Video	Inventory Part	250	0	0	Yes
Comedy	Comedy Video	Inventory Part	500	0	0	Yes
Drama	Drama Video	Inventory Part	450	0	0	Yes
CA Sales Tax	CA Sales Tax	Sales Tax Item	0	7.25%	0	No
Out of State	"Out-of-state sale exempt from sales tax"	Sales Tax Item	0	0%	0	

The other method QuickBooks uses to export data is in a file format with the extension **.IIF** at the end of the file name. The extension tells the programs using the file that it has been stored in Intuit Interchange Format. This is the format used in QuickBooks. Only lists may be exported in the .IIF file format. The .IIF format is also used to import lists from other programs into QuickBooks. To export lists from the File menu, click Export then click the list you want to export. Exporting the Item List would appear as follows:

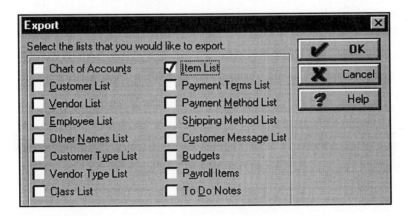

Once the list has been selected and the OK button clicked, QuickBooks will save the file on the disk you select using the name you specify and the extension .IIF.

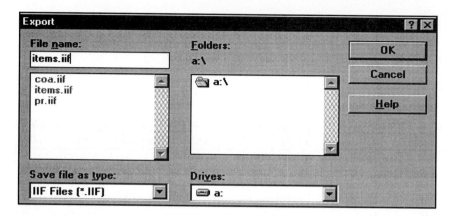

To export a template, such as a Customized Invoice, from one QuickBooks company to another, click the Lists menu, click Templates, click Customized Invoice, click the Templates button, click Export.

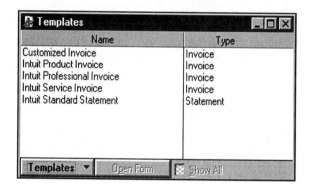

When the dialog box to Specify Filename for Export appears, enter a file name with the extension **.DES** or accept the filename provided by QuickBooks. Select the drive and folder or directory to which you want to export the file, then click OK. You may export the file to a floppy disk, or you may export it to the hard disk. If your template includes a company logo, you must also save the bitmap file containing the logo on the same disk and location you are using to export the file.

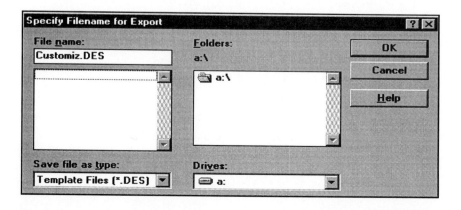

IMPORTING

You may import .IIF files and .DES files into QuickBooks. To import a file, click Import on the File menu, enter the file name, click OK. Importing the Items list stored in a file name **items.iif** would appear as:

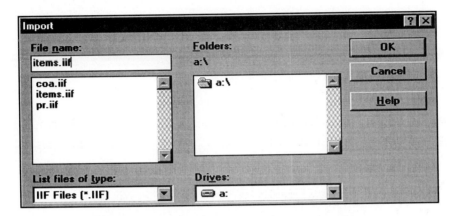

QuickBooks will give you a message stating "Your data has been imported." The list is ready for use. The same procedures would be used to import .DES files containing templates for a QuickBooks company.

The ability to import lists and templates and to export reports, lists, and templates gives you the flexibility to work with information in QuickBooks and in other programs.

QUICKBOOKS®
ON-LINE

QuickBooks is up-to-date in its on-line capabilities. It has integrated Internet access built into the program and provides the ability to perform on-line banking within the program.

INTUIT AND THE INTERNET

At Intuit's Web site you may get up-to-date information about QuickBooks and other products by Intuit. In addition, Intuit has a service that is free of charge and allows you to check the Web site to download messages and updates for QuickBooks. QuickBooks will remind you to do this at least once a month by displaying the following message:

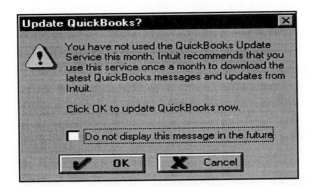

Not only does Intuit have a Web site, it is also accessible through QuickBooks by clicking Online on the menu bar.

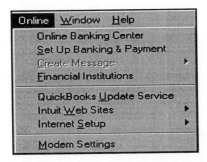

Pointing to Intuit Web Sites gives you choices for QuickBooks Small Business Online, Intuit Home Page, Payroll Tax Table Service, and QuickBooks Technical Support.

CONNECTING TO INTUIT INTERNET

Before connecting to Intuit's Web page, you must have the QuickBooks program and a company open. In addition, you must have a modem for your computer, and the modem must be connected to a telephone line. Once the modem is connected and QuickBooks and a company are open, you may establish your Internet connection.

QuickBooks has a step-by-step tutorial that will help you do this. Pointing to Internet Setup allows you to click on Internet Connection Setup and complete the tutorial. The first screen you see informs QuickBooks of your choice for your Internet connection. You may tell QuickBooks that you have an existing dial-up Internet connection, that you plan to use a direct connection through a network at school or work, or that you want to sign up for an Intuit Internet account with limited access. Because every computer may be different, this text will explore signing up for an Intuit Internet account. As in earlier chapters, you will need to click **Next** to go from one screen to another. Check with your instructor to see if you will be completing the Internet connection or simply reading this appendix.

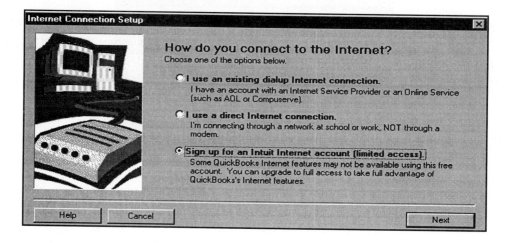

It is possible that you will need to have certain Windows files installed on your computer. If a screen appears instructing you to install files, see your instructor; or, if performing the connection from your home computer, refer to a Windows instruction manual to install the appropriate files.

The next screen that appears displays terms and conditions of use for the Intuit Internet account. Read through the terms, and click Yes if you agree to them. If you do not agree, click No to discontinue the setup. After agreeing to the terms, you will get a screen telling you about the steps that will be followed to set up your Internet access.

You will be required to provide some information on the next screen. You are requested to input your name, address, and day and evening telephone numbers. QuickBooks will not continue with the setup unless you provide this information. The minimum amount of information you can provide is your last name, zip code, and daytime telephone number.

When the above information has been provided, QuickBooks will search for your modem, display the information it found about your modem, and ask you to verify this information. After the modem has been verified, QuickBooks needs to know if your telephone is a pulse or tone, whether or not you have call waiting (this must be disabled before using the Internet), and your area code.

At this point QuickBooks will dial Intuit and register you as a user for the Intuit Internet. Once you have been registered as a user, you will receive a listing of access telephone numbers. Scroll through the list and select the number closest to your location. If you do not select a local telephone number, you may end up making a long-distance telephone call whenever you go on-line with QuickBooks.

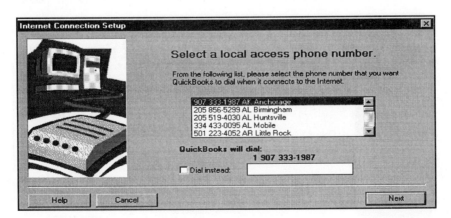

Once you select a local telephone access, Intuit will provide you with a user name and a password. The user name and the password will be required in order to access your account. Write down the user name and the password in a secure location. You do not want anyone else to have access to your account, and you do not want to lose your password.

After completing the tutorial to this point, you may be required to install Intuit's edition of Netscape. If so, follow the instructions provided. The next screen that appears allows you to send diagnostic data to Intuit when you access the Web page. Select either "Allow sending of data," or "Don't allow sending of data," then continue. Once these steps are complete, you get a screen telling you what you selected.

ACCESS INTUIT'S HOME PAGE

To access Intuit's Home Page, click Online on the menu bar, point to Intuit Web Sites, click on Intuit's Home Page. QuickBooks will connect you to the home page and will display the following during the dial-up and connection procedure:

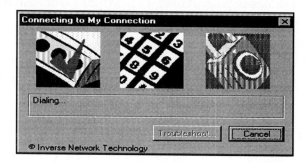

Once you are connected to Intuit's Web page, you will a see a screen similar to the following:

If you position the cursor on the right side of the screen on QuickBooks Product updates, the cursor will turn into a hand. This means you can click on the button for QuickBooks Product updates and get information about QuickBooks. On the left side of the screen, you can also access other Intuit topics, such as Intuit careers to receive information regarding careers with Intuit. In the center of the Web page, Intuit has several articles or items of information that you may read. When you access the Web page, scroll through it to see all the areas of information available.

QUICKBOOKS SMALL BUSINESS ONLINE (SBO)

If you click the button on the Web page for QuickBooks support and update, you will be taken to QuickBooks Small Business Online. You could also access this Web page by clicking on Small Business Online from the Online menu. This Web site contains information regarding the latest news about QuickBooks. It provides instant access to QuickBooks support information, and it provides answers to frequently asked questions. SBO allows you to check your tax tables and, if applicable, to download tax table updates. Tips for using QuickBooks and recent articles of general interest are provided on SBO. QuickBooks Small Business Online even has product information, and it gives you the ability to order products on-line.

When you access SBO, you may see a screen similar to the following; however, because Web pages are changed frequently, the screen that appears may be a bit different from the one shown below.

Scroll through the Web page to view the items available.

TAX TABLE UPDATES

Tax table updates are available for QuickBooks. The updates include new withholding tables for state and federal governments. Copies of and the printing setup for forms 941, 940, W-2, and 1099 Misc. are also included with the tax table update. You are entitled to one free update within the first 60 days of purchase. To ensure that you always have the most up-to-date tax tables, QuickBooks allows you to subscribe to its update service. The tax table update maybe downloaded along with any QuickBooks updates. In order to determine whether or not you have the most recent tax table, you may call Intuit's toll-free number, 1-800-771-7248, or visit Intuit's Web site, http://www.intuit.com/tts. QuickBooks also has a Payroll Notice dialog box to remind you to check your tax tables.

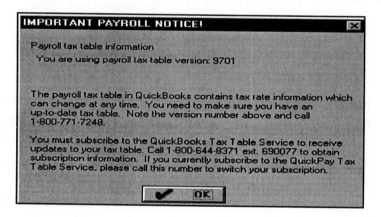

In fact, the screen for QuickBooks Small Business Online allows you check to see if your tax tables are up-to-date. Click "Make sure your '97 Tax Tables are up to date." QuickBooks will take you to Intuit's Tax Table Service. Scroll through the Tax Table Service screen, click "check to see if you have the latest tax table." QuickBooks will require you to provide information regarding the program you use, the program version you use, the tax table you use, the state taxes you pay, and any local taxes you pay. Once QuickBooks determines whether or not you have the latest version, it will tell you. At the time the text was written, the latest tax table was in use and the following tax table verification was given.

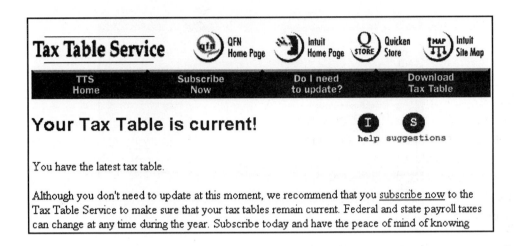

DOWNLOADING UPDATES TO QUICKBOOKS

Periodically, Intuit will provide a maintenance release that is available for downloading from the Web site. (Downloading means to get a copy of something, such as a program update from a Web site.) A maintenance release is issued if a problem is discovered and fixed after the original version of the program has been distributed. Intuit does not provide upgrades or new versions of the program for downloading. To download an update, choose QuickBooks Update Service from the Online menu. When you click Go Online, it may take up to 20 minutes to download the information from Intuit.

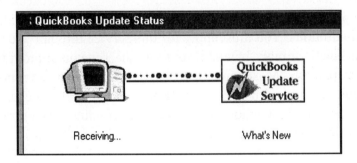

When you finish downloading the information, you will get a screen telling you about available updates and new updates.

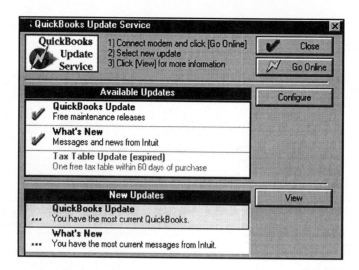

At the bottom of the screen, you are given information regarding the new updates QuickBooks has provided. If there is an update to QuickBooks, it must be installed before it is used. If the download contains news but not a maintenance release or a tax table, it does not need to be installed. To see the information from the download, simply click QuickBooks Update or What's News under New Updates, then click View.

ON-LINE BANKING AND PAYMENTS

On-line banking and payment services are offered through QuickBooks in conjunction with a variety of financial institutions. You must apply for this service through your financial institution. If you bank with or make payments to more than one institution, you must sign up with each institution separately. Most banks will charge a fee for on-line services and may not offer both on-line banking and on-line payment services. Intuit does not charge a fee for accessing on-line services through QuickBooks; however, if you sign up for Online Payment through QuickBooks, there is a charge.

In order to provide security and confidentiality in on-line services, you use a private network, *not* the Internet. You must have and use a Personal Identification Number (PIN) or password supplied by your financial institution. You may also use passwords within QuickBooks. High-level, state-of-the-art encryption is used to protect all information going to your financial institution.

As previously stated, you must apply to use on-line services through your financial institution. Sometimes this is done by submitting a paper application. In other instances you may be able to complete an Online Banking and Online Payment Setup Interview in QuickBooks and submit the application electronically. QuickBooks will provide a listing of financial institutions that allow electronic applications when you click the Online menu and Financial Institutions.

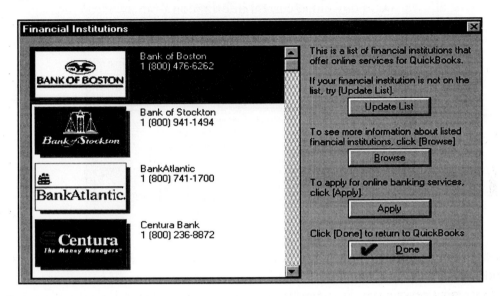

You may click the Update List button to get updated information regarding the different institutions and the services they offer. Sometimes services and fees will be detailed.

Because each institution is different regarding its procedures for setting up and using on-line services, this text will not actually subscribe to any of the on-line services but will discuss some of the features available.

ON-LINE BANKING

On-line banking allows you to download current information from and send messages to your financial institution. This can include transactions, balances, and on-line messages.

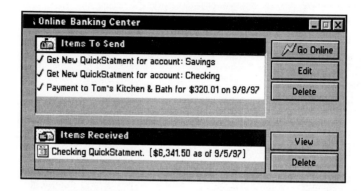

You can automatically compare the downloaded transactions with those in your register. QuickBooks will match downloaded transactions to those in your register and note any unmatched transactions so that they may be entered into your register.

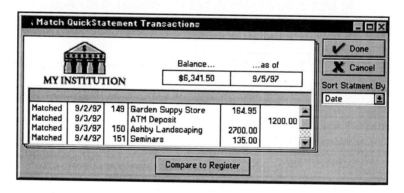

With on-line banking you may transfer money between two on-line accounts at the same financial institution.

ON-LINE PAYMENTS

You may use the on-line payment services to create on-line payment instructions for one or more payments, then send the instructions via your modem. You may schedule a payment to arrive on a certain date, inquire about on-line payments, and cancel them if need be.

To use on-line payments, you need to set up a payee. Once the payee is set up, you may either send an electronic funds transfer (EFT) to the payee's institution or have your financial institution print a check and send it to the payee. An electronic funds transfer deducts money from your account and transfers it into the payee's account electronically. This usually takes one or two business days. This is called lead time and must be considered when sending on-line payments. If you have your institution mail checks to payees, you should allow four days lead time. You may send any type of checks on-line except paychecks, liability payments, or sales tax checks.

If you are not using an on-line payment service, QuickBooks may ask you if you would like to receive information regarding on-line payment when you are paying bills.

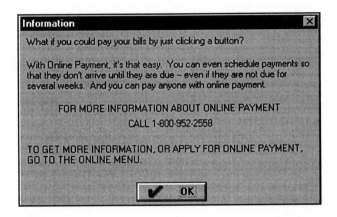

Intuit provides Online Payment but not Online Banking and charges a fee for the use of on-line payment.

INDEX